JUVENILE DELINQUENCY

Concepts and Control

FIFTH EDITION

ROBERT C. TROJANOWICZ

MERRY MORASH

School of Criminal Justice
Michigan State University

PRENTICE HALL, *Englewood Cliffs, New Jersey 07632*

Library of Congress Cataloging-in-Publication Data

Trojanowicz, Robert C. [date]
  Juvenile delinquency : concepts and control / Robert C.
Trojanowicz, Merry Morash.
    p.   cm.
  Includes bibliographical references and index.
  ISBN 0-13-511866-2
    1. Juvenile delinquency—United States. 2. Juvenile delinquency—
  United States—Prevention. 3. Juvenile delinquents—
  Rehabilitation—United States. I. Morash, Merry, [date]
  II. Title.
  HV9104.T76 1992
364.3'6'0973—dc20   91–29910
                                                                      CIP

Editorial/production supervision and interior design: Helen Brennan/Fred Dahl
Cover design: Marianne Frasco
Prepress buyer: Kelly Behr
Manufacturing buyer: Mary Ann Gloriande

 © 1992, 1987, 1983, 1978, 1973 by Prentice-Hall, Inc.
A Simon & Schuster Company
Englewood Cliffs, New Jersey 07632

Printed in the United States of America

10 9 8 7 6 5 4 3 2 1

ISBN 0-13-511866-2

PRENTICE-HALL INTERNATIONAL (UK) LIMITED, *London*
PRENTICE-HALL OF AUSTRALIA PTY. LIMITED, *Sydney*
PRENTICE-HALL CANADA, INC., *Toronto*
PRENTICE-HALL HISPANOAMERICANA, S.A., *Mexico*
PRENTICE-HALL OF INDIA PRIVATE LIMITED, *New Delhi*
PRENTICE-HALL OF JAPAN, INC., *Tokyo*
PRENTICE-HALL OF SOUTHEAST ASIA PTE. LTD., *Singapore*
EDITORA PRENTICE-HALL DO BRASIL, LTDA., *Rio de Janeiro*

Contents

DEC 1996

Preface

The main purpose of the fifth edition of *Juvenile Delinquency: Concepts and Control* is to provide the practitioner or the student interested in working with juveniles an overview of the juvenile delinquency phenomenon and the process involved in its causation, prevention, control, and treatment. Like the previous editions, this one emphasizes a multidisciplinary approach to the problem and updates information presented in the earlier editions, and includes as well new and important material related to the complex problem of juvenile delinquency.

The most popular and prevalent interdisciplinary issues, ideas, principles, and assumptions pertaining to the phenomenon are presented. The use of numerous examples facilitates the transition from complex theoretical principles to practical application.

Not only does the book provide an overview of the many variables related to delinquency, it points out the orientation, duties, responsibilities, and functions of the agencies in the juvenile justice system that deal with the juvenile delinquent. The orientation, programs, and procedures utilized by the various juvenile justice agencies are discussed to help the reader understand the processes the delinquent goes through from the initial contact with the police to the selection of a dispositional alternative. The description and discussion of the juvenile delinquency process will further facilitate the transition from theory to practice.

All of us, regardless of background or professional training, have our own theories about juvenile delinquency. Often practitioners amateur theorists demonstrate appropriate and sound logic, but because they are unaware of popular theoretical assumptions and current programs and practices they are unable to systematically compare their ideas with those of the "experts." This hinders the practitioner and the "amateur" from effectively replicating and refining their own most successful ideas and practices. In other words, many practitioners and aspiring practitioners "fly by the seat of their pants."

This book provides the reader with an exposure to the thinking of the experts in the field of juvenile delinquency, the process involved in the causation of this phenomenon, and examples of the most successful and most often used programs, procedures, and techniques for handling juveniles.

The strength of the book is that it points out the complexity of the juvenile delinquency phenomenon and the necessity of understanding the many variables related to its causation, prevention, treatment, and control—variables that range all the way from a knowledge of "normal" adolescent behavior to an understanding of processing procedures in handling delinquents.

The book recognizes racial, gender, and social class diversity in the adolescent population. New theories to explain girls' lawbreaking, examples of programs for girls, and information about how they are handled by the juvenile justice system are provided throughout the book. Special attention is focused on race and class as correlates of delinquency as well as biasing influences on official reaction to illegal behavior.

The establishment of effective juvenile delinquency prevention, treatment, and control programs can be accomplished only if the many variables identified in the book are understood, assimilated, and then initiated into action.

Part 1, "Introduction to the Study of Juvenile Delinquency," provides a framework for organizing the great amount of information we have about delinquency, and it reviews statistics on the delinquency problem. Chapter 1, "Issues in Understanding Juvenile Delinquency," lays the groundwork for understanding the interconnections between our beliefs about delinquency, assumptions about who the delinquents are, theories of delinquency causation, and delinquency control programs. The choice of one control program over another is often based on a combination of theories, assumptions, and beliefs. Without this recognition, it is difficult to make sense out of the complex network of programs intended to control adolescents' misbehavior.

Chapter 2, "Delinquents In and Out of the Juvenile Justice System," summarizes numerous research findings that tell us exactly which youths are most delinquent and which ones are most likely to be involved in the juvenile justice system. Because not all youths who break the law are apprehended or arrested, we cannot assume that those in court are actually the most delinquent. A number of recent surveys of nationally representative groups of adolescents are described, for they provide particularly useful estimates of the extent of illegal activity by youths.

In Chapter 2, many myths about the nature of the delinquent are challenged. Delinquency is found in all social classes. Despite newspaper and television accounts to the contrary, we are not currently besieged by extreme increases of juvenile delinquency or by large numbers of teenage gangs. Girls have become more delinquent than they formerly were, but mainly in typically "female" crimes, such as shoplifting. They are not nearly as violent as boys.

In the second part of the book, "Theories as the Basis for Program Design," the focus is on explanations of why adolescents break the law. Chapter 3 provides a survey of major sociological and psychological theories to explain delinquency. The chapter outlines new developments in theory, including research to explain females' delinquency, research on structural influences, efforts to integrate theories, and challenges to the beliefs on which some theories rest.

As a complement to the survey of a broad range of theories and related research in Chapter 3, Chapter 4, "The Family and Juvenile Delinquency," focuses just on information about the influence of families on delinquency. By narrowing attention to the family, the student is directed again to consider major theories and new developments, but in more depth than with the survey approach. Additionally, the interdisciplinary approach to understanding delinquency can be emphasized.

The concluding chapter on theory, Chapter 5, "The Adolescent," also uses an interdisciplinary approach, drawing from the disciplines of anthropology, history, sociology, and psychology. People from these fields have drawn attention to the special needs of delinquents which stem from their status as adolescents, and the role of their adolescent status in promoting delinquent behavior.

People working with juveniles tend to forget that the delinquent is an adolescent first and delinquent second. They are not familiar with the wide variety of adolescent disruptive behavior that is within the normal range. Often, most is expected of the delinquent than of the normal adolescent. Unfortunately, many prevention, treatment, and control programs are predicated on the "sickness" of the delinquent and not on the "healthiness" of the adolescent. It is important to understand the normal as well as the delinquent adolescent—as much may be learned from normality as from deviancy. Chapter 5 also examines the adolescent from many perspectives, including the historical, cultural, psychological, and sociological. Practical examples are given of methods of relating to the adolescent, and major areas for societal change in attitudes toward the adolescent are identified.

Although the focus in Chapters 2 through 5 is on theory, the interrelationships between theory, beliefs, and programs, and the issue of who the delinquents are remain central. These interrelationships are pointed out in the chapter material and are emphasized in discussion questions and projects.

In Part 3 of this book, "Treatment of the Delinquent," we give less emphasis to theories of juvenile delinquency and more to the programs and treatment methods which are commonly used. Chapter 6 reviews the organization and operation of the entire juvenile justice system—the police, court, and correctional agencies—as well as the laws which influence the system.

For youths who are involved with the juvenile justice system, and for some who are not, a multitude of programs have been developed over the years. A historical perspective of the most important of these programs is provided in Chapter 7 to give a sense of what has been tried and what has been successful. Additionally, many examples of frequently used contemporary programs are presented. Chapter 8 gives a more detailed understanding of the programs, whether old or new, by introducing the specific treatment methods which can be used in the various program settings.

The last two chapters of this section, Chapters 9 and 10, balance the overview of justice system operations, delinquency programs, and treatment methods. They are in-depth explanations of new and promising approaches to delinquency control. Like the overview, these two chapters stress the interplay between theory, beliefs, the treatment method, and the target population, and they present relevant research findings. They also give the student a detailed explanation of the steps involved in successful implementation of delinquency control efforts. Such organizational abilities are essential in effectively applying our theoretical understanding of delinquency and its control in real world settings.

"An Example: A Community-Based Treatment Program," Chapter 9, describes a halfway house program and discusses the input necessary for the establishment and operation of such a facility. The chapter uses many of the concepts relevant to prevention programs and methods which were stressed in Chapters 7 and 8.

Halfway houses are discussed more extensively than other juvenile facilities because (1) they are a prevalent type of community-based treatment facility for juveniles, often replacing institutions; (2) a discussion of the halfway house program lends itself to the incorporation of the theories, concepts, programs, and techniques that were discussed in the preceding chapters; and (3) the example of a halfway house program illustrates the numerous elements that have to be considered in successfully implementing a program to achieve its intended goals.

Chapter 10, "Delinquency Prevention through Citizen Involvement," emphasizes including the residents of the community in any decisions that relate to delinquency prevention, control, and treatment. Without community involvement, input and commitment to programs that are established to work with youngsters will be difficult to effect.

Part 4, "Juveniles with Multiple Problems," focuses on substance abuse and child abuse and neglect. In Chapter 11, "Alcohol and Drug Abuse," theories to explain abuse and special programs for its control are described. Many of the youths who are involved in the juvenile justice system abuse drugs and alcohol. Programs must take this into account in order to fully serve the delinquent.

"Child Abuse and Neglect," the topic of Chapter 12, is of great concern today for professionals in all phases of the juvenile justice system. The problem can no longer be viewed as "someone else's concern." Everyone, all the way from the investigating police officer to the judge who makes the final decision, must be aware of the seriousness of the problem and what can be done to remedy this unfortunate situation.

This book will give you the skills to recognize and analyze both historical and contemporary trends in juvenile delinquency theory and control. In the last chapter we apply these skills to pressing problems in coordinating various parts of the juvenile justice system and in implementing key policies. We also discuss the tremendous value of empirical research, which we have stressed throughout the book. As beliefs and theories about juvenile delinquency change, you will find that your own ability to understand juvenile delinquency insures a current and sophisticated appreciation of the field.

Finally, a complete bibliography with summaries and library call numbers is presented at the end of the book to provide an easy reference for both the student and the practitioner. An Instructor's Manual has been developed for the text to assist the teacher. It includes numerous case examples and related questions for discussion or essays, as well as test questions.

As with any endeavor, many people have contributed to the achievement of our goal. We would like to acknowledge some of the people who helped in completing this edition as well as earlier editions: Ray Valley, Suzanne (Pyzik) Jude, Thomas Schooley, Kathleen Williams, Bonnie Pollard, Jody Allen, Kathleen Adams, Victoria Schneider,

Lila Rucker, Robin Haarr and Mark Lanier for their research assistance; Dr. John Trojanowicz, Dr. Forrest Moss, and Sydell Spinner for their writing help; John Duhring, Steven Cline, Edward Francis, and Robert Weisman of Prentice Hall for their encouragement; Dr. Christopher Sower for his inspiration; and our families for their support and endurance.

1

Issues in Understanding Juvenile Delinquency

- DEFINITION OF DELINQUENT BEHAVIOR
- FOUR KEY ISSUES IN UNDERSTANDING DELINQUENCY
- THE USE OF RESEARCH
- AN EXAMPLE—DELINQUENTS, THEORY, PROGRAMS, AND BELIEFS
- SUMMARY

LEARNING OBJECTIVES

1. To define juvenile delinquency, and the related concepts of deviance and crime.
2. To know how an informed citizen, a parent, or a staff member in a juvenile justice agency can make a decision about the worth of various delinquency theories and programs.
3. To be aware that there are sociological, psychological, and other types of delinquency theory, and that programs are based on each type.
4. To understand that common beliefs about delinquency and its control affect everyone's reactions to adolescents who break the law.

In 1970, an innovative and ambitious administrator took charge of a county agency to handle delinquent adolescents who had been arrested. This agency, the Department of Juvenile Services, screened youths to decide which ones should go to court, prepared treatment recommendations for judges, and provided probation and parole programs. Because the agency was quite small, the administrator could personally supervise all staff members and develop new programs in the community. She was strongly committed to the state law's mandate to the department: to provide treatment, training, and rehabilitation for each offender. Therefore, she encouraged staff members to diagnose each offender's misbehavior, and to provide specialized treatment. Psychiatrists, psychologists, and social workers provided expert services in many cases. Nearly all offenders were "treated" in the community, and the administrator was very proud when an independent researcher found that the community-based services had not resulted in more recidivism than would have occurred if more offenders had been sent to locked institutions.

Today, the current administrator and staff show the effects of recent disillusionment with the effectiveness of delinquency programs, and public fear that juvenile delinquency is increasing and out of control. They advocate a "get tough" policy, which includes sending more offenders out of the community to secure institutional programs. One probation officer who had been at the department before the policy shift summed up the feelings of many staff: "We found out that the old treatment methods didn't work, so now we are trying something else." However, offenders and others from outside the department find it perplexing that treatment-oriented staff routinely diagnose and counsel delinquents alongside staff who, like the probation officer quoted above, have completely abandoned the treatment approach.

The above example illustrates the importance of understanding prior theories, practices, and beliefs in order to make sense of current efforts to control juvenile delinquency. The example also makes it very clear that there is a tendency to follow fads in juvenile delinquency programs. There is a need to carefully weigh research evidence against common sense beliefs, as well as against previously and currently favored methods of controlling delinquency.

The example further illustrates the rapid but incomplete change that has taken place in views of delinquency. Lamar Empey, a noted criminologist, sums up his observation of the change on a national scale:

> Remarkable changes in the American concepts of delinquency and juvenile justice occurred in the 1960s and 1970s. The reputation of the juvenile court has been badly tarnished; the rules that define delinquency have been altered; and faith in the concept of rehabilitation has been seriously eroded. In short, we are witnessing changes in our treatment of the young that are every bit as revolutionary as was the intention of the juvenile court in 1899, or the construction of prisons and reformatories almost a century before that.[1]

The degree to which the shift away from rehabilitation is incomplete, or in some cases has been reversed, is highlighted by the fact that several states (including Pennsylvania, Oklahoma, Louisiana, Colorado, and Oregon) are engaged in a new reform effort involving: (1) development of very small, treatment-oriented secure programs for violent offenders and (2) the replacement of large training schools with structured, community-based programs for non-

[1]Lamar T. Empey, "Revolution and Counterrevolution: Current Trends in Juvenile Justice," in *Critical Issues in Juvenile Delinquency,* eds. David Shichor and Delos H. Kelly (Lexington, Massachusetts: Lexington Books, D. C. Heath and Company, © 1980), p. 157.

violent offenders.[2] This shift back towards individualized treatment was pioneered by the states of Massachusetts and Utah, and it is given impetus by several court challenges of the constitutionality of the conditions in which many juveniles are confined.[3]

This chapter identifies four issues that must be resolved in order to make sense of today's juvenile delinquency theories, policies, and programs. A full understanding of these issues is essential to making judgments about the extent to which recent changes represent well-conceived programs, and as such, this understanding is a basis on which students can organize their own thoughts about delinquency. Before presenting these issues, it is necessary to provide a definition of delinquent behavior.

DEFINITION OF DELINQUENT BEHAVIOR

Delinquent behavior is prohibited by law and is carried out by youths approximately up to the age of eighteen. The exact lower and upper age limits differ from state to state, but age ten has been recommended by experts as the most logical cutoff point for children who are old enough to understand that their behavior is wrong.[4] The upper age limit varies between states, with some using 16 or 17, but most using 18.[5]

State laws legally prohibit two types of behavior for juveniles. The first includes behavior which is criminal for adults, such as the serious offenses of murder, rape, fraud, burglary, and robbery. Offenses which are criminal for adults but do not involve serious harm to other people, such as the offenses of trespassing and possession of drugs, are also included in this category. Status offenses are the second type of delinquent behavior, and they are not legally prohibited for adults. Running away from home, being out of the control of your parents ("unruly" or "ungovernable"), and being truant from school are the common status offenses.

The concept of juvenile delinquency has not always referred to the same type of behavior, and it has not even always existed. In a sense, the idea was invented in 1899 when the first juvenile court began to treat young offenders differently from those who were older.[6] Notions about what behavior should be defined as delinquency are not set and unchanging and, in fact, are frequently

[2]John Blackmore, Marci Brown, and Barry Krisberg, *Juvenile Justice Reform: The Bellwether States* (University of Michigan, School of Social Work: Ann Arbor, Michigan, 1988), p. vii.
[3]*Ibid.*

[4]Task Force on Juvenile Justice and Delinquency Prevention, *Juvenile Justice and Delinquency Prevention* (Washington, D.C.: U.S. Government Printing Office, 1976), p. 297.

[5]Charles P. Smith and Paul S. Alexander, *A National Assessment of Serious Juvenile Crime and the Juvenile Justice System: The Need for a Rational Response* (Washington, D.C.: U.S. Government Printing Office, 1980), p. xix.

[6]Don C. Gibbons, "Explaining Juvenile Delinquency: Changing Theoretical Perspectives," in *Critical Issues in Juvenile Delinquency*, eds. Shichor and Kelly, p. 9; and Lamar T. Empey, *American Delinquency: Its Meaning and Construction* (Homewood, Illinois: The Dorsey Press, 1978), p. 3.

questioned. In this vein, questions are now being raised as to the appropriateness of various delinquency definitions and the propriety of applying formal sanctions to such a wide range of juvenile behaviors, many of which are no more serious than general nuisances.[7] On the other side of the coin, many states have provisions to reclassify delinquent behavior as adult criminal behavior in cases where the offender is nearly old enough to be considered an adult and has committed a particularly serious offense.

FOUR KEY ISSUES IN UNDERSTANDING DELINQUENCY

In order to fully understand delinquency, four key issues must be considered. First, who are the adolescents with the most delinquent behavior? Second, which theories offer the best explanation of the causes of delinquency? These theories would provide the best basis for delinquency programs. Third, what programs and methods are effective in controlling delinquency? Fourth, what do different groups in our society believe about delinquency? That is, which adolescents do they see as delinquent, and which theories and programs do they think are best? These groups include professionals involved with delinquents, as well as various sectors of the general public.

As shown in the model of the interrelationships of four key issues (Fig. 1-1), each issue is related to the others. Our identification of certain youths as highly delinquent and our theories to explain their delinquency affect each other. Specifically, we often assume that we know which adolescents are the most delinquent, and we develop theories to explain why these youths differ from others. Alternatively it is possible to begin with a theory, and rely on it to make predictions about which youths are the most delinquent. Regardless of whether assumptions about who the delinquents are come before or after a theory is developed, the delinquency programs which we design are aimed at a "target population" of these youths.

Theories also suggest the problems that must be eliminated in order to stop delinquency, and thus have a direct bearing on the design of programs. However, it would be misleading to say that all, or even the majority of delinquency programs, are firmly grounded in theory. Beliefs also are a major influence on the interactions between predictions that certain youths are most delinquent, and theories, and programs. Very often, beliefs are the most important influence on our perceptions of which youths are the most delinquent, and on the choice of programs to use. Beliefs even influence our choice of one theory over another. This can occur regardless of research evidence showing the theory to be quite weak. Because the four key issues are so closely related, even chapters

---

[7]Ruth Shoule Cavan, ed., *Readings in Juvenile Delinquency,* 2nd ed. (Philadelphia: J. B. Lippincott Co., 1969); Margaret K. Rosenheim, "Notes on Helping Juvenile Nuisances," in *Pursuing Justice for the Child,* ed. Margaret K. Rosenheim (Chicago: University of Chicago Press, 1976), pp. 43–66.

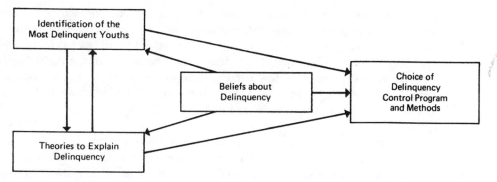

Figure 1-1 A model of the interrelationships of four key issues in understanding delinquency

in this book which focus on one issue will touch on the others. For this reason, a brief overview of each issue is provided in this introductory chapter.

Who Are the Delinquents?

D.C. Superior Court Judge Reggie B. Walton told a House panel on families yesterday that juveniles appearing before him now are younger, more violent and more immoral than ever.... "I have also seen a deterioration of remorse," said Walton, who is known for handing down harsh sentences and stern lectures from his Superior Court bench. "There just seems to be a lack of feeling about the violent acts that have been perpetrated."

The Washington Post, May 17, 1989, p. C3

One out of every eight people arrested for murder last year in Chicago was a kid. Four of every ten charged with robbery were kids.... "They have no rules. Everyone around them is using drugs," said Assistant State's Attorney Norma Reyes, a prosecuting supervisor in Cook County's Juvenile Court.
  "They live in a very violent environment and think nothing of stealing things that they want. Then they end up being violent themselves."

The Chicago Tribune, September 10, 1989, p. 1

There has been an alarming increase in delinquency in European Cities, and there is a danger of a similar increase in the city of New York.

The New York Times, August 2, 1918, p. 11*

Youth and intoxication are not legal palliations of a wanton murder. Law and common sense are both strained enough in these days to shield culprits, but if these excuses had been allowed to have weight, the whole community would literally have been at the mercy of the worst class of the population; for nearly all of our criminals are young men—in any other country they would be called boys—and nearly all are in the habit of drinking more or less every evening.

The New York Times, October 4, 1858, p. 4**

*© 1918 by the New York Times Company. Reprinted by permission.
**© 1858 by the New York Times Company. Reprinted by permission.

In the above list of quotations, the picture that the magazines and the newspapers draw of juvenile delinquents is startling, and even frightening. The public media suggest that there is a large and growing number of clearly identifiable teenagers who are dangerous, drug-using, gang-joining individuals. A close look at the list contains a few surprises, however. Some of the newspaper accounts are not recent, but are drawn from the 1800s and early 1900s. Are we really faced with an unprecedented increase in the number of dangerous delinquents?

As a first step in answering this question, keep in mind that every adolescent who breaks the law is not called a juvenile delinquent. Many are never caught, and of those who are, the majority are not treated as if they need special help or the severe punishment that a juvenile court can administer. People see a great deal of juvenile lawbreaking as childish pranks, "one-time" mistakes, and a normal part of "growing up." The decision to label a person as "delinquent" is somewhat arbitrary, for being delinquent is a matter of degree. Nearly all adolescents have broken the law at some time, but they vary markedly in how often, and how seriously, they break the law.

Official police or court records also are not perfect indicators of which youths are most delinquent. Research confirms that there is little overlap between the most serious offenders and the most punished offenders.[8] Police, court, and correctional program staff have a choice in how they treat youths who have broken the law, and sometimes they take action which results in no record of the offender's actions. This happens when police warn youths and take them home, or when court personnel handle a case informally. Official records tell us how program staff decided to handle juvenile delinquency cases, and they tell us which youths are most often handled severely—by an arrest, a court appearance, or a commitment to an institution. They do not tell us how often adolescents break the law.

Newspaper, television, and magazine accounts of juvenile delinquency are probably the least reliable information we have on how delinquent youths are. Mass media attention to gang delinquency, for example, has varied completely independently of the amount of gang activity.[9] Some people have concluded that as a result of the women's liberation movement, there is a marked change in the image of the female delinquent, but this media image is largely independent of any real change in the types of crime she is likely to commit.[10] In a final example of the inaccuracies of media accounts of delinquency, serious questions have been raised about the "monster" image of delinquents as violent

[8]Helene Raskin White, Robert J. Pandina, and Randy L. LaGrange, "Longitudinal Predictors of Serious Substance Use and Delinquency," *Criminology, 25*, no. 3 (August 1987), p. 727.

[9]Walter B. Miller, "Youth Crime in the Urban Crisis Era," in *Delinquency, Crime and Society,* ed. James F. Short, Jr. (Chicago: University of Chicago Press, 1976), pp. 91–128.

[10]Darrell J. Steffensmeir and Renee Hoffman Steffensmeir, "Trends in Female Delinquency: An Examination of Arrest, Juvenile Court, Self-Report, and Field Data," *Criminology, 18,* no. 1 (May 1980), p. 75.

and aggressive criminals. It may be more accurate to picture the majority as minor offenders, with a very small proportion occasionally committing a violent act.[11] In each of the examples given, it is clear that the popular image of juvenile delinquency trends, and of the juvenile delinquent, is open to question.

Theories and Programs

All delinquency programs used now and in the past are based on one or more theories to explain why adolescents are delinquent. Theories identify the causes of delinquency, and programs are designed to eliminate or counteract these causes. Biologists developed many of the earliest theories, in which genetic inheritance or other physical attributes were thought to cause crime. Though these early theories have been shown to be useless, they were important because they specified some measurable causes of delinquency. Therefore, it was possible to carry out research to show whether these causes were in fact predictive of delinquent behavior. By testing theories in this way, we can build up evidence that they either do or do not explain which youths are delinquent, and how delinquent they are.

The word "theory" can be used to refer to any explanation of delinquency. This general definition is often used by people who work in delinquency programs, and by the general public. The theory may not even be written down in descriptions of the program, or accepted by all program staff. Some theories, however, are carefully explained in scholarly books and articles, and these are formal theories of the type discussed in detail later in this book. Because formal theories are more carefully thought out, explained in writing, tested by research, and criticized and improved by many people, it is possible to make especially sound decisions about their worth as a basis for programs.

The majority of formal theories about delinquency causation have been sociological, psychological, or a combination of these orientations. The sociological approach to crime causation is concerned with the effects the social system or the environment has on the development of attitudes, group patterns of behavior, and other social factors. Translating these broad abstract concepts into variables that can give some indication of how the individual acquires criminal behavior is usually the domain of the psychologist. Theorists who make the connection between abstract general sociological theory and the more specific motivational aspects of psychological theory are called social psychologists. They integrate both social and psychological factors in their theories of crime causation.[12]

It is certainly not always the case that theories which research shows to be

[11]Donna Martin Hamparian, Richard Schuster, Simon Dinitz, and John P. Conrad, *The Violent Few: A Study of Dangerous Juvenile Offenders* (Lexington, Massachusetts: Lexington Books, D. C. Heath and Company, 1978), p. 130.

[12]Donald R. Taft, *Criminology* (New York: Macmillan Publishing Co., Inc., 1956), p. 84. Also Richard R. Korn and Lloyd W. McCorkle, *Criminology and Penology* (New York: Holt, Rinehart and Winston, Inc., 1966), pp. 273–274.

especially predictive of delinquency are the ones used in programs. Because personal beliefs play a large role in influencing the choice of theories, visitors, offenders, and personnel in the juvenile justice system are apt to find that several programs, based on very different theories, affect the lives of most delinquents. Police, for example, divert some juveniles from the court system by releasing them with a warning. The theory behind this action is that the deeper adolescents penetrate into the system, the more they will grow to see themselves as delinquents, and act as delinquents. This is a social-psychological theory, because it identifies the effect of one part of society (the juvenile justice system) on

Exhibit 1-1   Connections between research to describe delinquents, test theories, and evaluate programs

---

Testing Theories and Program Evaluation

Rehabilitation research must be guided by theory. . . . Greater efforts should be made to draw propositions from one of several complementary theories of crime into a causal model, employ that model as a guide in designing intervention strategies, and test the assumptions on which the programs are based.

SOURCE: Susan E. Martin, Lee B. Sechrest, and Robin Redner, eds., *New Directions in the Rehabilitation of Criminal Offenders* (Washington, D.C.: National Academy Press, 1981), p. 23.

Describing Delinquents and Targeting Programs

The overriding perception among many is that juvenile crime has sharply increased; juveniles are committing more serious violent crimes, like robberies and rapes; younger age groups are becoming involved in serious crimes, more females are becoming involved in serious crimes; and juveniles are using weapons more often. . . . These notions are often reflected in the popular media. Moreover, important policy is being introduced on the basis of these notions. . . . The issues stated above regarding juvenile crime are empirical questions and within the limited time frame of the NCS [National Crime Survey] data do *not* support the above.

SOURCE: John H. Laub, *Trends in Juvenile Criminal Behavior in the United States: 1973–1981* (Albany, New York: The Michael J. Hindelang Criminal Justice Research Center, Inc., State University of New York at Albany, 1983), pp. 9–10.

Describing Delinquents and Testing Theory

Our limited knowledge about the volume and distribution of delinquent acts in the American adolescent population has been one of the major stumbling blocks in our efforts to construct and test theories of delinquency and has undermined our efforts to accumulate a sound body of knowledge concerning delinquent behavior.

SOURCE: Delbert S. Elliott, Suzanne S. Ageton, David Huizinga, Brian A. Knowles, and Rachelle J. Canter, *The Prevalence and Incidence of Delinquent Behavior: 1976–1980* (Boulder, Colorado: Behavioral Research Institute, 1983), p. 1.

Issues for Discussion.   How are studies of the patterns of juvenile delinquency, program evaluations, and research to test delinquency theories dependent on each other? If we lack knowledge in one area—that is, on the patterns of delinquency, theory, or program evaluations—how can this mislead us in other areas?

---

adolescents' psychological makeup (adolescents' view of themselves as delinquents) as the cause of delinquency.

In contrast to the diversion approach, police may refer selected offenders to programs where they must pay restitution or work in payment for breaking the law. The theory behind this program is that such punishment will deter offenders, and other people who hear about the punishment, from breaking the law in the future. It would not be unusual to find the diversion- and the punishment-oriented programs operating side by side in the same police jurisdiction, for as theories become more or less popular, there is a tendency to add new and different programs without eliminating existing programs.

Consistent with the approach in this textbook, experts have stressed the important connections between research to describe delinquents, test theories, and evaluate programs (Exhibit 1-1). Understanding the connections is essential to the development of effective control efforts.

What Works?

Even if a program is based on a sound theory, evaluation research can reveal that the program does not work. Programs are considered effective when they accomplish one or more of several objectives, including: reducing recidivism, increasing restitution payment to victims, providing education or job training to offenders, and improving offenders' work records. The importance attached to the different types of objectives is dependent on personal values.

In 1974, an important debate began over whether any programs for offenders achieve the objective of reducing recidivism. Robert Martinson claimed that there were no successful programs for either juvenile or adult offenders.[13] In effect, he said that since the early 1900s, all programs thought to be effective in treating delinquency had failed.

As might be expected, several people strongly disagreed with Martinson. One of the most important arguments against Martinson's conclusion is that programs cannot be expected to be effective with every type of offender. Instead of searching for one perfect program, we should be trying to answer the question, "'Which methods work best for *which* type of offenders and under *what* conditions or in what type of settings?'"[14]

The need to match the offenders with programs has become more and more clear. John T. Whitehead and Steven P. Laub reviewed juvenile correctional treatment research published between 1975 and 1984. They concluded that, indeed, many of the interventions did not appear to "work."[15] However, when D. A. Andrews and his colleagues reviewed a similar set of studies, they reinforced the understanding that programs are effective when they are chosen

---

[13]Robert Martinson, "What Works? Questions and Answers About Prison Reform," *Public Interest, 10,* no. 35 (Spring 1974), pp. 22–54.

[14]Ted Palmer, "Martinson Revisited," *Journal of Research in Crime and Delinquency, 12,* no. 2 (July 1975), p. 150.

[15]John T. Whitehead and Steven P. Laub, "A Meta-Analysis of Juvenile Correctional Treatment," *Journal of Research in Crime and Delinquency, 26,* no. 3 (August 1989), pp. 276–295.

to meet the particular needs and learning styles of selected juvenile offenders.[16] For example, program evaluations show that, although programs designed to intervene with delinquents' families are generally successful, they do not work well with families that are extremely disorganized or if the offenders have extremely disruptive behavior.[17] A combination of several treatment methods may be most effective for some offenders.[18]

Many citizens and juvenile justice personnel are cynical about trying to help juvenile delinquents in special treatment programs. This is partly justified, because some programs are so overcrowded that it is impossible to treat most clients for a long enough time period. Another reason to be cynical is the frequent absence of resources and trained staff to put programs which could be effective into full operation. The popular media image of the dreadful increase in serious juvenile delinquency—even if it is not very accurate—makes taxpayers, police, court staff, and correctional workers alike feel helpless in their efforts to control delinquency. This cynicism has led some people to go along with Martinson, and recommend that we do not try to treat juvenile delinquency. Instead, we should treat delinquents as adults, and punish them for whatever they have done wrong.

Other people have resolved the question in different ways. One solution, which is mentioned above, is to try to figure out which treatment programs work for certain groups of delinquents, and invest the necessary resources to implement these programs. Another solution is to pay particular attention to evaluation studies which show that inexpensive programs are no worse than expensive ones. If a nonresidential program costs less than an institutional program, and it does not lead to increased recidivism, a solution is to choose the nonresidential program.[19] As a third solution, the humaneness of the program can be taken into account instead of cost. Using this approach, one expert concluded that although there was no difference between recidivism for delinquents in institutions and group homes, group homes were better because they provided more humane treatment.[20]

Beliefs About Delinquency

According to Walter Miller, there are two very extreme sets of beliefs which are held about delinquency, and crime in general.[21] He called these ex-

---

[16]D. A. Andrews, Ivan Zinger, Robert D. Hoge, James Bonta, Paul Gendreau, and Francis T. Cullen, "Does Correctional Treatment Work? A Clinically Relevant and Psychologically Informed Meta-Analysis," *Criminology, 28,* no. 3 (August 1990), pp. 369–404.

[17]Paul Gendreau and Bob Ross, "Effective Correctional Treatment: Bibliotherapy for Cynics," *Crime and Delinquency, 25,* no. 4 (October 1979), p. 471.

[18]*Ibid.*

[19]Lee Sechrest, Susan O. White, and Elizabeth D. Brown, eds., *The Rehabilitation of Criminal Offenders: Problems and Prospects* (Washington, D.C.: National Academy of Sciences, 1979), p. 33.

[20]Paul Lerman, "Evaluative Studies of Institutions for Delinquents: Implications for Research and Social Policy," *Social Work, 13,* no. 3 (July 1968), pp. 55–64.

[21]Walter B. Miller, "Ideology and Criminal Justice Policy: Some Current Issues," *Journal of Criminal Law and Criminology, 64,* no. 2 (June 1974), pp. 141–162.

tremes the "right" and the "left," and he wrote that most people have beliefs somewhere in the middle of the extremes. People on the right are concerned about:

1. excessive lenience toward lawbreakers;
2. favoring the welfare and rights of the lawbreakers over the welfare and rights of the victims, of law enforcement officials, and of the law-abiding citizen;
3. erosion of discipline and of respect for authority;
4. the cost of crime;
5. excessive permissiveness.

Along with these concerns, people on the right feel that offenders are responsible for their acts, and are not pushed into crime by unhappy living conditions or psychological illness (Exhibit 1-2). Furthermore, there is a clear guideline for what is acceptable behavior in society, and it is very important that this guideline be followed in order that others may feel safe.

People on the left are concerned about other issues:

1. too many laws, or overcriminalization;
2. unfairly labeling certain groups as offenders, and thereby stigmatizing them;
3. overusing correctional institutions;
4. overcentralization of delinquency control programs;
5. discriminatory bias in arresting, processing in court, and treating delinquents.

People who are on the left favor diversion programs to avoid stigmatizing adolescents and to keep them out of correctional institutions. Because they choose theories in which social conditions, such as poverty, are identified as the causes of delinquency, it seems unfair to punish the delinquents severely. The delinquents are not completely responsible for their actions. Instead, society should be reformed in an effort to prevent crime, and the juvenile justice system should be reformed to be less biased. Exhibit 1-3 presents an example of liberal beliefs about delinquency and its control.

Exhibit 1-2 A view from the right

"To Protect and To Serve." That's what the police role is supposed to be. But to protect and serve just isn't so. The only people protected and served are criminals. They get the breaks, not the victims, not the witnesses, not the good people. Sit in a courtroom sometimes and see who gets fucked around—cases continued, witnesses harassed and insulted, victims made out to be criminals, and plea bargaining. That's the worst! We could catch some dude coming out of a liquor store with a smoking gun in one hand and a bag of money in the other, and he'd walk out of court with ten days suspended for trespassing. Let me ask you, Who gets protected? Who gets served?

The opinion of a police officer, as cited in Robert M. Carter, "The Police View of the Justice System," in *The Juvenile Justice System*, ed. Malcolm W. Klein (Beverly Hills, California: Sage Publications, 1976), p. 122.

Exhibit 1-3 A view from the left

A juvenile may be labeled deviant anytime he/she socially interacts in a way which is disapproved of by society or possesses a characteristic viewed as abnormal by the educational system. . . . (L)abeling a juvenile is self-defeating and stigmatizing and may result in differential treatment by family, friends, and school officials.

Legislators should analyze their state statutes, remove outmoded or unfair laws and replace them with those suggested by the National Advisory Committee.

. . . (A)lternative methods should be developed with which to deal with juveniles accused of noncriminal misbehavior as a prevention measure. While family court jurisdiction over these acts may exist, alternatives to court intervention are to be preferred whenever possible. The acts these juveniles have committed are not crimes and seldom pose a threat to the community. Further, the stigma involved and the exposure to those more sophisticated in criminal activity can make the family court experience a negative one.

Excerpts from National Advisory Committee for Juvenile Justice and Delinquency Prevention, *Standards for the Administration of Juvenile Justice* (Washington, D.C.: U.S. Government Printing Office, 1980), pp. 65, 66, 67.

Traditional Beliefs. During the early periods of American history, delinquents were not believed to differ substantially from adult criminals, and therefore they were treated in the same way as adults, primarily with punishment.[22] By the 1900s, beliefs had changed considerably. As a result of greater urbanization and the emerging scientific theories of delinquency, the public became increasingly aware that youngsters should not be treated like adult offenders or incarcerated with them because of the contamination effect and the children's lack of life experience and lack of maturity.[23] Beliefs about delinquency in 1899 represented a position on the left, for they clearly located the blame for lawbreaking in the child's background, and suggested a nonpunitive approach to handling delinquency:

The conception of the delinquent as a "wayward child" first specifically came to life in April 1899 when the Illinois Legislature passed the Juvenile Court Act creating the first state-wide court especially for children. It did not include a new court; it did include most of the features that have since come to distinguish the juvenile court. The original act and amendments to it that shortly followed brought together under one jurisdiction cases of dependency, neglect and delinquency—the last comprehending incorrigibles and children threatened by immoral associations as well as criminal law breakers. Hearings were to be informal and nonpublic, records confidential, children detained apart from adults, a probation staff appointed. In short, children were not to be treated as criminals nor dealt with by the process used for criminals. A new vocabulary symbolized the new order: Petition instead of complaint, summons instead of warrant, initial

[22]Empey, *American Delinquency*, pp. 39–41.
[23]Robert G. Caldwell, "The Juvenile Court: Its Development and Some Major Problems," in *Juvenile Delinquency, A Book of Readings,* ed. Rose Giallombardo (New York: John Wiley and Sons, Inc., 1966), p. 356.

hearing instead of arraignment, finding of involvement instead of conviction, disposition instead of sentence. The physical surroundings were important, too: they should seem less imposing than a courtroom with the judge at a desk or table instead of behind a bench, fatherly and sympathetic while still authoritative and sobering. The goals were to investigate, diagnose, and prescribe treatment, not to adjudicate guilt or fix blame. The individual's background was more important than the facts of a given incident, specific conduct relevant more as symptomatic of a need for the court to bring its helping powers to bear than as prerequisite to exercise of jurisdiction. Lawyers were unnecessary—adversary tactics were out of place for the mutual aim of all was not to contest or object, but to determine the treatment plan best for the child. That plan was to be devised by the increasingly popular psychologists and psychiatrists: delinquency was thought of almost as a disease to be diagnosed by specialists.[24]

Consistent with the beliefs that delinquents are first and foremost children, and are therefore not fully responsible for their misbehavior, the concept of the juvenile court and the handling of youngsters was taken from the English concept of the role of the king acting as the parent when no parent existed to protect the rights of the child. The concept is better known as *parens patriae:*

> *Parens Patriae,* the state substituting for the king, invested the juvenile court with the power to act as parent for the child. The judge was to assume the fatherly role, protecting the juvenile in order to cure and save him. The juvenile court withheld from the child a procedure of safeguards granted to adults because it viewed him as having a right to custody rather than a right to liberty and juvenile proceedings were civil not criminal.[25]

In many ways, the American courts still perpetuate the concept of *parens patriae. Parens patriae* serves as a rationale for the court's strong intervention with youths who might become seriously delinquent, but who have up to this point committed only status or minor offenses. Numerous delinquency programs are based on the assumed appropriateness of court intervention, and the assumed location of the causes of delinquency in background experiences.

Beginning in 1961, there were a number of legal challenges to the informal, treatment-oriented approach which was a part of juvenile court procedures. In reaching a decision about the first case, *Kent* v. *United States,* the Supreme Court concluded:

> There is much evidence that some juvenile courts . . . lack the personnel, facilities and techniques to perform adequately as representatives of the State in a *parens patriae* capacity, at least with respect to children charged with law violation. There is evidence, in fact, that there may be grounds for concern that the child receives the worst of both worlds: that he gets neither the protections accorded

---

[24]*Task Force Report: Juvenile Delinquency and Youth Crime, Report on Juvenile Justice and Consultants Papers,* President's Commission on Law Enforcement and Administration of Justice (Washington, D.C.: U.S. Government Printing Office, 1967).

[25]Charles E. Reasons, "*Gault:* Procedural Change and Substantive Effort," *Crime and Delinquency, 16,* no. 2 (April 1970).

to adults nor the solicitous care and regenerative treatment postulated for children.[26]

Subsequent to this decision, several other important court findings have extended the due process protections which are normally provided to adults to juveniles.

Despite these legal constraints on the application of the *parens patriae* concept, the belief in this role for the courts remains deeply entrenched in the minds of many people who work within the system. However, other groups have argued for the complete abandonment of these beliefs and, as we have already explained, even for abandonment of all rehabilitation programs within the juvenile justice system.

A Challenge to Traditional Beliefs. Stimulated by the perception that juvenile delinquency is out of control, and impressions that our handling of delinquency is not punitive enough, people with beliefs tending to the right have advocated the handling of many delinquents within the adult court and correctional system, or at least harsher treatment within the juvenile system. Their reasoning is that we cannot and should not rehabilitate the offender within the juvenile justice system, but that we should develop a system of consistent punishments that can deter offenders and other youths from breaking the law.

A 1978 recommendation of a distinguished panel of experts, called the Twentieth Century Fund Task Force on Sentencing Policy Toward Young Offenders, provides one example of views found on the right.[27] The task force recommendations are intended to make the treatment of young offenders in juvenile courts more consistent with handling in adult courts, and to hold young offenders responsible for their actions. Thus, proposed handling of property offenders includes the use of punitive sanctions, such as fines and orders of restitution. Confinement is not recommended for these offenders.[28] For offenders who seriously harm other people, a gradually increasing set of penalties to be used for repeated offenses is recommended. Incarceration is considered to be an appropriate sanction for offenders who seriously threaten or harm others.[29]

There is no way to prove conclusively that some beliefs are better than others. Unlike theories and programs, beliefs are not easily tested by research, for they are reflections of value orientations. It is, however, very important to understand these beliefs, for they can explain the opinions and actions of police, court, and correctional personnel, as well as of different groups in the general public. Understanding your own beliefs can explain why you prefer some theories and programs, and may lead you to examine your preferences against research evaluating these programs.

---

[26]*Kent v. United States*, 383 U.S. 541, 16 L. Ed. 2d 84, 86 S. Ct. 1045 (1966).

[27]Twentieth Century Fund Task Force on Sentencing Policy Toward Young Offenders, *Confronting Youth Crime* (New York: Holmes & Meier Publishers, Inc., 1978).

[28]*Ibid.*, p. 87.

[29]*Ibid.*, pp. 96–98.

THE USE OF RESEARCH

At several points in the discussion of key issues in understanding delinquency, we have referred to the possible use of research in arriving at some resolution to these issues. Given the frequent appearance of fads in juvenile delinquency, and the constant development of new theories and programs, a major theme running through this book is that students must ultimately rely on their own thinking about delinquency. In this process, we stress the use of evidence from research, and every chapter will contain references to important research results.

Three types of research have a direct bearing on understanding delinquency and its control. First, there is descriptive research to provide information on the people who break the law, the types and numbers of offenses they commit, and the juvenile justice system. Second, there is research to test ideas expressed in delinquency theories. The third type is evaluations of programs to see if they bring about the desired results.

Tests of theories and program evaluations both involve attempts to show that delinquency is related to another factor. When theory is the focus, we want to show that the most delinquent youths have been exposed to the supposed causes of delinquency more than other youths. Evaluations try to show that those youths who go to a delinquency program are least delinquent afterward. Just showing that delinquency levels are associated with hypothesized causes or with not participating in certain programs does not prove conclusively that theories are sound or programs are good. It is still possible that something other than the hypothesized cause or the program affected delinquency levels. However, showing that these relationships at least exist is a crucial first step in assessing the worth of theories and programs.

Research results can be inconclusive for a number of other reasons. Delinquent behavior and factors thought to influence delinquency may be poorly measured. As noted earlier in this chapter, the definition of delinquency itself differs among people and at different historical periods. It is not even always possible to determine whether a youth has been exposed to a certain type of program. The youth may not have participated fully, or the program may have never been fully put into operation as intended.

Another common research problem involves sampling. It is intuitively clear that if research conclusions are based on a very small sample, even of one or two people, we will never know whether anything discovered is typical in a larger group. Furthermore, samples must always be taken so that there is a maximum chance that the people in the sample, and therefore in the study, are similar to those we want to consider in developing a sound theory or making a program recommendation.

Based on criticisms of previous research, new studies try to correct problems of measurement and sampling. Once such difficulties are reduced to a minimum, replications of the same research in different settings and with different samples make it possible to have considerable confidence in research results.

In order to encourage the best research possible, a panel of experts at

Exhibit 1-4 Guidelines for research on intervention

1. Rehabilitation research must be guided by theory.
2. Intervention programs and research should be developed jointly as a coordinated activity designed to test detailed theoretical propositions explicitly.
3. Intervention programs must be designed for and tested with a theoretically suggested, clearly specified target population.
4. In assessing any intervention program, the strength of the intervention should be systematically varied and evaluated.
5. The integrity with which an intervention program's intended activities or components are implemented must be carefully examined.
6. The timing of interventions in terms of the age and stage in the criminal career of the program client population requires further study.
7. A new strategy of search is needed to determine what interventions might work. The stages include (1) an initial program formulation, development, pilot testing, and modification phase; (2) a fuller test as a field experiment; (3) further modification and replication of the experimental model at the initial test site; and (4) replication under modified conditions at several additional sites.
8. Rehabilitation research must test interventions developed at multiple loci of interventions: the family, the school, the workplace, and the community, as well as the individual.

SOURCE: Susan E. Martin, Lee B. Sechrest, and Robin Redner, eds., *New Directions in the Rehabilitation of Criminal Offenders* (Washington, D.C.: National Academy Press, 1981), pp. 23–26.

Issues for Discussion. How can an intervention be "too weak" to prevent or correct delinquency? Why might a program be put into effect in a different way than originally intended? Why would some programs be more effective at the beginning of an adolescent's involvement in delinquency than when the adolescent has become a serious, repeat offender? What conditions might prevent a program that works with one group of offenders at one place from working with other youths in a different place? Why is a program with multiple interventions (family, school, and so on) most likely to be effective?

the National Science Foundation has established guidelines for research. The experts go beyond issues like sampling and measurement and recommend integrated study of target populations, theory, and programs (Exhibit 1-4).

AN EXAMPLE—DELINQUENTS, THEORY, PROGRAMS, AND BELIEFS

An example shows the need to know the distinction between how seriously delinquent an adolescent is, and the fact that he or she is classified as needing to attend a delinquency program. In the case presented here, it is possible to identify the theory underlying the program, the degree to which the program worked, and beliefs which would lead some people to use the program. Additionally, information from research on theory and to evaluate the program is described. This approach to thinking about juvenile delinquency and its control—an approach involving considering the four key issues emphasized in this chapter—can be applied to understanding the large number of delinquency theories and programs currently used in American society.

Juvenile Awareness Project Help

In 1976, the Lifers Group of offenders at Rahway State Prison began a program to control juvenile delinquency. This program was called the Juvenile Awareness Project Help (JAPH), and it was based on the idea that if youths knew the severity of imprisonment, they would not break the law.

Youngsters in JAPH were taken to a secure, adult prison where the "lifers" gave them a tour of the austere facility and discussed living conditions there. During the discussion, they learned about the high probability of being physically attacked, beaten, humiliated, and raped by other prisoners. The lifers spoke in frank, often profane, language about their experiences, and they sometimes verbally threatened the youths.

At a time when the media was proclaiming that juvenile crime was out of control, and it was increasingly becoming clear that there is no simple solution to delinquency, many people liked the idea of JAPH. The program was copied in a number of places. Even as it was adopted by others, research began to show that its effects were not as positive as hoped. In fact, one study of JAPH showed program participants were not particularly delinquent to start with and, once exposed to the program, they became more delinquent.[30]

Other research, not directly on the JAPH Program, has raised serious doubts about whether raising expectations of the serious consequences of breaking the law does reduce delinquency. It seems that youths who are likely to break the law know the consequences, but they assume that they will not be caught.[31]

Questions. How would you explain the popularity of the JAPH program? What explanation for delinquency seems to underlie the program? What arguments, based on beliefs, theories, and research, would convince someone to use this program? What arguments would convince someone not to use the program? What additional research in the area of theory, and of the program evaluation type, could be done to further our understanding of the JAPH program?

SUMMARY

The field of juvenile delinquency is marked by the simultaneous use of many different theories and programs, and by a tendency to adopt fads in the control

[30]*Scared Straight: A Second Look* (1337 22nd Street, N.W., Washington, D.C.: National Center on Institutions and Alternatives, 1980).

[31]Gary F. Jensen, Maynard L. Erickson, and Jack P. Gibbs, "Perceived Risk of Punishment and Self-Reported Delinquency," *Social Forces, 57,* no. 1 (September 1978), 57–78.

of delinquency. By considering four key issues, we have set the stage for reaching sound conclusions about theories and programs. The material we have presented shows that it is essential to have an accurate picture of who the delinquents are. Second, we must base programs on theories which are supported by research results. Third, evaluation research also is useful in determining which programs are most worthwhile. Finally, beliefs about juvenile delinquency exert a strong influence on how we picture and react to adolescents who break the law. Beliefs frequently outweigh research results in shaping ideas.

DISCUSSION QUESTIONS

1. What kinds of information would convince you that one delinquency program is better than another?
2. Explain why we do not have just one or two programs for delinquents, but a combination of many, sometimes conflicting, programs.
3. What questions about delinquency theory and programs can be answered through research?
4. At this time, are delinquency programs consistent with beliefs on the right or the left? Explain your answer.
5. How would you evaluate the "new reform" efforts to replace large institutions with a combination of small, secure programs for violent offenders and structured, community programs for nonviolent offenders?

PROJECTS

1. Locate a description of a delinquency problem or program in a newspaper or magazine. Identify the kinds of youths assumed to be most delinquent, the theories behind the programs, and the type of programs suggested. To what extent do beliefs and research results seem to be important?
2. Interview people who work with delinquents, such as police, court personnel, and social workers. Describe the way in which their beliefs about delinquency seem to influence how they picture the delinquent, the theories they favor, and the programs they like.
3. Locate several articles or books that evaluate programs for juvenile delinquents. Use the guidelines in Exhibit 1-4 to assess the quality of the evaluations. When you consider the highest-quality evaluations, which programs are most promising?

Delinquents In and Out of the Juvenile Justice System

- SOURCES OF INFORMATION
- OFFICIAL CONTACTS WITH THE SYSTEM
- TYPICAL DELINQUENTS
- SPECIAL GROUPS
- TRENDS AND REGIONAL DIFFERENCES

LEARNING OBJECTIVES

1. To be aware that the term "delinquent" has several definitions which vary in different types of research.
2. To be able to describe official records, the *National Crime Survey* of victims, and self-report studies as sources of information about delinquency.
3. To know the typical patterns of American adolescents' experiences with police and courts, and differences in the pattern of contacts of minor, violent, and chronic offenders.
4. To be aware of patterns of delinquency for special groups of offenders, specifically status offenders, drug users, gang members, and violent offenders.
5. To know which youths are most likely to be involved in various kinds of delinquency, and to be arrested, sent to court, and committed to institutions or other residential programs.
6. To be familiar with research on trends in delinquency, and on regional differences.
7. Based on research results, to be able to draw sound conclusions about which youths are most delinquent.

In Chapter 1, we provided a legal definition of *delinquent behavior,* and pointed out that this definition is not set, but is open to question and change. The definition of a *juvenile delinquent* is even less set, and it varies considerably from person to person. Some visualize juvenile delinquents as any children who have ever broken the law. Thus, they would classify the majority of adolescents as delinquents. Perhaps more common, the term juvenile delinquent can refer to youths who repeatedly commit serious offenses. Status offenders and minor offenders would be in a different category. In a third use of the term, juvenile delinquents are youths with an official police or court record.

For a number of reasons, it is essential to specify clearly whom we are talking about when we speak of juvenile delinquents. As emphasized in Chapter 1, we design programs to treat those youths whom we feel are the delinquents. Likewise, we develop theories to explain their behavior.

In developing a profile of the behavior of delinquent youths, we will rely on a number of research studies. Taken as a whole, these studies suggest that it is misleading to define juvenile delinquents as one homogeneous group. Instead, it seems that there is a large group of youths who occasionally commit minor offenses, and small groups who stand out as status, repeat, or violent offenders.

Sources of Information

There are three major sources of information on juvenile delinquents and their behavior. First, official statistics are available on the number of youths arrested, processed through juvenile court, and committed to institutions and other programs. These records are maintained by local police and courts, though in some cases they are summarized to provide a national picture. For example, local police departments send information on arrests and crimes reported to the FBI, where they are summarized in the Uniform Crime Reports. In a similar way, the local courts send reports to the National Center for Juvenile Justice, and these reports are summarized in an annual report of Juvenile Court Statistics.

Official statistics tell us who has been arrested and, subsequent to the arrest, what decisions are made about these youths. Specific decisions that can be made are to forward the case to a formal court hearing or to divert it out of the system, to determine that the child is delinquent or for some other reason should be under the supervision of the court, and to determine that youths under the jurisdiction of the courts should be on probation or in a residential program. Official statistics provide information about the movement of youths into, through, and out of the juvenile justice system.

A second source of information is the *National Crime Survey* of victims, in which a sampling of the people who live in selected cities are asked to report on situations when they were the victim of some offense. The victimization surveys tell us little about property offenders, because victims often have no idea of who stole or damaged their belongings. However, victims are asked to estimate the ages of offenders who have assaulted, robbed, or raped them. The victimization

Exhibit 2-1   Severity scores for different offenses

72.1 A person plants a bomb in a public building. The bomb explodes and 20 people are killed.

47.8 A parent beats his young child with his fists. As a result, the child dies.

35.7 A person robs a victim at gunpoint. The victim struggles and is shot to death.

24.8 A person intentionally shoots a victim with a gun. The victim requires hospitalization.

20.6 A person sells heroin to others for resale.

17.9 A person robs a victim of $10 at gunpoint. The victim is wounded and requires hospitalization.

17.5 A high school boy beats an elderly woman with his fists. She requires hospitalization.

15.9 A teenage boy beats his mother with his fists. The mother requires hospitalization.

11.7 Ten high school boys beat a male classmate with their fists. He requires hospitalization.

11.3 Three high school boys beat a male classmate with their fists. He requires hospitalization.

 8.8 A person sells marijuana to others for resale.

 7.9 A teenage boy beats his father with his fists. The father requires hospitalization.

 5.7 A theater owner knowingly shows pornographic movies to a minor.

 4.9 A person snatches a handbag containing $10 from a victim on the street.

 1.7 A person under 16 years old is drunk in public.

 1.6 A male, over 16 years of age, has sexual relations with a willing female under 16.

 1.4 A person smokes marijuana.

 1.1 A group continues to hang around a corner after being told to break up by a police officer.

 1.1 A person under 16 years old illegally has a bottle of wine.

 0.9 A person under 16 years old is reported to police by his parents as an offender because they are unable to control him.

 0.8 A person under 16 years old runs away from home.

 0.7 A person under 16 years old breaks a curfew law by being out on the street after the hour permitted by law.

 0.2 A person under 16 years old plays hooky from school.

SOURCE: Patsy Klaus and Carol B. Kalish, ''The Severity of Crime,'' *Bureau of Justice Statistics Bulletin* (Washington, D.C.: U.S. Department of Justice, 1984), pp. 2–4.

surveys estimate the proportion of violent offenses committed by youths as opposed to adults.

Self-report studies of delinquency are a third source of information. For these, a sample of adolescents are asked to report how frequently they have broken the law within some set length of time—for example, within the last year. Researchers have shown that self-report delinquency study results are quite reliable when checked against official records, reports of friends and relatives, and polygraph ("lie detector") tests.[1] Self-report studies tell us the frequency with which youths break different types of laws, and they tell us the prevalence of law breaking—that is, the proportion of youth who have broken the law at all. The information is not dependent on whether the youths were caught by the police, or on the decisions of police or court personnel.

[1]Lamar T. Empey, *American Delinquency: Its Meaning and Construction* (Homewood, Illinois: The Dorsey Press, 1978), pp. 141–166.

Seriousness of Delinquent Behavior

In a major contribution to making descriptive studies of the amount and nature of delinquent behavior meaningful, Marvin Wolfgang and Thorsten Sellin ranked delinquent acts according to seriousness.[2] They developed seriousness scores so that offenses could easily be compared on how much loss, damage, or personal injury resulted. The opinions of different groups in the society were taken into account in deciding how high a score to give each type of offense. Since Wolfgang and Sellin developed the idea of seriousness scores, increasingly sophisticated studies have been done to develop weighting schemes (Exhibit 2-1).

No source of information, and no scheme for ranking offenses by seriousness, can answer all questions about delinquency. However, by keeping in mind the type of information provided by each source, and the need to consider the seriousness of offenses, it is possible to develop a reasonably accurate picture of delinquents and their illegal activities. As you read the research results presented below, compare the image that emerges of the delinquent with the picture in media accounts, as well as with your own opinion.

DELINQUENTS IN THE JUVENILE JUSTICE SYSTEM

The Uniform Crime Reports

There is no doubt that a large amount of police effort is expended on the juvenile offender, and this is reflected by the Uniform Crime Reports. Police consider an offense cleared "when at least one person is arrested, charged with the commission of the offense, and turned over to the court for prosecution."[3] Clearance statistics are presented in Table 2-1. Of the offenses cleared in 1989, 20.3 percent of property crimes and 9.5 percent of violent crimes involved a juvenile. The violent offenses of robbery, aggravated assault, and forcible rape involved juveniles somewhat more often than did the offense of murder, for which 6.8 percent of cleared cases involved a juvenile. Over one third of arson cases cleared involved a juvenile.[4] This information about clearance rates provides an accurate picture of the types of juvenile cases handled by police and of police workload, and shows that police expend considerable effort on serious juvenile delinquency.

[2]Thorsten Sellin and Marvin E. Wolfgang, *The Measurement of Delinquency* (New York: John Wiley and Sons, Inc., 1964).

[3]*Crime in the United States, 1989* (Washington, D.C.: U.S. Government Printing Office, 1990), p. 169.

[4]*Ibid.,* p. 163.

Table 2-1   Victims' Reports of Personal Crimes of Violence, 1988, Percent Distribution of Multiple-offender Victimizations, by Type of Crime and Perceived Age of Offender.

	TOTAL	ALL UNDER 12	ALL 12 TO 20	ALL 21 AND OLDER	MIXED AGES	NOT KNOWN AND NOT AVAILABLE
Crimes of violence (1,444,450)	100.0%	0.4%[a]	38.9%	23.3%	29.4%	7.9%
Rape (9,630)	100.0[a]	0.0[a]	0.0[a]	0.0[a]	57.8[a]	42.2[a]
Robbery (454,710)	100.0	0.4[a]	39.8	28.0	24.7	7.1
Assault (980,190)	100.0	0.4[a]	38.9	21.3	31.4	8.0
Aggravated assault (441,750)	100.0	0.5[a]	38.4	21.3	29.9	10.0
Simple assault (538,440)	100.0	0.3[a]	39.4	21.4	32.6	6.4

Note: Detail may not add to total shown because of rounding. Number of victimizations shown in parentheses.
[a]Estimate, based on zero or on about 10 or fewer sample cases, is statistically unreliable.
Source: From *Criminal Victimization in the U. S., 1988* (Washington, D. C.: U. S. Government Printing Office, 1990), Table 47.

Juvenile Court Statistics

In 1987, courts with jurisdiction over juveniles handled an estimated 1,145,000 delinquency cases.[5] This means that for every 1,000 children aged 10 through 17, the courts handled 44.4 delinquency cases. Males were involved in most (80 percent) of the cases, and white youths were involved in 71 percent of the cases.

When the most serious charge is considered, the majority of cases involved a property offense (59 percent). Fewer cases involved a public order offense (19 percent), a person offense (16 percent), or a drug law violation (6 percent).[6] For both whites and nonwhites, the majority of cases involved a property offense, though nonwhites were somewhat more involved in person offenses than were whites.

Given that white youth make up 81 percent of the juvenile population, they were slightly underrepresented in the delinquency cases.* In contrast, nonwhite youth were overrepresented, particularly among the youngest juveniles and for delinquency involving drug law violations or offenses against people.

Not only are nonwhite youth more likely to have contact with juvenile courts, but also their cases are more often handled formally or waived to criminal court; they are more often detained; and, once adjudicated, they are most

[5]Howard N. Snyder, Terrence A. Finnegan, Ellen H. Nimick, Melissa H. Sickmund, Dennis P. Sullivan, and Nancy J. Tierney, *Juvenile Court Statistics: 1987* (Pittsburgh, Pennsylvania: National Center for Juvenile Justice, 1990), p. 5.

[6]*Ibid.*

*For most court jurisdictions, the majority of Hispanic youth are included in the white category.

likely to be placed outside of the home.[7] Some of the court statistics suggest that bias at least partially explains the more serious handling of nonwhite youth. For example, the 1987 estimates show that 21 percent of white youth and 48 percent of non-white youth charged with drug law violations were detained.[8] Chapter 6, Handling the Juvenile Delinquent within the Juvenile Justice System, will examine in some detail the issue of bias. Based on just the court statistics, however, we can conclude that minority juveniles are experiencing a disproportionate amount of the most serious reaction of the juvenile justice system.

Turning now to status offenses, in 1987 the juvenile courts handled an estimated 81,000 cases.[9] Status offenses are offenses that only apply to juveniles, and they include such behaviors as truancy and running away. Whereas racial differences were most pronounced for delinquency cases, the sex difference is pronounced for status offense cases. Compared with the much greater involvement of boys in delinquency cases, the number of cases involving girls and boys was more similar, with just under 60 percent of status offense cases involving boys. However, there were sex differences in the types of status offenses. Boys were more highly involved in liquor law violations, and girls with runaway incidents. Girls were more likely to be detained and placed outside of the home, apparently because they were more often runaways.

In addition to the insight provided by annual statistics on court cases, a recent study of youth born between 1962 and 1965 and referred to juvenile courts in Arizona and Utah is helping us to understand which youth are most likely to return to court, and who we should therefore target for intensive intervention efforts.[10] Youth who were first referred to juvenile court for burglary, truancy, incorrigibility, arson, motor vehicle theft, or robbery are most likely to return. Those initially referred for shoplifting, running away, and liquor offenses are least likely to return. (See Figure 2-1.)

In general, juvenile offenders who return to court are quite "versatile"— that is, they often come back for different offenses.[11] However, there is some specialization over time, especially after several returns and for certain status offenses, drug and alcohol offenses, and the property offenses of burglary and motor vehicle theft.

---

[7]Howard N. Snyder, *Court Careers of Juvenile Offenders* (Pittsburgh, Pennsylvania: National Center for Juvenile Justice, 1988).

[8]*Ibid.*, p. 9.

[9]Snyder, Finnegan, Nimick, Sickmund, Sullivan, and Tierney, *Juvenile Court Statistics: 1987*, p. 5.

[10]Howard N. Snyder, *Court Careers of Juvenile Offenders* (Pittsburgh, Pennsylvania: National Center for Juvenile Justice, 1988).

[11]David P. Farrington, Howard N. Snyder, and Terrence A. Finnegan, "Specialization in Juvenile Court Careers," *Criminology, 26,* no. 3 (August 1988).

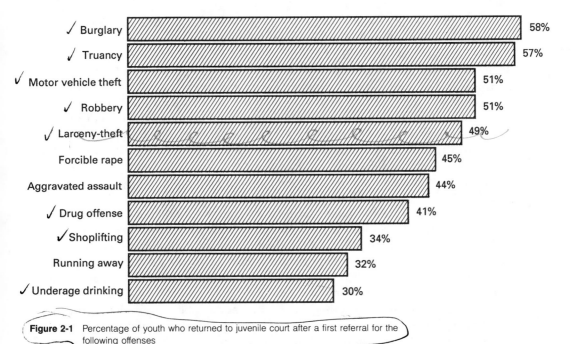

Figure 2-1   Percentage of youth who returned to juvenile court after a first referral for the
following offenses

Source: Office of Juvenile Justice and Delinquency Prevention, "Study Sheds New Light on Court Careers of Juvenile
Offenders," *OJJDP Update on Research* (August 1988), p. 3.

Survey of Youth in Custody

By the mid 1980s, on an average day 83,402 juveniles were in over 3,000
public and over 1,000 private juvenile facilities.[12] The typical offender being
held was male, white, non-Hispanic, between 14 and 17 years old, and had
committed a delinquent offense as opposed to a status offense.

For the juveniles held in long-term, state-operated institutions, the majority were involved in a property offense (45.6 percent), but many had also
committed a violent offense (39.3 percent).[13] Small proportions had committed a
drug offense (5.6 percent), public-order offense (7.2 percent), or a status offense
(just over 2 percent). Many had a history of repeated arrests, probation, and
commitments. Particularly for the youth in institutions, a history of repeated
serious offenses is common, characterizing 80 percent of those housed.[14]

[12]Office of Justice Programs, *Children in Custody, 1975–1985* (Washington, D.C.: Bureau of
Justice Statistics, 1989).

[13]*1989 Survey of Youths in Custody, Codebook* (Ann Arbor, Michigan: Criminal Justice Archives, 1990).

[14]Stephen A. Cernkovich, Peggy C. Giordano, and Meredith D. Pugh, "Chronic Offenders: The Missing Cases in Self-report Delinquency Research," *Journal of Crime and Criminology, 76,* no. 4 (Fall 1985), pp. 705–732.

There are some clear differences between the programs provided in public facilities, which include most of the long-term institutions and which are state operated, and private facilities, which are operated by nonprofit or for-profit organizations, usually with some contractual payment from the state.[15] Youth in public facilities are generally in training schools (51 percent) or in detention centers (28 percent), whereas those in private facilities are most often in halfway houses or group homes (53 percent) or at ranches, forestry camps, or farms (24 percent). As might be expected, the public facilities often have institutional environments with large (over 100) offender populations. Private facilities generally house small numbers in an open environment. Nearly 20 percent of the public facilities are overcrowded, in contrast to the 2 percent of private facilities.

The private and public facilities also differ in the types of youths served. Public facilities hold more of the delinquent youths, and private facilities house more of the status offenders. Given the high proportion of girls who are status offenders, more of them are in private facilities. Also, the private facilities have a higher concentration of white youth, leaving the public institutions to serve more of the black and the delinquent offenders.

It is not known whether the concentration of black offenders in the more restrictive institutions is fully explained by their greater delinquency. Given the more severe sanctioning of nonwhite offenders by the courts that we discussed above, it is possible that there is some racial bias. Even if there is little or no bias, there is still a question about whether the concentration of nonwhite offenders in the most institutional settings meets their needs for correction and, more generally, their developmental needs as adolescents.

States vary dramatically in the number of youths in custody. In 1985, in the District of Columbia, 684 youth for every 100,000 juveniles in the population were in a juvenile facility. In the same year, for West Virginia, just 107 youth for every 100,000 juveniles were in custody. The extreme differences between states would be expected if there were a related difference in crime rates, but this was not the case. Instead, the major explanatory factor appears to be the number of bed spaces available for detention and training school placement: Regardless of crime rates, youths living in states where detention and training school facilities are available will tend to be confined. Policy researchers have coined the phrase "justice by geography" to reflect the seeming injustice of a system with so much inequity.

The national statistical summaries that we have reviewed reveal the numbers of juvenile cases which police, courts, and correctional programs handle. Who are these youths who come into contact with the system? Do all adolescents have a few police contacts, or are the numbers high because a small group

---

[15]The following statistics on youth in custody are based on the publication, Office of Justice Programs, *Children in Custody, 1975–1985* (Washington, D.C.: Bureau of Justice Statistics, 1989).

are repeatedly arrested? Studies of birth cohorts and offenders' career patterns provide answers to these questions.

Birth Cohort Research

A *birth cohort* is a group of people who were born during the same year. Some juvenile delinquency research has provided descriptions of the number of police or court contacts by adolescents in one or more birth cohorts, and in at least one study, this information was supplemented with interviews once cohort members reached adulthood.

Marvin Wolfgang, Robert Figlio, and Thorsten Sellin provided detailed information about a birth cohort of all boys born in Philadelphia in 1945.[16] Each of the boys had lived in the city from the age of seven to eighteen. The research team gathered information on each boy from police and public school records. Of the total of 9,945 boys, 3,475 had a record of at least one police contact. These boys were responsible for 10,214 separate offenses known to the police. Nonwhites and youths from the lower-socioeconomic-class neighborhoods had three times as many police contacts as did others. They were also more likely to have a record for a violent offense. A much smaller group of 1,862 boys had committed 84 percent of the offenses, that is, 8,501 offenses.

An additional finding about the 1945 cohort is that the chronic juvenile offenders often become repeat and serious adult offenders. The chronic juvenile offenders made up 70 percent of the group that persisted in being involved with the justice system in both their adolescent and adult years. Thus, there was a clear tendency for the chronic juvenile offenders to be arrested repeatedly and for serious crimes when they became adults.

When the youths involved in the 1945 cohort study were age 26, a sample of them were located and interviewed face-to-face. The interview results allow for a unique comparison of official and self-report data, as well as special insights provided by the interviews themselves. Juvenile offenders who persisted in their illegal activity once they became adults tended to be from socially disadvantaged groups, a finding that suggests the importance of theories that explain why disadvantaged offenders break the law.[17] The age group most frequently involved in illegal activity was 16, and though racial and social class groups were similar in the number of delinquent acts, nonwhites reported more serious and violent offenses. As other research has shown, juvenile offenders did not seem to specialize in one type of delinquency, and they "committed their offenses in a rather spontaneous, unplanned fashion, with the support of others, especially if they were gang members."[18] The importance of interventions that address the

---

[16]Marvin E. Wolfgang, Robert M. Figlio, and Thorsten Sellin, *Delinquency in a Birth Cohort* (Chicago: University of Chicago Press, 1972).

[17]Marvin E. Wolfgang, Terence P. Thornberry, Robert M. Figlio, *From Boy to Man, From Delinquency to Crime* (Chicago: The University of Chicago Press, 1987), p. 196.

[18]*Ibid.*, p. 200.

community environment of the adolescent is suggested by the finding that the serious offender's "world appears to be characterized by almost random involvement in criminality, moving from one type of offense to another, without plan or design, being predator one day, prey the next."[19]

Results from a larger Philadelphia cohort of 13,811 males and 14,527 females born in 1958 confirms the earlier findings that chronic delinquents are few in number but commit a large proportion of the total crime.[20] Unlike the earlier study, the work on the 1958 cohort includes females, and it shows that very few (1 percent) of girls were chronic offenders with repeated contact with the juvenile justice system. Even among the chronic female offenders, serious crimes were rare. As in the earlier research, blacks were most likely to be delinquent, especially when assaultive offenses are considered. The 1958 cohort was generally more violent than the 1945 group, for they were more violently recidivistic at an early age, and they generally committed more Index Offenses (murder or non-negligent manslaughter, forcible rape, robbery, aggravated assault, burglary, larceny-theft, motor vehicle theft) before age 18. Taken together, the Philadelphia studies show that there is a persistent tendency for a small group of chronic male offenders to commit a large proportion of the serious juvenile crimes.

Another cohort study focused specifically on violent offenders in Columbus, Ohio.[21] Eight hundred eleven of the boys in the birth cohorts born between 1956 and 1958 had committed at least one violent offense. During their adolescence, youths in this birth cohort had police records of 3,393 offenses, but only 985 of these involved violent offenses. The vast majority (83 percent) of the youths who had a record of one violent offense were not rearrested for another violent act. Just over 12 percent were arrested twice, and just under 4 percent were arrested three or more times. Based on their findings, the researchers questioned the idea that juveniles are violent "monsters":

> The youthful monster idea is just that. For three birth cohorts of violent offenders, (811 subjects in all), just 22 youths could be classed as unusually violent, that is, media monsters.[22]

However, they do identify another problem group of teenagers:

[19]*Ibid.*, p. 201.

[20]Marvin E. Wolfgang, "Delinquency in Two Birth Cohorts," in *Prospective Studies of Crime and Delinquency,* eds. Katherine Teilmann Van Dusen and Sarnoff A. Mednick (Boston: Kluwer-Nijhoff, 1983), pp. 7–16.

[21]Donna Martin Hamparian, Richard Schuster, Simon Dinitz, and John P. Conrad, *The Violent Few: A Study of Dangerous Juvenile Offenders* (Lexington, Massachusetts: Lexington Books, D. C. Heath and Company, 1978).

[22]Simon Dinitz and John P. Conrad, "The Dangerous Two Percent," in *Critical Issues in Juvenile Delinquency,* eds. David Shichor and Delos H. Kelly (Lexington, Massachusetts: Lexington Books, D. C. Heath and Company, © 1980), p. 151.

The shortage of monsters is more than compensated by the large proportion of chronic offenders (272 of the 811), many of whom became chronic (five or more arrests) before reaching their fourteenth birthday.[23]

In both the Philadelphia and Columbus cohort studies, these chronic offenders were from the poorest, predominantly black areas. The overrepresentation of blacks can be explained as a result of their more constant exposure to socioeconomic conditions which result in crime, or of discriminatory arrest procedures.[24]

Delinquent and Criminal Careers

For some time, criminologists have recognized that the majority of offenders "peak" in their delinquent activities some time after age sixteen, and they do not become adult offenders. Arrest rates for property offenses fall off just after age sixteen, and then even more after seventeen and eighteen.[25]

Recidivism studies similarly show that people are rearrested less often once they become adults.[26] Moreover, self-report studies show that recruitment to delinquency becomes less common once individuals reach adulthood.[27] Though some of these tendencies may result from a police bias to arrest youths but not adults, this is unlikely for serious offenses. Several sources of information indicate that adolescents are truly more likely to break the law than adults.

DELINQUENTS DESCRIBED BY VICTIMS

Surveys of victims do not provide information about property offenders, since the victims frequently do not know who has stolen or damaged their belongings. However, they do give us some insight into violent crimes.

Of lone-offender violent victimizations, just under one-third (28 percent) are committed by people whom victims estimate to be between twelve and twenty.[28] Tables 2-2 and 2-3 summarize some of the information provided by victims about violent crimes in 1988. According to the victims, when there is just

[23]*Ibid.*, p. 151.

[24]Don C. Gibbons, *Society, Crime, and Criminal Careers: An Introduction to Criminology*, 3rd ed. (Englewood Cliffs, New Jersey: Prentice-Hall, Inc., 1977), pp. 116–117.

[25]Daniel Glaser, *Crime in Our Changing Society* (New York: Holt, Rinehart and Winston, Inc., 1978), p. 163.

[26]Wolfgang, Figlio, and Sellin, *Delinquency in a Birth Cohort*, 1972; Sheldon Glueck and Eleanor Glueck, *Later Criminal Careers* (New York: The Commonwealth Fund, 1937); and Daniel Glaser, *The Effectiveness of a Prison and Parole System* (Indianapolis: The Bobbs-Merrill Co., Inc., 1964), pp. 469–474.

[27]David F. Greenberg, "Delinquency and the Age Structure of Society," *Contemporary Crisis, 1*, no. 2 (April 1977), pp. 189–223.

[28]*Criminal Victimization in the U.S., 1988* (Washington, D.C.: U.S. Government Printing Office, 1990), Table 40.

Table 2-2 Victims' Reports of Personal Crimes of Violence, 1988, Percent Distribution of Lone Offender Victimizations, by Type of Crime and Perceived Age of Offender

| | | *PERCEIVED AGE OF LONE OFFENDER* | | | | | | |
| | | | *12–20* | | | | *21 and Over* | *Not Known and Not Available* |
Type of Crime	*Total*	*Under 12*	*Total*	*12–14*	*15–17*	*18–20*		
Crimes of violence (4,326,370)	100.0%	0.7%	27.8%	5.6%	10.0%	12.2%	67.8%	3.6%
Rape (115,820)	100.0	0.0ª	8.5ª	0.0ª	3.3ª	5.2ª	88.3	3.3ª
Robbery (568,510)	100.0	0.4ª	32.4	5.3	11.8	15.3	63.2	4.9
Assault (3,642,040)	100.0	0.8	27.8	5.8	10.0	11.9	68.1	3.4
Aggravated assault (1,238,200)	100.0	1.4	24.7	4.4	7.7	12.6	68.9	4.9
Simple assault (2,403,840)	100.0	0.5ª	29.3	6.6	11.1	11.6	67.6	2.6

Note: Detail may not add to total shown because of rounding. Number of victimizations shown in parentheses.

ªEstimate, based on zero or on about 10 or fewer sample cases, is statistically unreliable.

Source: From *Criminal Victimization in the U. S., 1988* (Washington, D. C.: U. S. Government Printing Office, 1990), Table 40.

Table 2-3   Number of Arrests per 100,000 Youth between 1970 and 1988

TYPE OF CRIME	ARRESTS					
	1965	1970	1975	1980	1985	1988
All types crime	3,354	4,150	5,244	4,865	4,334	4,490
Violent crime	304	460	616	638	568	613
Males	564	838	1,102	1,130	999	1,068
Females	36	67	114	125	118	135

Source: *Age-Specific Arrest Rates and Race-Specific Arrest Rates for Selected Offenses, 1965–1988*. Uniform Crime Reporting Program, FBI. 1990 American Statistical Index Microfiche 6224-7.

one offender, people aged twelve to seventeen commit 3.3 percent of all rapes, 17.1 percent of all robberies, and 15.8 percent of the reported assaults.[29] For the incidents that involve more than one offender, youths commit somewhat higher proportions of the violent crimes, reflecting a tendency for youths to break the law in groups more often than do adults.

The *National Crime Survey* of victims has provided information that is useful in explaining the discrepancy between official arrest statistics, which show black youths to be more seriously delinquent than others, and self-report surveys, which show few racial differences. It is possible that the arrest statistics reflect official bias rather than greater delinquency among blacks, or that the self-report studies are inaccurate due to the types of questions asked or the propensity of study participants to distort the truth. The survey of victims provides support for the official statistics, not the self-report studies. Black males, age eighteen to twenty, have the highest rate of committing violent offenses according to victim reports.[30] This finding does not mean that there is no bias in the juvenile justice system, but rather that any bias cannot completely explain why blacks are disproportionately represented in the official statistics. Also, it is most likely not race *per se* that is the cause of high delinquency rates, but the lower socioeconomic class and lack of opportunities associated with being of that class.

DELINQUENTS DESCRIBE THEMSELVES

Because not all delinquents are arrested, and victims do not always know the age of the assailants, self-report studies provide valuable descriptive information about delinquents and their behavior. Self-reported information can be collected through written questionnaires or through face-to-face interviews. Examples of the types of questions that might be asked are shown in Exhibit 2-2.

[29]*Ibid.*, p. 46.

[30]Michael J. Hindelang, "Variations in Sex-Race-Age Specific Incidence Rates of Offending," *American Sociological Review*, 46, no. 4 (August 1981), pp. 461–474.

Exhibit 2-2   Five questions from the *National Youth Survey*

	Once a Month	Once Every 2–3 Weeks	Once a Week	2–3 Times a Week	Once a Day	2–3 Times a Day
How many times in the *last year* have you:						
1. attacked someone with the idea of seriously hurting or killing him or her?	1	2	3	4	5	6
2. been paid for having sexual relations with someone?	1	2	3	4	5	6
3. used checks illegally or used phony money to pay for something? (includes intentional overdrafts)	1	2	3	4	5	6
4. sold marijuana or hashish? ("pot," "grass," "hash")	1	2	3	4	5	6
5. cheated on school tests?	1	2	3	4	5	6

SOURCE: Delbert S. Elliott, Suzanne S. Ageton, David Huizinga, Brian A. Knowles, and Rachelle J. Canter, *The Prevalence and Incidence of Delinquent Behavior: 1976–1980* (Boulder, Colorado: Behavioral Research Institute, 1983), pp. 540–544.

In one of the first self-report studies to rely on in-depth interviews, Martin Gold and his colleagues surveyed a sample of adolescents in Flint, Michigan.[31] Since Martin Gold's groundbreaking effort to provide an accurate picture of delinquency, the federal government has funded a major project, *The National Youth Survey Project,* to obtain self-report information from a representative national sample. Beginning in 1976, a large sample of youths, chosen to represent American adolescents nationwide, were asked to self-report their delinquency for five consecutive years. The large sample, the inclusion of youths during all of the adolescent years, and developments in the measurement techniques make the *National Youth Survey* an important addition to our information about delinquency.

According to the *National Youth Survey,* a majority of American youth between eleven and seventeen years old in 1976 admitted to some involvement in delinquent behavior.[32] Specifically, when a wide variety of minor and more serious offenses are considered, 67 percent of the youth population stated that they had committed one or more offenses. Consistent with the information from

[31]Martin Gold, *Delinquent Behavior in an American City* (Belmont, California: Brooks/Cole Publishing, 1970), p. 115.

[32]Delbert S. Elliott, Suzanne S. Ageton, David Huizinga, Brian A. Knowles, and Rachelle J. Canter, *The Prevalence and Incidence of Delinquent Behavior: 1976–1980* (Boulder, Colorado: Behavioral Research Institute, 1983), pp. 52–58.

other research, as the youths matured fewer were involved in the serious crimes against persons and general theft. In contrast, more of them reported status offenses, public disorder offenses, and illegal services. A few serious offenses were considerably more characteristic of the youths as they became older, and these were carrying a concealed weapon and selling marijuana and hard drugs. In sum, although many youths commit minor offenses, particularly as they grow older, few are involved in the most serious kinds of delinquency. Indeed, the finding that less than six percent of youths reported any one of the Index Offenses that are catalogued in the Uniform Crime Reports is quite consistent with other research that leads us to believe that much serious crime is committed by a small group of adolescents.

When sex, race, social class, and urban/rural subgroups are compared, it is clear that some youths are more prone to be involved in delinquency than are others. When the most serious forms of delinquency are considered, males are consistently more likely to be involved and are more often involved than are females.[33] The only exceptions were for the use of hard drugs and school delinquency in some years. The finding of girls' lower levels of delinquency is perhaps the most firmly established piece of information that we have about juvenile delinquency, and it has been confirmed in numerous studies.[34] Another gender difference in delinquency is that, unlike the males whose serious offenses peaked toward the end of adolescence, with the exception of theft, the *National Youth Survey* found a more level involvement among the females.[35]

Although females differed markedly from males in serious offenses, the differences were less extreme for the minor types of delinquency. In no case did the females report a higher rate of involvement than did the males. Offenses with only minimal differences between girls and boys included running away, lying about age, cheating on school tests, skipping classes, hitting parents, practicing credit card fraud, writing bad checks or counterfeiting, panhandling, and making obscene calls.[36]

Subgroup differences are less pronounced for race, social class, and urban/rural divisions than for gender, but they do exist. More blacks than whites reported a violent offense in the early years of the study, but this difference was not found by 1980.[37] On the other hand, whites were more likely to be involved in certain minor offenses, particularly minor theft, general theft, hard drug use, public disorder, and school delinquency.[38] Class differences were most pro-

---

[33]*Ibid.*, p. 63.

[34]Gary F. Jensen and Raymond Eve, "Sex Differences in Delinquency: An Examination of Popular Sociological Explanations," *Criminology, 13*, no. 4 (February 1976), p. 429.

[35]Delbert S. Elliott, Suzanne S. Ageton, David Huizinga, Brian A. Knowles, and Rachelle J. Canter, *The Prevalence and Incidence of Delinquent Behavior: 1976–1980*, p. 67.

[36]Delbert S. Elliott and Barbara J. Morse, "Drug Use, Delinquency and Sexual Activity" (Boulder, Colorado: Behavioral Research Institute, 1985), p. 9.

[37]Delbert S. Elliott, Suzanne S. Ageton, David Huizinga, Brian A. Knowles, and Rachelle J. Canter, *The Prevalence and Incidence of Delinquent Behavior: 1976–1980*, p. 75.

[38]*Ibid.*, p. 72.

nounced for the violent and serious offenses, with lower-class youth reporting especially high rates of assaults, and working-class youths reporting high rates of thefts.[39] Finally, the urban rural differences were small but consistent: Urban youth were more likely than others to report some involvement in delinquency.[40] It is well known that race, social class, and urban/rural differences are interrelated with each other. For example, minority group members tend to be concentrated in the lower classes. Further analysis is needed to determine whether each of the demographic variables has an independent influence on patterns of delinquency, or whether various combinations of race, class, and region account for lawbreaking patterns. Nonetheless, the *National Youth Survey* clearly pinpoints select groups of adolescents who are most at risk for being involved in the different types of delinquency.

Status Offenders

There is quite a bit of controversy over the characteristics of status offenders. Some people have argued, based partly on police and court records, that status offenders are a totally different group from other delinquents.[41] Using police or court records from different areas of the country, others argue that status offenders and other delinquents are no different from one another, or that status offenders progress to more serious delinquency.[42] One group of researchers concluded from their own study of official records that it is true that the majority of youths with a status offense on their record have not previously had a contact with the police, and will probably not be arrested for either a delinquent or status offense.[43] A much smaller group of youths who are charged with a status offense have a prior record of some type. Even among these youths, just about half do not return to court again.[44]

Self-report studies reveal that some status offenders do not commit other types of offenses, and that some do. Joseph Weis examined the data collected in six self-report studies, including Gold's study, and concluded that whether a child holds the legal status of a status offender tells us very little about his or her behavior. He summarizes his findings:

[39]*Ibid.*, p. 83.

[40]*Ibid.*, p. 91.

[41]Stevens H. Clarke, "Some Implications for North Carolina of Recent Research in Juvenile Delinquency," *Journal of Research in Crime and Delinquency, 12,* no. 1 (January 1975), pp. 51–60.

[42]Charles W. Thomas, "Are Status Offenders Really So Different? A Comparative and Longitudinal Assessment," *Crime and Delinquency, 22,* no. 4 (October 1976), pp. 438–455; Maynard L. Erickson, "Some Empirical Questions Concerning the Current Revolution in Juvenile Justice," in *The Future of Childhood and Juvenile Justice,* ed. Lamar T. Empey (Charlottesville, Virginia: University Press of Virginia, 1979), pp. 277–311.

[43]Solomon Kobrin, Frank R. Hellum, and John W. Peterson, "Offense Patterns of Status Offenders," in *Critical Issues in Juvenile Delinquency,* eds. Shichor and Kelly, pp. 203–235.

[44]*Ibid.*, p. 230.

In short, there are petty offenders and serious offenders, and both engage both in status offenses and delinquent behavior. But the latter do so more frequently and commit more serious property and violent crimes.[45]

It is not possible to predict what a child will do after once committing a status offense. Some do become more seriously delinquent, though the majority do not.

Drug Abusers

Drug abuse by adolescents is considered a problem because it is itself illegal, it can pose a health risk, and it may be linked to other types of criminal activity. (The risks of drug use and its link with other types of delinquency are discussed in Chapter 11.) Alcohol and marijuana use is very widespread, as revealed in a national monitoring and reporting program entitled *Monitoring the Future: A Continuing Study of the Lifestyles and Values of Youth.*[46] For the *Monitoring the Future* research, a sample of high school seniors has been taken each year since 1975. The high school seniors have been chosen so that they represent youths across the nation, and they are questioned about their drug use as well as their beliefs and values and the circumstances in which they use drugs.

Some of the findings that reveal widespread use of illicit drugs and both alcohol and cigarettes are

47.2 percent of high school seniors reported using marijuana at least once
23.1 percent of the seniors had used marijuana within the last year
12.1 percent had used the potent drug, cocaine, at least once[47]

In considering drug use among high school seniors, it is important to keep in mind that use is more common among dropouts, and thus the numbers for high school students underestimate the use among all adolescents.

The figures that we have reported refer to one-time use. Fewer youths report daily use of the various drugs. The most frequent and serious drug use is concentrated in densely populated urban areas rather than rural areas. Males and youths who do not have college plans also are more likely to report serious drug use.[48] Nevertheless, there is some use of dangerous drugs in all subgroups,

---

[45]Joseph G. Weis, *Jurisdiction and the Elusive Status Offender: A Comparison of Involvement in Delinquent Behavior and Status Offenses* (Washington, D.C.: U.S. Government Printing Office, 1980).

[46]Lloyd D. Johnston, Patrick M. O'Malley, and Jerald G. Bachman, *Highlights from Drugs and American High School Students: 1975–1983* (Rockville, Maryland: National Institute on Drug Abuse, 1984).

[47]Lloyd D. Johnston, Patrick M. O'Malley, and Jerald G. Bachman, as cited in *Sourcebook of Criminal Justice Statistics, 1989*, eds. Timothy J. Flanagan and Kathleen Maguire (Washington, D.C.: U.S. Government Printing Office, 1990), p. 356.

[48]Johnston, O'Malley, and Bachman, *Highlights from Drugs and American High School Students: 1975–1983*.

and American adolescents experience one of the highest, if not the highest, rates of drug use in comparison to youths in other nations.

Gang Members

It is commonly believed that gang members account for a considerable amount of serious juvenile crime,[49] and research has attempted to show that gang members are a strong influence on each other to break the law.[50] There is some agreement among law enforcement and social work personnel who work with gangs that these groups share some common characteristics. Members recurrently congregate outside of their homes and primarily with each other; they see themselves as having rights to a "territory" close to their homes and meeting place; they are structured partly according to age, have a well-defined leadership, and they engage in a wide range of activities together.[51] The popular media image of juvenile gangs committing violent offenses as a group has been combined with the ideas of theorists and practitioners into a belief that if we can solve the "gang problem," we can eradicate much serious crime.

Delinquent youth known to the police and juvenile corrections staff self-report rather high levels (though less than 50 percent) of gang membership. In the 1989 *Survey of Youths in Custody*, 31 percent of youths said that they had regularly associated with a gang in the year before commitment.[52] Similarly, 34 percent of Philadelphia youth born in 1945 and with at least one police contact indicated gang membership.[53]

The high prevalence of gang membership for youth in contact with the juvenile justice system is not necessarily a cause of delinquency, for it is possible that gang members are investigated and "processed" through the system more than other juveniles, or that social or other conditions cause both delinquency and gang membership. Even if gang membership does not cause delinquency, the juvenile justice practitioner must adjust treatment and control approaches to the reality that the gang often has some influence on offenders in the system, and thus interventions oriented towards peer relations are particularly appropriate.

[49]Walter B. Miller, *Violence by Youth Gangs and Youth Groups as a Crime Problem in Major American Cities* (Washington, D.C.: U.S. Government Printing Office, 1975); and Jackson Toby, "Delinquency in Cross-cultural Perspective," in *Juvenile Justice: The Progressive Legacy and Current Reforms,* ed. Lamar T. Empey (Charlottesville, Virginia: University Press of Virginia, 1979), pp. 105–149.

[50]C. Jack Friedman, Fredrica Mann, and Howard Adelman, "Juvenile Street Gangs: The Victimization of Youth," *Adolescence, 11,* no. 44 (Winter 1976), pp. 527–533; and Walter B. Miller "Lower-Class Culture as a Generating Milieu of Gang Delinquency," *Journal of Social Issues, 14,* no. 3 (Summer 1958), pp. 5–19.

[51]Walter B. Miller, *Violence by Youth Gangs and Youth Groups as a Crime Problem in Major American Cities.*

[52]*1989 Survey of Youths in Custody, Codebook* (Ann Arbor, Michigan: Criminal Justice Archives, 1990).

[53]Alicia Rand, "Transitional Life Events and Desistance from Delinquency and Crime," in *From Boy to Man, From Delinquency to Crime* eds. Marvin E. Wolfgang, Terrence P. Thornberry, and Robert M. Figlio (Chicago: University of Chicago Press, 1987), pp. 155–156.

Although many juvenile offenders in contact with police and correctional agencies are involved with gangs, even in high delinquency areas, the majority of adolescents are not members. For black suburban Chicago youth in the 1970s, just 10 percent of youth were in street gangs.[54] More recently, in California barrios known for their gangs, the majority of adolescents are not members.[55]

Also, despite increasing concern about the lethal nature of gang violence involving weapons, it is important to keep in mind that a rather small proportion of all violence is committed by gang members. The small proportion is reflected in several available statistics. For example, it was estimated that, in San Diego, 4 percent of 1982 violent offenses would involve gang members.[56] Between 1967 and 1981, police categorized 5.5 percent of Chicago homicides as gang related.[57] Most recently, at a time when gangs were being blamed for cocaine-related violence, research found that violence was very rare in cocaine arrests, and in fact most cocaine dealing did not appear to be the exclusive activity of gang members.[58]

Ideas about gangs are as much a product of the media and popular opinion as of careful research, and common beliefs can lead us astray in understanding and targeting delinquent youths for the purposes of delivering prevention and correctional services. One recent study in Boston found that youths who belonged to peer groups that fit the common image of a gang were no more delinquent than other adolescents.[59] Also, boys in self-report studies have indicated that they do not usually commit serious offenses with gang members. If they are with other people, it is just one or two other youths.[60] The *National Crime Survey* of victims similarly found that offending by groups of three or more is much less common than is offending alone, though it is more common among juveniles than adults.[61]

[54]John W. C. Johnstone, "Youth Gangs and Black Suburbs," *Pacific Sociological Review, 24,* no. 3 (July 1981), pp. 355–375.

[55]Diego Vigil, "Street Socialization, Locura Behavior, and Violence Among Chicano Gang Members (undated mimeo).

[56]Susan Pennell and Christine Curtis, *Juvenile Violence and Gang-Related Crime* (San Diego, California: San Diego Association of Governments/Criminal Justice Evaluation Unit, 1982), p. 3.

[57]Irving Spergel, "Violent Gangs in Chicago: In Search of Social Policy," *Social Service Review, 58,* no. 2 (June 1984), pp. 204–205.

[58]Malcolm W. Klein, Cheryl L. Maxson, and Lea C. Cunningham, *Gang Involvement in Cocaine 'Rock' Trafficking* (Los Angeles, California: Center for Research on Crime and Social Control, Social Science Research Institute, 1988), p. 9.

[59]Merry Morash, "Gangs, Groups, and Delinquency," *The British Journal of Criminology, 23,* no. 4 (October 1983), pp. 309–335.

[60]Maynard L. Erickson, "Group Violations and Official Delinquency: The Group Hazard Hypothesis," *Criminology, 11,* no. 2 (August 1973), pp. 127–160; and Michael J. Hindelang, "With a Little Help from Their Friends," *British Journal of Criminology, 16,* no. 2 (April 1976), pp. 109–125.

[61]John H. Laub, *Trends in Juvenile Criminal Behavior in the United States: 1973–1981* (Albany, New York: The Michael J. Hindelang Criminal Justice Research Center, Inc., State University of New York at Albany, 1983), pp. 29, 33.

Additionally, there is no indication of an increase in offenses by multiple offenders in recent years, or of an increased victimization rate for young adult males, who would be most at risk in gang fighting.[62] Such evidence does not mean that no serious offenses are committed with the support of gangs, but it does raise questions about how important or common the gang influence is relative to other factors. Any increase in violence due to gang activity appears to be localized and limited to the extent that it has no effect on national statistics.

At this point, estimates of the number of gangs and their influence on members remains controversial. Walter Miller, a long-time expert on delinquent gangs, noted that cliques and other kinds of groups may be important in passing a delinquent orientation to members, but the types of gangs we commonly picture as delinquent are found only in a few large cities.[63] In the future, it would be helpful to study the influence of all different kinds of peer groups, including the gang as commonly pictured, on members' delinquency.

Violent Juvenile Offenders

Another category of offenders that is of interest is the violent juvenile offender. Although there is disagreement about who should be placed in the violent category, work completed through a cooperative agreement of the National Council of Crime and Delinquency and the Office of Juvenile Justice and Delinquency Prevention has concluded that, for the purpose of concentrating resources on the most frequent and destructive youthful offenders, the category should be limited to adolescents with at least two adjudications for violent crime, specifically murder, rape, armed robbery, kidnapping, or arson of an occupied structure.[64]

TRENDS IN JUVENILE DELINQUENCY AND ITS CONTROL

Despite media and other claims to the contrary, it is not established that today's youth are markedly more delinquent or violent than they have been over the last fifteen years. The number of youth arrested per 100,000 youth in the population did seem to be increasing until the mid 1970s, but this rate of arrest seems to

---

[62]*National Crime Survey Statistics, 1978 through 1987* (Washington, D.C.: U.S. Government Printing Office).

[63]Walter B. Miller, "Gangs, Groups, and Serious Youth Crime," in *Critical Issues in Juvenile Delinquency,* eds. Shichor and Kelly, pp. 115–138. Also refer to Carl S. Taylor, *Dangerous Society* (Michigan State University Press).

[64]Robert A. Matias, Paul DeMuro, and Richard S. Allinson, *Violent Juvenile Offenders: An Anthology* (San Francisco, California: National Council on Crime and Delinquency, 1984), pp. 44–46.

have leveled off by the end of the 1980s. [See Table 2-3] This pattern holds for violent crime, and it remains to be seen whether claims of increased youth delinquency and violence in the 1990s are truly part of a trend.[65]

Besides the national statistics, a study focused on the city of Baltimore confirms the stability in homicide rates for juveniles. Between 1974 and 1984, the absolute number of juvenile homicides, the proportion of juveniles involved in homicide, and the number of homicides per 100,000 juveniles in the population remained stable.[66]

In the past, some theorists and the media expressed concern that girls were "catching up with boys" in the numbers involved in delinquent behavior, and that their delinquent behavior is increasingly serious. The conclusion from a review of thirteen self-report studies at different time periods was that girls may have increased their involvement in damaging property and theft of items worth less than ten dollars more rapidly than have boys. However, they are not catching up with boys in "joyriding, running away, fist fighting, gang fighting, carrying a weapon, strongarm theft, and major theft."[67] Even claims that official statistics show girls to be more like boys have been challenged. Most increases in girls' property offenses are in the area of shoplifting, which has traditionally been considered to be a crime committed by females. Increases in arrests for violent, officially recorded crimes are primarily in the category of "other assaults," many of which are "relatively nonserious in nature and tend to consist of being bystanders or companions to males involved in skirmishes."[68]

For both girls and boys, self-report studies provide evidence that, for many years, delinquency has not increased dramatically. In Martin Gold's survey, boys were similar for the years 1967 and 1972, though girls reported a slight increase in marijuana use in 1972.[69] The more recent *National Youth Survey* confirmed that there was no increase in the number of delinquent youths, but provided a more complex picture of the change. Between 1976 and 1980, the proportion of adolescents (fifteen to seventeen years old) who took part in many forms of delinquency actually decreased, but the number of delinquent acts reported by the group as a whole did not change.[70] It seems that fewer youths were involved in delinquency, but those who did break the law committed a greater number of illegal acts in 1980 than in 1976.

---

[65]Laub, *Trends in Juvenile Criminal Behavior in the United States: 1973–1981*, pp. 1–2.

[66]Derral Cheatwood and Kathleen J. Block, "Youth and Homicide: An Investigation of the Age Factor in Criminal Homicide," *Justice Quarterly, 7*, no. 2 (June 1990), pp. 205–292.

[67]Darrell J. Steffensmeir and Renee Hoffman Steffensmeir, "Trends in Female Delinquency: An Examination of Arrest, Juvenile Court, Self-Report, and Field Data," *Criminology, 18*, no. 1 (May 1980), p. 77.

[68]*Ibid.*, p. 70.

[69]Martin Gold and Donald J. Reimer, "Changing Patterns of Delinquent Behavior Among Americans 13–16 Years Old: 1967–1972," *National Survey of Youth, Report No. 1* (Ann Arbor: Institute for Social Research, University of Michigan, 1974).

[70]Elliott, Ageton, Huizinga, Knowles, and Canter, *The Prevalence and Incidence of Delinquent Behavior*, p. 105.

Exhibit 2-3 Encouraging results from the *Monitoring the Future* research

A growing number of American young people are showing common sense and good judgment when it comes to using alcohol, cigarettes, and illicit drugs, a University of Michigan research team reports.

In their 1984 nationwide survey of high school seniors, the researchers found that illicit drug use is continuing the gradual decline which began in 1980.

The proportion of seniors smoking marijuana regularly (twenty or more times in the previous month) dropped in 1984, this time from 5.5 percent to 5 percent, well below the peak level of nearly 11 percent in 1978. Nearly nine out of ten students said they disapprove of regular marijuana use.

Occasional marijuana use also declined: the 25 percent of seniors reporting use in the prior month was approximately one-third lower than the peak level of 37 percent recorded in 1978.

Lloyd D. Johnston, Jerald G. Bachman, and Patrick M. O'Malley, the three social psychologists who conduct the surveys at the U-M Institute for Social Research, report that marijuana use is increasingly viewed as risky and unacceptable behavior by American youth.

The proportion of seniors who disapprove of regular marijuana use has risen from about 65 percent in 1977 to 85 percent in 1984, while the number of seniors who see regular use as entailing a ''great risk'' to the user has grown from about one-third to two-thirds of all seniors during the same period.

SOURCE: News and Information Services, The University of Michigan, January 7, 1985.

The *Monitoring the Future* research on adolescent drug use for high school seniors is consistent with the *National Youth Survey,* for it shows an overall decline in illicit drug use among adolescents. Although there is a drop for most drugs except cocaine, the greatest change occurred because fewer youths have ever used marijuana. The drop occurred between 1979, when 51 percent of youths stated they had used marijuana at some time, and 1987, when 50 percent of youths made this statement. Despite the overall trend towards decreased drug use, increases in the uses of particular drugs, like cocaine, alert us to the potential for a large number of youths to use a currently popular dangerous drug. Also, while drug use has declined among males, it has increased slightly for females, and the percentage of females smoking at least one-half a pack of cigarettes has increased to the point that it is equal to the percentage for males.[71]

Even though there is no dramatic increase in delinquency over time, there is indication of some increase in assaults, and also in the arrest rate (though not necessarily the rate of offending) for shoplifting. Between 1975 and 1985, the *Monitoring the Future* data for seventeen-year-olds showed that an increasing

[71]Lloyd D. Johnston, Patrick M. O'Malley, and Jerald G. Bachman, *Illicit Drug Use, Smoking, and Drinking by America's High School Students, College Students, and Young Adults, 1975–1987* (Washington, D.C.: U.S. Government Printing Office, 1989).

proportion of youth self-reported assaults, and *Uniform Crime Report* data showed a similar rate of increase in arrests for assault.[72] During the same period, the proportion of youth involved in other offenses was fairly stable, though because of the declining youth population, the numbers of arrests decreased. One exception was that rates for shoplifting arrests, though not self-reported shoplifting, increased, but this most likely results from better detection by stores.

Despite the decrease in the "at risk" population of juveniles and the minimal changes in the juvenile crime rate, there has been a dramatic increase in the proportion of juveniles in custody. Just between 1976 and 1984, for instance, the number of juveniles in public and private facilities per 100,000 youth in the population increased 30 percent.[73] The increase is greatest for the private facilities, but it is also occurring in the more institutional public facilities. For an increasing proportion of adolescents, institutionalization or some other residential placement has become a part of "growing up."

The increase is due to a longer average stay of the juveniles who are institutionalized, for fewer youths are incarcerated. Of the youths who are incarcerated, an increasing proportion of them are black and Hispanic. The youths who are incarcerated in public facilities are more often male, for there have been sharp declines in the incarceration of females, probably as a direct result of efforts to remove status offenders from public facilities for delinquents.

Although it is clear that large numbers of status offenders and youths who are neglected and dependent are no longer in juvenile correctional institutions, there is a growing concern that some of them are being shifted to equally restrictive mental health, drug, and alcohol programs. One study showed that status offenders in Minnesota continued to be incarcerated in the mental health and substance abuse programs despite their removal from the correctional system.[74] Because Minnesota has been a leader in the development of mental health and substance abuse programs, these findings may not hold for the rest of the nation. However, policy makers and researchers need to remain alert to the possibility that the removal of status offenders as well as neglected and dependent children from juvenile institutions does not always mean that they are in their own families or in open settings, such as group homes or foster care.

REGIONAL DIFFERENCES

Official records which are compiled for the nation as a whole have the advantage of providing information about delinquents and their behavior throughout the

[72]D. Wayne Osgood, Patrick M. O'Malley, Jerald G. Bachman, Lloyd D. Johnston, "Time Trends and Age Trends in Arrests and Self-Reported Illegal Behavior," *Criminology, 27,* no. 3 (August 1989), pp. 389–417.

[73]Office of Justice Programs, *Children in Custody, 1975–85: Census of Public and Private Juvenile Detention, Correctional, and Shelter Facilities* (Washington, D.C.: Bureau of Justice Statistics, 1989), p. 2.

[74]Ira M. Schwartz, Marilyn Jackson-Beeck, and Roger Anderson, "The 'Hidden' System of Juvenile Control," *Crime and Delinquency, 30,* no. 3 (July 1984), pp. 371–385.

country. Furthermore, many of these reports describe smaller areas to reflect delinquents' police and court contacts in regions, states, cities, and counties. Thus, from the Uniform Crime Reports we know nationally what proportion of youths are arrested, and we can compare this proportion to smaller areas to see where youths are more or less likely to be arrested. Similarly, court statistics inform us of national proportions of youths involved, and we can compare the average to the proportion for cities and towns of interest.

The *National Crime Survey* of victims, beginning in 1973, has consistently shown that there is a higher rate of juvenile offending in personal crimes in large urban areas. For example: "In 1981, the rate of offending in personal crimes for juveniles was 5,404 per 100,000 juveniles in the United States, 8,936 per 100,000 juveniles in urban areas, and 12,726 per 100,000 juveniles in places with 1,000,000 or more persons."[75]

In contrast to official records and the *National Crime Survey*, the self-report studies are not generally conducted on a national basis. That is why we have been careful to note the area in which each piece of research was completed. Findings for one type of city, or a rural area, may not hold in other areas. Speaking about the cohort study of violent offenders in Columbus, Ohio, the authors commented on this problem:

> This 1956–1958 cohort of 811 subjects constitutes the sum total of all arrestees for violent crime in the age-eligible population. This number is laughably small when compared to similar cohorts in the South Bronx, North Philadelphia, East Los Angeles, South Chicago, and other celebrated cores of poverty and disorganization.[76]

Self-report study findings apply to the areas where they were conducted, and to similar cities and counties. In some cases, many studies in different places produce the same results. Then we can be more certain that results represent a more general state of affairs.

The city of Columbus seems to experience fewer crimes of violence than larger cities, such as New York and Chicago. Likewise, rural areas report fewer adult and juvenile crimes, and the crimes are of a less serious, less sophisticated nature.[77] Another difference is that official police contacts are not as concentrated among the lower classes in rural areas as in urban areas,[78] but instead all classes have about the same frequency of police contact.

[75]Laub, *Trends in Juvenile Criminal Behavior in The United States: 1973–1981*, p. 1.

[76]Dinitz and Conrad, "The Dangerous Two Percent," p. 144.

[77]Christine Alder, Gordon Bazemore, and Kenneth Polk, "Delinquency in Nonmetropolitan Areas," in *Critical Issues in Juvenile Delinquency*, eds. Shichor and Kelly, pp. 48–50; Robert Lyerly and James K. Skipper, Jr., "Differential Rates of Rural-Urban Delinquency: A Social Control Approach," *Criminology, 19*, no. 3 (November 1981), pp. 385–399.

[78]Alder, Bazemore, and Polk, "Delinquency in Nonmetropolitan Areas," p. 52.

CONCLUSIONS

In an effort to accurately describe juvenile delinquents and their typical patterns of behavior, we have presented research findings from official records, victimization surveys, and a number of self-report studies. It is clear that the adolescents who could be called delinquents differ considerably from each other, and different sources of information provide contradictory impressions of which youths are most delinquent. The picture that you accept of delinquents depends on your prior orientation, as well as the degree to which you think the sources of information about delinquency are valid.

One group of experts was called together to consider much of the research we have presented above, and to draw conclusions about the delinquency problem. These experts were a part of the Task Force on Sentencing Policy Toward Young Offenders, and they stressed the need to know who the delinquents are before formulating any policies about how to control them. They included people who have devoted their lives to the study of crime and delinquency, such as Marvin Wolfgang. A summary from their report presents the conclusions that they drew from existing research:

> Most young persons violate the law at some point during adolescence; relatively few young persons are repetitive, serious criminals.
>
> Most youth crime is not violent crime; offenses involving property outnumber violent crimes by more than ten to one . . .
>
> Most violent crime by the young is committed against young victims; a substantial amount of violence also spills over to the other age groups, and about 10 percent of all robbery by young offenders involves elderly victims.
>
> Most young persons who commit serious offenses will outgrow the propensity to commit crime in the transition to adulthood; a significant minority of serious young offenders will persist in criminal careers.
>
> Most young offenders who commit acts of extreme violence and pursue criminal careers come from minority ghettos and poverty backgrounds; so do their victims.[79] [This is more a function of socioeconomic class than of race.—*Author's note*]

SUMMARY

This chapter has described three important sources of information on delinquents, and thereby addressed one of the four central issues which we identified in Chapter 1: Who are the delinquents? Official reports tell us who was arrested and processed through the juvenile court and correctional systems. Victimiza-

---

[79]Twentieth Century Fund Task Force on Sentencing Policy Toward Young Offenders, *Confronting Youth Crime* (New York: Holmes & Meier Publishers, Inc., 1978), p. 4.

tion surveys tell us about instances when victims reported to interviewers that they had been threatened or harmed. Self-report studies provide information about juveniles' own descriptions of themselves and their behavior.

Juveniles do account for a larger proportion of arrests than do an equivalent number of adults. This drops off for property offenses after age sixteen, and for violent offenses after age twenty. Recidivism, victimization, and self-report studies show that this pattern cannot be explained by any bias in arrest procedures which favor adults.

Studies have consistently shown that females are less delinquent than males. They are not becoming more like males, in the sense of becoming either more delinquent or violent. The areas in which females have increased the most in delinquency appear to be marijuana use and shoplifting.

A small number of boys commit a large proportion of crimes, since they are chronic offenders. The vast majority of boys with one contact with the police would be classified as minor offenders. Status offenders are no more likely to become violent or chronic offenders than any other youths. It is unclear whether gang members are more seriously delinquent than other adolescents.

Several different sources of information confirm that there have not been dramatic changes in delinquency in recent years. However, there have been some shifts. Females have decreased in violent and theft crimes, and blacks are generally less delinquent. These decreases are offset by increased personal offenses by white males. On the whole, fewer youths are involved in delinquency, but those who are involved commit more illegal acts than did youths in prior times.

Studies of the juvenile justice system inform us that arrests have declined. Still, large numbers of adolescents are in institutional settings, because in many places delinquents are detained and incarcerated for a longer time than was usual in the past.

It is likely that regions, cities, and counties differ considerably from each other in amount and type of delinquency. Small cities have fewer arrests for violent crimes than do larger ones. Rural areas experience less serious and frequent juvenile crime, too.

DISCUSSION QUESTIONS

1. In planning delinquency prevention and treatment programs, how could you use information from official records, victimization surveys, and self-report studies?
2. If you were interested in discovering trends in delinquency in your community during the next ten years, what type of information would you want? Explain why this information would be most helpful.
3. Basing your answer on research findings, identify the groups of delinquents who appear to need special programs to control their lawbreaking behavior.

PROJECTS

1. Survey people who are not taking this course about their impressions of trends in delinquency. Compare the results of your survey to research findings in this chapter. How do you account for differences or similarities?

2. Working with a research librarian, find local Uniform Crime Report, National Court Statistics, and if they exist, locate the results of victimization surveys for the area where you live, or for a city or county of interest to you. Compare these to national statistics.

3. Review local newspapers in your library for articles about juvenile delinquency and drug use among teenagers. Do the articles accurately portray recognized tendencies and trends as revealed in this chapter? How can such media reports help or hinder efforts to design sound policies and programs for adolescents?

———————————3—

Theories of Delinquency Causation

- MAJOR TYPES OF THEORY
- SOCIOLOGICAL THEORIES
- RECENT ADVANCES IN SOCIOLOGICAL THEORY
- PSYCHOLOGICAL THEORIES
- RECENT ADVANCES IN PSYCHOLOGICAL THEORY
- THEORIES AND DELINQUENCY CONTROL

LEARNING OBJECTIVES

1. To know the difference between theories which were developed within the classical school and those in the positive school.
2. To understand that theories differ in the extent to which they recognize that people have free will, and the extent to which they recognize that there is intergroup conflict in society.
3. To be familiar with the major sociological and psychological theories which have been and continue to be used as a basis for delinquency control programs.
4. To know which theories are best supported by empirical research.
5. To know about current efforts to improve theories, including efforts to integrate the best ideas from different theories and to develop theories to explain female delinquency.
6. To be aware of the differences in the theories generally used by police, court, and correctional personnel.

This chapter will discuss the many aspects of criminology that are referred to as *theories of causation*. The reader will be exposed to several major views, taken mostly from the fields of sociology and psychology, which are important contributions to the understanding of delinquency causation. Additionally, there is a discussion of important strengths and weaknesses of each theory, and of evidence from research to test the theories. Recent advances are also reviewed, along with commentary on the areas most in need of more theoretical development and research. This wide-ranging survey provides a starting point for using existing knowledge as a basis for decisions about how to control delinquency. With this information, students can reassess their own understanding of delinquency, as well as the understanding of other people.

Before the last half of the nineteenth century, little scientific research was done to investigate the many factors that contribute to delinquency and crime. Most attempts at criminological explanation took the form of moralistic pronouncements or unscientific personal generalizations. Not until the end of the nineteenth century did scientific criminological inquiry begin to emerge in this country. With the onset of the discipline of sociology, academic courses that dealt with crime and criminality began to appear. Even at the present time the major discipline concerned with criminality and delinquency is the field of sociology, although in the latter part of the nineteenth century, psychology, psychiatry, and to a lesser degree other related disciplines became more concerned with the problem and interested in its causation, control, prevention, and treatment.[1]

Because of the variety of disciplines studying criminology, there are many different and often opposing explanations of delinquency and crime. To help clarify the different orientations, we shall discuss briefly the two major schools of criminological thought and the orientation that each takes when viewing the criminal offender. These two schools of thought, which give the *classical* and the *positive* views of criminology, provide the basis for past and contemporary criminological assumptions and principles of delinquency and criminality.

Classical and Positive Criminology

The differences in the theoretical orientation of the classical and positive schools of thought have implications for the way offenders are perceived and "treated."

The *classical* school of thought, developed by Cesare Beccaria, an Italian nobleman (1738–1794), conceived of people as free agents, pursuing hedonistic aims, and able to rationally decide on all or most courses of action.[2]

Offenders were viewed as possessing free will and being no different from nonoffenders except that they "willed" to commit crimes. As a natural consequence of this philosophy punishment was expected to be harsh and imme-

---

[1]Donald R. Cressey, "Crime," in *Contemporary Social Problems*, eds. Robert K. Merton and Robert A. Nisbet (New York: Harcourt, Brace and World, Inc., 1966), p. 160.

[2]George B. Vold, *Theoretical Criminology* (New York: Oxford University Press, 1968). See Chapter 2.

diate so that offenders would "unwill" to commit future crimes. The offenders' mental makeup, background, and extenuating circumstances were irrelevant.[3]

Because offenders were viewed as being very rational, the pleasure-pain principle was invoked as the major method of dealing with them. The pleasure-pain principle proposed that if the punishment for the particular act produced negative consequences that were more severe than the pleasures derived from committing the act, potential offenders would be discouraged from being deviant. Offenders were presumed to be rational enough and to have enough "good sense" to choose right from wrong, since most of their behavior was supposedly guided by the desire to seek pleasure and to avoid pain. If the punishment produced enough pain, then the potential offenders would decide not to become involved in unlawful behavior. The punishment was also supposed to fit the crime, and such factors as offender age or background characteristics were not to be considered. If a person was apprehended for committing an illegal offense, not only was the punishment painful, it often included incarceration so that the offender could contemplate and decide—or "unwill"—to commit future crimes.[4]

Succinctly stated, the classical school said that

> crime involves a moral guilt, because it is due to the free will of the individual who leaves the path of virtue and chooses the path of crime, and therefore it must be suppressed by meeting it with a proportionate quantity of punishment.[5]

The purpose of the classical orientation was to make the system of criminal prosecution and punishment rational and consistent, so that society could be protected and the offender could "change his ways."

The *positive* school of criminology, founded by Cesare Lombroso (1835–1909), emphasizes the criminal offender's personal and background characteristics rather than just the rational thought process and "free will."

> The positive school of criminology maintains, on the contrary, that it is not the criminal who wills; in order to be a criminal it is rather necessary that the individual should find himself permanently or transitorily in such personal, physical, and moral conditions, and live in such an environment, which becomes for him a chain of cause and effect, externally and internally, that disposes him toward crime.[6]

The positive school rejected the classical school's belief that people exercise reason and are capable of choice and free will, and that offenders are no different from nonoffenders.[7]

---

[3]Martin R. Haskell and Lewis Yablonsky, *Crime and Delinquency* (Chicago: Rand McNally and Co., 1970), p. 344.

[4]*Ibid.*

[5]Enrico Ferri, *The Positive School of Criminology,* ed. Stanley E. Guipp (Pittsburgh: University of Pittsburgh Press, 1968), p. 54.

[6]*Ibid.,* p. 24.

[7]David Matza, *Delinquency and Drift* (New York: John Wiley and Sons, Inc., 1964), p. 11.

In effect, offenders are "sick" and their behavior merely reflects the various determinants in each person's background. The determinants would be the offender's biological, psychological, sociological, cultural, and physical environments.

Treatment would include altering one or more of the determinant factors that contributed to the unlawful behavior. Even though almost all modern theories have emanated, in one way or another, from the positive school, Lombroso's work did not incorporate sociological and psychological considerations as we know them today. His *scientific investigations* emphasized the biological differences of offenders.

Basically, Lombroso felt that (1) criminals were a distinctive type at birth, (2) they could be recognized by certain stigmata, that is, such distinguishing characteristics as "a long, lower jaw," and "a low sensitivity to pain," (3) these stigmata or physical characteristics did not cause crime but enabled identification of criminal types, and (4) only through severe social intervention could born criminals be restrained from criminal behavior. The Lombrosian school of thought relied heavily on *biological determinism.*[8]

As pointed out earlier, there are other determinants of behavior that extend beyond biological determinism. For example, Gabriel Tarde refuted Lombroso's biological emphasis by focusing on *social determinism.* In other words, criminal behavior was the result of factors in the environment of the offender, and not due to biological makeup. The disagreement between Lombroso and Tarde, however, related solely to what factors determined or caused the criminal behavior. They did not disagree on the question of free will versus determinism. They both agreed that explanations of criminal behavior should extend beyond the classical school's free will emphasis. They parted ways when it came to specifically identifying which deterministic behavior (biological or social) provided the key for explaining criminal behavior.[9]

CONTEMPORARY THEORIES OF CRIMINALITY: AN OVERVIEW

The preceding discussion has attempted to illustrate briefly the transition and historical development criminology has taken from the older classical school of thought to the present emphasis on theories in which the assumptions are based on the positive school of criminology. This section will present the views of the major sociological and psychological theorists who have contributed to the present body of criminological knowledge.

Albert Cohen points out that sociological explanations of criminality do not oppose psychological explanations in that they are not rival answers to the same question, but they answer different questions about the same sort of behavior. Psychological theories are concerned mainly with motivation and those fac-

[8]Haskell and Yablonsky, *Crime and Delinquency,* p. 345.
[9]Cressey, "Crime," p. 161.

tors that contribute to the individual manifesting behavior in either deviance or conformity.

> Sociological inquiry or theory is concerned with identifying variables and processes in the larger social system that in turn shape those that are involved in motivation and that determine their distribution within the system . . . actions are not only events in the biographies of individuals (psychological theory)— things that people do; they are also events located somewhere in a social system or structure—in a family, a neighborhood, a city, a region, an organization, a country. Different kinds of deviant acts are variously distributed within a given social structure, and these distributions differ from one time to another and from one structure to another. It also makes sense to ask: What is it about social structures—their organization, their cultures, their histories—that accounts for differences within and between them?[10]

To simplify the distinction between psychological and sociological theories, it may help the reader to remember that the psychologist takes a more individualistic, specific view of human behavior and the personal internal factors that contribute to criminality. The sociologist takes a more general view, looking at the external environment in which the individual lives. The sociologist is concerned with the distribution of crime within the environment and the factors in the system that affect the crime rates. The sociologist can usually predict the amount of crime that will be committed in certain areas, but is unable to pinpoint specific potential offenders.

Determinism and Modern Theory

Modern crime causation theory, in the main, is all deterministic insofar as it posits a statistical relationship among an individual, the environment, and deviant activity. One criticism of positivist theory is that it ignores free will, and represents people's behavior as a product of circumstances. In the extreme view, circumstances such as economic conditions, family interactions, and psychological makeup determine whether a person breaks the law. In this view, the offender takes no part in deciding to break the law.

Positive theory need not and does not always attack the concept of free will directly, since most theory is stated in the form of probabilistic propositions. In probabilistic terms, people who are exposed to the causes of delinquency or who have the personality makeup of a delinquent are more likely to break the law than people who are not exposed. This is quite different from saying that they are certain to break the law. An explanation for the uncertainty is that potential offenders exercise their free will, and some of them thereby counteract influences toward delinquency. In choosing between theories, some people base

[10]Albert K. Cohen, *Deviance and Control* (Englewood Cliffs, New Jersey: Prentice-Hall, Inc., 1966), pp. 45–47. Also Forrest M. Moss, "Contemporary Theories of Criminality: An Overview," unpublished paper, Michigan State University, East Lansing, Michigan, 1976.

their decision partially on the extent to which the theory makes it clear how and when free will comes into play. Your own standing on this issue, and the importance you attach to it, are largely a matter of personal beliefs about human nature.

The effect of beliefs about free will on theories about delinquency is a good example of the way that the model of the interrelationships of four key issues works (see Fig. 1-1). As this model shows, beliefs about free will have an important influence on each theorist's explanation of delinquency.

Conflict and Order

Each theorist, and each of us, also differs in beliefs about the amount of conflict between racial, social class, and other groups in American society, and the importance of this conflict. The effect of beliefs about conflict on delinquency theories is another good example of the way the model in Chapter 1 works. Some people downplay this conflict, and stress order within society. They assume, for example, that most Americans hold the same values, and are equally accepting of the legitimacy of most laws.[11] In the order-oriented theories, social conflict and disagreement do not have a part in causing crime.

Theorists who stress the amount and importance of conflict in society emphasize discrimination in the enforcement of laws, disagreement over what behavior should be illegal, and the tendency for people in power to have laws enacted to protect their own interests. These conflict-oriented theorists have paid less attention to the causes of crime,[12] and it is not clear that they would explain all types of crime as resulting from deep-seated conflicts in society. However, a central theme in the conflict-oriented theories is that society must change in order that crime be reduced.

For some time, positive sociological and psychological theories have received the most attention in research and have most often been applied in program settings. The various psychological and sociological theories differ considerably from each other in their focus on the individual or society, in the degree to which they recognize free will, and in their emphasis on either conflict or order.

Although the psychological and sociological theories are most often the basis for delinquency control programs, two other types of theories have received recent attention. Within the positive school, there is a renewed interest in

---

[11]John Horton, "Order and Conflict Theories of Social Problems as Competing Ideologies," *American Journal of Sociology, 71,* no. 6 (May 1966), pp. 701–713; Don C. Gibbons and Peter Garabedian, "Conservative, Liberal and Radical Criminology: Some Trends and Observations," in *The Criminologist: Crime and the Criminal,* ed. Charles E. Reasons (Pacific Palisades, California: Goodyear Publishing Company, Inc., 1974), pp. 51–65.

[12]Don C. Gibbons and Joseph F. Jones, *The Study of Deviance: Perspectives and Problems* (Englewood Cliffs, New Jersey: Prentice-Hall, Inc., 1975), p. 102. Also William Selke, "Beyond Social Determinism," unpublished paper, Michigan State University, East Lansing, Michigan, 1976.

biological causes.[13] And, consistent with the classical orientation, deterrence research has focused on the degree to which the severity, certainty, and swiftness of punishment affect the decision to break the law.[14] This focus on punishment is, of course, an elaboration of the theme that individuals weigh the pain of punishment against the pleasure gained from the crime. Because biological and deterrence theories increasingly guide the thinking of some people about how to predict, react to, and treat juvenile delinquency, the research support for these approaches is presented before the discussion of sociological and psychological theories.

DETERRENCE THEORY

Our contemporary understanding of deterrence has grown beyond the simple notion that the speed, certainty, and severity of punishment will stop illegal behavior. It is recognized that punishment can have the effect of either *absolute deterrence,* which is preventing future offenses completely, or *restrictive deterrence,* which is reducing the frequency and seriousness of illegal behavior so as to avoid detection.[15] It also is recognized that punishment is just one influence on delinquency, and it cannot completely counterbalance the influence of family, community, and societal conditions on youth.

An example of the contemporary approach to understanding deterrence is Raymond Paternoster's study of tenth-grade students. He found that the perceived severity of punishment did not explain either involvement or frequency of involvement in minor forms of delinquency. However, juveniles who perceived a high certainty of apprehension delayed using marijuana and alcohol, and they committed most forms of minor delinquency less frequently. Even though punishment appeared to have some influence, Paternoster reminds us that the effect is marginal in comparison to effects of the availability of delinquent opportunities, absence of censure from significant others, moral inhibitions, and involvement in legitimate activities.

Aside from the issue of multiple influences on delinquency, several other considerations must be kept in mind to understand deterrence. First, it is not so

[13]Curt R. Bartol, *Criminal Behavior: A Psychosocial Approach* (Englewood Cliffs, New Jersey: Prentice-Hall, Inc., 1980), pp. 18–50; Susan E. Martin, Lee B. Sechrest, and Robin Redner, *New Directions in the Rehabilitation of Criminal Offenders* (Washington, D.C.: National Academy Press, 1981), pp. 56–62, 289–303.

[14]Gwynn Nettler, *Explaining Crime,* 2nd ed. (New York: McGraw-Hill Book Company, 1972), pp. 189–205; Maynard L. Erickson and Jack P. Gibbs, "Punishment, Deterrence, and Juvenile Justice," in *Critical Issues in Juvenile Delinquency,* eds. David Shichor and Delos H. Kelly (Lexington, Massachusetts: Lexington Books, D. C. Heath and Company, 1980), pp. 183–202; Susan E. Martin, Lee. B. Sechrest, and Robin Redner, *New Directions in the Rehabilitation of Criminal Offenders,* pp. 53–56.

[15]Raymond Paternoster, "Absolute and Restrictive Deterrence in a Panel of Youth: Explaining the Onset, Persistence/Desistence, and Frequency of Delinquent Offending," *Social Problems, 36,* no. 3 (June 1989), pp. 289–309.

much the objective level of punishment that is used in a family, court, or correc-tional setting, but the youth's *perception* of the speed, certainty, and severity of punishment that are likely to be related to breaking the law. Regardless of how certain punishment is in a certain jurisdiction, if a juvenile thinks there is a low likelihood of getting caught and being punished, there can be no deterrence. Many juveniles think that since they are under the jurisdiction of the juvenile courts, they will not be severely punished.[16] Also, there is some indication that juveniles do not consider incarceration, for example, a jail sentence, as much more "severe" than the loss of spending money or the imposition of an early curfew.[17]

A second problem for researchers is to measure the deterrent effect accurately. It is very difficult to determine a youth's perception of risk at the time the offense is being considered.[18] Perceived risk that is measured at some time period before the offense occurs can be changed dramatically through interac-tions with peers and experiences in breaking the law. Thus, the finding of little or no connection between perceived risk and delinquency may be a result of a sudden change in perceived risk just before the offense is committed. It is impor-tant not to overlook possible deterrent effects until research has ruled out the possibility of a sudden change.

BIOLOGICAL THEORIES

There are two key ways in which recent research has considered the effect of biology on delinquency.

- Youth may inherit genetic predispositions that make them prone to delinquency.
- Neurological deficits can play a part in delinquency causation.

In many cases the research designs to study biological causes are flawed, so that no firm conclusions can be drawn about cause and effect. Also, it is clear that most people with each of the biological predispositions do not become delin-quent, and even fewer become serious offenders.

Heredity

It is very difficult to untangle the effects of heredity from environment, because families often live in similar social situations, and even in the same

[16]Barry Glassner, Margaret Ksander, Bruce Berg, and Bruce Johnson, "A Note on the Deterrent Effect of Juvenile vs. Adult Jurisdictions," *Social Problems, 31,* no. 2 (December 1983), pp. 219–221.

[17]Maynard Erickson and Jack Gibbs, "Punishment, Deterrence, and Juvenile Justice," in *Critical Issues in Juvenile Delinquency,* eds. David Schichor and Delos H. Kelly (Lexington, Massachusetts: Lexington Books, D. C. Heath and Company, 1980), pp. 183–202.

[18]Steven Klepper and Daniel Nagin, "The Deterrent Effect of Perceived Certainty and Severity of Punishment Revisited," *Criminology, 27,* no. 4 (November 1989), pp. 721–746.

community, from generation to generation. Thus, parent and child may be affected by similar conditions of poverty, levels of neighborhood violence, and negative school environments. As will be discussed in Chapter 4, The Family and Juvenile Delinquency, the parent can also pass values and coping strategies on to the child that predispose the child to delinquency.

In a thorough review of the research on the connection of heredity and delinquency, Glenn D. Walters and Thomas W. White point out that adoption studies may be the best way to separate hereditary from environmental effects.[19] If the criminality of the biological parents predicts the adopted children's delinquency, there is compelling evidence of a link. Unfortunately , existing studies are not conclusive. Often only the biological mother's (but not the biological father's) criminality is considered; in some cases, the child remained with the biological mother for months before the adoption; and it is possible that delinquency results indirectly through inheritance of intelligence. Also, no differentiation is made between minor and serious forms of illegal activity, and often illegal behavior is not even measured, but instead such characteristics as "antisocial personality" are assumed to indicate delinquency or parental criminality.

Studies of families to detect passage between generations and studies of twins are also far from conclusive about the genetic explanation of delinquency. In family studies, it is particularly difficult to separate environmental from biological causes. Many biological outcomes, such as neurological deficits, can be traced to environmental conditions, such as lack of nutritious food during pregnancy. The difficulty with studies of twins is similar. These studies address the question of whether identical (monozygotic) twins are more similar in criminality than nonidentical (dizygotic) twins. Gordon Trasler found that the better the sampling and testing procedures in studies of twins, the less the similarity between siblings for both monozygotic and dizygotic twins.[20] Monozygotic twins are more similar in offending than are dizygotic twins, but the difference is not extreme.[21] Although heredity may play a role in the causation of delinquency, neither a strong nor a frequent effect has been supported in research.

Neurological Deficits

Because the appropriate data to study the link between neurological deficits and delinquency are rarely available, the studies that we have are scattered across different times and countries. For example, a study in the early 1970s in New Zealand revealed that verbal, visuospatial-motor integration, and memory deficits explained self-reported, early delinquency beyond what could

---

[19]Glenn D. Walters and Thomas W. White, "Heredity and Crime: Bad Genes or Bad Research?" *Criminology, 27,* no. 3 (August 1989), pp. 455–485.

[20]Gordon Trasler, "Biogenetic Factors," in *Handbook of Juvenile Delinquency,* ed. H. C. Quay (New York: Wiley, 1987).

[21]Odd Steffen Dalgard and Einar Kringlen, "Norwegian Twin Study of Criminality," *British Journal of Criminology, 16,* no. 3 (July 1976), pp. 213–232.

be explained by social disadvantage.[22] Terrie Moffitt's review of research on neurological problems and delinquency points to the many challenges involved in establishing a clear link, but it does suggest that there is a role for brain dysfunction, particularly as indicated by verbal and self-control deficits, in the causation of antisocial behavior.[23]

As with punishment and heredity, it is critical to understand that biological predispositions are not being proposed as sole or even major causes of delinquency. Instead, they may "tip the scale" in the favor of delinquency in a negative family, school, or community environment. A seven-year follow up on boys incarcerated in the Connecticut Training School illustrates the point. It was the combination of "vulnerabilities"—cognitive, psychiatric, and neurological—with a history of abuse and/or family violence, that distinguished between the boys who did or did not go on to adult violence.[24]

It is also critical to understand that, even when it is uncertain that various neurological problems are a major influence on delinquency, they may be prevalent among delinquents and thus require intervention. Among juveniles aged 6 to 17 who were referred to a multidisciplinary team by the Cook County, Illinois Circuit Court, fifty-five percent exhibited attention deficit disorder, and fifteen percent were classified as retarded.[25] The specialists at the court pointed to the need for testing, medication, special education, parental management training, behavioral family therapy, and cognitive skills training.

MAJOR SOCIOLOGICAL THEORIES

As pointed out earlier, sociology was the first major discipline to study criminology and crime causation. Several competing sociological theories are in use today. Decisions about which of these is "best" rest on their usefulness in explaining the actual distribution of delinquency today, and the amount of research evidence that supports the theory. Judgments about whether a theory is too deterministic or whether it correctly assumes that social life is mainly characterized by conflict or order usually rest on personal beliefs, and are therefore a matter of opinion. As you read about each of the positive theories, you may want

[22]Terrie E. Moffitt and Phil A. Silva, "Neuropsychological Deficit and Self-reported Delinquency in an Unselected Birth Cohort," *Journal of the American Academy of Child and Adolescent Psychiatry, 27,* no. 2 (March 1988), pp. 233–240. Also see: Terrie E. Moffitt, "The Neuropsychology of Juvenile Delinquency: A Critical Review," in *Crime and Justice: A Review of Research,* vol. 12, eds. Michael Tonry and Norval Morris (Chicago: University of Chicago Press, 1990), pp. 99–169.

[23]*Ibid.*

[24]Dorothy Otnow Lewis, Richard Lovely, Catherine Yeager and Donna della Femina, "Toward a Theory of the Genesis of Violence: A Follow-up Study of Delinquents," *Journal of the American Academy of Child and Adolescent Psychiatry, 28,* no. 3 (May 1989), pp. 431–436.

[25]Robert Zagar, and others, "Developmental and Disruptive Behavior Disorders among Delinquents," *Journal of the American Academy of Child and Adolescent Psychiatry, 28,* no. 3 (May 1989), pp. 237–240.

to use your own system to reach your opinion about the worth of each theory. The theories are arranged below to give a sense of the order in which they were developed, and to illustrate that new theories often improve on prior attempts to explain delinquency.

Social Structure and Anomie—Robert Merton

The main thrust of Merton's efforts was "in discovering how some social structures exert a definite pressure upon certain persons in a society to engage in nonconformist rather than conformist conduct."[26] He built on the work of Emile Durkheim, who was one of the earliest sociologists to talk about the social system and how it affects the individual.[27] Durkheim focused his attention on *anomie*—a situation in which individuals feel disconnected from any group and are isolated from the mainstream of interaction and positive peer support. According to Durkheim, anomie—a feeling of isolation or normlessness—is related to one deviant behavior, suicide. Robert Merton extended Durkheim's contribution by developing a similar explanation for illegal behavior.

Merton's explanation considers three concepts: (1) the cultural goals or aspirations that people learn from their culture, (2) the norms that people employ when attempting to achieve the goals, and (3) the institutionalized means that are available for goal achievement.[28] When there is a discrepancy between the institutionalized means available and the goals to which an individual aspires, strain or frustration is produced, norms break down, and deviant behavior can result. For example, if a lower-class child is exposed by the mass media to success symbols and a lifestyle that are difficult to attain because of lack of institutionalized means—such as adequate schools and employment opportunities—this, Merton feels, will create strain and frustration that leads to illegal behavior.

All societies differ in the way wealth is distributed and in the way opportunities present themselves. Merton saw our society as being extremely productive, but at the same time creating frustration and strain because all groups do not have equal access to the institutionalized means of legitimately achieving goals. He charts the alternative modes of behavior that can result when there is a disjunction between goals, means, and institutionalized norms, and when there is an overemphasis on goals or means. When both societal goals and institutional means are adhered to, there is *conformity*. If the means are followed but the goal is lost sight of, there is *ritualism*. *Innovation* is emphasis on the goal and disregard for the institutionalized means. *Retreatism* is rejection of both goals and means, and *rebellion* is withdrawal of all allegiance to the social system and an attempt to reconstruct a new one. Innovation and retreatism are most pertinent to our

---

[26]Robert Merton, "Social Structure and Anomie," *American Sociological Review*, 3, no. 5 (October 1938), p. 672.

[27]Emile Durkheim, *Suicide: A Study in Sociology*, translated by John A. Spaulding and George Simpson (Glencoe, Illinois: The Free Press, 1951).

[28]Merton, "Social Structure and Anomie," pp. 672–674.

interest in juvenile delinquency, for one form of innovation is illegal activity, and retreatism can be accomplished through involvement in a drug-oriented group.

Merton's approach is essentially sociological because he does not discuss individual motivational factors as they relate to the selection of a particular alternative. His emphasis is on the strain produced by the system and the culture, and on the position occupied by individuals, which will depend on the alternative they are forced to select. Merton's theory increases our understanding of the possible effects of strain produced by the system, but it does little to increase our understanding of why all persons in similar situations do not choose the same alternative, that is, why only some become involved in illegal activity.

Gang Theory—Frederick Thrasher

At about the same time that Merton was positing his views on deviant behavior, Frederick Thrasher was exploring the subject of group delinquency. Many theorists have studied the group and its effect on delinquent behavior. Processes whereby a group takes on certain behavior characteristics and then transmits them to its members are intriguing for both the theorist and the layman. Although other theorists, such as Cohen, Ohlin and Cloward, and Miller, include gang behavior in their studies on delinquency, Thrasher is considered the foremost authority on gang behavior because of his extensive research on the subject. Thrasher's study

> is not advanced as a thesis that the gang is a cause of crime. It would be more accurate to say that the gang is an important contributing factor facilitating the commission of crime and greatly extending its spread and range. The organization of the gang and the protection which it affords, especially in combination with a ring or a syndicate, makes it a superior instrument for the execution of criminal enterprises. Its demoralizing influence on its members arises through the dissemination of criminal techniques and a propagation through mutual excitation of interests and attitudes which make it easier (less inhibited) and more attractive.[29]

Thrasher felt that gangs originate naturally during the adolescent years from spontaneous play groups. The major factor that transforms a play group into a gang is conflict with other groups. As a result of the conflict, it becomes mutually beneficial for individuals to band together in the form of a gang to protect their rights and to satisfy needs which their environment and their family cannot. By middle adolescence, the gang has distinctive characteristics, such as a name, a particular mode of operation, and usually an ethnic or a racial distinction.

Thrasher is probably best known for the systematic way he analyzed gang activity and gang behavior. His rigorous attempt at analyzing all facets of gang activity has probably never been equaled. He studied the local community

[29]Frederick Thrasher, *The Gang* (Chicago: University of Chicago Press, 1936), p. 381.

to determine what influence it has on gang behavior. He found that the environment is permissive, lacks control, and facilitates gang activity. The presence of adult crime within these communities also influences gang behavior because many of the adults who have high status in the community are adult criminals. Even though most of the gang's activities are not illegal, the environment is supportive of illegal gang behavior. Local businessmen will act as fences for stolen goods, and local citizens are readily available customers for the stolen property. Local politics also contribute to gang behavior—political pull was often the only way that rewards could be obtained because of the extreme poverty conditions that existed at the time of this study.

Thrasher also studied gangs at the level of the adolescent and determined what activities are normal for adolescents and what activities are unique to gang members. He showed that gang behavior is enticing, rewarding, and supported within the environment. He emphasized that not all gang activities are necessarily deviant and that much of the gang members' time is spent in normal athletic activities as well as in other teenage endeavors. Yet, Thrasher's theory had direct implications for the prevention and control of delinquency (Exhibit 3-1).

Thrasher, like Durkheim and Merton, described how the environment can be conducive to delinquent behavior. The more the environment is supportive of and conducive to delinquency, the more delinquency will exist. The following theorists attempted to shed some light on why crime rates and criminal activity are inordinately high in certain environments and sections of the community.

Cultural Transmission and Social Disorganization—Clifford Shaw and Henry McKay

In attempting to account for the distribution of delinquency in American cities, Shaw and McKay concluded that because the high rate of delinquency that existed in Chicago from 1900 to 1906 had not changed a great deal from 1917 to 1923, even though demographic changes had taken place, delinquency and crime were learned and transmitted from one group to another and from one generation to the next and were fairly stable within the central part of large cities.[30]

There were two core ideas in the Shaw-McKay theory. One: extreme economic deprivation results in neighborhood mobility and a varied neighborhood population, which in turn result in social disorganization. Neighborhoods with such disorganization lack both informal and formal social controls over potential lawbreakers. Two: crime is transmitted through personal and group contacts.

According to Shaw and McKay, economic status has a great deal to do

[30]Clifford R. Shaw and Henry D. McKay, *Juvenile Delinquency and Urban Areas* (Chicago: University of Chicago Press, 1969).

Exhibit 3-1   Excerpts from Thrasher's notes

When the new garage of the F__ Company was opened, a small group of boys made it about as unpleasant for the company as they possibly could. The building had a wide expanse of glass and it was this shining mark that attracted the attention of two score or more active urchins in the neighborhood. They worked out an organized scheme of attack whereby they were enabled to elude watchmen, employees, and specially detailed police. Annoyance and property loss were continual and efforts to stop the trouble were ineffectual.

At length the president of the company had the Scout movement brought to his attention. He ruminated over the matter for some time and finally called upon the Scout Commissioner and enlisted the co-operation of one of the finest Scout Masters in the city.

In a casual way, this Scout Master made friends with the boys and one day suggested in an offhand manner that the Boy Scouts were a jolly bunch of boys and it might be fun to organize a troop. The suggestion made a big hit and the troop was formed.

Soon the "Holy Terrors," as the gang was often called, were so busy with their first aid, their endeavors to fathom the mysteries of signaling, and their study of Scoutcraft that there was no time for throwing stones. More than that, the inclination seemed to have vanished. Now with an old gang leader in command, they were as proud of their new task of defending all the property in the neighborhood as they used to be of their clever schemes for making trouble.

All the officers of the company have become deeply interested in the youngsters. Several times the Scouts have had turned over to them two or three of the company's coaches and have gone off for a day's practicing in the country.

The important point to be noted is that where the gang is broken up, the social world of the boy disintegrates and a new one must be substituted for it—not of the artificial type found in an institution, but one which will provide for a redirection of his energies in the habitat in which he must live.

SOURCE: Frederick M. Thrasher, *The Gang: A Study of 1,313 Gangs in Chicago*, abridged and with a new introduction by James F. Short, Jr. (Chicago: University of Chicago Press, 1963), pp. 351–353. © 1927 by The University of Chicago. Abridged edition © 1963 by The University of Chicago.

with the rates of delinquent behavior. The greater the economic deprivation, the greater the delinquency. The less the economic deprivation, the less the delinquency. Like Durkheim and Merton, Shaw and McKay feel that persons living in disadvantaged environments often have the same material aspirations as persons living in areas that have social and economic advantages. Residents in disadvantaged areas soon learn, however, that legitimate access to their goals is difficult. The disparity between their goals and the means available for legitimately achieving them therefore creates a situation conducive to deviancy, delinquency, and crime in urban areas. The authors sum up their propositions as follows:

It may be said, therefore, that the existence of a powerful system of criminal values and relationships in low income urban areas is a product of a cumulative process extending back into the history of the community and of the city. It is related both to the general character of the urban world and to the fact that the population in these communities has long occupied a disadvantageous disposition.[31]

Shaw and McKay do acknowledge that other factors may cause certain youngsters to become involved in delinquent activities, but they feel that these individual factors are secondary to the economic and social factors that exist in the community and have little bearing on actual rates of delinquency.

Today, Shaw and McKay's theory is seen as having a number of serious flaws. Probably most important, Shaw and McKay assumed that if a person lives in a neighborhood that is heavily populated by one type of person and has a high crime rate, this means that the person is likely to be criminal. This has been shown to be untrue by examples and through statistical reasoning.[32] The mistake in reasoning is called the "ecological fallacy." Other weaknesses are that zones around a city are not really neighborhoods, and the case histories used by Shaw and McKay may describe atypical delinquent youth. Also, since official police and court records are used to indicate delinquency, Shaw and McKay's research may show that inner-city youths are most likely to come into contact with police, but not necessarily that they are more delinquent.

Shaw and McKay did make a major contribution to our understanding of crime by emphasizing that it is learned while living in an environment conducive to deviant activity. This idea was further defined and elaborated in a theory developed by Edwin Sutherland.

Differential Association—Edwin Sutherland

Sutherland's theory of differential association is probably one of the most systematic and complete theories of delinquency causation that has yet been constructed. The theory states that (1) criminal behavior is learned; (2) criminal behavior is learned in interaction with other persons in the process of communication; (3) the principal part of learning of criminal behavior occurs within intimate personal groups; (4) when criminal behavior is learned, the learning includes not only techniques for committing the crime, which are sometimes very complicated, sometimes very simple, but also a specific direction of motives, drives, rationalizations, and attitudes; (5) the specific direction of motives and drives is learned from definitions of legal codes as favorable and unfavorable—in American society, these definitions are almost always mixed and consequently there is culture conflict in relation to the legal codes; (6) a person becomes delinquent because of an excess of definitions favorable to

---

[31] *Ibid.*, p. 321.

[32] W. S. Robinson, "Ecological Correlations and the Behavior of Individuals," *American Sociological Review*, 15, no. 3 (June 1950), pp. 351–357.

violation of law over definitions unfavorable to violation of law; (7) differential association may vary in frequency, duration, priority, and intensity; and (8) the process of learning criminal behavior by association of criminal and anticriminal patterns involves all of the mechanisms that are involved in any other learning.[33]

An important principle of differential association is that delinquent behavior will be predictable if there is an excess of definitions within the environment favorable to the violation of laws versus those definitions that are unfavorable to the violation of laws. When the former set of definitions takes precedence over the latter, the stage is set for the commission of crime. If individuals associate mostly with criminals, chances are that they will become involved in delinquent activity. Conversely, if they associate mostly with noncriminals, chances are that they will not become involved in delinquent activity. Sutherland's concepts of *frequency, duration, priority,* and *intensity* in relation to the quality and quantity of relationships help explain the effects of differential association. If individuals have many contacts with criminals over a long period of time and if these contacts are important, as well as intense, they will probably become involved in delinquent activity. Sutherland saw his theory as the basis for the design of delinquency control programs (Exhibit 3-2).

The major criticism of Sutherland's theory is that it is difficult to empirically test the principles and objectively measure "association" and the priority, intensity, duration, and frequency of relationships. In their book, *Principles of Criminology,* Sutherland and Cressey admit that "the statement of differential association process is not precise enough to stimulate rigorous empirical test, and it therefore has not been proved or disproved. This defect is shared with broader social psychological theory."[34] Even though Sutherland's theory of differential association is one of the most complete and systematic theories that exists regarding the way criminality is learned and transmitted, he does not adequately handle the problem of why some persons in the same environment incorporate and assume criminality as a mode of behavior while their peers do not. Role theory provides a part of the explanation and adds another piece to the puzzle of delinquency causation.

Self-Role Theory—George Herbert Mead

Mead lends new insight into why an individual takes on certain types of behavior (roles), becomes comfortable with them, and develops a characteristic lifestyle.[35] Role theory helps explain why only a limited number of persons assume criminal identities while the majority of people remain law abiding. Cohen adequately sums up the concept of role theory when he states that

[33]Edwin Sutherland, *The Sutherland Papers,* eds. Albert K. Cohen, Alfred R. Lindesmith, and Karl F. Schuessler (Bloomington: University of Indiana Press, 1956), pp. 8–10.

[34]Edwin Sutherland and Donald R. Cressey, *Principles of Criminology* (New York: J. P. Lippincott Co., 1966), p. 98.

[35]George Herbert Mead, "The Psychology of Punitive Justice," *American Journal of Sociology, 23,* no. 5 (March 1918), pp. 577–602.

Exhibit 3-2 Sutherland's theory and delinquency control

The most effective means for the control of juvenile delinquency lie almost exclusively in the local community and its personal groups. The family is doubtless the most important of these personal groups, but the recreational group and, for older children, the occupational group are very important. Unless the family is extraordinarily efficient, it does not keep its children from delinquency when the standards of the play groups and other groups conflict with the standards of the family. The proposition that the control of delinquency lies almost entirely in the local community is based on demonstrated knowledge regarding the causes of juvenile delinquency. The child lives his life in the personal groups within a community and in those groups acquires his standards of behavior and his conception of himself. He acquires these largely by oral definitions of the behavior which is proper and the behavior which is improper. This is illustrated by the difference between the boy delinquency rate and the girl delinquency rate. In the United States, in general, 80 per cent of the delinquency cases are boys and only 20 per cent girls. Boys and girls, in general, have equally ignorant and inefficient parents, and are equally lacking in organized recreational facilities, with the boys having better facilities than the girls when there is a difference. Also, boys and girls are approximately equal in the proportion of those who are feeble-minded, who are not wanted at home, and who are rejected by parents, and are approximately equal in emotional disturbances. Hence they cannot differ in delinquency because of such gross situational factors. They differ rather because parents and other intimate associates define one kind of propriety for girls and another for boys, and exercise one kind of supervision over girls and another over boys.

SOURCE: Edwin H. Sutherland, *On Analyzing Crime*, ed. Karl Schuessler, The Heritage of Sociology, series ed. Morris Janowitz (Chicago: University of Chicago Press, 1973), pp. 132–133. © 1973 by The University of Chicago.

it assumes, like differential association theory, that we do not learn anything without first being exposed to it. It also assumes, however, that whether we take notice of it, remember, and make it our own depends on whether it matters to us. . . . from the standpoint of role theory, the central issue in the problem of learning deviant behavior becomes the process of acquiring and becoming committed to roles.[36]

Hence, becoming delinquent and assuming a criminal identity involves more than merely associating with law violators. The associations have to be meaningful to the individual and supportive of a role and self-concept which the individual wants to become committed to.

Durkheim, Merton, Thrasher, and Shaw and McKay all emphasize the effect that the environmental system has on producing strain and, ultimately,

[36]Cohen, *Deviance and Control*, p. 101.

deviant behavior. Sutherland explains how criminality is learned and transmitted. Mead tells us why it is incorporated into an identity and perpetuated as a role. The following theorists build upon the contributions of the above-mentioned theorists and blend them with their own.

Working-Class Boy and Middle-Class Measuring Rod—Albert Cohen

Cohen feels that the problem of delinquency is mainly a working-class, male phenomenon. He states that

> the working class boy, particularly if his training and values be those of the working class, is more likely than his middle class peers to find himself at the bottom of a status hierarchy whenever he moves into the middle class world whether it be of adults or children. To the degree to which he values middle class status either because he values the good opinion of middle class persons or because he has, to some degree, internalized middle class standards himself, he faces the problem of adjustment and is in the market for a solution.[37]

He further states that

> a delinquent subculture is a way of dealing with the problems of adjustment. . . . These problems are chiefly status problems; certain children are denied the respect of society because they cannot meet the criteria of the respectable status system. A delinquent subculture deals with these problems by providing criteria of status which these children can meet.[38]

In other words, Cohen feels that working-class boys have not been equipped to deal with the competitive struggle that takes place in middle-class institutions. They have not learned the type of behavior that will contribute to their success, and therefore are not comfortable when they come in contact with these institutions. As a result of this frustration, they react against those institutions that they feel represent an environment that is too demanding, given the preparation they have received. "The hallmark of the delinquent subculture is the explicit and wholesale repudiation of middle class standards and the adoption of their very antithesis."[39]

Group or gang delinquent activity legitimizes and supports aggression against middle-class institutions. The collective support of the group is important to the boy if he persists in delinquent activity, because he is not convinced, at least unconsciously, that his hostile reaction is normal. As long as the group supports his actions, he can continue to blame the external middle-class institutions and ward off internal feelings of inadequacy.

[37]Albert Cohen, *Delinquent Boys, The Culture of the Gang* (Glencoe, Illinois: The Free Press, 1955), p. 119.
[38]*Ibid.*, p. 121.
[39]*Ibid.*, p. 130.

Cohen's work is an important example of an attempt to bridge the gap between psychology and sociology. However, the theory can be criticized because there is little empirical support for the key idea that working-class boys reject middle-class values.[40] Thus, even though the theory serves as a stepping stone in the development of our understanding, it may not be relevant to contemporary program design.

Success Goals and Opportunity Structures— Lloyd Ohlin and Richard Cloward

To cope with some of the discrepancies presented by anomie theory, role theory, and differential association, Ohlin and Cloward expand upon these precise concepts to give a more comprehensive explanation of the types of alternatives available as a result of strain. They also point out that the environmental system produces strain as a result of a lack of legitimate alternatives to satisfy needs.

> The disparity between what lower class youths are led to want and what is actually available to them is a source of a major problem of adjustment. Adolescents who form delinquent subcultures have internalized an emphasis upon conventional goals. Faced with limitations on legitimate avenues of access to these goals, and unable to revise their aspirations downward, they experience intense frustrations and exploration of nonconformist alternatives may be the result.[41]

Ohlin and Cloward go on to say that

> when pressures from unfulfilled aspirations and blocked opportunity become sufficiently intense, many lower class youth turn away from legitimate channels adopting other means beyond conventional mores, which might offer a possible route to successful goals. . . . Discrepancies between aspirations and legitimate avenues thus produce intense pressures for the use of illegitimate alternatives. Many lower class persons, in short, are the victims of a contradiction between goals toward which they have been led to orient themselves and socially structured means of striving for these goals. Under these conditions, there is an acute pressure to depart from institutional norms and to adopt illegitimate alternatives.[42]

Ohlin and Cloward describe three forms of behavior adaption to environmental strain. First, the criminal subculture exists in areas where there is a strong adult criminal culture and where youth learn patterns of criminality at an early age and then graduate to adult criminal circles. The illegitimate response

[40]Don C. Gibbons, *The Criminological Enterprise: Theories and Perspectives* (Englewood Cliffs, New Jersey: Prentice-Hall, Inc., 1979), p. 107; a similar conclusion is reached by Ruth Rosner Kornhauser, *Social Sources of Delinquency: An Appraisal of Analytic Models* (Chicago: University of Chicago Press, 1978).

[41]Lloyd Ohlin and Richard Cloward, *Delinquency and Opportunity, A Theory of Delinquent Gangs* (New York: The Free Press of Glencoe, 1960), p. 86.

[42]*Ibid.,* p. 105.

to strain in these neighborhoods takes the form of criminal apprenticeship programs. Second, the conflict subculture is similar to the criminal subculture in that it offers limited access to goal achievement through legitimate channels; however, no strong ties with the adult criminal subculture exist, resulting in a lack of even illegitimate opportunities for goal achievement. Criminality is more individually oriented in these neighborhoods, and behavior is more violent, and less structured and systematic. Criminal apprenticeships do not generally exist. The third form of behavioral adaption is the retreatist subculture, in which neither avenue of opportunity, legitimate or illegitimate, exists. In addition, an individual may also have certain moral inhibitions about becoming involved in a criminal type of behavior. The conflict may be resolved if the person withdraws from the environment and retreats to a drug culture.

Ohlin and Cloward, Cohen, Durkheim, Merton, Shaw and McKay, and Thrasher have all either stated or implied that crime is the result of strain produced by a lack of environmental opportunity, and is therefore more prevalent among the lower socioeconomic classes. The hostile manifestation of criminal behavior is generally felt to be a reaction to economic and social conditions, as well as to those institutions that set normative standards. The next theorist, Walter Miller, proposes that delinquent behavior may not necessarily be a reaction to strain or a rebellion against middle-class institutions, but simply behavior that is contrary to the middle-class standards because of different learned patterns of conduct acquired from the lower-class culture.

Lower-Class Boy and Lower-Class Structure— Walter Miller

According to Miller,

> in the case of gang delinquency, the cultural system which exerts the most direct influence on behavior is that of the lower class community itself—a long established distinctively patterned tradition with an integrity of its own—rather than a so-called "delinquent subculture" which has arisen through conflict of middle class culture and is oriented to the deliberate violation of the middle class norms.[43]

The lower-class culture that Miller mentions has come about as a result of the processes of immigration, migration, and mobility. Those persons who are left as a result of these processes comprise the lower class and have developed a pattern of behavior which is distinct to that class and not necessarily reactive against any other class. Miller states that

> expressed awareness by the actor of the element of rebellion often represents only that aspect of motivation of which he is expressively conscious; the deepest and most compelling components of motivation—adherence to highly mean-

---

[43]Walter Miller, "Lower Class Culture as a Generating Milieu of Gang Delinquency," *Journal of Social Issues, 14,* no. 3 (1958), p. 6.

ingful group standards of toughness, smartness, excitement, fate, and autonomy are often unconsciously patterned. No cultural pattern as well established as the practice of illegal acts by members of lower class corner groups could persist if buttressed primarily by negative, hostile, or rejective motives; its principal motivational support, as in the case of any persisting cultural tradition, derives from a positive effort to achieve what is valued within that tradition and to conform to its explicit and implicit norms.[44]

Miller also discusses, in addition to distinctive lower-class traits (toughness, autonomy, and so on), the effects female-based households in lower-class families have on the adolescent boy's sexual identification. The street group provides him with an opportunity to act tough, become involved in other masculine activities, and reject the female orientation that has been the greater part of his life up to that point. Many of the boy's delinquent activities revolve around his desire to become a "real man." Furthermore, the excitement and free life of the streets and the gratification received from "acting out" by means of the group provide a greater return for the effort expended than can be gained by adopting the more sedentary behavior that is normative to the other socioeconomic classes.

Miller has presented his ideas on delinquency and its relation to the lower class. Many detached worker programs based on his theory and research have been developed in an attempt to prevent and control delinquency (Exhibit 3-3).

During the 1970s and 1980s, research interest seemed to turn away from gangs. This was in part due to empirical evidence. For example, the specialized gangs described by Cloward and Ohlin were uncommon, and research evidence did not support Miller's ideas about female-dominated households and lower-class focal concerns.[45]

Delinquency and Drift—David Matza

David Matza attempted to blend the classical school's concept of "will to crime" with positive assumptions and methods of scientific investigation. He disagrees with the theories of Merton, Cloward and Ohlin, and Sutherland on the grounds that they are overly deterministic. He feels they present delinquent behavior as caused almost entirely by emotional and environmental factors, and fail to consider free will.

Matza acknowledges that environmental and emotional factors can have an effect on the individual's behavior, but he feels that other aspects contribute to making one youngster choose the delinquent route while another youngster in the same general environment does not. Matza feels that people are neither

---

[44]*Ibid.*, p. 19.

[45]Don C. Gibbons, *The Criminological Enterprise: Theories and Perspectives* (Englewood Cliffs, New Jersey: Prentice-Hall, Inc., 1979). Also see Ruth Rosner Kornhauser, *Social Sources of Delinquency: An Appraisal of Analytic Models* (Chicago: University of Chicago Press, 1978).

Exhibit 3-3   Detached worker programs in Boston

[the Project executed] action programs directed at three of the societal units seen to figure importantly in the genesis and perpetuation of delinquent behavior—the community, the family, and the gang.

The community program involved two major efforts: (1) the development and strengthening of local citizens' groups so as to enable them to take direct action in regard to local problems, including delinquency, and (2) an attempt to secure cooperation between those professional agencies whose operations in the community in some way involved adolescents (e.g., settlement houses, churches, schools, psychiatric and medical clinics, police, courts and probation departments, corrections and parole departments).

Work with families was conducted within the framework of a "chronic-problem-family" approach; a group of families with histories of repeated and long-term utilization of public welfare services were located and subjected to a special and intensive program of psychiatrically-oriented casework.

Work with gangs, the major effort of the Project, was based on the detached worker or area worker approach utilized by the New York Youth Board and similar projects. An adult worker is assigned to an area, group, or groups with a mandate to contact, establish relations with, and attempt to change resident gangs.

SOURCE: Walter B. Miller, "The Impact of a 'Total-Community' Delinquency Control Project," *Social Problems, 10*, no. 2 (Fall 1962), pp. 168–169.

totally free, as the classical school assumes, nor totally constrained or determined, as some positive theories assume. He feels that everyone is somewhere between being controlled and being free and that everyone drifts between these two states.

> Drift stands midway between freedom and control. Its basis is an area of the social structure in which control has been loosened, coupled with the abortiveness of adolescent endeavor to organize an autonomous subculture, and thus an independent source of control, around illegal action. The delinquent transiently exists in a limbo between convention and crime, responding in turn to the demands of each, flirting now with one, now the other, but postponing commitment, evading decision. Thus, he drifts between criminal and conventional action.[46]

According to Matza, psychological makeup and environmental factors do not destine an individual to become delinquent. There is, however, a movement between convention and crime, and impinging factors, one of them being the individual's "will," can influence which route is ultimately chosen.

Even though most of a youngster's activities are law abiding, he or she

[46]David Matza, *Delinquency and Drift* (New York: John Wiley and Sons, Inc., 1964), p. 28.

can periodically drift into delinquency because the normal conventional controls that usually inhibit delinquent behavior become neutralized as a result of the drifting process. When the youngster does become involved in difficulty, this is not an irreversible process. The youngster can and usually does drift back to conventionality. When the youngster does drift into delinquency and when the moral commitment to conventionality is neutralized, this is when the element of "will to crime" plays an important part. "I wish to suggest that the missing element which provides the thrust or impetus of which the delinquent act is realized is will."[47]

Bond of the Individual to Society—Travis Hirschi

Unlike most other theorists, Travis Hirschi did not set out to explain why some adolescents do break the law, but he tried to explain why some do not.[48] He challenged the image of delinquents in prior alternative theories, for he did not agree that the delinquent was a frustrated striver who was forced to break the law, nor did he see the delinquent as an "innocent foreigner" who didn't have the necessary knowledge to obey the law.

Hirschi developed the theory that youths do not generally take part in exciting but illegal activities because they generally have a strong bond to conventional society. The bond consists of attachment to parents, commitment to educational or other legitimate goals, involvement in conventional activities, and belief in legitimate values. Hirschi empirically tested his theory with a survey of 4,000 high-school students in California. His study, which has been replicated by other researchers, provided considerable evidence to support the social control explanation of delinquency. Regardless of their social class, the most delinquent youths were least attached to their parents, as reflected by low levels of parent-child intimacy and communication. Beliefs reflected by such things as lack of respect for the police and the law, and lack of involvement with homework were other predictors of delinquency. By both developing and empirically testing an explanation of delinquency, Hirschi considerably advanced our understanding.

Since Hirschi published his major findings in 1969, other theorists have remained interested in his ideas and have revised and refined the theory. At present, efforts are underway to integrate social control theory with other explanations, and to fill some of the voids.[49] Although social control theory can explain some of the differences between youths in levels of delinquency, it does not predict why certain adolescents exhibit particular patterns of delinquency. For example, why do some youths become chronic serious offenders, but others engage in occasional minor delinquency? Why do some youths commit only

[47]*Ibid.*, p. 181.

[48]Travis Hirschi, *Causes of Delinquency* (Berkeley, California: University of California Press, 1969).

[49]Michael Hindelang, "Causes of Delinquency: A Partial Replication and Extension," *Social Problems, 20*, no. 4 (Spring 1973), pp. 471–487; Marvin D. Krohn and James L. Massey, "Social Control and Delinquent Behavior: An Examination of the Elements of the Social Bond," *Sociological Quarterly, 21*, no. 4 (Autumn 1980), pp. 529–543.

status offenses? Also, there is a need to explain how bonds are developed in some but not all youths. The knowledge of the factors that influence the formation of bonds to society in the first place can serve as a basis for early prevention programs. Finally, several studies have revealed that the peer group, and in some cases a delinquent peer group to which a youth is strongly committed, plays an important part in the development of delinquent behavior. This information needs to be taken into account in the theoretical explanation.

The Labeling Perspective—Edwin Lemert

Edwin Lemert is usually seen as the most important contributor to what is called the *labeling perspective* on criminology.[50] In the labeling perspective, the emphasis is on explaining why certain laws are passed and enforced, and why police and court personnel officially process some people, but not others. As a part of this focus on the reactions to people who break the law, Lemert developed the idea that the reactions are in themselves causes of delinquency.

Lemert wrote that many individuals commit acts of *primary deviance* as a result of the various causes which the traditional theories have identified. Such people are not officially recognized as "delinquent," for their acts are undetected. Detection, and the official labeling by police and court personnel, has a direct effect on the offender's self-concept. Once official labeling occurs, others react to the offenders as delinquents, and the offenders begin to define themselves as delinquents. This change in self-concept leads to *secondary deviance*. The idea of secondary deviance builds on Mead's understanding that people act in accord with their self-concepts. To the extent that adolescents identify themselves as delinquents, they act like delinquents.

The labeling perspective is quite different from the traditional theories which we have reviewed, for it implicates police and court efforts to control delinquency as a negative influence. The perspective is not called a theory, because it includes several separate explanations of why and how officials react to delinquency, as well as of the cause of delinquency.

The labeling explanation of delinquency causation, unfortunately, has been oversimplified by some people. In this simplified form, the juvenile justice system contact inevitably damages the self-concept and leads to delinquency. Additionally, there is no delinquency until there is an official reaction.

One criticism of the simplified labeling explanation is that it ignores the possibility that offenders can reject labels, thereby exercising their free will.[51]

---

[50]Edwin M. Lemert, *Human Deviance, Social Problems, and Social Control,* 2nd ed. (Englewood Cliffs, New Jersey: Prentice-Hall, Inc., 1972); Edwin M. Lemert, *Social Action and Legal Change: Revolution Within the Juvenile Court* (Chicago: Aldine Publishing Company, 1970); and Edwin M. Lemert, *Social Pathology: A Systematic Approach to the Theory of Sociopathic Behavior* (New York: McGraw-Hill Book Company, 1951).

[51]David J. Bordua, "Recent Trends: Deviant Behavior and Social Control," *Annals of the American Academy of Political and Social Science, 369* (1969), pp. 149–163; Peter K. Manning, "Deviance and Dogma," *British Journal of Criminology, 15,* no. 1 (January 1975), pp. 1–20; and Edwin M. Lemert, "Beyond Mead: The Social Reaction to Deviance," *Social Problems, 21,* no. 4 (April 1974), pp. 457–468.

For example, youths who see court procedures as invalid reject negative labels by judges.[52] Youths also can ignore the labels placed by juvenile justice personnel because these personnel are unimportant to them, or are not believed.[53]

Research has produced conflicting findings about the effect of official labeling. Several studies have shown that arrest or court processing do not influence youths to see themselves as delinquent.[54] However, other research tells us that, at least for the youths who are not yet seriously involved in delinquent activity, official labeling does produce a delinquent self-concept.[55] Even if we agree that labeling results in negative self-concepts for minor delinquents, it is unclear whether self-concept changes produce increased delinquency. There is some research to show that youths with a delinquent self-concept are most delinquent.[56] However, it is not known whether the self-concept results in delinquency, or the delinquent lifestyle results in an accurate view of oneself as delinquent. There is a continuing need for a fuller understanding of the effects of official labeling before we could argue that programs to reduce labeling would have much influence on delinquent behavior.

Despite the problems of oversimplification and contradictory research findings, the labeling perspective has influenced us to carefully examine society's reactions to people who break the law. It also has served as the basis for recommended solutions to the delinquency problem (Exhibit 3-4). To be a more useful explanation of the cause of delinquency, the simplified version must be abandoned. Instead, the focus should be on identifying the types of people most affected by official labels. Furthermore, the tendencies of certain people to accept labels, whereas others reject them, can be documented.

[52]Ann Rankin Mahoney, "The Effect of Labeling upon Youths in the Juvenile Justice System: A Review of the Evidence," *Law and Society Review, 8,* no. 4 (Summer 1974), pp. 583–614; and Charles Wellford, "Labeling Theory and Criminology: An Assessment," *Social Problems, 22,* no. 3 (February 1975), pp. 332–345. For other criticisms see Gibbons and Jones, *The Study of Deviance,* 1975; and Walter R. Gove, ed., *The Labeling of Deviance,* 2nd ed. (Beverly Hills, California: Sage Publications, 1980).

[53]Morris Rosenberg, "Which Significant Others?" *American Behavioral Scientist, 16,* no. 6 (July/August 1973), pp. 51–82; and Merry Morash, "Juvenile Reactions to Labels: An Experiment and an Exploratory Study," *Sociology and Social Research, 67,* no. 1 (October 1982), pp. 76–88.

[54]Herman Schwendinger and Julia Siegel Schwendinger, *Adolescent Subcultures and Delinquency* (New York: Praeger, 1985).

[55]Leonard E. Gibbs, "Effects of Juvenile Legal Procedures on Juvenile Offenders' Self-Attitudes," *Journal of Research in Crime and Delinquency, 11,* no. 1 (January 1974), pp. 51–55; Peggy C. Giordano, "The Sense of Injustice? An Analysis of Juveniles' Reactions to the Justice System," *Criminology, 14,* no. 1 (May 1976), pp. 93–112; John R. Hepburn, "The Impact of Police Intervention Upon Juvenile Delinquents," *Criminology, 15,* no. 2 (August 1977), pp. 235–262.

[56]Gary F. Jensen, "Delinquency and Adolescent Self-Conceptions: A Study of the Personal Relevance of Infraction," *Social Problems, 20,* no. 1 (Summer 1972), pp. 84–103; Suzanne Ageton and Delbert Elliott, "The Effects of Legal Processing on Self-Concepts," *Social Problems, 22,* no. 1 (October 1974), pp. 87–100; Gary F. Jensen, "Labeling and Identity: Toward a Reconciliation of Divergent Findings," *Criminology, 18,* no. 1 (May 1980), pp. 121–129.

Exhibit 3-4 Radical nonintervention and labeling theory

We can now begin to see some of the meanings of the term "radical noninterven-tion." For one thing, it breaks radically with conventional thinking about delin-quency and its causes. Basically, radical nonintervention implies policies that accommodate society to the widest possible diversity of behaviors and attitudes, rather than forcing as many individuals as possible to "adjust" to supposedly common societal standards. This does not mean that anything goes, that all behavior is socially acceptable. But traditional delinquency policy has proscribed youthful behavior well beyond what is required to maintain a smooth-running society or to protect others from youthful depredations.

Thus, the basic injunction for public policy becomes: *leave kids alone when-ever possible.* This effort partly involves mechanisms to divert children away from the courts but it goes further to include opposing various kinds of intervention by diverse social control and socializing agencies. Radical nonintervention represents, perhaps, a more thoroughgoing and expanded version of the policy Lemert has termed "judicious nonintervention." Subsidiary policies would favor collective action programs instead of those that single out specific individuals; and voluntary programs instead of compulsory ones. Finally, this approach is radical in asserting that major and intentional sociocultural change will help reduce our delinquency problems. Piecemeal socioeconomic reform will not greatly affect delinquency; there must be thoroughgoing changes in the structure and the values of our society. If the choice is between changing youth and changing the society (including some of its laws), the radical noninterventionist opts for changing the society.

SOURCE: Edwin M. Schur, *Radical Nonintervention: Rethinking the Delinquency Problem* (Englewood Cliffs, New Jersey: Prentice-Hall, Inc., 1973), pp. 154–155.

Adolescent Subcultures and Capitalistic Economic Structure—Herman Schwendinger and Julia Siegel Schwendinger

Based on lengthy first-hand observations and interviews carried out be-ginning in the 1950s and extending into the 1980s, Herman Schwendinger and Julia Siegel Schwendinger have developed a comprehensive theory to explain delinquency.[57] Their work rejects many of the other theoretical perspectives that

[57]Jay R. Williams and Martin Gold, "From Delinquent Behavior to Official Delinquency," *Social Problems, 20,* no. 2 (Fall 1972), pp. 209–229; Delbert S. Elliott and Suzanne S. Ageton, "Reconciling Race and Class Differences in Self-Reported and Official Estimates of Delinquency," *American Sociological Review, 45,* no. 1 (February 1980), pp. 95–110; Michael Hindelang, Travis Hirschi, and Joseph G. Weis, *Measuring Delinquency* (Beverly Hills, Cal-ifornia: Sage Publications, 1981).

we have discussed. For example, they observed that few youths were concerned with future job opportunities and, therefore, strain produced by the disjuncture of goals and opportunities could not account for illegal behavior. Similarly, they observed that contrary to Hirschi's social control theory, youths (called *wheels*) who were committed to legitimate academic objectives as shown by their high levels of involvement in school activities were nevertheless quite delinquent. In developing an alternative explanation, the Schwendingers seek to identify the economic conditions under which there is development of peer groups that are likely to support delinquency among members. A capitalistic economic system is the context in which certain social class relationships are reflected in individuals' places in the labor force. Currently, adolescents in the United States are concentrated in public schools, where resources are allocated to developing the skills necessary for eventual participation in the labor force. However, schools do not allocate their resources equally to all types of youths. Some youth benefit more than others because of the economic and cultural advantages that are passed on to the members of certain ethnic, racial, or occupational strata, or because of the compensatory time and energy expended on them by self-sacrificing parents.[58]

At the same time that some youths benefit most from school programs, youths who initially lack motivation to achieve or who lose their motivation when they experience academic failure benefit least. Early in life, they focus their concern on personal consumption values and informal relations instead of legitimate work and family relations. In effect, they are marginalized or set apart from the mainstream of school activities and often, eventually, from the mainstream of participation in the labor force, for they do not develop the cognitive and other traits that make it possible for individuals to succeed in school or in the labor force.

In the context of a school environment that favors some youths over others, three major forms of adolescent peer group can develop. At one extreme are the marginalized youths or the streetcorner youths. At the other extreme are youths who focus their attention on academic pursuits. Another sizable number of adolescents belong to groups of "in" adolescents, "socialites," who invest their energy in leisure-time activities, for example, parties.

Adolescent peer groups are characterized by three stages of development that are important to delinquency. For both socialite and streetcorner groups, the first stage is characterized by delinquent acts that continue throughout adolescence:

> It consists of a constellation of delinquent activities including petty thievery, vandalism, truancy, alcohol abuse, individual fighting, and other garden variety of delinquent acts often referred to as "less serious" than others. The generalized modality also includes a variety of acts, such as "party crashing" or verbal abusiveness to peers and adults, that deviate from conventional rules of moral conduct; however, some of these latter acts, while irregular, are not unlawful.[59]

[58]Herman Schwendinger and Julia Siegel Schwendinger, *Adolescent Subcultures and Delinquency* (New York: Praeger, 1985).
[59]*Ibid.*, p. 184.

In the second stage, groups become quite competitive, and delinquency extends to fighting between individuals and groups, vandalism motivated by group rivalries, harmful pledging and hazing practices, and placing graffiti everywhere—on walls, stones, and bridges—proclaiming the superiority and power of collective identity.[60]

The exact form of the intergroup conflict varies depending on the type of group, the community, and the social class of group members, among other things.

Towards the middle of adolescence, youths can add a third form of delinquent activity to those common in stages 1 and 2 of group development. These youths may become involved in illegal markets, the particular type depending, in part, on the group to which the youths belong. For example, socialites tend to steal clothes and other items primarily to satisfy their individual needs, but streetcorner youths, especially those from deprived areas, steal goods that they can sell for money. Both socialites and streetcorner youths can earn money through loan-sharking, gambling, and prostitution.

Because the Schwendingers rely heavily on their detailed, first-hand knowledge of adolescents, they recognize that youths exercise considerable free will. Despite limitations on group membership that result from race, gender, and social class, to some extent adolescents choose the groups that they join; thus they are not compelled by the group to become delinquent. Also, groups can change their orientation by spending time in different localities, and people can leave a group to join or form another.

The Schwendingers' explanation of delinquency is an important contribution to the development of juvenile delinquency theory. Like Thrasher, they based their understanding on first-hand knowledge of adolescent peer groups. The fact that they observed similarities in peer groups that have existed from the 1950s to the 1980s suggests that their theory is valid over time. Another strength of the theory is the attempt to understand delinquency causation at several levels—including economic-structural, group, and individual levels. Finally, the theory links a tendency towards the formation of certain types of peer groups to certain community and economic conditions, thus explaining class differences, but not insisting that social classes are inevitably different.

RECENT ADVANCES IN SOCIOLOGICAL THEORY

In the discussion above, we have noted a number of difficulties with each of the existing theories of juvenile delinquency. Based on current research efforts, these theories continue to be revised, or in some cases parts of the theory which are unsupported by research are discarded. Sometimes certain groups of theorists, as well as other people, feel that an existing theory cannot be reformulated, but must be completely replaced. Such a major challenge to existing theories

[60]*Ibid.*, p. 185.

takes place when there is overwhelming evidence that the theory fails to explain a substantial amount of lawbreaking, or when there is a shift in assumptions about free will or conflict and order in society.

Efforts to test many of the theories described so far in this chapter continue into the present. Although Merton's theory (Social Structure/Anomie) did not focus on the individual, it is the basis for research showing that a lack of fit between economic goals and educational means is a moderate predictor of a child's delinquency,[61] or more generally that the inability to escape legally from aversive situations contributes to delinquency.[62] Recent research has provided support for Hirschi's social control theory, which has the advantage of applying to all social classes and to both females and males. Experts have used research results to back their recommendations that prevention and treatment programs should improve educational and other opportunities. Also, recommended program efforts include improving the school and other institutions with which youths can form a bond, and assisting youths in developing this bond.[63]

There are two additional areas in which we are seeing considerable effort to improve sociological theory to explain delinquency. One of these is new theory to correct prior misunderstandings and ignorance about girls and delinquency. The other is theory to build on the work of Shaw and McKay in an effort to explain the connection between destitute communities and delinquency.

Females—Traditional and New Theories

Because many of the original theories used to explain delinquency were based on research limited to boys, these theories need to be modified, replaced, or supplemented to answer three questions:

· Do the influences on delinquency in existing theories explain girls' and boys' behavior equally well?
· What special things about the lives and circumstances of girls must we recognize in order to understand their delinquency?
· Why are girls so much less delinquent than boys?

A number of criminologists are working to answer these types of questions, and some promising new answers are emerging.

---

[61]Margaret Farnworth and Michael J. Leiber, "Strain Theory Revisited: Economic Goals, Educational Means, and Delinquency," *American Sociological Review, 54*, no. 2 (April 1989), pp. 263–274.

[62]Robert Agnew, "A Longitudinal Test of the Revised Strain Theory," *Journal of Quantitative Criminology, 5*, no. 4 (December 1989), pp. 373–387.

[63]Joseph Weis and J. David Hawkins, *Reports of the National Juvenile Justice Assessment Centers, Preventing Delinquency* (Washington, D.C.: U.S. Department of Justice, 1981); Joseph Weis and John Sederstrom, *Reports of the National Juvenile Justice Assessment Centers, The Prevention of Serious Delinquency: What to Do* (Washington, D.C.: U.S. Department of Justice, 1981); Delbert S. Elliott, David Huizinga, and Suzanne S. Ageton, *Explaining Delinquency and Drug Use.*

Different or Similar Explanations
for Boys' and Girls' Delinquency

There is a need for additional research to help us determine whether the major delinquency theories also explain girls' behavior. Criminologist Josephina Figueira-McDonough has carried out important research to resolve this question, particularly as it pertains to the most common, minor forms of delinquency. She finds that social control theory explains girls' and boys' behavior equally well. For both, attachment to parents and attachment to school influence both norms and self-concept, which in turn explain minor delinquency.[64] Similarly, Professor Figueira-McDonough's work has shown that the predictors suggested by strain theory work equally well for girls and boys. These predictors include low social class, low legitimate aspirations, low school achievement, low grades, and high social activity.[65] The one unique explanation that Figueira-McDonough has found for girls pertains to school structure: in schools that are closed to gender-egalitarian values, girls who are aggressive and success-oriented are somewhat more involved in minor delinquency because other outlets are blocked to them.[66] In sum, there is considerable evidence that, for the most common forms of delinquency, the causative factors are the same for girls and boys.

If the *causes* of delinquency are the same for members of both sexes, the explanation for girls' lesser delinquency is that they experience these causes to a lesser degree. That is, girls are less delinquent because they do not have an excess of definitions favorable to breaking the law, they are not labeled, or they do not experience blocked opportunity as frequently as do boys.

Some experts have predicted that as the female gender role changes in our society, girls will become more and more like boys in their delinquency, with girls acting more violent and taking part in activities like gang fighting.[67] One explanation for the change is that the emancipation of women has resulted in girls adopting a male role.[68] Another is that boys' and girls' roles are becoming increasingly similar.[69] On the whole, theories linking delinquency with sex-role changes have been discredited. Rose Giallombardo summarizes the reasons:

[64]Josephina Figueira-McDonough, J. William Barton, and Rosemary Sarri, "Comparing Female and Male Offenders," in *Comparing Female and Male Offenders*, ed. Margerite Q. Warren (Newbury Park, California: Sage, 1981), pp. 17–45; William H. Barton and Josephina Figueira-McDonough, "Attachments, Gender and Delinquency," *Deviant Behavior*, 6, no. 2 (1985), pp. 119–144.

[65]*Ibid.*

[66]Josephina Figueira-McDonough, "School Context, Gender and Delinquency," *Youth and Adolescence*, 15, no. 1, (February 1986), pp. 79–98.

[67]Freda Adler, *Sisters in Crime: The Rise of the New Female Criminal* (New York: McGraw-Hill Book Company, 1975).

[68]*Ibid.*

[69]Nettler, *Explaining Crime*, pp. 123–128.

Changes in female sex-role behavior do not encourage violation of the existing laws. Indeed, as the major socializing agents in American society, females may be an instrumental force to deemphasize violence in American life on the basis that it is not role enhancing for males and females alike. The far-reaching effects of such socialization practices may in the long run function to decrease male crimes of violence.[70]

Additionally, research has shown that girls with the most feminist attitudes are the least delinquent,[71] and information in Chapter 2 raises serious questions about whether girls have changed very much in the type of crimes they commit.

Although there do not seem to be different causes for boys' and girls' minor delinquency, we do need to increase our understanding of girls' running away and other status offense behavior. This is essential because such a high proportion of the girls who are involved with the juvenile justice system are status offenders (see Chapter 2). Meda Chesney-Lind based a new theoretical explanation on her own research and the research of others.[72] According to her model of female delinquency, girls often run away in response to physical abuse, including sexual victimization by the father, stepfather, or another family member. Once they are "on the streets," several negative outcomes are possible. Parents can file a complaint with the juvenile court and have the girl returned home or punished by the court. This practice criminalizes victimized girls' survival strategies. The outcome is also negative for girls who remain on the streets, where they are viewed in terms of the profit that they can bring through prostitution.[73] It is necessary to understand such special circumstances of girls charged with status offenses or offenses such as prostitution and larceny. Many girls are motivated to commit such offenses so that they can survive when they run away from abusive families. Prostitution and larceny are, in a sense, allowed or even encouraged for girls, for they are consistent with gender stereotypes. Only by recognizing the reason for girls' offenses can police and court staff respond in a manner that will improve the life chances of runaway girls rather than narrow them further.

Traditional sociological theories have not only neglected explanations of why some girls are delinquent, but also of why girls are so much less delinquent than boys. At this point in time, there are no well-tested theories to answer this question. Theories are just being developed, and some examples illustrate that

[70]Giallombardo, "Female Delinquency," p. 79.

[71]Jennifer James and William Thornton, "Women's Liberation and the Female Delinquent," *Journal of Research in Crime and Delinquency, 17*, no. 2 (July 1980), pp. 230–244; and Peggy C. Giordano, "Girls, Guys and Gangs: The Changing Social Context of Female Delinquency," *Journal of Criminal Law and Criminology, 69*, no. 1 (Spring 1978), pp. 126–132.

[72]Meda Chesney-Lind, "Girls' Crime and Woman's Place: Toward a Feminist Model of Female Delinquency," *Crime and Delinquency, 35*, no. 1 (January 1989), pp. 5–29.

[73]Daniel S. Campagna and Donald L. Poffenberger, *The Sexual Trafficking in Children* (Dover, Delaware: Auburn House, 1988); Eleanor Miller, *Street Woman* (Philadelphia, Pennsylvania: Temple University Press, 1986).

many traditional ideas are being incorporated into these new theories. In one newly developed theory, the emphasis is on the fact that women are socialized to believe that their problems result from their own mental or physical defects.[74] This belief leads women to be self-destructive or to endure their problems, rather than striking out at other people through aggressive acts or stealing. In a second theory, which builds on Cloward and Ohlin's work, girls' lack of opportunity to break the law accounts for their limited delinquency.[75] A third theory is a variation of self-role theory: because girls know that other people do not expect females to break the law, they do not expect this of themselves.[76] Furthermore, girls' minimal contact with the juvenile justice system reduces the possibility that labeling will contribute to the development of a delinquent self-concept. The future development in understanding females' delinquency is likely to involve testing and improvement in these new theories of delinquency, as well as in the traditional theories.

Economic Marginalization and Social Disorganization

A number of theorists have identified major characteristics of contemporary American society that cause delinquency. The Schwendingers, whose theory was explained earlier, take this position when they point to the importance of a capitalistic society in stimulating delinquency. Nettler also identifies criminogenic conditions that cause crime throughout our society.[77] These include such influences as the physical relocation of large masses of people, crowding, child neglect and misuse of youth, and mass media.

The special position of adolescents in our society also has been identified as a cause of delinquency. According to one theory, there are structural forces keeping youths out of the labor force.[78] This leads to anomie, as Durkheim described it, isolation and a feeling of not being a part of the community. Adolescents are in this state of anomie because they do not participate in meaningful interactions, called *role relationships,* in work and other settings:

> An absence of these role relationships means a greater probability of "differential association" with youth or, in Sutherland's terms, greater priority being given to deviant patterns. In other words, the youth group becomes the only meaningful role relationship.[79]

[74]Richard Cloward and Francis Fox Piven, "Hidden Protests: The Channeling of Female Innovations and Resistance, *Signs, 4,* no. 4 (Summer 1979), pp. 651–669.

[75]Simons, Miller, and Aigner, "Female Delinquency," p. 10; and Joseph G. Weis, "Liberation and Crime: The Invention of the New Female Criminal," *Crime and Social Justice, 6* (Fall/Winter 1976), pp. 17–27.

[76]Giordano, "Girls, Guys and Gangs."

[77]Nettler, *Explaining Crime,* pp. 339–347.

[78]Paul C. Friday and Jerald Hage, "Youth Crime in Postindustrial Societies: An Integrated Perspective," *Criminology, 14,* no. 3 (November 1976), pp. 347–368.

[79]*Ibid.,* p. 365.

The structure of society such that it excludes youths from many types of role relationships, then, ultimately leads to delinquency.

As we move into the 1990s, it is apparent that some communities are cut off from the mainstream of legitimate economic opportunity. They are faced with long-lasting, high rates of unemployment. In addition, they possess minimal resources for meeting the need for adequate housing, education, and recreation. The term *underclass* is sometimes used to describe the residents of such communities. The underclass has developed as a result of major changes in the U.S. economy, which have had a negative effect on many groups, but especially minorities and recent immigrants. In the North Central and Eastern regions of the United States, industries that previously provided work for the unskilled have moved.[80] For Hispanics, unlike the situation faced by many immigrant groups earlier in the 1900s, there are communities in which unemployment and underemployment have persisted in some families across generations. The problems are compounded by limited assimilation and a continuous influx of new immigrants.[81] Finally, in many urban areas there has been a proliferation of "informal businesses," which operate unregulated, often require work at home, and which have the effect of creating a workforce of marginally employed people, often immigrants.[82]

One of the results of the shriveling of legitimate job opportunities has been the increased involvement of adolescents, as well as adults, in illegal markets. A particularly dramatic example is the distribution of crack cocaine. It is true that the ease of producing and obtaining crack cocaine is one attraction to this method of making money. However, it is critical not to lose sight of the effect of both community disorganization and lack of alternative means for earning income.

Both legal and illegal opportunities to make money continue to shape the delinquency of gangs and other youth cliques. A modern-day example of the influence of opportunity is evident in reserach by Mercer Sullivan, who compared New York City boys from varying backgrounds. Included in his study were: (1) boys of Puerto Rican heritage in a deteriorating, poor neighborhood (La Barriada), (2) boys in a predominantly black housing project (Projectville), and (3) boys in a working-class white area where most fathers were present in the household and employed (Hamilton Park).[83]

In each of the communities that Sullivan studied, opportunities influenced the form of delinquency. In La Barriada and Hamilton Park, theft from

[80]William Julius Wilson, *The Truly Disadvantaged: The Inner City, the Underclass, and Public Policy* (Chicago: University of Chicago Press, 1987).

[81]Joan W. Moore, Virgil Diego, and Robert Garcia, "Residence and Territoriality in Chicago Gangs," *Social Problems 30,* no. 2 (December 1983), p. 188.

[82]Sassen-Koob, "New York City's Informal Economy," in *The Informal Economy: Studies in Advanced and Less Developed Countries,* eds. A. Portes, M. Castells, and L. A. Benton (Baltimore: Johns Hopkins Press, 1989).

[83]Mercer Sullivan, *"Getting Paid": Youth Crime and Work in the Inner City* (New York: Cornell University Press, 1989).

local factories provided a source of income during midadolescence. In Projectville, the absence of factories and the physical structure of the project itself resulted in the frequent use of robbery, first from project residents, and later in the form of subway gold-chain snatchings. Regardless of how much or how little effort the boys invested in their educations, it was the availability of legitimate jobs that influenced them to continue in their delinquent patterns after age fifteen or sixteen. The availability of jobs depended heavily on a network of personal contacts that allowed many older boys in Hamilton Park to earn spending money. In La Barriada and Projectville, where the boys did not have the needed personal contacts, systematic burglary and subway chain snatching continued to be important sources of income. Sullivan's specific finding that a lack of legitimate employment opportunity is related to illegal behavior has been confirmed in other studies. For example, Richard McGahey found that neighborhoods without job opportunities are most likely to experience predatory crime.[84]

Many urban communities with limited employment opportunities have a similarity to the Chicago areas described by Shaw and McKay. That is, they are marked by high levels of disorganization. The lack of jobs makes it difficult for mothers and fathers to maintain a household. As a result, many families are headed by the mother only. Robert Sampson has additionally pointed out that rapid rates of population turnover and increased density result in neighborhoods where people tend to be strangers.[85] The combined effects of inadequate adult supervision (due to absent fathers); a community comprised of strangers; limited social controls provided by deficient schools, and minimal social service programs all set the stage for delinquency.

Recent data collection efforts have confirmed the importance of neighborhood context in explaining delinquency. Ora Simcha-Fagan and Joseph E. Schwartz found that delinquency was most likely in areas with such characteristics as low community attachment, social disorder, and an illegal economy.[86] In another study of urban settings, Leo Schuerman and Solomon Kobrin documented the combined effects of social disorganization at the community level and a lack of jobs on crime and delinquency. Population change resulting from a shift from owner-occupied to rental units, an increased proportion of father-absent households, and a loss of semiskilled and unskilled jobs from the area resulted in increases in illegal behavior.[87] This pattern is consistent with the

---

[84]Richard McGahey, "Economic Conditions, Organization, and Urban Crime," in *Communities and Crime*, eds. Albert J. Reiss, Jr., and Michael Tonry (Chicago: University of Chicago Press, 1986), pp. 67–100.

[85]Robert J. Sampson, "Communities and Crime," in *Positive Criminology*, eds. Albert J. Reiss, Jr., and Michael Tonry (Chicago: University of Chicago Press, 1987), p. 10.

[86]Ora Simcha-Fagan and Joseph E. Schwartz, "Neighborhood and Delinquency: An Assessment of Contextual Effects," *Criminology 24*, no. 4 (November 1986), pp. 667–703.

[87]Leo A. Schuerman and Solomon Kobrin, "Crime and Urban Ecological Processes: Implications for Public Policy," paper presented at the American Society of Criminology Meetings (Denver, Colorado, November 1983).

explanation that disorganization reduces the community level controls that keep illegal behavior in check, and that a lack of legitimate jobs provides a motivation for illegal behavior.

As we confront contemporary concerns with delinquency, there is a renewed recognition that social and economic structure have an important effect. The status of adolescents in our society may itself play a part in stimulating delinquent behavior. In urban neighborhoods where delinquency is particularly serious, we are using refined versions of opportunity theory and social disorganization explanations of delinquency to explain the amount of lawbreaking. Given the nature of current concerns about delinquency, it is appropriate to direct our attention to such structural causes of delinquency, both in our theory development and in the design of prevention and control programs, a topic that will be discussed in later chapters.

CONCLUSIONS FROM SOCIOLOGICAL THEORIES

The preceding section provides a general view of the major sociological theories of juvenile delinquency, as well as recent advances. All these theories have their strengths and their weaknesses. Merton and Durkheim have shown how the discrepancy between institutional means available and goals desired can produce strain which can in turn lead to delinquency. Thrasher, in a more general sense, also alludes to strain as a result of poverty and points out that an environment is conducive to delinquent behavior when ineffective social controls and inadequate models for identification exist. Shaw and McKay's and Sutherland's work also stress the importance of the environment for determining delinquent behavior. They also point out how delinquency and crime are transmitted from one group to another and how stable criminal patterns can result because of this learning process. George Herbert Mead sheds some light on how a delinquent role is incorporated into a lifestyle. If delinquent behavior is supportive of a person's identity, the person will incorporate it and use it. Ohlin and Cloward's and Cohen's work is similar to that of all the aforementioned theorists in that they too emphasize strain from the social system. However, the delinquent behavior they describe takes on more of a reactive nature against the dominant middle-class system and its social institutions and much of the delinquency is hostile and nonutilitarian and is used solely to vent aggression. Miller relates delinquency to lower-class status. David Matza is important to the discussion because of his attempt to combine the most relevant concepts of both the classical and positive schools of criminology. His realistic description of the "drift" process also helps place the delinquency phenomenon in its proper perspective. Travis Hirschi has taken a different path in the development of theory: He seeks to explain why some people do not break the law as a result of individuals' bonds and commitments to conventional society.

Ongoing empirical research has not provided much support for the subcultural theories of Ohlin and Cloward, Miller, and Cohen. Although Matza's

Table 3-1 A Summary of Contemporary Sociological Theories of Criminality in the Positive School

The Theory and Theorists	What Does the Theory Explain?	Causes of Crime Identified in the Theory	ASSUMPTIONS OF THE THEORY		Supporting Research
			Recognition of Free Will	Recognition of Conflict in Society	
Anomie Theory Durkheim	Rates of suicide and other deviance	Anomie, which is a feeling of isolation from the mainstream of society	no	no	weak
Strain Theory Merton	Deviance throughout society	A breakdown in norms resulting from a discrepancy between desired goals and institutional means	no	no	weak
Gang Theory Thrasher	Delinquency by gang members in poor city neighborhoods	A lack of control over youths *plus* transmission of delinquent values by gangs *plus* environmental support for illegal behavior	no	conflict between neighborhood groups	limited to data from early 1900s
Cultural Transmission Theory Shaw and McKay	Delinquency rates in the central city	Personal and group contacts in disadvantaged environments *plus* ineffective social control	individual choice has some effect	no	weak
Differential Association Theory Sutherland	Criminality of individuals	Learning of definitions favorable to breaking the law through interaction in intimate groups	no	no	weak

(continued)

Table 3-1 (Continued)

The Theory and Theorists	What Does the Theory Explain?	Causes of Crime Identified in the Theory	ASSUMPTIONS OF THE THEORY		
			Recognition of Free Will	Recognition of Conflict in Society	Supporting Research
Self-Role Theory Mead	Deviance of individuals	Commitment to a learned criminal role and self-concept	individuals choose to learn some roles	no	moderate
Working-Class Boy Cohen	Working-class boys' delinquency	Inability of working-class boys to succeed in middle-class institutions, especially schools	no	conflict with authority figures	weak
Opportunity Theory Ohlin and Cloward	Lower-class youths' delinquency	Delinquent subcultures formed in response to the discrepancy between goals and means	no	no	weak
Lower-Class Structure Miller	Lower-class boys delinquency	Lower-class cultural system	no	no	weak
Drift Theory Matza	Delinquency by individuals	Neutralization of normal conventional controls	people have some free will	no	weak
Bond of Individual to Society Hirschi	Why some youths do not break the law	Lack of a strong bond to conventional society	yes	no	strong
Labeling Perspective Lemert	Deviance by individuals	Official labeling by police and court personnel	not in simplistic versions	no	weak
Adolescent Subcultures, Capitalism Schwendinger and Schwendinger	Adolescent peer-group formations and their relationship to delinquency	Peer groups common in capitalistic society	yes	yes	moderate

theory is quite appealing as a method to integrate the classical and positive approaches, it too is not well supported by research. The labeling perspective advances beyond the traditional sociological theories by bringing our attention to the negative influence of juvenile justice system contact. Efforts are under way to build onto the overly simplified descriptions of the labeling process, and develop a more comprehensive explanation of delinquency causation. Ongoing research includes the application of traditional theories to female delinquents, and the development of new theories to account for the low levels of female delinquency, as well as the experiences of girls labeled as status offenders. As an alternative to theories which focus on just one social class, racial group, or sex, some people have attempted to identify things about our society which cause delinquency. The radical theorists, including the Schwendingers, focus specifically on the economic structure, and they are in this last group.

This abbreviated discussion of the major sociological concepts, which is summarized in Table 3-1, does not of course include all the theorists who have contributed to an understanding of juvenile delinquency. Chapter 4 will examine other concepts related to juvenile delinquency and the family.

Compared with sociological theorists, fewer psychologists seem to be interested in theorizing about juvenile delinquency and adult crime. Psychologists did not become interested in delinquency and criminality as a specific field of study until fairly recently. Even at the present time the study of delinquency and criminality is often considered only a secondary manifestation of the larger category of behavior termed *mental illness,* and the emphasis has been on studying mental illness in general in the psychology discipline.

MAJOR PSYCHOLOGICAL THEORIES

Whereas sociologists emphasize the environment of the social structure and its effect on crime rates and crime causation, psychologists take a more specific approach and consider the individual's motivational patterns in an attempt to describe delinquency and criminality. The present discussion will focus on psychological factors, and the sampling of theorists will range from those who operate under Freudian assumptions to those who use testing as their major method of criminological investigation. Just as all sociologists cannot be grouped into a single category, all psychologists do not as a group emphasize the same areas of investigation. Some sociologists are more psychologically oriented than some psychologists, and vice versa. For descriptive purposes, however, it will be assumed that both fields have a distinct body of knowledge and method of investigation and that if people call themselves either sociologists or psychologists certain assumptions can be made about their orientation to delinquency and criminality.

There are varying opinions about the quantity and the quality of the impact that psychological factors have on the causation of juvenile delinquency. At one extreme, Alex Inkeles argues that all sociological analysis should attempt to integrate ideas from psychology.[88] This can be done by identifying certain personality types which reject or accept the influences in the environment, by demonstrating how the personalities of members affect groups and organizations, or by incorporating psychological explanations of learning into sociological theories.

At present there is no single psychological theory (just as there is no single sociological theory) that has been tested empirically and totally explains, for all circumstances, juvenile delinquency and criminality. In addition, unsubstantiated overgeneralizations of human behavior have been made.

> This does not mean, however, that the search for valid hypotheses based upon demonstrated proof is not moving forward nor does it mean that the work in the field of delinquency may not be an important step in the development of an adequate personality theory.[89]

Regardless of the particular individual-based theory, delinquency and crime are viewed as an outgrowth of the maladaptive experience of the particular individual. There are numerous professionals and professions—that is, psychiatry, psychology, psychoanalysis—that use the individual approach. Generalizations will be made to include all the various groups so that discussion of psychological theories will be facilitated and a comparison between sociology and psychology will be made easier for the reader.

Psychoanalytic Theory—Sigmund Freud

Originally developed by Sigmund Freud, psychoanalytic theory asserts that all relevant personality formation is concluded very early in childhood, based on interaction between the child and the adult environment. The child goes through a series of sexual stages (oral, anal, phallic, and so on), during which the focus of attention is on resolving conflicts between unconscious drives and the demands of the adult world.[90] As the child develops, a three-part personality structure forms of the id, the ego, and the superego. These parts correspond to the primitive instincts (id), the sense of self (ego), and the conscience (superego), respectively. When drives to satisfy sexual desires are repressed or the level of control over them is abnormally low, various behavior disorders develop. Thus, some individuals become socially aggressive, others completely passive; some are unable to control particular impulses to action. The range of

---

[88]Alex Inkeles, "Sociological Theory in Relation to Social Psychological Variables," in *Theoretical Sociology*, eds. John C. McKinney and Edward A. Tiryakian (New York: Appleton-Century-Crofts Educational Division Meredith Corporation, 1970), pp. 403–431.

[89]Herbert A. Bloch and Frank T. Flynn, *Delinquency* (New York: Random House, 1956), p. 84.

[90]Gerald S. Blum, *Psychoanalytic Theories of Personality* (New York: McGraw-Hill Book Company, 1953).

deviation is immense. When the personality mechanisms are badly warped, anti-social actions, including juvenile delinquency, can occur.

August Aichhorn was an early theorist to apply the basic ideas of psycho-analytic theory in his comprehensive study and practice with juvenile delinquents. According to Aichhorn:

> psychoanalysis enables the worker to recognize the dissocial manifestations as a result of an inner play of psychic forces, to discover the unconscious motives of such behavior and to find means of leading the dissocial back to social conformity.[91]

Because of the conflicts that exist within delinquents, Aichhorn feels that first there has to be an understanding of the three dynamic components of the personality—the id, the ego, and the superego. As a result of understanding the interplay of these three dynamic components, conflicts can be diagnosed and the reasons for dissocial behavior understood. After this has been accomplished, psychoanalytic treatment methods and positive living experiences can be used to facilitate recovery. Since dissocial children have inadequate conscience structures, new positive identification models have to be provided so that the child's faulty identification with criminal parents or unacceptable persons in the environment can be altered.

Since Aichhorn made his initial contribution, there have been several adaptations of Freudian theory to delinquency, some of which deviate considerably from the work of both Freud and Aichhorn. For example, Erik Erikson focused on adolescents' need to achieve ego identity, which is a clear sense of their selves and beliefs.[92] Some youths do not achieve ego identity, and they are easily influenced by peers who lead them into delinquent activity. In another development of psychoanalytic theory, David Abrahamsen stressed the influence of conflict between the ego and superego, and the related inability to control impulsive, pleasure-seeking drives.[93] Seymour Halleck pinpointed youths' feelings of oppression and powerlessness as the root cause of delinquency.[94] He wrote that oppression and powerlessness can be counteracted by the excitement, a chance to use skills, and other benefits of delinquent actions. These and other psychoanalytic theories place a heavy emphasis on the family experiences that result in unconscious, internal conflicts at an early age, and that can explain delinquency. When the psychoanalytic theory was most popular, experts recommended that early psychiatric intervention be used on a wide scale to prevent illegal behavior (Exhibit 3-5).

[91]August Aichhorn, *Wayward Youth* (New York: The Viking Press, Inc., 1953), p. 3.

[92]Erik Erikson, *Identity, Youth and Crisis* (New York: Norton, 1968).

[93]David Abrahamsen, *Crime and the Human Mind* (New York: Columbia University Press, 1944).

[94]Seymour Halleck, *Psychiatry and the Dilemmas of Crime* (Berkeley, California: University of California Press, 1971).

Exhibit 3-5 A purely psychoanalytic approach to delinquency prevention

I have no hesitation in saying that the crux of the whole approach to the problem of murder and the problem of prevention or punishment lies in an adequate attack at the right point. The right point is theoretically at any age, from birth upwards, but in practice between the ages of 2½ and 8. There should be an adequate service of child guidance, including the use of batteries of tests; and we feel fairly convinced that although you would not recognize all the potential murderers, that would be a foolish claim, you would strike seriously to the root of the problem of murder and its prevention.

There are so-called projective techniques of examination which are valuable, because they eliminate subjective bias on the part of the examiner and of the case examined. They have now arrived at a state of, not perfection, but adequacy, so that it is possible to take a child who is to all appearances merely an inhibited child, without any history of bad behavior, and discover that he is potentially violent.

SOURCE: An interview with Dr. Glover, British psychiatrist and psychoanalyst, quoted in Michael Hakeem, "A Critique of the Psychiatric Approach to the Prevention of Juvenile Delinquency," *Social Problems*, 5, no. 3 (Winter 1957–58), p. 196.

Recently, there has been less emphasis on psychoanalytic theories of delinquency than on sociological or other psychological approaches. Even when research links family interactions and circumstances to delinquency, it is difficult to demonstrate that the family's effect is through an influence on unconscious motives, because the workings of the unconscious are not amenable to scientific measurement:

A methodology under which only the patient knows the "facts" of the case, and only the analyst understands the meaning of those "facts" as revealed to him by the patient, does not lend itself to external, third person, impersonal verification or to generalizations beyond the limits of any particular case.[95]

Also criticized is the emphasis on biological motivation, early childhood experiences, sexual drives, and the related deemphasis of both social factors and conscious motivations to break the law.[96]

The following theorists, although they are not considered to be psychoanalysts, also used individual, psychological principles to study delinquency and crime.

Multifactor Approach—Sheldon and Eleanor Glueck

Eleanor and Sheldon Glueck attempted to select all those factors that they felt explained some part of criminal behavior, regardless of whether the

[95]Vold, *Theoretical Criminology*, p. 125.

[96]Don C. Gibbons, *Society, Crime, and Criminal Careers: An Introduction to Criminology*, 3rd ed. (Englewood Cliffs, New Jersey: Prentice-Hall, Inc., 1977), pp. 164–165.

principles originated from psychology or sociology. Although the multifactor approach can make a valuable contribution to the understanding of criminal behavior, it is generally acknowledged that no one body of knowledge can be considered a theoretical base for this approach. Criticisms have been made of the multifactor approach—namely, that it is too loosely defined and that it is no more than superficial generalizations. A brief exposure to the multifactor point of view will be helpful, however, in providing a wider base of understanding of the delinquency phenomenon and how it is viewed by certain theorists.

The Gluecks state that

> persistent delinquency can be the result, not only of one specific combination or pattern of factors that markedly differentiate delinquents from nondelinquents, but of each of several different patterns. The concept of plurality of causal combinations immediately throws light on a host of puzzling problems in the study of crime causation. Just as the fact of a boy's death, although always and everywhere the same terminal event, may nonetheless be the result of various preceding sequences of conditions, so the terminal event of persistent delinquency may have in its causal pedigree and background a variety of different sequences leading to the same ultimate result of habitual antisocial behavior.[97]

In relation to the practitioner,

> many probation and parole officers, teachers, school attendants, officers, and others seem to want specific answers to the "why" of causation; that is, they want to know what the "ultimate cause" of a child's misbehavior is and how it came about. But the ultimate cause is something like a mirage. The more you approach it, the farther it seems to recede.[98]

The Gluecks used the multifactor approach in comparing five hundred delinquents with five hundred nondelinquents. The delinquents were matched by residence in underprivileged areas, age, ethnic origin, and intelligence. The Gluecks considered sociological variables (the environment) and psychological variables (internal dynamic processes). In addition, they administered tests. They concluded that the delinquency of the youngsters could not be blamed on any one set of factors. The delinquent behavior was the result of a combination of intellectual, social, temperamental, and physical factors. To pinpoint any particular one would be difficult. They summarized their findings as follows:

> It is particularly in the exciting, stimulating, but little controlled, and culturally inconsistent environment of the urban underprivileged area that such boys readily tend to give expression to their untamed impulses and their self-centered desires. . . . It will be seen that virtually all the conditions enumerated are of a kind that in all probability preceded the evolution of delinquent careers, and in respect to sequence of events in time may legitimately be regarded as causally connected.[99]

[97]Sheldon and Eleanor Glueck, *Venture in Criminology* (Cambridge, Massachusetts: Harvard University Press, 1967), p. 16.

[98]*Ibid.*, p. 17.

[99]*Ibid.*, p. 27.

Delinquency, then, is the result of an interplay of many different and diverse variables as viewed from the multifactor approach. In all of the psychological theories reviewed thus far, personality characteristics account for delinquency. Representing a different branch of psychology, the social learning theorists have instead stressed the importance of training to teach youths law-abiding behavior.

Operant Conditioning—Hans Eysenck

Hans Eysenck explains delinquency as a product of the interaction of a person's biological makeup and training. Focusing first on biological makeup, he contends that the personality is made up of three parts. One part is a tendency toward either extroversion or the opposite, introversion. This reflects the make-up of the central nervous system. The second part is a tendency toward neuroticism or stability, which reflects the peripheral nervous system. The third part, which is not explicitly linked to the nervous system, is psychoticism. People who are characterized by psychoticism exhibit "cold cruelty, social insensitivity, unemotionality, disregard for danger, troublesome behavior, dislike for other people, and a liking for the unusual."[100]

Training involves giving rewards for desired behavior and punishment for undesired behavior, as well as people to act as models whose behavior can be imitated. Eysenck stresses the reward and punishment aspect of training, as is evident in his description of the role of punishment:

> In every society there is a long list of prohibitions of acts which are declared to be bad, naughty, and immoral, and which, although they are attractive to him [the child] and are self-rewarding, he must nevertheless desist from carrying out. As we have pointed out before, this is not likely to be achieved by any formal process of long-delayed punishment, because what is required to offset the immediate pleasure derived from the activity must be an immediate punishment which is greater than the pleasure and, if possible, occurs in closer proximity to the crime. In childhood it is possible for parents, teachers and other children to administer such punishment at the right moment of time; the child who does something wrong is immediately slapped, sent off, sent upstairs, or whatever the punishment may be. Thus, we may regard the evil act itself as the conditioned stimulus and we may regard the punishment—the slap, the moral shaming, or whatever the punishment may be—as the unconditioned stimulus which produces pain or, at any rate, some form of suffering and, therefore, of sympathetic response. On the principle of conditioning, we would now expect that after a number of repetitions of this kind, the act itself would produce the conditioned response; in other words, when the child is going to carry out one of the many activities which have been prohibited and punished in the past, then the conditioned automatic response would immediately occur and produce a strong deterrent, being, as it were, unpleasant in itself.[101]

[100]Bartol, *Criminal Behavior*, p. 40; see also Hans J. Eysenck, *The Biological Basis of Personality* (Springfield, Illinois: Charles C. Thomas, 1967); and Hans J. Eysenck, *Crime and Personality* (London: Routledge and Kegan Paul, 1977).

[101]Hans J. Eysenck, *Fact and Fiction in Psychology* (London: Penguin Books, 1965), pp. 260–261. © 1965 by Penguin Books Ltd. Reprinted by permission of Penguin Books Ltd.

Just as punishments for certain behavior come to be anticipated, children develop an internal sense that previously rewarded behavior is pleasurable. This process of learning through training is called *operant conditioning.*

Eysenck combines his ideas about biological predispositions with those about training by identifying certain of the predispositions which make it difficult to train a child. Thus, in his theory, extroverts are considered to be difficult to train through operant conditioning. They may become delinquent, regardless of what would be considered normal parental efforts in training them. Additionally, Eysenck felt that lower- and working-class parents were particularly unable to use operant conditioning effectively, which accounted for the concentration of delinquency in these classes.

The biological part of Eysenck's theory has been strongly refuted on the grounds that there is little research support.[102] Nevertheless, there are studies supporting some of Eysenck's ideas, and this suggests the need to further test the theory. Eysenck's attempt to link personality types with the results of training efforts, in particular, may be a promising avenue for future research.[103]

Modeling—Alberta Bandura and Richard Walters

Albert Bandura and Richard Walters stress the importance of modeling in their social learning theory of delinquency. Thus, they move away from Eysenck's emphasis on biological makeup and training through reward and punishment. In their view, children copy the behavior of people whom they hold in high esteem and who have been providing rewards. These people typically include parents, and can include siblings, peers, and others.

In their own research, Bandura and Walters have concentrated particularly on understanding aggression. They have discovered a tendency to copy aggressive behavior from models who are rewarded when they are aggressive, and from those who are not punished:

> The role of models in the transmission of novel social responses has been demonstrated most extensively in laboratory studies of aggression. Children who have been exposed to aggressive models respond to subsequent frustration with considerable aggression, much of which is precisely imitative, whereas equally frustrated children who have observed models displaying inhibited behavior are relatively nonaggressive and tend to match the behavior of the inhibited model. . . . Children who observe an aggressive model rewarded display more imitative aggression than children who see a model punished for aggression.[104]

---

[102]M. S. Hoghughi and A. R. Forrest, "Eysenck's Theory of Criminality," *British Journal of Criminology,* 10, no. 3 (July 1970), pp. 240–254; J. F. Allsopp, "Criminality and Delinquency," in *A Textbook of Human Psychology,* eds. Hans J. Eysenck and Glenn D. Wilson (Baltimore: University Park Press, 1976), pp. 241–253; and M. Philip Feldman, *Criminal Behavior: A Psychological Analysis* (New York: John Wiley and Sons, Inc., 1977).

[103]Bartol, *Criminal Behavior,* pp. 47, 48.

[104]Albert Bandura and Richard H. Walters, *Social Learning and Personality Development* (New York: Holt, Rinehart and Winston, Inc., 1963), pp. 106–107.

In some cases children learn behavior entirely from observation, which can extend to television and movie characters. Although children can learn aggressive and other behaviors from the media, parents usually maintain a key role in reinforcing or punishing this newly learned behavior.[105]

There is considerable research support for the idea that modeling is the key to the learning of delinquent behaviors. In research laboratories, children act more aggressively after viewing films of adults acting aggressively. Other parts of the theory are supported by studies which show that children with a history of failure are most likely to copy violent models,[106] and that the child's other unique personality characteristics influence whether or not modeling takes place.[107] It should be noted that many of these studies are conducted in research laboratories. The conditions leading up to modeling, and the effects of modeling may be much more complicated in real-life situations.

Cognitive Developmental Theory—Jean Piaget*

In our discussion of the major psychological theories, we have already described three general perspectives which utilize a psychological approach to explain delinquency: the psychoanalytic theory (Freud), the multifactor approach (Glueck and Glueck), and the social learning theories (Eysenck, Bandura, and Walters). These three perspectives are nearly always discussed in the literature on juvenile delinquency. A fourth perspective, cognitive developmental theory, is less often discussed because its conceptualization has not been refined as an explanation of delinquency. However, since it holds considerable promise as an explanation of delinquency, we have included information on the theory here.

Cognitive developmental theory proposes that the human organism develops from conception in an orderly, sequential manner. Jean Piaget thus described intellectual development[108] and both Piaget and Kohlberg[109] presented

---

[105]Eleanor E. Maccoby, "The Development of Moral Values and Behavior in Childhood," in *Socialization and Society*, ed. John A. Clausen (Boston: Little, Brown and Company, 1968), pp. 229–271.

[106]Louise M. Soares and Anthony T. Soares, "Social Learning and Social Violence," *Proceedings*, 77th Annual Meeting of the American Psychological Association (Washington, D.C.: The Association, 1969).

[107]Mary A. Rosenkrans, "Imitation in Children as a Function of Perceived Similarity to a Social Model and Vicarious Reinforcement," *Journal of Personality and Social Psychology*, 7, no. 3 (November 1967), pp. 307–315; and Louise M. Soares and Anthony T. Soares, "Social Learning and Disruptive Social Behavior," *Phi Delta Kappan*, 82–84 (October 1970), pp. 82–84.

*NOTE: This section on *Cognitive Developmental Theory* was written by Vincent J. Hoffman, School of Criminal Justice, Michigan State University.

[108]Jean Piaget, trans., *The Origins of Intelligence in Children* (New York: International Universities Press, 1952).

[109]Jean Piaget, trans., *The Moral Development of the Child* (London: Routledge and Kegan Paul, 1965), pp. 197–199; Lawrence Kohlberg, "Stage and Sequence: The Cognitive Developmental Approach to Socialization," in *Handbook of Socialization Theory and Research*, ed. Donald A. Goslin (Chicago: Rand McNally, 1969).

an explanation of moral development, Kohlberg goes further and holds that an arrest in development in moral reasoning at certain stages can explain delinquency in some youth.[110]

The theory suggests that child development is predictive, normative, and positive in a normal environment or one in which the child's developmental needs are generally met. If the child's developmental needs are met, the youth is able to accomplish specific developmental tasks. There are levels or stages of development, and the child will exhibit a repertoire of behaviors which are appropriate to his or her developmental level. For example, a youth of fourteen should show intellectual and moral reasoning processes which are more developed than a child of six.

The prerequisites for a child's development include controls, security, knowledge of control boundaries, dependence on significant others and consistent interactions with them. The child also needs to develop competence through success experiences which relate to the child having an effect on the environment.

Related to the developmental needs are tasks. For the adolescent, the tasks include accepting one's physique and sexual role, establishing new peer relationships, attaining emotional independence from parents, achieving assurance of economic independence, choosing and preparing for an occupation, developing intellectual skills and concepts necessary for civic competence, acquiring socially responsible behavior patterns, preparing for marriage and family life, and building conscious values that are harmonious with the youth's environment.[111]

To the degree that the developmental needs are not met and the developmental tasks are not completed, the youth will experience behavior problems. The problem behavior may go against norms set up in the youth's environment and could relate to authority figures (parents, teachers, police), to peers, to family, and to agencies (school, place of employment).

Bronfenbrenner comments on alienation of youth from adults.[112] He writes that this alienation results in the youth's lack of direction and ignorance of boundaries and controls, which can be provided only by adults who are invested in the youth. The youth's lack of knowledge, resulting from this alienation and his or her attempts to obtain direction from peers or noninvested adults, quite often can be the occasion for the youth becoming involved in delinquent acts. In addition, if his or her needs for controls, attachment, and effective support are not met, the youth may simply give up attempts to exhibit acceptable behavior.

Another facet of this normative approach to deviance in youth revolves around ignorance by parents and other authority figures of what is normal

[110]Lawrence Kohlberg, "The Development of Modes of Moral Thinking and Choice in Years 10 to 16" (unpublished Doctoral dissertation, Harvard University, 1958).

[111]Ruth Havighurst, *Developmental Tasks and Education* (New York: Longmans Green, 1951), pp. 30–55.

[112]Urie Bronfenbrenner, "The Origins of Alienation," *The Scholastic,* 5 (Spring 1974), pp. 57–61.

developmental behavior. **Ferguson** describes the normal developmental behavioral practices of adolescents that often make adults at least defensive, and even punitive, toward youth. These behaviors include the adolescent's need to confront authority, make moves toward independence, and attempt to emulate adult behavior. Any one or a combination of these healthy adolescent behaviors, if they are exhibited at all in some cases or in a manner adults deem inappropriate, can cause the wrath of the adult world (oftentimes including the juvenile justice system) to descend on the reckless youth.[113]

Much more research must be done to spell out and clarify this developmental approach to understanding youth deviance. The efforts may be worthwhile, for the theory not only predicates normal motivation and behavior in the average youth, but also assumes that these developmental tendencies are strong and healthy.

RECENT ADVANCES IN PSYCHOLOGICAL THEORY

Several of the advances in psychological theory parallel, or are actually a part of, advances in sociological work. As in sociology, there is an ongoing effort to develop research support for each theory. Additionally, several people have pointed out and attempted to correct the inadequacies of existing psychological explanations of females' delinquency. There have been some attempts to integrate the best supported ideas from psychology and sociology. Similar to some trends in sociology, there also have been some radical challenges to traditional psychological explanations of behavior, including delinquency.

Empirical Research

Of the psychological theories reviewed, the psychoanalytic theories building on Freud's work and social learning theory as exemplified by Bandura and Walter's work continue to have considerable influence on delinquency programs. The amount of research evidence differs considerably for these two branches of psychological theory. Summarizing the research on psychoanalytic theory, Gibbons writes that

> no convincing evidence of psychological forces, particularly in the form of aberrant personality patterns and the like, has yet been uncovered. At the same time, it is clearly a non sequitur to imply, as many criminologists have done, that research results demonstrate that personality factors play no part in criminality. It is entirely conceivable that there are important psychological forces that have yet to be uncovered.[114]

[113]Lucy Ferguson, *Personality Development* (Belmont, California: Brooks/Cole, 1970), pp. 170–174.
[114]Gibbons, *The Criminological Enterprise*, p. 214.

In contrast, evidence presented so far indicates that there is considerable support for the theory that learning does occur through conditioning and modeling, and that this learning process can result in delinquent behavior.

Integration of Sociological and Psychological Theories

A major failure in the majority of criminological theories, which are the sociological ones, is that they have "not succeeded in resolving the issue of psychological forces and personality factors in crime and delinquency."[115] An early exception was the work of Frank Scarpitti, Ellen Murray, Simon Dinitz, and Walter Reckless, who combined sociological and psychological explanations.[116] Consistent with other sociologists, they were interested in the effect of "bad neighborhood" environments on delinquency. However, they felt that internal factors such as lack of esteem and feelings of inadequacy contribute to delinquent behavior. More specifically, an adequate self-concept (feeling worthwhile) can be an insulating factor in repelling delinquency, and can explain the existence of "good boys in bad neighborhoods."

Since Scarpitti and his colleagues focused attention on the possibility that individual differences could alter sociological influences on delinquency, several other theorists have attempted to show the joint effect of individual and sociological factors.[117] The *National Youth Survey*, which Chapter 2 described as an important source of data on adolescents, is one recent example of research that is designed to test integrated sociological and psychological theory.

The *National Youth Survey* considered the combined and separate effects of influences identified in a variety of theories. These influences included (1) the strain introduced by a failure to achieve aspirations for family functioning and school success, (2) conventional bonding to family and school, and (3) bonding to deviant peers. A key finding of the research is that once prior delinquency was taken into account, the only variable with a direct effect on delinquency was involvement with delinquent peers. Strain and conventional bonding did have some indirect influence on delinquency, for the youths who were least able to achieve their aspirations had the lowest levels of conventional bonding, and low levels of conventional bonding seemed to contribute to a tendency to become involved with delinquent peers (see Fig. 3-1). It may be that social learning from peers is of particular importance in predisposing youths to delinquency, especially if those youths do not have strong conventional bonds.

---

[115]*Ibid.*, p. 212.

[116]Frank R. Scarpitti, Ellen Murray, Simon Dinitz, and Walter Reckless, "Good Boys in a High Delinquency Area: Four Years Later," *American Sociological Review, 25,* no. 4 (August 1960), pp. 555–558.

[117]Delbert S. Elliott, David Huizinga, and Suzanne S. Ageton, *Explaining Delinquency and Drug Use* (Beverly Hills, California: Sage Publications, 1985).

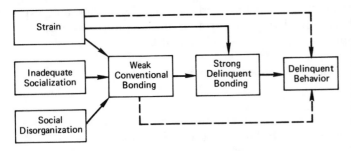

Figure 3-1 An integrated model to explain delinquency

SOURCE: Delbert S. Elliott, David Huizinga, and Suzanne S. Ageton, *Explaining Delinquency and Drug Use* (Beverly Hills, California: Sage Publications, 1985), p. 146. Copyright © 1985 by Sage Publications. Reprinted by permission of Sage Publications, Inc.

As shown in Figure 1-1 and Exhibits 3-1 through 3-5, theory has very important implications for the design of delinquency prevention programs. Thus, the researchers who conducted the *National Youth Survey* outlined the programmatic implications of their theoretical findings. In considering the many programs that target adolescent groups and gangs, they conclude:

> A key implication of our findings is that normal peer group processes facilitate delinquent as well as conventional behavior; and because these treatment groups rarely include any nondelinquent youth, it is unreasonable to expect that a group of serious chronic offenders will somehow generate a pro-social set of values and group norms by interacting with one another.[118]

They go on to recommend programs that influence potential delinquents to join peer groups in which members reinforce prosocial behavior. The programs also could focus on building stronger bonds to the family, school, and other conventional groups.

Under the sponsorship of the federal government, recommendations based on a similar integration of strain, social control, and social learning theories have been set forth for the treatment of violent juvenile offenders.[119] The integrated theory to explain juvenile violence suggests that interventions should focus on goals and opportunities as well as bonding to conventional society. Also, there is a need for programs to influence the conditions of social learning, and to consider predisposing psychosocial factors that can override other influences, specifically, violence in the family, a lack of empathy, and emotional disturbance. Again, the trend is to combine sociological and psychological theories into an explanation of delinquency, and to use the integrated result as the basis for developing a multipronged intervention to prevent juvenile delinquency.

Following another path in the integration of theory, some people have proposed that a combination of individual differences and immediate circum-

---

[118]*Ibid.*, p. 149.

[119]Jeffrey A. Fagan and Sally Jo Jones, "Toward a Theoretical Model for Intervention with Violent Offenders," in *Violent Juvenile Offenders: An Anthology*, eds. Robert A. Mathias, Paul De Muro, and Richard S. Allinson (San Francisco, California: National Council on Crime and Delinquency, 1984), pp. 53–69.

stances can best explain delinquency.[120] The types of immediate circumstances that might come into play include the physical characteristics of a neighborhood, such as lighting and the degree to which residents can get a clear view of adolescents' activities. Situational variations can provide

1. the material conditions which make crime possible;
2. features which constitute inducements to crime, and
3. elements which ensure that the benefits of crime can be obtained at low risk.[121]

Thus, a combination of personal traits with the availability of equipment needed to carry out a burglary, attractive goods to steal, and homes with entrances hidden from public view are likely to result in a juvenile breaking and entering offense. Whether the emphasis is on social structure or situation, there is a growing recognition that regardless of a person's individual makeup, she or he will be most likely to break the law when subjected to certain stresses or when exposed to particular circumstances.

Females—The Psychological Theories

In contrast to the failure of traditional sociological theories to consider females' crime, there have been several psychological theories with this focus. In most, there is an underlying assumption that the females' biological makeup causes psychological characteristics, which in turn lead to law-violating behavior. Carol Smart explains why many people consider this assumption sexist:

> It is sexist not because it differentiates between the sexes but because it attributes to one sex socially undesirable characteristics which are assumed to be intrinsic or "natural" characteristics of that sex."[122]

Furthermore:

> Myths about the "inherent" evil in women or their lack of intelligence and ability and their "natural" passivity therefore abound in these studies and they are used uncritically to supply "evidence" for either the greater or lesser involvement of women in crime.[123]

Lombroso's theory illustrates this problem. According to Lombroso, females are "naturally" less criminal because of their biological makeup. However, there are

[120]Michael Rutter and Henri Giller, *Juvenile Delinquency: Trends and Perspectives* (New York: Penguin Books, 1983), pp. 260–261.
[121]*Ibid.*, p. 260.
[122]Carol Smart, *Women, Crime and Criminology: A Feminist Critique* (Boston: Routledge and Kegan Paul Ltd., 1977), p. 91; see also Dorie Klein, "The Etiology of Female Crime: A Review of The Literature," *Issues in Criminology, 8,* no. 2 (Fall 1973), pp. 3–30.
[123]Smart, *Women, Crime, and Criminology,* p. 91.

some "born" female offenders who lack a "mother sense." Later in his career, Lombroso wrote that female offenders were born as psychologically more horrid and cruel than male offenders.[124]

Although Lombroso's biological orientation to explain males' crime has been abandoned, his influence persists in the explanation of females' crime:

> By shifting the focus of emphasis from causal factors in the environment to causal factors in individuals, the basis was laid for our present procedure of diagnosis and treatment of individual delinquents that views delinquency in terms of individual abnormality or psychological maladjustment.[125]

Specifically, in some theories, being female, along with the personality characteristics assumed to be related to this biological fact, is the cause of delinquency. For example, Gisela Konopka[126] attributed female delinquency, in part, to the dramatic physical changes experienced by girls at puberty, and special difficulties which girls have in identifying with their mothers. She does additionally identify social conditions as causes: the lack of opportunities girls see to move into meaningful adult roles, the lack of a legitimate outlet for aggressive drives, resentment of the sexual double standard, and the expectation that girls are passive. In another theory, Cowie, Cowie, and Slater assume that there is a "natural" personality difference between boys and girls, and therefore they have different sex roles. In their view, delinquency is a rebellion against the female sex role. Rebellion occurs in girls who have masculine physical traits.[127] Contrary to these theories in which special psychological characteristics of girls are the causes of delinquency, numerous studies confirm that female delinquents do not have different personalities than male delinquents.[128]

Social learning theorists explain sex-related differences in delinquency as a result of different socialization of boys and girls. Specifically, through rewards, punishments, and modeling, "girls are taught not to lash out, not to fight physically, but rather to deal with anger and frustration indirectly or verbally."[129]

The social learning theorist's position is challenged to some extent by modern-day theories and research that consider biological causes. These theories do not assume that biological makeup affects personality, but that it directly affects behavior. For example, studies have shown that the male hormone testos-

[124]Marvin E. Wolfgang, "Cesare Lombroso (1835–1909)," in *Pioneers in Criminology,* 2nd ed., ed. Hermann Mannheim (Montclair, New Jersey: Patterson Smith, 1973), pp. 232–291.

[125]Giallombardo, "Female Delinquency," p. 64.

[126]Gisela Konopka, *Adolescent Girl in Conflict* (Englewood Cliffs, New Jersey: Prentice-Hall, Inc., 1966).

[127]John Cowie, Valerie Cowie, and Eliot Slater, *Delinquency in Girls* (London: Heinemann, 1968).

[128]Thomas M. Achenbach, *Developmental Psychopathology* (New York: The Ronald Press Company, 1974).

[129]Bartol, *Criminal Behavior,* p. 279.

terone is related to aggression in males and females.[130] There is controversy about how much of aggression is caused by such factors, and how much by socialization.

Another area of controversy over the psychological theories is the relative influence of psychological causes as opposed to sociological causes. Several critics have argued that by focusing on the psychological factors responsible for females' delinquency, the girls' defective personalities or defective training is pinpointed for change. No recognition is given to possible inadequacies in society which may account for their delinquency.

CONCLUSIONS FROM PSYCHOLOGICAL THEORY

Like the sociological theories discussed, the psychological theories, which we have summarized in Table 3-2, add to an understanding and knowledge of deviant behavior, especially of the form that manifests itself in delinquency. As in sociological theory, there should be more scientific substantiation of the principles and assumptions utilized by psychologists and psychiatrists. Psychological theories and especially the psychoanalytic method have assumed certain universal uniformities about human behavior. The assumed "natural" differences between males' and females' personalities is one example of this. Generalizations have been made from these assumptions, and hence conclusions are not always applicable to all classes and types of behavior. Not all delinquents are mentally ill or deeply disturbed. More comparative studies using control and experimental groups have to be undertaken. Studies which investigate many different interacting variables, including social, psychological, and biological, will have to be performed.

THEORIES AND DELINQUENCY CONTROL

The criminologist Lamar Empey has developed a compelling argument that the way we define delinquency is an important influence on how we react to it.[131] Definitions of delinquency include perceptions of its extent and nature, as well as its causes. Thus, there is a direct relationship between theories of delinquency causation and the choice of methods and programs to control it. Understanding this relationship reveals the roots of police tendencies to base their actions on the classical school, and court and correctional personnel to use the positive school.

[130]Kenneth E. Moyer, "The Physiology of Aggression and the Implication for Aggression Control," in *The Control of Aggression and Violence*, ed. Jerome L. Singer (New York: Academic Press, Inc., 1971); and Harold Goldman, "The Limits of Clockwork: The Neurobiology of Violent Behavior," in *In Fear of Each Other*, eds. John P. Conrad and Simon Dinitz (Lexington, Massachusetts: Lexington Books, D. C. Heath and Company, 1977), pp. 43–46.

[131]Empey, *American Delinquency*.

Table 3-2 A Summary of Contemporary Psychological Theories of Criminality in the Positive School

The Theory and Theorists	What Does the Theory Explain?	Causes of Crime Identified in the Theory	ASSUMPTIONS OF THE THEORY		Supporting Research
			Recognition of Free Will	Recognition of Conflict in Society	
Psychoanalytic Theory Freud	Individual behavior, deviance	Unconscious motivations resulting from early childhood interactions with adults	no	conflict between the individual and society	weak
Psychoanalytic Theory Aichhorn	Delinquency by individuals	Unconscious motivations resulting from early childhood interactions with adults	no	conflict between the individual and society	weak
Multifactor Approach Glueck and Glueck	Delinquency by individuals	Many intellectual, social, temperamental, and physical factors	no	no	weak
Operant Conditioning Eysenck	Delinquency by individuals	Training *plus* biological makeup	no	no	moderate
Modeling Bandura and Walters	Delinquency by individuals	Modeling the behavior of others *plus* reward and punishment	no	no	strong
Cognitive Developmental Theory Piaget	Normal adolescent development	Unmet developmental needs	no	no	weak
Integrated Theory Scarpitti, Murray, and Dinitz	The behavior of "good boys" in a "bad neighborhood"	Bad neighborhood *plus* feelings of inadequacy and lack of esteem	yes	no	moderate
Integrated Model Elliot, Huizinga, and Ageton	Delinquency by individuals	Strain, bonding to family and school, bonding to deviant peers	no	no	strong
Circumstantial Explanation	Delinquency by individuals	Personality traits *plus* situational variations	no	no	weak

It also reveals the roots of different delinquency treatment methods used by personnel in the positive school.

It is understandable why police officers often subscribe to the classical school philosophy. Their profession is commissioned with dealing with the delinquent in a practical, legalistic, objective, and expedient manner. The police officer does not have the luxury of spending a great deal of time with the offender to talk about psychological dynamics and environmental background. He or she has to be practical because of the demands of the job. Many police officers have a limited familiarity with psychological and sociological theories of juvenile delinquency, most of which have emerged from the positive school of criminology. As a result, the classical school of criminology is most appealing to them.

Those professionals oriented to the positive school are usually in social work and social service professions. They feel that the offender is sick and needs social and personal treatment. Social agency professionals subscribe to the positive school of criminology for many reasons. They do not have to deal with the immediate problems of arresting, processing, and responding to the actual delinquent act within a community. They have more time to probe into the environmental and personal background of the offender to determine why his or her behavior has taken an antisocial channel. Also, social workers are more thoroughly grounded in the social sciences than are police officers. They have been exposed to the popular theoretical assumptions that have emerged from the positive school of criminology. As a result of these factors, most social workers quite naturally subscribe to the positive school.

The orientations of the additional community agencies in the criminal justice system in regard to criminological emphasis vary somewhere along the continuum between the classical and positive schools of criminology. Our emphasis will not, however, be focused as heavily on these agencies, because their orientation is not reflected in as extreme a manner as police and social work agencies. Also police officers and social workers are the professionals who come in most direct contact with the delinquent offender, and it is their handling of the offender that can have the most long-lasting effect on future behavior.

Chapter 10 will discuss the method of increasing interagency coordination and cooperation which can facilitate more effective delinquency prevention, control, and treatment. It should be mentioned here, however, that the establishment of training programs that are responsive to the feelings, orientation, and needs of both professions (police and social work) would be helpful in creating a more cooperative attitude between them. Each profession needs greater insight into the other's profession. New models for training would be conducive to developing joint efforts in order to produce more effective and coordinated programs.

SUMMARY

This chapter has presented a sampling of the most prevalent theories of crime and delinquency causation. These theories have different implications for the choice of appropriate juvenile delinquency control programs. If, for instance, it is assumed that societal structures facilitate the development of delinquency, practices and policies would logically be aimed at improving agencies and institutions so that a broad spectrum of youth might utilize the services. But if it is assumed that contact with formal official mechanisms is likely to aggravate the already present condition, policy would likely emphasize the restriction of exposure to the process. For example, two currently popular trends related to the labeling theory—diversion from formal processing and the removal of status offenses from the juvenile codes—are based on ideas which seem to be forging a new perception of delinquency and societal reactions to it. While it is not denied by advocates of these positions that individual and/or social factors might be related to delinquent behavior in a causal manner, the underlying notions of primary interest are the way in which delinquent behavior is defined and the manner in which these sanctions are applied in society.

Many shortcomings in juvenile justice can be traced to inadequately developed and tested theory, and the use of conflicting theories. Recent efforts to integrate sociological, psychological, and in some cases biological theories appear to have the greatest potential for pulling together a number of dangling concepts which are currently unaccounted for by delinquency theories. Only in this manner will a theory of delinquency evolve which comprehensively addresses both sides of the interactional process—the individual behavior and the societal reaction.

Because of the complexity of the problem, there is no single answer or "common cure." Many academic disciplines and theoretical approaches can contribute to a better understanding of the delinquency phenomenon and methods for its control, treatment, and prevention. Because a comprehensive knowledge of the problem necessitates an interdisciplinary approach, the next chapter uses the family as a focal point for analyzing juvenile delinquency and showing how sociological and psychological principles can be integrated and applied.

DISCUSSION QUESTIONS

1. How did the different theorists influence each other's thinking about delinquency? For example:
   a. Trace the influence of Freud's psychoanalytic approach on Aichhorn's work, and on explanations of females' delinquency.
   b. How did the subcultural gang theories of Ohlin and Cloward, Miller, and Cohen influence the direction of Matza's work?
   c. Which theories did Greenberg integrate in his own explanation of delinquency?
2. Which theories best explain official rates of delinquency, and which best explain self-reported delinquency?
3. Which theories are best supported by empirical evidence?
4. How do the theories vary in their recognition of conflict within our society, and in the degree to which they picture youths as having little or no free will?
5. For each theory, decide whether the control of delinquency should involve: (a) individual treatment, (b) changes in society, (c) emphasis on the amount and seriousness of punishment, or (d) some combination of these strategies.

PROJECTS

1. Think of an instance when, as an adolescent, you or someone you know broke the law. Which of the theories described in this chapter is the most helpful in explaining what took place?

2. Choose one theory and locate a number of journal articles in which the theory is tested. Explain your own conclusions about whether the theory is well supported.

3. Choose one of the explanations of delinquency that integrates more than one theory. What individual, situational, or social differences should a program based on this explanation focus on in controlling delinquency?

4

The Family and Juvenile Delinquency

- PSYCHOLOGICAL AND SOCIOLOGICAL THEORIES
- THE ENVIRONMENT OF THE FAMILY
- INTERACTION IN THE CONTEMPORARY FAMILY
- BELIEFS, THEORY, AND RESEARCH

LEARNING OBJECTIVES

1. To be aware that both the psychological and sociological disciplines contribute to our understanding of the family's influence on delinquency.
2. To be able to identify the many different family characteristics that are related to delinquency.
3. To recognize patterns of family interaction which are likely to result in delinquency.
4. To know that beliefs about the family have led some people to regard the family as the only influence on delinquency, and others to ignore the family's effect.
5. To be able to state your own position on the effect of the family and to use research findings to support your position.
6. To know that by drawing from different disciplines and from research to test different theories developed within these disciplines it is possible to develop a more comprehensive understanding of the causes of delinquency than if just one theory is used.

This chapter will present psychologists' and sociologists' views on an idea which many people accept without question—that the family is a major influence on the phenomenon of delinquency. The previous chapter has already briefly exposed you to several theories in which the family affects delinquency, and these theories are described more fully here. Several other theories also are introduced. The chapter describes research which is helpful in selecting the best supported of these theories. With this information, you can see how various psychological and sociological principles can be integrated into a meaningful framework. This interdisciplinary framework of theoretical ideas is relevant to understanding the distribution of delinquency in our society, and to selecting appropriate programs to control it. It is also useful to examine specific beliefs about the family's effect on delinquency against such a framework, with the idea that some common beliefs might require modification.

Regardless of the particular professional orientation or academic discipline, many people agree that the family plays an important part in youngsters'

Exhibit 4-1   Treatment of violent delinquents

The following is a statement by Daniel H. Jacobs, M.D. He is an assistant professor of clinical psychiatry at the Harvard Medical School and a former director of the Cambridge Court Clinic, which treats a large number of juvenile offenders.

Institutions also need to involve the families of these youths. Careful evaluation of the families from which the child has come, and if he's a fourteen year old, to which he may return, is essential. . . . For adolescents particularly, one needs to very carefully evaluate the kind of placement after the institution that is best for them. Can the boy's family provide the structure and support he needs? I think a good deal of family therapy would probably be indicated. Certainly a family evaluation by a social worker is essential.

You have to have outreach. What we've found in our outpatient clinic is, the parents are often so overwhelmed by social and emotional problems of their own, that they have practically nothing to give to the child. If you take that child away for a period, help him, but then return him to parents who have not been able to give him much and who are still overwhelmed by problems, the chance that he is going to regress is quite likely. My impression is these children, despite all their toughness, suffer from a great deal of separation anxiety. Often they haven't got enough good mothering in the first place. They, therefore, have a lot of trouble separating from their environment. What you would do in an institution is separate them temporarily. They may then look as though they're doing well because they can put a car together or because they learn, but you may not have dealt with their emotional attachments to the parents that raised them. Often the parents are not willing to let go of the children either, even though they may neglect them or abuse them, they have very strong ties to these children. Unless those ties are examined, and emotional separation and individuation for the adolescent aided, you may find that the delinquents leave after looking successful in the program and be right back into antisocial behavior.

SOURCE: Andrew H. Vachss and Yitzhak Bakal, *The Life-Style Violent Juvenile* (Lexington, Massachusetts: Lexington Books, 1979), pp. 296–297.

lives. The family institution provides children with their first experiences in social living, and these experiences have an effect on later development. What happens in the family is believed to have great impact on how children behave in other social institutions and on whether they become seriously delinquent.

Many theorists, ranging from those oriented to Freudian psychology to sociologists, consider the family the most significant factor in the development of juvenile delinquency. Socioeconomic status, peer group relations, class mobility, and delinquent subculture are also identified as important, but, if analyzed closely, each is either directly or indirectly related to the family environment. For example, youth with weak bonds to the family tend to be in delinquent peer groups.[1] Similarly, the youth who are most attached to gangs that support violent delinquency tend to come from families with the types of problems that are outlined in the pages that follow.[2]

An interdisciplinary effort, focusing on the family's role in delinquent behavior, can therefore be helpful in examining the delinquency phenomenon. We can incorporate concepts and variables from both the psychological and the sociological disciplines to give a more insightful understanding of delinquency and a comprehensive approach to the problem. Such a comprehensive approach to delinquency control is used by many practitioners, who stress the importance of family evaluation and treatment (Exhibit 4-1).

THE FAMILY AS A LINKING CONCEPT

Using the family as a focal point for examining delinquency is not a shift away from recognizing the influence of the broader environment, for instance, community conditions or opportunity structures. Nor does it require us to ignore the influence of the individual characteristics of juveniles. Rather, the family can be seen as an important linking concept, that is, an idea that helps us to organize and further develop our thoughts about how the environment has its influence on delinquency and about how individual predispositions towards delinquency are developed.

Research on the family is helpful in understanding the connection between the environment and delinquency. To illustrate this, we will consider the following findings:

- According to theories that identify minimal opportunity structure or disorganized neighborhoods as causes of delinquency, lower-class youth would be more delinquent than others (see Chapter Three, Theories of Delinquency Causation).

---

[1]Delbert S. Elliott, David Huizinga, and Scott Menard, *Multiple Problem Youth: Delinquency, Substance Use, and Mental Health Problems* (New York: Springer-Verlag, 1989).

[2]Peter Adler, Carlos Ouando, and Dennis Hoceuar, "Familiar Correlates of Gang Membership: An Exploratory Study of Mexican-American Youth," *Hispanic Journal of Behavioral Sciences 1*, no. 6 (March 1984) pp. 65–76.

- There is evidence that the connection between delinquency and social class is not particularly strong (see Chapter Two, Delinquents In and Out of the Juvenile Justice System).
- When official contact with the juvenile justice system is used as a measure of delinquency, the connection to social class is stronger than when self reports of delinquency are used.

How can knowledge of the family help us to explain the apparent incongruity of the above findings? How can such knowledge give us a clearer picture of how delinquency comes about?

In considering the effect of social class, it is important to recognize that child-rearing variables that affect delinquent behavior are similar in delinquents' families regardless of class.[3] Long before youth are affected by opportunity structures and negative community conditions, they are influenced by their families. A study by Robert Larzelere and Gerald Patterson showed that differences in how parents monitored and disciplined their children explained the greater early involvement in delinquency for lower-class boys in comparison to working-class boys. Lower-class families were more likely to have less monitoring and more negative forms of discipline, and thus there was a higher level of early delinquency for the lower-class boys. Larzelere's and Patterson's suggestions for interventions to prevent and control delinquency are useful. They point to the need to not only teach parenting skills, but also to improve the resources available to lower-class parents.

An additional insight provided by understanding the role of the family is that characteristics of the family that are unrelated to self-reported delinquency might still influence official records. In a study of over seven hundred high school sophomores, Richard E. Johnson found that juvenile justice officials are more likely to respond harshly to the misbehavior of children in mother-only families.[4] This tendency was greatest for families with girls, and it could not be explained by the youths' greater involvement in delinquency. Because mother-only families occur more frequently in the lower social classes, the greater *official* delinquency of lower-class children may be a result of official reaction.

The centrality of the family in understanding delinquency is illustrated by the research reviewed above. First, family differences can explain why demographic characteristics, such as social class, are moderately associated with delinquency. Second, family differences can explain official reactions to adolescents. As we will show in the pages that follow, family variables also result in many of the individual characteristics, such as lack of internal controls, that predispose adolescents to be affected by delinquent influences.

[3]Robert E. Larzelere and Gerald R. Patterson, "Parental Management: Mediator of the Effect of Socioeconomic Status on Early Delinquency," *Criminology, 28,* no. 2 (May 1990), pp. 301–324.

[4]Richard E. Johnson, "Family Structure and Delinquency: General Patterns and Gender Differences," *Criminology, 24,* no. 1 (February 1986), pp. 65–80.

PSYCHOLOGY AND THE FAMILY

Chapter 3 pointed out that psychological theories are mainly concerned with variables that relate to early childhood experiences which influence the formation of the personality or the learning of behavior. Psychologists who stress personality development feel that early emotional deprivation is directly associated with, and related to, later psychological disturbances and emotional problems. The greater the deprivation, the greater the emotional insecurity, and therefore the greater the chance for emotional problems or deviant behavior. Psychologists who stress learning feel that the inappropriate use of rewards and punishments, and the absence of models for appropriate behavior, can result in the learning of delinquent behavior. Children who are not adequately trained and who do not have warm and caring adult models will most likely become delinquent. In this section, we begin with a review of the ideas of psychologists who stress personality development.

Personality Development

In a variety of psychological theories, the family plays a key role in the development of personality that predisposes some youths to delinquent behavior. The Freudian theory discussed in Chapter 2 is one example of this type. Usually, very early childhood experiences are emphasized, and families that provide a continuously negative setting for the development of a "healthy" personality have the greatest effect on delinquent behavior.

As one example of an explanation based on the family's role in personality development, Sidney Berman stressed that delinquent children often have had difficulty in early relationships with parents.[5] This implies that these children have reacted adversely to certain early life experiences which other children have been guided through more adequately. The concern, therefore, is with the psychological factors which structure this morbid behavior.[6]

The early life experiences of the child in the family lay the groundwork for the type of future behavior and the development of attitudes, values, and a lifestyle. Parental hostility, rejection, and inconsistency can all contribute to delinquent behavior.[7] The family is the backdrop in which the child learns to deal with emotions and drives, and to handle problems in a socially acceptable manner. When the family does not help the youngster to adjust to the environment, he or she loses the most important means of psychological support and the most effective agent for socialization.

One type of explanation that is often offered for continuous delinquent behavior that eventually becomes adult criminality is that the individual has a

---

[5]Sidney Berman, "Antisocial Character Disorder," in *Readings in Juvenile Delinquency*, ed. Ruth S. Cavan (Philadelphia: J. B. Lippincott Co., 1964), p. 142.

[6]*Ibid.* p. 142.

[7]*Ibid.* p. 142.

psychopathic personality. Not all psychopaths are involved in illegal activity, but several of their characteristics predispose them towards breaking the law. These characteristics include a lack of true affection for others, a tendency to lie, and an inability to learn from their mistakes or from being punished.[8]

Neurological predispositions (particularly early childhood hyperactivity—also called attention deficit disorder) and family factors have been implicated in the causation of the psychopathic personality. William McCord and Joan McCord, for example, recognized the role of neurological damage, but also pointed to the effect of extreme emotional deprivation.[9] The kinds of family factors implicated include parental loss;[10] cold and distant parents; and capricious and inconsistent rewards, punishment and discipline.[11]

According to the personality development approach, early childhood experiences in the family determine in great part how the youngster will be molded and will eventually adapt to the external environment.[12] Delinquency is an expression of desires, drives, urges, and motivations that have been greatly influenced by early family experiences. If the family experiences have been positive, the adolescent will be able to handle the pressures and responsibilities of adjusting to the community with positive problem-solving skills.

Learning of Behavior

Instead of focusing on personality development, the learning psychologists use punishment by parents as a key concept to explain how the family influences delinquency. Explanations of learning of aggressive behavior provide a good illustration of the learning theorists' ideas. Families can encourage aggression by using certain types of punishment:

> A parent who is yelling at or slapping a child is certainly supplying that child with a model for aggression and, in light of the findings of innumerable laboratory studies, it should not be surprising to find the child behaving in the same way.[13]

The use of inconsistent discipline is another way that parents encourage aggression, or other forms of delinquency, for that matter:

[8]Hervey M. Cleckley, "Psychopathic States," in *American Handbook of Psychiatry*, ed. Silvano Arieti (New York: Basic Books, 1954), pp. 567–588.

[9]William McCord and Joan McCord, *The Psychopath* (Princeton, New Jersey: D. Van Nostrand, 1964), p. 8–10.

[10]Jane Oltman and Samuel Friedman, "Parental Deprivation in Psychiatric Conditions," *Diseases of the Nervous System, 28*, no. 5 (May 1967), pp. 298–303; Michael Craft, Geoffrey Stephenson, and Clive Granger, "A Controlled Trial of Authoritarian and Self-governing Regimes with Adolescent Psychopaths," *American Journal of Orthopsychiatry, 34*, no. 3 (April 1964) pp. 543–554.

[11]H. Buss, *Psychopathology* (New York: Wiley, 1966).

[12]Beatrice Simcox Reiner and Irving Kaufman, *Character Disorders in Parents of Delinquents* (New York: Family Service Association of America, 1959), p. 15.

[13]Gary C. Walters and Joan E. Grusec, *Punishment* (San Francisco, California: W. H. Freeman and Company, 1977), p. 145.

Inconsistent discipline usually also reflects inconsistent dispensation of reinforcement. This means that reproductions of the behavior would not be consistently strengthened or weakened in the home environment.[14]

Like the theories that stress the family's influence on personality development,
the learning theories suggest that certain family characteristics are at the root of
delinquent behavior.

SOCIOLOGY AND THE FAMILY

Whereas the psychologist is concerned with the identification of individual variables, such as motivation, drives, values, needs, and learned patterns of behavior,
the sociologist is concerned more with the general environment as it relates to
the distribution of crime, the factors in the system that affect crime rates, and the
functioning of the institutions of control that have been commissioned to deal
with the offender. In other words, sociology attempts to explain the manner in
which society acquires crime, the processes that contribute to crime causation,
and the mechanisms developed to deal with it. Underlying sociological investigation is the assumption that unfavorable environmental conditions in the social
system influence an individual's or family's actions and, in so doing, promote
delinquency. Even though sociology and psychology deal with different aspects
of the crime problem (sociology stresses the system; psychology stresses the
offender), both disciplines look at "control." Psychology emphasizes the process
of personal or internal control that is represented by the superego (conscience)
or the learning of behavior. Sociology emphasizes the institutions in the community that directly influence the external social control processes. Reiss views
delinquency as being the result of the failure of both personal and social controls
to produce behavior that conforms to social norms and is acceptable to the
community.[15]

> Delinquency results when there is a relative absence of internalized norms and
> rules governing behavior in conformity with the norms of the social system to
> which legal penalties are attached, a breakdown in previously established con-
> trols, and/or a relative absence of a conflict in social rules or institutions of which
> the person is a member. Hence, delinquency may be seen as a function or
> consequence of the relationship established among the personal and social con-
> trols.[16]

The chance of delinquency becomes greater when both personal controls and social controls break down. The family is extremely important because

[14]Curt R. Bartol, *Criminal Behavior: A Psychosocial Approach* (Englewood Cliffs, New Jersey:
Prentice-Hall, Inc., 1980), p. 121.
[15]Albert J. Reiss, Jr., "Delinquency as the Failure of Personal and Social Controls," *American
Sociological Review, 16*, no. 2 (April 1951), pp. 196–207.
[16]*Ibid.*, p. 196.

it can both influence the development of the internal control structure (conscience) and have an effect on the external control social process by its methods of direct control and discipline.[17] If the parents are not adequate models of identification, so that a positive conscience can develop, and if their methods of discipline are not effective, community social control institutions usually have to intervene.[18] Thus, if youngsters are going to refrain from delinquent behavior they must be guided by both internal and external control structures.[19]

THE ENVIRONMENT OF THE FAMILY

As Chapter 3 pointed out, sociological explanations of criminality and delinquency do not oppose psychological explanations because they are not rival answers to the same question but answer different questions about the same sort of behavior.[20] The same general question about the family can be addressed within both disciplines: What kind of family environment is most likely to encourage delinquency? Using theory and research from both disciplines, this section will discuss family environmental factors that can have an impact on producing delinquent behavior—broken homes, family tension, parental rejection, methods of parental control, parental emotional stability, and family economics.

As you consider each variation in the family environment and in family interactions that contribute to delinquency, keep in mind that no one factor is of much help in predicting which families will have delinquent children. Rather, combinations of these factors are helpful in predicting delinquency, especially when the child is young and parents have much more influence than peers.[21] Also, there is evidence that background influences—parental criminality, parental drunkenness, frequent moves—contribute to delinquency because they result in family situations marked by erratic punishment and lax supervision.[22] We cannot assume a causal relationship just because family background factors are related to delinquency.

We will begin this section with a discussion of a structural difference that has been stressed in the past and that still continues to be studied: the "broken home." Despite the emphasis that has been placed on the broken home in the past, research has repeatedly shown that just the structure of the family—that is the number of parents present—is of limited value in explaining delinquency.

[17]Nye, *Family Relationships and Delinquent Behavior*, p. 72.

[18]*Ibid.*, p. 23.

[19]Gold, "Status Forces in Delinquent Boys."

[20]Albert K. Cohen, *Deviance and Control* (Englewood Cliffs, New Jersey: Prentice-Hall, Inc., 1966), p. 47.

[21]Ralph Loeber and Thomas Dishion, "Early Predictors of Male Delinquency: A Review," *Psychological Bulletin, 94*, no. 1 (July 1983), pp. 68–99.

[22]John H. Laub and Robert J. Sampson, "Unraveling Families and Delinquency: A Reanalysis of the Gluecks' Data," *Criminology, 26*, no. 3 (August 1988), pp. 355–380.

What, then, are the differences between the families of delinquents and those of nondelinquents? Rolf Loeber and Magda Stauthamer-Loeber reviewed numerous studies and located consistencies in the types of family differences that seemed to account for delinquency.[23] They discovered that the delinquents' families stood out in terms of breakdowns in family socialization. Examples included: lack of parental supervision, rejection of the children by their parents, and a general failure of parents to be involved with their children's lives. Background variables, including parental criminality and conflictual marital relations, were less important factors although they still played a part in the process.

Broken Homes

There is a long-standing belief among many juvenile justice practitioners and criminologists that broken homes are conducive to the development of a pattern of delinquent behavior. In an early study of delinquents, Sheldon and Eleanor Glueck found that a much higher proportion of nondelinquents were exposed to households where there were minimal disruptions rather than those typified by parental separation, divorce, death, or parental absence. In a substantial number of the broken homes in which children became delinquent, the youngster was under five years of age at the time of the break.[24] Other experts similarly feel that the American family has its greatest influence over the younger children in the family, and hence it is most devastating to these children when the family becomes disrupted for whatever reason.[25] Because they have more autonomy and have developed coping skills, older children are not as adversely affected. This view corresponds with the psychological theories according to which a child's behavior patterns and psychic structure are almost completely formed by age five, and instability and physical and psychological deprivation at an early age can be devastating (for example, see the psychoanalytic and social learning theories described in Chapter 3). It is logical to conclude that broken homes can contribute to delinquency for they can result in economic hardships, the loss of some affection, the loss of proper role models necessary for socialization, and fewer barriers to the development of friendships with delinquents.[26] There is considerable empirical research that has linked the broken family to delinquency. Monahan[27] found that delinquents from broken homes were more likely to be recidivists than those from unbroken homes;

[23]Rolf Loeber and Magda Stauthamer-Loeber, "Family Factors as correlates and Predictors of Juvenile Conduct problems and Delinquency," in eds. Michael Tonry and Norval Morris, *Crime and Justice: An Annual Review of Research*, Vol. 7 (Chicago: University of Chicago Press, 1986).

[24]Sheldon Glueck and Eleanor Glueck, *Delinquents and Nondelinquents in Perspective* (Cambridge, Massachusetts: Harvard University Press, 1968), p. 12.

[25]Rodman and Grams, "Juvenile Delinquency and the Family," p. 196.

[26]Joseph H. Rankin, "The Family Context of Delinquency," *Social Problems*, 30, no. 4 (April 1983), p. 466.

[27]Thomas P. Monahan, "Family Status and the Delinquent Child," *Social Forces*, 35, no. 3 (1957), pp. 250–258.

Browning,[28] Gold,[29] Slocum and Stone,[30] and Peterson and Becker[31] also found that a significantly greater number of delinquents than nondelinquents were from broken or disorganized homes.

Despite the beliefs and research that support the idea that the broken home is of considerable importance in the development of delinquency, this conclusion is not shared by all people. Many of the studies cited above have been criticized for relying on official data. As indicated earlier in this chapter, there is evidence that juvenile justice system personnel treat youths from broken homes more severely than others even though they are no more delinquent. Thus, statistics on the link between official status as delinquent and the broken home may be created by personnel.

Aside from the shortcomings of official data, there is a failure of prior research to study the complex interrelationship between broken homes and discord. Sterne, for example, explains that the actual breaking up of the home is preceded by much disruption, disorganization, and tension.[32] Therefore, because negative factors existed before the formal separation, the broken home in itself was not the major contributing factor to delinquent behavior. The tensions and problems that created and contributed to the actual breakup are the real causative factors, with the eventual breakup being only the final link in a long line of disruptive activity.[33] Since Sterne set forth his reasoning, there has been quite a bit of research to indicate that it is not the breakup of the family alone, but the discord associated with it, that contributes to delinquency. The research has shown that:[34]

1. parental discord is associated with antisocial disorder in the children even when the home is unbroken;[35]

[28]Charles J. Browning, "Differential Impact of Family Disorganization on Male Adolescents," *Social Problems, 8,* no. 1 (Summer 1960), pp. 37–44.

[29]Gold, "Status Forces in Delinquent Boys."

[30]Walter Slocum and Carol L. Stone, "Family Culture Patterns and Delinquent-type Behavior," *Marriage and Family Living, 25,* no. 2 (May 1963), pp. 202–208.

[31]Donald R. Peterson and Wesley C. Becker, "Family Interaction and Delinquency," in *Juvenile Delinquency,* ed. Herbert C. Quay (Princeton, New Jersey: D. Van Nostrand Co. Inc., 1965), pp. 36–99.

[32]Richard S. Sterne, *Delinquent Conduct and Broken Homes* (New Haven, Connecticut: College and University Press, 1964), p. 21.

[33]*Ibid.,* p. 28.

[34]The review of the literature cited below is taken from Michael Rutter and Henri Giller, *Juvenile Delinquency: Trends and Perspectives* (New York: Penguin Books, 1983), p. 190.

[35]Maude M. Craig and Selma J. Glick, "Ten Years Experience with the Glueck Social Prediction Table," *Crime and Delinquency, 9,* no. 3 (July 1963), pp. 249–261; William McCord and Joan McCord, *Origins of Crime: A New Evaluation of the Cambridge-Somerville Study* (New York: Columbia University Press, 1959); Michael Rutter, "Parent-Child Separation: Psychological Effects on the Children," *Journal of Child Psychology and Psychiatry, 12,* no. 4 (December 1971), pp. 233–260; Michael J. Power, Patricia M. Ash, Elizabeth Schoenberg, and E. Catherine Sirey, "Delinquency and the Family," *British Journal of Social Work, 4,* no. 1 (Spring 1974), pp. 13–38; Beatrice Porter and K. Daniel O'Leary, "Marital Discord and Childhood Behavior Problems," *Journal of Abnormal Child Psychology, 8,* no. 3 (September 1980), pp. 287–296.

2. the extent of discord is associated with the likelihood of disorders even in groups in which all the homes are broken;[36]

3 children removed from home into the care of the local authorities because of family difficulties or breakdown already showed an excess of disturbed behavior before they were separated from their families;[37] and

4. family discord does not necessarily end when the family becomes "broken" by divorce or separation.[38]

If discord associated with the broken home is of primary importance in explaining delinquency, it would be useful to design programs that minimize family conflict and hostility.

Additional questions have been raised about the relationship of broken homes to delinquency by individuals who point to research showing little or no link. Rosen reanalyzed the data from seven studies of the broken home, including those of the Gluecks, Shaw and McKay, Nye, and Browning. He confirmed that delinquents do tend to come from broken homes, but the tendency is not very great.[39] Several studies conducted since 1970 have shown little or no link between the broken home and delinquency.[40]

What can we conclude from the conflicting findings about broken homes? Joseph Rankin attempted to answer this question by carrying out a more complex examination of data than had been done in prior studies. He looked at the relationship between *specific types* of delinquency and *specific types* of broken homes. Rankin disagrees with earlier conclusions that broken homes are unrelated to delinquency:

> Contrary to previous research that has found only weak relationships between broken homes and general delinquency, this study indicates that at least three

[36]E. Mavis Hetherington, Martha Cox, and Roger Cox, "Play and Social Interaction in Children Following Divorce," *Journal of Social Issues, 35,* no. 4 (Fall 1979), pp. 26–49; Robert D. Hess and Kathleen A. Camera, "Post-Divorce Family Relationships as Mediating Factors in the Consequences of Divorce for Children," *Journal of Social Issues, 35,* no. 4 (Fall 1979), pp. 79–96; Judith S. Wallerstein and Joan B. Kelly, *Surviving the Break Up: How Children and Parents Cope with Divorce* (New York: Basic Books, 1980).

[37]Wallerstein and Kelly, *How Children and Parents Cope with Divorce;* Lydia Lambert, Juliet Essen, and Jenny Head, "Variations in Behavior Ratings of Children Who Have Been in Care," *Journal of Child Psychology and Psychiatry, 18,* no. 4 (September 1977), pp. 335–346.

[38]Hetherington, Cox, and Cox, "Play and Social Interaction in Children Following Divorce"; Wallerstein and Kelly, *How Children and Parents Cope with Divorce;* Hess and Camera, "Post-Divorce Family Relationships as Mediating Factors in the Consequences of Divorce for Children."

[39]Lawrence Rosen, "The Broken Home and Male Delinquency," in *The Sociology of Crime and Delinquency,* 2nd ed., eds. Marvin E. Wolfgang, Leonard Savitz, and Norman Johnstone (New York: John Wiley and Sons, Inc., 1970).

[40]Rachelle J. Canter, "Family Correlates of Male and Female Delinquency," *Criminology, 20,* no. 2 (August 1982), pp. 149–167; Michael Hennessy, Pamela Richards, and Richard Berke, "Broken Homes and Middle-Class Delinquency: A Reassessment," *Criminology, 15,* no. 4 (February 1978), pp. 505–527; Lawrence Rosen, "The Broken Home and Male Delinquency," in *The Sociology of Crime and Delinquency,* eds. Marvin Wolfgang, Leonard Savitz, and Norman Johnson (New York: John Wiley and Sons, 1970), pp. 489–495; Richard E. Johnson, "Family Structure and Delinquency: General Patterns and Gender Differences," *Criminology, 24,* no. 1 (February 1986), pp. 65–84.

Exhibit 4-2   Broken homes and serious delinquency—implications for social policy

Since the association with delinquency is so weak, the effects of any change in family-household structure per se would be negligible. Thus, social programs aimed at "keeping families intact" will have little impact on delinquency rates or patterns. For instance, critics of assistance programs for single mothers and dependent children, who argue that such policies encourage broken homes (via financial incentives for remaining separated) and thus contribute to increased juvenile delinquency, are mistaken; their underlying assumption (that broken homes lead to delinquency) does not hold. We would conclude that such social policies may be valued or criticized on other pragmatic grounds, but not as a delinquency prevention strategy.

SOURCE: L. Edward Wells and Joseph H. Rankin, "Broken Homes and Juvenile Delinquency: An Empirical Review," *Criminal Justice Abstracts, 17,* no. 2 (June 1985), p. 269.

Issues for Discussion.   Regardless of contradictory research findings, will some people continue to insist that broken homes are a major and direct cause of delinquency? In what subgroups of society is this belief likely to persist? What are the implications for policy and program development? How could you as a policy maker, staff person in a juvenile justice agency, or a private citizen insure that programs and policies are based on sound social science research?

types of juvenile misconduct—running away, truancy, and auto theft—are strongly related to a *specific type* of broken home: those in which both biological parents are missing. Thus, earlier conclusions that broken homes are simply not an important etiological factor in delinquency are at best misleading, since my analysis shows that broken homes are differently related to different types of juvenile misconduct . . . and that the relationships may be stronger when broken homes are defined more explicitly than in previous research.[41]

Also contradicting prior findings that broken homes affected girls more than boys, Rankin discovered that the link between broken homes and delinquency was the same regardless of gender. It still may be that the link is due to discord, economic hardships, or other factors that are associated with the broken home, and it would be useful to more fully understand the nature of the link in order to design intervention programs to minimize the difficulties of adolescents in broken homes. Because the link between broken homes and serious delinquency is questionable, social policies and programs to preserve the family are unlikely to affect delinquency (Exhibit 4-2).

Family Tension

Sterne's statement that the cluster of events preceding the formal breakup is the major contributing factor to delinquent behavior is most illuminating because this is often overlooked in studies of broken homes.[42]

[41]Rankin, "The Family Context of Delinquency," p. 477.
[42]Glueck and Glueck, *Delinquents and Nondelinquents in Perspective,* p. 12.

Abrahamsen believes that family tension greatly contributes to delinquent behavior.[43] The tension that exists in many "intact" families of delinquents results from hostility, hatred, bickering, and the like. This type of tension-filled family environment is obviously not conducive to making the youngster feel secure and content. Long-term tension reduces family cohesiveness and affects the parents' ability to provide an atmosphere conductive to satisfactory child rearing and family problem solving.[44]

Andry found that tension in homes of delinquents is also manifested through intersibling quarrels.[45] Aichhorn states that

> the relationship [of children] to the parents has somehow become abnormal and the original relations of the children to one another, stressed as they are by competition, have not developed into a normal brotherly bond as they should have if they had been submitted to the influence of an equally divided affection toward the parents.[46]

In regard to family cohesiveness, McCord, McCord and Zola agree that cohesive homes produce few delinquents, whereas homes where tension and hostility exist are good breeding grounds for future delinquents.[47] When a great deal of tension and hostility exists in the home, the youngster is often forced to find "peace of mind" in groups outside the family environment. When the youngster seeks relief from the constant bickering and quarrels within the family, he or she often flees and "takes refuge in the street."[48]

According to McCord, McCord and Zola:

> Quarrelsome, neglecting families actually had a higher crime rate than homes in which a permanent separation had disrupted the family—conflict and neglect within the home predisposes a child to crime (even more so than broken homes).[49]

Nye shows a relationship between quarreling and delinquent behavior for girls, but not for boys.[50] He explains this by pointing out that the family is more of a focal point for girls than for boys and that the boy can often retreat to the streets or to other groups more readily than can his female counterpart.

[43]David Abrahamsen, *The Psychology of Crime* (New York: Columbia University Press, 1960), p. 43.

[44]*Ibid.*, p. 46.

[45]R. G. Andry, *Delinquency and Parental Pathology* (London: Methuen and Co., Ltd., 1960), p. 64.

[46]Aichhorn, *Delinquency and Child Guidance*, p. 154.

[47]William and Joan McCord and Irving Zola, *Origins of Crime* (New York: Columbia University Press, 1959).

[48]Aichhorn, *Delinquency and Child Guidance*, p. 164.

[49]McCord, McCord, and Zola, *Origins of Crime*, p. 83.

[50]Nye, *Family Relationships and Delinquent Behavior*, p. 48.

Disruptive, quarrelsome, and tension-producing relationships between parents not only affect the marital relationship but disrupt the entire family.[51] This total family disruption can often contribute to and even produce delinquent behavior. The Gluecks found that one in three delinquent families, as compared with one in seven nondelinquent families, were disrupted when one of the parents left the family because of a tension-filled and quarrelsome relationship.[52] Aichhorn found that in all the families that he worked with which had a delinquent youngster some kind of conflict or disturbance was present in the family relationships.[53] Slocum and Stone noted that 52 percent of delinquents studied, compared with 16 percent of nondelinquents, considered their families uncooperative—which can be another indication of conflict or tension.[54]

If, then, the family environment is unstable and if the parents quarrel most of the time and have difficulty getting along together, they will be unable to exert a positive influence on their children. When there is a great deal of conflict within the household, the child often bears the brunt of much of the parents' hostility. The youngster can get caught up in parental quarrels and be negatively affected by family disruption. The Gluecks point out that

> there is already evidence that the forces of disruption found excessively in the families of the delinquents were greater and stronger than those making for cohesiveness. In addition, it should be pointed out that less than two in ten in the families of the delinquents, compared to six in ten families of the control group, evidenced strong and steady affectional ties among the members, shared joint interests, took pride in their homes, and felt themselves to be "one for all and all for one." Thus, in the highly important quality that is both expressive of loyalty to the blood group and supportive of the individual in his sense of security and in devotion to others, the delinquents were far more deprived than nondelinquents.[55]

Even though some disagreement may exist as to the amount of influence that the divorced versus the hostile but nondivorced family has upon delinquent behavior, it is evident that marital adjustment, family cohesiveness, and the amount of tension existing in the family are directly related to juvenile delinquency.[56]

Parental Rejection

From the psychological standpoint, emotional deprivation as the result of lack of parental love has much to do with juvenile delinquency. Rejected or

---

[51]Rodman and Grams, "Juvenile Delinquency and the Family," p. 198.
[52]Glueck and Glueck, *Delinquents and Nondelinquents in Perspective*, p. 8.
[53]Aichhorn, *Delinquency and Child Guidance*, p. 33.
[54]Slocum and Stone, "Family Culture Patterns and Delinquent-type Behavior."
[55]Glueck and Glueck, *Delinquents and Nondelinquents in Perspective*, pp. 9–10.
[56]Rodman and Grams, "Juvenile Delinquency and the Family," p. 198.

neglected children who do not find love and affection, as well as support and supervision, at home, often resort to groups outside the family; frequently these groups are of a deviant nature. The hostile or rejecting parent is usually not concerned about the youngster's emotional welfare or about providing the necessary support and guidance. In many cases, parents become concerned about their children's activities outside the home only when the children are involved in difficulty which embarrasses them. The importance of rejection was confirmed by Lauber and Stauthamer-Lauber's reconsideration of prior studies.[57] Compared to other family influences, rejection had a strong effect on delinquency. Richard E. Johnson's research is one study showing the devastating result.[58] He discovered that parental love directly influences delinquency, and that it can also have an indirect effect through its influence on peers' influence on adolescents. His study of 734 Seattle, Washington, high school sophomores revealed that an adolescent's perception of greater parental love apparently decreases the desire for peer approval. None of the other variables measured were related to desire for peer approval. This finding suggests that there may be a several-step causal process through which parental love decreases the effects of negative peer influences, which in turn prevents juvenile delinquency.

Jenkins also found that parental rejection had a direct effect on the child's ultimate development and growth of a conscience.[59] He stated that the lack of an adequate conscience structure, combined with feelings of hostility for being rejected, led to general unsocialized aggression. On the other hand, socialized delinquent behavior would result when there was parental indifference rather than outright rejection. In other words, the form of aggression was less serious in those youngsters whose parents showed indifference than in those youngsters whose parents showed outright rejection.

According to Andry, delinquents were the recipients of less parental love both in quantity and in quality than were nondelinquents.[60] There was also less adequate communication between child and parent in homes of delinquents. If a strong positive emotional tie does not exist between parents and children, this can produce problems. A positive atmosphere in the home is conducive to effective modeling by the parents and also increases the amount of influence that parents exert over their children. The Gluecks found that in twice as many nondelinquent homes the father showed much more warmth and affection than in delinquent homes. In nondelinquent homes mothers also were much more affectionate than in delinquent homes.

> The extent to which the boy's father was acceptable as a figure with whom to identify is revealed in a finding that fewer than two out of ten of the delinquents,

[57]Lauber and Stauthamer-Lauber, 1986.

[58]Richard E. Johnson, *Juvenile Delinquency and its Origins: An Integrated Theoretical Approach* (Cambridge: Cambridge University Press, 1979), pp. 100–101.

[59]Richard L. Jenkins, "Motivation and Frustration in Delinquency," *American Journal of Orthopsychiatry*, 27, no. 3 (July 1957), pp. 528–537.

[60]Andry, *Delinquency and Parental Pathology.*

as contrasted with more than half of the nondelinquents, considered their father to be the kind of man that the boy himself would like to be and had respect for the father's vocational and social standing as well as having some sort of common understanding with him.[61]

Bandura and Walters, like the Gluecks, found a direct correlation between rejecting, hostile fathers and delinquent behaviors.[62] Fathers of delinquents spent far less time with their sons than did the fathers of nondelinquents. Their rejection and hostility can take both direct and indirect forms. The direct forms are obvious. Indirectly, however, the parents may reject the youngster by becoming so involved in other activities that they substitute the giving of material rewards for emotional affection and security. In addition, if parents are away from the home most of the time, either because of an occupation or because of outside activities, their exposure to their children is limited. They are unable to be adequate identification models. When this occurs, it is more difficult for the youngster to assume a socialized internal control structure (conscience).

Many professionals in the fields of both psychology and sociology agree that open rejection and hostility can directly affect youngsters and ultimately produce delinquency and that the family institution has the greatest influence on the youngster's behavior in the community. Parental control is both direct and indirect. Parents indirectly control their children through the identification process, which ultimately results in the development of an adequate conscience structure. Parents exert direct control by developing a system of rewards and punishments. The method of parental control is an important aspect of child rearing.

Methods of Parental Control.   Every parent uses some type of discipline in rearing children, even though it may differ from situation to situation and from child to child, as well as in content and form. L. Edward Wells and Joseph H. Rankin identified at least three ways in which parents exercise direct control:

- parents exert controls by specifying particular rules, constraints, and criteria for their children's behavior
- parents exert controls by monitoring their children's behavior, for example by keeping track of where they are or by watching them directly
- parents exert controls by punishing their children[63]

---

[61]Glueck and Glueck, *Delinquents and Nondelinquents in Perspective*, p. 14; also see Lauber and Stauthamer-Lauber, 1986, p. 372.

[62]Abrahamsen, *The Psychology of Crime*, p. 43.

[63]L. Edward Wells and Joseph H. Rankin, "Direct Parental Controls and Delinquency," *Criminology, 26*, no. 2 (May 1988), pp. 263–285. Also see Stephen Cernkovich and Peggy Giordano, "Family Relationships and Delinquency," *Criminology, 25*, no. 2 (May 1987), pp. 295–321.

In their own research, Wells and Rankin found that direct parental control is as important in explaining delinquency as the more indirect controls, such as parent-child communication and attachment to parents.[64]

One part of family discipline is a set of reasonable rules and criteria that are communicated to the child. Some families do not have rules about when children should be home or where they should go.[65] Children may be involved in many independent activities and allowed to "roam the streets" while parents are ignorant of their whereabouts.[66] There can be a lack of "house" rules that establish routines for meals or chores and that limit selected behaviors.[67]

It is important to recognize that reasonable rules—not extremely strict rules—are related to low levels of delinquency. Youth who report very strict parental rules as well as those who report very lax rules tend to be delinquent.[68] Research on early involvement in sexual activity shows a similar pattern: youth are least active if they view their parent's rules as being moderate as opposed to being either very lax or very strict.[69]

Aside from establishing reasonable rules, skilled parents also monitor their children through efforts to keep track of their whereabouts or even more directly by spending time with them.[70] Very lax monitoring is one of the family characteristics that makes a strong contribution to delinquency.[71]

Punishment is the aspect of direct parental control over children that has been the focus of the greatest amount of research. Every parent uses some type of punishment in rearing children, even though it may differ from situation to situation and from child to child. It is clear from research that there is no simple prescription for the "right" type of punishment, but there are some negative patterns that should be avoided.

McCord, McCord and Zola classified methods of disciplining youngsters

[64]Also see Stephen Cernkovich and Peggy Giordano, "Family Relationships and Delinquency," *Criminology, 25*, no. 2 (May 1987), pp. 295–321.

[65]Harriet Wilson, "Parental Supervision: A Neglected Aspect of Delinquency," *British Journal of Criminology, 20*, no. 3 (July 1980), pp. 203–235.

[66]*Ibid.*

[67]Gerald R. Patterson, *Coercive Family Process* (Eugene, Oregon: Castalia Publishing Co., 1982).

[68]L. Edward Wells and Joseph H. Rankin, "Direct Parental Controls and Delinquency," *Criminology, 26*, no. 2 (May 1988), pp. 263–285.

[69]Brent Miller, J. Kelly McCoy, Terrance Olson, and Christopher Wallace, "Parental Discipline and Control in Relation to Adolescent Sexual Attitudes and Behavior," *Journal of Marriage and the Family, 48*, no. 3 (August 1986), pp. 503–512.

[70]Wells and Rankin, "Direct Parental Controls and Delinquency," pp. 263–285; also see Boyd Rollins and Darwin Thomas, "Parental Support, Power, and Control Techniques in the Socialization of Children," in *Contemporary Theories about the Family*, Vol. 1 eds. Wesley Burr, Reuben Hill, F. Ivan Nye, and Ira Reiss (New York: The Free Press, 1979), pp. 317–364.

[71]Douglas Smith and Raymond Paternoster, "The Gender Gap in Theories of Deviance: Issues and Evidence," *Journal of Research in Crime and Delinquency, 25*, no. 2 (May 1987), pp. 140–172; Cernkovich and Giordano, "Family Relationships and Delinquency," pp. 295–321.

under six types: (1) *love-oriented discipline,* in which reasoning is used with the child and punishment involves withholding rewards or privileges; (2) *punitive discipline,* in which a great deal of physical violence is used and there is a great deal of anger, aggression, and threat; (3) *lax discipline,* in which neither parent exerts much control; (4) *erratic discipline,* in which one parent uses love-oriented methods and the other is lax or wavers between the two types; (5) *erratic discipline* (love oriented, lax, and punitive), in which both parents waver in using the three methods, so that all three are combined; and (6) *erratic discipline* (punitive and lax), in which one parent is punitive and one parent is lax, or both parents waver between the methods.[72]

McCord, McCord, and Zola found that lax or erratic discipline involving punitive methods was strongly related to delinquency, whereas consistent discipline, either by punitive or love-oriented methods, was significantly related to nondelinquency. The erratic nature of the discipline, not the amount involved, was the major variable in producing the delinquent behavior.

> Contrary to our expectations (and to findings of previous studies) we found no evidence that consistently punitive discipline leads to delinquency. In fact, we were surprised to discover that the 14 children who had been severely but consistently treated had the lowest rate of crime. Consistent use of love-oriented techniques also seems to produce noncriminality.[73]

A reanalysis of data on 500 delinquents and 500 nondelinquents during the 1940s further confirms that erratic punishment by either mother or father contributes to delinquency.[74]

As research has added to our understanding, there have been more and more studies to support the idea that the consistency of discipline is the essential element in establishing an atmosphere where delinquency is less likely to develop. Some parents do not follow through on their threats to punish unacceptable behavior; and they lack effective methods for resolving conflicts between themselves and their children, so that problems can escalate and remain unresolved.[75] When there is this type of inconsistent discipline and lack of cooperation between parents, an adequate control structure does not exist within the home. The child then often rejects the entire sphere of parental influence because of a loss of respect for the process of control utilized by the parents. Parents cannot present a united front if inconsistency and disagreement exist, and therefore the youngster will not be influenced by them, will often belittle their efforts, and will not develop an adequate superego (conscience). The youngster can also manipulate the inconsistent pattern of control to turn one parent against the other. The

---

[72]McCord, McCord, and Zola, *Origins of Crime,* p. 76.

[73]*Ibid.,* pp. 77–78.

[74]John H. Laub and Robert J. Sampson, "Unraveling Families and Delinquency: A Reanalysis of the Gluecks' Data," *Criminology,* 26, no. 3 (August 1988), pp. 355–380.

[75]L. Edward Wells and Joseph H. Rankin, "Direct Parental Controls and Delinquency," *Criminology,* 26, no. 2 (May 1988), pp. 263–285.

ultimate effect is that the youngster does not have the benefit of consistent guidelines and limits as assistance in behaving in a socially acceptable manner.[76] The attitude of "nothing can happen to me" will develop because the youngster learns that the parents' inconsistent discipline and demands are seldom translated into coordinated action. Consistency is extremely important, and a united approach by parents is desirable—but difficult to present if there is a broken home, a great deal of tension in the home, or parental rejection. All these factors can be important negative contributory variables in the delinquent's home. Another important aspect of the environment of the family, which can have a marked effect on how the child ultimately reacts in the community, is the parents' emotional stability.

Parental Emotional Stability

Delinquent behavior can often be directly traced to behavioral disturbances and emotional instability in one or both of the parents. Parents who have their own emotional sickness frequently "act out" the sickness or transmit it to their children. Freeman and Savastano found that, although some parents of delinquents wanted to give their children "adequate parenting," their own personality problems interfered with their effectiveness. If the only time a parent shows a great deal of tenderness is after punishing the child, the child will often deliberately misbehave for the express purpose of receiving the tenderness, even though it is not under the most optimal conditions. The erratic and misdirected tenderness provides an important motivation for the child's negative behavior.

If there is little love between the parents, the youngster can become the "love object" of one or the other. The inordinate amount of attention these youngsters receive because they are being used as a substitute for the rejected marital partner can be greatly confusing. Freeman and Savastano reported that marital conflict was frequently expressed in the parent-child relationship. The parent gives the child a great deal of love and affection, worries about the child constantly, and does not allow much freedom. The child can often exploit this situation by being disruptive, knowing it is possible to get away with a great deal of misbehavior. There is no control from the parent because the child has become a substitute love object in an entangled relationship. In addition, the lack of control creates uneasiness for the youngster because no limits or reference points are established to guide behavior. As a reaction to this type of situation, the child may "act out" further so that controls will be imposed and some type of structure developed. A negative cycle develops. The more acting out the child does, the more the parent is permissive, and then the greater the acting out in the hope that controls will be imposed. This type of abnormal relationship is not conducive to effective child rearing and can ultimately contribute to delinquent behavior. When the marital relationship between parents is not positive and the child is the recipient of inappropriate and exaggerated emotions, children learn

---

[76]Aichhorn, *Delinquency and Child Guidance*, p. 223.

that they are not loved for themselves, but are being used as objects by one or both parents to vent their hostility on each other.[77]

In households where parents do have behavioral disturbances and manifestations of emotional immaturity, instability, or insecurity, there is frequent loss of temper and the direction of inappropriate emotions to children. Where tension, hostility, and displaced emotions exist, the family environment will not be conducive to producing children who are themselves stable and who can function effectively. In families where one or both parents have emotional disturbances—or a disease such as alcoholism—the youngster runs a much greater risk of developing problems that often manifest themselves in a delinquent activity.

The effects of parental emotional instability can be indirect, that is, they can occur because emotional instability results in parenting practices that produce delinquency. An important example of such an indirect effect of parental emotional instability is provided by a recent reanalysis of the Gluecks' data.[78] The reanalysis showed that fathers and mothers with a history of alcoholism and criminality used force and inconsistent discipline on their sons, which in turn accounted for their sons' delinquency. Similarly, mothers with the problems of alcoholism and criminality provided poor supervision, which also contributed to delinquency.

In some psychological theories, the connection between parental emotional health and delinquency is more direct. For example, Reiner and Kaufman noted that parents of antisocial character disorder children often acted out their own unconscious parental wishes through their children.[79]

> Often a parent engages in overt delinquency or shows deviant attitudes that are a counterpart to the child's behavior. But even in such cases when the child gets in conflict with the law, the parent is enraged at the child's behavior. He does not condone the delinquency in the child or really condone it in himself. In some instances, one form of delinquency may be acceptable to the parent while another form is not acceptable. In these cases, we find that the parent is afraid that his own impulses, against which he has built a rigid reaction formation, will break through, and he projects this danger onto the child.[80]

Other theorists, such as Aldrich,[81] generally agree with Reiner and Kaufman's statement that many parents receive vicarious satisfaction when their children act out unacceptable impulses. These parents have emotional disturbances themselves and have never really worked out their internal conflicts. The

---

[77]Beatrice Freeman and George Savastano, "The Affluent Youthful Offender," *Crime and Delinquency, 16,* no. 3 (July 1970), pp. 264–272.

[78]John H. Laub and Robert J. Sampson, "Unraveling Families and Delinquency: A Reanalysis of The Glueck's Data," *Criminology, 26,* no. 3 (August 1988), pp. 355–380.

[79]Reiner and Kaufman, *Character Disorders in Parents of Delinquents.*

[80]*Ibid.,* pp. 15–16.

[81]C. Knight Aldrich, "Thief," *Psychology Today, 4,* no. 10 (March 1971), pp. 67–68.

major energy release for their own instability comes through their children's delinquent activities.

The unconscious transmission of negative attitudes of parents to their children has been a subject of much discussion. Although theorists disagree as to the amount and form that these transmissions take, they believe that much, if not most, early delinquent behavior is spawned in the family. Even though Bandura and Walters in their study of adolescent aggression found no evidence that parents had displayed "consistently blatant anti-social behavior," they did find that many of the fathers of the boys had provided aggressive models for imitation.[82] Parental emotional instability can have its effects either directly or indirectly, but regardless of how the effects occur, the result can be the promotion of illegal behavior.

Family Economics

Families of delinquents, regardless of socioeconomic status, usually have certain characteristics that are different from those of families of nondelinquents—disruptive homes with a great deal of tension and rejection, ineffective methods of parental control, and parental emotional instability. New analysis of the data that the Gluecks collected sheds some light on how family economics can contribute to delinquency.[83] The pressures of poverty—specifically economic dependence, crowding, and lack of mobility—apparently place parents at greater risk for using the erratic and harsh discipline that contributes to delinquency.

Also, a family's inability to provide for the material needs of an adolescent can affect the amount of control that the family exerts because youth can seek material support and acceptance outside of the home, in some cases from delinquent peers.[84] A very basic example of this pertains to the physical condition of the home, which can affect a youth's self-perceptions:

> The homes in which delinquents live tend to be dirty and rundown—the homes of delinquents are often disorderly and cluttered, present routines are weakly fixed, physical space is at a premium and privacy can best be had by leaving the house—there is little order in the model delinquent home. As a physical social stimulus the typical delinquent home acts mainly as a repellent, driving people away.[85]

INTERACTION IN THE CONTEMPORARY FAMILY

Research and theory to explain delinquency take into account many different family characteristics. Some of these, such as family economics and broken

---

[82]Albert Bandura and Richard H. Walters, *Adolescent Aggression* (New York: The Ronald Press Company, 1959), p. 355.

[83]Laub and Sampson, "Unraveling Families and Delinquency," pp. 355–380.

[84]Reiss, "Delinquency as the Failure of Personal and Social Controls," p. 198.

[85]Peterson and Becker, "Family Interaction and Delinquency," p. 67.

homes, are difficult to change, and their link to delinquency is difficult to interpret because of their relationship to other factors that are associated with delinquency. In contrast, an aspect of family life that can be influenced by probation officers, social workers, and other court and corrections staff is family interaction. Also, family interaction appears to be related to delinquency regardless of other conditions, for example, for families with differing levels of economic advantage and for families that are both broken and intact. We have already mentioned some delinquency-producing interactions in our discussions of family tension, parental rejection, parental control, and parental emotional stability. Since many existing programs try to change family interactions, we will give a more detailed description of the interaction patterns thought to produce delinquency.

Parenting Skills

An understanding of parenting skills holds promise as an explanation of delinquency. Much of our knowledge of parenting skills comes from studies of youths who display a wide variety of disturbances, including mental illness and acting-out behavior, as well as illegal activity. Since these various types of disturbance are very closely related to each other, our discussion will draw on research relevant to parenting skills that prevent a variety of youth problems.

One of the characteristics of families in which one or more children are disturbed is the inability of family members to work out difficulties without engaging in destructive arguments.[86] When family members talk together, they show high levels of negative feelings about each other and often they give conflicting messages. There are many fruitless disputes in which conflicting messages and negative feelings are expressed, and that escalate into shouting matches, but for which there is never any resolution. Day-to-day problems of living together, as well as more serious long-term difficulties, are never worked out, and thus the communication is "inefficient."

Considerable research has been carried out on parenting skills and delinquency by Gerald R. Patterson.[87] Patterson pointed out that many people take the ability to act as a parent for granted, but that this assumption is erroneous:

> increasing numbers of young parents function in isolated family systems, removed from modeling influences, informal sources, and support systems. Such being the case, then there will be wide variations among parents in performing parenting skills. Parenting skills describe a perfectly mundane set of operations that would include: (a) notice what the child is doing; (b) monitor it over long periods; (c) model social skill behavior; (d) clearly state house rules; (e) consistently provide sane punishments for transgressions; (f) provide reinforcement

[86]Michael Rutter, *Changing Youth in a Changing Society: Patterns of Adolescent Development and Disorder* (Cambridge, Massachusetts: Harvard University Press, 1980), p. 151.

[87]Gerald R. Patterson, "Children Who Steal," in *Understanding Crime: Current Theory and Research*, ed. Travis Hirschi and Michael Gottfredson (Beverly Hills, California: Sage Publications, 1980), pp. 73–90.

for conformity; and (g) negotiate disagreements so that conflicts and crises do not escalate.[88]

A failure to adequately carry out the operations of parenting that are listed by Patterson often leads to delinquent behavior.

Patterson has provided convincing clinical evidence of the lack of parenting skills among families with an antisocial child. The parents were not highly attached to their children, and thus they lacked the motivation to be effective. In addition, they lacked basic parenting skills. For example, in many cases when a child was stealing, the parents did not even accept that this was going on unless they observed the child directly. When other people informed them of the theft, the parents accepted a "story" from the child, and in a sense, failed to "notice what the child was doing." Instead of believing that the child had stolen, the parents tended to accuse other people of picking on their child.

The failure to notice inappropriate behavior was followed by other shortcomings in carrying out the operations of good parenting. The parents of children who stole did not consistently provide reasonable punishments for transgressions. Even when they did notice and accept that a child stole, they often did not follow through with punishment. When they did punish the child, they would "yell, scold, threaten, and occasionally physically assault the child,"[89] rather than using withdrawal of privileges or work details. Youths who stole at an early age and at a high rate often become involved with the police by the age of fourteen.

Patterson points out that he asks a question similar to the one posed by Travis Hirschi in the development of social control theory: The proper question concerning delinquency is *not* "Why do young children steal?"; the real question is "Why do older youth continue to do what is normal for two- and three-year-old children?" According to Patterson's own theory, which he calls *coercion theory*, "parents who cannot or will not employ family management skills are the prime determining variables."[90]

Weak Relationships

As we noted in our discussion of Patterson's work, it is not only the lack of parenting skill that can play a part in the development of delinquent patterns, but also weak relationships between parent and child. These weak relationships can manifest themselves in many ways. Families may not share in joint activities during leisure time.[91] They may not have intimate communication with each other, in that youths do not talk over their future plans with their parents, and

---

[88]*Ibid.*, p. 81.

[89]*Ibid.*, p. 87.

[90]*Ibid.*, p. 88.

[91]Gold, "Status Forces in Delinquent Boys"; Donald J. West and David P. Farrington, *Who Becomes Delinquent?* (London: Heinemann Educational Books, 1973).

they do not share their thoughts and feelings with their parents.[92] Parents may not typically explain rules or help children to understand things by answering their questions. When there are weak parent-child relationships, parents often feel that they cannot "get through" to their children and that the children are not a part of the family, for they stay in their own rooms or outside of the house much of the time.[93]

As with many family factors, it is difficult to determine whether weak relationships account for delinquency alone or because they are associated with the lack of sane discipline and other conditions that lead to illegal behavior. However, insofar as treatment is concerned, weak relationships are an essential factor in improving family interactions. It is quite difficult to motivate parents to improve their interactions when they do not feel strongly attached to their children.[94] Individuals who work with the families of delinquent youths often must begin by understanding the parents' lack of motivation to be effective parents, and in some cases it may not be possible to stimulate this motivation in time to correct the family interactions contributing to delinquency.

Overreliance on External Resources

The reliance on technical assistance from professionals and "outsiders" has become commonplace. Textbook knowledge and professional assistance is necessary, but any honest professional would be the first to point out that outside assistance should only be used to supplement the intuitive sensitivities, feelings, and judgments of parents. If parents depend exclusively on outside resources, they lose their ability to empathize and to communicate effectively with their children.

After reviewing the literature, it becomes evident that although much has been written about preadolescent child care and development, comparatively little has been written about the way parents should relate to their teenage children. Many specialists are willing to work with preadolescents, but few of them want to work with adolescents. This is unfortunate because the teenage years, the period of most juvenile delinquency, is a time of turbulence, and youngsters are attempting to determine who they are and what their goals in life should be. They are developing self-concepts and attempting to cope with the struggle of dependence versus independence. If parents have depended exclusively on child-rearing manuals during their children's early years, they have not learned to handle their children's problems through an honest direct relationship. Instead of communicating directly in accordance with the emotion that accompanies the particular confrontation or event, the communication pro-

---

[92]Hirschi, *Causes of Delinquency,* p. 90. Michael Rutter, Philip Graham, O. F. D. Chadwick, and W. Yule, "Adolescent Turmoil: Fact or Fiction?" *Journal of Child Psychology and Psychiatry, 17,* no. 1 (January 1976), pp. 35–56.

[93]Patterson, *Coercive Family Process.*

[94]*Ibid.*

cess becomes tempered and complicated with jargon and popular theoretical clichés. Parents often deny and repress the acceptable and common human emotions of anger and ambivalence. When these emotions are not expressed directly and honestly, they are often manifested in subtle forms that are difficult for the child to understand and accept.[95]

For example, a parent may be irritated at a child's behavior in a particular situation, but because the parent believes that the emotion of anger is abnormal, he or she does not express these feelings or set limits on the child's behavior. Instead, a parent may deny that the emotion exists. Denial is not totally effective, however, because invariably the feelings are expressed in some form which, if not expressed directly, usually takes a passive-aggressive (indirect) channel. The result is that the parents may "pick at" the child for such insignificant matters as haircuts, dress, and taste in music. The child cannot understand this and overreacts. Problems such as this can be avoided if parents can learn to handle the situation and their emotions on the spot. The child, if dealt with directly, can much more readily accept the parents' anger and understand the need for imposing limits and the rationale for the particular restriction. Expression of displaced emotions is not effective in problem solving. It only contributes to a denial of the problem and further widens the gap between generations.[96]

Parents are able to "get away with" their dependence on outside resources during the early years of the child's life because children are fairly predictable at this time and most of their difficulties revolve around physical rather than emotional problems. When the child reaches adolescence, however, there are not only limited outside resources (psychiatrists, reading material, etc.), but the child is no longer as predictable. If parents have not learned to use their intuitive feelings and good judgment to react spontaneously in a sensitive manner, they will be at a loss during the teenage period. The problem becomes increasingly severe as a result of their increased frustration and need for help during the teenage years. Patterson has called this type of parent the "perfect parent," who has an overreliance on external resources and an inability to directly express anger (Exhibit 4-3). Parents who have not learned to relate to their child become even more amenable to popular clichés and shallow jargon, and their effectiveness in preparing the youngster for interactions in the community becomes neutralized.[97]

Avoidance of Decision Making

Parents find that one of their most difficult tasks is decision making. Parents avoid making important decisions for their children in many ways. They can relegate their decision-making responsibility to others (outside resources), or

[95]Group for the Advancement of Psychiatry, *Normal Adolescence*, p. 98.

[96]Nye, *Family Relationships and Delinquent Behavior*, p. 73.

[97]Clyde E. Vedder and Dora B. Summerville, *The Delinquent Girl* (Springfield, Illinois: Charles C. Thomas, Publisher, 1970).

Exhibit 4-3 The perfect parent

The general picture presented is of a *perfect* middle-class family. It is as if one were observing a TV show; their lines are carefully chosen, the voices and feelings are carefully modulated. The parents speak of love and responsibility. The children are neatly dressed and are usually well behaved during the sessions.

The parents have usually read a number of books on the subject of child psychology or parent training. At first sight, the therapist may be enchanted, thinking: "Here, at last, are parents interested in our theory; this will be fun." If the therapist has a middle-class orientation, he or she may feel they can identify with this family. Some of the parents were subjected to brutal conditions in their own childhood experience, and they want to make sure that this does not happen to their children. After assiduous study, they set out to do what they believe middle-class parents do. They want to be *Perfect Parents* and raise perfect children.

. . . Some of these parents tend to drop the first person pronouns and substitute Mommy and Daddy. In talking to the child about transgressions of house rules, they do not say, "You took my car without asking, and that makes me mad." Such confrontations are avoided at all cost. The direct expression of anger is also avoided as long as possible. The communication comes out more like, "Mommy and Daddy feel there is still some misunderstanding about the car. As you know, you are still under age, and according to the law. . . ." They lecture their child, *but they do not confront him.* Sweet reason prevails. The child sits with downcast eyes, awaiting the lecture's end. If the child appears to listen, and if he claims to feel sorrow and repentance, then the parents are satisfied. The parents believe in reason, information-giving, and in the redeeming virtues of guilt. The child's weeping is accepted as a sign of guilt. The point is, *at no time* do the parents punish him for his behavior; instead, they lecture. During their discourse, one or both parents bring to bear much of their store of understanding about why children do what they do. They read, then reread, the child's intentions. When they are finished, not a blemish in the child's character remains unvarnished.

These are people who are trying to be rational. They don't usually hit their child, but sometimes their facade crumbles, and a beating ensues, or the child is ejected from the house. A major battle produces profound guilt reactions in the parents. This, in turn, is deftly utilized by the child to obtain even more freedom from parental control.

SOURCE: Gerald R. Patterson, *Coercive Family Process* (Eugene, Oregon: Castalia Publishing Company, 1982), p. 301.

they can simply avoid making decisions. Because an efficient and nonanxiety-provoking decision-making process is sought, simple answers to complicated child-rearing problems are often forthcoming.

Because parents do not know how to react to the adolescent struggle of dependence versus independence and are not confident in their own decision-making ability to take the adolescent problem as it comes on a case-by-case basis, they often tend to oversimplify the process by subscribing to either an extremely permissive or an extremely disciplinarian philosophy and approach to child rearing. Both extremes can have disastrous results. The strictly disciplined child rebels against the parents' stringent demands, while the "free-floating" child does not know where he or she is going and may react in a delinquent manner due to fears of the extensive freedom given so readily. Many practitioners have had delinquent adolescents tell them that they wished their parents had exerted more controls and set limits because they interpreted limits and controls as being an expression of love and concern. Extreme permissiveness can be harmful to, and misunderstood by, the child, and the family therefore becomes an ineffective agent of socialization. Extreme permissiveness and extreme discipline are merely different sides of the same coin. They are symptoms of the same problem—inadequate parenting. Excessive discussion and rationalizing of these symptoms may often only be a diversionary tactic that parents find useful when they do not want to examine their own motives for taking extremes rather than considering the youngster's individual situation, circumstances, and personality. Of course, when parents do take all these factors into consideration, the decision-making process becomes much more difficult than it would have been if they had merely adhered to either the permissive or the disciplinarian philosophy. It is much easier to say yes or no to the child than to analyze each situation for its merits and disadvantages.[98]

Unrecognized Immaturity

Technological advances and rapid social change have led many parents to believe that, because their youngsters seem more sophisticated intellectually and socially, they are also better equipped emotionally to handle complex problems. Parents often accept totally whatever their children say, but are not sensitive to their feelings and nonverbal communication. Adolescents may say they are grown up, may sound as if they are grown up, and may look as if they are grown up, but may still vacillate between wanting to be children and wanting to be adults. They may still seek assistance from their parents in planning and for guidance, but because the parents believe what children say, they react by giving the youngsters more freedom than they can handle. In other words, many youngsters grow physically and intellectually, but not emotionally. They believe that their parents want them to be sophisticated, and the parents believe that their youngsters want to be treated as sophisticated adults. This faulty communication process exists because parents have not relied on honest communication in respect to feelings, nor have they been sensitive to their children's needs and nonverbal communication. Too often parents give their children decision-making power under the guise of the children's right to individual freedom, self-destiny, and self-expression when, in fact, they want to reduce their own anxiety

[98]John and Valerie Cowie and Eliot Slater, *Delinquency in Girls* (London: Heinemann Educational Books, 1968).

Exhibit 4-4   The "sibling" parent

As much as possible, the mother functions as an equal, a friend. Sometimes the position is based on a misinterpretation of a laissez-faire, egalitarian philosophy. Many of these mothers seem cut off from other adults; the children are their primary source of support. There are few house rules, few schedules, few assigned roles, and no single person punishes antisocial behavior. Each family member defends his or her own territory. Sometimes a temporary vigilante committee may be set up to redress a wrong. Sometimes an older sibling will occupy a very tentative role as housekeeper, but usually this does not include rule setting. In doing away with the disciplinarian features of the parent role, the mother buys friendship from her children. This can often become a major problem in treatment. If she now attempts to set rules and enforce them, the mother fears the children may reject her. The mother's concern about such a rejection is overwhelming.

If some *Parent-Siblings* also hold delinquent values, then the therapists may find themselves in the interesting position of trying to convince the children *and* the mother that stealing is a reprehensible act. The *Parent-Sibling* and the children may form a xenophobic enclave that serves to protect its members from outsiders. In counterculture families we sometimes find both parents adopting this role. They assume little or no responsibility for any aspect of the child's behavior. The child simply fends for himself and, in some extreme cases, comes home only to sleep. The parents assume that if the child is left free to express his own wishes and desires, that gradually inner controls will emerge.

SOURCE: Gerald R. Patterson, *Coercive Family Process* (Eugene, Oregon: Castalia Publishing Company, 1982), p. 296.

and indecisiveness. Parents sometimes go so far as to act as a sibling to their children (Exhibit 4-4). They therefore relinquish their own decision-making responsibility and force it on their children. This gain is an undesirable assumption and process because only with the guidance of parents within a cohesive family unit can youngsters become astute decision makers.[99]

Unconscious Parental Transmissions

The subtle negative ways in which parents can influence their children's behavior can also contribute to delinquent behavior, and they are often the result of the parents' own emotional instability and neurotic method of problem solving. As was pointed out earlier, these undesirable transmissions from parents to children can be a contributing factor in the youngster's acting out the parents' feeling in an antiauthority, antisocial manner. When parents transmit only negative feelings or attitudes without assisting their youngsters in developing the accompanying frustration tolerance and self-control, problem situations can oc-

[99]McCord, McCord, and Zola, *Origins of Crime.*

cur. Youngsters cannot usually handle these transmissions without support. They have not learned the accompanying controls because they have not been exposed to the necessary life experiences and are not familiar with the decision-making processes that can assist them in analyzing the total situation. Most human behavior is the result of an "attitude set," plus an evaluative process and then a decision as to what mode of behavior will be appropriate. Children who pick up negative transmissions from their parents without the accompanying controls only have the benefit of one of the variables in the decision-making process—attitude.[100]

Parents can also transmit to children the attitude of individual rights and freedom of expression, two highly valued norms in a democratic society, without emphasizing personal responsibility and social consciousness. The use of drugs, a contemporary social problem, is an example of how children pick up their parents' transmissions without accompanying controls. Although most parents will subscribe to, and transmit to their children, the values of individual freedom of expression, most parents will not condone drug use by their children. Parents do not realistically discuss the constellation of factors involved in using drugs and may only transmit an attitude or feeling of individual freedom of expression. Youngsters can therefore logically conclude that individual rights and freedom of expression can be extended to the individual's right to use drugs and become involved in other self-gratifying behavior. The parents' transmission of feelings and attitudes without communicating the ramifications of these feelings and attitudes and the spectrum of their life experiences gives the child only half the picture.

Persons working with juvenile delinquents can also be guilty of the same phenomenon. For example, a probation officer may personally feel that drug laws should be liberalized and may either consciously or unconsciously transmit this to the child. The youngster, not having the accompanying controls, acts out the probation officer's feelings, uses drugs, is apprehended, and is convicted. The probation officer can receive vicarious satisfaction from the child's acting out against the establishment that has imposed the legal restrictions against the use of drugs. The probation officer, however, does not have to pay the penalty for the use of drugs. The delinquent youngster "pays the price"; the probation officer receives the satisfaction. If the probation officer in this example found it necessary to transmit the attitude, he or she should also have discussed the ramifications regarding the use of drugs, the logic behind the law, and the process for changing it. Again, as in the example of the parents and the child, the delinquent has been given only half the picture. The mere transmission of an attitude without accompanying explanations can initiate or perpetuate antisocial behavior.

Inconsistency Between Adults

In some families, one adult undermines the efforts of another adult to set limits on a child's behavior. Often, one of the adults, usually a parent, is harsh

---

[100]Reiner and Kaufman, *Character Disorders in Parents of Delinquents*, p. 15.

Exhibit 4-5 Patterns of inconsistency between adults

There are apparently a large number of variations on this theme. In one instance, it was the resident grandparent who functioned as the secret agent, actively sabotaging the efforts of the parents to set limits upon their child. When they attempted to set rules or punish deviant behavior, the grandparent served as the child's advocate and was sufficiently adept to cause confusion in the ranks of the parents' forces. The grandmother served as baby-sitter for more than a decade and, during that time, effectively prevented the parents from setting consequences for stealing, even when the child stole from her!

There is a more frequently occurring variation of this theme; it is the *My-Child and Your-Child* pattern. This is often found where a new step-parent joins the family. The wife is not allowed to punish her *husband's* child; he, on the other hand, is not allowed to punish *her* child. The children are, of course, eager participants in this game and feed mildly distorted reports of yesterday's battles to each parent. In one blended family of five children, when the stepfather objected to his wife's children using obscenity in his presence, the children simply repeated his objection to the mother. She launched into a vituperative attack upon him for attempting to punish *her* children. He, in turn, assiduously defended *his* children from her efforts to set limits. Both parents wanted the option of being overly permissive with their own brood. As a result, all five children were out of control and were in frequent contact with the local police. Later, when these parents separated, it was possible for them to effectively apply child management procedures to their own children.

SOURCE: Gerald R. Patterson, *Coercive Family Process* (Eugene, Oregon: Castalia Publishing Company, 1982), p. 299.

and punitive, and can exert some control over the child. The other parent disagrees with the harsh and punitive approach and is very warm and permissive, even when the child is misbehaving. Whenever the more strict parent is absent, the child is out of control. Patterson has found that multiple-offending adolescent delinquents come from families of this type in many cases[101] (Exhibit 4-5).

As a child grows older in a family in which the adults are inconsistent, she or he often can manipulate the parents to obtain favors or a relaxation of rules. The rule setter can become more and more physical, and after physical battles, the other spouse often withdraws psychologically. This leaves both parents without support from each other, and the rule setter is resentful of the child. When the rule setter leaves the house, the child asks the other parent for permission to leave the house, borrow the family care, or for money. These requests are granted out of guilt that the child has been beaten. The results is that rules are not consistently stated and enforced, and the child often breaks the "rules" outside of the home, becoming involved in various illegal activities.

[101]Patterson, *Coercive Family Process*, p. 299.

MULTIPLE INFLUENCES ON DELINQUENCY

Using an interdisciplinary approach, we have identified several of the characteristics of families of delinquents. A small but important body of research gives us some indication of the combined effects of different mixtures of these characteristics. For example, Johnstone describes a study by McCord and McCord:

> They found that when strong affectional ties existed between boys and both of their parents, different methods of discipline had no effect on delinquency. When affectional ties were strong with just one parent . . . erratic or lax discipline resulted in higher levels of delinquent behavior.[102]

Here the effect of one family characteristic, alternative methods of discipline, is weakened as long as children have strong affectional ties with both parents.

Another study by Joan McCord examined the combine effects of parent characteristics, child-rearing methods, social class, and broken homes on juvenile delinquency.[103] In particular, three measures of child rearing—mother's affection, supervision, and parental conflict—were quite predictive of the number of offenses an individual committed as both a child and adult. Other aspects of the home atmosphere were less predictive, but did still differentiate the youths who did and did not break the law. These were parental aggression, mother's self-confidence, and father's deviance. In keeping with what we have concluded from other research on the broken home, paternal absence was not a major factor differentiating youths who did not become involved with the juvenile and adult courts. Social class also was not a factor, but this may be because the youths were not extremely different from each other in social class, for they all came from a congested urban area. McCord's research is of considerable importance, for it is one of the few efforts to collect data beginning in a person's childhood and extending into adulthood.

Patterson noted that the failure to parent effectively sometimes results from structural conditions in the family, such as inadequate economics, a broken family with inadequate resources to provide for supervision of the child, and working parents who cannot or do not arrange for child care when they are out of the home.[104] The problem in these families is not neurotic conflict or a lack of warmth, but commitment to activities other than taking care of children or limitations on the amount of time and energy they can expend on the family. When the one or two parents in a family are in constant crisis, the family may be chaotic and disorganized, and the children are likely to be chronic delinquents. Such complete disorganization is an extreme, however, and in many cases parent

---

[102]John W. C. Johnstone, "Delinquency and the Changing American Family," in *Critical Issues in Juvenile Delinquency*, eds. David Shichor and Delos H. Kelly (Lexington, Massachusetts: Lexington Books, D. C. Heath and Company, 1980), p. 89.

[103]Joan McCord, "Some Child-Rearing Antecedents of Criminal Behavior in Adult Men," *Journal of Personality and Social Psychology*, 37, no. 9 (September 1979), pp. 1477–1486.

[104]Patterson, *Coercive Family Process*, p. 298.

involvement in child rearing can be improved, or other adult substitutes can be involved in caring for the child.

The effect of family characteristics also is weakened in certain situations, and for certain types of offenses. A study of Johnstone provides good examples of how the strength of the effect of family characteristics depends on other factors. He studied the influence of the following family characteristics: broken family, amount of shared parent-child activity, closeness of parent and child, parental authority, and the extent to which parent and child worked out rules together.[105] The other factors were family economics, community levels of poverty, and association with delinquents' peers. Recall that these last two factors were identified in the cultural transmission and the differential association theories reviewed in Chapter 3. Family characteristics had more influence on minor delinquency (status and drug infractions) than on serious delinquency (violence, burglary, and larceny). Poverty in the community was the major explanation of serious delinquency.[106] Youths from poorer families were slightly more likely than others to commit serious offenses, but family economics is just a minor influence compared to community poverty.[107] By considering variables that both sociologists and psychologists identify, Johnstone is better able to explain how strongly and when family characteristics affect delinquency. This clearly shows the utility of an interdisciplinary approach in understanding delinquency.

Recent research on multiple influences on delinquency has convinced some people that, although the family has an effect, it does not necessarily have the *major* effect on all kinds of delinquency, for both girls and boys, throughout the entire period of adolescence.[108]

As to the question of whether the family influences girls and boys equally in their tendencies to be delinquent, the evidence is somewhat contradictory. Perhaps because we believe that girls are more involved with and controlled by their parents than are boys, many people assume that girls are more affected by their parents than are boys. Some research has supported this view. For example, Gold and Petronio found that the family is less of an influence on boys' delinquency than is their involvement in the youth culture, for example, in dating.[109] However, girls' delinquency is more affected by their relationships with their fathers and their families in general.[110]

In contrast to research that supports the belief that girls are most influ-

---

[105]John W. C. Johnstone, "Juvenile Delinquency and the Family: A Contextual Interpretation," *Youth and Society, 9,* no. 4 (March 1978), p. 305.

[106]Johnstone, "Delinquency and the Changing American Family," p. 92.

[107]Johnstone, "Juvenile Delinquency and the Family," p. 311.

[108]Don C. Gibbons, *Society, Crime, and Criminal Careers: An Introduction to Criminology,* 3rd ed. (Englewood Cliffs, New Jersey: Prentice-Hall, Inc., 1977), p. 236.

[109]Martin Gold and Richard J. Petronio, "Delinquent Behavior in Adolescence," in *Handbook of Adolescent Psychology,* ed. Joseph Adelson (New York: Wiley-Interscience Publication, 1980), pp. 495–535.

[110]Susan K. Datesman and Frank R. Scarpitti, "Female Delinquency and Broken Homes: A Re-assessment," *Criminology, 13,* no. 1 (May 1975), pp. 33–56.

enced by the family, there is some indication that boys are as strongly if not more affected. The *National Survey of Youth,* which was described in Chapter 2, has helped us to understand the complexity of the relationship between family factors, delinquency, and gender. The *National Survey of Youth* gathered data on several aspects of the child-parent relationship.

- *Social integration,* which includes three factors: the amount of time spent with the family in an average week (*family involvement*); reports of family influence on thoughts and activities (*parental influence*); and ratings of parent importance (*family importance*).
- *Personal commitment,* which includes three factors: the personal importance of conventional goals (*family aspirations*); acceptability of deviant means to obtaining family goals (*family normlessness*); and feelings of being part of the family (*family social isolation*).[111]

For both girls and boys, the family differences were related to delinquency, especially status offenses and a general measure of all types of illegal activity. In contrast to some prior research and to the beliefs of many, family differences were most strongly linked to the delinquency of boys. The difference between girls and boys was most pronounced for serious crimes, suggesting that the family is of particular importance in explaining the delinquency of serious male offenders. Other research has shown that gender differences in the influence of the family on delinquency cannot be assumed. Specifically, even if family conflict is not the major influence on boys' serious delinquency, it does have some influence.[112] Conversely, girls are not *only* affected by the family, but also by peer-group influences.[113] Research has raised critical questions about assumed gender differences as well as the common belief that the family is the primary influence on delinquent behavior.

The effect of the family depends not only on gender and type of crime, but also on the age of the child. Gold and Petronio found that

> more of the variance in the frequency of younger boys' delinquent behavior was accounted for by their relationships with their mothers, while among older boys the relationship with their fathers was the most distinguishing variable. Among girls, the frequency of younger girls' delinquency behavior is also accounted for by their mothers, but among older girls, attitude towards school was the most distinguishing variable. Among older girls from urban environments, the degree of emotional warmth between fathers and daughters related significantly to delinquency.[114]

Richard Johnson also concluded that the effect of the family depends on the child's age. He considered school and peer group experiences as well as parental attachments and came to the conclusion that "by the time they reach adoles-

[111]Delbert S. Elliott, David Huizinga, and Suzanne S. Ageton, *Explaining Delinquency and Drug Use* (Beverly Hills, California: Sage Publications, 1985), p. 153.

[112]Stephen Norland, Neal Shover, William E. Thornton, and Jennifer James, "Intrafamily Conflict and Delinquency," *Pacific Sociological Review,* 22, no. 2 (April 1979), pp. 223–240.

[113]*Ibid.,* p. 237.

[114]Gold and Petronio, "Delinquent Behavior in Adolescence," pp. 511–512.

Exhibit 4-6 A promising program to improve family interaction

A focus on the systematic nature of parent-child interaction may have the greatest promise for developing technology for family intervention. Applications of social learning theory have generated a movement usually referred to as behavior modification. This approach is clinical in orientation, and in this context a variety of programs for changing or managing problem behavior on the basis of Skinnerian principles have been developed. These programs are designed for and tested and modified in real settings, including families, both in clinic visits and in the home. There are a number of such programs to manage the behavior of children who are disruptive in school or at home, although they are not specifically directed at what has been defined as predelinquent or delinquent behavior.

The best representative of this clinical-research literature is the continuing work of Patterson and his colleagues. . . . Because of its clinical nature, this research is necessarily based on small numbers of families. But even so, the record of success is impressive. Patterson begins with the twofold premise that continuing antisocial or disruptive behavior by a child is usually reinforced instead of suppressed in the home by the nature of the child's interactions with family members and that this pathological chain of socialization can be reversed if the interacting parents or siblings can be taught very specific responses that do not reinforce these disruptive behaviors. The child's behaviors that can be controlled in this way include aggression, disobedience, and various forms of self-victimization usually resulting in severe physical punishment. In short, the problem behavior is defined as part of an interaction routine that is continually repeated, thereby reinforcing the problem behavior.

This explanation is oversimplified, of course, particularly with respect to the variations on problem behavior that occur in real settings. But the behavioral principles involved are simple, and Patterson has developed a standardized set of training procedures for the parents and other social agents whose reinforcement behaviors he is seeking to change. Problem behaviors by the child are specified (usually some form of coercive behavior such as hitting), and reinforcement behaviors and patterns of reinforcement by parents and other socializers are identified. Procedures for tracking the child's aversive stimuli are then matched to a schedule of contingencies designed to terminate instead of escalate the interaction of aversive stimuli between child and control agent. The procedures not only show immediate results, but they also make clear to the control agent how much the behavior problems depend on the specific interactions.

Specific deficiencies in parental tracking and reinforcement of a child's behavior, such as low rates of contingent reinforcement for prosocial behavior and uneven rates of contingent reinforcement for antisocial behavior, are the focus of change. For example, a parent may fail to "track" a chain of behavior that normally ends in aggression unless the chain is disrupted. Tracking requires paying close attention to the child's behavior patterns and identifying the beginning stages

(Continued)

Exhibit 4-6   Cont.

of an aggressive chain. A parent can be trained to track properly and then intervene effectively. Payoff for the parent's newly learned skills is immediate, as is the effect of backsliding by a parent.

Such programs, in spite of their success, are not without problems for purposes of rehabilitation. The amenability factor may or may not be enhanced by the relative ease with which success can be shown. Violence in the family—both aggression by a child or children and physical punishment by parents in response— is one of the targets of these techniques. The clinics using the techniques obtain clients mostly by referral from schools and other settings where problem behavior has been identified. It is not known whether this referred and largely voluntary clientele can expand to a level where the effect on delinquency would be felt. If family intervention for the purposes of socialization or rehabilitation is to be proactive, amenability and receptivity will become important unknown factors.

A different kind of problem with this approach has to do with its potential effectiveness for suppressing delinquent behavior. These social engineering procedures have the advantage of being specific enough to standardize and articulate as a set of training procedures. But this very specificity is disadvantageous as well because the effects of a program are narrowed to the particular interactions that the program is designed to modify. While these programs are broadly applicable across many settings (e.g., family and school), it is unclear to what extent the modified behaviors transfer from one setting to another. The learning contingencies having to do with social control are theoretically the same from one setting to another, but there may be critical differences in techniques and how they are used in the social perception of the various settings. In short, a behavior modification program that successfully manages aggressive interaction in the family may not change a child's aggressive behavior outside the home.

SOURCE: Susan O. White and Murray A. Straus, "The Implications of Family Violence for Rehabilitation Strategies," in *New Directions in the Rehabilitation of Criminal Offenders,* eds. Susan E. Martin, Lee B. Sechrest, and Robin Redner (Washington, D.C.: National Academy Press, 1981), pp. 278–280.

Issues for Discussion.   How is the proposed program related to the principles of coercion theory as developed by Gerald Patterson (described earlier in this chapter)? Enumerate the factors that can make it difficult to successfully implement the proposed program. Given the uncertainty about whether the proposed program of family intervention will effectively prevent delinquency, should the program be tried? If you feel the program should be used, under what conditions and with which adolescents?

cence . . . these young people's situational decisions to abide by or break the law are almost unaffected by the nature of their ties with their parents.[115] Thus, we would conclude that early intervention aimed at improving family situations would be particularly important in preventing delinquency, but as adolescents

[115]Richard E. Johnson, *Juvenile Delinquency and Its Origins: An Integrated Theoretical Approach* (New York: Cambridge University Press, 1979), p. 141.

mature, programs would have to focus on a wider range of influences to effectively interrupt a pattern of delinquency (see Exhibit 4-6).

BELIEFS, THEORY, AND RESEARCH

Up to this point, we have presented research and theory to show the constellation of family characteristics, including interactions within the family, which contribute to delinquency. We also have pointed out some modifications of this idea by citing research showing that, although the family has an effect, other factors also influence delinquency. Additionally, the strength of the family's contribution to delinquency depends on age, sex, community, and type of offense. Some people have gone beyond these modifications, and said that the family does not contribute to delinquency in any meaningful way. This controversy is presented here, for it is a good illustration of a major idea emphasized in Chapter 1. Specifically, personal beliefs have an important influence on our understanding and control of delinquency.

Some people have argued that our very strong beliefs about the family and delinquency lead us to assume more or less of a connection than there is. Johnstone describes the controversy in the juvenile delinquency literature:

> Just as this literature is voluminous, so too is it inconclusive. In it one can discover positions ranging from the view that the family is the single most important determinant of delinquent behavior to the view that although some empirical associations may exist, there is no basis on which to posit any direct causal connection between the two.[116]

People who feel that the family does not play an important part in causing delinquency point out that, in many studies, the families of official delinquents are compared to the families of adolescents who are not in contact with the juvenile justice system.[117] It is possible that youths are arrested or sent to court because of their families' characteristics. To the extent that this is true, we cannot conclude that the family characteristics cause delinquency. Fortunately, there are some self-report delinquency studies which avoid this problem. In these particular studies, delinquency was related to family characteristics, but more weakly than in other research.[118]

At this time, there is no research evidence indicating that we should completely ignore the family as a cause of delinquency. Even if there were, it is unlikely that this would occur. Much of the public shares the belief that family characteristics and parent-child interactions are at the root of much delinquency. Some theorists and researchers also hold this belief, whereas for political reasons

[116]Johnstone, "Delinquency and the Changing American Family," p. 83.

[117]Josefina Figueira-McDonough and Elaine Selo, "A Reformulation of the 'Equal Opportunity' Explanation of Female Delinquency," *Crime and Delinquency*, 26, no. 4 (July 1980), pp. 333–343.

[118]Nye, *Family Relationships and Delinquent Behavior;* and Travis Hirschi, *Causes of Delinquency* (Berkeley, California: University of California Press, 1969).

others reject it.[119] Since research on the broken home began, conclusions about the effect on delinquency have been more influenced by popular beliefs than by actual research evidence.[120] Given this situation, it is important to carefully consider the quality of research, taking into account things like the use of official records rather than self-report delinquency measures. We must also look carefully at the amount of effect that family characteristics have, and the conditions under which they have an effect.

In drawing conclusions about families and delinquency, we also must avoid making erroneous assumptions about families. For instance, many people assume that teenage mothers cannot provide adequate care for their children. However, in many families this is not an issue, since teenage mothers live with their own parents, and other relatives take a major part in rearing the children.[121] There is not adequate research to tell us how this and other types of less typical family arrangements affect delinquency. Therefore, we cannot assume that the effect is negative.

CONCLUSIONS

The complexities of the family environment and the way they contribute to delinquency singly or in combination with other factors have been discussed. Specific problems in parent-child interactions also were delineated because they can influence the youngster's future behavior. In particular, poor parenting skills and parents' lack of motivation to improve their skills can promote a pattern of stealing and aggression at an early age, and these early patterns often result in youths' involvement with the juvenile justice system during their adolescence.

In their interactions with children, many contemporary parents have substituted cliches for feelings and have transmitted attitudes to their youngsters without accompanying explanations of the total picture. Parents often tell their children that when they were their age, they solved complicated problems very easily. This is not realistic. The problem-solving and decision-making processes, whether in the workaday world or in the family, are difficult processes at any age. A transmission to children that decision making is difficult and that only through mutual assistance can the process be effective will be helpful in presenting a realistic picture of the life process and in establishing an effective communication between child and parent. A realistic and empathetic approach to child rearing that includes assistance and guidance in daily decision making to prepare youngsters for future roles in their communities is much more effective

[119]Gwynn Nettler, *Explaining Crime*, 2nd ed. (New York: McGraw-Hill Book Company, 1978), p. 333.

[120]Karen Wilkenson, "The Broken Family and Juvenile Delinquency: Scientific Explanation or Ideology?" *Social Problems, 21*, no. 5 (June 1974), pp. 726–739.

[121]Andrew Billingsley, *Black Families in White America* (Englewood Cliffs, New Jersey: Prentice-Hall, Inc., 1968).

than a superficial or mechanical approach that substitutes material rewards for emotional security and support.[122]

SUMMARY

By focusing on the family, this chapter draws from both the sociological and psychological disciplines and points out the usefulness of blending the two disciplines for a more comprehensive understanding of the delinquency phenomenon. The sampling of material presented illustrates the factors in the family environment that contribute to delinquency and the importance of a healthy family atmosphere in influencing youngsters in socially acceptable ways.

Practical suggestions have been made for increasing the effectiveness of family interactions in the contemporary community. In particular, it is important to improve parenting skills in the areas of noticing inappropriate behavior, monitoring children's behavior over a long period, modeling social skill behavior, clearly stating house rules, consistently punishing youths for breaking the rules, providing reinforcement for following rules, and negotiating disagreements to avoid the escalation of conflicts.

There are numerous other ideas, theories, and assumptions about the influence of the family on delinquent behavior. Correctional and court personnel usually consider the family to be extremely important. Some research shows that family influence varies by gender, type of offense, and community prosperity. According to other people, the family has little or no influence. To a large extent, these different ideas about the family rest on strongly held personal beliefs. As a result, it is essential to consider existing sound research on the issue before reaching any conclusions.

Despite this controversy, it cannot be denied that the family is of some importance in influencing delinquency. Numerous studies have shown that there is a connection between family characteristics and delinquent status or behavior. The chapters of this book which focus on delinquency programs and treatment methods will reemphasize this point. First, however, the next chapter will focus on adolescence and the special experiences that accompany this stage of development.

DISCUSSION QUESTIONS

1. What family characteristics are most likely to result in delinquency? Use research findings described in this chapter to support your view.
2. State the major reasons why parents and their children have difficulty communicating when they interact.
3. What form of discipline by parents is most likely to guard against delinquency? Explain the extent to which your opinion is based on research findings or, alternatively, on your personal beliefs.

---

[122]Reiner and Kaufman, *Character Disorders in Parents of Delinquents*, p. 15.

4. Which youths seem to be most prone to becoming delinquent because of family characteristics? If economic pressures are at the root of some of the negative family dynamics that contribute to delinquency, what is the appropriate balance between family-oriented interventions to improve parenting skills, interventions to replace inadequate parenting, and interventions to improve the family's economic status? In developing an ideal plan for interventions, students should compare each approach on the timing of intervention, the probable short- and long-term costs and benefits, the feasibility in targeting services to the appropriate families, etc.

PROJECTS

1. Thinking about your own or another person's family, what patterns of interaction seemed to promote delinquency? What patterns seemed to guard against delinquency?

2. Survey classmates or other students about their views on the influence of the family on delinquency. How would you describe the beliefs which seem to underlie their views? Are these beliefs supported by research findings presented in this chapter?

3. Develop a community program that can help strengthen the families of delinquents.

5

The Adolescent

- THREE PERSPECTIVES ON ADOLESCENCE
- WORKING WITH ADOLESCENTS
- CASE STUDIES

LEARNING OBJECTIVES

1. To be aware that our modern-day beliefs about adolescence differ from the beliefs of people in different cultures and at earlier historical periods.
2. To see the relationship between beliefs about the adolescent stage of life and our treatment of youths, particularly delinquents.
3. To be aware of behavior that is considered "normal" for contemporary adolescents.
4. To understand how societal conditions, including one-to-one interactions with delinquents, can best promote a youth's adjustment.
5. To be able to analyze delinquents' circumstances, and identify those difficulties stemming from their status as adolescents as distinct from those resulting from other causes.

Like the previous chapter on the family, this one uses an interdisciplinary approach to add to our understanding of delinquency. We will concentrate on the adolescent stage of life and the place of adolescents in American society by drawing from the works of sociologists, psychologists, anthropologists, and historians. This interdisciplinary approach is particularly appropriate to the study of adolescence:

Marked social, psychological, and physical changes are characteristics of this age span and they do not occur unrelated to each other. The physical changes have definite effect on the social and psychological adjustments of the individual; social factors influence the psychological and physical changes. The psychological factors have repercussions both socially and physiologically.[1]

Furthermore, many social, psychological, and physical changes of adolescence are unique to modern-day American society. Youths stay in school longer and mature physically earlier, for example, than in previous historical periods. By comparing adolescence in other cultures and at earlier periods of time, we can become more aware of the special status and needs of contemporary American youths.

Since all juvenile delinquents are adolescents, it is necessary for students of delinquency and personnel who work in delinquency programs to understand the psychology of the adolescent.

Adolescence encompasses an extensive period of accelerated physical and psychological growth. Its onset can be determined by observation of physical changes—change usually begins at about the age of ten in girls and the age of twelve in boys. Clinical evidence shows that modifications of the psychological structure takes place at approximately the same time as the physical change occurs.[2]

Awareness of physical and related psychological changes is required to answer a number of questions. What is normal adolescent behavior? Can some delinquency be considered normal during adolescence? What special psychological needs do adolescents have? What rights and responsibilities are adolescents mature enough to handle?

Adolescents are set apart from other age groups not only because they themselves are different from adults and younger children. Their status in society is also unique. The expectations we have for adolescents, the things we encourage them to do or not to do, and the limits we set on their activities result in special adolescent experiences. For example, adolescents are expected to spend much of their time preparing for the future in school, are encouraged to avoid long-lasting and serious relationships with a person of the opposite sex, and are legally prohibited from living away from their parents. How is this unique status related to delinquency? Does it encourage delinquent behavior in some ways? We will present the answers of a number of scholars to these questions.

Anthropologists and historians provide a different perspective for the study of adolescents. By comparing adolescence at different times and in different cultures, they raise interesting questions about how adolescents should be

---

[1]Irene M. Josselyn, *The Adolescent and His World* (New York: The Family Service Association of America, 1952), p. 10.

[2]*Ibid.*, p. 5.

treated in society, and about whether our society has unnecessarily created special psychological needs during this period of life. Because this perspective provokes us to think through our beliefs about adolescents, we will begin with the cultural and historical viewpoints. As you read about contemporary adolescents described later in this chapter, you should keep in mind that their experiences and needs are very much influenced by modern-day beliefs.

A CULTURAL PERSPECTIVE

Margaret Mead, in her famous study *Coming of Age in Samoa,* concluded that adolescence and the characteristics peculiar to it are culturally determined— depending on the culture, adolescents will be happy or unhappy, constrained or uninhibited, and their experiences as adolescents will be almost solely determined by the culture in which they live.[3] Mead felt that the Samoan culture, unlike the culture in our country, was much more conducive to the youngster's experiencing less turmoil and adjusting satisfactorily to the environment.

Other Cultures

The Cavans point out that a shortening or even an omission of adolescence occurs in societies where there is a well-organized family controlled by family elders. In some cultures the child's entire behavior revolves around the family, and little outside assistance supplements the material and psychological support that the child receives from the family. The particular role that the youngster occupies in the family or in the community is well established, with little room for experimentation or mobility. When the youngster becomes physically mature, he or she is considered an adult and is given the privileges of adulthood as well as its responsibilities.[4]

The Cavans describe the traditional Eskimo society to show that some cultural groups lack both adolescence and delinquency.

> The child and youth was never physically separated from his family, either on a daily basis for education, employment or recreation, or on a yearly basis at college or for a prolonged journey. There were no hangouts on lighted street corners where youth might gather. As adult skills were learned, the child's status increased and in some groups special recognition was given as each new stage was reached. A special step toward adulthood was reached when a boy was given his own kayak, usually about the age of eight or nine, or when inland he brought down his first carabao at about age eleven or twelve. In some groups a killing of the first major meat animal called for a special celebration. As soon as the youth had killed at least one of each such animal he was considered ready for marriage.

[3]Margaret Mead, *Coming of Age in Samoa,* 4th ed. (New York: Dell Publishing Company, 1971).

[4]Ruth S. Cavan and Jordan T. Cavan, *Delinquency and Crime: Cross Cultural Perspectives* (Philadelphia: J. B. Lippincott Co., 1968).

Thus, step-by-step the boy made his way from childhood to adulthood always living and participating in the activities of family and community.[5]

Some cultures use ceremonies to clearly establish the point at which a child has become an adult. In one primitive culture, a special ceremony was used for boys:

> The younger teen-agers were sequestered from the community, starved for prolonged periods, then circumcised en masse. These ritualistic practices supervised and executed by the constituted authority of the gens or clan were probably assertions that the youth was not an independent entity, an island to itself, but belonged to his society (gens or clan). After the contemplation of these sadistic, humiliating, and impotenizing (castrating) rituals, the youngster was fully accepted into the fraternity of the males in his community. He had equal status with his elders in the men's house and participated on an equal basis with them in hunts and wars.[6]

In contrast to the tendency to initiate boys into the public sphere and to establish them as adults rather than children, girls are not considered to be dramatically different from children when they reach puberty. Instead, ceremonies are often used to impress

> on her the necessity for subduing her physical self in order to attain feminine virtue. Her body is scarified and molded. She is enclosed in a designated space within her own household or village, in a hogan or seclusion chamber, surrounded by a mound of earth, buried from her waist down in a pit of sand. Her separation from childhood does not require a removal in actual space. Like a caterpillar that must be enclosed in a cocoon and undergo a quiet, unseen metamorphosis to then emerge from the chrysalis as a butterfly, the girl undergoes transformations to maturity, but by way of imaginary adventures. . . . However far-reaching the imaginary journey, it takes place in a cocoon—the family nest or nearby hut.[7]

For both girls and boys, there is usually the assumption that as they enter adulthood, they will take on new roles in both the sexual and moral realms of life.

In other primitive cultures, ceremonies are not used to mark the transition to adulthood, but once a child reaches puberty the transition is smooth and there is no special social recognition. These cultures with and without recognition of puberty are distinguished from our own, which is marked by confusion about the transition, by a period called adolescence between childhood and adulthood, and by a delay of the transition to adult status well beyond puberty.[8]

---

[5]*Ibid.*, p. 23.

[6]S. R. Slavson, *Reclaiming the Delinquent* (New York: The Free Press, 1965), p. 7.

[7]Louise J. Kaplan, *Adolescence: The Farewell to Childhood* (New York: Simon and Schuster, 1984), pp. 31–32.

[8]Walter C. Reckless, *The Crime Problem* (New York: Appleton-Century-Crofts, 1967).

Consistent with the belief that adolescence is not a separate stage of life, in cultures other than our own, people of different ages are not separated from each other as they are in our culture. Fortas, for example, describes traditional African societies:

(T)he social sphere of adult and child is unitary and undivided. . . . Nothing in the universe of adult behavior is hidden from children or barred from them. They are actively and responsibly part of the social structure, the economic system, the ritual and ideological system.[9]

Adolescent-aged people are not treated differently from adults in all cultures, either. American Indian parents typically do not interrupt the activities of adults or children. They believe that people of all ages have the right to pursue their own activities and interests without interference, regardless of what is "best" for the child.[10]

These examples from other cultures illustrate that the adolescents' experiences depend upon how youths are perceived and what place there is in the society for them. Coleman states that

adolescence is not a time of stress and turmoil in all cultures. Where the adolescent has a well-structured role, contributes to the social group and has assured status, he does not suffer the insecurities and fears of our adolescents or exhibit the extreme behavior many of our adolescents manifest in their attempt to feel important and worthwhile. In proportion, then, as we encourage and plan for a useful part for our adolescents to play in their community, and insofar as we are able to solve our own uncertainties and provide a stable social and economic setting in which they can see a meaningful place as they reach adulthood, we shall be fostering mental health and preventing abnormal behavior.[11]

Contemporary American Culture

In industrialized and technologically advanced countries like the United States, the period of adolescence is much longer than it is in underdeveloped countries, according to some, because of the need for increased training and specialization and less dependence on the family as a total unit. Education of the adolescent is extended beyond the secondary grades and even well into the college years, which means that the period of adolescence is often prolonged and the dependence on the family, at least financially, becomes even more accentuated and the transition from adolescence to adulthood is delayed.

There are several other characteristics of the transition to adulthood which make our culture unique. Speaking of movement into adult work and

---

[9]M. Fortas, "Social and Psychological Aspects of Education in Ireland," in *From Adult to Child*, ed. John Middeton (Garden City, New York: Natural History Press, 1970), p. 14.

[10]Jimm Good Tracks, "Native American Non-Interference," *Social Work, 18*, no. 6 (November 1973), pp. 30–34.

[11]James C. Coleman, *Abnormal Psychology and Modern Life* (Glenwood, Illinois: Scott, Foresman and Company, 1956), p. 596.

occupational roles, and marriage and parenthood roles, and of emancipation from parental authority, Skolnick describes the differences:

> In all three ways the transition to adulthood in our culture is unusual. While our young people become adults relatively late in terms of their assumption of work and marital roles, they are emancipated from parental authority both abruptly and at an early age.[12]

In many other cultures, youths never become emancipated from parental authority, even after they have left their parents' home and become parents themselves.

Ruth Benedict pointed out that our culture is one of the few in which children are prepared for adulthood by encouraging them to act differently than adults:

> Children play while adults work; the child is supposed to be obedient, the adult dominant; the child is supposed to be sexless, while the adult is expected to be sexually active and competent.[13]

The demand that adolescents abandon childish behaviors and assume contradicting adult behaviors can lead to the turmoil during adolescence.

There are other ways in which our society may contribute to difficulties, including delinquency, during adolescence. Like most technically advanced societies, ours keeps adolescents out of the labor market for as long as possible, thus extending and accentuating the adolescent period. As mentioned earlier, increased training and specialization are the main reason for this delay; however, an individual's job or vocational skill is one of the major factors in achieving adult status and the rewards that go with it. If the youngster is kept out of the labor market because of the real or imagined need for educational diplomas and degrees, this has the effect of not only prolonging adolescence but, if the youngster quits school and cannot find a job, it can contribute to delinquent behavior.

Even groups which at one time had less confusion regarding the transition to adulthood are affected by the influence of modern-day working and living conditions on their traditional culture. One which we described above, the Eskimo community, has been affected by technology and change, and at present, as the Cavans point out, there are increasing signs of youthful male delinquency. The delinquency occurs in the towns and not in the rural settings that once typified Eskimo life. Eskimos in towns have more difficulty conforming to the traditional Eskimo behavior, and the function of the family is changed. Because many of the Eskimo youngsters want steady jobs so that they can earn money and have the same luxuries as other local ethnic groups, there is an increased

---

[12]Arlene Skolnick, "Children's Rights, Children's Development," in *The Future of Childhood and Juvenile Justice*, ed. Lamar T. Empey (Charlottesville, Virginia: University Press of Virginia, 1979) pp. 155–156.

[13]*Ibid.*, pp. 159–160.

"breaking of the bonds" between the youths and their families. The result is that the extended family exerts less control and has less influence over the youngster's behavior and actions, which in turn affects the delinquency rates:

> The family does not operate as a social, economic, or political unit. A child at an early age enters specialized agencies that compete for his loyalty and open many choices to him for present or future aspirations and goals. The passage from childhood to adulthood is now clearly and almost inevitably channeled toward a specific adult role. In the transition from early childhood in his family to later childhood in organized agencies, the child may escape incorporation into any conventional organized group and become a kind of "free lance" in his behavior lacking in self-discipline or clear orientation toward a goal.[14]

Our complex system of socialization has the positive benefits of opening different options to youths. At the same time, it can create confusion for many youngsters, and contribute to the delinquency of some of them.

A HISTORICAL PERSPECTIVE

Our discussion of different cultures makes it clear that there is no one universal view of adolescence, and therefore no one correct "place" for, or pattern of behavior among, adolescents in our society. This point also is made by historians who examine the history of childhood. The historical perspective also reveals the societal conditions leading up to our beliefs about adolescence, as well as conditions which may be contributing to changes in contemporary beliefs.

The History of Childhood

Scholars interested in the history of childhood have documented that before the fifteenth century, children, much less adolescents, did not hold a protected status.[15] Because most died during infancy, they were not treasured as individuals by their parents. Some historians have pointed out quite brutal aspects of childhood:

> While children were not segregated from adults . . . their status was at the bottom of the social scale. In antiquity, both boys and girls were sometimes placed in brothels, suffered castration and clitoridectomy, and then became the sexual playthings for adults. . . . The apprenticeship system . . . led to the exploitation

---

[14]Cavan and Cavan, *Delinquency and Crime*, p. 8.

[15]Philippe Ariès, *Centuries of Childhood*, trans. Robert Baldick (New York: Alfred A. Knopf, Inc., 1962); Robert H. Brenner, ed., *Children and Youth in America: A Documentary History*, 2 vols. (Cambridge, Massachusetts: Harvard University Press, 1970); John Demos, *A Little Commonwealth* (New York: Oxford University Press, 1970); John R. Gillis, *Youth and History* (New York: Academic Press, 1974); Lloyd de Mause, *The History of Childhood* (New York: Psychohistory Press, 1974); David Hunt, *Parents and Children in History: The Psychology of Family Life in Early Modern History* (New York: Basic Books, Inc., Publishers, 1970).

of child labor. Finally, methods of social control were often brutal and counte-
nanced severe beatings with whips, rods, and cudgels.[16]

Only in the fifteenth and sixteenth centuries did the idea develop that children
should be treated in a special way in order to prepare them, primarily morally,
for adulthood.[17] Religious influences were an important reason for this shift.

In America and other western countries, a second major shift in beliefs
occurred during the nineteenth century. Instead of seeing delinquency as a sin,
people viewed it as a result of family and community disruptions and disorder.[18]
This opened the door to reform the offender, either by changing the family and
community, or by replacing them with more positive influences. "Child-saving"
institutions were established, and eventually the state became heavily involved in
reforming delinquents through the juvenile court system. These changes are
referred to as the "child-saving movement."

The tendency for increased government involvement in bringing up
children, and thus in controlling delinquency, is part of a larger historical trend.
Research shows that, throughout the world, beliefs about children have
changed.[19] As beliefs changed, governments recognized childhood as a special
period of life and attempted to insure that children developed into adults who
could contribute to society. Thus, child labor regulations were passed, the government took an active role in providing education, and eventually education
was made compulsory.

Like childhood, the idea of adolescence has not always existed in our
culture, but it came into being along with the child-saving movement of the
nineteenth century. The invention of adolescence as a stage in life occurred in all
societies which became "advanced technological societies":

> The emergence of adolescence is related to the decline of the working family as
> the unit of economic production. In stable agricultural societies, where occupa-
> tions are passed on from father to son, one generation quietly merges into the
> next. The decline of this tradition opened up a gap between the experience of
> parents and children and transformed the teenage years into a time of occupa-
> tional choice. The prolongation of education and the removal of childhood from
> the labor market by means of compulsory education and child-labor laws also
> contributed to the adolescent experience.[20]

An important quality of this adolescent stage of life is that school is required, and
many types of work are prohibited. Youths who formerly might have been in

---

[16]Lamar T. Empey, "The Progressive Legacy and the Concept of Childhood," in *Juvenile
Justice: The Progressive Legacy and Current Reforms,* ed. Lamar T. Empey (Charlottesville,
Virginia: University Press of Virginia, 1979), pp. 13–14.

[17]*Ibid.,* p. 14.

[18]*Ibid.,* p. 24.

[19]John Boli-Bennett and John W. Meyer, "The Ideology of Childhood and the State: Rules
Distinguishing Children in National Constitutions, 1870–1970"; *American Sociological Review, 43,* no. 5 (December 1978), pp. 797–812.

[20]Arlene Skolnick, "The Limits of Childhood: Conceptions of Child Development and
Social Context," *Law and Contemporary Problems, 39,* no. 3 (Summer 1975), pp. 62–63.

"craft occupations" of "farming, baking, and shoemaking" or apprenticed to "lawyers, merchants, pharmacists, and administrators" in preindustrial Europe, were now prohibited from such activities.[21]

The implications of these changes have been somewhat different for females and males. In the middle ages when all children were relatively ignored, girls were more likely to be neglected, or even killed in their infancy as less useful in producing necessary material support for the family. Later, as all children became a center of attention and concern, this was particularly true for girls. The attention was in the form of protectiveness. Girls were excluded from schools or, in some cases, from more advanced education.[22] In the American colonial period, when boys were emancipated from their families so they might pursue employment, this was uncommon for girls: "'Letting go' of a daughter conflicted with the prevailing social attitudes towards the sheltering and protection of women."[23] During a subsequent historical period, the early twentieth century, "female juvenile delinquents often received more severe punishments than males, even though boys usually were charged with more serious crimes."[24] This trend was based on beliefs that delinquent girls must be controlled to limit the possibility that they would pass inferior genes onto offsprings. Furthermore, psychological theories of the day portrayed women as needing more controls than men, and a "modernization" of public attitudes about sexuality convinced some people that women were in great danger of becoming sexually "impure."[25]

Today's juvenile court system is influenced by traditions based on historical beliefs about adolescence. As we noted in Chapter 4, there is a strong emphasis in the juvenile court on supporting the family, or acting as the family if necessary. Juvenile delinquency laws define the status offenses as activities which are inappropriate for the childhood stage of life. Specifically, they require school attendance and they prohibit sexual behavior. And the juvenile courts have generally been particularly protective of females, using harsh control methods (institutions) for the relatively minor status offenses.

Recent Changes

As the historical account shows, the definition of adolescence is not "fixed," but within our culture it changes over time. We may now be in another period of major change in beliefs. Empey writes that in the past we moved from indifference to preoccupation with children, and now we are moving to a deem-

[21]*Ibid.*, p. 67.

[22]Empey, *Juvenile Justice*, p. 16.

[23]F. Raymond Marks, "Detours on the Road to Maturity: A View of the Legal Conceptions of Growing Up and Letting Go," *Law and Contemporary Problems, 39*, no. 3 (Summer 1975), p. 84.

[24]Steven Schlossman and Stephanie Wallach, "The Crime of Precocious Sexuality: Female Juvenile Delinquency in the Progressive Era," *Harvard Educational Review, 48*, no. 1 (February 1978), p. 65.

[25]*Ibid.*, pp. 81–91.

phasis on early childhood and adolescence. He calls this current thinking about children a period of attenuation.[26]

Skolnick describes a similar change:

> In a variety of ways the norms of conventional age grading appear to be losing their previous decisive influence. Although the adult world is still sharply marked off from the world of the child, there is certain blurring around the edges. "Adolescence" is spreading at both ends—younger children are absorbing teenage culture and attitudes, and many of those in their twenties and beyond are refusing to progress to "adulthood." Some of the indicators of separate status . . . such as dress and amusements, no longer distinguish children and adults as sharply as they once did. Current clothing styles are not only unisex, they are increasingly uniage.[27]

This contemporary challenge to traditional beliefs about adolescence is having some effect on the juvenile courts and related programs to control delinquency. This is most evident in the childs' rights movement, which will be discussed in some detail at the end of this chapter.

In addition to the change in beliefs about childhood, we have recently experienced a change in the size of the adolescent population relative to other age groups. In a 1979 article, Davis described this change:

> In 1890 only 4.0 percent of the American population were over 65. Today the figure is 10.9 percent. In the most probable projection of the Census Bureau, the proportion rises in the year 2000 to 12.2 percent. Simultaneously, the proportion of young people aged 15–19 has been generally shrinking. It was 10.5 percent in 1890, is 9.8 percent today, and will be, according to the Census Bureau's Series II projection, 7.8 percent in the year 2000.[28]

According to Davis, the population makeup explains the delinquency of the 1960s. He feels that because of the low ratio of adults to youths, there was less integration of the generations, and this led to conflict and disruption. Generally, the current generation of adolescents are growing up with a higher ratio of adults to themselves, which may in turn affect their behavior.[29] Of course, some adolescents—particularly in the poor urban areas characterized by the underclass—may not experience the shifting demographics, since in such neighborhoods adult males tend to be absent. But outside of such areas, we may be seeing less prominence of a "youth culture."

A SOCIAL-PSYCHOLOGICAL PERSPECTIVE

The cultural influences and historical trends that we have outlined ultimately affect the daily lives of adolescents, their development, and their personalities.

---

[26]Empey, *The Future of Childhood and Juvenile Justice*, p. 26.

[27]Skolnick, "The Limits of Childhood," p. 71.

[28]Kingsley Davis, "Demographic Changes and the Future of Childhood," in *The Future of Childhood and Juvenile Justice*, ed. Empey, p. 125.

[29]*Ibid.*, p. 132.

As part of this general trend, American cultural traditions and history affect the families, community institutions, and neighborhood experiences which in turn affect adolescents.[30] We will now turn our attention to some of the resulting characteristics of adolescents and their daily experiences which are considered to be a normal part of the teenage years.

The Normal Adolescent

The combined physical and psychological and social changes that take place during the adolescent period affect the adolescent's self-concept, the way that she or he feels, and the way other people react to the adolescent. However, contrary to the common belief that adolescence is always characterized by turmoil and unhappiness, research has shown that this is the case for only some youths. A study by Daniel and Judith Offer revealed at least three pathways to development for adolescent boys.[31] Some youths experienced *continuous* growth. They seemed to mature with a smoothness and with clear objectives. They had good relationships with parents and teachers, and they did not deviate from cultural and societal norms. As one might expect from the prior chapter on the family, youths with continuous growth were from stable, intact families and had parents who encouraged independence.

A second group of boys experienced *surgent* growth, that is, cycles of ups and downs between adjustment and personal growth alternating with periods of no growth or even some backsliding in development. Many of the boys characterized by surgent growth had experienced some type of family crisis, such as parent separation or divorce, or illness in the family.

A third group experienced *tumultuous* growth, showing continuous inner turmoil and related behavior problems. These youths did not trust adults and they often were unhappy. As we stressed in Chapter 4, communication with parents is quite important to child development. The boys with tumultuous growth had frequent and escalating conflict with their parents and were from families manifesting overt marital conflicts. They often relied heavily on their peers rather than their parents for support.

Researchers and theorists who have studied adolescence have often assumed that all youths go through a period of *tumultuous* growth. This assumption may be the result of the focus on much study on adolescents who have behavior problems, including patterns of delinquency. For example, Ackerman describes the adolescent:

> During adolescence, anxiety, emotional confusion, erratic social behavior, shifting concepts of self in the outer world, weakness of reality perception, vacillating moral standards, instability and irregularity of impulse control, and fickle ambivalent interpersonal relations may all be part of a normal transitional adapta-

[30]James F. Short, Jr., "Social Context of Child Rights and Delinquency," in *The Future of Childhood and Juvenile Justice*, ed. Empey, p. 183.

[31]Daniel Offer and Judith Offer, *From Teenage to Young Manhood* (New York: Basic Books, Inc., 1975).

tion. Transitory mild disturbances of these types may not constitute clinical pathology. Clinical diagnoses can in no way be based on intrinsic adolescent phenomena.[32]

Redl also focused on tumultuous development in his description of the normal teenager's behavioral constellation:

1. Conflict of double standards: individual child still parent loyal, peer group code basically "anti-adult." Result: new waves of guilt and shame in both directions.
2. Embarrassment about open submission to adult politeness and good manner codes.
3. Shamelessness in language and behavior bravado through flaunting of health and safety rules, special joy in risk taking.
4. Avoidance of too open acceptance of adults in official roles even of those very much liked (teachers and parents, for example).
5. Loyalty to peers and risk taking in their favor even when they are personally despised or feared.
6. Openly displayed freshness against authority figures.
7. Deep-seated revulsion toward any form of praise or punishment which seems to be perceived as "infantilizing."
8. Safety in homosexual groupings; view of the other sex as "hunter's trophy" rather than in terms of interpersonal relationships.
9. Negative loading of any form of official acceptance of help from adults; pride in "taking it bravely" at any price.
10. No prestige of verbal communication with a trusted adult; hesitation about communicating about feelings and emotions.
11. Apathy toward adult as partner in play life unless it is a group game situation.[33]

In our society, girls in particular are negatively affected when their reproductive organs become developed. According to one study:

> In seventh grade, white adolescent girls who have entered the new environment of junior high school appear to be at a disadvantage in comparison both to boys in general and to girls who do not have to change schools. Among the girls, the ones with lowest self-esteem appear to be those who have recently experienced multiple changes, that is, who have changed schools, have reached puberty, and who have started to "date." Among boys, in contrast, early pubertal development is an advantage for self-esteem.[34]

From our review of other cultures, we know that the physical fact of puberty does not consistently result in low self-esteem. The roots of the girls' turmoil are

---

[32]Nathan W. Ackerman, *The Psychodynamics of Family Life* (New York: Basic Books, Inc., Publishers, 1958), p. 231.

[33]Fritz Redl, "Adolescents—Just How Do They React?", in *Adolescence: Psychosocial Perspectives*, eds. Gerald Caplan and Serge Lebovici (New York: Basic Books, Inc., Publishers, 1969), p. 82.

[34]Roberta G. Simmons, Dale A. Blyth, Edward F. Van Cleave, and Diane Mitsch Bush, "Entry into Early Adolescence: The Impact of School Structure, Puberty, and Early Dating on Self-esteem," *American Sociological Review, 44,* no. 6 (December 1979), p. 948.

found in the reactions of other people as girls develop physically. Some adults, peers, and advertisements encourage them to look like an adult and to become sexually active. At the same time, in accord with our historical traditions, there is a countervailing encouragement to avoid sexual activity, and in some cases girls feel degraded because they look physically mature at an early age.

In developing a picture of the normal adolescent in contemporary American society, it is important to keep in mind that, just as there is no one normal type of behavior and personality for adolescents of different cultures, there is no one normal path to maturity within our own culture. Some youths may not pass through the turmoil and the searching for a self-concept, but pass directly from childhood to adulthood.[35] This is supported by research on working-class boys, who do not experience a long period of searching for self because they must move into the job market to survive economically.[36] Similarly, girls in a rural black culture move from childhood to adulthood quickly when confronted with pregnancy early in their adolescence.[37]

Although adolescence is not necessarily "pathological," and many adolescents make the transition to adulthood with few difficulties, we will concentrate on those youths who do experience problems. They are of particular interest to students and practitioners concerned with the control of delinquency. In fact, normal adolescent milestones may not be reached because of one type of delinquency—drug abuse—which makes it difficult to learn to tolerate others, resolve conflicts, and develop mature relationships with parents and peers.[38]

Our comments about the typical development of adolescents in American society are important for those persons working with juvenile delinquents. It is often easy to forget that youngsters are adolescents first and delinquents second, and that much of their behavior is considered normal for the particular age group. When working with delinquents, much of the behavior that is well within the range of "normal" limits for an adolescent may be interpreted as inappropriate and "abnormal." If the person working with delinquent adolescents is too quick in shutting off the normal adolescent expression of verbalizations and behavior, this can compound the problems for the delinquent youngsters. Delinquent youngsters should have at least the same amount of leeway as their nondelinquent counterparts. Practitioners who work with delinquents but do not understand the normal clusters of behavior typical of normal adolescents will have difficulty working effectively because they will often overreact to normal behavioral manifestations. This puts pressure on the youngsters to act in a

---

[35]Elizabeth Ann Molcomb Douvan and Joseph Adelson, *The Adolescence Experience* (New York: John Wiley and Sons, Inc., 1966); Daniel Offer, *The Psychological World of the Teenager: A Study of Normal Adolescent Boys* (New York: Basic Books, Inc., Publishers, 1969).

[36]Merry A. Morash, "Working Class Membership and the Adolescent Identity Crisis," *Adolescence, 15,* no. 58 (Summer 1980), pp. 313–320.

[37]Molly C. Dougherty, *Becoming a Woman in Rural Black Culture* (New York: Holt, Rinehart and Winston, Inc., 1978).

[38]Linda Golden and Marsha Klein Schwartz, "Treatment as a Habilitative Process in Adolescent Development and Chemical Dependency," *Alcoholism Treatment Quarterly, 4,* no. 4 (Winter 1988): 35–41.

manner that many see as abnormal for teenagers in general (quiet, sedentary, etc.). When the youngsters are unable to handle this pressure, they may release their energy in an exaggerated manner, including juvenile delinquency.

Although some adults feel that young people are a threat to the adult way of life, most youngsters are closely aligned with many adult values, and much of the behavior of the delinquent adolescent is well within the range of normal acceptance. It is not the purpose of the person working with the juvenile delinquent to change the youngster's entire personality and orientation, for much of his or her orientation, feelings, and expectations are the same as those of the normal adolescent. What does have to be altered are those aspects of behavior that go beyond the limits of acceptability.

Adolescent Development

During the period of adolescence—especially in a highly industrialized culture like ours—not only are physical and psychological changes taking place, but the youngster is attempting to develop a self-concept. This is a difficult process; therefore, the adolescent's behavior is contradictory, and vacillation from one mood to another is common.

> Today he may idealize a certain philosophy of life only to express tomorrow slavelike devotion to a completely contrasting approach to the problems of living. At one time he follows too rigidly an idealized code of conduct, the demands of which if he really met would deny him all human gratification. As if by a sudden metamorphosis of character he then violates—or more often talks of violating—even acceptable "behavior."[39]

The youngster's change in mood from day to day causes parents much concern. The contradictions in verbalizations or in behavior or the contradictions in both are, as Josselyn feels, the result of an attempt to find clear-cut answers to internal conflicts.

> He is attempting to avoid discord by choosing a variety of notes to play singularly. He does not know how to play several notes in harmony.[40]

This has important implications in working with the youngster. Adults often find it frustrating that the youngster fluctuates in moods and in behavior so readily and so easily. This frustration can be transmitted to the youngsters and can contribute to their insecure feelings. If the adult merely takes much of the youngster's erratic behavior in stride, the "testing" of the environment and parents will subside. With the guidance and support of the adult, more consistent orientations to problem solving can occur.

Coleman discusses the conflicts or problem areas that adolescent young-

---

[39]Josselyn, *The Adolescent and His World*, p. 10.
[40]*Ibid.*

sters have to deal with during adolescence.[41] He points out the main areas of adaptation that have to take place during this period if the youngster is going to handle problems with some semblance of order and ultimately be a productive citizen. First, the youngster struggles with the phenomenon of dependence versus independence. Up to the point of adolescence, children have generally been dependent on their parents for the satisfying of both emotional and physical needs. As they proceed through the adolescent period they become more independent, possibly by having a part-time job or by being able to spend an allowance with more flexibility. (Because the dependence-independence conflict is important, it will be elaborated upon later.)

Second, Coleman points out that the adolescent period is a transition from pure pleasure to reality. Before the adolescent period and in the infant stages, the youngster did not usually have to be concerned about "basics" such as food, clothing, and shelter. As a child progresses through adolescence, there is much pressure to start thinking about a future vocation and a role in life.

Third, Coleman describes the problem the youngster has transcending from incompetence to competence. Before the adolescent period, the youngster did not have to have specific skills either educationally or vocationally to survive. With the onset of adolescence, however, he or she has to become competent in order to be self-supporting in the future. In addition to this, the adolescent youngster has to consider what Coleman identifies as extending beyond himself to "other-centered activity" rather than merely self-centered activities. As adolescents start thinking about an adult role and vocation, they must extend beyond their own self-centeredness and egocentricity and learn to give as well as take. When they eventually prepare to raise their own families, this will necessitate involvement in "other-centered" projects to provide for their support.

Finally, Coleman mentions that the adolescent develops from a nonproductive to a more productive orientation. Before adolescence and, ultimately, adulthood, the youngster did not have to be productive and contribute to the social group as a whole. The family made a major investment and provided for the child's physical and emotional needs. The adolescent begins thinking about adult obligations and responsibilities, however, and must learn how to become productive. This is usually realized through a vocational or professional role which he or she attempts to prepare for. Obviously, not all these areas of adjustment that Coleman discusses are adequately handled by all adolescents.

> Although these pathways toward maturity characterize normal development, it is possible for development to be arrested or fixated at different points along the continuum from infancy to maturity. This might be the case with the middle-aged Don Juan whose sexual behavior resembles that of an adolescent or the developmental sequence may be reversed as in regression where the individual reverts to behavior which once brought satisfaction.[42]

---

[41]Coleman, *Abnormal Psychology and Modern Life*, p. 65.
[42]*Ibid.*, p. 66.

Ackerman feels that one of the greatest struggles for adolescents is to resolve their identification with parents and to build an identification and self-concept that is uniquely their own.

> Adolescence is a groping, questioning stage, a phase in which the adolescent condenses the values that will guide his social perspective for the major part of his life. It is exactly here that he confronts the challenge of bringing into harmony his view of self and his view of the world. He must now link his life-striving with a personal philosophy. The adolescent asks: What is life? Who am I? What am I good for? Where do I fit? Who are my real friends? Who are my enemies? What must I fight, with whom, against whom, for what life goals? And finally: Is life really worth the struggle? The kind of feverish, anxious, searching for identity, values and social orientation is paralleled by an expanding interest in social and economic conflicts, in religion and philosophy. In the service of this search the adolescent mobilizes his intellect and exploits it as a defense against his anxiety. Such struggle deeply affects the adolescent's choice of group association, in the time of testing of parental images and temporary dissolution of self, the adolescent seeks to identify with something larger than himself. His urge is to ally with a cause greater than his own.[43]

There is a push-and-pull phenomenon which creates many difficulties and conflicts for the adolescent. On the one hand, the parents and their expectations have been important since birth; on the other hand, the peer group, which begins to be important in childhood, becomes increasingly important during adolescence. Though most adolescents' peers are drawn from backgrounds similar to their own, the peer group can have a life style and a value system that are much different from those of the family, and, thus, problems can arise.

> The adolescent who loves his parents but who also wants to be accepted by his peers, may have a problem in deciding which standard will govern. Usually he makes some kind of compromise, letting parental standards govern some aspects of his behavior, and peer standards other aspects. But the peer group often has the edge in such contest partly because of the generally outward direction of social development, and partly because our culture places so much value on getting along with one's peers. This is less of a problem in other cultures. Young people in Germany, for example, are more concerned about maintaining good relations with their parents, whereas American youth tend to be more interested in getting others to like them—adolescents today, thanks to the general availability of part-time jobs and the generosity of their parents, are relatively free to do as they will, buy what they want and use time as they think best—all without being responsible to anyone.[44]

The increased freedom and material possessions, however, are often not much help when the youngster needs the guidance and assistance of mature adults and concerned parents.

In effect, then, adolescents do not have the protection that is given to

---

[43]Ackerman, *The Psychodynamics of Family Life*, p. 215.

[44]Henry Clay Lindgren, *Educational Psychology in the Classroom* (New York: John Wiley and Sons, Inc., 1967), p. 140.

younger children, nor do they have the rights and privileges that accompany adult status. It has been suggested that the only way to rectify this lack of status is to involve the adolescents in the decision-making processes of their community. The passing of voting rights bills and the granting of other privileges to youngsters are an attempt to involve at least the older adolescent in these processes. This should resolve one of the problems of status affirmation which is often lacking in Western society and makes it difficult for the adolescent to find a rightful place as a contributing member of the community.[45] Much of the futility and frustration that exists among teenagers can be reduced if they are involved in community problem solving and decision making. This not only will be a wise use of human resources but also will contribute to a more definite role definition for young people, and possibly reduce many of the problems associated with the transition from adolescence to adulthood.

Dependence Versus Independence

The prolongation of dependency relationships between parents and youngsters can have many negative ramifications. It is mandatory that parents understand the adolescent's conflict of wanting to be independent but becoming frightened when parental guidance and support are withdrawn too soon.

Parents often, either consciously or unconsciously, perpetuate the dependency relationship by never helping their child to become independent and self-sufficient through a mutual process of cooperation, communication, and assistance.

> Many parents while they consciously wish their child to grow up actually are resistant to this process. Perhaps they cannot face the vacuum that will exist when the child is no longer dependent on them. Sometimes they are jealous of the child entering early adulthood with all its apparent glamour when their own adulthood seems tarnished.[46]

If the child is forced into prolonged dependence of if the parents do not allow for development into an eventual productive citizen, the child will often rebel through delinquent activity. Once delinquent behavior has become manifest and the child has come in contact with the criminal justice system, it becomes much more difficult to bridge the communication gap between the youngster and the parents. When communication between them breaks down, the adolescent's perception of all adults can become negative.

> He perceives adults as agents bent on denying pleasures and frustrating consummation of sexual urges which are now at their height. He views adults as determined to restrict his awakening striving for self-direction and autonomy. While the adolescent attempts to defend himself against infantile strivings, he also feels

[45]*Ibid.*
[46]Josselyn, *The Adolescent and His World*, p. 29.

with increasing anxiety, the strain of pressures of making his way into the wider world of which he knows he must become a part.[47]

In its extreme form, when problems snowball and when communication lines are broken between parents and the youngster, the situation becomes so severe that the youngster may completely dissociate from the family and make his or her own way in the community or in the delinquent group. Parents are then viewed as a necessary evil to provide the "basics" and material satisfactions.[48]

The precipitating factor that often directly contributes to faulty communication between the youngster and the parents is the youngster's attempt to achieve some independent status within the community and within the family constellation. Parents do not realize that the search for an independent identity is normal, as is the vacillation between dependence and independence. As Chapter 4 pointed out, when parents react in an extreme manner, such as overpermissiveness or authoritarianism, this does not solve the adolescent's struggle. It only accentuates it.

> As a result [of the struggle of dependence versus independence] he is apt to make demands for dependence which he has not made since he was a small child. At the time, he wants advice about what clothes to wear, what hours to keep, what food to eat, what political party to respect, or what ethical or moral formula to embrace.[49]

Adolescents who find themselves slipping into dependency on their parents may overreact by acting in a very independent manner. The parents' understanding of the dependent-independent dilemma will prevent overreactions and will transmit to the youngster that the parents have the situation under control. When parental overreaction occurs, the youngster often retreats to the peer group for support and guidance.[50] The peer group may be negatively oriented and may therefore contribute to delinquent behavior.

THE SEXUAL BEHAVIOR OF ADOLESCENTS

It is of considerable importance that people who work with juvenile offenders differentiate between normal adolescent sexual behavior, problems that can result from normal sexual behavior (for example, pregnancy, adolescent parenthood), and illegal sexual behavior (for example, sexual assault). Historically, the juvenile court has defined what many individuals and groups consider to be normal sexual behavior as an indication of waywardness and thus have con-

---

[47]Slavson, *Reclaiming the Delinquent*, p. 11.

[48]Lindgren, *Educational Psychology in the Classroom*, p. 141.

[49]Josselyn, *The Adolescent and His World*, p. 38.

[50]Coleman, *Abnormal Psychology and Modern Life*, p. 595.

cluded that there is a need for intervention into the lives of young people. This was primarily true for girls, who in the late 1800s and early 1900s were considered to be in danger of drifting into prostitution and other criminal activity if they showed any signs of being "immoral" or sexually active.[51] These signs included characteristics and behaviors such as spending leisure time with peers and away from the family, suggestive dress, masturbation, disobedience to parents, and being in the company of older men. Many of these characteristics and behaviors were common, especially to youths in the less advantaged social groups, with the result that a large number of females were at risk of being selected by either their parents or others as candidates for reform, in some cases in restrictive institutions.

It now is recognized that it is not abnormal for adolescents to have an interest in sexual activity and to engage in a variety of behaviors ranging from kissing to sexual intercourse (Exhibit 5-1). Our previous review of anthropological and historical information revealed that whether or not a certain activity is seen as normal for adolescents depends on the historical period and the culture, not on any absolute rule about what is appropriate. Nevertheless, the juvenile court's early efforts to control the sexual behavior of young women continue to be reflected in some contemporary practices and policies. It is sometimes assumed that sexual behavior is characteristic of every girl who has broken the law, for instance by shoplifting or assaulting someone.[52] Similarly, in some juvenile institutions all girls are required to submit to gynecological exams.[53] Although some people in our society view adolescent sexuality as healthy, normal, and safe due to the availability of contraceptives and abortions, others continue to view it as sinful and dangerous, and thus as a reason for juvenile court intervention.

Although we would advocate *against* the efforts of the court to control typical sexual development and behavior of adolescents, it is necessary for juvenile justice personnel to be aware of the pattern of normal development as well as the problems of sexually active adolescents. Often workers in the juvenile justice system see clients with the usual conflicts and needs of any adolescent who is developing sexually. The youths in the juvenile justice system are probably somewhat more sexually active than others, and thus more at risk of pregnancy and venereal disease, for there is a correlation between a variety of delinquent activities and sexual activity. It is not certain why this correlation exists. One strong possibility is that the factors that contribute to delinquency also contribute

[51]Steven Schlossman and Stephanie Wallach, "The Crime of Precocious Sexuality: Female Juvenile Delinquency in the Progressive Era," *Harvard Educational Review, 48,* no. 1 (February 1978), pp. 65–94.

[52]Allan Conway and Carol Bogdan, "Sexual Delinquency: The Persistence of a Double Standard," *Crime and Delinquency, 23,* no. 2 (April 1977), pp. 131–135; Meda Chesney-Lind, "Guilty by Reason of Sex: Young Women and the Juvenile Justice System," in *The Criminal Justice System and Women,* eds. Barbara Rafel Price and Natalie Sokoloff (New York: Clark Boardman Company, 1982), pp. 77–103.

[53]*Ibid.*

Exhibit 5-1   Sexual involvement and normal adolescent development

A Male Describes His Experience. I started going steady with a girl in my junior year. By my senior year I was getting tired of just looking. The girl with whom I was going steady had the same moods and was as straight as I was. She was getting tired of it too—her curiosity was beginning to overtake her. So after hinting around about it one night, we decided to let each other discover the other's body. It was an experience we'll never forget. . . . There was only one limitation though. We had agreed we wouldn't have sexual intercourse until after we got married. We felt that we couldn't handle the responsibility if she did become pregnant, and "we wanted to leave something for marriage."

A Female Describes Her Experience. I had been going "steady" with a boy since eighth grade and in tenth grade he moved to another town. One weekend I went to visit him at his house. We had been swimming and decided to take a shower together in his basement. I couldn't bring myself to take my swimsuit off so we took the shower with them on. I remember being really turned on and thought that we were doing a very sexy and daring thing. Later that night I went to my room and he came with me. We started to watch TV and then started kissing. We were on the bed lying down and it felt very nice. . . . I thought of that weekend for the rest of the summer, redreaming that one moment.

SOURCE: Eleanor Morrison, Kay Starks, Cynda Hyndman, and Nina Ronzio, *Growing Up Sexual* (New York: D. Van Nostrand Company, 1980), pp. 98, 95.

to early sexual activity, a failure to use contraceptives, unexpected pregnancy, and the birth of a child during adolescence. These factors include poverty and racism, which lead to a sense of having little control over or interest in the future.

A number of different studies have shown that delinquent youths are more sexually active than others, but that many sexually active youths are not delinquent. Shirley and Richard Jessor found that high school nonvirgins sometimes shared the same attitudes with youths who used drugs and alcohol and broke the law in other ways: They valued independence and deviance, their parents appeared to accept their behavior, and their peers accepted and modeled the illegal and sexual behavior.[54] It may be that there are different patterns of adolescent sexual activity, only some of which are associated with delinquent orientations. For example, Robert Sorensen divided sexually active high school students into those with multiple partners (sexual adventurers) and those with only one partner (sexual monogamists).[55] Most of the adventurers were males, and they were likely to have poor communications with their parents and to have difficulties in forming close interpersonal relationships. We would expect that the sexual adventurers would be more delinquent than others.

[54]Shirley L. Jessor and Richard Jessor, "Transition from Virginity to Nonvirginity among Youth: A Social-Psychological Study Over Time," *Developmental Psychology, 11,* no. 4 (July 1975), pp. 473–484.

[55]Robert C. Sorensen, *Adolescent Sexuality in Contemporary America.* (New York: World, 1973).

Table 5-1 summarizes research on the factors related to nonmarital intercourse among adolescents. These factors do not necessarily cause nonmarital intercourse, but they can be used to predict which youths are likely to be sexually active.

Not only do delinquent youths tend to be more sexually active than others, but there has been a general increase in the sexual activity of all adolescents.

Since the early 1970s, increased numbers of adolescents have had sexual

Table 5-1 Summary of Major Factors Apparently Associated with Nonmarital Intercourse Among Adolescents

FACTORS	MALES	FEMALES
Social Situation		
Father having less than a college education	unknown	yes, especially for blacks
Low level of religiousness	yes	yes
Norms favoring equality between the sexes	probably	yes
Permissive sexual norms of the larger society	yes	yes
Racism and poverty	yes	yes
Migration from rural to urban areas	unknown	yes
Peer-group pressure	yes	not clear
Lower social class	yes (probably)	yes (probably)
Single-parent (probably low-income) family	unknown	yes
Residence in western states	unknown	yes (for whites)
Psychological		
Use of drugs and alcohol	yes	no
Low self-esteem	no[a]	yes[a]
Desire for affection	no[a]	yes[a]
Low education goals and poor educational achievement	yes	yes
Alienation	no[a]	yes[a]
Deviant attitudes	yes	yes
High social criticism	no[a]	yes[a]
Permissive attitudes of parents	yes[a]	yes[a]
Strained parent-child relationships and little parent-child communication	yes	yes
Going steady; being in love	yes[a]	yes[a]
Steady love partner with permissive attitudes	—	—
Risk-taking attitudes	yes[a]	yes[a]
Passivity and dependence	no[a]	yes[a]
Aggression; high levels of activity	yes	no[a]
High degree of interpersonal skills with opposite sex	yes[a]	no[a]
Lack of self-assessment of psychological readiness	no[a]	yes[a]
Biological		
Older than 16	yes	yes
Early puberty	yes	yes

[a]Variables supported by only one or two small studies. Other variables are supported by a number of investigations.

Source: Catherine S. Chilman, *Adolescent Sexuality in a Changing American Society: Social and Psychological Perspectives for the Human Services Professions* (New York: John Wiley and Sons, 1983), p. 99.

intercourse.[56] At the end of the 1980s, one-quarter of 15-year-old girls were sexually experienced, and two-thirds of 18-year-old females were sexually experienced. It should be noted that these proportions are even higher for boys.[57] Boys receive more peer pressure to have sex, and less parental pressure to avoid sex, which may explain their higher involvement.[58] It is ironic that females have been the subjects of long-standing and continuing control efforts by the juvenile courts in an effort to control sexual behavior, but males have been the more sexually active. No doubt, the court reflects the widely recognized "double standard" that permits males considerably more sexual freedom than females.

Before moving on to a discussion of problems experienced by some sexually active adolescents, it is important to point out that homosexual behavior is quite common, especially during childhood and adolescence. The small amount of research on the incidence of homosexual behavior reveals

> It appears that homosexual contacts are most common before age 15 and that the incidence is higher for boys than girls. Sex play, consisting of exhibitionism, voyeurism, and mutual masturbation occurs fairly frequently in groups of boys between the ages of 8 and 13. About 10 percent of boys and 5 percent of girls may engage in sex relations with the same sex at least once during early adolescence.[59]

The number of adults who are exclusively homosexual is smaller than the number of adolescents who are involved in homosexual relationships. Homosexual behavior used to be regarded as sinful or as a sign of mental illness. These views have been rejected by many elements of society, most notably psychiatrists and psychologists. Yet, there remain laws against soliciting another person to be involved in homosexual relationships. Regardless of these laws, the prevailing view among professionals in the human services is that homosexual involvements are often a part of normal adolescent development, and many adults who remain exclusively homosexual have no mental health problems. In addition to understanding that sporadic homosexual relationships are common, human services professionals need to recognize the special difficulties for exclusively homosexual youths in a society that often stigmatizes them and provides no clear guidelines for accepted homosexual relationships.[60]

[56]Cheryl D. Hages. *Risking the Future*. Washington, D.C.: National Academy of Sciences Press.

[57]Kristin A. Moore and Thomas M. Steif, "Changes in Marriage and Fertility Behavior: Behavior Versus Attitudes of Young Adults," *Youth and Society, 22*, no. 3 (March 1991), p. 365.

[58]*Ibid.*, p. 367.

[59]Catherine S. Chilman, *Adolescent Sexuality in a Changing American Society: Social and Psychological Perspectives for the Human Services Professions* (New York: John Wiley and Sons, 1983), p. 60.

[60]Paul H. Paroski, "Health Care Delivery and the Concerns of Gay and Lesbian Adolescents," *Journal of Adolescent Health Care, 8*, no. 2 (March 1987): 188–192.

Issues for Discussion.   Which of these factors associated with nonmarital intercourse also are factors associated with delinquency? For your answer, draw on the research presented in Chapters 3 and 4. Should juvenile justice personnel take an active role in attempting to control adolescent sexual development and behavior? Should they be prepared to offer referral and other services to sexually active adolescents?

Contraceptives, Pregnancy, and Early Marriage

When we look at the statistics on the proportion of young women who do not use contraceptives regularly, it is not surprising that many adolescents become pregnant.

> Only about 45 percent of sexually active adolescent females studied in 1976 and 1979 said they used any form of contraceptive at their first intercourse. About 33 percent had never used any form of birth control, and another 33 percent said they always used a method of birth control when they had coitus.
> Only a few local studies of contraceptive use by males have been made. [One] . . . found that 89 percent of the black males and 69 percent of the white males in their high school study population said they had had unprotected intercourse at least once.[61]

We have already explained that juvenile justice system populations are particularly likely to be sexually active. They also are particularly likely not to use contraceptives, for the community conditions and individual traits that characterize delinquents also characterize adolescents who do not use contraceptives.

There are many reasons why individual youth fail to use contraceptives. Some think they will be "lucky" and can avoid pregnancy.[62] Others feel they are powerless to control their lives, so they leave things to fate. Open and regular communication with parents is extremely important in insuring that adolescents obtain needed information. Because girls usually have more responsibility for the use of contraception in our society, mother-daughter communication is of particular importance. Joyce Ladner found that in a black, urban ghetto, mothers discouraged their daughters from using contraception, and many girls did become pregnant.[63] Although poor communication can occur in any type of family, feelings of powerlessness and a lack of control over one's future are more characteristic of poorer families. The result is that poor youths are more likely than others to become pregnant.

Given the increasing number of sexually active adolescents and the infrequency of contraceptive use, it is predictable that a growing proportion of adolescents have become pregnant. Since the late 1970s, the pregnancy rate for

---

[61]*Ibid.,* p. 108.

[62]*Ibid.,* p. 110.

[63]Joyce A. Ladner, *Tomorrow's Tomorrow: The Black Woman* (Garden City, New York: Doubleday, 1971).

teens has remained at 11 percent, and although nearly 50 percent of the pregnancies are terminated with an abortion, an increasing number of the girls who have their babies do not marry.[64] A large number of youths are faced with the difficult decision of dealing with an unplanned pregnancy, and whether abortion, single parenthood, or marriage is the choice, the pregnant girl and her partner often require special counseling and health and educational services. Pregnancy often results in a girl's dropping out of school and poor job prospects. For adolescents who marry, the divorce rate is high, family size is large, and the children have poor health.[65] Special services can offset many of these disadvantages, but these are often difficult to locate or unavailable from any one source, a situation which involves juvenile justice personnel in helping clients find and use appropriate supports.[66]

In one of the few national surveys to determine the characteristics of adolescent parents, several predictors were identified:

> These include being black and of lower socioeconomic status, and having low cognitive development scores, few intellectual interests, unclear educational goals, and measured personality characteristics that indicate high levels of impulsivity and lower scores on items having to do with being "mature, calm, cultured, vigorous and leadership oriented."[67]

As we have found for early sexual behavior and use of contraceptives, the factors associated with early childbearing are similar to those associated with delinquency, thus accounting for the fact that many delinquent youths will also be among those adolescents who become parents.

Just as juvenile justice system personnel, including social workers, probation officers, and workers in institutions, may find themselves in the position of referring youths for services related to contraception and pregnancy, they may find it necessary to make referrals to services for youths they suspect of having a sexually transmitted disease (a venereal disease). The most common

---

[64]Kristin A. Moore and Thomas M. Steif, "Changes in Marriage and Fertility Behavior: Behavior Versus Attitudes of Young Adults," *Youth and Society, 22,* no. 3 (March 1991), p. 368.

[65]Charles H. Wright, "The Prevention of Teenage Pregnancy: The Only Answer," *Journal of the National Medical Association, 72,* no. 1 (January 1980), pp. 11–13; Henry P. David and Wendy P. Baldwin, "Child Bearing and Child Development: Demographic and Psychosocial Trends," *American Psychologist, 34,* no. 10 (October 1979), pp. 866–871; Arthur B. Elster and Elizabeth R. McAnarney, "Medical and Psychological Risks of Pregnancy and Childbearing During Adolescence," *Pediatric Annals, 9,* no. 3 (March 1980), pp. 89–94; Gail H. Henderson, "Consequences of School Age Pregnancy and Motherhood," *Family Relations, 29,* no. 2 (April 1980), pp. 185–190; T. Allen Merritt, R. A. Lawrence and Richard L. Naeye, "The Infants of Adolescent Mothers," *Pediatric Annals, 9,* no. 3 (March 1980), pp. 100–110; Darlene Russ-Eft, M. Sprenger, and A. Beever, "Antecedents of Adolescent Parenthood and Consequences at Age 30," *Family Coordinator, 28,* (April 1979), pp. 173–178.

[66]Wendy Baldwin and Virginia S. Cain, "The Children of Teenage Parents," *Family Planning Perspectives, 12,* no. 1 (January/February 1980), pp. 34–43.

[67]Chilman, *Adolescent Sexuality in a Changing American Society,* p. 137.

and serious of these are syphilis, gonorrhea, chlamydia, and herpes simplex virus type II. All but herpes simplex virus type II have a known cure, but even for that disease, adolescents should obtain appropriate treatment and counseling to reduce symptoms and avoid spreading infection. Adolescents often avoid seeking help with suspected sexually transmitted diseases out of embarrassment, but they usually can obtain sympathetic treatment at youth-oriented health department programs or Planned Parenthood offices.

AIDS

Practitioners in the juvenile justice system should be aware of adolescents' risk for contracting Acquired Immune Deficiency Syndrome (AIDS), a fatal disease transmitted through heterosexual and homosexual intercourse, intraveneous drug use, and other situations in which bodily fluids are intermingled. As of January 1991, just 479 AIDS cases had been reported for individuals aged 13 through 19.[68] This figure is an underestimate of the actual number of adolescents with AIDS, since some cases are contracted during the teenage years but not diagnosed and reported until after age 19.

For several reasons, adolescents in general, and those likely to be in contact with the juvenile justice system, may be a high-risk group for acquiring the disease.[69] Compared with adults, a higher proportion of adolescents are exposed to AIDS through heterosexual intercourse as opposed to sharing needles or homosexual relations.[70] Placing delinquent adolescents at risk are the general propensity of many youth to avoid using condoms, which prevent the spread of AIDS, as well as the involvement of delinquent adolescents in intraveneous drug use. Particularly for urban minority youth, who are overrepresented in the juvenile justice system, risk is increased by incomplete information about AIDS and resulting risky behavior.[71] Youth in the juvenile justice system are in need of education and other prevention programs oriented towards AIDS, and thus juvenile justice practitioners must assume direct responsibility for meeting this need when youths are in court custody, or for arranging appropriate referral.

---

[68]Centers for Disease Control, *HIV/AIDS Surveillance Report*, Atlanta, Georgia: Centers for Disease Control (February 1990) pp. 1–18.

[69]On the designation of juveniles—particularly those involved in drug use, prostitution, and runaway behavior—as a high-risk group, see Mark M. Lanier and Belinda R. McCarthy, "AIDS Awareness and the Impact of AIDS Education in Juvenile Corrections," *Criminal Justice and Behavior, 16,* no. 4 (December 1989), pp. 395–411.

[70]Karen Hein, "Lessons from New York City on HIV/AIDS in Adolescents," *New York State Journal of Medicine, 90,* no. 3 (March 1990), 143–145.

[71]Douglas Bell, Andrew Feraios, and Tanis Bryan, "Adolescent Males' Knowledge and Attitudes about AIDS in the Context of Their Social World," *Journal of Applied Social Psychology, 20,* no. 2, part 2 (March 1990), pp. 424–448; Ralph J. DiClemente, "The Emergence of Adolescents as a Risk Group for Human Immunodeficiency Virus Infection," *Journal of Adolescent Research, 5,* no. 1 (January 1990), pp. 7–17.

Sexual Aggression

It is not possible to provide an in-depth discussion of illegal sex-related activities, particularly rape, prostitution, and pornography, in which adolescents become involved. Compared to the number of youth who are sexually active and even to the number who do not use contraceptives and become pregnant, the number who are involved in clearly illegal activities, either as perpetrators or as victims, is much smaller. There is one type of illegal activity that is more common, though, and this is sexual aggression, usually by a male and against a female. Technically, many acts of sexual aggression could be defined as sexual assault, but they are not, for both girls and boys view males' acts of persuasion and even force as normal. In keeping with our interest in describing usual adolescent sexual experiences, we will describe the pattern of sexual aggression that is increasingly coming to light through research efforts.

Jacqueline Goodchilds and her coworkers studied 432 Los Angeles teenagers, half of whom were male and the other half of whom were female.[72] The most common age was 16, and black, Anglo, and Hispanic racial groups were represented about equally. The researchers found that in many situations the youths thought it was "okay" for a male to force a female to have sex. For example, when questioned about situations where "the girl had led the guy on" or "the couple had dated a long time," just 34 percent of both males and females said it was never okay "for a guy to hold a girl down and force her to have sexual intercourse." In our society, there is a prevailing attitude that forced sex is acceptable under some situations, and adolescents share this viewpoint.

Whereas the research by Goodchilds was not specific to youths who were particularly likely to be delinquent, the work of Julia and Herman Schwendinger (discussed in Chapter 3) provides us with some insight into the sexual aggression typical of all types of peer groups.[73] Girls with a "bad reputation" are seen as "fair game" for a variety of persuasive or forceful methods of involving them in sexual activities. However, in the streetcorner groups, which you recall are the most delinquent, the exploitation of the girls is unchecked by countervailing forces.

> Alongside conceptions of women that imply quite different social relationships based on respect, friendship, and love, the sexist exploitation of girls is common to all stradom formations. However, the girls themselves, to some degree, resist this exploitation, although their success varies depending on stradom conditions. For instance, during junior high school, the groups rapidly developing into

---

[72]Roseann Giarrusso, Paula Johnson, Jacqueline Goodchilds, and Gail Zellman, "Adolescents' Cues and Signals: Sex and Assault," paper presented at the Western Psychological Association Meetings (San Diego, April 1979); Gail Zellman, Paula B. Johnson, Roseann Giarrusso, and Jacqueline D. Goodchilds, "Adolescent Expectations for Dating Relationships: Consensus and Conflict Between the Sexes," paper presented at the American Psychological Association Meeting (New York, September 1979).

[73]Herman Schwendinger and Julia Siegel Schwendinger, *Adolescent Subcultures and Delinquency* (New York: Praeger, 1985).

female socialite formations frequently exert greater control over sexual relationships with boys than do groups developed by streetcorner girls. Never developing anything comparable to the complex sorority club systems that anchor
socialite formations among girls during high school, the girls from streetcorner
formations have less effective support from peers. Lacking such group support,
the streetcorner girl's relations with the boys are much more determined by the
boy's interest in sexual by-play and intercourse. By middle adolescence, sexual
by-play and promiscuity also exist among the socialites, but it continues to be
more extensive and exploitative in the streetcorner domains. Like many other
conditions that are outside their personal control, such relations become interpreted by the girls as the "way things are," and even as a sign of acceptance or
status by others.[74]

The Schwendingers' observations of adolescent peer groups are very helpful in
emphasizing that an adolescent's decision to become sexually involved is complex, and it is strongly influenced by peer pressure and support. Sexual aggression by males is condoned in cases where girls come to be seen as "pigs" and
"whores," though in our society this type of sexual aggression is often overlooked.

WORKING WITH ADOLESCENTS

Drawing on several disciplines, we have presented material which is the basis for
two strategies for working with adolescent delinquents. In the first, the emphasis
is on rethinking and redefining the place of adolescents in contemporary society.
People who are concerned with this approach frequently advocate the extension
of either children's rights or responsibilities, or of both. Some argue that such
changes can reduce delinquency by clarifying meaningful and appropriate behavior for adolescents, and bringing them into the mainstream of society.

The second strategy involves interacting with individual delinquents
with sensitivity to the fact that the delinquent is an adolescent first and a delinquent second. If this is forgotten, the practitioner in the criminal justice system
may have difficulty relating to the youngster as a teenager and be guilty of
perpetuating the labeling process and viewing the delinquent as "extremely
different." (See Chapter 3, "Theories of Delinquency Causation.")

The first of these strategies, the move toward increasing children's
rights, attempts to change typical reactions to adolescents, expectations of them,
and activities we make readily available to them in the society. The second strategy, involving one-to-one interactions with adolescents, is based on our understanding of the special dilemmas of youths in contemporary society. It is
intended to alleviate (or at least not aggravate) problems, including delinquency,
which are shared by many youths because of their special position in our society.

[74]*Ibid.*, p. 167.

Children's Rights

The cultural, historical, and social-psychological perspectives, which we reviewed at the beginning of this chapter, make it clear that considerable diversity is possible during the adolescent years, and that in our society we have limited this diversity in a way that can create special problems for youths. Individuals who are a part of the children's rights movement stress the need to change the nature of adolescence in our society.[75] The major change would be to extend the rights of youngsters. Children's rights advocates are not an organized group, and they differ considerably from each other. However, they agree that many current conditions common during the adolescent stage of life limit adolescents' rights and stunt development and increase problems such as delinquency.

Zimring identifies four beliefs that underlie arguments to increase children's rights.[76] One belief is that adolescents can make judgments as wisely as adults in many cases. After all, in earlier historical periods and in other cultures, the majority of youths worked and assumed familial responsibilities. A second belief is that by limiting intervention into youngsters' lives, we avoid doing unintended harm. A third belief is that by extending rights, we can accomplish other important objectives. The right to an attorney in juvenile court, for example, promotes achieving the objective of fairness in judicial proceedings. Fourth, some believe that adolescents should have the right to "learn by doing." Zimring describes this as the "learning permit" view of adolescence:

> This image of adolescent life would suggest that policies should be avoided that permanently impair the life chances of an adolescent: when the young violate the law, permanent labels, exile from the community, and exclusion from school and other paths of opportunity should be viewed with disfavor. In the economic sphere, work experiences would be encouraged, but not at the cost of pushing the young away from even greater skill development or the ability to change directions. Likewise, necessary experiments with sex and affection should be shielded, insofar as is practical, from lifetime commitment.[77]

Although each of these four beliefs are held by some advocates of children's rights, the last "learning permit" approach is particularly common in our society.[78]

There are different types of rights that some people would like to extend to children:

[75]Beatrice and Ronald Gross, eds., *The Children's Rights Movement: Overcoming the Oppression of Young People* (Garden City, New York: Anchor Press/Doubleday, 1977); Richard Farsen, *Birthrights* (New York: Macmillan Publishing Co., Inc., 1974).

[76]Franklin E. Zimring, "Privilege, Maturity, and Responsibility: Notes on the Evolving Jurisprudence of Adolescence," in *The Future of Childhood and Juvenile Justice,* ed. Empey, p. 320; also see Gary B. Melton, "Toward 'Personhood' for Adolescents: Autonomy and Privacy as Values in Public Policy," *American Psychologist, 38,* no. 1 (January 1983), pp. 99–103.

[77]Zimring, "Privilege, Maturity, and Responsibility," p. 331.

[78]*Ibid.,* pp. 330–331.

1. "rights against the state," such as adequate housing and parental care;
2. greater state protection from abuse by parents, by other authority figures, and even by such adults as television advertisers;
3. constitutional protections in actions involving the state, such as the right to legal counsel in juvenile court proceedings, due process in school expulsions, or First Amendment rights to wear armbands or to distribute pamphlets; and
4. the right to challenge parental authority—to act independently of parents, to seek legal redress against parental demands, or to have the freedom to obtain abortions and other medical services without the need for parental consent.[79]

The first two of these rights emphasize "nurturance," that is, "the provision of services for children," whereas the third and fourth emphasize "self-determination," or "the right of children to have control over various aspects of their lives." The extent to which a person desires to extend rights in the nurturance of self-determination areas depends heavily on his or her beliefs about adolescents—for example, the beliefs outlined by Zimring.

We have already seen a trend toward extending legal rights to youths:

> The voting age, a symbol of citizenship, has shifted from age twenty-one to age eighteen, and the minimum age for valid marriage, after drifting upward for an extended period, has now been reduced for males in those states that previously had higher minimum ages of marital eligibility for males than females. Where age-related prohibitions are still enforced, as in alcoholic beverage control, the age of permissible purchase has drifted downward in many states from twenty-one to nineteen or eighteen over the last decade. During the same period courts have held that "mature minors" may obtain abortions without parental consent and may be given access to contraceptive devices without parental notice....
>
> Within the juvenile court there is a powerful movement to deprive the court of jurisdiction to intervene coercively in the lives of disobedient and truant minors, and a growing consensus that enforcement of age-related prohibitions on smoking, drinking, and other victimless behaviors should be de-emphasized. Modern reform proposals for the juvenile court often include giving children the right, having run away from home, to stay away from home in defiance of parental wishes. Meanwhile, the courts have given recognition to the rights of minors to free expressions in school settings . . . , and accused delinquents in juvenile court proceedings have been accorded the right to an attorney to pursue the child's interests as the child perceives them.[80]

Another way to extend the rights and opportunities for adolescents is to advocate for them individually in a counseling or casework context, or as a group. Adolescents are not an effective political group. As they make up a decreasing proportion of the population, they must compete with larger groups for limited resources, including employment, educational, medical, and recreational services. In this situation, advocates who assist youths in getting resources and gaining access to desired programs are essential. Advocates can work on three different levels: they can intervene and "straighten out" individual youths' prob-

---

[79]Skolnick, "Children's Rights, Children's Development," p. 141.
[80]Zimring, "Privilege, Maturity, and Responsibility," pp. 317–318.

lems with other people, such as parents or peers; they can help youths gain access to needed resources; or they can advocate general changes in public policies which would help all youths.[81]

A third way to extend teenagers' rights is to alter basic social institutions. The school experience can be altered to overlap with active participation in the job market. For example, "schools might become communities in which children would carry out responsible service activities, but also would include time for learning."[82] Or families can provide adolescents with meaningful tasks. Several of these alternatives are discussed in Chapter 7.

Besides the extension of rights to adolescents, counseling is another common delinquency control method.

Counseling Delinquents

Lubell points out that the existence of a youth subculture diametrically opposed to adult lifestyles, ideals, and values is probably exaggerated, and that there are many more youngsters who share the viewpoints of their parents than those who do not.

> The dominant impression left by the term generation gap is that of a unified younger generation that is breaking drastically from both its elders and society in almost every conceivable way. Actually, though, my interviewing over the last four years on how young people differ in their thinking from their parents suggests that: (1) much more continuity than gap exists between the two genera-tions; [and] (2) parents have not been rendered obsolete but continue to exert an almost ineradicable influence on their children.[83]

Even though the differences between generations may not be as great as is sometimes portrayed, there are at least some differences, especially between delinquent youngsters and law-abiding adults. The practitioner in the juvenile justice system not only has to be aware of these differences, but has to be willing to communicate honestly with these youngsters so that problem solving can be facilitated.

Adolescents in general are very difficult to work with, and delinquent adolescents present an even greater challenge. Slavson states that during the adolescent period

> there is doubt about sexual and social adequacy and self-regard is at a low ebb. To a large extent the adolescent adopts as a defense against these self-doubts a stance of self-maximization and employs antiphobic attitudes of omnipotence so

---

[81]Robert B. Coates, Alden D. Miller, and Lloyd E. Ohlin, *Diversity in a Youth Correctional System* (Cambridge, Massachusetts: Ballinger Publishing Company, subsidiary of J. B. Lip-pincott Co., 1978), pp. 179–180.

[82]Skolnick, "The Limits of Childhood," p. 72.

[83]Samuel Lubell, "That Generation Gap," in *Confrontation*, eds. Daniel Bell and Irving Kristil (New York: Basic Books, Inc., Publishers, 1968), p. 58.

that he may maintain an image of strength. He thus wards off hopelessness and depression. To admit to doubts, vacillation, conflicts and especially inability to deal with problems on his own and to have to seek help, constitutes a source of severe narcissistic injury against which the adolescent defends himself. This complex of feelings constitutes one of the main sources of resistance to therapy, only second in intensity to the rise of awareness of inadequacy.[84]

A major purpose of this section has been to point out the dynamics and conflicts that exist in the developmental period called adolescence, and the cultural and historical factors contributing to them. Even if the youngster does not become involved in delinquent activity, there are still many problems and conflicts. It is necessary that the practitioner understand the dynamic processes and conflicts of adolescence in order to be successful in delinquency prevention and rehabilitation efforts. Practitioners should remember their own adolescence and their conflicts and frustrations (such as the struggle for independence) during that time. The conflicts and frustrations may take a different form of expression today, but the basic need to develop an adequate self-concept, feel worthwhile, and be accepted by the group is not much different from that of past generations. To be effective in working with young people, Anthony states,

> adults need to recognize that adolescents are people, and particular people at that. It is important to remember that the stereotypes that have been cultivated are not necessarily even true of a minority of adolescents and that adolescents are not all delinquent, irresponsible, hypersexual or simpleminded creatures in pursuit solely of a good time. As long as these stereotypes persist, adolescents will respond by setting up barriers to communication, excluding the adult by the conspiracy of silence or by a language and culture of their own. The adults are then narcissistically affronted that the youth want to act and look and talk differently from them and then interpret this as rebellion, overlooking the fact that the adolescents want to act and look and talk differently from the children and are as deeply engaged in delineating their identities as in revolting against authority.[85]

The concept that adolescents are people with feelings and problems, as well as with a unique status in life, must also be extended to the delinquent youngster, who in addition to having the normal problems of adolescence often has severe economic, social, and psychological problems.

Caplan aptly points out that parents should look at their teenagers in the context of total development:

> If the adult remembers how much of himself has gone into the making of the adolescent he would be able to sympathize and empathize to an extent that should make for a partnership based on mutual respect and affection.[86]

---

[84]Slavson, *Reclaiming the Delinquent,* p. 11.

[85]James Anthony, "The Reactions of Adults to Adolescents and Their Behavior," in *Adolescence: Psychosocial Perspectives,* eds. Caplan and Lebovici, p. 82.

[86]*Ibid.,* p. 77.

The practitioner in the juvenile justice system dealing with the juvenile delinquent should also understand the problems and dynamics of the adolescent. This chapter will conclude with two case studies of adolescents which clarify the utility of the many ideas presented in this chapter for developing and applying an effective strategy for working with adolescents who are delinquent.

CASE STUDIES

The case studies presented here illustrate special difficulties that are common to delinquents and that are related to their status as adolescents. Personnel working with delinquents could use different strategies to assist the youths. The choice of one strategy over the others rests in part on each staff member's use of this book's discussion of the cultural, historical, and social-psychological perspectives on adolescence.

Case Study I

The first case study describes a girl who is similar to many who are involved with juvenile authorities. She is fifteen, her name is Ann, and she might have been brought to the attention of the juvenile authorities by parents who think she is out of their control.

> [Ann] had an "identity crisis" concerning her desire to go out with a boy of fifteen. It was an identity crisis because the previous instructions about dating given to her were all family demands. What should she do? She was not expected to date at all: "You're too young," "Wait until you are older," "We'll tell you when we think you are old enough to date." She knew all this very well, and as long as her sense of self was based on her family role, she was fine. But she also knew that "people" expected her to "grow up." These people represented societal demands. They included, "What's the matter with you, are you a baby or something?" and "you've got to start going out with boys sometime."
> If Ann went out with John, few societal authorities would be upset. If Ann understood "make your own decisions" literally, she might let John "go all the way." She would quickly find both her peer group—through the bad reputation tactic—and societal authorities—through allegations of immaturity, loss of control, and impulsiveness—didn't mean that she should make her own decisions at all. What they meant was: make the decisions *in terms of* societal rules and standards, not in terms of familial rules and standards.[87]

Questions. How do your personal beliefs about normal adolescent behavior for Ann compare with the beliefs of others presented in this chapter? How does contemporary American culture contribute to the confusion Ann is experiencing? Should the juvenile justice system intervene in this type of a situation? What different strategies can be used by juvenile justice personnel and

[87]Ted Clark, *The Oppression of Youth* (New York: Harper Colophon Books, Harper and Row, Publishers, 1975), p. 20.

other programs to intervene in Ann's problem, or to prevent similar difficulties in the future?

Case Study II

The second case study describes a youth charged with receiving four dollars of stolen money.

> [Herb] was quite upset because he had been arrested and taken to Juvenile Hall. He stated that Jack had owed him some money and, even though he knew receiving stolen property was in violation of the law, he had the money coming to him. The point of receiving stolen property was discussed with Herb and, even though he seemed intellectually capable of accepting responsibility, we could not believe that he felt emotionally, or with conscience, that he was doing anything wrong.

According to Herb,

> he has a steady girl friend, who is the mother of his child. His supervising probation officer was aware of this relationship and the child, and stated that the birth of the child created quite a disturbance, but that both the girl's mother and Herb's parents decided that it was best that they did not marry.
>
> Herb has many problems insofar as his future is concerned. He wants to enter the professions or jobs that require a great deal of education, such as electrical engineering or interior decorating. The sad fact is that Herb is quite limited intellectually.[88]

Questions. What are the inconsistencies in the expectations of other people that Herb will accept responsibility for his own behavior? What rights does Herb have to make decisions about his life circumstances? What opportunities does Herb seem to need and want in order to assume his responsibilities? What are the advantages and disadvantages of an individual counseling strategy to help Herb, and one that would more generally change the status of adolescents in our society? What special needs does Herb have because he is an adolescent?

SUMMARY

This chapter has discussed the period of development termed *adolescence* from the perspective of the anthropologist, historian, and social psychologist. A number of the unique features of contemporary society, including the exclusion of adolescents from the work force, demands to prepare for adulthood, and age segregation from adults create difficulties during the teenage years. Juvenile

---

[88]Louis B. Wies, *From the Probation Officer's Desk: Case Histories of Delinquents, with Analysis of Causes and Cures* (New York: Exposition Press, 1965), pp. 51–52.

delinquents may break the law as a result; even if social status as an adolescent does not cause the youth to break the law, the youth may present many special problems of adolescence to be dealt with in the juvenile justice setting.

Proponents of children's rights argue that society-wide changes would benefit adolescents, and particularly delinquents. The extension of increased legal rights to adolescents is one way to allow youths more participation in work and other activities, and to protect them from abuse, neglect, and interference. Another way to assist youths is to advocate for them as individuals or as a group, and a third is to alter social institutions affecting them.

In working with delinquents we must be aware of needs which they share with all adolescents. These include a recognition of their possible conflict over dependence versus independence, and their sense of isolation from both child and adult life styles.

DISCUSSION QUESTIONS

1. What evidence is there in this chapter, or from other sources, to support your own beliefs about the capabilities, rights, and responsibilities of adolescents?
2. What changes in laws, schools, work opportunities, and family life could reduce delinquency? Support your views with information from this chapter.
3. Of the various strategies for working with adolescents, are some more easily used by juvenile justice personnel than others? Why?

PROJECTS

1. Obtain descriptions of several different programs for delinquents. (You may want to use some of the descriptions in Chapter 7, "Delinquency Prevention Programs," of this book.) Which of these programs most fully protect the rights of the participants? Which meet their developmental needs—for example, the need for independence?
2. Review the course descriptions in different departments at the school you are attending. Develop a list of courses which would help you better understand adolescents, and therefore delinquents.
3. Develop a sourcebook of services for sexually active adolescents in your community. Write a set of guidelines to assist juvenile court personnel in helping sexually active youths. Specifically, what counseling and other strategies should they use, when should they formally intervene, and what rights do adolescents have to a private sexual life? Explain your reasons for including each guideline.

6

Handling the Juvenile Delinquent within the Juvenile Justice System*

- ORIGIN AND DEVELOPMENT OF THE JUVENILE COURT
- THE POLICE AND THE JUVENILE
- THE JUVENILE COURT—INTAKE AND PROCESSING
- BIAS IN DECISION MAKING
- A CASE STUDY

LEARNING OBJECTIVES

1. To trace the development of today's juvenile justice system.
2. To know the stages of juvenile justice processing, and the options for handling the juvenile at each stage.
3. To be aware of the juvenile's legal rights, and procedures for protecting these rights, at each stage of processing.
4. To be aware of recent changes in juvenile law and in the operation of the police and court agencies.
5. To understand the debate about the appropriate role of the juvenile court and the law in responding to status offenders.
6. To be aware of discrimination in police and court decision making.
7. To be aware of key dilemmas facing police and court personnel, including social workers who work within the system or who accept referrals from employees of the system.

This chapter will emphasize the major components of the juvenile justice system—the police department, the intake division of the juvenile court, and the

*Note: Ray C. Valley provided assistance with this chapter.

juvenile court. It will focus on the juvenile bureau of the police department, where the delinquent first comes in contact with the system and is either released or processed forward; the intake division of the probation department, where, again, the delinquent is either released or processed to the juvenile court; and the juvenile court, whose options range from outright release to incarceration. We will examine their philosophy, their duties, and the processes they use, individually and jointly, when handling the delinquent. We also will review important court decisions that affect juvenile justice processing.

Several different occupational groups are involved in the processing of juvenile offenders. The police have the major role of maintaining public order and safety, as well as enforcing laws. Juvenile court intake, probation, and parole officers are called upon to carry out a variety of functions, including "diagnosing" the cause of juvenile offending, recommending an appropriate rehabilitative plan, recommending and/or carrying out a plan intended to provide appropriate punishment, and providing counseling and monitoring. The specific emphasis that juvenile court workers place on each of these tasks depends on the jurisdiction and the job assignment. Social workers and other mental health professionals often come into contact with juvenile offenders, either in the court setting or through referrals from the court, and they provide additional diagnostic and treatment services. Government prosecutors file charges against youth and represent the state at hearings, and defense lawyers represent the interests of the juvenile.

The judge makes a determination, based on legal considerations, that a delinquent act has been committed. This determination depends on various pieces of information, including "facts" gathered by the police and court personnel as well as assessments that may include formal testing by mental health professionals. Often, intake and probation workers in the court setting are oriented towards applying social science principles to develop a recommendation for the judge. Increasingly, the judge must also consider state laws and administrative procedures that limit judicial discretion in order to make sentencing proportionately severe to the offense and the offender's prior record.

ORIGIN AND DEVELOPMENT
OF THE JUVENILE COURT[1]

The legal basis for the juvenile court can be traced back to the concept of *parens patriae,* mentioned in Chapter 1. This Latin phrase literally means "the parent of the country" and refers to the belief that the state, as the ultimate authority, has both the right and the obligation to direct and protect those of its citizens who, because of some impediment, demonstrate a need for such direction and protection. The impediment might be age, infirmity, mental incompetence, or, in the

[1]Most of the research for this section on the origin and development of the juvenile court was accomplished by John M. Thomas in a graduate paper presented to Robert C. Trojanowicz, School of Criminal Justice, Michigan State University, East Lansing, Michigan.

case of minors, immaturity. The nature of the intervention was conceived to be in the manner of parental guidance and admonition, with the strong emotional ingredient of familial concern. This attitude derived from the personal, individual manner of handling family disputes as opposed to the cold, legalistic justice of the criminal court.

A further legal basis of the juvenile court derived from the presumed innocence of children under seven years of age, which had long constituted an important feature of common law. Children were thought to be incapable of committing a criminal act since their immaturity precluded the presence of one of the most important prerequisites: guilt intent (*mens rea*). This principle of common law was later extended to older age groups and remains an integral component of the philosophy of the juvenile court.

Other developments heralded the advent of the juvenile court. As early as 1825, for example, special institutions were established for children. Probation, which from its inception was employed in the handling of both adult and juvenile offenders, was first used as an alternative to incarceration in Boston in 1841. Both of these reforms sprang from the work and experimentation of the pioneering Swiss educators Jean Jacques Rousseau (1712–1778) and Johann Heinrich Pestalozzi (1746–1827), who concluded that children are distinct from adults, both physically and psychologically. Heretofore, children had been conceived of merely as "imperfect" adults or as "adults in miniature," who thus were expected to be able to adhere to adult standards of behavior. The humanitarian movement begun by these two giants culminated in the progressive educational reforms of John Dewey (1859–1952) in the United States at the turn of the nineteenth century. The movement spilled over into all areas concerned with children.

There is some disagreement concerning who actually established the first juvenile court. Some contend, for example, that the first children's courts were instituted in south Australia, by executive order in 1889 and by statute in 1895. Others credit the United States with the first juvenile court act. Since the controversy is limited to the English-speaking world, however, the authors suspect that a record search of the non-English-speaking world might produce some surprising findings.

Whoever passed the first act, the Colorado legislature passed the "Compulsory School Act" on April 12, 1899. Chapter 136 reads as follows:

> Every child between the ages of 8 and 14 who absents himself habitually from school, or is incorrigible, vicious or immoral in conduct or who habitually wanders about the streets and public places during school hours, having no business or lawful occupation, shall be deemed a juvenile disorderly person subject to the provisions of this Act.[2]

Although this act contains some of the basic elements of a full-blown juvenile court act, especially in reference to status offenses, its primary concern is

[2]Colorado Laws, Chapter 136, p. 342 (1899).

truancy. Therefore, the first comprehensive juvenile court act is considered to be the bill passed by the Illinois legislature on July 1, 1899, called "An Act to Regulate the Treatment and Control of Dependent, Neglected and Delinquent Children." It mandates the institution of a juvenile court in all counties with a population of over 500,000. Only one such court was established, since Cook County (Chicago and environs) was the only county populous enough to be required to comply. The act included the following features:

1. gave jurisdiction over dependent, neglected, and delinquent children;
2. emphasized guidance, protection, and rehabilitation as opposed to punishment;
3. eliminated the adversary tactics of formal criminal procedures, establishing a "summary" proceeding;
4. instituted a new vocabulary, that is, "State in the interests of Child" replaced the "complaint" of "State v. Child," "summons" was used instead of "warrant," "initial hearing" instead of "arraignment," "finding of involvement" instead of "conviction," and "disposition" instead of "sentence";
5. specially appointed judges in separate courtrooms with physical surroundings different from those of criminal courts;
6. ordered the separation of children from adults whenever both were confined in the same institution;
7. forbade committing a child under twelve to a jail or police station;
8. provided for probation officers, who would investigate cases and supervise children placed on probation.

The professed objective of the juvenile proceeding was not to contest a criminal charge but to determine what could be accomplished in the best interests of the child. The proceeding followed the character of a civil case, which virtually negated the child's basic constitutional rights of notice of the charges, the right to counsel, the right to a confrontation and cross-examination of the witnesses, the right to protection against self-incrimination, and the observance of the rules of evidence.

An informal and flexible procedure of the nature described above was thought to be in the best interests of the child; it would cause less trauma to and labeling of the child and would therefore be more conducive to rapport, cooperation, and rehabilitation.

Following the Illinois example, a juvenile statute was passed in Colorado in 1903. By 1909 twenty states and the District of Columbia had passed similar bills. By 1920 all but three states had juvenile court acts on the books. Wyoming was the last to follow suit in 1945. (There are no federal juvenile courts. Children under eighteen who violate federal laws not punishable by death or life imprisonment may be sent to state juvenile courts or processed as delinquents in a federal district court.)

Initially, juvenile courts of various jurisdictions developed differently, especially as related to procedures and facilities. Nevertheless, the Illinois act was copied more or less accurately in several of its major features:

1. the age at which a child could be declared a criminal was raised, usually from seven to approximately sixteen;

Exhibit 6-1 A social scientist's view

Social scientists familiar with the juvenile court and its problems in the main agree that one of the great unwanted consequences of wardship, placement, or commitment to a correctional institution is the imposition of stigma. Such stigma, represented in modern society by a "record," gets translated into effective handicaps by heightened police surveillance, neighborhood isolation, lowered receptivity and tolerance by school officials, and rejections of youth by prospective employers. Large numbers of youth appearing in juvenile court have lower class status or that of disadvantaged minorities, whose limited commitments to education already puts them in difficulties in society where education increasingly provides access to economic opportunity. Given this, the net effect of juvenile court wardship too often is to add to their handicaps or to multiply problems confronting them and their families.

SOURCE: Edwin M. Lemert, "The Juvenile Court—Quest and Realities," in *Task Force Report: Juvenile Delinquency and Youth Crime* (Washington, D.C.: U.S. Government Printing Office, 1967), pp. 93–94.

2. a child declared a delinquent was subject to the jurisdiction of the juvenile court;
3. the juvenile court extended the doctrine of *parens patriae* to all children who were in need of state protection.

As the juvenile court movement spread, definitions of delinquency were broadened, and the court's jurisdiction was expanded to include nondelinquency cases, such as illegitimacy and mental defectives. There also existed a tendency to raise the upper age limit of juveniles, subject to the court's authority, in some states to as high as twenty-one. The court was given authority over adults in certain cases involving juveniles, such as neglect, child abuse, and contributing to the delinquency of a minor. The juvenile court in the essential form established in 1899 remained operant and free of serious challenge until 1966.

The population explosion subsequent to World War II led in the sixties to a dramatic rise in juvenile crime. The overworked juvenile courts came under increasingly close scrutiny. Legal scholars and appellate courts especially began to doubt the wisdom of the flexible, informal procedures of the juvenile courts. At this same time, social scientists were developing the labeling theory, which identifies the experience of court processing as a cause of subsequent delinquent behavior. Information about the labeling theory was shared with many law and policymakers in the widely distributed government publication, the *Task Force Report: Juvenile Delinquency and Youth Crime*.[3] In a part of this report, which was prepared by the President's Commission on Law Enforcement and the Administration of Justice, Edwin Lemert drew on sociological theories as a basis for recommending changes in the juvenile court (Exhibit 6-1). Criticisms of juvenile

[3]Edwin M. Lemert, "The Juvenile Court—Quest and Realities," in *Task Force Report: Juvenile Delinquency and Youth Crime* (Washington, D. C.: U.S. Government Printing Office, 1967), pp. 91–106.

court operations culminated in three U.S. Supreme Court decisions, which threatened to alter radically the nature of the handling of juveniles in the future.

In *In re Gault*, 387 U.S. 1 (1967), the first juvenile court case in history to be decided on constitutional grounds, the commitment of fifteen-year-old Gerald Gault to a state industrial school for the duration of his minority, for allegedly making an obscene telephone call, was overturned. In light of the due process clause of the Fourteenth Amendment, the Supreme Court ruled that Gault had been denied the following basic rights:

1. notice of the charges;
2. right to counsel;
3. right to confrontation and cross-examination of the witnesses;
4. privilege against self-incrimination;
5. right to a transcript of the proceedings;
6. right to appellate review.

In reference to this case, Justice Fortas wrote "under our Constitution, the condition of being a boy does not justify a kangaroo court."[4]

The Supreme Court's decision in the *Gault* case had the effect of diluting the doctrine of *parens patriae* and the informal procedures of the juvenile court by suggesting that all the technical rules of evidence were to be adhered to.

This same general trend was continued in the 1970 decision *In re Winship*, 397 U.S. 358 (1970). The Supreme Court ruled that due process required the juvenile courts to follow the criminal court standard of "beyond a reasonable doubt" as opposed to the civil court standard of "preponderance of the evidence" in establishing guilt. Justice Brennan listed a number of reasons for the Court's position, among which were:

1. the youth's interest in not losing his liberty;
2. society's concern for not convicting an accused when reasonable doubts concerning his guilt exist;
3. the need to insure the community of the fairness of the criminal law.[5]

In his dissenting opinion in the *Winship* case, Chief Justice Warren Burger does express a continued adherence to the principle of *parens patriae:*

> What the juvenile court needs is not more but less of the trappings of legal procedures and judicial formalism; the juvenile court system requires breathing room and flexibility in order to survive, if it can survive the repeated assaults from this court.[6]

The majority of Supreme Court rulings do not fully reject the idea of *parens patriae* but require the extension of due process along with the principle of *parens patriae.*

[4]387 U.S. 1, at 28 (1967).
[5]397 U.S., at 361–364 (1970).
[6]397 U.S. 358, at 376 (1970).

This dual emphasis is evident in the 1971 and 1975 Supreme Court rulings regarding juveniles. The first, in *McKeiver* v. *Pennsylvania,* confirms the *parens patriae* principle. In this case the Supreme Court considered "whether the Due Process Clause of the Fourteenth Amendment assures the right to trial by jury in the adjudicative phase of a state juvenile delinquency proceeding."[7] Writing for the majority, Justice Blackmun upheld the state court decisions, holding that the concept of due process of law as applied to juvenile court proceedings does not include the right to trial by jury.

With the exception of the McKeiver case, over the last two decades the Supreme Court has granted juveniles the same due process protections as are afforded to adults. Yet, in the 1984 case *Schall* v. *Martin,* the Court again decided that juveniles did not have the same protections as adults, for they could be denied bail and held for the protection of themselves and society.[8] Thus, even though the majority of juvenile cases have been decided so as to protect due process, the Court continues to make its decisions on a case-by-case basis, recognizing that juveniles should not always be accorded the same rights as adults.

A Trend Towards "Just Deserts"

There is a growing trend to revise juvenile justice statutes that have traditionally emphasized rehabilitation as the primary purpose of court intervention. The traditional emphasis on rehabilitation is seen in the Illinois Juvenile Court Act:

> The purpose of this act is to secure for each minor subject hereto such care and guidance, preferably in his own home, as will serve the moral, emotional, mental and physical welfare of the minor and the best interests of the community; to preserve and strengthen the minor's family ties whenever possible, removing him from the custody of his parents only when his welfare or safety or the protection of the public cannot be adequately safeguarded without removal; and, when the minor is removed from his own family, to secure for him custody, care and discipline as nearly as possible equivalent to that which should be given by his parents, and in cases where it should and can properly be done to place the minor in a family home so that he may become a member of the family by legal adoption or otherwise. . . . This Act shall be administered in a spirit of humane concern, not only for the rights of the parties, but also for the fears and the limits of understanding of all who appear before the court.[9]

In place of the focus on rehabilitation, several states have adopted determinate sentencing policies so that the sentence is set not so much to meet the needs of the child, but to fit the amount of punishment to the seriousness of the juvenile's

[7]403 U.S. 528, at 530 (1971).
[8]*Schall v. Martin,* 104 S. Ct. 2403 (1984).
[9]*Illinois Criminal Law and Procedure for 1976.* Illinois Revised Statutes 1975 and Supplement. Brought to date through all laws enacted by the Regular Session of the 79th General Assembly, PA 79-1192 (St. Paul, Minn.: West Publishing Co., 1976), Chapter 37, "Juvenile Court Act," Section 701–2, p. 6.

offense and past record. This fitting of the punishment to the offense is referred to as a policy of "just deserts."

The increased emphasis on "just deserts" has been documented by Law Professor Barry C. Feld.[10] He found that in at least ten states, preambles to the juvenile law have been changed to focus on "public safety, punishment, and individual accountability" as objectives. In state-level appeals that have challenged the goal of punishment as inconsistent with the goal of rehabilitation, the courts generally have allowed the shift to punishment.[11] The court decisions have been based on the reasoning that punishment is itself "rehabilitative."

Professor Feld described four ways in which the juvenile courts have become less oriented to rehabilitation. One is the use of determinate sentences, which involve maximum and minimum limits based on seriousness of the offense and prior record. A second is the use of mandatory minimum sentencing statutes, which allow, or in some cases require, a judge to set a minimum amount of time to be served, most often for very serious offenses or repeat offenders. Finally, in some states the department of corrections or the juvenile parole authorities use administrative guidelines for fitting the punishment to the offense.

As a result of the shift, there are several examples of court procedures that differ sharply from the early image of the juvenile court as providing "treatment" that is individualized according to the juvenile's need.

- In Washington State, legislature creates serious, middle, and minor offense categories, and judges follow guidelines for length of sentencing to institutions that are based on offender age, the prior record, and the category of seriousness.[12] At the extreme, the most serious offenders *must* be institutionalized for at least one hundred twenty-five weeks.
- According to a 1988 revision of Texas law, the most serious offenders (for example, those charged with murder or aggravated sexual assault) are sentenced through a determinate process which allows for a jury trial, a sentence of up to thirty years, and transfer to the Texas Department of Corrections.[13]
- The Illinois Juvenile Court Act of 1987 requires that judges commit certain serious offenders to the Department of Corrections, with no possibility of parole, until they are twenty-one years old.[14]
- When the Youthful Offender Parole Board in California sets a time for release, the seriousness of the offense is the most important consideration.[15]

---

[10]Barry C. Feld, "The Juvenile Court Meets the Principle of Offense: Punishment, Treatment, and the Difference it Makes," *Boston University Law Review,* 68, *no.* 5, pp. 821–915 (November 1988). B.U.L. Rev.—Boston University Law Review ENGPER S-3N

[11]*State* v. *Lawley,* 91 Wash. 2d 654, 591 P.2d 772 (1979); *In re Steven Minors,* 99 Nev. 427, 664 P.2d 947 (1983).

[12]B. Fisher, M. Fraser, and M. Forst, "Institutional Commitment and Release Decision Making for Juvenile Delinquents: An Assessment of Determinate and Indeterminate Approaches, Washington State—A Case Study," 1985.

[13]Tex. Fam. Code Ann. §§53.045,54.04(d)(3) (Vernon Supp. 1988).

[14]Ill. Ann. Stat. ch. 37, #805-35 (Smith-Hurd Supp. 1988).

[15]Private Sector Task Force on Juvenile Justice, *Final Report 1987,* p. 71.

In each of these examples, the choice of sentence type and length are not based on the immediate needs of the child. Instead, the guiding principle is "just deserts".

The most extreme example of the shift towards treating juveniles more like adults is found in cases that have been waived to adult court and for which the juvenile has been sentenced to death.[16] In seven states, the death penalty can be used for youths sixteen or seventeen years old, and in nineteen states there is no minimum age. As of the mid 1980s, 281 juvenile offenders had been executed since 1642, the time of the first documented execution.[17] The permitting of the death penalty for juveniles in the U.S. is unusual by international standards. It is not permitted in any European country, or in most other countries, for that matter.

In 1988, the ruling on a Supreme Court case, *Thompson* v. *Oklahoma*, reaffirmed that immaturity remains as a potential mitigating factor in sentencing decisions. In *Thompson* v. *Oklahoma*, the court considered whether the death penalty was a "cruel and unusual punishment" for a fifteen-year-old who had committed a heinous murder. The sentence of a death penalty was overruled based on the "lack of experience, perspective, and judgment" characteristic of adolescents. Thus, even though the death penalty is legally allowed, it must be applied with some consideration for the juvenile's maturity.

Debates Over Handling Status Offenders

All states currently have laws prohibiting some status offenses. In some jurisdictions, status offenses are handled through usual juvenile court procedures, but in others the petitions and proceedings are separate for youth designated as Persons or Children in Need of Supervision (PINS or CHINS) because they are truant, runaway, or out of control of their parents.

The 1974 Juvenile Justice and Delinquency Prevention Act specified that states' receipt of federal funds for delinquency programs was dependent on reform in the handling of status offenses. Specifically, status offenders were to be removed from institutions.[18] The 1976 report of the *Task Force on Juvenile Justice and Delinquency Prevention* further emphasized the need to reform the juvenile court procedures for status offenders.[19] Their guidelines include recommendations to "discard the vague labels that have formed the basis for court jurisdic-

---

[16]For example, see *Thompson* v. *Oklahoma*, 108 S. Ct. 2687 (1987); *Eddings* v. *Oklahoma*, 455 U.S. 104 (1982).

[17]Victor L. Streib, "Persons Executed for Crimes Committed while under Age Eighteen," *Augustus*, 9, (1986), pp. 20–25.

[18]*Public Law*, pp. 93–145 (1974); in 1977, the law was extended to cover dependent and neglected youths.

[19]National Advisory Committee on Criminal Justice Standards and Goals, *Juvenile Justice and Delinquency Prevention* (Washington, D.C.: U.S. Government Printing Office, 1976), p. 311.

tion and some serious abuses up to now." They define just five status offense behaviors as deserving of judicial intervention:

1. School Truancy
2. Repeated Disregard for or Misuse of Lawful Parental Authority
3. Repeated Running Away from Home
4. Repeated Use of Intoxicating Beverages
5. Delinquent Acts Committed by a Juvenile Younger than 10 Years of Age.[20]

They also recommend that the child's entire family be placed under the jurisdiction of the court. The treatment of status offenders in programs, including institutions, for juveniles is condemned as unwarranted and damaging.

Several national groups went much farther than the 1976 Task Force report in their criticism of the laws governing status offenders, and have recommended that status offenses be completely removed from the jurisdiction of the juvenile court. These groups include the National Council on Crime and Delinquency, the International Association of Chiefs of Police, and the Institute of Judicial Administration and American Bar Association Joint Commission on Juvenile Justice Standards.[21] Arguments for completely decriminalizing status offenses are: The juvenile courts could concentrate resources on serious offenders; status offenders are not a danger to others; and existing treatment of status offenders is stigmatizing and can promote more serious delinquency.

In the last decade, most states have limited the detention or incarceration of status offenders, with the overall result being a significant drop in the number of status offenders in secure pretrial detention and in correctional facilities with delinquent offenders.[22] Some states, for example, Washington and Maine, have moved towards full divestiture of status offenses from juvenile court jurisdiction. When full divestiture occurs, even if some action seems to be in the best interest of a status offender, no official requirements can be imposed on the child or that child's family.

Opponents of the removal of status offenses from the jurisdiction of the juvenile court claim that such action produces a situation in which no agency would be empowered to detain a runaway child, for instance, against his or her will. No agency would be able to require treatment or behavioral change of any kind, which would remove an important source of protection for both the juvenile and for society as a whole (Exhibit 6-2). A significant number of status offenders are either unwilling or unable to seek help on their own initiative. If running away, for example, is no longer an offense, to whom will a concerned

---

[20]*Ibid.*, p. 312.

[21]Joseph G. Weis, *Jurisdiction and the Elusive Status Offender: A Comparison of Involvement in Delinquent Behavior and Status Offenses* (Washington, D.C.: U.S. Government Printing Office, 1980), p. 9.

[22]Solomon Kobrin and Malcolm W. Klein, *National Evaluation of the Deinstitutionalization of Status Offender Programs—Executive Summary* (Los Angeles: Social Science Research Institute, University of Southern California, 1982); Barry Krisberg and Ira Schwartz, "Rethinking Juvenile Justice," *Crime and Delinquency, 29,* no. 3 (July 1983), pp. 333–364.

Exhibit 6-2   A Dilemma: Youths who are a danger to themselves

---

Penny ran away from home when she was 11 years old. She was placed in a residential home in the Los Angeles area and ran away again. She moved into an apartment with another minor and three adults, but was accidentally discovered when authorities showed up with an eviction notice. She returned to the residential placement and ran away again. A short time later, Penny turned herself over to the police. Once again, she was placed in a residential home and, once again, Penny ran away.

In June of 1983, Penny was living in a disreputable Hollywood "crash pad." A common type of haven for runaways, "crash pads" are adult residences that house children for purposes of sexual exploitation. Later in the year, Penny was arrested for theft. The authorities did not prosecute and she again found her way back to the street. Within a period of 3 years, Penny received six placements and ran from each one.

The handling of Penny's case was based on California's compliance with the Federal deinstitutionalization mandate. As a result of the State bill passed in 1976, local runaways cannot be securely held for more than 12 hours. Runaways from another country or State can be held for 24 to 72 hours, depending on the proximity of their homes to the jurisdiction where they are picked up. Once a runaway has been confined for the maximum amount of time allowed by law, the authorities are required to release them to a nonsecure facility.

The Los Angeles County police have even less authority to deal with runaways than State law provides. The County has never opened a secure facility to hold runaways for the few hours California's deinstitutionalization bill allows. Instead of secure confinement, the County probation department contracts private homes to serve as temporary shelters under the design of the Status Offender Detention Alternatives Program (SODA). Runaways are free to stay at SODA facilities until they are returned home or until other permanent arrangements can be made. Unfortunately, they are free to leave as well, and many of them do. . . .

Penny was within her legal rights every time she walked away from her placements. The Los Angeles County authorities could not hold her simply because she was a runaway living on the streets. That was not reason enough. In time, however, Penny came up with a reason good enough to warrant confinement in a secure facility. She was arrested for prostitution, reclassified from status offender to delinquent, and detained in Juvenile Hall.

Detective Delores Schley of the Los Angeles Police Department has followed Penny's case since 1981. According to Schley, the fate of a runaway like Penny can be attributed to the national deinstitutionalization effort. She believes that "truancy and running away are predelinquent acts. These are the kids who are likely to become delinquents." Yet the current policy is to ignore them until they do. Schley said that the police tend to "view picking up runaways as a wasted effort. It takes a good 4 hours of an officer's time to process a juvenile runaway, and the kids are sometimes back out on the street before the officers finish their reports."

SOURCE: Office of Juvenile Justice and Delinquency Prevention, "Runaway Children and the Juvenile Justice and Delinquency Prevention Act: What Is the Impact?" *Juvenile Justice Bulletin* (Washington, D.C.: U.S. Department of Justice, no date), p. 3.

---

parent turn for assistance in locating a runaway child? They further claim that there is no such thing as a juvenile who specializes in status offenses; juveniles who commit one kind of offense, status or otherwise, are assumed to be more likely to commit any of the other offenses.

The removal of status offenses would cause the prosecution of many more serious offenses, claim opponents; a status offense charge at present is often the result of plea bargaining, in which a more serious charge is reduced on the promise that the offender will seek help. Status offenses are also easier to prove, and a conviction enables the court to require treatment. With the removal of status offenses, the police, neighbors, teachers, and so on, will no longer need to be concerned about runaway, truant, or misbehaving youths until they have committed a serious offense, which action would thereby eliminate an important delinquency prevention strategy.

A current difficulty of the courts is the unwillingness of the community to provide alternatives to detention for their juvenile offenders. Will these same communities be more willing to provide these and even additional services when status offenses are repealed? ask opponents.

The Result of Changes in Juvenile Laws and Procedures

In assessing the effect of the diverse legal changes, Anne Larason Schneider's research on the state of Washington is of considerable interest, for that state is unique in simultaneously enacting legislation to divest status offenses, require diversion of minor delinquents, and set sentencing guidelines to establish a pattern of graded punishments for serious offenders. A member of the Washington State House of Representatives explained the intent of the changes:

> It [the law] is meant to limit the courts to their judicial function, to require them to deal more consistently with youngsters who commit offenses, and to identify social resources outside the court for handling non-criminal behavior. In terms of the philosophical polarities that have characterized the juvenile court debate for a century, the bill moves away from the *parens patriae* doctrine of benevolent coercion, and closer to a more classic emphasis on justice.[23]

How, then, has the move away from the *parens patriae* doctrine affected adolescents in Washington?

The success of the Washington reforms are mixed and, in some cases, uncertain. It does not appear that the intended change to a system in which youths would be deterred by increasing severity of treatment for repeated serious violations fully occurred. Schneider's research showed that many of the delinquents were faced with an increase in the certainty of minor sanctions and a

---

[23]Anne Larason Schneider, "Divesting Status Offenses from Juvenile Court Jurisdiction," *Crime and Delinquency, 30,* no. 3 (July 1984), p. 351.

decrease in the certainty of a severe sanction.[24] Other youths were less likely to be referred to court by the police, but if they were referred, they were almost certain of being incarcerated. It is not known whether the change in legislation, changes in law enforcement policies, or some other factors were responsible for the observed effects on the youths.

Even though youths in Washington State could no longer be referred to court for just a status offense, they could be referred if they had broken a law in addition to committing the status offense. Thus, some status offenders did appear in court after the legislative changes had occurred. Yet, the number was reduced by half of those who appeared before legislative changes, and therefore divestiture did produce some reduction in contacts with the court.[25] In some jurisdictions, youths with both a status and delinquent offense were treated more severely than those with just a charge of delinquency. Finally, it is questionable that the large network of alternative services that was to assist status offenders outside of the juvenile justice system has indeed met the challenge. The complexity of decision making and the related labeling process in the juvenile justice system has, at least in part, made it difficult to translate legislative intent into reality.

Impediments to legislative reform also are found with the New York juvenile offender law, passed in 1978. The New York law was intended to "get tough" with serious delinquents by requiring the prosecution of juveniles as adults for fifteen serious offenses. Between 1978 and 1983, 6,951 New York City youths were arrested under the law, but contrary to the law's intent, 68.6 percent were dismissed, diverted, or otherwise disposed of before they ever reached the end of the adult criminal justice process.[26] The youths who were sentenced under the law usually did not receive particularly long sentences, even if the cases involved extreme violence. Overall, there were many steps in applying the law, the resources to help youths in family court were not available to the serious juvenile offenders, and the youths were often rejected as clients by both juvenile and adult programs and institutions. "Get tough" legal reform did not prove to be a panacea for serious juvenile crime in either New York or Washington.

The cases of legal reform provide instructive examples of the interplay between beliefs, theory, and research. Shifts in legislation result from a number of different trends in thinking about adolescents. Teilmann and Klein identified the children's rights movement as one of the influential trends.[27] Another is the

---

[24]Anne Schneider, "Sentencing Guidelines and Recidivism Rates of Juvenile Offenders," *Justice Quarterly, 1,* no. 1 (March 1984), pp. 107–124.

[25]Schneider, "Divesting Status Offenses from Juvenile Court Jurisdiction," pp. 347–370.

[26]Elizabeth T. Schack and Hermine Nessen, *The Experiment that Failed: The New York Juvenile Offender Law—A Study Report* (New York: Citizens' Committee for Children of New York, 1984).

[27]Katherine S. Teilmann and Malcolm W. Klein, "Juvenile Justice Legislation: A Framework for Evaluation," in *Critical Issues in Juvenile Delinquency,* eds. David Shichor and Delos H. Kelly (Lexington, Massachusetts: Lexington Books, D.C. Heath and Company, 1980), pp. 29–44.

"war on crime," including federal, state, and local efforts to control the serious repeat offender.

THE POLICE AND THE JUVENILE

The police are the first major component in the justice system to deal with the juvenile delinquent. Current statistics show that a large percentage of arrests, including a significant number of those for serious offenses, involve juveniles. The police also handle many nondelinquent juvenile matters, such as neglect, abuse, domestic problems, and so on. The specialized police unit for handling juvenile cases has come into increasingly widespread use. The necessity for the specialized juvenile unit has derived from the increasing complexity of our communities and the impersonality of many of the organizations that serve community residents. In former times police officers lived in their districts, knew local residents, and therefore shared and could identify with their problems. Because of the intensity of the officer's involvement with the inhabitants of a particular district, it was possible to handle many problems informally and personally. Increased urbanization, however, soon brought with it increasing caseloads, leading to the routinization and impersonalization of police functions. This and other practical matters led to the formation of the specialized juvenile unit.

The juvenile unit varies in size depending on the type of police department and the size and nature of the community. In those areas where there is a low volume of juvenile crime, certain officers may be assigned part time to work with juveniles. In other departments, the juvenile bureau can be a very large unit with the concomitant resources and personnel. Although the juvenile officer's responsibilities depend to a great extent on the size of the department, some features of such work are common to most departments. For example, the officer is usually charged with dealing with all offenses that involve juveniles, as well as family cases involving neglect and abuse. Routine duties will include contacting and interviewing juveniles, their friends, their parents, teachers, employers, the complainant, and so on, determining the circumstances surrounding an offense, maintaining juvenile records, and appearing in juvenile court. In more sophisticated departments, the juvenile officer is also involved in preventive-type activities, such as giving speeches to schools and coordinating programs with other agencies in the community. The juvenile officer may also attempt to influence the members of the department by making them aware of the special problems that exist when dealing with juveniles and the appropriate methods for processing them.

The police have a great deal of discretionary power, ranging all the way from the option of releasing the juvenile at initial contact in an unofficial manner to making a referral to the juvenile court, which may result in detention. The officer can also refer the youngster to a community agency, such as a big brother or big sister program, or a mental health clinic. The youngster also can be apprehended and taken to the police department.

Figure 6-1 illustrates the steps followed when a police officer comes upon an "event" or receives a complaint. This is the beginning of the process that ultimately determines whether the youngster will come into contact with the court or be released. At the time of the event or the complaint, the officer may decide that the offense is minor and does not necessitate further investigation;

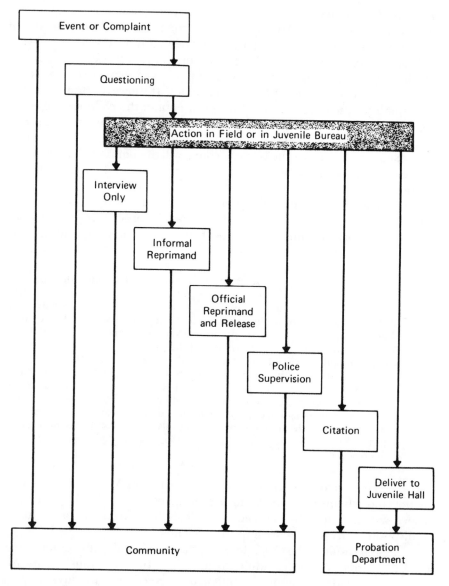

Figure 6-1   Decision points in police handling of juveniles

SOURCE: From James T. Carey, Joel Goldfarb, Michael J. Rowe, and Joseph D. Lohman, *The Handling of Juveniles from Offense to Disposition,* U.S. Department of Health, Education, and Welfare (Washington, D.C.: U.S. Government Printing Office, 1967), p. 26.

the child may therefore be released on the spot. If additional information is necessary, the officer can briefly interview the youngster, perhaps decide that the situation does not warrant further discussion, and release the child to the parents. If the officer considers the offense or complaint serious enough to warrant further investigation and discussion, the child can be referred to the police department's juvenile bureau. The options of the juvenile bureau are illustrated in Figure 6-1. A juvenile bureau officer can interview and release the child with an informal reprimand. An official or recorded reprimand may be the officer's choice. Another option, although used infrequently, is to release the youngster with police supervision. In all these cases the child is released to the community, which usually means to the parents. The process in these cases would end with the juvenile bureau of the police department. If, however, the juvenile officer feels that the situation warrants further attention, the child can be referred to the juvenile court for a determination. Before a determination, however, the youngster can be delivered to a juvenile home or a detention facility. The *intake* unit, usually a division of the probate court, will then make a determination as to whether the process should end at intake or continue further in the juvenile court.

Because of the great number of delinquent offenses, as well as the wide range of discretionary powers held by the police, procedures vary considerably from community to community. Other factors also enter into the decision-making process:

> Decisions are generally based on the nature of the offense, the appraised character of the youth, which in turn is based on such facts as his prior police record, age, associations, attitude, family situation, the conduct of his parents, and the attitude of other community institutions such as his school. The external community may exert pressure on the police department which may affect the disposition of any case. Here attitudes of the press and the public, the status of the complainant or victim, the status of the offender, and the conditions which prevail in the available referral agencies (the length of the waiting list, the willingness of the social agencies to accept police referrals) are all of consequence. Internal police department pressure such as attitudes of coworkers and supervisors and the personal experience of the officer may also play an important part in determining the outcome of any officially detected delinquent offense. These factors also indirectly determine the officially recorded police and court delinquency rates.[28]

Many factors, therefore, determine whether a youth is to be processed or not and whether he or she may eventually end up in the formal juvenile justice system. The police procedure for handling juveniles from initial contact to disposition involves many important elements.

As a result of the *Gault* decision, the police are legally required to extend the safeguards granted to adults to juveniles. Juveniles must be informed of their rights, evidence cannot be unlawfully served, and the juvenile's rights in

---

[28]*Task Force Report: Juvenile Delinquency and Youth Crime*, p. 419.

Exhibit 6-3 Michigan Juvenile Court Rules

Conditions under which an officer can take custody:

1. When a child is found violating any law or ordinance.
2. Conditions exist which make an arrest lawful, if the child were an adult.
3. The officer reasonably believes the child is evading the person or proper authority having legal custody.
4. Conditions or surroundings under which the child is found are such as to endanger his health, morals, or welfare.
5. The officer continues a lawful arrest made by a private citizen.

SOURCE: Michigan Juvenile Court Rules of 1969, Rule 2, Section 2.

any other areas must be protected. To make the police officers' job even more complex, not only must they deal with delinquent youngsters, but they must also be astute in determining child abuse and neglect. (Because the problem of child abuse and neglect is so prevalent today and offers one of the greatest challenges for juvenile justice professionals, a later chapter in this book focuses on this topic.) The following procedures are of special importance to police officers when handling juveniles.

Detaining and Taking into Custody

In most states the law of arrest is the same for juveniles and adults, and thus an officer must have *probable cause* to believe that the suspected juvenile has committed an offense. Mere suspicion is not in itself probable cause, but absolute certainty is not required either. The rules for determining probable cause are more stringent for misdemeanor cases, in which the police officer must actually see the crime. Exhibit 6-3 is an example of the rules defining the conditions under which an officer may take a juvenile into custody without a court order.

After the juvenile has been taken into custody, certain procedural rights and safeguards must be considered. As a result of the 1964 *Escobedo* v. *Illinois* decision, police officers are required to notify suspects, including juveniles, of their right to legal counsel at the time of arrest.[29] The 1966 *Miranda* v. *Arizona* decision requires that suspects be advised of their rights before interrogation; otherwise their confessions cannot be used in court.[30] The officer must advise the suspect of the right to remain silent and to speak to an attorney, and must provide the information that the state will provide an attorney to those who desire but cannot afford one. Finally, all suspects must be told that anything they say may be used against them. The court has the responsibility to determine whether the youth who waived these rights understood what this waiver meant. If the youth is processed further and comes into contact with an intake probation

[29]*Escobedo* v. *Illinois*, 378 U.S. 478 (1964).
[30]*Miranda* v. *Arizona*, 384 U.S. 436 (1966).

officer, this officer should also read the *Miranda* warnings, thereby providing added assurance that the child's legal rights have been protected.

In most states, the officer who takes the child into custody is also responsible for notifying the child's parents.[31] There has been considerable controversy about whether juveniles are competent to waive their *Miranda* rights, particularly without the aid and counsel of a parent. In one U.S. Supreme Court case, *People v. Lara,* it was decided that the legal competence of a juvenile to waive her or his rights should be determined by the "totality of the circumstances doctrine," in other words, by a consideration of not only age, but also factors such as intelligence, education, and comprehension.[32]

At the same time that the courts have been trying to establish criteria for judging juveniles' competence to waive their rights to silence and legal counsel, social scientists are trying to provide research evidence to shed light on the issue. Thomas Grisso considered competence in a psychological sense, defining incompetence as the failure to demonstrate a sufficient level of performance on a criterion measure of understanding or the perception of rights.[33] Using this definition, Grisso concluded:

1. As a class, juveniles of ages 14 and below demonstrate incompetence to waive their rights to silence and legal counsel. This conclusion is generally supported across measures of both understanding and perception . . .
2. As a class, juveniles of ages 15 and 16 who have IQ scores of 80 or below lack the requisite competence to waive their rights to silence and counsel.
3. About one-third to one-half of juveniles 15 and 16 years of age with IQ scores above 80 lack the requisite competence to waive their rights when competence is defined by absolute standards . . .
4. Race is a relevant variable for consideration in weighing juveniles' competence to waive rights, for two reasons. First, a greater percentage of black juveniles than of white juveniles perform in the lower IQ range noted above. Second, black juveniles in lower socioeconomic classes may have greater difficulty translating the *Miranda* warnings than do whites in lower socioeconomic classes.
5. Indexes of the amount of prior court experience (for example, number of prior felony referrals) bear no direct relationship to the understanding of *Miranda* warnings *per se.*[34]

Grisso's research raises questions about the indirect ways in which police practices and legal procedures can introduce a bias against some youths. Whether or not his research will have any influence on the design of police practices or on future court decisions remains to be seen.

In the two remaining decisions that we will discuss, the Supreme Court supported the actions of the police in following due process procedures to pro-

---

[31]Mark M. Levin and Rosemary C. Sarri, *Juvenile Delinquency: A Study of Juvenile Codes in the U.S.* (Ann Arbor: University of Michigan Press, 1974).

[32]67 Cal.2d 365, 62 Cal. Rptr. 586, 432 P.2d 202 (1967).

[33]Thomas Grisso, *Juveniles' Waiver of Rights: Legal and Psychological Competence* (New York: Plenum Press, 1981), p. 194.

[34]*Ibid.*, pp. 193–194.

tect the rights of juveniles. The first case, *Fare* v. *Michael C.,* involved a suspect who asked to call his probation officer, but who did not request an attorney.[35] The youth incriminated himself during interrogation, and later his case was appealed on the basis that his rights had been violated when he was not allowed to speak with his probation officer. The Court found that asking to speak to a probation officer is not equivalent to asking to speak with an attorney, and the original conviction was upheld. In the second case, *California* v. *Prysock,* there was a question about the timing of the police informing a young murder suspect of his rights to an attorney.[36] The Court also upheld that conviction, ruling that regardless of when it was given, the *Miranda* warning was clear and could easily be understood by a juvenile. Thus, in recent years some Court rulings reflect the recognition that due process concerns are met when the police follow reasonable interrogation procedures for adolescents.

After parents have been notified, the juvenile still has the same constitutional right as an adult—the right to contact an attorney or have any one of his or her choosing present during an interview. The basis for this is the 1963 Supreme Court decision which ruled, on an appeal case of *Gideon* v. *Wainright,* that new trials could be demanded by anyone convicted of a crime without legal counsel.[37] The *Gideon* decision, the *Escobedo*[38] decision, and the *Miranda*[39] decision all apply to both adults and juveniles.

Search and Seizure

The law governing search and seizure is essentially the same for both adults and juveniles. According to the Fourth Amendment:

> The right of the people to be secure in their persons, houses, papers, and effects, against unreasonable searches and seizures, shall not be violated, and no warrants shall issue, but upon probable cause, supported by oath or affirmation, and particularly describing the place to be searched, and the person or things to be seized.

If evidence is obtained from an illegal search, a child's lawyer can make a pretrial motion to suppress the evidence, and in most cases the court will rule that the evidence is inadmissible.

The one area of controversy that pertains to adolescents but not to adults is the right of school officials to search students and their belongings on school property. For example, school officials may feel that in order to protect other people in the school, they must search for drugs, weapons, or stolen property. On the one hand, some people argue that the school can act *in loco*

[35]442 U.S. 23, 99 S.Ct. 2560 (1979).
[36]453 U.S. 355, 101 S.Ct. 2806 (1981).
[37]*Gideon* v. *Wainright,* 372 U.S. 335 (1963).
[38]*Escobedo, idem.*
[39]*Miranda, idem.*

parentis and, in the interest of protecting other children and teachers, can not only search a child and that child's belongings, but can also turn the child over to the police. On the other hand, others argue that this is illegal search and seizure, and that *Miranda* warnings often are not given before the child is questioned by either the school administrator or the police.

In one New York State case, *People* v. *Overton,* police came to a high school with a search warrant and, after finding no marijuana on the person of two students,[40] asked for the administrator's permission to search the students' lockers. The police discovered marijuana, and the trial court ruled that despite the defect in the original warrant, the police could obtain evidence from the lockers because the administrator gave permission for their search, and the lockers were the property of the school.

When a school official rather than the police is involved in a search, although students are protected from illegal searches, school officials are not constrained in the same way that police are. School officials, according to the Supreme Court ruling in *New Jersey* v. *T.L.O.,* do not need "probable cause" to conduct a search, just reasonable grounds to believe the student has broken a school rule or the law.[41]

Fingerprinting, Photographing, Lineups, and Keeping Records

Fingerprinting and photographing juveniles, as well as keeping records, are sources of controversy. Even though these may be important tools for the police in detecting crime and preventing delinquency, they nevertheless must be used with discretion. Records can be helpful for both the community and the juvenile when they are used properly. They are useful for providing background information on offenders so that the agencies in the juvenile justice system can best protect the community and provide treatment and rehabilitation for the youngster.

The controversy about records revolves around the question of who is to see them and what data should be recorded. The President's Task Force on Juvenile Justice and Delinquency Prevention (1977) recommended that juvenile fingerprints and photographs be used only by the police department which collects them, only to solve specific crimes, and that they be destroyed once the investigation is complete.[42] About one-half of the states limit the power of police to take fingerprints or photographs. The most common prohibition is against providing fingerprints to the Federal Bureau of Investigation for its use in centralized files.[43] These guidelines and laws, as well as local police department

[40]24 N.Y.2d 522, 301 N.Y.S.2d 479, 249 N.E.2d 366 (1969).

[41]*New Jersey* v. *T.L.O.,* 105 S.Ct. 733 (1985).

[42]National Advisory Committee on Criminal Justice Standards and Goals, *Juvenile Justice and Delinquency Prevention,* pp. 221–223.

[43]Levin and Sarri, *Juvenile Delinquency,* pp. 26–27.

policies (see the Illinois Juvenile Court law referred to earlier), are intended to protect juveniles from stigmatization at an early age.

If a juvenile is requested to appear in a lineup, a counsel is entitled to be present as a result of the decision of *U.S. v. Wade*, which requires the presence of counsel at a lineup for adult prisoners.[44]

Many persons object to photographing, fingerprinting, and keeping records on juveniles because it is too akin to adult criminal proceedings. As pointed out earlier, however, juvenile procedures are becoming more and more closely aligned with adult procedures. This is just one of the many dilemmas facing the professionals who work with juveniles.

Disposition of Offenders Taken into Custody

After taking a juvenile into custody and abiding by the legal safeguards and procedures outlined above, it must be determined whether the child should return home without a court referral or whether court action is necessary. The decision will be based on the police officer's investigation, which will include the circumstances surrounding the offense, the offense itself, and an assessment of the youngster's family situation (as well as available alternatives within the community). The juvenile will generally be released to the parents if the offense is minor, there is no habitual delinquency pattern, and the parents are deemed capable of providing a positive influence in the situation.

The U.S. Supreme Court has not decided many cases relevant to the disposition of offenders taken into custody, so it is only state legislation and case law that govern the pretrial process, including detention. The Michigan law is typical in requiring a hearing on detention for any child who is taken into custody. Section 712a.15 of the compiled laws of Michigan, 1948, states:

Detention pending hearing shall be limited to the following children:

A. Those whose home conditions make immediate removal necessary.
B. Those who have run away from home.
C. Those whose offenses are so serious that release would endanger public safety.
D. Those detained for observation, study and treatment by qualified experts.

In addition to following state law, a number of jurisdictions have adopted an important decision from the case *Moss v. Weaver.*[45] The Fifth Circuit Court of Appeals held that children who are to be detained for a lengthy time are entitled to a hearing to determine that there is probable cause that they have actually committed a crime. If a child is detained, the right to bail varies from state to state.

One U.S. Supreme Court decision that has bearing on the pretrial re-

[44]*U.S. v. Wade*, 338 U.S. 218 (1967).
[45]525 F.2d 1258 (5th Cir. 1976).

lease concerns *preventive detention,* which is the right of a judge to detain a suspect until trial because the suspect is a danger to others or self. In contrast to the usual illegality of preventive detention for adults, the Court found in *Schall* v. *Martin* (1984) that it was legal for a child to be detained for the protection of self and others.[46]

THE JUVENILE COURT—INTAKE AND PROCESSING

As mentioned earlier, there is a juvenile court in every state of the union. It is usually a specialized unit of the state judicial system and is based in the local community. Most juvenile courts are part of the circuit, district, superior, county, common pleas, probate, or municipal courts. The jurisdiction generally includes delinquency, neglect, and dependency cases; however, adoption, appointment of guardians for minors, determination of custody, and termination of parental rights are also included in juvenile court jurisdiction. The age of the juvenile processed by the court is usually up to age eighteen, but in some states it ends at sixteen or can be extended up to age twenty-one.

The juvenile court can receive funding from both the state and local jurisdiction. Financing depends on the particular jurisdiction. Also depending on the state, there are various appeal procedures available to a disgruntled juvenile client. The judge is elected or appointed, and the police, the schools, and other agencies make referrals to the juvenile court.

There are considerable variations in the philosophy, structure, and procedures of juvenile courts across the country.[47] The court often operates under unsatisfactory fiscal conditions, which is conducive neither to an orderly operation nor to the provision of services to the client and the community:

> The court's dilemma in coping with such critical pressures is sharpened by its dependence on local agencies or publics for support and cooperation. Many local units must be relied upon to provide assistance in case handling and service. The resources of police departments, schools, social agencies, welfare bureaus, the bar association, and the medical societies are needed to supplement those of the court. The dilemma also has more general terms of reference. The election of the judge and the basic operating budget necessitate maintenance and good will from a broad range of local units and interest groups. Certain organizations, furthermore, play crucial roles in validating court performance among the general public. Police judgments, in particular, but also those of schools, welfare agencies, and professional associations are taken as more or less authoritative evaluations of juvenile court activity and the risk of public challenge from these units must be taken into account as the court deals with individual cases.[48]

---

[46]104 S.Ct. 2403 (1984).

[47]Rosemary Sarri and Yeheskel Hasenfeld, eds., *Brought to Justice? Juveniles, the Courts, and the Law* (Ann Arbor: University of Michigan Press, 1976).

[48]Robert D. Vinter, "The Juvenile Court as an Institution," *Task Force Report: Juvenile Delinquency and Youth Crime,* pp. 86–87; also see Anne Rankin Mahoney, *Juvenile Justice in Context* (Boston, Massachusetts: Northeastern University Press, 1987).

In the juvenile court, we would expect to see the results of legal protections like those provided by *In re Gault.* Certainly defense lawyers are involved, but there is research evidence that in some states, half or more of the delinquent and status offenders—some of whom received severe dispositions—did not have a lawyer.[49] In contrast, in certain states, for example California and New York, most youth have representation. Particularly in light of the trend towards a "just deserts" approach to sentencing, adequate representation would seem to be essential. Otherwise, the child can receive the worst of two worlds: The child does not receive the procedural safeguards guaranteed in adult criminal courts, nor the individualized treatment that was the original intent of the juvenile court movement.[50]

Even though the juvenile court's original intent was to rehabilitate rather than punish, a lack of resources, lack of cooperation, and lack of insight have often turned it into a second-rate agency for processing juveniles. Ideally, the court should be able to guarantee the child's legal rights through procedural safeguards without losing sight of the individualized treatment approach, which is the avowed purpose of juvenile court philosophy.

THE INTAKE DIVISION OF THE JUVENILE COURT

The procedure of the juvenile court begins with a *petition* against the child, which usually originates with a law enforcement agency, although it can be initiated by other sources. School authorities, for example, can refer truancy and vandalism cases. Other agencies may also make referrals, but most referrals come from the police.

Most juvenile courts employ a well-defined routine in processing juveniles who are brought before them on a petition alleging delinquency, dependency, or neglect. The *intake* or initial screening is usually performed by an intake unit, controlled and supervised by the juvenile court, which consists of one or more probation officers. Often the intake unit performs court functions other than those of initial screening. The interest in diverting minor offenders before adjudication has created a new responsibility and a new challenge for many intake units. Thus the initial screening might result in a diversion of the child from the court into programs run by expert child-serving institutions, such as "youth service bureaus" or "child advocacy centers." To quote the President's Commission on Law Enforcement:

> Intake is essentially a screening process to determine whether the court should take action and, if so, what action or whether the matter should be referred

---

[49]*Kent v. U.S.* 383 U.S. 541 (1966).

[50]Barry C. Feld, "*In re Gault* Revisited: A Cross-State Comparison of the Right to Counsel in Juvenile Court," *Crime and Delinquency, 34,* no. 4 (October 1988), pp. 393–424; also see David P. Aday, Jr., "Court Structure, Defense Attorney Use and Juvenile Court Decisions," *Sociological Quarterly, 27,* (Spring 1986), pp. 107–119.

elsewhere. Intake is set apart from the screening process used in adult criminal courts by the pervasive attempt to individualize each case and the nature of the personnel administering the discretionary process. In adult criminal proceedings at the post-arrest stage, decisions to screen out are entrusted to the grand jury, the judge or usually to the prosecutor. The objective is screening as an end in itself: attempts to deliver service to those screened out are rare. . . . At intake in the juvenile courts, screening is an important objective, but referral is an additional goal. Thus, the expressed function of intake is likely to be more ambitious than that of its criminal law counterpart and the function is performed chiefly by persons who are neither legally trained or significantly restricted in the exercise of their discretionary authority by procedure requirements comparable to those of the criminal law.[51]

The National Advisory Commission on Criminal Justice Standards and Goals recommends that an intake unit should:

1. make the initial decision whether to place a juvenile referred to the court in detention or shelter care;
2. make the decision whether to offer a juvenile referred to the court the opportunity to participate in diversion programs; and
3. make, in consultation with the prosecutor, the decision whether to file a formal petition in the court alleging that the juvenile is delinquent and ask that the family court assume jurisdiction over him.[52]

Figure 6-2 illustrates the process of alternatives that exist at the intake phase. The intake unit, if it is part of a large organization, assigns an intake worker to screen the incoming cases. The intake worker reviews the case and the circumstances, verifies the facts, and usually prepares a brief social history for the court. The case often goes no further than this, and the determination is made to dismiss and release the child, to admonish and dismiss or possibly to require informal probation supervision by one of the probation officers.

In summary, after the intake process, then, there can be outright dismissal, admonishment and dismissal, informal supervision by the probation staff, referral to a community agency for mental health services, or other types of nonjudicial sources. Many courts promote the philosophy that it is far better to handle the youngster who needs supervision in an informal manner or by a nonjudicial community agency, in order to avoid contact with the formal juvenile justice court processes. This approach is often grounded in the labeling theory (see Chapter 3 on theory). According to the labeling theory, the further the child proceeds through the juvenile justice system, the greater are the chances that he or she will be labeled delinquent, which has negative ramifications for the child both in the immediate situation and in the future.

The intake and screening process is an important aspect of the juvenile justice system. When used properly, it can effectively curtail or interrupt much

---

[51]*Task Force Report: Juvenile Delinquency and Youth Crime*, p. 14.

[52]*National Advisory Commission on Criminal Justice Standards and Goals, Task Force on Courts* (Washington, D.C.: U.S. Government Printing Office, 1973), p. 296.

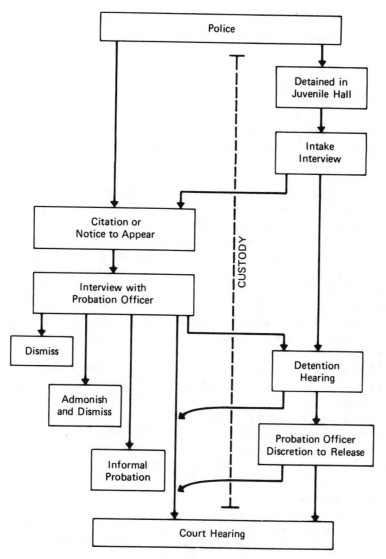

Figure 6-2 Decision points in probation handling of juveniles
SOURCE: From James T. Carey, Joel Goldfarb, Michael J. Rowe, and Joseph D. Lohman,
The Handling of Juveniles from Offense to Disposition, U.S. Department of Health,
Education, and Welfare (Washington, D.C.: U.S. Government Printing Office, 1967), p. 26.

delinquent behavior before it becomes serious. The intake process can also stimulate community agencies to help parents to better understand their children's behavior and the measures needed to prevent future delinquent acts.

If the child is released at intake and no further processing takes place, there should still be a follow-up after any referral to a community agency by either the police or the intake unit. Follow-up not only facilitates the rendering of services to the child, but also promotes closer cooperation between the agencies involved.

JUVENILE COURT PROCESSING BEYOND INTAKE

If the intake unit has placed the child on informal probation, but the child is having difficulty and it is deemed necessary that further action be taken, the probation officer can initiate the *petition*. For those cases that the intake unit feels further action is deemed immediately necessary after a police referral, a petition will be originated without first putting the child on informal probation. The petition, which states the circumstances of the child's situation, precedes the *preliminary hearing*, which takes place in the presence of a judge. The reason for the preliminary hearing is to decide if there are enough facts to warrant court action. The petition that originates this action can request a declaration of delinquency, dependency, neglect, or any other type of juvenile disposition. The petition can be signed by any authorized person: a police officer, the probation officer who was supervising the child on informal probation, or a citizen. The parents are notified of the action. At the preliminary hearing, a juvenile's case can be transferred to criminal court. The increased use of such transfers is discussed later in this chapter.

The *Gault* decision states that there must be adequate notice in writing of the charge, and verification of the child's right to counsel at the hearing must be made unless it was intelligently waived. There is also a privilege against self-incrimination unless intelligently waived and, in the absence of valid admission, determination of delinquency rests upon sworn testimony in open court. If at the preliminary hearing the judge decides that the facts warrant court action, the case will be scheduled for an adjudication hearing.

Adjudication Hearing

At the adjudication hearing, which is considered a part of the preliminary hearing, the youth is questioned about the offense, the circumstances, and the facts that have been presented. The petition may be dismissed at this hearing if there is not enough evidence. If there is a finding of delinquency (or neglect, and so on), a new court date is set for the *disposition hearing*.

The National Advisory Commission on Criminal Justice Standards and Goals recommends that the following procedures be employed at the adjudicatory hearing:

> At the adjudicatory hearing, the juvenile alleged to be delinquent should be afforded all of the rights given a defendant in adult criminal prosecution, except that trial by jury should not be available in delinquency cases.
> In all delinquency cases, a legal officer representing the State should be pres-

ent in court to present evidence supporting the allegation of delinquency. If requested by the juvenile, defense counsel should use all methods permissible in a criminal prosecution to prevent determination that the juvenile is delinquent. He should function as the advocate for the juvenile, and his performance should be unaffected by any belief he might have that a finding of delinquency might be in the best interests of the juvenile. As advocate for the juvenile alleged to be delinquent, counsel's actions should not be affected by the wishes of the juvenile's parents or guardian if those differ from the wishes of the juvenile.[53]

Disposition Hearing

There is supposed to be enough time between the adjudication hearing and the disposition hearing to allow the probation officer to make a social investigation. At the disposition hearing, the judge uses this investigation to decide what alternatives will be most appropriate for the child. The social investigation includes an evaluation of the child's environment, the interrelationships of child and family, the child's attitude and behavior in neighborhood, community, and school, the circumstances regarding the difficulty, and the ability of the parents to provide supervision and guidance at home. The probation officer can consult neighbors, school counselors, teachers, and any other persons who may know the youngster. After the judge has studied the social investigation, he or she may also question the parents or the probation officer to acquire additional material that may not be a part of the social investigation. After considering all the relevant facts in the case, the judge makes a disposition. Alternative dispositions are

1. Release the child to the parents (with possible referral to a community social agency).
2. Place the child on probation.
3. Commit the child to an institution.
4. Utilize a foster home placement.
5. Make the child a ward of the court in order to provide necessary medical services or other supervision, especially in cases of neglect.

In severe cases of neglect, the court can also terminate some parental rights. This option is not often used: the removal of children from their natural parents is a very difficult decision to make.

In several states, the court has granted youths the right to due process protections in the disposition stage of processing. Also, several cases have dealt with the actual disposition, requiring, for example, that community resources be exhausted before a youth is committed to a state institution.

Probation, the most commonly employed dispositional alternative, is a service provided by the court which compels the child to meet certain requirements established by the court and carried out under the supervision of a proba-

---

[53]*Ibid.,* pp. 302, 474.

tion officer. The major requirement is that the youngster meet with the probation officer regularly for a specified period of time. Probation is a trial period during which the youngsters attempt to mobilize their own resources as well as those of the community, and, under the supervision of the probation officer, become rehabilitated. The length of probation can range from a few months to a few years. While the youngster is on probation, it is expected that the resources made available will be utilized and that the supervision and guidance which are not provided in the home will help the youngster to succeed not only on probation but also in the community after release from probation.

If the probationer abides by the rules set by the court and satisfactorily completes the requirements, probation is terminated. If the youth is not successful on probation and becomes involved in recurring difficulties, another plan may be made. This plan could include incarceration in an institution or placement in a setting that would provide more stringent supervision and guidance— for example, a halfway house.

Chapter 7, "Delinquency Prevention Programs," discusses institutional facilities. Chapter 9, "An Example: Community-Based Treatment Program," discusses services such as halfway houses. Upon release from an institution or another residential facility, the child is often supervised by an aftercare worker, a parole officer, or some person with a similar title. The supervision is equivalent to what the child would have received had he or she been placed on probation and not been incarcerated.

In some states the court has jurisdiction over aftercare services, while in other states they are the responsibility of such organizations as the Department of Youth Services or Social Services. Regardless of the administrative structure, the basic purpose is to provide supervision and guidance on the assumption that the youngster is not ready to experience total freedom in the community.

In most of the states, there are procedures through which a juvenile can be transferred (or waived) to criminal court.[54] The reasons for using waiver have typically been that the juvenile justice system lacks the means to provide treatment or to protect the community from the offender. In reality, the result of waiver is an immediate increase in the severity of response to the juvenile: "an extended detention stay, a protracted adjudicatory process, a felony conviction resulting in social and legal sanctions, and a lengthy sentence in a secure correctional facility."[55] In more than thirty states, the law requires a waiver for youth of a certain age who have committed particularly serious offenses, for example armed robbery. A smaller number of states allow waiver at the discretion of the juvenile court. There also is a growing number of states that allow waiver at the

---

[54]Barry C. Feld, "The Juvenile Court Meets the Principle of the Offense: Legislative Changes in Juvenile Waiver Statutes." Presented at the Annual Meeting of the American Society of Criminology, Atlanta, Georgia.

[55]Cary J. Rudman, Eliot Hartstone, Jeffrey A. Fagan, and Melinda Moore, "Violent Youth in Adult Court: Process and Punishment," *Crime and Delinquency, 32,* no. 1 (January 1986), pp. 75–96. Jeffrey Fagan, Martin Forst, and T. Scott Vivona, "Racial Determinants of the Judicial Transfer Decision: Prosecuting Violent Youth in Criminal Court," *Crime and Delinquency, 33,* no. 2 (April 1987):259–286.

discretion of the prosecutor or, for serious felonies, when a grand jury indicts the juvenile. Greater use of waiver is part of the trend towards a "just deserts" approach to juvenile justice.

When a judge is involved in deciding on waiver, the juvenile's rights are protected, in part because of prior Supreme Court decisions. One of these decisions is *Kent* v. *United States,* in which the Supreme Court reversed the conviction of a sixteen-year-old youth who had been tried as an adult for housebreaking, robbery, and rape. The high court held that the waiver to criminal court was procedurally invalid because the youth had been denied a hearing with the assistance of counsel and a statement of the juvenile court concerning its reasons for the waiver to criminal court. In its ruling, the Supreme Court demonstrated that the *parens patriae* philosophy of the juvenile court was "not an invitation to procedural arbitrariness,[56] and further:

> There is evidence, in fact, that there may be grounds for concern that the child receives the worst of both worlds: that he gets neither the protection accorded to adults nor the solicitous care and regenerative treatment postulated for children.[57]

The extension of due process to juveniles is emphasized in the 1975 case, *Breed* v. *Jones*.[58] There, the Court ruled that it was in violation of the double jeopardy clause of the Fourteenth Amendment to prosecute a seventeen-year-old in a criminal court following adjudicatory proceedings in a juvenile court.

Even when legal protections are provided through the court process, there have been criticisms. One problem is that, since minorities are overrepresented among serious offenders, any negative effects of handling in the criminal justice system will mainly fall on these groups.[59] Also, research has shown that at least some jurisdictions automatically waive all seventeen-year-olds, and thus they alter the original intent of the law.[60] A third criticism is that waiver is increasingly being used for recidivist property offenders rather than violent offenders.[61] A very different criticism of the use of waiver is that in some jurisdictions, where serious juvenile offenders are treated harshly, waiver has re-

---

[56]383 U.S. 541, at 541 (1966).

[57]383 U.S. 541, at 556 (1966).

[58]421 U.S. 519 (1975).

[59]Jeffrey A. Fagan, Martin Forst, and T. Scott Vivona, "Racial Determinants of the Judicial Transfer Decision: Prosecuting Violent Youth in Criminal Court," *Crime and Delinquency, 33,* no. 2 (April 1987):259–286.

[60]Jeffrey A. Fagan, J. Rudman, E. Hartstone and K. V. Hansen, "System Processing of Violent Juvenile Offenders: An Empirical Assessment." in *Violent Juvenile Offenders: An Anthology.* R. Mlakthias et al., eds. *(San Francisco: National Council on Crime and Delinquency,* 1984).

[61]*Dean J. Champion,* "Teenage Felons and Waiver Hearings: *Some Recent Trends, 1980–1988," Crime and Delinquency, 35,* no. 4 (October 1989), pp. 577–585. On less severe sentence, also see David Reed, *Needed: Serious Solutions for Serious Juvenile Crime* (Chicago: Chicago Law Enforcement Study Group); Elizabeth T. Schack and Hermine Nessen, *The Experiment that Failed: The New York Juvenile Offender Law—A Study Report* (New York: Citizen's Committee for Children of New York, Inc.).

sulted in a lower rate of conviction and less severe punishment.[62] Also, when the increased use of transfer to criminal court has been evaluated, there has been no reduction in the juvenile crime rate.[63]

The transfer of juveniles through prosecutorial decisions has been particularly controversial, for standards are often vague and prosecutors are typically more oriented towards punishment than the juvenile court's original objective of rehabilitation.[64] A study of Florida's use of prosecutorial transfer between 1979 and 1987 suggests that there may be reason for criticism. The cases that were transferred at the discretion of the prosecutor often did not appear to be particularly serious, and many very serious cases were not chosen for transfer. In some cases, it seemed that youth were transferred primarily because they were nearing age eighteen, when they would no longer be under the jurisdiction of the juvenile court. Possible reasons for the transfer of seemingly inappropriate cases include the lack of juvenile treatment facilities and the absence of clear guidelines regarding who should be transferred.

BIAS IN DECISION MAKING

At each stage of processing, juvenile justice system employees choose between several options for handling the alleged offender. The police decide whether to warn a youth and avoid further processing or, at the other extreme, to file a petition in juvenile court. The intake division, probation officers, and judges all have a part in choosing between different options. One of the most important contributions of theorists who work within the labeling perspective is to our understanding of how these decisions are made, and the degree to which they reflect a bias against some groups in society.

In response to the striking overrepresentation of minority youth in the juvenile justice system, many people have raised the possibility that there is bias in the decision-making process. More specifically, at one or more of the decision points, minority and/or lower class youth are more likely than others to be treated harshly than majority youth with similar offense patterns. An early example of this was the finding of Irving Piliavin and Scott Briar that a "recalcitrant demeanor," which the police frequently attributed to black youth, played an important part in influencing police to stop and arrest a youth.[65] Since Piliavin and Briar first drew attention to the potential for racial bias, numerous

---

[62]*Ibid.*

[63]Simon I. Singer and David McDowall, *Criminalizing Delinquency: The Deterrent Effects of The New York Juvenile Offender Law* (Buffalo, New York: State University of New York, 1987).

[64]Donna M. Bishop, Charles E. Frazier and John C. Henretta, "Prosecutorial Waiver: Case Study of a Questionable Reform," *Crime and Delinquency, 35,* no. 2 (April 1989), pp. 179–201.

[65]Irving Piliavin and Scott Briar, "Police Encounters with Juveniles," *American Journal of Sociology, 70,* no. 2 (September 1964), pp. 206–214.

studies have been conducted on not only police but on the many other decision makers in the juvenile justice system, and the results have been mixed.

In an effort to untangle the findings about racial bias in juvenile justice decisions, the Office of Juvenile Justice and Delinquency Prevention funded a major research initiative.[66] When all prior research was considered, about two-thirds of the studies found harsher treatment of racial minorities at some decision-making point. In some cases, race had an influence in just selected jurisdictions of the state, and in others it had an influence because the jurisdictions with larger minority populations responded more harshly to juveniles than did other jurisdictions. Discrimination was found in at least some studies for each of the decision points, and, in some places, discrimination accumulated as a youth moved through the system, with the result that it was most obvious at the later stages of justice system processing.

Although race has some effect on decision making, it is important to keep in mind that this is just one influence. For police decisions, demeanor continues to be important, along with seriousness or nature of the offense, prior juvenile record, and the victim's preference.[67] After arrest, the type and seriousness of the juvenile's offense is the strongest influence on intake and court decisions, with the harshest outcomes for youth who are dependent or neglected, abused or victimized, or involved in a robbery.[68]

Given the multiple influences on juvenile justice decisions, how serious a problem is racial discrimination? The potential negative outcome is illustrated by a study of 50,000 juvenile cases in Florida.[69] Youth who are at the adjudication stage have already gone through a recommendation for formal processing that treats blacks more harshly than whites. The problem is compounded at the adjudication stage, where black minor offenders are more often designated as delinquent than are white minor offenders with similar records. The bias is again compounded at the disposition stage, where blacks are more likely than similarly delinquent whites to be institutionalized or transferred to criminal courts. Since prior dispositions often result in harsher treatment, processing after a rearrest will continue to place black youth at risk for the most severe court handling.

Combined with the "just deserts" trend, discriminatory treatment can place minority youth at very high risk for the serious consequences of adult

[66]Carl E. Pope and William H. Feyerherm, "Minority Status and Juvenile Justice Processing (Part I)," *Criminal Justice Abstracts, 22,* no. 2 (June 1990), pp. 327–335; Carl E. Pope and William H. Feyerherm, "Minority Status and Juvenile Justice Processing (Part II)," *Criminal Justice Abstracts, 22,* no. 3 (September 1990), pp. 527–542.

[67]Charles P. Smith, T. Edwin Black, and Adrianne W. Weir, *A National Assessment of Case Disposition and Classification in the Juvenile Justice System: Inconsistent Labeling.* Vol. 2: Results of a Literature Search (Washington, D.C.: U.S. Government Printing Office, 1980).

[68]Charles P. Smith, T. Edwin Black, and Fred R. Campbell, *A National Assessment of Case Disposition and Classification in the Juvenile Justice System: Inconsistent Labeling.* Vol. 1: Process Description and Summary (Washington, D.C.: U.S. Government Printing Office, 1979), p. xv.

[69]Donna M. Bishop and Charles E. Frazier, "The Influence of Race in Juvenile Justice Processing," *Journal of Research in Crime and Delinquency, 25,* no. 3 (August 1988), pp. 242–263.

processing. The negative impact of racial as well as gender bias is found in the use of the New York Youthful Offender designation. In New York State, juvenile jurisdiction ends at age 15, and youth as young as 13 are held responsible for certain serious offenses. But, if a young criminal offender is designated as a Youthful Offender, incarceration in adult facilities and other severe treatment is avoided. However, Ruth Peterson found that black and Hispanic males were the least likely to be placed in the Youthful Offender category, and thus the "get tough" laws in New York had the greatest impact on them.[70]

Research conducted by Daniel J. Curran also sheds some light on the nature of bias against females. Curran identified three periods in the development of the Philadelphia Family Court System: (1) a "paternalistic" period (1960–1967), during which female delinquents were harshly treated by the courts "for their own good"; (2) a "due process" era (1968–1976), which reflected the spirit of the *Gault* decision; and (3) a "law and order" phase (1977–1980), during which the court adjusted to the new conservatism of the late 1970s.[71] During the phase of conservatism, which has continued into the 1980s, fewer girls are diverted from the formal court process, and the progress made in dismissing minor cases that had come with the *Gault* decision is largely reversed.

Christine Alder, in a final example of research that exposes gender bias in the processing of delinquents, discovered that on the whole, diversion programs have tended to draw more female than male minor offenders into the system from those youths who normally would not have been involved at all.[72] Her finding did not hold for all diversion programs, but the trend did exist.

Gender bias is complicated by countervailing tendencies for different kinds of offenses. There is a reverse bias against boys in the area of detention decisions:

> For more serious offenses involving violence or property damage, males are more likely to be detained than females; for less serious offenses, females are more likely to be detained.[73]

Boys are additionally more likely to be arrested for serious offenses than are girls.[74] We can state with some certainty that beliefs about appropriate and expected behavior for boys and girls does lead to quite different treatment based on the gender of the offender. Also, police are influenced by many factors

---

[70]Ruth D. Peterson, "Youthful Offender Designations and Sentencing in the New York Criminal Courts," *Social Problems 35*, no. 2 (April 1988), pp. 111–130.

[71]Daniel J. Curran, "The Myth of the 'New' Female Delinquent," *Crime and Delinquency, 30*, no. 3 (July 1984), p. 386.

[72]Christine Alder, "Gender Bias in Juvenile Diversion," *Crime and Delinquency, 30*, no. 3 (July 1984), p. 400.

[73]Smith, Black, and Weir, *A National Assessment of Case Disposition and Classification in the Juvenile Justice System*, p. xviii.

[74]Susan K. Datesman and Frank R. Scarpitti, "Unequal Protection of Males and Females in the Juvenile Court," in *Juvenile Delinquency: Little Brother Grows Up*, ed. Theodore Ferdinand (Beverly Hills, California: Sage Publications, 1977), p. 67.

besides the seriousness of the offense. For this reason, some groups are disproportionately represented as the "clients" in the juvenile justice system, but they
are not necessarily the most seriously delinquent youths in the community.

CONCLUSION

A look at the origin, development, and present state of juvenile justice processing reveals both lasting tendencies and recent changes. There is no doubt that
"just deserts" is receiving more attention than ever before in many states, and
that increasing numbers of juveniles are being transferred to the criminal justice
system, where some of them are incarcerated in adult correctional institutions.
There is no clear evidence that these changes have reduced juvenile delinquency,
and there is concern that the severe treatment may be experienced most by
minorities.

Despite the shift towards "just deserts," juvenile court operations as well
as Supreme Court rulings reinforce a belief that juveniles, including very serious
offenders, lack the maturity of judgment of adults; and the juvenile court does
have a critical role to play in rehabilitation. In the juvenile court setting, the
sources of youths' problems are diagnosed and many youth continue to be handled informally, often through referral to a variety of community agencies.
There are, however, limited financial resources and problems of court organization that interfere with these traditional activities of the juvenile court. It is
possible that the focus on "just deserts" will place yet another constraint on the
effective delivery of the promise of care and rehabilitation.

To say the least, there are many and varied philosophies on how the juvenile
court should operate. The following case study will provide the reader with an
opportunity to see how the theories and beliefs about the juvenile court are used
in practice.

A CASE STUDY*

The case involves a youngster whom we will call John Smith. John is fifteen years
of age and lives in Marquette, Michigan. The contact John has with the Lansing,
Michigan, police is the result of his being stopped for a traffic infraction. John is
unable to produce a driver's license or a registration for his vehicle. The officers,
because they are suspicious, make a quick radio check with their headquarters
and determine that the car was stolen in John's hometown. John is apprehended
for unlawfully driving away an automobile (felony), for failing to stop at a red
light, and for not having an operator's license or a vehicle registration on his
person.

*Developed and coordinated by Ray C. Valley, Michigan State Police, East Lansing, Michi-
gan.

After a short conversation, John tells the officers that he stole the car in Marquette and that he would like to talk about the incident.[75] At this point the officers are obliged to (1) advise John of his constitutional rights, (2) determine his age, which in this case is easily learned through other identification that John has on him, (3) obtain the address of John's mother and father because it is necessary to contact them immediately and notify them of the detention of their child, who is four hundred miles away from home. A record of the notification is also made.[76]

The officers make contact with John's parents, and the parents give a verbal waiver which allows the officers to interview John. The local probate court is contacted, and the judge gives verbal agreement that custody and detainment is advisable in this case and that a petition will be signed later in the morning.[77]

The vehicle John is driving has the original license plates on it, as determined by a check of the owner, who lives in Marquette. The owner is advised that the vehicle is being held in Lansing. The owner states that John has taken the automobile without permission, hence verifying that the vehicle was stolen.

The officers take John to the juvenile home where he is lodged, and a custody statement is filed.[78]

John, acting somewhat remorseful, states again that he would like to talk about the circumstances under which he stole the automobile. The officers again advise him of his constitutional rights before interviewing him and request that he sign a waiver. The officers make the determination that he is sophisticated and intelligent enough to make this waiver.[79]

The next morning a probation officer is assigned by the local judge to act as John's guardian until he is returned to his home community.[80] The probation officer decides to advise John against further interviews by the police officers, and all interviews are terminated.[81]

Arrangements are made for John to meet with the probate judge that morning at 10:00 A.M., at which time the officers request an authorization for a petition. The petition is authorized, it is signed by the officers, and the following charges are made before the judge: (1) unlawful driving away of an automobile, (2) no operator's license, (3) no vehicle registration, (4) failure to stop for a red light. The petition must allege the facts with particularity.[82]

[75]*Miranda* v. *Arizona*, 384 U.S. 436 (1966).

[76]Officer's custody statement and record of notification to parent, guardian, or custodian (the specific form used in this case and following examples will depend on the state).

[77]*People* v. *Roberts*, 364 Mich. 60 (duty to take before court, 1961); *in re Mathers*, 371 Mich. 516 (adequacy of petition, 1964).

[78]*Obinetz* v. *Buddo*, 315 Mich. 512 (statement of custody, 1967).

[79]*Hailing* v. *U.S.*, 295 Fed. 161 (use of admissions following waiver, 1961); *Reddick* v. *U.S.*, 326 Fed. 650 (admissibility of conversations with police, 1964); *Gault, idem.*

[80]Michigan juvenile code, 12A, 14 (juvenile in custody; detention areas. ". . . child to be completely isolated so as to prevent any verbal, visual or physical contact with any adult prisoner").

[81]*Kent, idem; Gallegos, idem.*

[82]*Gault, idem.*

The preliminary inquiry is held before the judge. John, the officers, the probation officer, and John's parents are present. At this time the judge decides that, since the automobile was stolen in another community, John should be tried and a disposition should be made in that community. John is then returned to Marquette by juvenile authorities of that community.[83]

If the judge had determined that John could return with his parents, a bond might have been required to assure that John would appear before his home court.[84]

It is determined before John's leaving for home that fingerprints and a photograph will be helpful, and permission is granted by the court.[85]

Summary of procedures so far:

1. Custody was taken when subject was apprehended for a felony and misdemeanors.
2. Juvenile was advised of his constitutional rights.
3. Parents were contacted and notified of apprehension, and the time was recorded.
4. Probate court was contacted: detention was requested and was granted by the court.
5. Waiver was obtained before interviewing the juvenile.
6. Request for a petition was made and granted.
7. Petition was signed, and alleged facts were set forth with particularity.
8. After the judge had considered all the facts, John was transferred to his home community.
9. Petitions for fingerprinting and photographing were approved by the court.
10. John was returned to his home community.

In Marquette the juvenile authorities are presented with the information that has been compiled thus far by the Ingham County Probate Court. After reviewing the information and again being advised of his constitutional rights, John is released to his parents. The parents sign a written release assuring the court that John will be present when a time is designated.[86]

The preceding steps taken in court are part of the preliminary hearing, which must be held forty-eight hours from the time the juvenile is taken into custody. Since the purpose of the hearing is to determine if there are enough facts to support court action and if protection or supervision of the court is necessary, in most cases the hearing is informal and a lawyer is not required. Where a felony has been committed, however, such as in the present case, an attorney can and probably will be called.[87] There are two more phases of court hearings, an adjudication hearing and a disposition hearing.[88]

[83]State statutes relating to the transfer of juveniles.

[84]State statutes relating to right to bond.

[85]State statutes relating to fingerprinting and photographing juveniles.

[86]State statutes relating to duty to release the juvenile upon assurance of parents that the child will appear before court when requested.

[87]*Escobedo, idem* (right to counsel); *Gault, idem* (right of child and parent to be notified).

[88]*Gault, idem; in re Mathers,* 371 Mich. 516 (1964).

The adjudication hearing is considered a part of the preliminary hearing, and both this hearing and the disposition hearing usually have stenographic equipment to record what takes place. States differ in their requirements, but if no specific law exists, there is usually a probate rule or a written memorandum referring to the use of stenographic or mechanical equipment.

The adjudication hearing determines whether the child will come under the jurisdiction of the court. The child and the parents or a guardian are present. All witnesses and evidence or facts are now brought before the court. The juvenile may waive the right to counsel or retain counsel at this time. If the juvenile does not understand his or her constitutional rights, the judge appoints counsel. The judge does this if it seems that the child will not adequately be represented by the parents. The request for an attorney is made in writing, stating the names of the parties represented. The attorney is furnished copies of all pleadings.[89]

At the adjudication hearing for John, the facts presented are sufficient and a disposition hearing date is set. The probation department is requested to do a social investigation of John to provide the judge with adequate information so that a meaningful disposition can be made. If a youngster pleads guilty to an offense and if the parents and attorney consent, the disposition phase can sometimes be held immediately.

The plea of guilty has much more significance in adult court. In juvenile cases the emphasis is not on guilt or innocence, but on individualized justice. There is concern not only with the incident, but with the future welfare of the child as well. The social investigation is important in contributing to this end.

In the case of John, a probation officer conducts a social investigation, including the factors that were mentioned earlier in the chapter.

The dispositional hearing determines what measures the court will take in selecting an alternative that will be most beneficial to John. The allegations are read and presented, and John and his parents are again advised of their right to counsel. John is also advised of his right to remain silent and of his right to cross-examination. A record of the proceedings is also made.[90]

After all the facts are considered, the judge makes a determination as to the disposition of the case. The alternatives open to the judge were mentioned earlier.

Probation is usually the alternative selected and, in the present case, John is placed on probation. It is determined that his offense is not an indication of a pattern of delinquent or criminal behavior, and that he can be helped at home and guided and supervised by a probation officer. In John's case, it is concluded that he stole the car upon a dare from friends after they had been involved in "drinking." John and his friends were only going to take the car for a short ride, but they were having so much fun driving the automobile that they impulsively decided to take it out of town. John is to report to a probation officer

[89]*Gault, idem.*
[90]*Gault, idem.*

for two years, and he cannot apply for a driver's license until he is released from probation.

SUMMARY

This chapter has focused on the processing and handling of juveniles through the various components of the juvenile justice system. The three major components discussed were police, the intake division of the juvenile court, and the juvenile court. A case study was utilized to illustrate the procedure involved.

It cannot be assumed that merely because an agency has as part of its function the prevention, control, and treatment of delinquency, the goal will necessarily follow the good intentions of the initiators of the particular program. All agencies that deal, either directly or indirectly, with delinquents have the potential for perpetuating and in fact sometimes producing the delinquency, as well as reducing it.[91]

The Police

Police agencies can contribute to the perpetuation of delinquent behavior. Many times the first contact that a child has with the juvenile justice system is with a police officer. Many young people, delinquents in particular, have problems with authority because of poor authority relationships in their past. If a child's first contact with a police officer is negative and the police officer exerts authority in an arrogant manner, this can support the child's already negative concept of authority and contribute to further acting out against authority within the community. However, an officer who impresses the child as being an understanding but firm adult who will be fair, can have a positive impact and can be one of the major factors in influencing children to alter their behavior and divert their energy into socially acceptable channels.

The Juvenile Court

The juvenile court also has the potential for producing and perpetuating delinquency. If the court is not responsive to the needs of the total community, and in fact indiscriminately prosecutes and processes children from limited segments of the community, the indiscriminate labeling can affect both children's attitudes toward themselves and the community's attitude toward them. The social ostracism and the negative self-concept can contribute to their antisocial behavior in the community. Court procedures should be equitable and sensitive to the possible negative ramifications of hasty labeling. Realistic, humane, and

---

[91]Walter Miller, "Inter-Institutional Conflict as a Major Impediment to Delinquency Prevention," *Human Organization, 17* (Fall 1958).

appropriate methods of processing and treating juveniles are necessary, if the court is to be an effective component in the juvenile justice system.

Prosecutors and Defense Attorneys

As a result of many Supreme Court and lower court decisions, defense attorneys have become participants in the juvenile court process. However, depending on the state and the local jurisdiction, the degree to which they participate in protecting the rights of the child varies considerably. States where defense attorneys represent low proportions of the serious offenders, or where juveniles are most often represented by inexperienced attorneys, need to improve their public defender systems. Otherwise, the legal safeguards provided by the courts cannot have their full impact.

In some states, prosecutors now play a key role in deciding whether a youth should be transferred, or waived, to criminal court. A combined absence of legal safeguards and the existence of vague guidelines raises serious questions about the benefits of change in this direction. Because prosecutors traditionally emphasize punishment rather than rehabilitation, their increased power in the juvenile justice system could seriously threaten the ideal of rehabilitation.

Social Service Providers

Whether working in the court, or as specialists to which the courts refer youth, social workers, mental health specialists, and other similar professional groups deliver services to many youth. It is essential that these service providers understand the complexity of the local juvenile justice system, and recognize the dual and potentially conflicting objectives of providing treatment and matching a punishment to an offense. It is essential that social service providers reinforce the notion that youth are responsible for their actions, while at the same time making sure that appropriate supports are provided to prevent further illegal activity.

DISCUSSION QUESTIONS

1. How would the various stages of juvenile justice system processing be different if the courts did not adhere to the idea of *parens patriae?*
2. Based on the research information in Chapter 2, is there justification for special handling of status offender cases? For each stage of processing, how should status offenders be handled?
3. What beliefs about children, and the differences between girls and boys, are the basis of juvenile law and of police and court procedures?
4. What are the dilemmas facing police and court personnel, including social workers, as they try to provide individual treatment to each child and to protect each child's legal rights?
5. Some people have argued that since the juvenile court is moving towards a "just deserts" approach, it should be abolished. The criminal court can take age into account as a mitigating factor just as well as the juvenile court, and the criminal court provides better protection of the offender's rights. Develop a list of points in support and not in support of this position.

PROJECTS

1. Determine how your state's law has changed (or not changed) in the emphasis on "just deserts" and the handling of waiver decisions. How does your state compare to general trends for changes in the law?

2. Using the information presented in this chapter, develop questions about the dilemmas and conflicts experienced by police officers, court staff, attorneys, and social service providers who work with juveniles. Interview one type of professional, and share the responses with other members of the class.

7

Delinquency Prevention Programs*

- PURE PREVENTION PROGRAMS
- EARLY PREVENTION PROGRAMS
- FEDERAL PREVENTION EFFORTS
- CONTEMPORARY LOCAL PREVENTION—POLICE, SCHOOLS, AND COMMUNITY
- ALTERNATIVES TO COURT PROCESSING
- REHABILITATIVE PREVENTION
- REHABILITATION IN THE COMMUNITY
- THE MASSACHUSETTS COMMUNITY-BASED SYSTEM
- INSTITUTIONS
- CONCLUSION

LEARNING OBJECTIVES

1. To be aware of the variety of past and current delinquency prevention programs.
2. To know of the link between the classical school of criminology and practices in punishing the offender, as well as the link between the positive school of criminology and prevention programs.
3. To understand that theories of delinquency causation underlie the design of prevention programs.
4. To know of the major federal efforts which are pure prevention programs.

*Note: The introductory material to this chapter was written by John M. Trojanowicz.

5. To know of a wide variety of pure and rehabilitation prevention programs, and to be aware of modern-day tendencies to use certain types of programs more often than others.
6. To recognize the special difficulties surrounding the development of constructive programs in institutional settings.
7. To appreciate the extent to which research has informed us, or in some cases failed to inform us, of the effectiveness of various programs.

Every society requires a greater or lesser degree of conformity to its behavioral norms or laws. It invariably responds in some fashion when these are violated. The nature of the response varies widely according to the act and from society to society. Moreover, it is subject to a development which parallels the state of a society at a given period. One act might be considered gravely serious at one point in time and relatively harmless at another. A society threatened by an external enemy, for example, is likely to react to behavioral deviations differently than it would in a time of peace and prosperity. In addition to fluctuations in response due to alternating periods of stress and calm, societal responses to illegal behavior evolve historically in roughly the same manner as do societies themselves.

In preliterate societies, a high degree of cooperation was required if the group was to survive. Every group member had his or her function to perform according to ability and status. Some members hunted while others fashioned weapons. Some prepared the food and tended the fire, others sewed clothing, and so on. In these primitive organizations, there existed a high degree of immediate, mutual dependence. If one member failed to perform a task satisfactorily or in any way disrupted the equilibrium of the group, the survival of all was threatened. Since a very high degree of conformity was necessary under such conditions, practically every aspect of life became ritualized. Violations of the rituals, which included witchcraft and sacrilege as well as treason and poisoning, were responded to either by the annihilation or the banishment of the offending member. The offender was considered unclean and was removed as a social hygiene measure. Offenses against private individuals of different families, such as assault, murder, and theft, were avenged by the relatives of the victim in blood feuds and were not considered sufficiently grave to require societal response. Injuries to other members of the same family were dealt with totally within the family. Thus, the responses to deviant and what would now be termed criminal or delinquent behavior were not punitive in the modern sense but arose from a desire to annihilate an enemy of the group, to offer sacrifice to appease or otherwise avert the wrath of the gods, to cleanse the community of pollution, to avenge cases of private injury, and to show surprise and disgust at one who would offend a family member.

As societies became larger, more complex, and subject to a central authority in the person of a king, reaction to wrongs came to be viewed as collective or social, as offenses against the group as well as against the victim. If an offender were executed, it was to protect against potential danger to other members of the group. A person's hand was cut off not for the purpose of inflicting pain or deterring others with similar intentions, but to incapacitate the offender and thereby prevent him or her from breaking the law again. Fines were levied with a view toward restitution of the victim, rather than as a method of punishing the offender.

It was not until the modern period, beginning roughly in the second half of the seventeenth century, that the inflicting of pain on an offender came to be regarded as having value in the deterrence of crime. The classical school (mentioned earlier), which included such noteworthy adherents as Rousseau, Montesquieu, Voltaire, and Beccaria, maintained that the individual calculates pleasures and pains in advance of action. Thus, society's response to crime should be calculated in a fashion that would render the punishment of an illegal act more painful than the pleasure accruing from it. It was hoped that the fear of pain would exceed the anticipated pleasure of the act, and that the individual would therefore opt for socially acceptable behavior. Also, pain served to repay society for the deviant acts, considered an offense against the group. The inflicting of pain as a societal response to illegal acts has remained up to the present the most prevalent of the several alternatives. In modern, industrial societies, fines and removal from the group by imprisonment are the most frequently employed methods.

In the late eighteenth and early nineteenth centuries, the prison, which up to that time had been used primarily for debtors, political prisoners, and criminals awaiting other dispositions, became the major correctional vehicle. Imprisonment is ideally suited to the retribution-pleasure-pain deterrent theories since its length can be varied with the crime. Parole and probation can be viewed as modified extensions of imprisonment.

Chapter 3 pointed out that the positive school of criminology advocated by Lombroso, Ferri, Garofalo, and others held that criminality arises from a multiplicity of factors, including heredity and environment. This position denied individual responsibility for criminal acts, thereby eliminating the justification of punishment as a response. According to this school of thought, criminals should be treated with a view toward reform. Society, however, must be protected from those who cannot be salvaged; they must be maintained in segregation. Segregation, however, should be the last resort.

Prevention, as it is known today, is a relatively new concept, though it grew out of the positive school of criminology. Prevention efforts rest on the assumption that the causes of delinquency, whether biological or sociological or psychological, can be identified and removed. The many prevention programs now in existence are designed to remove one or more of the several hypothesized causes of delinquency. A number of these causes are identified in the theories which were reviewed earlier in this book. Other prevention programs are based on assumptions about human behavior which do not have such a firm basis in theory, but instead reflect popular beliefs.

Delinquency Prevention

Early efforts at delinquency prevention and establishment of programs and strategies were usually local endeavors initiated by privately supported family-centered agencies and groups. Urbanization necessitated that both private and public agencies become involved in delinquency prevention because of the immensity of the problem and the complexities of the urban society.

During the 1900s, a wide variety of community, state, and national agencies became involved in delinquency prevention, control, and treatment. Most of these efforts, however, were independent and uncoordinated.

> By the mid-1950's, the delinquency prevention effort in virtually every large city was like a jigsaw puzzle of services involving important government departments which had heretofore operated with relative independence. The agencies concerned with delinquency prevention included the schools, recreation departments, public housing authorities, public welfare departments giving family service and administering child welfare, private social agencies, and health departments and other medical facilities (including psychiatric hospitals and clinics). The size, shape, and strength and position (role in the community) of the various pieces of the delinquency prevention picture varied greatly from one city to another—the format for delinquency prevention services varied from city to city partly because the coordinating agency in each city is the one which happened to be the strongest.[1]

From the beginning, prevention programs suffered from a lack of interagency communication and the interprogram conflicts that resulted from the diverse disciplines—including sociology, psychology, and psychiatry—that influenced the prevention approach.[2]

In reviewing the many prevention efforts in both the past and present, we will consider two major categories of program: *pure prevention*, or primary prevention, which attempts to inhibit delinquency before it takes place; and *rehabilitative prevention*, or secondary prevention, which treats the youngster who has come in contact with the formal juvenile justice system. Rehabilitative prevention, if effective, can also be considered a preventive mechanism if the treatment provided deters future delinquent behavior. Pure prevention therefore deals primarily with youngsters who have not been adjudicated delinquent, whereas rehabilitative prevention deals with youngsters who have been adjudicated delinquent.

J. David Hawkins and his coauthors have developed a detailed typology of twelve prevention program strategies. They relate each strategy to a different theory of delinquency causation:

A. BIOLOGICAL/PHYSIOLOGICAL strategies assume that delinquent behavior derives from underlying physiological, biological, or biopsychiatric conditions. They seek to remove, diminish, or control these conditions.

B. PSYCHOLOGICAL/MENTAL HEALTH strategies assume that delinquency originates in internal psychological states viewed as inherently maladaptive or pathological. They seek to directly alter such states and/or environmental conditions thought to generate them.

C. SOCIAL NETWORK DEVELOPMENT strategies assume that delinquency results from weak attachments between youth and conforming members of society. They seek to increase

---

[1] *Juvenile Delinquency Prevention in the United States*, U.S. Department of Health, Education, and Welfare, Children's Bureau, 1965, p. 12.
[2] *Ibid.*, p. 17.

interaction, attachments, and/or involvement between youth and nondeviant others (ps, parents, other adults) as well as the influence which nondeviant others have on potentially delinquent youth.

D. CRIMINAL INFLUENCE REDUCTION strategies assume that delinquency stems from the influence of others who directly or indirectly encourage youth to commit delinquent acts. They seek to reduce the influence of norms toward delinquency and those who hold such norms.

E. POWER ENHANCEMENT strategies assume that delinquency stems from a lack of power or control over impinging environmental factors. They seek to increase the ability or power of youth to influence or control their environments either directly or indirectly. . . .

F. ROLE DEVELOPMENT/ROLE ENHANCEMENT strategies assume that delinquency stems from a lack of opportunity to be involved in legitimate roles or activities which youth perceive as personally gratifying. They attempt to create such opportunities. To meet the conditions of role development, roles developed or provided must be perceived by youth as worthwhile. . . .

G. ACTIVITIES/RECREATION strategies assume that delinquency results when youth's time is not filled by nondelinquent activities. They seek to provide nondelinquent activities as alternatives to delinquent activities. . . .

H. EDUCATION/SKILL DEVELOPMENT strategies assume that delinquency stems from a lack of knowledge or skills necessary to live in society without violating its laws. Education strategies provide youth with personal skills which prepare them to find patterns of behavior free from delinquent activities, or provide skills or assistance to others to enable them to help youth develop requisite skills.

I. CLEAR AND CONSISTENT SOCIAL EXPECTATIONS strategies assume that delinquency results from competing or conflicting demands and expectations placed on youth by legitimate organizations and institutions such as media, families, schools, and communities which impinge on the lives of youth. . . . These strategies seek to increase the consistency of the expectations from different institutions, organizations, and groups which affect youth.

J. ECONOMIC RESOURCE strategies assume that delinquency results when people do not have adequate economic resources. They seek to provide basic resources to preclude the need for delinquency.

K. DETERRENCE strategies assume that delinquency results because there is a low degree of risk or difficulty associated with committing delinquent acts. . . . They seek to increase the cost and decrease the benefit of criminal acts through restricting opportunities and minimizing incentives to engage in crime.

L. ABANDONMENT OF LEGAL CONTROL/SOCIAL TOLERANCE strategies assume that delinquency results from social responses which treat youth's behaviors as delinquent. These strategies seek to remove the label "delinquent" from certain behaviors.[3]

This typology illustrates the wide variety of possible delinquency prevention strategies, as well as the close connection between program design and theory. In the first chapter of this book, we emphasized this connection as very important to understanding juvenile delinquency control efforts. It is necessary, though, to understand that although prevention strategies *can* be closely linked

[3]J. David Hawkins, Paul A. Pastor, Jr., Michelle Bell, and Sheila Morrison, *A Typology of Cause-Focused Strategies of Delinquency Prevention* (Washington, D.C.: U.S. Government Printing Office, 1980), pp. 11–25.

to theories of delinquency causation, in practice the theoretical basis for programs is often unstated or misunderstood by program clients, staff, and the general public.

Although the pure prevention and rehabilitation prevention dichotomy, as well as the more detailed descriptions of types of prevention programs, were selected to facilitate discussion, it is difficult to pigeonhole prevention efforts into such neat categories because many programs include youths varying considerably in the seriousness of their delinquency. Most programs range in the continuum from pure prevention to rehabilitative prevention, and many use a combination of strategies.

An overview of both pure prevention and rehabilitative prevention programs follows. For the overview, we have chosen programs to illustrate a wide variety of the strategies identified in Hawkins' typology. Whenever possible, programs which have been rigorously evaluated were chosen.

Since the 1930s there have been several shifts in the types of prevention programs which are most often used. The need to illustrate these shifts was another consideration in the choice of programs to describe. These shifts roughly parallel changes in the delinquency causation theories which were in vogue at different periods of time. As juvenile justice practitioners and citizens who influence the choice of prevention programs, you should know of prior efforts and the degree to which their success or failure is documented by research. It also is instructive to be aware of the way in which certain types of prevention programs have become very popular for a period of time, and then have been replaced by new approaches. The replacement is never complete, so that today we have many different types of programs in use, though some are more common than others.

As well as being influenced by current theories of delinquency causation, changes in program emphasis result from changes in political climate:

> While prevention has become recognized as an important aspect of juvenile crime control, debate regarding the best prevention methods currently remains intense. Juvenile delinquency is a complex issue influenced by family, school, peer, employment, community, physiological, psychological, and legal variables. The field of delinquency prevention has been marked by the clamor of competing advocates for a variety of approaches targeting different combinations of these variables.[4]

In developing your own opinions about the adequacy and desirability of a prevention strategy, you will be less influenced by fads if you use your judgment to assess the worth of the theory underlying each program. Earlier chapters of this book emphasized the development of this skill. You should also pay close attention to the evidence from evaluation research as a guide to form your opinion about the worth of a particular type of prevention program.

[4]*Ibid.*, p. 1.

PURE PREVENTION PROGRAMS

There are several general types of pure prevention programs, including national federal efforts to offer services to individual youths, local efforts to strengthen the communities with high delinquency rates, and local programs that try to identify and treat individuals. Chapter 8 provides a detailed review of individual treatment methods that are used in pure prevention and rehabilitation programs. Federal and community programs are described below, and available research on their effectiveness is presented. Unfortunately, relatively little funding has been available to evaluate pure prevention efforts, so their success is uncertain.[5]

Early Community-Based Programs

The early community-oriented delinquency prevention programs are of considerable interest today, for they attempted to change the environmental settings that are conducive to delinquency. After the early emphasis on community programs waned, individual treatment programs grew in popularity. However, numerous studies have shown that the roots of the delinquency problem do not reside in individuals, but rather in the larger social problems in communities, families, and schools.[6] It may be that some of the early community intervention models provide the most useful starting point for the design of new prevention efforts.

The Chicago Area Project. One of the earliest projects to deal with the problem of juvenile delinquency as well as other social problems was the Chicago Area Project. This project was based on the causation theories of Shaw and McKay (Chapter 3), and Shaw himself took an active role in implementing and designing the project. Shaw viewed immigrant parents in the slums of the 1930s

as people who needed help in developing a sense of community and in finding ways to adjust more effectively to a totally different culture. Delinquency and other social ills might be prevented if parents and neighborhoods could learn to control their own children and could provide them with educational and other resources, so that as they grew up they would be better adapted to urban industrial life than their parents.[7]

[5]William E. Wright and Michael C. Dixon, "Community Prevention and Treatment of Juvenile Delinquency: A Review of Evaluation Studies," *Journal of Research in Crime and Delinquency, 14,* no. 1 (January 1977), pp. 35–67, p. 36.

[6]For a summary of this research, see Gayle Olson-Raymer, "The Role of the Federal Government in Juvenile Delinquency Prevention," *Journal of Criminal Law and Criminology, 74,* no. 2 (Summer 1983), pp. 594–595.

[7]Lamar T. Empey, *American Delinquency: Its Meaning and Construction* (Homewood, Illinois: The Dorsey Press, 1978), p. 257; see also Solomon Kobrin, "The Chicago Area Project—a Twenty-Five-Year Assessment," in *Juvenile Delinquency: A Book of Readings,* ed. Rose Giallombardo (New York: John Wiley and Sons, Inc., 1966), pp. 473–482.

The project concentrated its efforts in areas of high delinquency and crime in an attempt to mobilize the support of the community so that delinquency could be prevented and new opportunity structures provided for area residents. Such programs as the sponsorship of recreation projects, a campaign for community improvement, and other efforts directed at helping youngsters were initiated. Both professional and volunteer workers provided personalized services, and the concentration of resources in the area was felt to contribute to more effective problem solving. Even though objective research on the success of the program is minimal, this was a very early attempt to mobilize community resources in high-crime areas. It was felt that if legitimate opportunities were provided for youngsters, much of the frustration and strain that exist in the disadvantaged areas of large cities could be reduced, and this could have a direct impact on reducing crime and delinquency.

In an analysis of historical archives, Steven Schlossman and Michael Sedlak have provided new insights into the activities and the effects of the Chicago Area Project.[8] They concentrated on the records of the Russell Square committee, one of the more effective neighborhood organizations that attempted to prevent delinquency. The Russell Square committee was concerned with preventing delinquency through recreation, including a boys' club program; through community self-renewal efforts such as improvement in the neighborhood's physical appearance and restriction of bars, brothels, and fences; and through "curbstone counseling" of youths and coordination with the school and parole officials. Even though scholars have debated the degree to which the Russell Square committee reduced delinquency, the program is unique in its creative implementation of prevention efforts.

The Midcity Project. The Midcity Project was initiated in a lower-socioeconomic class district of Boston in 1954 to reduce the amount of illegal activity engaged in by local adolescents.[9] The focus was somewhat similar to that of the Chicago Area Project because of its thrust in a large inner-city area to reduce and prevent crime and delinquency. This multifaceted program had as one of its major goals the improving of coordination and cooperation between the existing social agencies of the community. In addition, the project attempted to identify and work with chronic problem families within the area who had histories of long use of public welfare services and other government programs. Workers were assigned to the area to develop positive relations with juveniles so that problem solving could be facilitated. Between June 1954 and May 1957 seven project field workers maintained contact with approximately four hundred youngsters between the ages of twelve and twenty-one.

A summary of the findings and an evaluation of the project indicate that there was no significant measurable inhibition of either law violation or unethical

---

[8]Steven Schlossman and Michael Sedlak, *The Chicago Area Project* (Santa Monica, California: Rand, 1983).

[9]Walter Miller, "The Impact of a 'Total Community' Delinquency Control Project," in Giallombardo, *Juvenile Delinquency,* p. 493.

behavior as a consequence of project efforts. However, the cooperation and communication between residents and agencies had been improved.

South Central Youth Project. The South Central Youth Project was established by the Community Welfare Council of Hennepin County, Minneapolis.[10] The project was directed by a planning committee, which included executives of both public and private agencies. Like the Midcity Project, one of its major objectives was to make community agencies more responsive to community residents' needs. In addition, because of many interagency problems, services were not being adequately provided to youngsters and families within this area. The goal of the project was to detect the beginning stages of delinquency and to improve interagency communication and agency cooperation with community residents. Although it was felt that some of the existing agencies within the community were effective, many residents were not receiving the benefit of community resources. These residents lived in the south-central area of Hennepin County.

Most of these residents were socially and economically disadvantaged and did not know how to utilize community resources or operate within large bureaucratic structures. The project focused on identifying those families that needed help but were not getting it, so that resources could be provided. This project, like other programs mentioned, has not undergone rigorous evaluation. One of the conclusions reached as a result of the South Central Youth Project was that agencies established to service community residents are often ineffective. There is a lack of cooperation between the agencies themselves as well as a lack of communication between the agencies and the community residents. New insights were gained as a result of this project in regard to the process of developing linkage between the agencies and the community residents.

The Central Harlem Street Club Project. The Central Harlem Street Club Project was operated under the guidance of the Welfare Council of New York City.[11] The council, a volunteer organization, was created in 1925 to act as a coordinating and planning center for welfare and health services in the boroughs of New York City. Financial support for the project was obtained from such varied sources as individual contributions and foundations. The project began in 1947 and ended in 1950. The target population was four gangs, whose membership ranged from thirty-five to over one hundred. Workers involved in the project contacted about three hundred members and frequent contact was made with about half of this number. The gangs selected were the most antisocial in the area, and they were involved in many delinquent activities within their communities. There was also much intergang conflict and fighting. Many boys joined gangs because of their need for the protection provided by the gang.

[10]Gisele Konopka, "South Central Youth Project: A Delinquency Control Program (1955–57)," *Annals of the American Academy of Political and Social Science,* 322 (1959), pp. 30–37.

[11]D. Molamun and J. R. Dumpson, *Working with Teenage Gangs* (New York: Welfare Council of New York City, 1950).

Much of the activity in a gang included loitering and was conducive to the development of unproductive and negative personal habits. The workers in the project attempted to influence gang members so that their activities would be more socially acceptable. Developing a relationship with the youngsters was often difficult because of the conditions that existed in Harlem and the resentment of the youngsters in the area.

This program was limited because of a lack of funds. Lack of resources hindered an intensive evaluation of the program, although the accomplishments listed showed that at least some negative behavior was altered because of the youngsters' relationship with the workers. Also, in some cases, more appropriate alternative modes of environmental adaptation were presented to the youths.

The community-based programs that have been presented so far have some characteristics in common. They were all initiated in areas of high crime and delinquency, and attempts were made to link community resources to area residents. The theories underlying these programs emphasized the influences on delinquency of poverty, the disorganization of poor communities, and gangs in these slum areas. The programs were major efforts intended to eradicate these causes or, in some instances, to help youths and their families avoid the negative effects.

Community-Based Programs in the 1960s

The early emphasis on preventing delinquency by mobilizing the efforts of community residents in community problem solving grew under the auspices of the federal government during a major national effort to combat poverty. Under the influence of President John F. Kennedy, federal agencies were heavily involved in a "War on Poverty," during the 1960s. The Community Services Administration, which we have described, is the modern-day remnant of this massive effort. This involvement continued during Lyndon Baines Johnson's presidency. The emphasis is exemplified by four programs that received support from the Office of Juvenile Delinquency and Youth Development of the Department of Health, Education, and Welfare. (This department was subsequently divided into the Department of Health and Human Services and the Department of Education.) Similar to the Chicago Area Project, these programs were based on the assumption that social, structural, and environmental pathology were major causes of youthful deviance. The opportunity theory developed by Cloward and Ohlin was an additional basis for many program designs intended to open up new opportunities for poor people.

> The projects varied greatly in size, geography and programs—efforts were directed to the evaluating and examining of a variety of issues relevant to community organizations represented within the six projects.[12]

[12]These six programs are described in Charles Grosser, *Helping Youth, A Study of Six Community Organization Programs,* U.S. Department of Health, Education, and Welfare, Office of Juvenile Delinquency and Youth Development.

Mobilization for Youth.   One of the main objectives of the Mobilization for Youth project was to overcome the apathy and defeatism of the slum dweller through a system of self-help programs which attempted to organize the unaffiliated residents of the target area.

> The rationale was that youth could not be successfully integrated into socially constructive community life unless their adult role models (parents, etc.) themselves were a part of the community.[13]

The target selected was a sixty-seven-square-block area on the east side of New York, with a population of one hundred thousand persons. The goal of the project was to organize the various groups in this area into an effective source of power. It was felt that individuals in the community were unable to deal with poor housing, poor schools, inadequate police protection, and other issues themselves, and that in a coordinated group effort many of these problems could be dealt with and solved through pressure exerted by the "people's" organizations. This project met with resistance from one of the city's largest newspapers, as well as from many government officials. There was little cooperation or open acceptance by many government units and public officials within the community, and an investigation of the program did turn up irregularities, such as administrative difficulties.

United Planning Organization.   The United Planning Organization project focused on a high-delinquency area of Washington, D.C. A strong relationship between juvenile delinquent activity and socioeconomic conditions was thought to exist in this area, which contained many youngsters who had come in contact with the juvenile justice system. Because the opportunity structure within this area was obviously not conducive to the youngsters' achieving their goals and satisfying their needs in a socially acceptable manner, it was felt that better community coordination and more efficient delivery of services from community agencies would solve many of the problems.

The development of self-help organizations and the involvement of citizens in community decision making were encouraged. Citizen involvement in problem solving was felt to be one of the answers to developing awareness of the problems and fostering community participation.

Neighborhood centers were developed to filter information about the problems of the community to residents and serve as headquarters for disseminating information. One of the strategies of the project was to change the attitudes of both the residents and the institutions established to serve them. It was estimated that at the peak of the project there were twenty-five block clubs as well as many other organizations working to solve the problems of the area. Better leadership and more active citizen involvement resulted in some projects being more successful than others.

---

[13]*Ibid.,* p. 7.

The decentralized approach to decision making and administration was felt to be more conducive to citizen involvement than a centralized orientation. A shortcoming of the decentralized approach, however, was that communication channels were often garbled and therefore coordination between different projects and citizen groups was difficult. One of the most interesting aspects of the program was the wide acceptance and use of credit unions owned and operated by community citizens who lived within the target area. Before the United Planning Organization, there was only one credit union for the poor. After the success of the community-operated credit union, similar credit unions emerged in the community and were supported by the residents.

This project also emphasized the solving of practical problems such as housing and unemployment. One of the major efforts was the development of a housing project. United Planning Organization did encounter some administrative difficulties, as did the Mobilization for Youth program.

Action for Appalachian Youth.   The Action for Appalachian Youth program focused on an area near Charleston, West Virginia. The basic premise was that value conflicts between urban and rural society were a source of much tension, strain, and frustration. This supposedly creates a system where there is a lack of "meshing" between persons within the same environment, and this lack of meshing creates conflicts, which in turn contribute to social problems, such as delinquent behavior.[14]

The residents of the target areas were difficult to reach because of such geographical factors as mountains, ridges, and creeks. It took a great deal of physical endurance even to make contact with the residents. Furthermore, because of long years of isolation, the people had developed a lifestyle much different from that of "conventional persons," which made communication very difficult. Each target "hollow" was assigned a neighborhood worker. The worker's presence was difficult to explain because there was no precedent for such a program. It took a long time to become acquainted with the residents.

Some of the main concerns of the residents were the need for better roads and increased recreational facilities. As a result of assistance provided by the worker, various improvement associations evolved with elected officers, committees, and regular meetings.

Numerous problem issues were raised and discussed at these meetings, and petitions were circulated to elicit public opinion and support.

Each neighborhood improvement association sent delegates to a general council which functioned on a countywide basis. A technique of the neighborhood staff worker was one of nonintervention—a nondirective approach was used with the community. Some workers questioned this role because they felt that a more active, aggressive approach was needed to help solve problems in these isolated backward areas. The project and the contact of the worker with

[14]*Ibid.*, p. 37.

the community facilitated communication, problem delineation, and in some cases problem solving.

The HARYOU ACT. The HARYOU ACT (Harlem Youth Opportunities, Unlimited, Associated Community Teams) was initiated in Harlem, New York, a target area of a quarter-million people, 94 percent black, living in a three-and-a-half-square-mile urban area. The program attempted to increase the chances for the youth in the community to lead productive lives and develop socially acceptable types of behavior.[15]

Even though the goal of the program was commendable, it did encounter difficulties in administration and pressures were exerted by various interest groups. There was also competition within the program itself, and "too much was expected too fast."

The massive problems that existed in the Harlem area, along with the administrative and pressure group difficulties, hindered the effective operation of the program.

The Impact of Programs in the 1960s. Unfortunately, many of the potential positive results of the last four programs described were neutralized by inefficient administration, internal problems, and conflict between community interest groups. The actual positive results are also difficult to determine because the areas in which the programs were focused had many massive problems.

Ideally, programs of this kind could do much to solve community ills and help reduce crime and delinquency; however, many of the goals initially established were not achieved. If methods of research and project evaluation were built into all projects dealing with community improvement and crime and delinquency problem solving, the positive and negative aspects could be clearly identified. When program results are not identified, it is difficult to induce community involvement and obtain financial support from the government structure. When there are not sound methods of administrative control and a clearly defined goal orientation, many internal difficulties arise and overall sponsorship of the necessary government and private units is difficult to obtain.

In some cases, there are indications that certain program strategies used in the early programs should be avoided. The clearest example of this is the research finding that work with gangs can increase members' solidarity, which *increases* the potential for delinquency.[16]

All the programs discussed so far are pure prevention efforts, in that their major focus is an attempt to alleviate conditions that breed crime and delinquency by involving community residents in problem solving and decision making. The youngster is assisted before there is any contact with the formal juvenile justice system.

---

[15]*Ibid.*, p. 44.

[16]Malcolm W. Klein, "On the Group Context of Delinquency," *Sociology and Social Research*, *54*, no. 2 (July 1969), pp. 63–71.

Federal Prevention Efforts

For many years, the federal government has made vigorous attempts to prevent delinquency and has provided financial support through its various departments. By 1980, federal efforts had reached a peak.[17] Since that time, there has been reduced federal support and a shift in focus has occurred. This shift is summed up in the phrase, "Not Social Problems but Justice." As noted in Chapter 6, Handling the Juvenile Delinquent within the Juvenile Justice System, due process and punishment are now emphasized in many states. This emphasis is mirrored at the federal level. The change in emphasis is apparent when we examine the history of federal efforts since the 1970s.

The Juvenile Justice and Delinquency Prevention Act of 1974 (P.L. 93-415) provided for the coordination of federal delinquency programs, and established juvenile delinquency prevention as a national priority. The act established an Office of Juvenile Justice and Delinquency Prevention (OJJDP) and, within that office, a National Institute for Juvenile Justice and Delinquency Prevention (NIJJDP) as its research, evaluation, and information center. OJJDP is located in the Department of Justice. There are several provisions in the act that ensure a coordinated interagency and interdisciplinary approach to the delinquency problem. It established overall objectives and priorities and created a coordinating council on juvenile justice and delinquency prevention and the National Advisory Committee on Juvenile Justice and Delinquency Prevention. The coordinating council has representatives of federal agencies and is chaired by the attorney general. The advisory committee is composed of private citizens appointed by the President, over one-third of the members being under the age of twenty-six at the time of their appointment.[18]

Not only is OJJDP responsible for coordinating other federal efforts and establishing national guidelines and objectives, but it funds several delinquency prevention and control programs across the country. These programs are demonstrations of innovative approaches and attempts to implement major federal policies at the state and local levels. In the past, funds have been allocated to initiate diversion programs, alternatives to institutions, and special services for status offenders. Other funded efforts include programs to keep youths in school and prevent unwarranted suspensions and expulsions, restitution programs, and programs for particularly serious offenders. Projects which replicate successful programs also have received funds, particularly those which are designated as "Exemplary Projects" by a panel of experts who advise OJJDP.

The 1984 Report of the National Advisory Committee for Juvenile Justice and Delinquency Prevention recommended a changed emphasis for re-

[17]Olson-Raymer, "The Role of the Federal Government in Juvenile Delinquency Prevention," p. 581.

[18]National Advisory Committee for Juvenile Justice and Delinquency Prevention, *Standards for the Administration of Juvenile Justice* (Washington, D.C.: U.S. Government Printing Office, 1980).

search and for the Exemplary and other programs.[19] In essence, the report suggests that the prior federal emphasis has been on status and other minor offenders, and has not been directed at the serious, repeat offender who commits most of the crime and is therefore the greatest threat to the public. The report does acknowledge that prior efforts to deinstitutionalize status offenders and divert youths from the system have produced some good results. Yet, there is a need to invest most current resources in the understanding and control of the chronic offender. Programs are needed to better identify, apprehend, prosecute, treat, or incarcerate the most serious delinquents.

The Habitual Serious and Violent Offender Program is one of the initiatives that the federal government has supported as part of its response to serious offenders.[20] Serious and repeat juvenile offenders were to receive intensive attention from experienced prosecutors, and victims and witnesses also have been provided with special services. In addition to the procedural changes intended to increase the chances that a youth would be found delinquent, the program provides for special diagnostic assessment, treatment plans, and case management after the finding of delinquency. Despite the provision for follow-up treatment, the primary focus of the program is to improve the probability of conviction. For example, this program makes it possible for prosecutors to remain with a case until it has moved through all steps of court contact; it discourages plea bargaining, and it supports victims and witnesses. Just one-third of the funding was allocated for corrections, and only a small proportion of program participants actually received correctional services.

Besides the focus on Habitual Serious and Violent Offenders, the OJJDP and the U.S. Department of Education have jointly supported the growth of the National School Safety Center (NSSC). The activities of the Center are to:

- Promote interagency cooperation and replication of exemplary school safety techniques and programs.
- Expand training resources in school safety and delinquency prevention to provide appropriate skills development for law enforcement and other criminal justice personnel.
- Instruct educators in school safety issues, including organizational management, law in the school, child abuse reporting, and law-related educational curriculum development.
- Assist schools in developing techniques to involve business leaders, criminal justice professionals, and community leaders in school safety and delinquency prevention.
- Collect and disseminate information on school safety and delinquency prevention, criminal law, rules, and procedures in federal, state, and local jurisdictions.[21]

The NSSC has stimulated numerous schools to develop school crime prevention

---

[19]National Advisory Committee for Juvenile Justice and Delinquency Prevention, *Serious Juvenile Crime: A Redirected Federal Effort* (Washington, D.C.: U.S. Government Printing Office, 1984).

[20]Robert C. Cronin, Blair B. Bourque, Jane M. Mell, Frances E. Gragg and Alison A. McGrady, "Evaluation of the Habitual Serious and Violent Juvenile Offender Program: Executive Summary," (Washington, D.C.: U.S. Department of Justice, January, 1988).

[21]Verne L. Speirs, "School Safety Programs," *NIJ Reports,* (July 1986), pp. 8–11.

and control programs. Consistent with the general thrust of contemporary federal efforts, many of these programs include strong law enforcement components, though some also provide prevention and treatment.

Besides state and local efforts, several federal departments besides OJJDP have, at one time or another, been involved in delinquency programming. Despite decreased federal involvement since the mid-1980s, many of these programs continue in reduced form or have been taken over by state or local governmental units.

Department of Labor. The United States Department of Labor Manpower Administration operates youth-serving activities under the Employment and Training Administration. The Job Corps is one of these programs:

> The in-school program provides part-time employment, on-the-job training and useful work experience for youths still in school or in need of money to remain in school. The out-of-school program provides work and training and sufficient supportive services to obtain meaningful employment for unemployed or underemployed low-income persons. The summer program is designed to offer training, work experience and income to help disadvantaged students to return to school in the fall.[22]

In 1977, the Youth Employment and Demonstration Projects Act authorized four additional programs, which are the Youth Employment and Training Programs, the Youth Community Conservation and Improvement Projects, the Youth Incentive Entitlement Pilot Projects, and the Young Adult Conservation Corps. These programs are generally oriented toward groups of youths who are experiencing the most severe difficulties entering the job market, and they often include educational and training components to improve participants' skills.

Research has not clearly demonstrated that Department of Labor programs are effective in the control of delinquency. A major study that was carried out between 1975 and 1977 found that work support did little to decrease delinquent activities.[23] The root of the problem was that youth felt the program could not prepare them for entry level jobs or careers.

Community Services Administration. The Community Services Administration also provides services that either directly or indirectly relate to delinquency prevention. The programs under the Community Services Administration, like those under the Department of Labor, are an effort by the government to funnel resources into areas with high rates of crime and delinquency, as well as other social problems, in an attempt at social problem solving. Resources funneled into areas of high crime and delinquency rates can be effectively utilized to

---

[22]*Annual Report of Federal Activities in Juvenile Delinquency, Youth Development and Related Fields,* U.S. Department of Health, Education, and Welfare, Social and Rehabilitation Service, 1971, p. 109.

[23]Manpower Demonstration Research Corporation, *Summary and Findings of the National Supported Work Demonstration,* 1980.

develop favorable alternatives in behavioral adjustment for youngsters who are not exposed to an adequate opportunity structure. Cooperative endeavors by the federal government and local communities can facilitate the development of pure prevention programs, which will improve community conditions and help reduce delinquency and crime.

Because they are based on a philosophy of local involvement, Community Services Administration programs are frequently unique efforts at the community level. Project Uplift is one example of such an effort, for it combines community concern for both the juvenile delinquent and the elderly victim:

> Project Uplift, operated by the Peoria (Ill.) Commission on Economic Opportunity, aims at reducing juvenile crime while at the same time reducing the fear of the community's elderly of being victimized. An Elderly Escort Service operating in conjunction with a new Youth Center was established during the first year. (Local police officials actively advise on the program.) During its second year, the project expanded its escort service to more closely relate the youths to the older escortees through clean-up projects plus a job training program for actual and potential juvenile delinquents.[24]

The National Youth Sports Program is sponsored by the Community Services Administration in a number of different communities:

> The program provides an opportunity for economically disadvantaged youths to benefit from sports skills instruction, engage in sports competition and improve their physical fitness. In addition, each participant must receive a minimum of three hours per week of enrichment activities which include drug/alcohol abuse education and instructions on job responsibilities. They also receive medical exams, counseling in study practices, positive attitudes and career opportunities.[25]

Whether a Community Services Administration program is originated in the community or at a national level, it is intended to strengthen the basic community structure by creating economic and other opportunities or by alleviating social problems. For this reason, these programs are of considerable importance in the prevention and control of delinquency.

Department of Education.   The activities of the Department of Education range from the funding of state and local programs to educational research and training programs. Some programs funded under the Youth Act of 1980 are highly targeted basic skills programs for youths in grades 7 through 12. Among these programs are alternative education and work projects for out-of-school youths, and vocational educational coordination.

Similar to the federal efforts we have discussed already, those sponsored by the Department of Education are oriented toward providing opportunities

---

[24]*Community Services Administration: Creating Opportunity,* Annual Report Fiscal Year 1979 (Washington, D.C.: Community Services Administration, 1980), p. 12.
[25]*Ibid.,* p. 37.

and are targeted to the very populations which are frequently delinquent. In particular, youths who have difficulties in school and who cannot find status through employment are often the very youths who are involved in delinquent activities.

Department of Agriculture. Federal extension services under the Department of Agriculture provide programs for youngsters which can often indirectly contribute to reducing juvenile delinquent activities. The 4-H program operated under the Federal Extension Services branch of the Department of Agriculture has become increasingly involved in preventing delinquency in urban areas:

> Cooperative Extension Service agents work through schools, churches, service clubs, public housing directors, juvenile correctional institutions, neighborhood councils and centers, community action panels, etc., to introduce 4-H programs and methods. Professional Extension staff are assisting in the programs through the use of paid program assistance and by volunteer adult and teen-age leaders.[26]

For example, in Saginaw County, Michigan, a special preventive juvenile delinquency program called *Outreach* uses high-risk, wilderness adventure experiences to increase youths' self-confidence, and in this way to reduce delinquency. Several of the 4-H Clubs of Michigan sponsor a personal development and drug prevention program in both rural and urban areas:

> *High on Myself* approaches substance abuse prevention through a process that helps young people develop skills that they can use to help themselves. It focuses on the emotional development of the individual and opportunities for growth. The strategy is to provide experiences where young people can develop the positive skills and feelings they need to become a mature person. The activities include self-concept building, communication skills, values clarification, problem-solving skills, decision-making skills, and stress reduction. The activities are experiential in that they provide opportunities for growth by allowing the individual to actively participate in his/her own learning. *High on Myself* is a program involving both youth and adults, with adults doing things with kids, not for or to them.[27]

These programs which focus on troubled youths or which are preventive, including those in urban areas, build on a nationwide interest in delivering delinquency prevention services through the 4-H model.

Federal extension programs under the Department of Agriculture have mainly served rural youths, but because of an increased awareness of the many problems that exist in urban areas an attempt is being made to provide resources to the cities so that many of these problems can be eliminated or alleviated. The

---

[26]*Annual Report of Federal Activities*, p. 107.

[27]Judy Ann Goth-Owens, *High on Myself: A 4-H Substance Abuse Prevention Program* (East Lansing: Cooperative Extension Service, Michigan State University, 1979), p. 1.

resources provided by the government to these communities can be helpful in identifying problems and initiating programs for their solution.

Contemporary Local Prevention—Police, Schools, and Community

For a number of reasons, there has been a shift away from community change-oriented programs such as those described above. They are still used, and in South Chicago, where the Chicago Area Project first operated, the Mexican Community Committee continues in the tradition of Shaw's original plan.[28] The Mexican Community Committee consists of community residents who volunteer substantial time to the community treatment of juvenile misconduct and crime. Close relationships exist between the committee and schools, the juvenile court and the police, and every effort is made to convince these institutions that the community can rehabilitate most of the Hispanic delinquents in South Chicago. Even though there are some important differences between the present-day efforts in South Chicago and the early Chicago Area Project, the community continues to demonstrate an interest in diverting and handling large numbers of community youth who come into contact with the juvenile justice system. Despite the continuity of the Chicago Area Projects, in general community efforts are not the most predominant type of pure prevention program. Richard Lundman and Frank Scarpitti concluded from an extensive review of the literature on prevention programs:

> With but a few exceptions, we found that previous delinquency prevention efforts reflected psychological understandings of the causes of juvenile delinquency. As a consequence, attention has been directed toward treatment of individuals.[29]

A number of the individual treatment methods used in prevention and rehabilitation programs are reviewed in the next chapter.

Here, we will focus attention on contemporary prevention programs which do not stress individual treatment. In order to provide a balanced view of the range of programs, we will describe a community development program staffed by police, school programs, and a community-based effort to improve the financial resources available to programs for youths. We have already discussed prevention programs aimed at the family (Chapter 4).

The Flint Neighborhood Foot Patrol Program. The Flint Police Department operated solely with motorized or preventive patrols until January, 1979, at

---

[28]Beryl Schlossman, Gail Zellman, and Richard J. Shavelson, *Delinquency Prevention in South Chicago: A Fifty-year Assessment of the Chicago Area Project.* (Santa Monica, California: Rand, 1984), p. 32.

[29]Richard J. Lundman and Frank R. Scarpitti, "Delinquency Prevention: Recommendations for Future Projects," *Crime and Delinquency, 24,* no. 2 (April 1978), p. 214.

which point the Charles Stewart Mott Foundation provided funding for the implementation of an experimental community-based foot patrol.[30]

Flint's Neighborhood Foot Patrol Program was unique in a variety of ways. It emerged from an initiative which integrated citizens into the planning and implementation process through citywide neighborhood meetings in 1977 and 1978. It attempted to ameliorate three distinct problems: (1) the absence of comprehensive neighborhood organizations and services; (2) the lack of citizen involvement in crime prevention; and (3) the depersonalization of interactions between officers and residents. The program began in 1979 with twenty-two foot patrol officers assigned to fourteen experimental areas which included about 20 percent of the city's population. The activity and efforts of the foot officers addressed seven basic goals:

1. To decrease the amount of actual or perceived criminal activity.
2. To increase the citizen's perception of personal safety.
3. To deliver to Flint residents a type of law enforcement service consistent with the community needs and the ideas of modern police practice.
4. To create a community awareness of crime problems and methods of increasing law enforcement's ability to deal with actual or potential criminal activity effectively.
5. To develop citizen volunteer action in support of, and under the direction of, the police department, aimed at various target crimes.
6. To eliminate citizen apathy about reporting crime to police.
7. To increase protection for women, children, and the aged.

The Flint program's salient features were a radical departure from both preventive patrol and traditional foot patrol models. Flint's foot patrol officers did not limit their activities to downtown or business areas. They were based in and accessible to all types of socioeconomic neighborhoods. Their crime prevention efforts went beyond organizing neighborhood watches. They attempted to serve as *catalysts* in the formation of neighborhood associations which articulate community expectations of the police, establish foot patrol priorities, and initiate community programs. Foot patrol officers also worked in partnership with community organizations and individual citizens to deliver a comprehensive set of services through referrals, interventions, and *links* to governmental social agencies.

The foot patrol officers reconciled their role with the reality of policing; they not only provided full law enforcement services, as did their motorized counterparts, but they made a conscious effort to focus on the social service aspects of their job, bringing problems to a resolution. Since they patrolled and interacted in the same areas day after day, week after week, they develop a degree of intimacy with residents which translated into an effective cooperative relationship.

---

[30]Robert C. Trojanowicz, et al., *An Evaluation of the Neighborhood Foot Patrol Program in Flint, Michigan* (East Lansing, Michigan: The National Neighborhood Foot Patrol Center, Michigan State University, 1982.)

The Flint Police Department's two forms of patrol operated on the basis of relatively distinct organizational objectives and managerial patterns. Foot officers mobilized citizens in order to provide a matrix within which communities can identify and deal with many of their own problems, including—but not exclusively—crime. With the advice, consent, and direction of citizens, foot officers targeted, addressed, and resolved specific community-level concerns— juvenile alienation, victimization of the aged, neighborhood safety and security, and so on. By comparison, motor officers continued to adhere to the narrowly oriented preventive strategy of "crime control," reacting to events after they occurred.

Motor patrol officers perceived social service as an annoying interlude between periods of "real" police activity—pursuit, investigation, arrest; foot officers enjoyed a comprehensive, integrated, and realistic sense of their role in their emphasis on social service as part of community-based crime control. Where motor officers were subject to alternating bouts of inactivity and intense, frenzied periods, foot officers were able to maintain a consistent level of activity. During "down" periods, motor officers did not utilize their skills on a proactive basis; foot officers not only exercised their proactive skills continuously, but they developed and nurtured new talents in their community organizer, linkage, and catalyst capacity.

Supervisory personnel within the Flint Police Department adapted their methods according to the form of patrol for which they were responsible. Motor patrol supervisors continued to measure success primarily in terms of the number of calls made and response time. They adhered to the semimilitary model of authority, with some supervisors infrequently interacting with officers, either individually or collectively. Roll call remained an impersonal exercise which averaged twelve minutes and involved all officers and sergeants on a given shift. Sergeants did not necessarily assume responsibility for a stable pool of officers, because shift rotations and sector assignments changed frequently. Sergeants reviewed officers monthly. They were compelled to interact with individual officers directly only when performance seemed to be deficient.

Sergeants responsible for foot patrol officers encouraged a participatory mode of supervision. Supervisors meet daily with the eight officers assigned to a specific sector. The briefings, which average thirty-one minutes, were used to exchange information and to develop community-based strategies. The sergeants were familiar with the individual officers and knew their accomplishments well. When necessary, sergeants assisted and supplemented individual efforts, but did not interfere with the autonomy each officer enjoyed in defining community problems and programs. The decision-making freedom which sergeants permitted foot patrol officers was reflected in the availability of flexible or "flex" time. Although scheduled for either morning or afternoon shifts, foot patrol officers elected to work an evening or two instead. The only constraint on such flexibility is that the officer's alternate schedule had to be responsive to the community's needs.

The supervisory and management role in foot patrol was less directed and uniform. Supervisory and command personnel served as resources and conduits for foot patrol officers and their communities. They became the repository for citywide information, which facilitated community involvement in the crime-prevention and -solving process. Under ideal circumstances, supervisors coordinated and prioritized community activities according to available resources and community needs. They did not impose cumbersome bureaucratic procedures on either foot patrol officers or on community residents.

Some of the results of the Flint experiment have been reported elsewhere. Briefly, the Neighborhood Foot Patrol Program reduced crime rates by 8.7 percent. More dramatic were the reductions in calls for service, which decreased by 42 percent over the period 1979–1982. Citizens began handling minor problems themselves, or the foot officer acted as mediator on an informal basis, negating the need for a formal complaint.

Although the impact on calls for service alone was significant, additional evidence indicated that citizens felt safer, were satisfied with the program, felt that it had impacted the crime rates, and that it had improved police-community relations. There was much closer interaction between the foot officers and citizens. Over 33 percent of neighborhood residents knew their foot patrol officers by name, and 50 percent of the rest could provide accurate descriptions of foot officers. Citizens also felt that foot officers were more effective than motor officers in encouraging crime reporting, in involving citizens in neighborhood crime-prevention efforts, in working with juveniles, in encouraging citizen self-protection, and in following up on complaints. The foot patrol officers themselves felt well integrated into the communities they served, minimizing their sense of isolation, alienation, and fear. The foot patrol experiment was so successful that the citizens of Flint passed a tax millage increase in August, 1982 which extended the program to the entire city. A three-year tax renewal was passed in June, 1985 and again in 1988.

From the inception of the program, work with juveniles was an integral part of the foot patrol officer's job. Officers were expected to have preexisting relationships with adolescents and their families and to participate in such activities as the Police Athletic League, school programs and other prevention efforts. The expected involvement with juveniles was in sharp contrast to the usual role of the police officer, in which work with juveniles is viewed as a nonessential and low-priority aspect of the job.[31]

Although the designers and administrators of the Flint Neighborhood Foot Patrol Program considered work with juveniles to be highly important, the officers were reluctant to do this work in the early stages of the project. Many felt that work with juveniles was the proper task of social workers, not police officers. Through training and supervision, efforts have been made to overcome the aversion to working with juveniles. The evaluation of the foot patrol program

[31]Egon Bittner, "Policing Juveniles: The Social Context of Common Practice," in *Pursuing Justice for the Child*, ed. Margaret K. Rosenheim (Chicago: University of Chicago Press, 1976), pp. 69–93.

indicates that there has been a shift in working with juveniles. In general, foot patrol officers were extensively involved with juveniles in their areas. This is particularly true in a public sense. That is, foot patrol officers conducted field trips to amusement parks, accepted speaking engagements, and participated in such activities as the Police Athletic League. At the same time, however, the evidence also suggested that foot patrol officers were somewhat reluctant to become involved with juvenile offenders and their families in the private setting of the home.

The Flint Neighborhood Foot Patrol Program stands as an unusual example of a program that altered the role of police to emphasize the prevention of juvenile and other crime instead of reaction to crimes that have already occurred.

Evaluation research results showed that community residents felt that the Flint foot patrol officers were more effective in handling juvenile-related problems than were motor patrol officers. Further, the foot patrol officers were able to organize and support numerous neighborhood associations throughout the city, and these associations in turn played a key role in directing police efforts to work with juveniles. Presently, Flint has a greatly reduced foot patrol effort due to financial constraints. With an increase in crime, officers are having difficulty responding to serious crime. If the economic conditions in Flint improve, foot patrol will again be emphasized.

The School and Pure Prevention.   There is increased awareness of the central role that schools can play in preventing delinquency. Every youngster spends a considerable amount of time in school, and many acts of delinquency are committed within the school setting. Research has shown that

> while family and other variables may be important at earlier stages of the development process, among high school students experiences of academic failure, weak commitments to educational pursuits and attachments to school, and association with delinquent peers appear more closely related to delinquency than do family, community, or social structural variables.

Therefore,

> school-based prevention efforts should seek to (1) increase students' experiences of academic success, (2) stimulate student attachment and commitment to school, and (3) stimulate attachments between students and non-delinquent peers as well as between students and teachers.[32]

Although the school can be viewed as an institution that could prevent delinquency, we must be aware of its role in delinquency causation and as a setting for

---

[32]J. David Hawkins and John S. Wall, *Alternative Education: Exploring the Delinquency Prevention Potential* (Washington, D.C.: U.S. Government Printing Office, 1980), pp. 9–10; see also Delbert S. Elliott and Harwin L. Voss, *Delinquency and Dropout* (Lexington, Massachusetts: D.C. Heath and Company, 1974).

delinquency. Without this awareness, it is impossible to realistically design and implement effective school-based prevention programs.

More than one of the theories that are reviewed in Chapter 3 point to the school as a factor in explaining delinquency. (Refer to Chapter 3 and to Table 3-1 for a summary of these theories.) Early in the development of sociological explanations of delinquency, Robert Merton and later Lloyd Ohlin and Richard Cloward (Opportunity Theory) tied delinquency to the experience of blocked educational and occupational goals, two factors that are closely related to the school experience. Albert Cohen (Working-Class Boy) described the frustration and anger that working-class boys felt when confronted with the expectations of middle-class teachers. It is well known that schools routinely divide youths into different achievement groups, usually tracking some of them for college and others for working-class or lower-status jobs. Edwin Lemert's analysis (Labeling Perspective) would suggest that the common practice of tracking would stigmatize youths and play a role in the development of secondary deviance, that is, a pattern of delinquent activity. Most recently, the work of Herman and Julia Schwendinger (Adolescent Subcultures, Capitalism) points to the unequal allocation of school resources as an influence on some youths to take part in delinquent peer groups and to experience failure in learning basic skills necessary in our society. Although each of the theories noted above differs from the others, they all do agree that the school plays a critical role in fostering either legal or illegal behavior.

The idea that schools do not uniformly provide a positive atmosphere for adolescent development has considerable empirical support. Many of the youths who are seriously delinquent find their school experiences to be very negative.[33] Consistent with labeling theory, these are the youths who are in school programs geared to educate students tracked into the nonacademic low-status pathways leading into occupations requiring limited skills. A study by one of the authors examined the atmosphere in junior and senior high schools in Boston.[34] Student relationships with key staff members (primarily teachers) were more formal, task-oriented, superficial, and unequal than in other kinds of community programs. In response to a series of open-ended questions, 11 percent of the youths said that in school they did not like the staff, and 16 percent volunteered that staff were not helpful or understanding. The student responses suggest that schools are often unable to provide the ties to the community that could control delinquency. Even though there are undoubtedly some communities that have the resources to provide outstanding school programs, it is realistic to assume that most delinquents attend schools where meaningful involvements are not the norm (Exhibit 7-1).

---

[33]William T. Pink, "Schools, Youth, and Justice," *Crime and Delinquency, 30,* no. 3 (July 1984), p. 444.

[34]Merry Morash, "Two Models of Community Corrections: One for the Ideal World, One for the Real World," in *Evaluating Juvenile Justice,* ed. James R. Kluegel (Beverly Hills, California: Sage Publications, 1983), pp. 47–66.

Exhibit 7-1 Problems in American high schools

Ridgefield High has much in common with most high schools from coast to coast. It is neither trouble free nor terrible. Classes are at times inspired, occasionally dreadful, and, most often, routine. A few students tackle ideas as if they were in a college seminar. Most graduate without being stretched to their potential. At Ridgefield and elsewhere, there is a kind of unwritten, unspoken contract between the teachers and the students: Keep off my back, and I'll keep off yours.

Ridgefield, along with most other high schools in the nation falls somewhere in the middle ground of academic quality. Exceptional institutions are at either end. At one extreme are the very bad, trouble-ridden schools that hold few, if any, academic goals for students; at the other are outstanding institutions—supportive and demanding—where students receive a first-class education.

Troubled high schools frequently are in inner cities where problems of population dislocation, poverty, unemployment, and crime take priority over education. They also may be found in decaying suburbs or in rural communities racked by poverty and neglect.

Students in failing urban schools often jam into battered buildings with wire-covered windows and graffiti-covered walls. Tile and other hard surfaces reflect the glare from naked light bulbs hanging in protective cages of wire.

Changing classes is like the morning rush hour in Manhattan. Students push and shove in crowded stairways, or ride dangerous elevators and escalators often brought to a quick halt by pranksters. Neighboring residents complain of noise, vandalism, and drugs.

Security guards patrol the halls, attempting to keep order. When violence breaks out, teachers often turn away. They're afraid. On a good day in such a school, the attendance is 50 percent.

Once inside the classroom, students pay little attention to the teacher, who, in turn, expects little from the students. In one such school we heard the teacher say, "I'll write on the blackboard what you need to know." In another, "Helium, we won't worry about that." In still another, "Don't worry, we won't have any hard problems on the test."

Many students are two or more years below grade level in reading and math. Few have a sense of real accomplishment. Heroic teachers can be found, but generally the faculty feel discouraged; some have given up. A handful of kids are high achievers. Most are bored, restless, and rebellious. About half drop out. Those who do graduate get odd jobs or are unemployed. Few go on to college.

SOURCE: Ernest L. Boyer, *High Schools: A Report on Secondary Education in America* (New York: Harper & Row, Publishers, 1983), pp. 15–16. Copyright © 1983 by The Carnegie Foundation for the Advancement of Teaching. Reprinted by permission of Harper & Row. Publishers, Inc.

Issues for Discussion.   Is it realistic to expect the nation's public schools to prevent delinquency? What are the pros and cons of placing delinquency prevention programs in schools? How could effective programs be implemented?

Not only do schools contribute to the general problem of delinquency, but they often are the site of much delinquent activity. The National Institute of Education sponsored the Safe Schools Study, which revealed that:

- Over 61,000 teachers were physically assaulted in 1976.
- Each month an estimated 282,000 junior and senior high school students are attacked and 112,000 are robbed.
- Although teenage youth aged 12 to 19 spend 25 percent of their waking hours in school, 40 percent of the robberies and 36 percent of the assaults (on them) occur while in school; for the 12 to 15 year age group alone these figures are 68 percent and 50 percent. The estimated annual costs of school vandalism range from $50 million to $600 million, with most estimates clustering at $100–200 million.[35]

In interpreting the findings of the Safe Schools Study, it is important to keep in mind the differences between urban and suburban or rural schools. As Robert Rubel pointed out, only about 8 percent of the school administrators reported serious problems in their schools, and most administrators felt that at the end of the 1970s, violence and vandalism leveled off.[36] Still, there is considerable violence and vandalism in urban schools, for the averages are misleading. A higher proportion of students and teachers in urban schools are victimized than in other areas, and in these urban schools the fear of crime and disruption to education pose serious threats to the learning process. Before we can even begin to consider urban schools as sites for delinquency prevention programs, it is necessary to get a handle on the illegal activity that occurs inside schools (see Table 7-1).

Three different approaches have been proposed to control delinquency inside schools or to use the schools as a site for preventing adolescents from becoming involved in delinquency in any setting. There are *legislative reform*, *improvement of existing school programs*, and the *provision of alternative education*.

There have been two general types of *legislative reform*, one aimed at changing the atmosphere within the school setting, and the other at changing the requirements for compulsory education. The National School Safety Center described state legislation aimed at the school setting:

Bills have been passed ranging from broad education reform including improved disciplinary programs to specific crime-related actions including the curtailment of drug trafficking in and about schools, and increased penalties for campus-related crime. For example, in 1984 a bipartisan coalition of legislators passed, and the governor signed, a package of bills called "California Safe Schools Program." The program will: (1) increase penalties for campus crimes; (2) require courts to notify school administrators, teachers and counselors of

[35]National Institute of Education, U.S. Department of Health, Education and Welfare, *Violent Schools—Safe Schools: The Safe School Study Report to the Congress, 1* (Washington, D.C.: U.S. Government Printing Office, 1977).

[36]Robert J. Rubel, "Analysis and Critique of HEW's Safe School Study Report to the Congress," *Crime and Delinquency, 24,* no. 3 (July 1978), pp. 257–265.

Table 7-1 Estimated Number and Percentage of Victimizations Taking Place in Schools in 1982

Type of Victimization	TOTAL		INSIDE SCHOOL	
	Number	Percent	Number	Percent
Rape and attempted rape	154,131	100	2,730	2
Robbery	980,400	100	21,944	2
Robbery and attempted robbery with injury	354,385	100	3,703	1
Serious assault	174,026	100	1,386	1
Minor assault	180,359	100	2,317	1
Robbery without injury	365,602	100	9,111	2
Attempted robbery without injury	260,414	100	9,130	4
Assault	3,690,648	100	198,465	5
Aggravated assault	1,282,421	100	36,666	3
With injury	457,464	100	18,104	4
Attempted assault with weapon	824,956	100	18,561	2
Simple assault	2,408,228	100	161,799	7
With injury	690,829	100	60,614	9
Attempted assault without weapon	1,717,399	100	101,185	6
Personal larceny with contact	507,172	100	22,164	4
Purse snatching	132,254	100	1,352	1
Attempted purse snatching	44,380	100	—	—[a]
Pocket picking	330,537	100	20,812	6
Personal larceny without contact	12,987,502	100	2,042,799	16

[a]Too small a number to accurately estimate.

Source: Timothy J. Flanagan and Maureen McLeod, *Sourcebook of Criminal Justice Statistics—1982* (U. S. Department of Justice, Bureau of Justice Statistics. Washington, D.C.: U. S. Government Printing Office, 1983), pp. 320–321.

students who have committed violent crimes; (3) require the attorney general to prepare a concise criminal and civil law summary pertinent to campus crime, violence and discipline and delineate differences between campus crimes and mere disruptive behavior; (4) require standardized reporting of school crime and evaluation of crime prevention programs; and (5) discourage disruptive "outsiders."[37]

There is a question about whether schools can be improved in isolation from the communities where they are located. Students, who are the major perpetrators of delinquency in schools, bring problems fostered by family interactions, peer group experiences, and community conditions into the school setting. It remains to be seen whether legislation, staff training, or changes in school discipline can really be effective in controlling the difficulties that have their roots outside of the school.

The proposal for eliminating mandatory school attendance has not been enacted, and it is very controversial. Jackson Toby examined the statistics on

[37]National School Safety Center, *School Safety and the Legal Community* (Sacramento, California: National School Safety Center, 1985), p. 5.

school crime and came to the conclusion that if youths were not required to attend school against their will, there would be a marked decrease in violence.[38] He noted that the rates of assault on, and robberies of, students by students is higher in junior high schools than in senior high schools. He reasoned the junior high students are more likely to be involuntary students, whereas by the high school years, such students drop out. Toby notes that prior attempts to persuade youths to attend school have not been successful, and even compulsory education has little effect, for it does not guarantee either attendance or involvement in school activities. His solution is to allow disinterested and alienated students to leave school, and in fact to prohibit them from entering school once they have officially dropped out.

We turn now to programs oriented toward altering the curriculum, atmosphere, and structure of existing schools. The *social development approach*, as developed by Joseph G. Weis and his associates, stands as an instructive example of the potential for prevention through school change as well as the many difficulties in bringing about such change. Recognizing the crucial tie between empirically tested theory and the design of prevention programs, Weis, Sederstrom, and Hawkins began with a review of the available research in an effort to identify the major causes of juvenile delinquency. Drawing on the research to test social control and cultural deviance theory (described in Chapter 3), they proposed that the process of social development rested on opportunities for involvement and interaction with legitimate institutions and people.[39] If these opportunities were coupled with a youth's skills for involvement and rewards to the youth, then involvement would follow and lead to the commitment, attachment, and beliefs conducive to nondelinquent behavior. Also, a youth who was positively involved would choose to associate with nondelinquent peers. The end result would be the prevention of delinquent behavior (see Fig. 7-1).

Weis's project attempted to bring about institutional change in the school setting in order to foster the involvement that can prevent delinquency. Specific areas for change included:

1. Increase all students' chances for educational success, for example by developing curricula and educational materials relevant to students and by avoiding labeling certain youths as incapable of learning.
2. Make the school curriculum relevant to the occupational market, especially for students who will not go to college.
3. Develop a means of generating and sustaining the commitment of youth to the educational system and to community standards of behavior, for example by including youths in planning and decision making within the school.
4. Locate and reintegrate students who are not achieving or behaving.

[38]Jackson Toby, "Violence in Schools," *National Institute of Justice: Research in Brief* (Washington, D.C.: U.S. Department of Justice, December 1983).

[39]Joseph Weis and J. David Hawkins, *Reports of the National Juvenile Justice Assessment Centers, Preventing Delinquency* (Washington, D.C.: U.S. Department of Justice, 1981); Joseph Weis and John Sederstrom, *Reports of the National Juvenile Justice Assessment Centers, The Prevention of Serious Delinquency: What to Do?* (Washington, D.C.: U.S. Department of Justice, 1981).

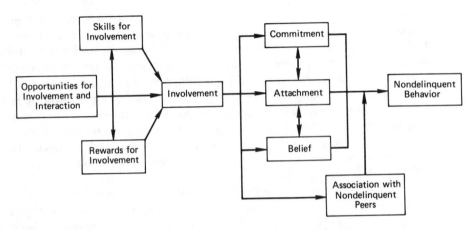

Figure 7-1 A model of the process of social development used as the basis for school innovation

SOURCE: Joseph Weis and John Sederstrom, *Reports of the National Juvenile Justice Assessment Centers, The Prevention of Juvenile Delinquency: What to Do?* (Washington, D.C.: U.S. Department of Justice, 1981), p. 37.

5. Bring about close cooperation and coordination among the schools, family, and community agencies.[40]

Besides changes in the schools, work with families, community organizations against delinquency, the disruption of delinquent groups, and the encouragement of ties to conventional groups are recognized as essential to delinquency prevention.

Federal funding was provided to operate a research and development project to change the schools in Seattle, Washington, and in essence to put the social development theory to the test.[41] After considerable negotiation, seven schools were involved in the project, and in many ways the problems in these schools typified those in schools throughout the country. Many of the students were alienated from school activities, and many teachers showed symptoms of "burnout," tending to be preoccupied with their own welfare and discouraged by a difficult and often unrewarding work environment. The delinquency prevention project promised to change the negative atmosphere of the school by bringing new monetary and other resources, establishing a comprehensive training program, and supplying leadership in the innovative educational methods that we outlined as potentially useful in preventing delinquency. Unfortunately, teachers showed considerable resistance to using the new methods or even to attending training sessions. Staff turnover was high at both the administrator and teacher levels, so even when individuals became involved in the project, they

[40]Weis and Sederstrom, *The Prevention of Serious Delinquency,* p. 41.
[41]Douglas M. Kerr, "Changing Schools to Prevent Delinquency," a paper presented at the 1984 meetings of the American Psychological Association, Toronto, Ontario.

frequently left. In many cases, the administrators and teachers saw no reason to accept innovative changes, and the project was never fully implemented.

Project PATHE (for Positive Action Through Holistic Education) is a more successful example of a school-based program using the social development approach. Between 1980 and 1983, in the Charleston County, North Carolina, public schools, the program combined direct intervention with high-risk youth and changes in the school environment. Specifically:

> It sought to create a climate of mutual respect and cooperation and a sense of belonging among teachers, administrators, and students; to increase effective communication; to increase student and faculty involvement in planning for and implementing school change efforts; to increase the clarity, fairness, and consistency of school rule enforcement, and to increase teachers' classroom management skills.[42]

The program differs from the usual school program, which tries to change the individual, through its emphasis on changing the school environment.

The program design was consistent with social control theory, for it was intended to promote attachment to the school and give the students something to lose if they misbehaved. Increased participation in school activities and greater academic success were also objectives. Unlike the Seattle experiment, Project PATHE was well managed and was implemented as intended. An evaluation showed that, consistent both with program intentions and with social control theory, "increases in students' sense of belonging in the school accompanied (small) decreases in delinquent behavior and misconduct . . . [and] commitment to education also increased."[43] At least in some settings, it does appear that public school interventions can prevent delinquency.

Besides changing existing school programs, *alternative education programs,* which can be physically located either in traditional school buildings or in other settings, hold promise for providing potentially delinquent students with a sense of worth and competence by involving them in nontraditional activities.

The *Childcare Apprenticeship Program* is one example of such a program. Between 1975 and 1976, this program operated at the Robert W. White Alternative School in Boston. The program involved disturbed and delinquent teenagers in apprenticeship child care work with much younger children, many of whom were autistic or schizophrenic. A key feature of the program was careful screening of the apprentices; only teenagers who showed the ability to empathize with the young children were allowed to participate. The program participants took part in truly needed child-care activities, and thus they could "experience feelings of competence and responsibility."[44] The child-care activities replaced

[42]Denise C. Gottfredson, "An Empirical Test of School-Based Environmental and Individual Interventions to Reduce the Risk of Delinquent Behavior," *Criminology, 24,* no. 4 (November 1986), pp. 705–731.

[43]*Ibid.,* p. 726.

[44]Hayden Duggan and John Shlien, "The Childcare Apprenticeship Program: An Experiment in Cross-Age Intervention," in *School Crime and Disruption,* eds. Ernst Wenk and Nora Harlow (David, California: Responsible Action, 1978), p. 188.

an afternoon educational program which was considered to be boring by many students. The staff of the program reported a reduction in delinquency and disruption in the school setting.[45]

A school-based prevention program attempted to reduce youths' general levels of delinquency in a Quincy, Illinois, junior high school. Twenty boys took part in an alternative educational experience within the school. The boys were poor students, were considered to be behavior problems, or had police and court records. Gold and Petronio have described this program:

> The teachers of the two alternative classes were chosen not on the basis of any special training, but rather because of their interest in and sympathy for this kind of child. The curriculum was based on individual, small-group, and classroom projects developed out of the students' interests. Classroom procedures were informal and the relationships between teachers and pupils were warm and friendly.[46]

An experiment was conducted to compare the twenty boys in the alternative classroom program with twenty in regular classes. Although the two groups were similar in academic achievement, those in the alternative classroom liked school better and had better attendance. Most important,

> the behavior records of the school and the police records in the community documented that their disruptive and delinquent behavior had declined by more than one-third, while the official delinquency of the boys in the control group tripled. Furthermore, a follow-up study demonstrated that the boys in the special classes made better transitions to the world of work as indicated by their employers' ratings and the length of time for which they held jobs.[47]

The Quincy program resembles the Childcare Apprenticeship Program in its provision of "autonomy and potency," or a chance to succeed. Gold and Petronio have concluded from this research, as well as their own studies, that school programs which help teenagers in this way are most successful.[48]

In general, alternative education programs which are successful share a number of other features:

1. Individualized instruction with curricula tailored to students' learning needs and interests, clear learning goals, and an individually paced learning program.
2. Clear rewards for individual improvement in academic competency.
3. A goal-oriented work and learning emphasis in the classroom.
4. Small student population in the program.
5. Low student-adult ratio in the classroom.

---

[45]*Ibid.*, p. 197.

[46]Martin Gold and Richard J. Petronio, "Delinquent Behavior in Adolescence," in *Handbook of Adolescent Psychology*, ed. Joseph Adelson (New York: Wiley-Interscience Publication, 1980), p. 519.

[47]*Ibid.*, p. 520.

[48]*Ibid.*, p. 521.

6. Caring, competent teachers.
7. Strong, supportive administrator.[49]

There is growing concern over the contribution of negative school experiences to delinquency, and the amount of violence and other lawbreaking within the school setting. For this reason, many experts recommend that schools develop programs with the qualities listed above, and in that way take a major role in pure as well as rehabilitative prevention.

The Chicago Youth Alliance. We began this section on pure prevention programs by noting that some community programs are still in use. One of these is the Chicago Youth Alliance, which was funded as a demonstration prevention program by a branch of the Justice Department, the Office of Juvenile Justice and Delinquency Prevention.[50] Beginning in 1976, the program operated in three parts of Chicago, and it involved the formation of an alliance between a wide variety of youth-serving agencies. Though on the surface there are similarities between this program and the earlier community efforts, there is a major difference. The Chicago Youth Alliance was intended to organize and obtain services for youths rather than to work directly with them.

In one community, Uptown, youth-serving agencies were experiencing considerable problems. They were not allowed to rent needed office and program space, and they were denied needed short-term emergency bank loans. These difficulties resulted from a community-wide struggle to concentrate resources on well-to-residents and successful businesses, and to discourage less prosperous people from remaining in the area.

Once the agencies organized, they publicized their combined economic contribution to the area. This included their employment of neighborhood residents, their purchase of supplies, and their use of banking services. They threatened to boycott banks and businesses which did not cooperate with them. As a result, considerable community cooperation was obtained by the youth-serving programs. The Chicago Youth Alliance stands as an example of a program based largely on radical criminological theory, according to which a person's position in the economic system is a major influence on human interactions.

Table 7-2 summarizes the pure prevention programs in the community and schools that we have discussed. At this time, you could find examples of all of these types of programs in operation. In forming your own judgment about the worth of these programs, you will want to consider three pieces of information in the table. The first is the description of predelinquents served by the program. Based on the information in Chapter 2, you can determine the degree to which each program serves an appropriate group. The second piece of information to consider is the assumed causes of delinquency, or the theory underly-

---

[49]Hawkins and Wall, *Alternative Education,* p. vi.

[50]Joseph Bute, Jr., "Practicing from Theory: Work with Youths and Reflections on Radical Criminology," *Crime and Delinquency, 27,* no. 1 (January 1981), pp. 106–121.

Table 7-2 A Summary of Pure Prevention Programs in the Community and Schools

PROGRAMS FROM THE 1930s TO THE PRESENT	WHO ARE THE PRE-DELINQUENTS SERVED BY THE PROGRAM?	WHAT ARE THE ASSUMED CAUSES OF DELINQUENCY, OR THE THEORIES, UNDERLYING THE PROGRAM?	RESEARCH EVIDENCE OF PROGRAM SUCCESS
Early Community-Based Programs • Chicago Area Project • Midcity Project • South Central Youth Project • Central Harlem Street Club Project	Poor youths in high-crime areas	Social, Structural and Environmental Pathology Cultural Transmission Theory—Shaw and McKay Gang Theory—Thrasher	weak
Community-Based Programs in the 1960s • Mobilization for Youth • United Planning Organization • Action for Appalachian Youth • The HARYOU ACT	Poor youths in high-crime areas	Social, Structural, and Environmental Pathology Cultural Transmission Theory—Shaw and McKay Gang Theory—Thrasher Inadequate Opportunity Structure Success Goals and Opportunity Structure—Cloward and Ohlin	weak
Contemporary Pure Prevention Programs • Continuation of Chicago Area Project	Poor youths in high-crime areas	Social, Structural, and Environmental Pathology Cultural Transmission Theory—Shaw and McKay Gang Theory—Thrasher	weak
• Flint Neighborhood Foot Patrol Program	Youths in neighborhoods with varying social class and racial groups	Community Involvement and Individual Youth Problems	moderate
• Social Development Approach-Seattle Schools • Project PATHE	Youths in school	School Curriculum, Atmosphere and Structure Social Development Theory—Weis and colleagues	moderate if implemented as intended

(continued)

Table 7-2 *(Continued)*

PROGRAMS FROM THE 1930s TO THE PRESENT	WHO ARE THE PRE-DELINQUENTS SERVED BY THE PROGRAM?	WHAT ARE THE ASSUMED CAUSES OF DELINQUENCY, OR THE THEORIES, UNDERLYING THE PROGRAM?	RESEARCH EVIDENCE OF PROGRAM SUCCESS
Contemporary Alternative Education Programs • Childcare Apprenticeship Program	Unadjusted public school students	Inadequate Opportunity Structure Success Goals and Opportunity Structure—Cloward and Ohlin Individual Adjustment Psychological Theories	strong
Contemporary Community-Based Programs • The Chicago Youth Alliance	Poor youths in inner-city areas	Discrimination against lower social classes Radical Theory	weak

ing the program. Not every program is clearly related to a specific theory. At the least, we can usually determine that a program is based on either sociological or psychological theories. You can use the information from Part 2 regarding the quality of sociological and psychological theories in general as well as specific theories to decide whether programs are based on sound understanding of the causes of delinquency. The third piece of information in the table to consider is a conclusion about the research evidence that the program prevented delinquency. In some cases the evidence is weak because research has not been completed. By weighing all the information, you can draw your own conclusions about which programs are most promising.

ALTERNATIVES TO COURT PROCESSING

Police officers and probation staff (usually intake workers) have always diverted some youths from formal court action. The image of the police officer who sternly warns a minor offender and then returns the youth to the parents' supervision is firmly entrenched in most people's minds, and those who are familiar with the operations of the juvenile court realize that many youth are similarly warned and released by probation staff. Beginning in the 1960s and extending to the present, empirical research has confirmed that the police screen out well over half of all youths with whom they have contact.[51] There also is considerable empirical evidence that over half of the youths who were referred by the police or others to the court were not formally petitioned to juvenile court. Augmenting the general pattern of diversion in the juvenile justice process, a rapid expansion in the use of more complex diversion programs began in 1967.

In 1967 the President's Commission recommended increased reliance on the new breed of diversion programs. At that time, Lemert's theory of the negative effects of labeling served as the theoretical basis for the recommendation. It was generally believed that court processing reinforces a youth's negative self-image, and that this leads to increased delinquency. Through its funding programs and publications, the federal government encouraged local groups to develop diversion programs that would provide a very wide variety of services to youths; now there are many such programs in operation.

The Sacramento Diversion Project

The Sacramento, California, Diversion Project stands as an important early example of the programs that were encouraged at the federal level. It was designed in 1970 to provide services for runaways, youths "beyond control" of their parents, and other troubled adolescents[52] (see Exhibit 7-2). Youths participating in the project are referred by the police, family, or the schools, and immediately after the referral to the intake division, a family meeting is arranged. During this meeting, which usually takes place within a few hours after referral, the emphasis is on the importance of the family's tackling the problem as a group. Every effort is made to arrange for the child to return home with the family, and detention is avoided whenever possible. If a return home is not feasible, a temporary foster care placement or voluntary placement with another family or relatives is encouraged. Up to four follow-up counseling sessions are arranged with the family on a voluntary basis.

Beginning in 1972, the program was expanded to include minor offenders. For both the status offenders and the minor offenders, the project resulted in a decreased number of court petitions, fewer informal probations, and less recidivism. The youths in the project had less recidivism than a similar control group of youths who did not receive project services. Although the project youths had less recidivism, the recidivism rate for those in the project and the control group was quite high. In a one-year period, 54.2 percent of the control group youths and 46.3 percent of the project participants were rebooked for a

[51]Irving Piliavin and Scott Briar, "Police Encounters with Juveniles," *American Journal of Sociology,* 70, no. 2 (September 1964), pp. 206–214; Donald Black and Albert J. Reiss, Jr., "Police Control of Juveniles," *American Sociological Review,* 35, no. 1 (February 1970), pp. 63–77; Richard J. Lundman, Richard E. Sykes, and John P. Clark, "Police Control of Juveniles: A Replication," *Journal of Research in Crime and Delinquency,* 15, no. 1 (January 1978), pp. 74–91.

[52]Roger Baron and Floyd Feeney, *Juvenile Diversion Through Family Counseling* (Washington, D.C.: U.S. Government Printing Office, 1976).

Exhibit 7-2 A typical case diverted by the Sacramento Diversion Project

---

Johnny G., a somewhat retarded and chubby 14-year-old with a smile and winning way, was brought to the Juvenile Hall as being "beyond the control of his parents." This was the fourth time to the Hall for this "offense." Twice previously he had been placed on informal probation and had only recently completed his stint. Johnny's father is a 41-year-old truck driver and his mother a 30-year-old housewife. There are no other children. The father says the problem is that Johnny sometimes steals from his parents, never goes to sleep at a decent hour, rarely gets up in time for school and "just doesn't listen." The father says that he has to go to bed early, usually by 10 P.M. because his work requires him to get up early in the morning. The mother . . . likes to stay up late and does not get up until after Mr. G. has gone to work and Johnny to school . . . on those occasions when Johnny does get up in time for school. . . . Both mother and father indicate that Johnny has no specific bed time and virtually none of the family rules are consistently enforced with respect to Johnny.

SOURCE: Floyd Feeney, "The PINS Problem—A 'No Fault' Approach," reprinted with permission from Teitelbaum and Gough's *Beyond Control: Status Offenders in the Juvenile Court* (Cambridge, Massachusetts: Ballinger Publishing Company, 1977), Ch. 8, pp. 251–252. Copyright 1977, Ballinger Publishing Company.

---

penal code violation. Unfortunately, it is unclear from the research exactly why recidivism decreased. As others have pointed out, the Sacramento project not only provided counseling to family and youth, but participants were less often detained overnight, and were less often referred to court.[53] Is it the counseling, the detention practices, the referral pattern, or some combination of these factors that explains the reduction in recidivism?

Despite the uncertainty of the reasons for its success, the Sacramento program was replicated in many communities, including eleven in California, where it was used not only with the white females who predominated in Sacramento, but also with more blacks and Hispanics who were males with a history of criminal offenses.[54] Evaluation of the replication efforts showed that the diversion project continued to reduce recidivism slightly, even when used with more serious delinquent offenders.

Questions about Diversion

In addition to questions about the reduction in recidivism in the Sacramento and similar programs, there have been more general criticisms of the rapid development of diversion programs. Lemert, whose work on labeling

[53]Robert M. Carter and Malcolm W. Klein, eds., *Back on the Streets: The Diversion of Juvenile Offenders* (Englewood Cliffs, New Jersey: Prentice-Hall, Inc., 1976), p. 329.

[54]Ted Palmer, Marvin Bohnstedt, and Roy Lewis, *The Evaluation of Juvenile Diversion Projects: Final Report* (Sacramento, California: Division of Research, California Youth Authority, Winter 1978).

theory has been a basis for these programs, is one of the critics.[55] He points out that diversion programs were intended to limit children's contacts with the police and courts. Because many so-called diversion programs are managed by police and court personnel, they do not accomplish this goal. In fact, some programs bring more youths into frequent contact with the juvenile justice system, since they accept only the least serious offenders as clients. If the diversion program did not exist, it is likely that these offenders would have been warned and released, rather than intensively counseled. This problem has been recognized by many people who describe it as a process of "widening the net" of official control over youths.[56]

A criticism related to net widening is that many diverted youth have not been found to have broken the law, but are "diverted" before any formal processing occurs, and thus before they are in contact with a defense attorney.[57] It is possible that youth who would not be found delinquent through formal processing "volunteer" for diversion programs because they fear the unknown outcome of formal processing.[58] Thus, there are no due process protections, and there is more involvement in the system than if there were no diversion. Such a result can be criticized not only on the grounds that it is unfair for the youth, but also because juvenile justice system resources are shifted away from the most serious offenders to those who find themselves in the diversion programs.

In response to criticisms of the diversion effort, the Office of Juvenile Justice and Delinquency Prevention provided funding for a National Evaluation of Diversion Projects. Programs in Kansas City, Missouri, Memphis, Tennessee, Orange County, Florida, and New York City were funded based on their willingness to carry out an experiment to determine the effectiveness of diversion. An experiment in which there is a control group of youths who do not attend the program provides the most convincing evidence of whether a program works or not. The special diversion projects were similar to the Sacramento approach, for the primary services were individual and family counseling. Some of the programs did provide additional services, such as recreation. Three groups of youths were compared: those released with no action, those diverted into the special program, and those referred for additional court processing. Unlike the Sacramento research, the study revealed no major difference between the groups.

Richard Lundman has tried to explain why the national evaluation of diversion did not provide as positive results as the earlier California evalua-

[55]Edwin M. Lemert, "Diversion in Juvenile Justice: What Hath Been Wrought," *Journal of Research in Crime and Delinquency, 18,* no. 1 (January 1981), pp. 34–46.

[56]For evidence that diversion increases contact with the juvenile justice system, see Charles E. Frazier and John K. Cochran, "Official Intervention, Diversion from the Juvenile Justice System and the Dynamics of Human Services Work: Effects of a Reform Goal Based on Labeling Theory," *Crime and Delinquency, 32,* no. 2 (April 1986), pp. 157–176.

[57]Feeley, Malcolm M., *Court Reform on Trial: Why Simple Solutions Fail* (New York: Basic Books, 1983).

[58]S. P. Lab, *Crime Prevention: Approaches, Practices and Evaluations* (Cincinnati, Ohio: Anderson Publishing, 1988).

tions.[59] He suggested that many of the youths in the California programs would never have been arrested at all, but more of the clients of the programs in the national evaluation would have been arrested. Thus, the national evaluation focused on programs serving more delinquent youths than did the California evaluations. Perhaps the programs were effective only with the least delinquent adolescents.

Refining the Diversion Strategy

We have seen the crucial role of theory in stimulating the interest in diversion programs. Also, evaluation research has been important in raising questions about both the programs and the theory. An extensive research project carried out by Ted Palmer and Roy Lewis sheds additional light on the way in which a theory-based program can be studied and refined to make it more effective.[60]

The research by Palmer and Lewis has several strengths. It focuses on fifteen California Youth Authority sponsored, community-based diversion programs; it uses the same outcome measures to determine whether the programs are effective. Exhibit 7-3 includes descriptions of four of the programs that Palmer and Lewis studied.

Multiple goals are considered. Does diversion reduce recidivism? Are youths really diverted? Does diversion save money? Also, the differences in programs and clients are considered. The projects offered a wide range of alternatives to initial and subsequent processing; some were located in, some outside the formal justice system. Youths differed in their prior record, the source of referral, and reasons for referral. Because Palmer and Lewis had a strong research design and fully understood the complexity of the diversion programs, their research results give us some very useful guidance in the design of future diversion programs.

Palmer and Lewis concluded that no single diversion program is ideal for all youths under all conditions, or even for most youths under most conditions. The ideal system would match individuals to particular kinds of programs for the purpose of optimizing the various outcomes (less justice system contact, less recidivism, etc.) that are desired. For most youths, the best time for involvement in a diversion program is after the second, or in some cases the third offense. Diversion programs are equally effective for status offenders and for those who have committed more serious offenses. Besides the findings of Palmer and Lewis, there is evidence from other sources that the most successful diversion programs use some method of behavior change (see Chapter 8, "Methods of Treatment"). In the case of diversion, research has provided quite specific guidelines for the design of effective programs.

[59]Richard L. Lundman, *Prevention and Control of Juvenile Delinquency* (New York: Oxford University Press, 1984), pp. 97–98.
[60]Ted Palmer and Roy V. Lewis, *An Evaluation of Juvenile Diversion* (Cambridge, Massachusetts: Oelgeschlager, Gunn and Hain, 1980).

Exhibit 7-3   Diversion programs studied by Palmer and Lewis

El Centro (Imperial County Delinquency Intervention/Diversion)

This project was designed to provide diversion services to clients within the target area, and to develop new alternatives to traditional justice system processing. It was operated by the Imperial County Probation Department and its largest single referral source (40%) was probation. Project activities usually consisted of counseling and recreation. Of the clients who were sampled by EJDP, 50% were between the ages fourteen and sixteen and 9% had a prior arrest record.

Irvine (Pre-Trial Intervention and Diversion Project)

This project was designed to (1) provide access to a wide range of services for predelinquent youths, (2) assure continuity of treatment for individual youths and families, and (3) provide long-term follow-up on every case. It was sponsored by the city of Costa Mesa and administered by a management board that represented a number of local police departments. Most referrals (80%) were from the police department. PIDP used four main treatment modalities: contingency contracting, parent-child communication, coping skills, and community involvement. These were usually implemented by family counseling, individual counseling, and referral to other resources. Of the clients sampled by EJDP, 59% were between ages fourteen and sixteen and 17% had a prior arrest record.

Simi Valley (Project Interface)

Project Interface was designed as a community outreach counseling service for youths and families with drug-related problems. It was sponsored by Ventura County and administered by a management board that represented various groups and agencies within the county. Target areas included the following communities: Simi Valley, Moorpark, Newbury Park, and Thousand Oaks. The largest single referral source (40%) was law enforcement. Principal services were family and group counseling. Of the clients sampled by EJDP, 56% were between ages fourteen and sixteen and 20% had a prior arrest record.

Yreka (Siskiyou County Juvenile Diversion Project)

This project was designed to serve youths classified as 601 cases, especially runaways or minors beyond parental control. It operated under the Siskiyou County Probation Department and its largest single source of referrals (80%) was law enforcement. SCJDP's policy was to divert youths by providing intensive crisis counseling to minors and/or their parents at the earliest point of contact. Other activities included individual, group, and family counseling. Of the clients sampled, 61% were between fourteen and sixteen and 19% had a prior arrest record.

SOURCE: Ted Palmer and Roy V. Lewis, *An Evaluation of Juvenile Diversion* (Cambridge, Massachusetts: Oelgeschlager, Gunn and Hain, 1980), pp. 38–43.

REHABILITATIVE PREVENTION PROGRAMS

Most community and government efforts at delinquency prevention and crime prevention emphasize rehabilitative prevention. The reason for the greater emphasis on rehabilitative prevention is not only because of the lack of commitment to, and the lack of resources for, pure prevention programs but also because many of the pure prevention programs have not had adequate evaluations, nor have they been objectively researched to determine their effectiveness. It is often difficult to convince the community legislators and the funding agencies that pure prevention programs should be initiated and developed, and therefore rehabilitative prevention programs receive most of the attention. Rehabilitative prevention, although at present necessary, would not be needed on a large scale if pure prevention efforts were prevalent and successful. Rehabilitative prevention also suffers from a lack of resources, and community programs are often merely sporadic attempts to deal with the problem once it has occurred. Because the problem has progressed to a very serious point by the time rehabilitative prevention is initiated, it is often difficult to successfully help the youngster.

All the following programs are rehabilitative programs. Some have been evaluated and researched and definite conclusions can be drawn. Others have not been rigorously evaluated, and therefore it is difficult to measure their successes and failures.

REHABILITATION IN THE COMMUNITY

The most common alternatives to institutionalization, *probation* and *parole,* derive from the positive school of crime causation. Adherents to the positive school maintain that an offender has social, intellectual, or emotional deficiencies that can and should be corrected so that he or she may assume a productive role in the community.

Probation

Probation is a tool of rehabilitative prevention. According to Haskell and Yablonsky:

> The correctional system provides for the treatment and supervision of offenders in the community by placing them on probation in lieu of confinement in a custodial institution. In most cases probationers serve the sentence of the court under the supervision of the probation officer assigned by the court. The judge has broad powers in this situation and can set the conditions of probation and the length of supervision. He maintains the power to order revocation of probation, usually for a violation of one of the conditions set by him or his agent or for

the commission of another offense. The effect of revocation is to send the prisoner to a custodial institution.[61]

The specific administration of the probation program depends upon the state and the jurisdiction. Although in many states probation is a part of the court—a juvenile court, probate court, or some other court jurisdiction—one probation department may be quite different from another. In most states, juvenile courts administer probation services, while in the other states there is a variation.

The probation officer can use a variety of techniques in counseling the youngster—for example, vocational guidance or personal counseling (see Chapter 8). It is obviously difficult for the probation officer to adequately serve a caseload of seventy-five or more individuals. In many cases it is necessary to establish a priority list to determine which youngsters are in greatest need of assistance and must be taken care of first. In many jurisdictions, the probation officer's major problem is "putting out fires." There is little time for counseling, other than on a superficial level. It is, unfortunately, unusual for the probation officer to have sufficient time and resources to serve a caseload adequately.

Volunteer Probation Counseling Program, Lincoln, Nebraska. Pilot programs have been initiated which have attempted to provide sufficient resources so that the probation officer can be more effective as a result of a reduced caseload. For example, in Lincoln, Nebraska, the Volunteer Probation Counseling Program is an important part of regular probation services.[62] Once youths are adjudicated as delinquent for misdemeanors, evaluations are conducted to determine if they are "high risk," that is, likely to commit another serious offense. These youths are placed on probation for one year, and during the first two months they receive intensive counseling by a probation officer and attend court-operated education classes. For the remaining ten months of probation, many of the high-risk youths are assigned to a community volunteer for one-to-one counseling outside of the court setting.

A psychologist carefully matches volunteers with probationers, based on the needs and abilities of each. If there is any doubt about a volunteer's ability to work directly with an offender, the volunteer is offered another type of job. The psychologist also is responsible for training the volunteers, though there is an emphasis on using the existing talents and caring attitude of each volunteer.

The volunteer-probationer relationships usually center on the sharing of recreation and sports experiences, and on active problem solving. Educational and employment problems were the most common, and many volunteers located jobs for their probationers.

A comparison of youths in the program with those who were not as-

---

[61]Martin R. Haskell and Lewis Yablonsky, *Crime and Delinquency* (Chicago: Rand McNally and Co., 1970), p. 432.

[62]Richard Ku, *The Volunteer Probation Counselor Program* (Washington, D.C.: U.S. Government Printing Office, 1975).

signed to a volunteer showed that the participants in the Volunteer Probation Counseling Program had fewer new offenses during the probationary period. Their new offenses were also less serious.

Project CREST, Gainesville, Florida.

Project CREST (Clinical Regional Support Teams) in Gainesville, Florida, is another volunteer program to assist probationers.[63] The volunteers are assigned to work with serious offenders, including repeat misdemeanants and felons. Probation officers place restrictions on the youths and monitor their compliance. At the same time, the volunteers develop supportive relationships with the youths in an attempt to work through the youths' problems and develop caring relationships. In this way, a dual emphasis in treatment is provided.

The volunteers are students in the counselor education program at the University of Florida. They are trained during an intensive twelve-hour workshop before they meet with clients. Thereafter, regular meetings are held for professional supervision and additional training, as well as coordination of efforts between the regular probation officer and the volunteer. Research on Project CREST demonstrates that the participants do recidivate less often than do other youths.

The Volunteer Probation Counseling Program and Project CREST are examples of how communities are attempting to serve probationers better by providing the necessary resources to deal with the problem. In both programs the use of volunteers is prevalent. The use of volunteers is becoming acceptable in other communities throughout the country. This is one method of reducing the pressure on probation officers and involving citizens in the criminal and juvenile justice systems processes.

Restitution Programs.

Restitution is often used in combination with probation, although it may be the focus of an independent program or a part of a diversion program.[64] In 1978, OJJDP stimulated the use of restitution by funding 41 local programs, which in just the first two years of operation served 17,354 offenders. At that time, over one-third of the offenders were serious or chronic delinquents who had committed crimes such as arson, burglary, robbery, or assault. Most were asked to pay monetary restitution. By 1985, there were 400 formally recognized restitution programs for juvenile offenders.[65]

In some cases youths are not required to pay monetary restitution, but instead must complete community service projects. The community service project might be tailored to the offense. For example, a youth who vandalizes a school playground could be required to spend time cleaning up schoolyards. Or

[63]William DeJong and Carolyn Stewart, *Project CREST,* Gainesville, Florida (Washington, D.C.: U.S. Department of Justice, 1980).

[64]Anne L. Schneider, ed., *Guide to Juvenile Restitution* (Washington, D.C.: U.S. Department of Justice, 1985).

[65]Anne L. Schneider, "Restitution and Recidivism Rates of Juvenile Offenders: Results from Four Experimental Studies," *Criminology, 24,* no. 3 (August 1986), pp. 533–552.

a shoplifter could be asked to spend time working in an animal shelter to "pay back the community" for the higher prices that result from shoplifting activity. Proponents of restitution programs believe that it is rehabilitative to pay back individuals or society for damages resulting from illegal activity, for the youth learns to accept responsibility for her or his misbehavior. When community work is involved, there might be other benefits, such as positive involvements with people and institutions that develop at the work site.

Critics of restitution programs view them as part of the move to treat juveniles severely. They point out that restitution is actually retribution—that is, punishment aimed at getting even with the offender. Many of the youth in restitution programs would be sanctioned less severely or not at all if the programs did not exist.[66] Also, indigent youth may be at an unfairly high risk for sanctions if they do not pay their restitution.

There is, however, some evidence of positive outcomes from restitution programs. First, there is no doubt that victims do receive some benefit. According to a federally funded evaluation of eighty-five programs over a two-year period, the victims received over two-and-one-half million dollars, and the offenders contributed over three hundred fifty thousand hours of community service work, and over six thousand hours of work for the victims.[67] Second, compared with traditional dispositions (for example, short-term detention and probation), some restitution programs result in less recidivism.[68] For instance, youth in Washington, D.C. who were assigned to the restitution program averaged about ten fewer offenses for each one hundred youth per year in comparison to similar youth assigned to probation.[69] It is not clear exactly why restitution has its influence, but Anne Schneider, who has evaluated many of the restitution programs, suggests several reasons: the positive benefits of "real job" situations, less stigma, the experience of being "held accountable," inability to rationalize about the negative effects of the offense, a deterrent effect, or intensive supervision.[70]

Intensive Probation. In many jurisdictions, seriously delinquent youth are placed in small probation caseloads and provided with close supervision, monitoring, and other services. For example, they may be required to make phone contact with the probation officer at specified times each day, to spend certain hours in a school or job program, and to meet with the probation officer several times each week. Intensive probation is sometimes provided by regular probation workers who are given a small caseload, or it can be provided through a contract with a private program.

[66]Barry Krisberg and James Austin, "The Unmet Promise of Alternatives to Incarceration," *Crime and Delinquency, 28,* no. 3 (July 1982), pp. 374–409.

[67]Peter Schneider, "Research on Restitution: A Guide to Rational Decision Making," in *Guide to Juvenile Restitution,* ed. Anne L. Schneider.

[68]Anne L. Schneider, ed., *Guide to Juvenile Restitution* (Washington, D.C.: U.S. Department of Justice, 1985).

[69]*Ibid.,* p. 550.

[70]*Ibid.,* pp. 550–551.

When intensive probation is used for youth who would otherwise be sent to an institution, it can dramatically reduce costs for the juvenile justice system and eliminate negative effects of the institutional environment and of the disruption of any positive community involvement. There are some indications that intensive probation does not increase recidivism, and it may even result in less recidivism in comparison to institutionalization.[71]

Parole

Parole (also called aftercare) is similar to probation in that they both handle offenders in the community and are generally organized along the same lines, although the populations of offenders are quite different. Parolees have been incarcerated and subjected to the institution "code" and all that implies. As might be expected, success rates of probationers are considerably better than those of parolees.

Although the decision to grant a parole is in theory based on an inmate's improved attitudes and behavior and on potential for success in the community, the paroling authority is seldom in a position, either by training or knowledge, to make an informed, individual evaluation. More important, statutes often limit the discretion of the paroling authority so that an offender must serve a certain minimum sentence before being eligible for parole, regardless of his or her attitudes and behavior. Moreover, community pressure is exerted on the parole board which prevents it from acting solely in the interests of the offender.

The use of parole varies considerably from one jurisdiction to another; some employ it extensively and others hardly at all.[72]

Generally, both parole and probation have three major functions to perform. The primary function is that of *surveillance*. The officer must maintain contact with the offender, the family, the school, and/or place of employment to determine adherence to the correction plan, to gauge progress, and generally to show interest and concern. Supervision of this nature should constitute more than a mere threat. Properly applied, it can aid the offenders in determining their responsibilities and the expectations that society places upon its functioning members so that they will not repeat the mistakes of the past. Second, the officer must make the offender aware of those *community services* that are available to help in solving individual problems. Third, the officer must *counsel* the offender and family and other important persons to help them understand the conditions that led to the original deviant behavior with a view toward eliminating its underlying causes.

---

[71]William H. Barton and Jeffrey A. Butts, *Intensive Supervision in Wayne County: An Alternative to State Commitment for Juvenile Delinquents. Final Report* (Ann Arbor, Michigan: Institute for Social Research, University of Michigan, 1988); Lynn Sametz and Donna Hamparian, *Innovative Programs in Cuyahoga County Juvenile Court: Intensive Probation Supervision and Probation Classification* (Cleveland, Ohio: Federation for Community Planning, 1989).

[72]U.S. Department of Justice, Federal Bureau of Prisons, National Prisoner Statistics: Prisoners in State and Federal Institutions for Adult Felons, 1964, *National Prisoner Statistics Bulletin*, 38, no. 11 (November 1965).

On the whole, research has not shown traditional parole services to be effective in reducing recidivism.[73] However, certain innovative parole efforts have more positive outcomes, even with very serious offenders.

The Violent Juvenile Offender (VJO) Program. The VJO Program assisted chronic, violent juvenile offenders in developing social bonds to the legitimate community (social control theory) and in "unlearning" delinquent behavior (social learning theory). The link between the program elements and various theories can be seen in the program principles:

- *Social networking:* the strengthening of personal bonds (attitudes, commitment, and beliefs) through positive experiences with family members, schools, the workplace, or nondelinquent peers.
- *Provision of opportunities for youths:* the strengthening of social bonds (attachments and involvement) through achievement and successful participation in school, workplace, and family activities.
- *Social learning:* the process by which personal and social bonds are strengthened and reinforced. Strategies include rewards and sanctions for attainment of goals or for contingent behaviors.
- *Goal-oriented behaviors:* the linking of specific behaviors to each client's needs and abilities, including problem behaviors and special intervention needs (for example, substance abuse treatment or psychotherapy).[74]

Youth were initially placed in a *multiple-phase residential program* that allowed for movement from a restrictive placement to community living as positive behaviors were learned. Then, *reintegration services* were provided to reinforce the learning that had taken place in the residential programs. And, a *case management* procedure was followed so that service plans could be reviewed and revised on a regular basis.[75]

The VJO Program was established in four sites. In the two sites where implementation was the most consistent with the original program plan, there was a lower failure rate than for traditional correctional programming. A short confinement followed by quality parole services seems to have considerable promise in comparison to the usual approach, which is to provide lengthy incarceration and minimal parole services.

Closing Comments on Probation and Parole. The current trend is to maintain heavy use of parole and probation. However, there is doubt that these strategies can realize the potential that is suggested by research on intensive probation programs or the VJO Program described above. The treatment afforded to juveniles on probation and parole is usually far from intensive, since resources are very scarce and large caseloads are common.

---

[73] Patrick Jackson, *The Paradox of Control: Parole Supervision of Youthful Offenders* (New York: Praeger, 1983).

[74] Jeffrey A. Fagan, "Treatment and Reintegration of Violent Juvenile Offenders: Experimental Results," *Justice Quarterly,* 7, no. 2 (June 1990), pp. 233–263.

[75] *Ibid.,* p. 233.

Community Programs

Often, in conjunction with probation and parole services, various community programs exist for the purpose of rehabilitating juvenile offenders. Some community programs are operated directly by state agencies, including the juvenile authorities, but others are private and take referrals (often under contract) from the courts or juvenile authorities.

__Foster Homes and Group Homes.__   Foster home placement has long been utilized as an alternative to incarceration as well as a routine aspect of juvenile aftercare. Increasing dissatisfaction with foster homes over the years as well as their unavailability has led to the development of group homes in a number of states. *Achievement Place* in Lawrence, Kansas, is one of the more successful of these.

Achievement Place is a residential treatment program in Lawrence, Kansas, which is designed to rehabilitate delinquent and neglected youths. It operates on the premise that youthful deviant behavior is based on a lack of social, academic, self-help, and vocational skills rather than on psychopathology. After being placed in the program by the courts, youths learn needed skills with the help of specially trained married couples who are "teaching parents." Six to eight youths live with the teaching parents in a family-sized home located in their own community which permits them to maintain contact with their own families and to attend classes in local schools. The teaching parents are trained to work closely with the parents, teachers, and other members of the community.[76] Another component of the program is a token economy in which youths are rewarded with points for good behavior. The points can be traded for desired objects or privileges. Each part of the program seems to be necessary for success, for attempts to copy just one part—for instance, the token economy—have met with failure.[77]

When Achievement Place participants were compared to youths in a training school, contacts with the police and the courts were the same before and during placement, but they were considerably lower for the Achievement Place boys after placement. A group of probationers with relatively infrequent contacts with the police and courts had more frequent contacts than the Achievement Place youths after finishing the probation program.

__The Halfway House.__   The "halfway house" was originally conceived of as an institution "halfway out" to help incarcerated offenders make the difficult transition from the rigid control of the penal institution to the freedom of the

---

[76]"Youth Program Expansion Funded by Federal Government," *Juvenile Justice Digest,* 2, no. 10 (October 1974), pp. 5, 6.

[77]Elery L. Phillips, Elaine A. Phillips, Dean L. Fixson, and Montrose M. Wolf, "Achievement Place: Behavior Shaping Works for Delinquents," *Psychology Today Magazine,* 7, no. 1 (June 1973), pp. 75–79.

community. Now it is viewed as a potential alternative to imprisonment, an intermediate solution between probation and institutional control.

Some halfway houses are large, single-family dwellings, while others are located, for example, in a YMCA hotel. Most are in neighborhoods with mixed land usage, racial integration, and nearby transportation. Residents wear civilian clothes, secure work or attend school in the community, and gradually earn more freedom in the form of leaves and excursions until they are finally permitted to move out—although they might still be required to return for conferences with greater or lesser frequency, depending upon individual progress and the court order. Regular individual counseling and group sessions form an integral part of the treatment program. (Chapter 9 expands on the halfway house concept.)

Learning Centers. A number of communities have established "learning centers" as an alternative to institutionalization. The basic objectives of the centers are to maintain the offender in the community, thereby reducing the possibility of further alienation, and to enhance treatment by integrating the attitudes of parole counselors, who are primarily concerned with treatment, protection of the parolee's rights, and crisis intervention, and educators, whose primary interests are attendance, task completion, and appropriate behavior. The centers should permit concentration on the common goal of teaching new skills.

The *Providence Education Center* in St. Louis, Missouri, is one example of this type of program.[78] Boys between twelve and sixteen years of age who have committed a serious offense and have a history of failure in school are accepted into the program. The program provides individualized instruction in academic areas, with an emphasis on remedial assistance in reading and mathematics. The student-teacher ratio is very low, just six-to-one. Counseling, and aftercare assistance in continuing education or locating work in the community, are other services of the program.

Because the program is nonresidential, the cost is much lower than training school placement. The program is successful in reducing recidivism; participants break the law less often after enrollment than before. Students also are less truant, better behaved, and make progress in academic achievement.

St. Louis Home Detention. The St. Louis home detention program was designed as a rehabilitative alternative to institutionalization. It places youths, who would otherwise be incarcerated, under the supervision of a community worker. The youthful offenders are either returned to their families or placed in surrogate homes. No more than five youths are assigned to a community youth worker, who comes from the offender's community. Delinquents are placed in the program sometime between their arrest and the formal disposition of their cases. The objectives of the youth workers are to keep their charges available for appearance in court and to structure individual programs as they see fit. They

[78]*Providence Educational Center* (Washington, D.C.: U.S. Government Printing Office, 1974).

work under the direction and supervision of the assistant superintendent of detention and are required to develop close working relationships with the probation staff.

The youth workers function in two-person teams, which permits them to relieve each other in individual cases; they are assigned to specific areas of the city. They are required to maintain daily contact with each youth as well as with other persons with whom the youth has frequent contact. In addition, they are responsible for involving and supervising their assignees in various kinds of activities such as attendance at sports events, movies, bowling, and so on. A telephone answering service keeps the workers on call twelve hours per day.

During the course of the demonstration project, which ran from September 30, 1971, to July 1, 1972, there was not one instance of a youth not being available to the court. Only 5.15 percent of the youths committed new offenses, none of which was violent; 21 percent had to be returned to detention because their programs were not working, even though they did not commit new offenses. The estimated cost per childcare day of the home detention program was $4.85 as opposed to $17.54 in the detention facility. Moreover, the program was well received by the community.[79]

The Provo Experiment. The Provo Experiment in delinquency rehabilitation was begun in 1956 in Provo, Utah, by a volunteer group of professional and lay people known as the Citizen Advisory Council to the juvenile court.[80] The program was funded by the court, and the research was financed by the Ford Foundation. The program accepted boys from all the major communities around Provo. Only habitual offenders fifteen to seventeen years of age were assigned to the program, and not more than twenty boys were admitted at any one time. The length of stay was specified by the court, and release usually came some time between four and seven months. The boys lived at home and spent only part of each day at Pine Hills, the program center. Otherwise they were free to interact in the community and participate in community activities. The program did not utilize any testing, gathering of case histories, or clinical information. The experiment was initiated because it was concluded that

1. The greatest part of delinquent activity takes place in a group—a shared deviation which is a product of differential group experience in a particular subculture.
2. . . . because most delinquents tend to be concentrated in slums or to be the children of lower-class parents their lives are characterized by living situations which limit their access to success goals.[81]

[79]Paul W. Kene and Casimir S. Zantek, "The Home Detention Program of St. Louis, Missouri," *Delinquency Prevention Reporter*, U.S. Department of Health, Education, and Welfare (September-October 1972), pp. 3–6.

[80]Lamar T. Empey and Jerome Rabow, "The Provo Experiment in Delinquency Rehabilitation," *American Sociological Review, 26* (October 1961), pp. 679–695.

[81]*Ibid.*

The treatment system of the Provo Experiment consisted of two phases. Phase one, the "intensive treatment phase," was an effort to create a social system oriented to the task of producing change. Phase two, "the community adjustment phase," was an effort to maintain reference group support for a boy after the intensive treatment of phase one. The boy continued to meet with his group periodically for discussions. Treatment was continued on an intensive basis, unlike traditional methods such as probation or parole, where only periodic visits take place.

The Provo Experiment was an attempt to treat the youngster in an intensive manner while allowing him the freedom of the community. It was different from probation in that the treatment orientation was mainly group counseling and group interaction. The youngsters assisted each other in problem solving, and they learned that the gang or group had a great deal of influence on their behavior. This understanding, it was felt, would help the boys avoid negative peer group situations. Also, because many of the youngsters who participated in the Provo program belonged to the same gangs, much of the delinquent activity of these groups would be neutralized. The boys began to use positive peer pressure to influence each other to become involved in more socially acceptable activities. An evaluation of the program indicated that recidivism rates for boys in this program appeared to be significantly lower than those for comparable boys who had been committed to training schools.[82]

The Highfields Project. The Highfields Project was started in New Jersey in 1950 because there was no adequate facility for youngsters on a short-term basis. It was believed that short-term treatment (not to exceed three months) would be more appropriate than long-term institutionalization for many juveniles. Guided group interaction was the major treatment method and was supplemented with a work and recreation program. The program of guided group interaction and exposure to work experience was directed toward providing the boys with increased work skills and broadening their perspective and alternatives to problem solving.[83]

Two evaluations have been made of the Highfields Project. In the first evaluation, which was made by McCorkle and others, it was determined that although 18 percent of the Highfields boys violated parole, 33 percent of the control group violated parole. The Highfields boys adjusted better over extended periods of time up to five years after release.[84]

In the second evaluation, which was made by H. Ashley Weeks, the Highfields boys were also compared with boys who had been sent to the Annandale Reformatory. Whereas 63 percent of the Highfields boys made a good

---

[82]The President's Commission on Law Enforcement and the Administration of Justice, *Task Force Report: Corrections* (Washington, D.C.: U.S. Government Printing Office, 1967), p. 39.

[83]Lloyd W. McCorkle, Albert Elias, and F. Lovell Bixby, *The Highfields Story* (New York: Holt, Rinehart and Winston, Inc., 1958).

[84]*Ibid.*, p. 143.

adjustment in the community, only 47 percent of the control groups succeeded on parole.

> The whole Highfields experience is directed toward piercing through the strong defenses against rehabilitation, toward undermining delinquent attitudes and toward developing a self-conception favorable to reformation. The sessions on guided group interaction are especially directed to achieve this directive. Guided group interaction has the merit of combining the psychological and the sociological approaches to the control of human behavior. The psychological approach aims to change the self-concept of the boy from a delinquent to a nondelinquent. This process involves changing the mood of the boy from impulses of lawbreaking to impulses to be law-abiding.[85]

The success of the Highfields Project was one of the major reasons the Provo Experiment was started. An evaluation of the Provo Experiment indicated that 29 percent of the experimental group violated parole after fifteen months, while 48 percent of the control group which did not have the benefit of the treatment were parole violators. Even though there are positive indications of the success of the Highfields Project, some questions remain because the subjects in the two comparison groups differed in age, schooling, and delinquent history. It is possible that these differences explain the positive outcome.

Conclusions About Community Programs

Table 7-3 summarizes information on several rehabilitative prevention programs in the community. As with Table 7-2, this information can be used to form personal judgments about the worth of these programs.

There is some research evidence of the positive effect of using community corrections programs. For example, research on community programs in Utah revealed that although recidivism was high (over 70 percent) in community placements, the rate of breaking the law went down considerably from the rate before placement.[86] Similarly, in Illinois, a study found that community treatment had a positive effect, and thus should not be replaced by a "just deserts" approach in which institutionalization would become more common.[87] The use of community placements instead of institutions does not appear to increase danger to the public, and it seems to have positive outcomes.

Even for the chronic and serious juvenile offenders, there is an effort to develop innovative community programs so that institutional treatment can be avoided. According to Peter Greenwood, the most frequently used alternatives

---

[85]*Ibid.*, p. v; also H. Ashley Weeks, *Offenders at Highfields* (Ann Arbor: The University of Michigan Press, 1963).

[86]James Austin and Barry Krisberg, *The Impact of Juvenile Court Intervention* (San Francisco, California: National Council on Crime and Delinquency, 1987).

[87]John D. Wooldredge, "Differentiating the Effects of Juvenile Court Sentences on Eliminating Recidivism, *Journal of Research in Crime and Delinquency, 25*, no. 3 (August 1988), pp. 264–300.

Table 7-3 A Summary of Rehabilitative Prevention Programs in the Community

CONTEMPORARY PROGRAMS AND THEIR SERVICES	WHO ARE THE PRE-DELINQUENTS SERVED BY THE PROGRAM?	WHAT ARE THE ASSUMED CAUSES OF DELINQUENCY, OR THE THEORIES, UNDERLYING THE PROGRAM?	RESEARCH EVIDENCE OF PROGRAM SUCCESS
Volunteer Probation Counseling Volunteers counsel youths recreational activities	"High risk" misde-meanants	Inability to Solve Educational and Employment Problems Psychological Theories	strong
Project CREST Volunteers counsel youths	Serious and repeat misdemeanants and felons	Absence of Caring Adult Plus Personal Problems Psychological Theories Family-Oriented Theories	strong
Restitution Programs Youths pay mone-tary restitution or do community service	Varies by program	Lack of Responsibility for Actions Psychological Theories Deterrence Theory	weak
Achievement Place Counseling Residential care	Court-referred youths	Lack of Social, Academic, Self-Help, and Vocational Skills Psychological Theories	strong
Providence Education Center Remedial education Counseling Recreation	Serious male offenders with school failures	Educational Deficiencies plus Personal Problems Psychological Theories	strong
St. Louis Home Detention Community worker supervision	Youths eligible for in-carceration	Lack of Supervision Psychological Theories Family-Oriented Theories	strong
The Provo Experiment Positive peer pressure	Habitual male offenders	Delinquent Peer Pressure Differential Association Theory—Sutherland	strong
The Highfields Project Group treatment Employment skill education	Boys requiring short-term residential placement	Individual Problems Psychological Theories	moderate

to institutional placement are: wilderness challenges, small secure units with no more than fifteen residents, group homes, and tracking programs in which case workers monitor only one or two youth at a time.[88]

The alternatives to institutions which we have reviewed so far are for the most part relatively small, local programs. They serve a limited geographic area, usually one city or court jurisdiction. Massachusetts has carried out a large-scale effort to replace institutions for juvenile offenders. This effort is reviewed below.

THE MASSACHUSETTS COMMUNITY-BASED SYSTEM

The factors influencing the closing of the Massachusetts Training Schools have been well documented by thorough research efforts. In particular, Lloyd Ohlin, Robert Coates, and Alden Miller have studied the steps leading up to the closing of the institutions.[89] They have additionally studied the effects of the new programs on youths who are involved in the state correctional system.

In the 1960s and early 1970s, there was widespread public criticism of the Massachusetts institutions. Recidivism rates for youths in the institutions were quite high, and poor physical conditions of the facilities as well as instances of brutality by staff against inmates influenced politicians to sponsor a major reform effort. Initially, Jerome Miller, who was employed as the commissioner of youth services, had the mandate to reform the institutions. After three years, he felt that such reforms were impossible, and he disbanded the institutional programs completely. He began to establish a system of regionalized, community programs, which has grown considerably during the last several years. In 1985 the number of youths in secure state-financed programs was limited to 170, as compared to over one thousand before Jerome Miller was employed.

A very complex and diversified collection of private programs has developed to provide services to Massachusetts delinquents (see Exhibit 7-4). For most of these, the state Division of Youth Services (DYS) purchases either nonresidential or residential services for a specific number of youths placed into the programs. The services purchased include all of the types reviewed in our above discussion of the different types of rehabilitative programs, as well as many innovative programs. Although the new system is diversified, there are some general characteristics of the new programs:

1. They are small and individualized rather than large and impersonal.
2. They are humane and therapeutic rather than punitive and custodial.

[88]Peter W. Greenwood, "Promising Approaches for the Rehabilitation or Prevention of Chronic Juvenile Offenders," *Intervention Strategies for Chronic Juvenile Offenders: Some New Perspectives* ed. Peter W. Greenwood (New York: Greenwood Press, 1986), pp. 207–274.
[89]Robert B. Coates, Alden D. Miller, and Lloyd E. Ohlin, *Diversity in a Youth Correctional System: Handling Delinquents in Massachusetts* (Cambridge, Massachusetts: Ballinger Publishing Company, subsidiary of J.B. Lippincott Co., 1978), see also Yitzhak Bakal and Howard W. Polsky, *Reforming Corrections for Juvenile Offenders: Alternatives and Strategies* (Lexington, Massachusetts: Lexington Books, D.C. Heath and Company, 1979).

Exhibit 7-4   The Massachusetts system in 1984

Today 92 percent of the 1,800 youths in DYS custody are cared for daily in a community-based program, at home, or on aftercare status. Eight percent are housed in small, locked secure treatment facilities. The ideal size of a secure program is fifteen (15) youths.

Massachusetts pioneered the Purchase of Service System for juvenile offenders in the early seventies. The agencies we contract with today are third generational. You can appreciate the influence of the private provider on the Commonwealth when you consider that sixty percent of DYS' thirty-seven million dollar budget is allocated to contracted programs. . . . Programs for serious juvenile offenders are evenly divided between the state conducted and contracted programs. . . . By the Spring of 1985 the Department's Capital Expansion Project will be complete and its secure capacity for serious offenders will be at 170. Because the Department of Mental Health had limited success in serving a disturbed and violent juvenile offender, DYS assumed that responsibility and recently contracted with one of its providers to conduct a 15-bed secure unit for that segment of our population.

SOURCE: Edward J. Loughran, ''The Serious Youthful Offender in Massachusetts.'' A paper presented at the 1984 Serious Youthful Offender Conference, Philadelphia, Pennsylvania, pp. 2–3, 4.

---

3. The placement process involves the youth and the family, rather than imposing a decision upon them.
4. The alternatives tend to depend upon and use resources from the community, rather than becoming self-sufficient.

Important features of the Massachusetts community-based system are the matching of youths to programs best suited to meet individual needs, careful tracking of youth to make sure they are adequately supervised, and case management so that youth who have difficulties in a program can be rematched to three, four, or even five different placements in an attempt to find the ideal constellation of services and security.

The transition to the Massachusetts community-based system has not been smooth. From the beginning, there were strong critics in the judiciary and the legislature. Many judges were skeptical of the ability of DYS to control youths without extensive use of secure facilities. When the institutions were first closed, alternative programs were not immediately available, and some youths did not receive the supervision or treatment that they required. Even after the dramatic expansion of resources available in the community, in 1981 a group of politically active conservatives proposed legislation that would have lowered the age for criminal arraignment, provided for automatic waiver of juveniles to superior court, allowed judicial sentencing of juveniles instead of having DYS establish the length of sentence, and required secure confinement of second-time property offenders.[90] The proposed legislation has been compared to the 1978 New York Juvenile Offender Law (see Chapter 6).

In response to the proposal for legislation that would drastically limit the involvement of DYS in the treatment of serious offenders, DYS staff worked to educate the public to the fact that there is not a crime wave in Massachusetts. In fact, the rate at which youths were being arraigned was decreasing faster than the youth population was falling. The decreased arraignments could be due to cutbacks in the police force, increased use of station-house adjustments and diversion, the passage of the Children in Need of Supervision Law to divert status offenders, or the availability of special education programs for all youths in need. Or the decrease could be a result of the shift to the community-based system. Whatever the cause, however, the case can be made that deinstitutionalization has not resulted in dramatic increases in crime. In addition to pointing to decreasing arraignment rates, DYS officials established clear guidelines for minimum sentences to be applied for specific serious crimes after a case-by-case consideration of mitigating factors.

The legislation to increase the severity in reaction to juvenile offenders did not pass, but there is a shift toward the "get tough" philosophy. A system of deciding on placement based on the fit between offender needs and treatment program services is being supplemented, and perhaps changed, to incorporate a consideration of risk.[91] Youth are being classified according to five risk levels as well as treatment needs, and there is pressure to ensure that the many private programs maintain specified levels of security. An initial assessment of the fit between available placements and risk levels suggested that more secure placements are needed. The degree to which Massachusetts will be able to maintain its leadership role in emphasizing appropriate treatment in the face of pressures to focus more on control remains to be seen.

Another dilemma is posed by the shift of resources to violent offenders. The positive outcome of this shift has been that Massachusetts is able to provide secure, nontraumatic settings with great depth and breadth of services. The negative outcome, though, is that community placement alternatives have fewer resources. The "back to justice" trend in the 1980s has not left Massachusetts untouched.[92]

Because of the dramatic nature of the shift to community corrections, researchers showed considerable interest in Massachusetts. A thorough documentation of the change was carried out during the early years after deinstitutionalization. Coates, Miller, and Ohlin summarize their findings about recidivism:

[90]Edward M. Murphy, "Deinstitutionalization: Myth and Reality." Remarks at the Annual Congress of the American Correctional Association, San Antonio, Texas, 1984.

[91]Susan Guarino-Ghezzi and James M. Byrne, "Developing a Model of Structured Decision Making in Juvenile Corrections: The Massachusetts Experience," *Crime and Delinquency, 35*, no. 2 (April 1989), pp. 270–302.

[92]Susan Guarino-Ghezzi, "Initiating Change in Massachusetts' Juvenile Correctional System: A Retrospective Analysis," *Criminal Justice Review, 13*, no. 1 (Spring 1988), pp. 1–11.

When looking at indicators of recidivism over time, representing the training-school system of the late sixties and the community-based system of the middle seventies, we saw that the absolute rate had increased slightly. Numerous explanations are possible for this increase, reflecting changes in the makeup of the DYS population over time, broader societal trends in youth crime, changing attitudes towards females, and changes in police and court resources. Nonetheless, it is clear that the reforms in DYS did not bring about a decrease in the recidivism rate, and it is equally clear that the reforms did not generate an explosive youth crime wave.[93]

Evaluation of the Massachusetts system in the mid 1980s shows lower recidivism than in the earliest years of the reform. The 51 percent recidivism rate for a twelve-month period is comparable to other states, if not better.[94]

The major shift toward community corrections has neither solved the many difficulties in providing effective programs for delinquent youths, nor has it resulted in a large increase in juvenile crime. It has resulted in a greater proportion of youths being in programs which encourage the development of ties to legitimate elements of the community and which provide a home-type living environment.

REHABILITATION IN INSTITUTIONS

Institutions which house thousands of juveniles have become considerably more humane over the years. The lock-step, rules of silence, physical punishments, lengthy banishment to solitary confinement, and so on have either been abolished or considerably modified. In many modern institutions, residents are permitted to have radios and see movies regularly, are fed well, and receive good medical and dental care. Visitation policies have been liberalized and, in general, the resident is less isolated from family and community.

The nature of incarceration varies considerably from one jurisdiction to another in terms of the size, the architecture of the institution, the resources available for programs and facilities, and the nature of the resident population. Institutional populations range from several hundred to several thousand residents. The most common American prison for adults is surrounded by high walls and topped by gun towers at strategic intervals; it houses its inmates in tiered cell blocks and provides dining halls and work and recreation areas where prisoners are handled in mass fashion. The number of youth under age 18 but in prison is growing due to the increased use of waiver to criminal court. Most of the juveniles in adult prisons are property offenders, not violent offenders, as might have been expected.[95]

[93]Coates, Miller, and Ohlin, *Diversity in a Youth Correctional System*, p. 172.

[94]Barry Krisberg, James Austin, and Patricia A. Steele, *Unlocking Juvenile Corrections: Evaluating the Massachusetts Department of Youth Services* (San Francisco, California: National Council on Crime and Delinquency, 1989).

[95]Office of Juvenile Justice and Delinquency Prevention, *Juvenile Justice: Before and After the Onset of Delinquency: United States Paper for the Sixth United National Congress on the Prevention of Crime and the Treatment of Offenders* (Washington, D.C.: U.S. Government Printing Office, 1980), pp. 30–31.

Training schools are used only for juveniles. They are ordinarily considerably smaller than adult prisons and are organized along different lines. They normally have no walls and a dozen or more juveniles are housed in a number of smaller dormitory-like buildings called "cottages." These are complemented by a variety of additional structures, such as a school building and vocational shops. Most residents are placed in an academic or vocational program; some work in the maintenance of the institution.

The largest number of institutional employees work in custodial activities. Business, clerical, and bookkeeping personnel manage the flow of goods and supplies into and out of the correctional institution. Usually a small group of workers are designated as treatment personnel. Of these, an even smaller number are actually assigned to activities that might be termed rehabilitative in nature. These include psychiatrists, psychologists, social workers, chaplains, and teachers.

All states have at least one facility for the treatment of youngsters within an institutional setting. Michigan, for example, has a complex of institutional arrangements which are a division of the Department of Social Services. Institutions are located at various sites in the state, and there are varying degrees of custodial supervision, depending upon the needs of the youngster and the seriousness of the behavior problem. There is a closed facility at Whitmore Lake, Michigan, where youngsters who have severe behavior problems are housed. There are also more open facilities for youngsters who do not need the intense supervision necessary under the Whitmore Lake program.

Subsequent to incarceration, an offender, either juvenile or adult, is usually assigned to a diagnostic center or classification unit to be interviewed and tested. The individual's record is reviewed so that the appropriate decision regarding custodial and program assignments can be made.

There is a considerable variation in the proportion of youths who are incarcerated in different states. Robert Vinter found that "(t)here was a ninety-one-fold difference between the state with the highest rate and that with the lowest."[96] This difference is unrelated to state crime rates. Between 1970 and 1974, for example,

> there was no association between states' annual rates of juvenile institutionalization and their rates of either total index crime or violent crime. Surprisingly, there was no association with property crime, which is reported to be the most common type of juvenile law violation; nor was any correlation found with other categories of crime.[97]

Vinter also reports that in sixteen institutions chosen for study, "there were twice as many misdemeanants and status offenders in the institutions as youths who had committed crimes against persons,"[98] although there is a trend to deinstitu-

---

[96]Robert D. Vinter, "Trends in State Corrections: Juveniles and the Violent Young Offender," *Crime and Delinquency, 25,* no. 2 (April 1979), pp. 145–161.

[97]*Ibid.,* p. 149.

[98]*Ibid.,* p. 153.

tionalize status offenders. State policies and practices are the primary influence on a youth's chances of being institutionalized. Crime rates and the type of offense a youth has committed are not major influences when states are compared. Thus, the programs for youths in institutions will affect many minor offenders as well as the more serious delinquents, particularly in states which favor incarceration.

Conditions in Juvenile Institutions

A number of studies have been conducted of the conditions in juvenile institutions, and in most cases this research has revealed many negative aspects of life in the typical large training school (Exhibit 7-5). Often custodial staff and treatment workers work at cross-purposes with one another, the former primarily concerned with security and considering the latter a threat to it. In some cases, treatment workers consider a preoccupation with security measures detrimental to rehabilitation. Relations between staff and treatment workers are confusing at best and are often actually hostile. Staff decision making tends to be routinized, focused on the criminal act rather than on treatment needs of the offender.[99]

A code of resident conduct, similar to that of adult prisoners, frequently inhibits relations between the juveniles and their keepers and treaters. The "code" generally requires residents to cooperate with one another in defiance of institution authority. The delinquent peer group in the institution is a significant determinant of both the form and the results of treatment.

In many institutions, the victimization of residents is a common occurrence. For example, Clemens Bartollas, Stuart J. Miller, and Simon Dinitz examined life inside of "what outwardly appears to be a fine, modern, humane, well-kept, well-staffed juvenile training school" in Ohio.[100] They found that exploitation and victimization were inherent aspects of institutional life. In many cases, staff used youths who exploited others to "keep the peace." The appropriation of property was the most common form of exploitation, but coerced sexual relations, while not as common, did occur. Sexually exploited youths were treated as pariahs by both staff and residents, making their lives very difficult. A classification system that the staff used to label dangerous and emotionally disturbed youths actually made it easier for exploitation and victimization to occur, for dangerous youths were expected to exploit, and other youths were seen as natural victims. Bartollas, Miller, and Dinitz concluded that there is no way to adapt to institutional life and at the same time experience therapy or rehabilitation. In extreme cases, youths adapt by running away, attempting suicide, or resorting to drugs.

---

[99]Philip L. Reichel, "Getting to Know You: Decision-Making in an Institution for Juveniles," *Juvenile and Family Court Journal, 36*, no. 1 (1985), pp. 5–15.

[100]Clemens Bartollas, Stuart J. Miller, and Simon Dinitz, *Juvenile Victimization: The Institutional Paradox* (Beverly Hills, California: Sage Publications, 1976), p. 260.

Exhibit 7-5   The atmosphere of a secure institution

Before gaining entrance into the internal environs of the institution, one must sign in at the switchboard to obtain the necessary permission and escort. After the arrival of the escort and a brief discussion of the purpose of the visit, a switchboard operator pushes the buzzer that opens one of two heavy, reinforced glass doors, allowing the visitor to enter a twenty-foot hallway. At the end of this hallway is yet another door, and upon ringing a buzzer, an officer pushes a button admitting the visitor into the main part of the institution. Once inside, the visitor is faced with two long and empty corridors, one of which leads to the chapel, the gymnasium, and the educational and vocational areas. The second corridor, extending approximately a quarter of a mile away from the main switchboard and patrolled by an officer in an electric golf cart, contains storage rooms, the nurse's office, the canteen, and, finally, the eight cottages in which the youths live.

SOURCE: Lindsay M. Hayes and Robert Johnson, *Confining Wayward Youths: Notes on the Correctional Management of Juvenile Delinquents* (Washington, D.C.: National Center on Institutions and Alternatives, 1980), pp. 5–6.

Issues for Discussion.   How can the secure institution help or hinder learning that can be transferred to the community? What feelings and perceptions of self is an inmate of a secure institution likely to develop? What types of inmate-staff relations are fostered? What would working conditions be like for the staff?

Although it is always difficult to establish a positive atmosphere in a large institution, some are more successful than others. Barry C. Feld studied state-wide efforts in the Massachusetts juvenile correctional institutions to operate treatment programs.[101] The programs used a variety of approaches, including individual counseling, group meetings, and social work services. Other programs within the institutions did not use any treatment methods, but instead stressed custody. All of these programs operated in various "cottages" on the state training school grounds.

The custody programs were characterized by a lack of communication between staff and inmates, and an emphasis in the youth subculture on fighting. Youths did not inform staff of fighting, and even when the staff were aware of aggressive acts, they frequently did not intervene. In some cases, staff encouraged fighting on the grounds that youths should be able to protect themselves.

In treatment programs, the staff encouraged youths to inform them of fighting or threats of physical aggression. There was usually an elaborate system of rewards and punishments, consisting of the granting or taking away of various privileges. This system was used to discourage fighting and to encourage open communication. Sharing information about fighting was often a part of treatment activities, such as regular group meetings. Youths did not feel that

[101]Barry C. Feld, *Neutralizing Inmate Violence* (Cambridge, Massachusetts: Ballinger Publishing Company, subsidiary of J.B. Lippincott Co., 1977).

they had to fight in order to survive, and they relied on staff to control aggression. Feld reports that once youths left the treatment programs, they were less likely than those leaving the custody cottages to be rearrested for violent acts.

In addition to contending with the general atmosphere, staff and youths in institutions must often contend with a lack of resources and trained personnel. The level of resources depends to a great extent on outside pressures. In times of economic stress, pressures for punitive measures are greater and funds are less available for quality treatment programs with ample staff, equipment, and facilities.

The failure of juvenile institutions to provide adequate programs is particularly serious in institutions for girls. Very often the types of programs available to girls are severely limited by popular beliefs about "appropriate" roles for females in our society. The *Survey of Educational and Vocational Programs in State Juvenile Correctional Institutions* provides strong evidence that this problem is widespread. For this survey, the Female Offender Resource Center studied twenty-two female, thirty male, and fifty-five coeducational institutions. The Resource Center found that

> the male institutions offered a larger variety of vocational training programs than the female institutions. The programs most commonly offered in male institutions are auto shop, welding, and small engine repair. In female institutions, they were cosmetology, business education, nurses' aide instruction and food services. If the young women were allowed to work at a job while incarcerated, they were more likely to be unpaid than the young men, and if paid, it was almost always at a lower rate. Academic education was generally poorer quality in female institutions than male institutions, as were other specialized institutional services such as those in the areas of counseling, religion, and medicine.[102]

The seriousness of this problem is aggravated by the tendency to use institutions for female delinquents who have committed relatively minor crimes, in part because there are fewer alternatives to institutions for females.[103] The net result of these practices is that many minor female offenders are placed in highly restrictive programs with a paucity of educational and treatment opportunities.

Minority group males and females also are disproportionately affected by any inadequacies of institutional programs. By 1982, minority youth were incarcerated at a rate three or four times higher than majority youth, and they were more often placed in public training programs as opposed to private correctional programs in the community.[104]

As we showed in our review of the literature on which youths are most

---

[102]Lee H. Bowker, *Women, Crime and the Criminal Justice System* (Lexington, Massachusetts: Lexington Books, D.C. Heath and Company, 1978), p. 230.

[103]Robert D. Vinter, *Time Out: A National Study of Juvenile Correctional Programs* (Ann Arbor: The University of Michigan Press, 1976).

[104]Barry Krisberg, Ira Schwartz, Gideon Fishman, Zvi Eisikovits, Edna Guttman, and Karen Joe, "The Incarceration of Minority Youth," *Crime and Delinquency, 33,* no. 2 (April 1987), pp. 173–205.

delinquent (Chapter 2), these differences are not fully explained by the claim that minority group adolescents are more delinquent than others. At least part of their overrepresentation in institutional programs is due to their being incarcerated more often than white youths, regardless of their delinquency records.

Effectiveness of Treatment in Institutions

In recent years, research has provided us with some understanding of the effectiveness of treatment in institutions. A study by William McCord and Jose Sanchez is unique because it followed up on training school residents over a twenty-five-year period.[105] The residents had gone to two different training schools, one that was oriented to punitive discipline and strict rules, and the other which provided milieu therapy. Milieu therapy, which will be discussed in more detail in the next chapter, encourages self-government and a "community of understanding." McCord and Sanchez found that until the age of twenty-four, the youths in the treatment-oriented program had much lower crime rates than those in the punitive program. However, as the youths matured past age twenty-four, there was less difference. After twenty-four, ethnicity was the greatest influence on recidivism, probably because youths in minority ethnic groups had the most difficult time locating jobs and achieving a successful status in their twenties. The findings that McCord and Sanchez report give us evidence that the quality of the treatment program in an institution makes a great difference on the recidivism of youths. The findings also remind us that, as many of the theories of delinquency indicate, social structural and economic conditions have an impact on criminality that cannot be completely overcome by individual treatment.

Not only does the availability of a sound treatment program affect the success of institutionalization, but careful matching of youths with institutional treatment has an influence. In the initial phase of the California Treatment Program, from 1961 to 1969, 802 boys and 212 girls were assigned either to an intensive probation service or to an institution.[106] On the average, the youths had been in trouble with the law six times before, but none had committed a robbery, assault with a deadly weapon, or forcible rape.

Youths assigned to probation were supervised in small caseloads of twelve or under. Jesness's I-Levels of interpersonal maturity were used to categorize the youths. Additionally, youths were classified as neurotics, power oriented, or passive conformists. The probation officers specialized in working with youths at a certain I-Level and of a certain type, and they provided differential treatment suited to these youths' special needs.

---

[105]William McCord and Jose Sanchez, "The Treatment of Deviant Children: A Twenty-Five Year Follow-Up Study," *Crime and Delinquency, 29,* no. 3 (April 1983), pp. 238–253.

[106]Ted Palmer, "The Youth Authority's Community Treatment Project," in *Effective Correctional Treatment,* eds. Robert R. Ross and Paul Gendreau (Toronto: Butterworths, 1980), pp. 255–278.

The largest group of boys were the neurotics. They recidivated much less often in the probation program than in institutions.

In contrast, the power-oriented youths recidivated more often in the probation program than those who were sent to institutions. The results were mixed for the passive-conformist boys and for all types of girls.

Ted Palmer, who played a major role in conducting the California research, concludes from these studies:

> Delinquent behavior can probably be reduced in connection with community and residential programs *alike*, by means of careful diagnosis and subsequent placement of individuals into appropriate rather than inappropriate or less than optimal settings and programs. In short, it might be said that it matters *which* youths (or types of youths) are placed into *which* type of setting, and that careful selection may lead to higher rates of success for residential and community-based programs alike.[107]

In looking at evaluations of juvenile delinquency programs, it is crucial to take into account the type of youth that participates. In some cases, it is possible that research may conclude that a certain program does not work, but if the program had been used with another type of youth, the results could be more positive.

One additional piece of research on institutions has provided evidence of effectiveness. Charles Murray and Louis Cox studied youths sent to St. Charles Training School and the Valley View Training School in Illinois.[108] The boys were compared with others who were in alternative programs, including nonresidential treatments, group homes, wilderness programs, out-of-town residential camps and the Illinois Psychiatric Institute. All of the boys were serious offenders with a long history of delinquency. Murray and Cox found that youths in the institution committed 68 percent less delinquency after release than they did before being institutionalized. However, the other programs also produced a reduction. For example, the youths in nonresidential programs committed 53 percent fewer delinquent acts after release than they committed in a similar time period before attending the program.

Lundman has reviewed the findings of the study by Murray and Cox, and tried to reconcile them with our information about the negative atmosphere and conditions in juvenile institutions and common sense judgment that institutions are unlikely to rehabilitate youths.[109] He considered the results of evaluations of the Provo Experiment and the Silverlake Experiment, both of which compared the effects of institutional and community treatment. The Provo Experiment showed that both institutions and community treatment reduced youths rates of breaking the law, but the effect was greater and lasted much longer for the youths experiencing community treatment. In the Silverlake Experiment, institutions and community treatment resulted in similar levels of

---

[107]*Ibid.*, p. 271.

[108]Charles A. Murray and Louis A. Cox, Jr., *Beyond Probation: Juvenile Corrections and the Chronic Offender* (Beverly Hills, California: Sage Publications, 1979).

[109]Lundman, *Prevention and Control of Juvenile Delinquency*, pp. 209–212.

recidivism. Thus, as Lundman points out, when the three comparisons are considered together, it appears that community treatment is at least as good as institutions in producing a reduction in the number of delinquent acts that a youth commits, and in the long run community treatment may be better.

Our knowledge of conditions in juvenile institutions and the results of research lead to the conclusion that the use of institutions on a large scale is not justified if the goal is to treat and rehabilitate the offender. Some argue that it is justified as "just deserts" for the harm caused by illegal activity, but that is another issue. When institutions are used, their effectiveness can be maximized by careful screening of selected youths to be committed and by careful design of educational and therapeutic programs.

The Future of Institutions

In view of the above realities concerning institutions, plus the statistics on recidivism, which show that incarceration tends to promote and harden offender attitudes and behavior rather than to rehabilitate, thinking has evolved more and more to the position that institutions, as they are now constituted, are hardly appropriate settings for therapeutic endeavors. According to some experts, the best that can be expected of institutions is that they successfully implement programs which are valuable adjuncts to treatment, such as humanitarian handling of inmates, vocational and educational training, religious activities, recreational participation, and prerelease planning. The actual treatment, which constitutes a basic modification of behavior and attitudes, is probably best effected outside institutional walls. Whenever possible, alternatives to incarceration are recommended, and if incarceration is used, it should be for a short period during which adequate treatment is available. The 1980 report of the National Advisory Committee on Juvenile Justice and Delinquency Prevention, for example, recommends the following:

> Whenever there is a choice among various alternatives, the option which least intrudes upon liberty and privacy should be preferred—"when you swat a mosquito on a friend's back, you should not use a baseball bat."[110]

The institutions of the future, as envisioned by the National Advisory Committee, should strive to remove many of the isolating effects of incarceration, thereby facilitating the difficult transition back into the community for those who have been imprisoned. The committee summed up a number of its major recommendations:

> The standards urge that residential facilities, other than camps and ranches, be in or near the communities from which they draw their population and recom-

[110]National Advisory Committee on Juvenile Justice and Delinquency Prevention, *Standards for the Administration of Juvenile Justice* (Washington, D.C.: U.S. Government Printing Office, 1980), p. xiv.

mend a low treatment staff-to-youth ratio and access by juveniles placed in residential facilities to a full range of educational, counseling, health, mental health and recreational programs. The increased costs which may result from the implementation of these recommendations can be substantially offset, through the utilization of community rather than in-house services, and through placing fewer juveniles in residential programs and reducing the length of their stay in such programs in accordance with the principle, emphasized throughout these standards, of employing the least restrictive alternative.[111]

Other standards emphasize the need to provide noninstitutional programs for status offenders and to protect the rights of juveniles who are in all types of correctional programs. Acceptable methods for disciplining program participants also are recommended, and these include the establishment of grievance procedures and ombudsman positions.

Experimentation in the handling and treatment of both adult and juvenile inmates has suggested some beneficial changes for institutional settings. Following are descriptions of a few of the more interesting and progressive institutional programs that have been started. Not all the programs described can be considered treatment in the strict sense. Some are merely adjuncts to treatment, but they illustrate reforms in North American juvenile institutions.

Canadian Training School for Females.   The staff in a Canadian training school for girls initiated a program to stop inmates from prevalent types of self-mutilation.[112] The girls had a high incidence of burning and carving themselves. Traditional treatment methods, such as counseling, punishment, education, or isolation, were not successful in stopping the mutilation. Instead, an effective treatment program was established by giving the girls a role in operating it. Staff report that the previously common problem of mutilation was markedly less frequent.

Twin Pines and Verdemont Ranch Programs.   Twin Pines Ranch for Boys and Verdemont Ranch for Boys are California state correctional programs. The boys live at the ranches for ten months, though they are allowed to return home on some weekends or for shorter visits. After the ten-month period, four months of aftercare are provided.

The Twin Pines program emphasizes work as an important rehabilitative tool for juveniles. Inmates are trained to carry out physical and personal duties related to hygiene, food preparation, upkeep of living quarters, ranch work, recreation, and sports.

The Verdemont Ranch program is in a similar setting, but the emphasis is quite different. Individual and group counseling are used extensively to teach families better communication skills. A variety of activities also are provided to improve family unity.

[111]*Ibid.*, p. 371.
[112]Robert R. Ross, *Self-Mutilation* (Lexington, Massachusetts: Lexington Books, D.C. Heath and Company, 1979).

Michael B. Maskin used an experimental approach to compare the effects of these different types of correctional programs.[113] During the youths' ten months in the programs, only four of thirty of those at the ranch emphasizing family communication were rearrested, but half of the thirty youths in the work program were rearrested. In the four-month aftercare program, participants in the family communication counseling continued to be less frequent recidivists. Although the sample of youths studied in these programs was quite small, family counseling for incarcerated youths does appear to be a more promising strategy than work.

Preston Training School, California. Carl F. Jesness has developed an elaborate scheme for categorizing youths according to their maturity in interacting with other people (I-Level), and as one of nine delinquent subtypes. The subtypes are: unsocialized and aggressive, unsocialized and passive, conformist and immature, conformist in a delinquent culture, manipulator, neurotic and acting out, neurotic and anxious, situational emotional reaction, and cultural identifier. At one training school, half of the youths were assigned to cottages with delinquents in the same categories as themselves.[114] Staff were assigned to these cottages according to their personal interests and abilities in working with a certain type of youth. The remaining half of the youths were assigned to regular training school cottages.

Regardless of the youths' characteristics, there were no differences between those in the special cottages and those in the regular program. The two groups were the same in recidivism after fifteen and twenty-four months.

Ward Grievance Procedure, California Youth Authority. The California Youth Authority operates a grievance procedure in all of its institutions.[115] Any youth who has a grievance is entitled to a hearing by representatives of staff and other youths in the institution. The youth has the right to appeal any decisions to other groups within the state system or, if the youth is still not satisfied, to a panel that is not associated with the Youth Authority. Lawyers who are trained as professional arbitrators voluntarily chair these outside panels. Grievances are handled in a timely fashion, and youths always receive a written statement of decisions.

The youths in the institutions handle all of the paperwork for the program. Both staff and youth participants are fully trained to review grievances and take part in joint decision making.

Between September 1973 and April 1975, 70 percent of the dispositions

[113]Michael B. Maskin, "The Differential Impact of Work-oriented vs. Communication-oriented Juvenile Correction Programs upon Recidivism Rates in Delinquent Males," *Journal of Clinical Psychology, 32,* no. 2 (April 1976), pp. 432–433.

[114]Carl F. Jesness, "The Preston Typology Study: An Experiment with Differential Treatment in an Institution," *Journal of Research in Crime and Delinquency, 8,* no. 1 (January 1971), pp. 38–52.

[115]Ward Grievance Procedure, California Youth Authority (Washington, D.C.: U.S. Government Printing Office, 1975).

favored the youth filing the grievance, or provided some type of compromise settlement. Just 2 percent of the grievances had to be resolved by the outside panel, which suggests that the state system was able to provide some satisfactory resolution in all but a few cases.

The inventory of innovative institutional programs for delinquents could be continued almost *ad infinitum,* a fact which should suffice to illustrate that correctional staff are making efforts to treat youths in institutional settings. Table 7-4 summarizes the effects of several rehabilitative prevention programs. Although some of these programs have produced more humane living conditions in the institutions, none have been highly effective in reducing recidivism to any considerable degree once the youths leave the institutions. For this reason, considerable efforts have been made to treat offenders in the noninstitutional settings that we have already described.

CONCLUSION

This chapter has presented a sampling of the various prevention efforts that have been tired and are being used to prevent, control, and treat juvenile delinquency. Several of the programs discussed were *pure* prevention efforts—pre-

Table 7-4 A Summary of the Effects of Institutional Rehabilitative Prevention Programs

PROGRAMS TO BE COMPARED	EFFECTS DURING INCARCERATION	EFFECTS AFTER INCARCERATION
Massachusetts Training School Programs		
Custody programs	Strong and violent inmate culture	More violent recidivism
Treatment programs	Weak, less violent inmate culture	Less violent recidivism
Canadian Training School for Females		
Counseling, punishment, education, and isolation	Continued self-mutilation	Not Known
Inmate run program	Reduced self-mutilation	Not Known
Twin Pines and Verdemont Ranch Programs		
Twin Pines work program	More rearrests on home visits	More recidivism
Verdemont family communications program	Fewer rearrests on home visits	Less recidivism
Preston Training School		
Placement based on I-level	Not known	No change in recidivism
Ward Grievance Procedure		
Inmate run grievance procedure	Satisfactory grievance resolution	Not known

venting delinquency before it occurs. Other programs were a combination of pure prevention and rehabilitative prevention—treating both youngsters who have come in contact with the juvenile justice system and those who have not. Other types of programs described were those established mainly for youngsters who have come in contact with the juvenile justice system and who need rehabilitation and treatment so that future delinquent behavior will not be manifested in the community. We also have presented information on diversion programs which attempt to provide rehabilitative services to youths outside of traditional police and court programs.

The need to match offenders with programs has become more and more clear. John T. Whitehead and Steven P. Lab reviewed juvenile correctional treatment research published between 1975 to 1984, and they concluded that, indeed, many of the interventions did not appear to "work."[116] However, when D. A. Andrews and his colleagues reviewed a similar set of studies, they reinforced the understanding that programs are effective when they are chosen to meet the particular needs and learning styles of selected juvenile offenders.[117]

The next chapter, "Methods of Treatment," will discuss treatment approaches, counseling methods, and other therapeutic strategies. Just as it was pointed out in this chapter that there are many prevention-type programs, the next chapter will examine a variety of approaches and techniques of treatment that have been tried and are being used with youngsters.

DISCUSSION QUESTIONS

1. Differentiate between *pure* and *rehabilitative* prevention.
2. It is recognized that pure prevention is more effective in dealing with delinquency than rehabilitative prevention. Why, then, are there not more pure prevention programs?
3. Compare the advantages and the disadvantages of community programs versus institutionalization. Cite research findings reviewed in this chapter to support your views.
4. What are the pros and cons of the different strategies to deal with the problem of delinquency and its relation to schools?
5. Do the benefits of diversion programs outweigh the possible disadvantages?
6. What are the special problems that females and minority youths experience in institutional correctional programs?
7. Consider the possible explanations for positive outcomes of restitution programs. Given your understanding of the best supported theories to explain delinquency, which explanation(s) do you think are most feasible and why? Explain how you would design a restitution program to avoid the criticisms but to provide any benefits.
8. Assume that your job is to prioritize spending areas for a state budget for the prevention and control of delinquency. Consider the limited amount of money available, the needs of the juveniles, and public safety. What percent of your budget would you spend for pure prevention, diversion, tradi-

[116]John T. Whitehead and Steven P. Lab, "A Meta-Analysis of Juvenile Correctional Treatment," *Journal of Research in Crime and Delinquency, 26,* no. 3 (August 1989), pp. 276–295.

[117]D. A. Andrews, Ivan Zinger, Robert D. Hoge, James Bonta, Paul Gendreau, and Francis T. Cullen, "Does Correctional Treatment Work? A Clinically Relevant and Psychologically Informed Meta-Analysis," *Criminology, 28,* no. 3 (August 1990), pp. 369–404.

tional probation and parole, special probation and parole programs, various community programs, and juvenile institutions? Justify your answer based on your knowledge of who is in the juvenile justice system, the results of research to test theory, and the results of program evaluation research.

PROJECTS

1. Classify each of the many programs reviewed in this chapter according to whether it is based on sociological or psychological theories of crime causation. Can you identify the specific crime causation theory on which some of these programs are based?

2. According to your understanding of the types of youths who are most likely to be delinquent (Chapter 2), classify the programs described in this chapter according to their capacity to focus services on the most delinquent youths.

3. Describe an ideal network of community-based programs for youths in your community.

4. Review newspaper stories and editorials and contact legislators' offices and public-interest groups to identify pressure groups (a) for the increased use of institutions and (b) against the use of institutions in your state.

8

Methods of Treatment

- INDIVIDUAL TREATMENT METHODS
- GROUP TREATMENT METHODS
- COMPARING TREATMENT METHODS

LEARNING OBJECTIVES

1. To know about the many different treatment methods that are currently used with delinquents.
2. To be familiar with how these methods are used, and the skills that staff using each method must have.
3. To be aware of the research showing that the various methods are or are not effective.
4. To be familiar with programs that use a combination of methods.

Specific methods of treatment in handling the juvenile are used both in pure prevention and rehabilitative prevention programs, as well as in diversion programs and in the agencies that deal with troubled youths in the community. Many approaches and methods can be used in treating the delinquent in these programs. Most of the methods have a theoretical orientation, and they relate to the theories and assumptions about human behavior that were discussed in previous chapters. For example, the psychoanalytic and psychiatric methods of treating the youngster is the outgrowth of research that emphasized the intrapsychic interplay of the dynamics of the individual and the forces that determine behavior.

   The various treatment methods to be described are strategies that attempt to change those conditions thought to be causative factors in juvenile delinquency.[1] Even though an approach can take many forms, it can usually be classified as either an individual approach to treating the offender or a group approach where offenders are treated within the constellation of a group and among their peers. A third category of treatment, punishment, is not as prevalent today as in the past. Although those who prescribe punishment as a method of treatment in itself feel they can justify their position, it will not be considered in this chapter as a viable technique of treatment. The rationale underlying the use of punishment is that pain serves as a deterrent to further criminal action. Punishment, as an end in itself, is often used when staff are untrained and when more appropriate methods of treatment are unknown. In the context used in the present discussion, punishment is not to be equated with the setting of limits or the transmission of expectations with resulting enforcement of restrictions or reprimands if reasonable expectations are not adhered to. The setting of limits and restrictions and reprimands is a necessary element in any method of treating and handling the youngster. They can be effective supplements to the major treatment approach utilized. It is when punishment or restriction becomes an end in itself that it cannot be justified or regarded as effective "treatment."

The two basic approaches, then, in dealing with youngsters, are the individual and the group method of treatment. The individual method is generally used by psychiatrists, psychologists, and social workers, while the group method involves schoolteachers, recreation specialists, and social workers. It is difficult, however, to classify professions by method because psychologists often use the group method, while social workers and even some sociologists use the individual method. There is also a blending of the individual and the group work approach, with the possibility that the same person will be using both the individual and the group method. The method that therapists or counselors select usually fits their professional training, personality, and clientele. Even though a combination of approaches will generally be used, one major orientation will be taken, with specific assumptions about the causes of human behavior.

Knowledge of the various approaches for treating and rehabilitating the delinquent or the predelinquent is important for the professional within the juvenile justice system. Regardless of the phase of juvenile justice that he or she is involved in (police work, social work, courts, probation, parole, corrections, research), an awareness of treatment methods and strategies will provide familiarity with the many approaches, the current terminology, and the assumptions about human behavior made by other professionals in the juvenile justice system.

Although the police officer, for example, may not use or be trained to use many of these methods and may not even agree with their orientation, knowledge of them will provide greater insight into the reasons why professional counterparts in other agencies take their particular orientation to delinquent behavior problem solving. Furthermore, exposing all the different professionals within the juvenile justice system to the various treatment approaches and strat-

[1] Paul Lerman, *Delinquency and Social Policy* (New York: Frederick A. Praeger, Inc., 1970), p. 37.

egies may be instrumental in the development of an orientation that will be generally normative and acceptable to all the various professions. A more coordinated and normative orientation to treating the delinquent would be conducive to providing a consistent approach to delinquency problem solving.

Because of the many treatment methods, the professional soon learns that there is no "right way" to treat the youngster and that many approaches have merit. This allows the professional to select the approach or the parts of many approaches that seem to be most effective and beneficial.

As pointed out earlier, it is difficult to correlate specific approaches with a particular academic orientation—sociologists usually take a "social engineering" approach to delinquency prevention and treatment, while psychologists treat the individual. In other words, sociologists attempt to determine the conditions of the social structure that breed delinquency, while psychologists emphasize the individual and interpersonal dynamics. Sociology has typically been regarded as a theoretical discipline researching the causes, rates, and effects of crime and delinquency. The profession of social work is the "practical arm" of the sociologist. The social worker attempts to put into practice the assumptions that have been posited by sociologists. However, social workers base much of their actual treatment of clients on psychological and psychiatric theories and principles.

The social worker, then, translates the theories and assumptions of both psychological and sociological theory into action. This is one of the main reasons why individual and group approaches to treatment are often blended.

In addition to theorizing about causes of delinquency, the psychologist, like the social worker, often becomes involved in the specific use of treatment methods. The sociologist is usually oriented to the more massive problem of "social engineering."

The majority of treatment methods in use are based on the psychological and, to a lesser extent, the social-psychological theories of crime causation.

> The rise of the rehabilitation orientation in corrections has centered, for the most part, around the growth of individual treatment policies and theories arguing that offenders are emotionally "sick." Prison programs, probation services, guidance clinics, juvenile courts, and other treatment agencies have considered the lawbreaker as an emotionally disturbed person in need of psychotherapeutic treatment, almost to the exclusion of any other tactic.[2]

Rosemary Sarri's survey of 35 group homes, institutions, and day treatment centers revealed that 85 percent used individual counseling, 79 percent group counseling, 71 percent reality therapy, 68 percent behavior modification, 59 percent family therapy, and 56 percent psychotherapy.[3] Additionally, 80 percent

---

[2]Don C. Gibbons, *Society, Crime and Criminal Careers: An Introduction to Criminology,* 3rd ed. (Englewood Cliffs, New Jersey: Prentice Hall, Inc., 1978), pp. 156–157.

[3]Rosemary Sarri, "Service Technologies: Diversion, Probation, and Detention," in *Brought to Justice? Juveniles, the Courts, and the Law,* eds. Rosemary Sarri and Yeheskel Hasenfeld (Ann Arbor: The University of Michigan Press, 1976), p. 141.

of institutions used religious counseling, and 30 percent of group homes used educator therapy. Youths on probation most often received individual counseling (44 percent) or group counseling (38 percent). About one-third of youths received work placement, academic or remedial education, or vocational education.[4] All of these predominant treatment methods attempt to change the child, and they ignore the social structural causes of delinquency which are identified in sociological theories. The majority of people who work within the juvenile justice system and provide direct services intended to eliminate delinquency use the psychological theories as their basis for action.

The terminology used for the particular treatment method and the label used for the treater can be confusing. Some treatment approaches are similar but have different names. Also, the function and the role of the treater can be similar for the various methods, but he or she may be called a counselor, caseworker, therapist, or psychotherapist.

A discussion of the individual and group methods of treatment follows. Although it is difficult to assign a particular academic discipline or profession to the many approaches, the professionals who utilize the following methods are generally psychologists, psychiatrists, and social workers. There are approaches, however, that such professionals as the police and school counselors can use, and these approaches will also be emphasized.

PSYCHOTHERAPY

Both Kolb[5] and Wolberg[6] define *psychotherapy* as a method of treatment of emotional and personality problems by psychological means. The aim of this method is to remove or retard symptoms or behavior patterns that are contributing to dysfunctional behavior. The promotion of personal growth is the end product. Nikelly states that

> any form of psychotherapy involves change in the client's attitude as well as his feelings and such change will ultimately be reflected in the client's value system. The therapist should not hesitate to disclose that he too has values and that his and the client's values may occasionally clash. Such a conflict can actually form a landmark during the process of psychotherapy because the client must examine his own values carefully in order to understand why they fail to help him function effectively as an emotionally healthy and adjusted person.[7]

Psychotherapy is an outgrowth of Freudian psychoanalytic and psychiatric assumptions. One of the basic concepts of psychotherapy is the phe-

---

[4]*Ibid.*, p. 162.

[5]Lawrence C. Kolb, *Noyes' Modern Clinical Psychiatry* (Philadelphia: W. B. Saunders Co., 1968), p. 346.

[6]Lewis R. Wolberg, *The Techniques of Psychotherapy* (New York: Grune and Stratton, Inc., 1967), p. 3.

[7]Arthur G. Nikelly, "Basic Processes in Psychotherapy," *Techniques for Behavior Change* (Springfield, Illinois: Charles C. Thomas, Publisher, 1971), p. 31.

nomenon of *transference,* the redirecting of feelings from the client to the therapist, which in turn enables the therapist to probe the attitudes, thoughts, and feelings about significant persons in the client's past through his or her own relationship with the client. Many times the therapist will represent an authoritative figure of the client's early past and, in the case of a delinquent, the therapist often represents a parental figure. Aichhorn, who was one of the first people to attempt psychotherapy with delinquents, felt that transference was one of the most important elements in treating the juvenile delinquent.[8] Through his research, he concluded that all the extremely aggressive boys in his institution had had similar life experiences with their parents, that is, constant quarrels between parents or parental figures. There is much hate between the youngster and parents because of these early relationships. Since the early relationship of the youngster and parents was not satisfactory, the youth's emotional development was often retarded, with the effect that a delinquent was often impulsive in an attempt to satisfy infantile urges not satisfied in the normal manner within the family. Satisfying these urges and impulses can take the form of antisocial behavior within the community.

One of Aichhorn's methods of handling youths who had grown up in such a situation was to utilize the method of transference and allow them to satisfy their impulses while under the guidance of a sympathetic adult (or parental substitute) whom the youngster could trust and rely on.

> If delinquency is to be cured and the asocial youth made fit again for life in society, the training school must provide him with new ties and induce him to attach himself to persons of his environment. We try to bring about such attachments by the kindly manner in which we treat our pupils.[9]

Aichhorn was explaining that the institutionalized child under his direction was allowed to operate in an atmosphere of love and acceptance and therefore did not have to fear severe rejection or physical punishment. The children, under these conditions, would learn to develop a satisfactory relationship, trust the adult figure, and satisfy their needs. Aichhorn felt that this trust, as a result of the warm friendly relationship, could be generalized to other adults and institutions in the community. This would eliminate much of the impulsive necessity to act out against authority substitutes.

Friedlander, whose orientation to human behavior is similar to that of Aichhorn, discovered that there were changes in behavior due to the transference established between youths and the counselor.

> The aggressiveness was not just acted out; the person of the educator (therapist) became an important factor in it. The boys clearly wanted to provoke him to punish them and were therefore specially destructive when in his presence. This punishment would have provided them with an instinctive gratification on the sadomasochistic level which they had been able to obtain in all their former

[8]August Aichhorn, *Wayward Youth* (New York: The Viking Press, Inc., 1963).
[9]August Aichhorn, *Delinquency and Child Guidance* (New York: International Universities Press, Inc., 1964), p. 29.

environments. When the punishment did not come, the boys grew dissatisfied. Not only did they not derive sufficient gratification when destroying inanimate things but the unforeseen reaction of their educators put them in a difficult position; there was no longer any justification for their hatred. They still tried to get what they wanted by being more and more aggressive but in the end they had to give in: they began to feel guilty (the first stage of superego development) and they broke down. Behind their aggressiveness and their wish to be punished, which has been transformed to the educators, there now appeared a fierce longing to be loved. This was still very untamed. Their demands for the affection of the leader were insatiable but they now had an emotional relationship to an adult which made education possible.[10]

The above quotation illustrates the transference phenomenon in operation. The clients generalized to the educator or the therapist their early attitudes and feelings toward adults. They expected the therapist to react the way their parents would have reacted. When they found that not all adults reacted the same as their parents, they began to evaluate their attitudes and their behavior and concluded that not all adults were the same. Thus, they did not have the generalized hatred for all adults or all adult institutions, and their acting out behavior began to diminish greatly.

Long and Kamada believe that in the initial therapeutic stages, it is essential to develop a basis of trust between the therapist and the youngster.[11] All youngsters, whether in a therapeutic situation or in the family constellation, constantly test to determine the limits of acceptable behavior and the reaction of the adult. If delinquents come from family situations where there was very little trust or emotional security, they are very skeptical in treatment situations. If therapists cannot establish themselves as trusting persons who will be unlike the youngster's brutal and insensitive parents, it will be difficult for the youngster to benefit from the treatment.

Holmes points out that many delinquent youngsters, even though they may be in their late teens, fantasize a great deal and have feelings of omnipotence.[12] Everyone is aware that a very young child, as a result of fantasizing, can pretend to be anybody, including strong and powerful individuals. Because delinquent youngsters have not had satisfying or emotionally secure environments, they utilize fantasy to increase their feelings of worthfulness, deny unpleasant circumstances, and avoid facing the reality of their environment and its demands and requirements. When the youngster's behavior is dealt with thoroughly and objectively by the therapist, this can be surprising to the youngster and can neutralize many fantasies about adult authority figures. Being treated fairly and objectively is often a new experience for a youngster, and when this does occur it is both unexpected and incongruent with earlier life experiences.

[10]Kate Friedlander, *The Psycho-Analytical Approach to Juvenile Delinquency* (London: Routledge and Kegan Paul Ltd., 1947), p. 243.

[11]Anna Marie Long and Samuel I. Kamada, "Psychiatric Treatment of Adolescent Girls," *California Youth Authority Quarterly*, 17, no. 2 (Summer 1964), pp. 23–24.

[12]Donald J. Holmes, *The Adolescent in Psychotherapy* (Boston: Little, Brown, and Company, 1964).

Holmes is emphasizing the importance of directness with the youngster. When the delinquent youngster manipulates and uses devious means to satisfy some needs, there is an expectation of the same type of reaction from adults within the environment. When this negative, manipulative, devious cycle is interrupted by the therapist, the youngster becomes aware of the negative cycle of behavior and realizes that some adults do react differently and do not always play dishonest games of manipulation. Holmes is also careful to point out the importance of going beyond merely making interpretations of behavior in psychotherapy. Interpretation in itself does not always alter behavior.

> If an adolescent boy prefers stealing cars to suffering the anxiety he would experience if he did not steal cars, he would probably not be helped by interpretation alone. The general principle is the same as in the treatment of addictions or perversions. It is virtually impossible to treat a chronic alcoholic successfully in a tavern.[13]

The therapist, then, interprets behavior to point out the negative dynamics, and must also point out the reality of the situation and of the behavior itself. For example, to merely explain to a youngster that stealing cars results from an unresolved oedipal conflict will not usually in itself contribute to diminished car stealing. This interpretation, however, along with pointing out the reality of the negative ramifications of car stealing and the long-range problems that will be created by it, can be helpful. The youngster will learn that the negative consequences of stealing cars and possible incarceration are not very pleasurable, and that other modes of behavior or other alternatives can be developed to satisfy desires and impulses. The therapist as the authority person can, in addition to making an interpretation, provide healthy alternatives and guidelines for the youngster.

Jurjevich points out that the therapist must help delinquent youngsters to be responsible for their own behavior even when they are in a supportive correctional setting.[14] From the many case histories that Jurjevich reviewed, he found that there were many difficulties in the youngsters' backgrounds, but he felt that these unfortunate circumstances could not be used by the clients as excuses to act irresponsibly because they would still be evaluated according to the normative criteria established by society, which its institutions of control would enforce. Thus his main direction was not focused on past traumas or injuries or personal handicaps, but in the direction of providing new alternatives for the youngsters so they could avoid future problems in the community.

The psychotherapeutic method is often ascribed an aura of mysticism. In very simple terms, psychotherapy is merely a method of conversation between the client and the therapist to allow them to get to know each other so that they can be comfortable in exchanging communication. The communication allows

---

[13]*Ibid.*, p. 185.

[14]Ratibor-Ray M. Jurjevich, *No Water in My Cup: Experiences and a Controlled Study of Psychotherapy of Delinquent Girls* (New York: Libra Publishers, 1968).

the client to begin to relate personal experiences, perceptions, ideas, and reasons for negative as well as positive behavior so that solutions will be forthcoming. The effective therapist will create an atmosphere where youngsters can be comfortable and can relate their feelings and attitudes but will always be provided a base or reference to reality. The emotionally secure and able therapist or counselor will provide these reference points even when they are not popular with the client but in the long run will be most effective for positive behavior.

Studies of the effectiveness of psychotherapy in interrupting a pattern of delinquent behavior have rarely shown this method to be successful, and in some cases youths in psychotherapy become more delinquent than others.[15] The exceptions involve programs that are used only for youths prejudged to be amenable to psychotherapy, and programs that use psychotherapy in combination with other treatment methods. One of these successful programs using a combination of methods was offered to boys in a correctional institution. They were encouraged to develop a warm interpersonal relationship with a therapist who took part in individual and group discussions of self-defeating behavior. Besides the psychotherapy, the therapists used negative reinforcement of inappropriate behavior and approval for appropriate behavior. Role playing also was used during the therapy session.[16] A second psychotherapy program which has been demonstrated to be effective used discussions with the youth as a first step in treatment.[17] Then the youths and therapists set behavioral goals, and the youths practiced the desired behavior in an educational setting. The counselor, who also worked as the classroom teacher, observed the youths' attempts to act in a positive way, and during a later counseling session discussed any needed modifications in behavior. Although psychotherapy is still widely used, we do want to stress that there is little research evidence that it is effective for a large number of delinquents, particularly when it is used as the sole treatment method.

In conclusion, psychotherapy emanates from the framework of psychoanalysis and psychiatric theory. The therapist evaluates the client's feelings, experiences, and inner dynamics. He or she attempts to point out faulty perceptions and provide positive alternatives to behavior adaptation. The therapist usually represents many adults in the youngster's past. Ideally, the new positive attitude of the youngster which results from his or her relationship with the therapist alters negative behavior in the community. The most successful psychotherapy programs are those which accept clients who are considered to be particularly amenable to treatment, and those which use psychotherapy in combination with other treatment methods.

[15]Dennis A. Romig, *Justice for Our Children: An Examination of Juvenile Delinquent Rehabilitation Programs* (Lexington, Massachusetts: Lexington Books, D. C. Heath and Company, 1978), p. 81.

[16]Roy W. Persons, "Psychological and Behavioral Change in Delinquents Following Psychotherapy," *Journal of Clinical Psychology*, 22, no. 3 (July 1966), pp. 337–340.

[17]Evelyn S. Thomas, "Effects of Experimental School Counseling of Delinquency-Prone Adolescents," *Dissertation Abstracts*, 28, no. 7–A (1968), p. 2572.

SOCIAL CASEWORK

Social casework, according to Tappan, is that phase of social work dealing directly with the maladjusted individual to determine the kind of help needed in coping with personal problems.[18] Ferguson feels that "when social work is primarily concerned with the fullest possible degree of personality development we call it social casework."[19]

Although similar in many respects, technically social casework should be considered different from psychotherapy. In fact, those social workers utilizing social casework often see themselves as therapists and feel that, even though they have been trained in social casework, the specific focus of their social casework training has been in the psychotherapeutic area. Regardless of the technical difference between the two, they both rely on developing a positive relationship with the client in order to provide assistance in problem solving. In casework, as in psychotherapy, the client relates on a one-to-one basis with the caseworker. This type of interaction can result in a joint effort at problem solving and the development of socially acceptable alternatives to community adjustment. The casework method is conducive to determining the conditions that contribute to deviant behavior and pinpointing the resources necessary to support clients in their efforts to become contributing members of society. The caseworker utilizes the social history to explore the client's background, environment, and relationship with family, friends, and peers. The social history, or case history, affords the caseworker, who may be a probation officer, parole officer, prison counselor, mental health worker, or school social worker, the opportunity to evaluate the personal strengths and weaknesses of the client as well as the environment so that a treatment plan can be devised and carried out. In terms of environmental manipulation, the youngster may be removed from the family or community and placed in a rehabilitative agency or treatment program for the purpose of minimizing severe pressures of the family or peer group who are contributing to the youth's negative behavior.

In working with delinquents, it is often difficult to obtain their cooperation because they are unwilling to trust the caseworker. The delinquent's family may also be resistant and may become defensive and feel threatened by the caseworker's "probing." Parents often fear that the negative dynamics of their family and their relationship with their youngster will become known and that they will be blamed for their youngster's predicament. Even though social casework, like many other methods, has been successful with neurotics, it has often not been successful with delinquents. Neurotics are usually motivated in the helping relationship, while delinquents are not. The intensity of the one-to-one relationship with the caseworker is also threatening. Some of the assumptions of social casework are not applicable in treating the delinquent. For example, the

[18]Paul W. Tappan, *Juvenile Delinquency* (New York: McGraw-Hill Book Company, 1949), p. 362.

[19]Elizabeth A. Ferguson, *Social Work: An Introduction* (Philadelphia: J. B. Lippincott Co., 1963), p. 9.

caseworker often takes a passive approach to treatment under the guise of client self-determination and the need for client involvement and commitment. Delinquents need a more direct and aggressive approach, which accelerates client involvement and joint problem solving.

In some cases the family refuses to become involved in the helping process even when the *aggressive casework* method is utilized; consequently, the caseworker may have to call upon an authoritative agency like the juvenile court to intervene in the problem situation.

> Steps toward the use of aggressive casework arise from the acceptance of a social philosophy that assigns to the community not only the right to protect children but the responsibility of taking vigorous action on their behalf when their behavior reflects a destructive process that the family itself cannot or will not control.[20]

Casework with delinquents can be viewed as a three-phased process. Initially and in less severe cases, the typical method of passive involvement with the clients can often be utilized. If, however, the youngster is a chronic offender, the passive processes of self-determination and cathartic verbalization have usually already been tried. The youth may be resentful and cynical of not only the process itself but also the adult who is using it. Furthermore, if the parents are contributing to and fostering the delinquent activity, the caseworker's passive methods will not be successful because of their hostility and unresponsiveness. Therefore, the second phase involves the use of aggressive casework in which the worker must be persistent and direct in approaching the problem. The worker confronts the parents and defines the problem, the consequences if the problem is not handled, and the alternatives for its solution. The worker must provide a great deal of support in the early stages of treatment so that the family will become involved in the problem-solving process and will be able to make realistic decisions and accept responsibility.[21] Finally, if the first phase of passive casework and the second phase of aggressive casework are not successful, an authoritative agency such as the juvenile court may have to be presented to the family as the only alternative, and it may have to intervene to insure that the parents and the youngster will begin to look at their problem realistically and attempt to seek solutions.

Frequently, regardless of whether the technique utilized is the passive approach or the aggressive approach, it is still difficult to work with youngsters and their families because the atmosphere is usually tense and pervaded with hostility and resentment toward the criminal justice system. Another form of casework called "directed friendship" was developed.[22] Paid nonprofessionals visit homes and schools for the express purpose of giving personal advice and

[20]Harry Manuel Shulman, *Juvenile Delinquency in American Society* (New York: Harper and Row, Publishers, 1961), p. 642.

[21]Alice Overton, "Aggressive Casework," in *Reaching the Unreached*, ed. Sylvan S. Furman (New York City Youth Board, 1952), p. 54.

[22]Edwin Powers and Helen Witmer, *An Experiment in the Prevention of Delinquency: The Cambridge-Somerville Youth Study* (New York: Columbia University Press, 1951).

Exhibit 8-1   The Cambridge-Somerville Youth Study

In 1935, Richard Clark Cabot instigated one of the most imaginative and exciting programs ever designed in hopes of preventing delinquency. A social philosopher as well as physician, Dr. Cabot established a program that both avoided stigmatizing participants and permitted follow-up evaluation.

Several hundred boys from densely populated, factory-dominated areas of eastern Massachusetts were included in the project, known as the Cambridge-Somerville Youth Study. Schools, welfare agencies, churches, and the police recommended both "difficult" and "average" youngsters to the program. These boys and their families were given physical examinations and were interviewed by social workers who then rated each boy in such a way as to allow a selection committee to designate delinquency-prediction scores. In addition to giving delinquency-prediction scores, the selection committee studied each boy's records in order to identify pairs who were similar in age, delinquency-prone histories, family background, and home environments. By the toss of a coin, one member of each pair was assigned to the group that would receive treatment.

SOURCE: Joan McCord, "A Thirty-Year Follow-Up of Treatment Effects," *American Psychologist, 33*, no. 3 (March 1978), p. 284.

Issues for Discussion.   What society-wide changes might have made the Cambridge-Somerville Youth Study more successful? Should a similar approach be used in the future? If yes, under what conditions?

guidance. A relationship with the youngsters is developed so that the "friendship person" can be a readily available source of advice, guidance, and support to the youngster before there is more difficulty with the law. This is a much different approach from waiting until the youngster becomes chronically involved in serious difficulty.

The Cambridge-Somerville Youth Study, which began in 1939, focused on the outcome of a major application of the directed friendship approach to social casework (see Exhibit 8-1). Youths and their families were provided with casework services for a ten-year period. The program was not a strong influence on recidivism except among a select group of youths. Successful program participants were from families with minimal emotional maladjustment and which desired help. Another key factor in program success was a close correspondence between the social work services and the sources of family difficulty. In a followup study, one of the original researchers, Joan McCord, examined the court, mental hospital, and alcoholism treatment center records for both the study participants and a similar group of youths who did not receive treatment. She found that "none of the . . . measures confirmed hopes that the treatment had improved the lives of those in the treatment group." In fact, there seemed to be negative side effects of the program, for the participants were more likely to commit a second crime, showed more signs of alcoholism and serious mental illness, died younger, had occupations with lower prestige, and reported that their work was not satisfying.[23] It is not possible to say for certain why there were negative results, but McCord suggests that the assistance of high-status caseworkers raised the expectations of program participants, and when the assistance was no longer available, the result was symptoms of dependency and resentment. This finding alerts us to the necessity of considering the effects of offering services that raise expectations without opening up opportunities to meet these expectations.

Evaluation research has not provided any clear indication that social casework is an effective treatment method for delinquency. In fact, some studies have shown that, when casework services are very intensive, youths are more like to recidivate.[24] These negative findings about such a frequently used treatment method make it clear that the treatment of delinquency is often experimental. We are by no means in a position to choose highly effective treatment for each delinquent youth. Even methods that have been used for many years have not been consistently demonstrated to be effective.

REALITY THERAPY

The major basis of the *reality therapy* approach is that all persons have certain basic needs. When they are unable to fulfill these needs, they act in an irresponsible manner. The object of reality therapy is to help the person act in a responsible manner—in the case of delinquents, to help them refrain from antisocial activity. A premise of this approach is that regardless of what the delinquent youngsters have done and the extenuating circumstances—for example, inadequate parents or negative environmental conditions—youngsters are still responsible for their behavior. The reality therapy method is an understandable, common-sense approach which its originator, Dr. William Glasser, holds can be utilized by all members of the criminal justice system ranging from the arresting officer to the counselor in the training school. Anyone who comes in contact with the delinquent can utilize this approach because it does not emphasize nebulous psychiatric terms, extensive testing, or time-consuming case conferences.

> The only case records needed are occasional notes about what has occurred that shows increased responsibility. If the boy fails, the reason is that we were not able to help him become responsible enough to live in society. We need no detailed record of this failure to explain why.[25]

[23]Joan McCord, "A Thirty-Year Follow-up of Treatment Effects," *American Psychologist, 33,* no. 3 (March 1978), p. 288.

[24]Romig, *Justice for Our Children,* p. 7.

[25]William Glasser, "Reality Therapy: A Realistic Approach to the Young Offender," in *Readings in Delinquency and Treatment,* eds. Robert Schasre and Jo Wallach (Los Angeles: Delinquency Prevention Training Project, Youth Studies Center, University of Southern California, 1965), p. 65.

In sharp contrast to the psychotherapeutic methods, reality therapy emphasizes the present behavior of the youngster and considers it the most important event. What happened in the past is insignificant because, regardless of how much is known about the past extenuating circumstances and the parent-child relationship, the past cannot be changed. The basis of psychotherapy is that a person cannot change present behavior unless he or she can clearly tie it to events in the past. Glasser states that delving into the past is "a fruitless historical journey—which leads to excusing the offender's present actions as an unfortunate culmination of his history."[26] The premise is that, since our past history cannot be changed or objectively reconstructed, we can never fully understand the reasons why we committed a certain act, and interpretations are often merely guesses as to causative relationships. Furthermore, if present behavior is merely a reflection and the sum total of all past experiences (as traditional psychotherapies propose), then when the present behavior is modified and changed this nullifies all past experiences.

Glasser believes that many therapists, caseworkers, and counselors feel that the youngster is unhappy because of past circumstances, and acting out within the community results from this unhappiness. Efforts to make the youngster happy invariably fail because the unhappiness is the result of irresponsible behavior (delinquent activity) and not the result of past personal and environmental circumstances. Since everyone wants to feel worthwhile and to be evaluated positively by peers, irresponsible delinquent behavior causes negative self-evaluations and hence feelings of worthlessness or unhappiness. The only way people can be made to feel worthwhile and fulfill their basic needs is by acting in a responsible manner, which means avoiding delinquent behavior.

The main objective of reality therapy is to make the individual a responsible person within the community, and this starts with a positive relationship and interaction with the therapist. If the therapist treats the youngster as responsible rather than an unfortunate youngster, this will transmit strength to the youngster. The therapist should be a warm and honest person who emphasizes the positive rather than the negative and strength rather than weakness, and should have confidence that the youngster will act responsibly. The youngster is expected to obey rules, but is not rejected for breaking one. The reality of the situation and the possible negative consequences of unlawful activity, are, however, pointed out. The therapist never asks why the youngster became involved in the activity. Only present events are considered.

> Open ended questions such as "Why did you do it?" should be avoided. Too much questioning, too much initial conversation gives him the opportunity to make excuses, to feel antagonistic toward authority, to justify in his mind that what he did was not very wrong or if wrong not really his fault.[27]

[26]*Ibid.*, p. 57.
[27]*Ibid.*, p. 53.

In reality therapy, the therapist always gives the client a great deal of support for acting in a responsible manner. The therapist always transmits to the youngster a certain set of expectations or rules, defines the limits of acceptable behavior, and follows through with any consequences that have been laid down in the "contract."

Reality therapy has been criticized because many feel that it is an over-simplification of human behavior, and that in some cases the transmitting of expectations to the youngster can have negative effects if the youngster came from a situation in which there were a great many expectations transmitted which were impossible to live up to and follow. Regardless of the criticism, however, there is evidence that the method can be effective not only in juvenile courts and in probation settings but also in institutions.[28]

Reality therapy, like other therapies, is only as good as the individual counselor or therapist who is using it. If it is not used correctly it can be a punitive technique when treating youngsters. For example, a therapist, in a coldhearted manner after a youngster has been apprehended, can say, "I don't want to know why you are involved in a difficulty. You are irresponsible and I will not become involved with you as your counselor until you react in a more responsible manner." This, of course, can be a very hostile attitude transmitted to the youngster under the guise of reality therapy. Any therapy, regardless of its techniques, can be used as a hostile, punitive mechanism by an inefficient therapist. Sufficient training is required for reality therapy to be used effectively.

As stated earlier, reality therapy can make an important contribution to the criminal justice system process. One of the major problems in handling and treating juveniles is *consistency.* Because the criminal justice system is composed of professionals from various backgrounds, training, and orientation, consistency is often lacking within the system.

In Chapter 4 we saw how inconsistency in the family can contribute to acting out behavior by the youngster. Inconsistent handling of the juvenile in the criminal justice system can also have negative consequences. Reality therapy can be effective in combating inconsistencies in treatment and handling and can provide the base for a more coordinated approach to treating the delinquent. With sufficient training, all types of professionals within the system can use the reality therapy method.

TRANSACTIONAL ANALYSIS

Transactional analysis, which can be utilized both individually and in groups, is mainly concerned with evaluating and interpreting interpersonal relationships and dynamic transactions between the client and environment. According to Berne, transactions between individuals can be viewed as "pastimes and

---

[28]A. R. Putnam and Charles R. Barnett, "Effects of Reality Therapy on Recidivism Rates in Gibault School for Boys," *Justice Professional,* 3, no. 1 (1988), pp. 107–125.

games."[29] In other words, much of the interaction that takes place with individuals can be viewed as games or game playing.

Transactional analysis is based on the following assumptions.

1. Human relationships consist of competitive acts or social maneuvers which serve a defensive function and yield important gratification which can be labeled "games."
2. All persons manifest three different "ego states": the *child*, a relic of the individual's past; the *parent*, whom he has incorporated through identification with his parents; and the *adult*, who is the mature and responsible self.
3. Each of these "ego states" perceives reality differently: the child prelogically, and parent judgmentally, and the adult comprehensively on the basis of past experience.
4. The three states operate constantly in response to the person's needs and the "games" in which he indulges at a given time.[30]

The major purpose of therapy is to point out the various games that the client plays and attempt to strengthen the adult component of the personality, displace the immaturities of the child component, and reduce the subjective judgment of the parental component. Before using transactional analysis, the therapist, through diagnosis of the patient's demeanor, gestures, vocabulary, and voice, attempts to determine the ego state responsible for the patient's symptoms and disturbances. For example, it may be pinpointed that much of an adolescent's behavior is manifested like an impulsive, immature child and this is the reason for delinquency. In other words, the individual's game playing results from the dynamic child component, and the major portion of the individual's time is spent in these childish activities which ultimately result in hedonistic, impulsive behavior within the community. After the initial diagnosis and interpretation, the individual may have sessions with the therapist to further pinpoint the game playing and those components that are most manifest. The person may also be placed in a group where the transactions and game playing become more revealing in interaction with others.

Even though this method has primarily been used with adults, Berne feels that it has a special value for adolescents because of their typical resistance to psychotherapy. In one of the few research reports on transactional analysis with delinquents, in fact, Jesness did report a successful use of the method in a California training school. The method was successful with youths who were diagnosed as neurotic and aggressive or unsocialized passive, but not as manipulators.[31]

Berne has explained the apparent success of the transactional analysis method with adolescents. He notes that not only are adolescents resistant to psychotherapy, but delinquent adolescents are even more so:

[29]Eric Berne, *Transactional Analysis in Psychotherapy* (New York: Grove Press, 1961).
[30]Wolberg, *The Techniques of Psychotherapy*, p. 257.
[31]Carl F. Jesness, "Comparative Effectiveness of Behavior Modification and Transactional Analysis Programs for Delinquents," *Journal of Consulting and Clinical Psychology, 43*, no. 6 (December 1975), pp. 758–779.

Since the majority of teenage patients are sent or brought to treatment, the relationship of the therapist is not an autonomous one so that there is a strong temptation to rebellion, withdrawal, or sabotage. In effect, the therapist becomes a delegate of their parents which under the usual contract puts him at a great disadvantage from the beginning. The sought for "cure" too often resembles a prescription written by the parents, who visualize the therapeutic relationship as a *Parent-Child* one, and the patient tends to do the same. The situation can be decisively altered at the social level by explicitly setting up an *Adult-Adult* contract, whereby the therapist offers to teach the patient transactional analysis, with the provision that the patient can do as he pleases with what he learns.[32]

In this situation, the adolescent or the delinquent adolescent does not necessarily take a subservient role but is taught the method of transactional analysis. The major principle learned is how to identify the three dynamic components of the personality. Therapists can point out that they too have components of the *parent* and the *child* as well as the *adult*. They can also illustrate to the youngsters in what cases their own *child* component, or childishness, is manifested. The child then does not have to operate as a subservient, but can learn the method and apply it without the direction of the therapist. Transactional analysis can be effective by teaching the youngster a method of evaluating behavior and categorizing it as adult oriented, parent oriented, or child oriented. In most cases the youngster can make the final determination as to the appropriateness of certain behavior and the category into which it falls. If youngsters constantly evaluate their behavior and actions as childish, through their own awareness of the method and "diagnosis," they can alter the impulsive childish component of their personalities and emphasize the more acceptable adult characterizations.

Cognitive Problem-solving Therapies

One type of therapy used with juvenile offenders focuses on teaching them to think through a situation before taking any action.[33] Participants are taught to think logically, objectively and rationally; and they are taught not to overgeneralize, distort facts, or blame others for their actions or for what happens to them.[34] Many offenders do not know how to delay their actions while they think through and analyze the consequences, and they often lack skill in making long-range plans in how to best satisfy their desires.[35] They may be

---

[32]Berne, *Transactional Analysis in Psychotherapy,* p. 355.

[33]Robert R. Ross and E. A. Fabiano, *Time to Think: A Cognitive Model of Delinquency Prevention and Offender Rehabilitation,* (Johnson City, Tennessee: Institute of Social Sciences and Arts, Inc., 1985); Paul Gendreau and Robert R. Ross, "Revivification of Rehabilitation: Evidence from the 1980s," *Justice Quarterly, 4,* no. 3 (September 1987), pp. 349–396.

[34]Rhena L. Izzo and Robert R. Ross, "Meta-analysis of Rehabilitation Programs for Juvenile Delinquents: A Brief Report," *Criminal Justice and Behavior, 17,* no. 1 (March 1990), pp. 134–142.

[35]*Ibid.*

unable to analyze interpersonal problems because they cannot understand other people, they cannot see the connection between their own behavior and the reactions of other people, and they cannot picture alternatives to an aggressive reaction to conflict situations.[36] Each of these deficits in thinking through a situation is corrected through discussion either on a one-to-one basis or in a group setting.

Lawrence Greenberg explained why offenders often need cognitive problem-solving therapy.[37] Highly violent and aggressive people are often cut off from others, and they have a distorted view of social interaction in which any conflict is met with an aggressive action. As time goes on, the distorted view of the world becomes less and less open to change, and there is a need to learn how to understand the interactions of other people and how to think through reactions to these people.

As an example, the cognitive problem-solving approach was used for a select group of juveniles in a Kansas state treatment facility.[38] They were taught a problem-solving strategy for a typical selection of situations that might result in delinquent behavior, and they were given instruction in impulse control for a second set of problems. Hypothetical situations were presented in individual sessions that were held twice a week for four weeks. For the very small number of youth exposed to the treatment, it did appear that they had learned some new ways of thinking through situations and that they were able to apply these approaches to new scenarios that had not been discussed with the therapist.

Once a child learns the basic skills of problem solving, the therapist must provide opportunities for role modeling and behavior rehearsal under supervision. For instance, a situation involving peer pressure to break the law or of temptation to shoplift might be "acted out" in a group. The therapist might first take the role of the potential offender and interact with the peers, or verbalize thoughts about carrying through the shoplifting. Then each of the offenders would take the primary role, with others taking the parts of the friends in the situation involving peer pressure. Programs that do provide role modeling situations and that give the youth repeated chances to practice the appropriate thinking and behavior do improve problem solving skills, even in high-risk adolescents.[39]

---

[36]*Ibid.*

[37]Lawrence S. Greenberg, "Constructive Cognition: Cognitive Therapy Coming of Age," *The Counseling Psychologist, 16,* no. 2 (April 1988), pp. 235–238.

[38]Anthony A. Hains and Ann Higgins Hains, "Cognitive-behavioral Training of Problem-solving and Impulse-control with Delinquent Adolescents," *Journal of Offender Counseling, Services and Rehabilitation, 12,* no. 2 (Spring 1988), pp. 95–113.

[39]Alan E. Kazdin, Karen Esveldt-Dawson, Nancy French and A. S. Unis, "Problem Solving Skills Training and Relationship Therapy in the Treatment of Antisocial Child Behavior," *Journal of Consulting and Clinical Psychology, 55,* no. 1 (February 1987), pp. 76–85; and John Lochman, Louise Lampron, Peter R. Burch, and John F. Curry, "Client Characteristics Associated with Behavior Change for Treated and Untreated Aggressive Boys," *Journal of Abnormal Child Psychology, 13,* no. 4 (December 1985), pp. 527–538; Izzo and Ross, cited above.

VOCATIONAL COUNSELING

Vocational counseling is different from the preceding therapeutic methods and does not necessarily attempt to understand the interpersonal dynamics of human behavior or spend a great deal of time on diagnosis. It is similar, though, in its emphasis on changing the youthful offender rather than the larger social structure; for example, the types of jobs available to youths. The main purpose of vocational counseling is to increase the client's knowledge of career choices, job specifications, and qualifications and training needed for successful employment. The vocational counselor can help young people identify their interests by questioning them about their attitudes toward work in general and the specific types of employment that appeal to them. Aptitude and interest testing may also be used. This experience is often a whole new area for delinquent adolescents, because they have never held a job and hence have never experienced the problems that exist or the positive rewards that can result. The positive attitudes, skills, and habits that the youngsters develop and refine in the work situation can be carried over to the community and can positively affect their relationships with others.

> Perhaps the most crucial problem to tackle in helping young people prepare for the adult world of work is in positively influencing their attitudes toward work. Many characteristics typical of the delinquent youth militate against a ready adjustment to employment. Typically the delinquent lacks self-confidence. He knows that he will make serious mistakes on the job. He goes forth expecting not to be liked, looking for slights and unfairness. He seeks immediate gratification of his impulses and has difficulty in working toward goals which are as remote as a pay check which comes only once a week. Basic skills are important primarily because they influence a child's attitude toward work and self-confidence. It is upon the development of constructive attitudes toward and reactions to work that emphasis should be placed. This means that an analysis of each child's interest, aptitudes, and capacity to tolerate the demands of the assignment should be made before work and shop assignments are made. His initial experience should be carefully structured to assure some sense of achievement and to avoid too much frustration.[40]

The work situation can provide a realistic environment where behavior can be evaluated and many of the youngster's problems can be resolved. The astute counselor can utilize problem situations that occur in the work environment to point out interpersonal difficulties that the youngster has, which usually also exist outside the work environment. The personal relationships that exist between youngsters and their work supervisors or work peers can be critical in altering attitudes and behavior and in facilitating solutions to problems.

> Whether or not a boy or girl becomes particularly skilled on the work assignment is one factor but more important is the satisfaction he realizes from a working

[40]National Conference of Superintendents of Training Schools and Reformatories, *Institutional Rehabilitation of Delinquent Youth: Manual for Training School Personnel* (Albany, New York: Delmar Publishers, Inc., 1962), pp. 106–107.

relationship. If he can gain confidence in his supervisor he has made the first step toward placing confidence and trust in other individuals—IF the training can reconcile the child's aptitudes and personality needs with the basic rules of society then it has accomplished this rehabilitation and indeed trained and educated him for life in the community.[41]

A positive identification model can frequently be the most effective means of influencing the youngster to develop positive alternatives to problem solving.

Job placement and job-related programs which successfully reduce delinquency share one important element. They provide youths with jobs which are not "dead end," but which allow for career advancement. For example, a GED program coupled with job placement had a greater effect on recidivism than a job placement program used alone. The GED program facilitated delinquents' advancement in their careers of interest, as evidenced by their higher-paying jobs once they received the GED.[42] In a similar way, training in data processing is a very effective vocational program because participants are able to locate jobs relevant to their training, and they can advance in their careers.[43] Romig explains the success of such programs:

> When an individual finds meaning, status, and opportunity for learning and advancement in a job, negative behaviors such as delinquency decrease. Jobs and job placement do *not* necessarily make a significant difference. However, jobs that have value to the individual and provide an opportunity for advancement can help reduce crime and delinquency.[44]

Because younger youths in our society are excluded from work situations, it can be difficult if not impossible to develop this type of meaningful work experience, which includes the possibility of movement up the career ladder, for them. To be fully effective, job placement programs must often include efforts to develop jobs with upward mobility for the teenager, as well as the counseling for the teenager. This type of job placement program would have the dual focus of changing the individual and the larger opportunity structure in society.

The astute counselor (therapist, caseworker, and so on) is also aware of the existing resources in the community and the programs available to help train and retrain youngsters so that they can become more effective citizens and successful workers. Helping the youngster adjust to the work environment is as much a part of therapy or counseling as the communication and interpretation of interpersonal dynamics that take place within the context of therapeutic intervention.

---

[41]*Ibid.*, p. 108.

[42]Brian Neal Odell, "Accelerating Entry into the Opportunity Structure: A Sociologically Based Treatment for Delinquent Youth," *Sociology and Social Research, 58,* no. 3 (April 1974), pp. 312–317.

[43]Romig, *Justice for Our Children,* p. 45.

[44]*Ibid.*, p. 47.

Vocational Guidance

Vocational guidance programs that involve vocational counseling have often been effective in redirecting the energy of delinquent youngsters into positive channels. Experimental projects have been developed to encourage youngsters to stay in school so that they can acquire a vocational goal and increased skills which will contribute to a more positive self-image and success in the community. Various attempts have been made both with individuals and with groups to encourage youngsters to develop needed skills and discuss their attitudes about work and the problems that they perceive or encounter in the work world. One such project attempted to encourage youths to discuss their perceptions of work. This was accomplished through the group process of discussion meetings.

> The only regulations voiced at the very onset were that the participants must not damage or destroy any of the office property and not do bodily violence to any member of the group. These regulations were accepted and respected throughout the group sessions.[45]

The meetings were set up to discuss various situations that the youths encountered at work and the relationships they had with work supervisors, work peers, and other persons within the environment. In other words, the entire constellation of factors that related to work assignments, work skills, and activities and duties were covered. The open discussions were

> not merely an outpouring of hostility because as the meetings progressed some of the boys interpreted the behavior of others in the group. They began to be critical of themselves. At first their hostility was directed towards school authorities and then to their parents, representatives of the law, and peers. Finally they began to realize that they were also involved.[46]

The main point is that the effective counselor can utilize the group itself to solve problems and increase the awareness of individual members in the group of their involvement in the interpersonal work processes. In addition, new alternatives for behavioral adaptation can be developed for the work environment and the community in general.

Programs like the Neighborhood Youth Corps (see Chapter 7) have been effective in combining work training with vocational and interpersonal counseling.

> It is work focused so that all aspects of the youth's life are dealt with in terms of their relevance for his career. Counseling is concerned primarily with helping the youth examine his desires, feelings, and attitudes, his day-to-day problems

---

[45]Frederick Weiner, "Vocational Guidance for Delinquent Boys," *Crime and Delinquency, 11,* no. 4 (October 1964), p. 368.

[46]*Ibid.*, p. 369.

and his behavior in the counseling situation itself. The group is used as a reference group and all are expected to help each other.[47]

Many people in our society consider a large number of occupational choices to be inappropriate for females. This belief can result in special problems in providing vocational guidance for girls. The *Youth Women's Company* is a particularly innovative program in Tucson, Arizona. Its purpose is

> to prevent delinquency and to provide young women between the ages of fourteen and eighteen with vocational counseling, skill training in nontraditional areas, and job placement.[48]

Vocational guidance is used to familiarize the clients with career opportunities, including those which are and are not considered to be typical for women, and to build self-confidence to learn new skills. Workshops in skill areas such as plastering and carpentry are one part of the program. The program employs methods that are essential to reducing delinquency. Participants are assisted in clarifying their own interests and values as they pertain to work, and are given the skills to find jobs which provide a career ladder. They also learn the meaning of various vocational titles and classifications, and the average salary and work conditions characteristic of each.

The Youth Assistance Program, which is described in Exhibit 8-2, is a vocational guidance program that uses labor union volunteers to assist youths aged 16 and over. This type of vocational guidance program can play an important part in preventing delinquency and rehabilitating a youngster who has been labeled delinquent.

BEHAVIOR THERAPY

Behavior therapy, or behavior modification, is based on the assumption that delinquent behavior is learned. This type of therapy is closely linked with the social learning theory described in Chapter 3. Maladaptive behavior usually has to be modified through the development of new learning processes. Generally, behavior therapy assumes that behavior will change in direct proportion to the amount of rewards or punishments that exist as reinforcement—negative or unpleasant reinforcement will reduce or eliminate much negative behavior, whereas positive or pleasant reinforcement will tend to maintain or even increase positive behavior. If positive behavior is adequately rewarded, it will be perpetuated. Conversely, if negative behavior is not rewarded, it will eventually subside.

[47]Beryce W. MacLennon and Naomi Felsenfeld, *Group Counseling and Psychotherapy with Adolescents* (New York: Columbia University Press, 1968), p. 148.

[48]Angela Atkinson, "The Young Women's Company: Stepping Away from Occupational Segregation," in *Teenage Women in the Juvenile Justice System: Changing Values,* eds. Ruth Crow and Ginny McCarty (376 South Stone Avenue, Tucson, Arizona 85701: New Directions for Young Women, Inc., 1979), p. 136.

Exhibit 8-2 The Youth Assistance Program

When a client is referred by a probation officer, he or she comes to the project office and is seen by one of the social workers. An assessment is made of the client's readiness and motivation for different kinds of program activity, involving staff and volunteers, over a period of several meetings. At each session, the client is assisted in exploring his or her feelings and toward a clarification of options in the often alien and unfamiliar worlds of work, training, and education.

The social worker introduces the client to the notion of working with a union volunteer, when the client appears ready for such a relationship. The volunteer is provided with all available information about the client and the client is told about the specific volunteer. When both are ready, they are brought together. They may meet evenings or weekends, or other times at mutual convenience. Every volunteer is working and a union member, so that much of his or her special contribution to the client involves the volunteer as a representative of the world-of-work and of the unions as organizations which function on behalf of workers.

Before the client is assigned to a volunteer, the staff has made efforts to upgrade the clients' job readiness, social skills, knowledge of public transportation, sensitivity to employers' expectations of appearance, punctuality, communication skills, and related matters. The staff will, together with the youth, plan the education, training, or job situation most appropriate for his/her situation, abilities, and interests. It will make a vigorous effort to involve the client in some union-sponsored activity. Formal apprenticeship programs usually require a high school diploma or its equivalent, so that most clients are not eligible for them. The staff attempts to find other union-related work or training openings for which the client can be qualified. Sometimes, a client may require substantial long-term preparation before entering the world of work and accepting new values. Some youths do not even have social security numbers and others do not know how the public transportation system works. Many youths have urgent immediate needs which must be met; a few clients, for example, have no place to live and sleep in doorways or subways.

SOURCE: Charles Winick and Elias B. Saltman, "A Successful Program Utilizing Labor Union Volunteers with Young Adult Probationers," *Journal of Offender Counseling, Services and Rehabilitation, 7,* no. 2 (Winter 1982), pp. 19–20.

Issues for Discussion. What characteristics of the job market make it difficult to offer effective vocational guidance to youths with limited educational and job skills? What are the strengths of the Youth Assistance Program?

Shah states that according to the behavioral approach the therapist must deal with clear and observable aspects of behavior so that objective conclusions and evaluations can be made.[49] Thorp and Wetzel point out that observable behavior, whether positive or negative, can be reinforced or punished according-

[49]Saleem A. Shah, "Treatment of Offenders: Some Behavioral Concepts, Principles and Approaches," *Federal Probation, 23,m* no. 3 (September 1959), p. 29.

ly.[50] The client can be made aware of the sequence of events that culminates in particular types of behavior. Negative behavior like delinquent activity can be pinpointed, and negative reinforcements like restrictions can be implemented. Positive behavior, like success on the job and in school, can be positively reinforced and rewarded.

Dressler points out that, if the therapist is going to be effective in accomplishing behavior modification, it is necessary to first determine each individual's "reinforcers."

> A youngster's reinforcers may be determined by carefully observing his behavior, since each child has his own list of reinforcers which can be ranked for importance. Candy for the quite young and money for those who are older are generally in the category of reinforcers but, aside from these, reinforcers usually cannot be accurately determined without observation of the child and inquiry of him and significant others, such as family, peers, and teachers. The investigator wants to know what people, things, and events motivate the particular individual. What does he want to get out of them?[51]

Reinforcers, then, are those aspects that are deemed important by youngsters, which they will strive to achieve so that they will gain personal satisfaction. Praise, attention, money, food, and privileges can be considered positive reinforcers. Threats, punishment, confinement, and ridicule are negative reinforcers. Even though both types can be employed in modifying behavior, research has shown that positive reinforcements tend to produce more effective and enduring behavioral changes.[52]

The therapist, in an attempt to achieve a desired goal, tries to shape the behavior of the youngster by employing slow and gradual changes beginning with the individual's existing level of performance—the therapist determines the behavioral level of the client. For example, the youngster may be a chronic delinquent who has been involved in much delinquent activity. The "treatment" has to begin at this point. Because the therapist proceeds at a very slow pace and behavior modification is attempted in only small doses, success is a gradual process and the little successes become steppingstones to larger achievements.

> Each appropriate or correct move toward the goal is provided external or extrinsic reinforcements (praise, approval, prizes, candy, good grades, etc.). Such progress may also generate internal or intrinsic reinforcements for the individual.[53]

In other words, as the behavior is modified and as rewards are provided, the delinquent activity is reduced, allowing the individual to develop a self-image of

---

[50]Ronald G. Thorp and Ralph J. Wetzel, *Behavior Modification in the Natural Environment* (New York: Academic Press, Inc., 1969), p. 186.

[51]David Dressler, *Practice and Theory of Probation and Parole* (New York: Columbia University Press, 1959), pp. 229–230.

[52]*Ibid.*, p. 230.

[53]Shah, "Treatment of Offenders," p. 32.

Table 8-1   Examples of Point Consequences

BEHAVIOR	POINTS
Social	
Citizenship	
Participation in family conference (new boy)	+ 1,500
Reading (depending on ability)	+ 10–100/pg
Special news (T.V.)	+ 20/min
Elected or candidate for school office	+ 3,000
Aggressiveness	
Fighting (second person objects)	− 10,000
Hitting (second person doesn't object)	− 1,000
Temper (yelling, slamming objects, stomping, etc.)	− 3,000
Teasing (name calling, annoying gestures, etc.,	− 2,000
if second person objects)	
Teasing (if second person doesn't object)	− 500
Noise and rowdiness	− 3,000
Arguing (peers)	
Minor	− 300
Major	− 3,000
Arguing (adults)	
Minor	− 500
Major	− 5,000

Source: John L. Levitt, Thomas M. Young, and Donnell M. Pappenfort, "Achievement Place: The Teaching-Family Treatment Model in a Group-Home Setting," *Reports of the National Juvenile Justice Assessment Centers* (Washington, D. C.: U. S. Department of Justice, 1981), p. 8.

being able to achieve personal satisfaction in a socially acceptable manner. If the youngster is able to stay on the job and receive gratification through receiving a paycheck, this may be a new experience and the satisfaction and the positive reinforcements can affect his or her internal self-concept and result in altered behavior in the community.

A point system is often used as a part of behavior modification treatment. For example, at a group home it has been used to give rewards for desired behavior and punishments for negative behavior (Table 8-1). Youths can use any points they accumulate to obtain privileges and various items (Table 8-2).

In general, behavior modification treatment has not led to reduced recidivism, but has influenced youths to behave positively while they are in a program.[54] The use of the behavior modification method at the Fred C. Nelles School, a training school for delinquent boys in California, illustrates both the advantages and limitations of the treatment method. All staff, including those involved in either custody, teaching, or treatment, were trained to provide

[54]Robert R. Ross and Bryan McKay, "Behavioral Approaches to Treatment in Corrections: Requiem for a Panacea," in *Effective Correctional Treatment*, eds. Robert R. Ross and Bryan McKay (Toronto: Butterworths, 1980), p. 47.

Table 8-2 Privileges that can be Earned with Points
on the Weekly Point System

PRIVILEGES	PRICE IN POINTS (WEEKLY SYSTEM)
Basics	5,000
Snacks	3,000
T. V.	3,000
Hometime	6,000
Out of Saturday's work	6,000
Allowance $1 (1)	3,000
Allowance $2 (2)	6,000
Bonds	1,500
Specials	Negotiated

Source: John L. Levitt, Thomas M. Young, and Donnell M. Pappenfort, "Achievement Place: The Teaching-Family Treatment Model in a Group-Home Setting," *Reports of the National Juvenile Justice Assessment Centers* (Washington, D. C.: U. S. Department of Justice, 1981), p. 13.

Issues for Discussion. Does a point system violate the rights of children? What are the differences and similarities between the point system and reward and punishment in a family setting? Would the point system result in a change in behavior after the youth leaves the program?

positive reinforcements to youths. Program participants were better behaved than a comparable group in another training school. The positive results continued while the boys were in the training school, but they did not carry over to affect recidivism after release.[55]

The *Behavioral-Employment Intervention Program* is one of the few demonstrations that behavior modification can not only change behaviors in a correctional program setting, but also can affect arrests and frequency of institutionalization. All youths in the program were placed in a job. Employers were trained to give positive reinforcement for good behavior, and they were instructed to praise and reward youths' appropriate behavior. The experimenter received written reports of the youths' performance, and for the first phase of the treatment they gave additional praise to youths during a weekly group meeting. All youths were trained in skills related to adapting to the work world, including performance and grooming. A final part of the treatment was a written agreement of the expectations that the experimenter, the youth, and the employers held for each other. This combination of treatment methods resulted in better job attendance and reduced recidivism. It is not known whether the behavior modification method would have been effective if used alone, but,

[55]Romig, *Justice for Our Children*, p. 15.

when used in conjunction with skill training, job placement, and a written state-ment of expectations, it was clearly effective.[56]

Behavioral modification has been used successfully to alter negative be-havior and encourage positive achievements. The family is the first "institution" that either directly or indirectly uses the behavior modification approach. The juvenile soon learns how to respond to the environment. Parents who have been consistent in their reward and punishment system can influence their children to act in a socially acceptable manner. If parents are inconsistent or lack warmth in their approach to child rearing, they will not be successful in positively influenc-ing their children.

Behavior modification is simply a method of establishing or reestablish-ing an effective reward and punishment system to help the youngster become more compatible with the expectations and demands of the environment.

BEHAVIORAL CONTRACTS

Behavioral contracting (also called contingency management) has become a very popular and useful method of working with delinquent adolescents. The as-sumptions of behavior modification contracting have proven useful in graphical-ly illustrating to the client the expectations of the counselor and the conse-quences of client behavior. The client is actively involved in developing the contract and, in effect, it is a partnership between counselor and client.

Rutherford explains that

> behavioral contracting involves the systematic negotiation between mediator (parent, teacher, probation officer, social worker, unit counselor, or supervisor) and a target (delinquent adolescent) of the behaviors to be performed within a given environment, and the specific reinforcing consequences or "payoffs" to be provided when performance requirements are met. Behavioral contracting is based upon an applied behavior analysis model whereby the environment dy-namics which maintain behavior are assessed. In behavioral contracting, a behav-ioral analysis involves specifying: (A) the antecedents which will cue the contract behavior, (B) the contract behavior to be developed, and (C) the consequences which will maintain the contract behavior [see Fig. 8-1]. The "antecedents" are events which are present in the environment to cue behaviors. They include those stimuli, cues, directions, or prompts that set the occasion for a given behavior and a specific, predictable consequence. The antecedent cues for doing 20 arithmetic word problems at home may be a math book, a sharp pencil, 3 sheets of paper, directions at the top of the page, and a quiet, well lighted room. These cues may signal that the "consequences" of completing the "contract be-havior," e.g., math problems done correctly by 9:00 a.m. the following morning, will be positive. The positive consequences may be a higher letter grade, praise from teacher and parents, and/or a specifically contracted item or event such as a coke or 20 minutes of free time at midday. Behavioral analysis makes the assumption that consequences which are positive will result in an increase in the frequency of the desired behavior.

[56]Timothy L. Walter and Carolyn M. Mills, "A Behavioral-Employment Intervention Pro-gram for Reducing Juvenile Delinquency," in *Progress in Behavior Therapy with Delinquents*, ed. Jerome S. Stumphauzer (Springfield, Illinois: Charles C. Thomas, Publisher, 1979).

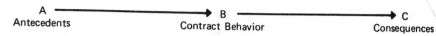

Figure 8-1 Behavioral analysis of contract behavior

In summary, behavioral analysis involves planning before the fact and behavioral programming after the fact of a given behavior. Sound behavioral contracts specify systematically each of the three steps of the behavioral analysis mode.[57]

To enhance the usefulness of contracts between youth and correctional staff, contracts can also be developed between youth and parents. Exhibit 8-3 is a family contract for 15-year-old John, who lived with his mother and siblings. He had poor school attendance and was not completing school assignments. Other problems were his violation of curfew and his selling of cigarettes that his mother gave him in an attempt to win his confidence. On the positive side, John was motivated to take a driver's education course, and he had been repairing cars with a neighbor.

A number of studies have shown the effectiveness of using behavior contracts in correctional programs.[58] This treatment method also appears to be effective in community settings. In one program, the staff trained teachers and parents to develop contracts with youths. The contracts outlined expected behavior and consequences.[59] This treatment method was most effective when the contracts provided a very clear definition of the expected behavior and identified positive goals that the youth strove to achieve. Behavior contracts have also been effective in reducing arrest rates by 31 percent for 1,200 young offenders. To bring about this reduction, parents and youths were trained to use the contracting approach to improve home, school, and neighborhood behavior. These applications of behavior contracts fully involved the youths in choosing the goals to be outlined in the contract, and they involved important adults in rewarding achievement of these goals.[60]

These successful uses of behavioral contracting, and others which we have not reviewed here, closely follow several steps that Rutherford has identified as essential to insure success. Most noteworthy are the following. There must be an analysis of the client's behavior to determine the antecedents and

[57]Robert Bruce Rutherford, Jr., "Establishing Behavioral Contracts with Delinquent Adolescents," *Federal Probation, 39*, no. 1 (March 1975), p. 29.

[58]Curtis J. Braukmann, Dean L. Fixsen, Elery L. Phillips, and Montrose M. Wolf, "Behavioral Approaches to Treatment in the Crime and Delinquency Fields," *Criminology, 13*, no. 3 (November 1975), pp. 299–331; and Alexander F. Douds, Michael Engelesjord, and Thomas R. Collingwood, "Behavior Contracting with Youthful Offenders and Their Parents," *Child Welfare, 56*, no. 6 (June 1977), pp. 409–417.

[59]Richard B. Stuart, Sirinka Jayaratne, and Tony Tripodi, "Changing Adolescent Deviant Behavior Through Reprogramming the Behavior of Parents and Teachers: An Experimental Evaluation," *Canadian Journal of Behavioral Science, 8*, no. 2 (April 1976), pp. 132–143.

[60]Richard B. Stuart and L. A. Lott, Jr., "Behavioral Contracting with Delinquents: A Cautionary Note," in *Annual Review of Behavior Therapy and Practice, 8*, eds. Cyril M. Franks and G. Terence Wilson (New York: Brunner/Mazel, Publishers, 1973).

Exhibit 8-3   Family contracts are often used to bring about changes in behavior

---

CONTRACT

Date_____

1A. For each day that John attends all classes, he will earn the privilege of ten (10) cigarettes per day or one (1) package of cigarettes every other day.

1B. For each day that John does not attend all classes, ten (10) cigarettes per day will not be earned.

2A. If John attends 90 percent of the *full* school days between Monday, May 21, 1973, and Friday, June 14, 1973 (20 days), he will earn one (1) driver's education course. The driver's education course will begin on June 18, 1973.

2B. If John does not attend school for 90 percent of all classes between May 21, 1973, and June 15, 1973 (20 days), the privilege of the driver's education course will be withdrawn.

3A. For each take-home assignment that John turns in to his teachers between Monday, May 21, 1973, and Friday, June 15, 1973, John will earn one evening out on the weekend, provided his mother knows his whereabouts and the time that he will return home.

3B. For each take-home assignment that John does not turn in to his teachers between Monday, May 21, 1973, and Friday, June 15, 1973, John will stay in one evening during the weekend.

As negotiator and overseer of this contract, Mr. Rick Blackley will see that all sections of this contract are followed and that said consequences will be paid.

As representative of the Central High School, Mr. Tom Anderson, counselor, will act as the monitor of the behaviors in the school (i.e., attending classes and turning in assignments).

_____   _____
Mr. John Wright, Student   Mrs. Judy Wright, Mother

_____   _____
Mr. Rick Blackley,   Mr. Tom Anderson,
Negotiator   Counselor

SOURCE: Robert Bruce Rutherford, Jr., "Establishing Behavioral Contracts with Delinquent Adolescents," *Federal Probation,* 39, no. 1 (March 1975), pp. 28–32.

Issues for Discussion.   Describe situations in which behavior contracts could be used to help youths with school- or job-related problems. What skills do family and delinquents need to use the behavior contract method? Could behavior contracts be used in institutional settings?

---

consequences of behavior. The behavioral contract must not only be fair and formal, but it must precisely state the conditions of the agreement. In addition, the contract should be stated in positive terms and implemented with positive rewards for positive behavior.

CRISIS INTERVENTION

Even though *crisis intervention* has not been utilized extensively with youngsters in the past, Villeponteaux believes that it can have great therapeutic value in dealing with acting out adolescents.[61] The basis of the theory is that when people experience a crisis, their psychological resources may become overtaxed, making them vulnerable to further breakdown. The resolution of the current crisis may lead to the solution of older problems, as well, because of the reawakening of fears and repressed problems that recur during time of crisis. Redl and Wineman describe it as "emotional first aid on the spot." they go on to say that

> problem situations in the child's day-to-day life have strategic and therapeutic importance when they can be dealt with immediately before or immediately after they occur and even more when the person who deals with them has witnessed the incident.[62]

The delinquent often expresses aggression by acting out in the community and coming in conflict with the law. If the therapist witnesses or is told how the youngster handles and expresses aggression and reacts to frustration and strain, the therapist can use the immediate situation to help the youngster develop new methods of adaptation. Villeponteaux provides an example of the techniques used at Horizon House, a program for boys:

> A minor infraction of a rule could be handled in one of several ways. For example, a boy might (and in fact, often did) come late to the program. If he was three or four minutes late, the worker could simply overlook this tardiness, or could reprimand, or warn him, or "make an issue" of it.[63]

If the therapist wanted to "make an issue" of the boy's behavior, he or she could emphasize the problem by pointing out in an objective manner how the boy was functioning. The immediate problem could then be related to the way the boy functioned in other situations in the past. The present situation or crisis can be used for problem solving because it is probably part of a pattern of behavior that the youngster uses in relating to the environment. This pattern often contributes to delinquency. The successful resolution of the crisis in the immediate situation can be generalized to similar situations in the future and can be helpful in acquainting the child with a new problem-solving process that will contribute to more appropriate behavior.

In some cases, crisis intervention involves the family as well as the youngster. This family approach was used as the key treatment method in the Sacramento Diversion Project, which was described in Chapter 7 of this book. Another example of crisis intervention involving the family is described in Exhibit 8-4.

Handling problems when they are at the crisis stage and when there is a great deal of anxiety can contribute to problem solving. Because youngsters who are involved in chronic delinquent behavior often do not experience anxiety and guilt, it is difficult to rehabilitate them or motivate them enough so that they want to get involved in the change process. The anxiety that exists in the crisis

---

[61]Lorenz Villeponteaux, Jr., "Crisis Intervention in a Day School of Delinquents," *Crime and Delinquency, 16,* no. 3 (July 1970), pp. 318–319.

[62]*Ibid.*, p. 319.

[63]*Ibid.*, p. 320.

Exhibit 8-4   Crisis intervention in the Intensive Intervention Project

---

The Intensive Intervention Project (IIP) is a demonstration program funded by the State Law Enforcement Planning Agency under the sponsorship of the Family Court of the First Circuit of Honolulu. Conceptually, it is similar to the Sacramento Diversion Project. The purpose of the project is to provide effective diversion of those adolescents from the court system who are referred for the first time for behaviors, such as runaway, incorrigibility, need for supervision, and first time minor law violations.

The core of intervention *strategies* used by the IIP includes five components: (1) immediate response to referrals, which is intended to capitalize on the motivation because of a family crisis situation with respect to contact with the juvenile justice system (police and court); (2) intensive but time-limited outreach services, where the time and place of counseling meetings, their duration, and their frequency are accommodated to the family situation to reduce client resistance; (3) a focus on the family as a system which is functioning maladaptively and which requires change as a unit for long-term remediation to be effected; (4) use of counseling teams consisting of a male and female, typically of similar ethnic extraction to act as role models and to increase the probability that all family members will be able to relate to the counselors; and (5) frequent reliance on adjunct agencies for accepting referrals to maintain changes initiated by intensive counseling.

The . . . crisis intervention techniques which are utilized begin with the present problem, but then shift to family interactions in a system, that is, how patterns of interaction maintain the situation that led to the crisis. These techniques include seven components: (1) intellectual understanding of causal relationships between parental and adolescent behaviors; (2) clarification of values and demands of family members regarding critical issues; (3) active involvement of counselors as models, with expression of feelings and thoughts to the family; (4) training family members in expressing themselves clearly and completely; (5) exploration of previous coping methods and their inadequacies; (6) focusing on the present and future to facilitate active, goal-oriented problem solving; and (7) use of behavioral contracts and training in negotiating skills to foster clearly stated rules and consequences for family members' actions and compromises over disagreements.

SOURCE: Terry C. Wade, Teru L. Morton, Judith E. Lind, and Newton R. Ferris, "A Family Crisis Intervention Approach to Diversion from the Juvenile Justice System," *Juvenile Justice, 28,* no. 3 (August 1977), pp. 43–51.

Issues for Discussion.   Is the crisis intervention program likely to have much effect on preventing further delinquency? Base your judgment on your understanding of Chapter 4, "The Family and Juvenile Delinquency." Which types of families are most and least likely to benefit? What skills do counselors using this method need in order to be effective?

Table 8-3 A Summary of Individual Treatment Methods for Delinquents

TREATMENT METHOD	INTERVENTION USED TO PROMOTE CHANGE
Psychotherapy	Conversation and therapist-client relationship leading to changes in values, attitudes, and feelings
Social Casework	Social work concerned with environmental change and individual change to promote personality development
Reality Therapy	Conversation to help the delinquent act responsibly
Transactional Analysis	Conversation to point out various games the client plays and to strengthen the adult part of the personality
Cognitive Problem Solving Therapies	Discussion and role playing to improve understanding of others and logical thinking through of a situation before taking action
Vocational Counseling	Education regarding career choices, job specifications, and qualifications and training needed
Vocational Guidance	Encouragement to acquire vocational goals and skills
Behavior Therapy	Rewards and punishments to change behavior
Behavioral Contracts	Agreements about expectations; rewards and punishments for specific behavior
Crisis Intervention	Resolution of a current crisis in order to resolve old problems
Counseling	Support and reeducation

situation can be used as a motivating force for change. Crisis intervention, as a technique for dealing with problems on the spot, can be effective in producing change and helping the delinquent develop new methods for handling strain, frustration, and aggression in crisis situations.

INDIVIDUAL AND GROUP COUNSELING

Counseling can be used with both groups and individuals. Usually, the major goals of counseling are support and reeducation.

> The counseling procedure involves the client's understanding of his immediate situation and the solving of a problem which affects him and others. No attempt is made to effect a fundamental change of the client's personality—when a person needs reorientation to a particular situation, counseling is indicated. If the problem is of a long-standing duration, psychotherapy is recommended.[64]
> The American Correctional Association defines the technique as follows:
> Counseling is a relationship in which one endeavors to help another understand and solve his problems of adjustment. It is distinguished from service or admonition in that it implies *mutual* consent.[65]

[64]Nikelly, "Basic Processes in Psychotherapy," p. 28.
[65]The American Correctional Association, *Manual of Correctional Standards* (Washington, D.C.: The Association, 1966), p. 422.

These quotations illustrate an important principle. Methods of treatment can be viewed on a continuum. The many individual treatment methods for delinquents are summarized in Table 8-3. Vocational counseling and individual and group counseling are sometimes considered superficial approaches to interpersonal problem solving. Their main objective is usually to help the client handle immediate practical problems. No major attempt is made to restructure the personality or make extensive diagnostic evaluations. More sophisticated methods, such as social casework and psychotherapy, are used for intensive personality evaluation and treatment. Approaches like transactional analysis and reality therapy fit somewhere between the more superficial counseling methods and the more intensive psychotherapeutic methods. A youngster could conceivably be receiving assistance simultaneously from professionals using the various methods mentioned. For example, a school counselor or vocational counselor could be providing help in handling the day-to-day problems that occur in school and on the job, while a probation officer could be providing help through the use of principles extracted from reality therapy, behavior therapy, or transactional analysis. At the same time the youngster could also be evaluated and even treated by a psychiatrist who used psychotherapeutic techniques. Although this example would not be typical, it would be possible.

The most prevalent group treatment approach in institutional settings and juvenile court programs is called *group counseling,* which involves the sharing of personal concerns, problems, and day-to-day experiences within the group.[66]

Sharp notes that the group approach often is successful in teaming up with individualized services.[67] Together, they provide a complementary orientation to individual and group problem solving. In the counseling situation,

> the counselor establishes and operates within an atmosphere which is open and accepting. It is only when the child is free from the feeling that he must defend himself that he is also free to explore himself openly with a degree of candor. . . . The counselor is an "enabler"—not a judge or an instrument of retribution.[68]

In group counseling or group therapy, which is discussed below, it is important to select those youngsters who can benefit from the group but who will not be scapegoated. Some youngsters, for personality reasons or for other reasons such as extreme passiveness and dependency, can be harmed by the group because of the hostility that will be directed toward them and the scapegoat role that they may be forced into.

Role playing may be a highly effective component of group counseling because it enables youngsters to view situations as others do. The participants in the group have to be comfortable enough with one another so that the role

---

[66]Rosemary C. Sarri and Robert D. Vinter, "Group Treatment Strategies in Juvenile Correctional Programs," *Crime and Delinquency, 11,* no. 4 (October 1965), p. 330.

[67]E. Preston Sharp, "Group Counseling in a Short-Term Institution," *Federal Probation, 23,* no. 3 (September 1959), p. 8.

[68]*Ibid.,* pp. 8–9.

playing will come naturally and so that they will not feel self-conscious or inhibited by the role-playing process. The basic concept of role playing is that because behavior of an individual is mainly the result of a reaction to what other people think of a person or what a person believes they think, the assuming of different roles will allow the youngster to test out perceptions in a nonthreatening situation. The counselor or the group leader can objectively evaluate the role-playing behavior and the responses of the group to it. New insights which can be carried over to real-life situations can then be fostered.

> In these processes, the group members are given an opportunity to try on the psychological shoes of others. They are exposed to processes which may give them some idea about how others may feel or think. A lack of awareness or caring about how others think or feel may be one of the major causal factors of delinquent behavior. It has been found that many delinquent children cannot realistically appraise or react to the feelings and thoughts of others.[69]

Many formats can be followed when utilizing the role-playing method. An actual skit can be developed, with participants placed in various roles. The role playing can also be spontaneous as a result of suggestions by either the members of the group or the leader. Sharp relates a case study in which boys were constantly complaining about the staff and their mistreatment of the boys.[70] The boys were asked to reverse roles and play the parts of the supervisors. As a result of this reverse role playing, the boys soon learned how to look at problems through the supervisors' eyes and were able to understand their roles. Likewise, the supervisors were able to understand the boys' position, and this mutual understanding contributed a great deal to the formation of increased positive relationships between the boys and the staff. Chandler is another person who has reported the successful use of role playing. He used this treatment method with seriously delinquent youths who had difficulty understanding and anticipating other people's behavior, and who tended to be self-centered in their thinking. After a series of role-playing sessions, the youths were less egocentric in their thinking, and they were only half as delinquent as similar youths who did not receive the treatment.[71]

It often becomes difficult to manage these group sessions because of the very nature of the participants' personalities and the hostility that is often directed at the group leader.

> A leader needs to have some concept of what is the therapeutically effective activity on the part of the group and when it is utilizing the time efficiently toward moving in that direction. (This is determined by the degree of expression of feeling, the group interaction, sincere interest in helping each other, the

[69]*Ibid.*, p. 10.

[70]*Ibid.*, p. 11.

[71]Michael J. Chandler, "Egocentrism and Antisocial Behavior: The Assessment and Training of Social Perspective-Taking Skills," *Developmental Psychology, 9*, no. 3 (November 1973), pp. 326–333.

feeling of group intensity, evidence of insight being developed, attitude changes, etc.)[72]

There does have to be some initial structure from the group leader. The leader should point out that the major purpose of the group is to solve problems through the understanding of each other's viewpoints and the expression of ideas, feelings, and alternatives. The group leader is mainly an objective observer who can give the group direction. He or she should not be an authoritarian and should be open to a variety of topics within a broad framework. It is the group's responsibility to initiate subjects that will be worth listening to and of interest to other group members. Even though the group leader will manage the discussion to provide some direction, it is up to the group to keep the discussion going. The two major results of the group discussions will be the expression of feelings and ultimately a concerted effort at problem solving by the entire group.[73]

 Although some group counseling programs have been effective in reducing recidivism and in improving other behaviors, many have not. Based on his review of several of the research reports on counseling, Romig concluded:

> Youths who experienced group counseling with therapists offering high levels of empathy, nonpossessive warmth, and genuineness were able to spend more time out of the institutions than the control group.[74]

As with many of the methods we have already reviewed, group counseling is often effective when used in combination with other treatments, such as teaching interaction skills and the behavior modification method.[75]

GROUP THERAPY

Differentiating between *group therapy, group counseling, group psychotherapy, guided group interaction,* and *social group work* can be confusing. Sarri and Vinter, in summarizing juvenile group treatment strategies, include psychotherapy, guided group interaction, and social group work under *group therapy.*[76] They maintain that these various methods are distinguished only by the type of worker who performs the service. Gazda feels that the terms *group therapy* and *group psychotherapy* are generally used synonymously.[77]

[72]Glenn J. Walker, "Group Counseling in Juvenile Probation," *Federal Probation, 23,* no. 4 (December 1959), p. 34.

[73]*Ibid.,* p. 35.

[74]Romig, *Justice for Our Children,* p. 73.

[75]*Ibid.,* p. 73.

[76]Sarri and Vinter, "Group Treatment Strategies in Juvenile Correctional Programs," p. 332.

[77]George M. Gazda, *Basic Approaches to Group Psychotherapy and Group Counseling* (Springfield, Illinois: Charles C. Thomas, Publisher, 1968), p. 4.

Parole and probation agencies have been experimenting with group methods in recent years. Rather loose and ambiguous terminology has resulted. The terms group therapy, group counseling, group guidance, and guided group interaction are employed variously and often interchangeably. Almost anything undertaken with more than one individual at a time is likely to be termed group work or group therapy.[78]

Some writers feel that group therapy is a more intense process than social group work, and that the emphasis is still on the individual while the group is used as a mechanism to better understand the individual and that individual's behavior. Because the delinquent often manifests behavior as a part of a group or a gang, it is felt that the group therapy situation is the natural vehicle in which to view the way the youth reacts to the group and the group's influence on each member's behavior. Furthermore, the one-to-one relationship with a therapist in social casework or individual psychotherapy can be very threatening to adolescents, since they are more comfortable interacting with their peers and being a part of a group. The adolescent often acts much differently outside the natural environment of the group. In addition, in individual counseling there is a more obvious superior—subordinate relationship. This situation is neutralized in the group where youngsters can receive a great deal of support from their peers. The "naturalness" of the group and the interaction are often conducive to the leader's making more valid judgments about the youngsters, their patterns of interaction, and their methods of problem solving.

The group process does not in itself solve all the problems of resistance to treatment. Just as there is resistance to the individual method, there is resistance to the group method. The groups generally pass through various phases with distinguishable characteristics and processes. In the initial stages of the group meetings, some youths will not talk at all, while the more verbal members will try to monopolize the conversation with trivia. The group manipulators attempt to justify their involvement by making the leader and the group members believe that the group cannot function without them and that they are the leaders. Many times these pseudotherapists attempt to manipulate the group to the point where meaningful and relevant problem situations are never discussed.

> The therapist has to recognize the mood of the group and the corollary role that the con man is playing. He tries to elicit general feelings and tries to open up the hitherto silent members of the group. These sleepers often provide the therapist with a clue as to what is going on at the moment.[79]

Once the "con man," or manipulator, can be controlled to the point where more significant group verbalization and discussion can take place and

[78]Dressler, *Practice and Theory of Probation and Parole*, p. 183.

[79]Robert S. Shellow, Jack L. Ward, and Seymour Rubenfeld, "Group Therapy and the Institutional Delinquent," *International Journal of Group Psychotherapy, 8*, no. 3 (July 1958), p. 267.

where the other group members are finally able to express their feelings, the group begins to open up and their ideas and gripes begin to be manifested. The youngsters soon find that they can make their ideas known and can express their feelings without the threat of retaliation by other group members or by the group leader. Manipulators in the group constantly try to test the group leader's authority and position. In the early stages of the group meetings, the group members do not want the spotlight focused on them. Hence the reason for the expression of hostility toward the leader and the attempt to divert the group processes into unproductive channels. The astute group leader, however, is not easily manipulated and understands the group process and the phases that the youngsters have to go through before meaningful dialogue, discussion, and problem solving can take place.

Throughout the group sessions and especially in the initial and middle stages, there is also considerable ambivalence toward the authority figure who is the group leader. Although group members often want to receive the guidance of the leader in problem solving, they are not sure whether the leader can be trusted because of their past negative experiences with adults. The group leader has to recognize this and allow the youngsters to go at their own pace.

Ideally, the group will advance to the point where the expression of honest feelings will become commonplace. Once positive feelings begin to be expressed about the group leader, it is an indication that the group is progressing to the point where they will begin to look at their problems in a realistic manner and assist one another, with the help of the leader, in arriving at successful alternatives and solutions to common problems.

The group method does not always follow the sequence that has been described—the discussion of trivia, the expression of hostility toward the adult authority figure, the phase of acceptance of the authority figure, and then problem solving. There are peaks and valleys, and often when the group seems to be progressing well, there are backward trends or regression to earlier phases. However, the regression does not last long, and if the leader can ride out the storm, the group begins to progress again and can attain new levels of interaction and understanding.

Of the many variations of the group method, Allen describes an approach in which there are two group leaders, one of whom is a "silent observer." Allen feels that this facilitates problem solving.

> The silent observer method is a variation on traditional dual therapy techniques. It is hypothesized that group interaction might be improved by the adoption of a dual therapy technique in which the role of the second therapist was modified to that of a silent observer. Among the potential advantages of the new method was the fact that the observer being less involved with the group than the therapist himself would be in an excellent position to make objective observations about the group.[80]

[80]James E. Allen, "The Silent Observer: A New Approach to Group Therapy for Delinquents," *Crime and Delinquency, 16,* no. 3 (July 1970), p. 325.

Even though the observer does not react directly, he or she can evaluate the dynamic interplay taking place in the group. The observer is also not placed "on the defensive" or "on the spot" like the primary group leader. After the group meeting, the observer can provide the primary therapist or the leader with new insights regarding the dynamics of interaction and alternatives for problem solving. Allen feels that the use of the silent observer not only accelerates and enhances the treatment process in the group but also provides a training laboratory for new group leaders. The training aspect of the silent observer role may well be the most important benefit of the method.

Like most other methods discussed, the specific orientation (within a general structure) that the group leader takes toward the goal of helping youngsters will vary depending on the leader's training, personality, and client group. The various group methods, just like the individual methods, do allow for individual variation and experimentation.

SOCIAL GROUP WORK

Ferguson defines *social group work* as social work "focused on the individual in a group setting," which attempts to help each group member function more effectively in groups and derive greater satisfaction from this participation.[81] According to Dressler, social group work is differentiated from social casework by its additional goal of furthering the group's accomplishment of a social purpose as a group;[82] its similarity to social casework is evident in its goals of improving the individual's relationships and subjective responses to the social environment.[83]

The social group work method operates under many of the same assumptions as social casework, although it is more complex because of the number of group members and the increased interpersonal dynamics. It is possible for an individual to be involved in both social casework and social group work at the same time, but not all clients are capable of this dual involvement. Konopka lists some of the principles of social group work:

1. The worker's function is helping and this helping is perpetuated to establish purposeful relationships with group members.
2. The worker must be warm, understanding, and spontaneous, but yet be able to maintain and enhance group direction.
3. The worker has to accept group members without accepting their behavior and often "limits" have to be utilized but in a constructive manner.
4. The worker has to manage the group while at the same time not forgetting the uniqueness of the individual.[84]

[81]Ferguson, *Social Work*, p. 13.

[82]Dressler, *Practice and Theory of Probation and Parole*, p. 162.

[83]Tappan, *Juvenile Delinquency*, p. 366.

[84]Gisela Konopka, "The Social Group Work Method: Its Use in the Correctional Field," *Federal Probation, 20*, no. 1 (March 1956), pp. 25–31.

In summary, the worker has to be able not only to empathize and understand individual problems, but also to visualize and conceptualize how the group processes can contribute to problem solving. The worker must also be both sympathetic and consistent in the way he or she manages the group so that there will be a structural framework that will facilitate goal achievement.

Pierce visualizes the group as a "social laboratory" in which the individual group members experiment with new patterns of social functioning.[85] The individuals can then evaluate their new patterns of behavior by the reactions of the group members. If there is a satisfactory response, they may try them in their relationships with peers outside the groups or in institutions in the community.

> As group members develop a sense of the group as something more than a collection of individuals interacting, they are able to use this identification with the group as a force for modifying their own behavior and attitudes. Often one is able to risk change or growth because "the group is behind me."[86]

Of the many different types of group work and group therapy, one particular variation that has been used is what is called the "detached" group work method. Some youngsters do not have the desire to come to an agency to participate in formal group meetings; therefore, the group worker has to extend beyond the confines of the agency and develop relationships with youngsters "on the street."

> Group workers act on a tolerant basis and accept the gang members as individuals while making clear that they do not go along with their delinquent behavior. This gain and acceptance requires time. In time, the group worker hopes to get the gang to modify its role in the community and the priority of the individual's role. The aim is to reduce the individual gang member's role as a delinquent.[87]

The detached worker attempts to reduce antisocial behavior within the community, broaden the group members' social horizons, provide the individual group member with new alternatives to social behavior both with peers and with community institutions, and generally improve each member's personal and social adjustment.

Although there is no doubt that the "detached" group work method involves the social worker with youths who would often not come to a program in an agency setting, there have been some serious problems in using the method. Most youth peer groups are not particularly well organized. The assignment of a detached worker to peer groups has in some instances helped them to become

---

[85]F. J. Pierce, "Social Group Work in a Women's Prison," *Federal Probation, 27,* no. 4 (December 1963), pp. 37–38.

[86]*Ibid.*, pp. 33–38.

[87]Mabel A. Elliott, "Group Therapy in Dealing with Juvenile and Adult Offenders," *Federal Probation, 27,* no. 3 (September 1963), p. 54.

better organized and more cohesive. As a result, they are *more* delinquent than before the detached worker was assigned.[88]

Some studies of the effects of the detached method have been negative. For example, the Chicago Youth Development project used detached workers in one section of the city for six years. In addition to the detached worker, the program operated a boys' club and used community organization to reduce delinquency. The staff were particularly skilled in empathizing with and relating to youths. Still, an evaluation showed no reductions in delinquency or school dropout, and no increases in employment, for the youths in the program.[89]

The social group work method is intended to help delinquent youngsters to understand their deficiencies and to develop new and more productive patterns of interaction in the community. At one time, this method was widely used by detached workers, and it is still used in some areas. Detached workers should be aware of the potentially negative effects of increasing group organization and cohesiveness, and should develop strategies to avoid this possibility.

GROUP PSYCHOTHERAPY

Even though there is a blending of the various therapeutic approaches and it is often difficult to differentiate between them, a separate discussion of each is helpful because it illustrates, at least numerically, the descriptive approaches that exist. *Group psychotherapy,* when compared with other group methods, is usually thought of as having more ambitious goals, such as deep insight development and personality restructuring. Many of the techniques utilized, however, are similar to other group methods, and the major difference is in the *degree* of "probing" and the intensity of the relationship.

When working with adolescents, it is often difficult to develop group unity and common goals in the group treatment. Often little commonality exists between group members, although this can be somewhat controlled with adequate selection procedures. Even in groups that have many similar characteristics, it is difficult for group members to empathize with one another.

> This may be particularly true of delinquents who are notoriously self-centered. They form groups not out of friendship, but for mutual security against the adult world which is perceived as hostile.[90]

Schulman states that the components necessary for an effective group psychotherapy situation, such as personal interaction, cooperation, and toler-

---

[88]Malcolm W. Klein, "Gang Cohesiveness, Delinquency, and a Street Work Program," *Journal of Research in Crime and Delinquency, 6,* no. 2 (July 1969), pp. 135–166.

[89]Martin Gold and Hans W. Mattick, *Experiment in the Streets: The Chicago Youth Development Project* (Springfield, Virginia: National Technical Information Service, 1974).

[90]Marvin Hersko, "Group Psychotherapy with Delinquent Adolescent Girls," *American Journal of Orthopsychiatry, 32,* no. 1 (January 1962), pp. 170–171.

ance, are in direct conflict with the dissocial, antagonistic, and exploitive orientation of delinquents.[91] He feels that traditional therapeutic techniques must be modified when working with the delinquent. To facilitate group identification, it is important to point out the common benefits that can be gained by all group members by their participating in the group. Even though group members will initially be skeptical of the benefits they can receive, once the group is in progress, the secondary benefits of associating with the group and socializing with their peers will contribute to greater cooperation and goal achievement.

Group therapy is based on the assumption that one of the major problems that delinquents have in their communities is that their behavior and demands are not realistic. In other words, they are not very effective at "reality testing." Their personalities, in many cases, have been retarded at early impulsive levels of functioning, and they often do not have adequate reality reference points. Group psychotherapy, as well as some other group methods discussed, help the delinquent to test reality and the attitudes and reactions of the leader and the other group members before extending into the "uncertain waters" of the community.

For increased effectiveness with delinquent youngsters, it is helpful if the parents also receive some type of treatment. It is discouraging to treat the youngster if the family contributes to further delinquent behavior. Parents who tend to subvert the efforts of the therapist with their youngsters and who contribute to their acting out behavior in the community often have to be confronted and dealt with on the same therapeutic basis as their youngsters.

Through *family therapy,* parents are made aware of the often hidden and distorted negative aspects of their relationship with their youngsters. The therapist can point out these negative dynamics and patterns of behavior so that they will be recognized and altered.

Regardless of whether the therapy involves a group of family members or a group of delinquent youngsters, the techniques are similar in that the group is used as a vehicle to foster expression of feelings, to involve the members in problem solving, and to observe the interaction and interplay of group participants. The positive insights and the behavioral modification that take place in the group can then be transferred on a more permanent basis outside the group to the community.

As with many methods commonly used to treat delinquents, there is no clear research evidence that group psychotherapy is effective. In fact, some studies have shown that it can even result in increased problems. Boys participating in one program showed more disturbances on a follow-up personality test, and they were not any different in recidivism from youths who did not receive group psychotherapy.[92] In another program for delinquents in a mental hospital

---

[91]Irving Schulman, "Modifications in Group Psychotherapy with Antisocial Adolescents," *International Journal of Group Psychotherapy,* 7, no. 3 (July 1957), p. 310.

[92]W. J. O'Brien, "An Experimental Use of Modified Group Therapy in a Public School Setting with Delinquent Adolescent Males." *Doctoral dissertation,* University of California, Berkeley, 1963.

setting, boys received group psychotherapy.[93] They also took part in a self-government council and work, and were rewarded for positive behavior. Compared with youths who were more strictly supervised and who received individual treatment, those receiving group psychotherapy had higher recidivism. These findings reinforce a point we have made repeatedly—there is a need for considerably more research on commonly used treatment methods for delinquents.

ACTIVITY THERAPY

Many clients do not have the verbal ability necessary to communicate effectively in a conventional individual or group therapeutic situation. Very young children and resistant subjects such as delinquents and predelinquents are especially suited to the *activity therapy* method. A group of six to eight children are gathered or invited to meet at a specific time and place to engage in play, such as group games or some artistic endeavor like modeling clay. The atmosphere is permissive, and the youngsters can use their time as they wish.

> A moderately neurotic child finds great release in a permissive environment where he can act out his repressed hostility and aggression in creative work, play, mischief, and hilarity. Because his behavior does not call for retaliation, punishment, or disapproval, pent-up emotions find appropriate discharge. Perhaps of even greater value is the fact that he sees other children act freely without dire or destructive consequences. This has the effect of reducing guilt about hidden impulses of hate and feelings of being bad or worthless. Not only are the blockings to free expression through unrestricted acting out removed by *activity catharsis*, but the individual psychotherapy with these patients is facilitated as a result. The child communicates more freely and is less protective and less suspicious of the caseworker and psychiatrist.[94]

Slavson points out that only certain types of children can effectively utilize activity therapy as a substitute for the more verbal orientation of conventional group therapy or individual psychotherapy.[95] The open aggression and hostility that is permitted within a permissive situation can create anxiety in some neurotic children and overwhelm them to the point where the activity group experience can become devastating. Typologies can range all the way from the accidental or situational offender to the chronic character disorder offender. Each of these diagnostic classifications often necessitates special consideration and specific therapeutic techniques. For example, because the neurotic offenders suffer from anxiety and guilt, their delinquent behavior is merely a symp-

---

[93]Michael Craft, Geoffrey Stephenson, and Clive Granger, "A Controlled Trial of Authoritarian and Self-Governing Regimes with Adolescent Psychopaths," *American Journal of Orthopsychiatry, 34*, no. 3 (April 1964), pp. 543–554.

[94]S. R. Slavson, quoted in Tappan, *Juvenile Delinquency*, p. 368.

[95]*Ibid.*

tom of their attempts to resolve this inner conflict; whereas the character disorder offenders have a minimum amount of anxiety and guilt, and their acting out is a result of a lack of conscience structure, or superego. Thus, methods of treatment will have to vary considerably between the two diagnostic categories. Anxiety and guilt should not be clinically induced in those neurotic children who already suffer from them, but methods that use even the minimal amounts of anxiety felt by the character disorder client can be the motivating force for the youth's seeking inner change and new modes of adaptation.

Even though the pure categories of *neurotic* offender or *character disorder* offender may not actually exist, those youngsters whose personality structure can be evaluated as predominantly neurotic would probably benefit most from such insight-type methods of treatment as psychotherapy and casework. The character disorder offenders would probably benefit most from such methods as reality therapy and behavior modification because they do not have as much motivation, anxiety, or desire to develop deep insight into their problems—the main goal is to interrupt their negative cycles so that they cease to come in contact with the law. Any insight that they gain into their problems is a bonus.

Not only is it important to select youths for activity therapy carefully, but it is essential to take care in choosing appropriate activities. Shraga Serok and Arthur Blum have recommended that games be used in work with delinquent activity groups. Games of strategy, but not games of chance, can be utilized as:

1. a means of teaching problem-solving behaviors,
2. a vehicle for teaching youngsters how to channel and control aggression,
3. a means of teaching youths to accept social responsibility and to anticipate the consequences of their behavior.[96]

The use of games in therapy is based on the idea that play is of considerable importance in socializing delinquents. Through play activities, children learn how to behave according to rules, and they learn to interact with other people. The counselor has an important role in game-oriented activities:

> In the context of the game plan, counselors can discuss the need for rational problem solving, the need to weigh alternative courses of action, the control of impulsive actions—all for the immediate purpose of demonstrating how it is possible to gain greater control over the game's outcome. Later, this learning must be transferred to real-life situations; however, games may provide a useful starting point for the transfer process.[97]

Certain types of activity therapy can therefore be useful for some youngsters. It is most useful when followed up by application of learning to real-life situations. Regardless of the therapeutic technique utilized, a careful evaluation has to be made regarding its appropriateness for the particular client. Not all

[96]Shraga Serok and Arthur Blum, "Games: A Treatment Vehicle for Delinquent Youths," *Crime and Delinquency*, 25, no. 3 (July 1979), pp. 358–363.
[97]*Ibid.*, p. 361.

clients can benefit from the same technique, and in fact a combination of techniques is often required.

GUIDED GROUP INTERACTION

Guided group interaction is basically similar to group therapy or group psychotherapy in that it is also based on the assumption that through the group and its processes delinquents can solve their problems. The group is the major vehicle for change. It has been a factor in the success of some institutional programs.

According to McCorkle, guided group interaction assumes that delinquents will benefit from the freedom to discuss and analyze problems and their own roles and relationships within the group.[98] McCorkle feels that guided group interaction operates most effectively in an informal atmosphere where most of the social controls evolve from the group itself and where meaningful interaction of group members can ultimately produce insight and new patterns of adaptation to the community.

> The object is to develop a group culture in which those involved will make themselves responsible for helping and controlling each other. The assumption is that a delinquent is more likely to be influenced by his peers than by professional staff. The individual member is not likely to manipulate others nor will he be able to lie or alibi himself out of uncomfortable situations in front of his peers. They have all been down the same road and they are not easily hoodwinked.[99]

This description of guided group interaction is not much different from the description of group psychotherapy and group therapy. The group can exert a great deal of pressure on its individual members after the group has been stabilized and the leader trusted, and meaningful dialogue has taken place. The peer group has extensive power over the individual members and can impose sanctions if one of the members does not become meaningfully involved. Empey and Rabow relate that at Pine Hills, a facility for delinquent boys, the group is permitted to use sanctions, within the confines of the treatment system, on members who do not cooperate. The ultimate sanction is refusal to release a boy from the program.[100]

The process described for guided group interaction in regard to the structure of the group and the means it takes to achieve meaningful dialogue, communication, and expression of feelings is similar to the group processes

[98]Lloyd W. McCorkle, "Group Therapy with Offenders," in Johnston, Savitz, and Wolfgang, "The Sociology of Punishment and Corrections," p. 518; see also Lamar T. Empey and Steven Lubeck, *The Silverlake Experiment* (Chicago: Aldine Publishing, 1971); and H. Ashley Weeks, *Youthful Offenders at Highfields* (Ann Arbor: University of Michigan Press, 1958).

[99]Dressler, *Practice and Theory of Probation and Parole*, p. 202.

[100]Lamar T. Empey and Jerome Rabow, "The Provo Experiment on Delinquency Rehabilitation," in *Juvenile Delinquency: A Book of Readings*, ed. Rose Giallombardo (New York: John Wiley and Sons, Inc., 1966), p. 541.

discussed earlier. The group leader plays an important role in directing and managing significant aspects of the interaction, although he or she attempts to do this according to a democratic model of group participation, discussion, and ventilation of feelings. The initial stages of the group are used to vent hostility and aggression. Initially, the group members are self-centered and unable to realistically or meaningfully involve themselves or their peers in the problem-solving process. Later, as the group progresses and the group members see that their group peers have similar problems and backgrounds, empathy and group identification is facilitated.

> Simultaneously, the behavior of the group becomes more orderly and the leader finds increased support for its earlier definitions. If the initial anxieties and resistances have been adequately handled, warmer, friendlier relations replace the earlier aggressive, destructive, hostile responses. With the release of hostile, aggressive feelings and some understanding of the origin of these feelings, deeper levels may be reached.[101]

McCorkle gives the following criteria for selecting a youth for a group and for using when the group is in actual operation: the youth should be able to contribute to group maintenance, and members should be suited to each other. Generally, group members should be of the same age, educational level, and intelligence, and participation should be on a voluntary basis. The group should meet at regular intervals and at specified times and should not exceed twenty in number.[102]

Guided Group Interaction has been used in a wide range of program settings, including institutions, community programs, and even in schools. After reviewing the research on Guided Group Interaction, Gary Gottfredson concluded that, in the community, the approach provides a cost-saving alternative to institutional placement.[103] Also, compared to traditional probation, it results in less recidivism. However, guided group interaction in the school setting may result in increased delinquency, and in all settings there is a need for well-designed experiments to clarify exactly when and for whom the method is effective.

MILIEU THERAPY

Whether the youngster is in an institution, a halfway house, or some other controlled or semicontrolled setting, *milieu therapy* attempts to produce an environment that will facilitate meaningful change, increased growth, and satisfactory adjustment.

---

[101]McCorkle, "Group Therapy with Offenders," p. 522.

[102]*Ibid.*, p. 523.

[103]Gary D. Gottfredson, "Peer Group Interventions to Reduce the Risk of Delinquent Behavior: A Selective Review and a New Evaluation," *Criminology, 25*, no. 3 (August 1987), pp. 671–714.

Slavson feels that milieu therapy is suitable for persons whose deviant behavior is a reaction to unfavorable life conditions.[104] If the milieu, or environment, is carefully planned so that deviant adaptation will not be needed, fostered, or encouraged, delinquent behavior will be modified or eliminated. Kane feels that the milieu consists of everything happening to the child in the therapeutic environment, whether it is the institution, a halfway house, or some other controlled setting.

> It is as subtle as the attitudes of staff and the kinds of controls administered and the purpose of those controls, constructive or punitive. If one is to single out the essence of a therapeutic milieu, I would say that it is found in the quality of relationships between the children and the direct contact staff.[105]

Because their environment is, in fact, the therapeutic setting, daily activities, including both failures and successes, are the topics of discussion between clients and those persons who are a part of their milieu. Fenton and others define the correctional milieu and the goals of milieu therapy in this setting.

> The correctional community is a method of social therapy in which staff and inmates make a conscious effort to utilize all the experiences in all areas of the group existence in a therapeutic manner. This program bridges a communication gap between staff and inmates typically found in correctional institutions and also utilizes inmate peer influence—the self-help concept—to help inmates gain self-awareness and a more responsible outlook. Inmates who live and work together meet with the staff regularly with an expressed goal of improving postrelease performance. By employing, under staff direction, open communication, confrontation, as well as other treatment methods, inmate participants can model and adjust their behavior through learning, testing, and fixating newer and more effective modes of perceiving and relating to others.[106]

Although research has not always shown that milieu therapy is successful, it was effectively used at the National Training School, which is for youths who have broken both state and federal laws.[107] The milieu therapy was used for older teenagers along with group and individual counseling, and youths in the program had relatively informal and therapeutic contacts with staff and other inmates. Compared with youths in the regular training school programs, participants exposed to milieu therapy committed less serious offenses after leaving the program. They received a similar number of misconduct reports while in the program, but reported for sick call less often.

We have already reviewed the results of another evaluation of milieu therapy: McCord and Sanchez's twenty-five year follow-up of training school

[104]S. R. Slavson, *Reclaiming the Delinquent* (New York: The Free Press, 1965), p. 17.

[105]Joseph H. Kane, "An Institutional Program for the Seriously Disturbed Delinquent Boy," *Federal Probation, 30*, no. 3 (September 1966), pp. 42–43.

[106]Norman Fenton et al., *Explorations in the Use of Group Counseling in the County Correctional Program* (Palo Alto, California: Pacific Books, 1962).

[107]Craft, Stephenson, and Granger, "A Controlled Trial of Authoritarian and Self-Governing Regimes with Adolescent Psychopaths."

inmates who were in two programs, one using milieu therapy and the other characterized by punishment and discipline (see Chapter 7).[108] McCord and Sanchez found that the training school inmates who were exposed to milieu therapy recidivated less often until the age of twenty-four, but as they grew into adulthood the initial differences were not maintained.

Milieu therapy takes a more general orientation to treatment than guided group interaction, group therapy, social casework, and the other methods because it focuses on the total environment of the individual and is viewed as the major therapeutic agent. Milieu therapy is generally utilized in controlled or semicontrolled environments where the client's behavior, actions, and experiences can be somewhat regulated. The many other techniques discussed in this chapter, such as casework and group therapy, can be used to supplement the milieu therapy approach.

INTERVENTION WITH FAMILIES

Attempts have been made to treat aggressive youngsters in their own homes by training their parents to deal with the behavioral problems, and this approach is recommended by many experts (Exhibit 8-5). The Oregon Research Institute initiated a series of investigations using the direct home intervention approach with Patterson, Reid, and Hendriks elaborating on many of the methods and techniques. In Chapter 4, we examined the theory behind these family intervention techniques, which include provision of an incentive for the family to change, extensive training in intrafamily relations, parent training to monitor or track their children, and programs to alter the antisocial behavior itself. Family intervention techniques are consistent not only with Patterson's specific theory but also with the control and social learning theories.

A careful evaluation of Patterson and his coworkers' intervention with the families of youth with antisocial behavior showed that some parents have been able to alter their own behavior and their childrens' behavior, not just in the treatment setting, but also in the home.[109] Positive changes depend on several factors in addition to teaching the parents effective parenting skills. These factors include the clinical skills of trained therapists and an unlimited time for the therapy to continue. Long-term follow-up treatment is particularly important with children who steal and those who are chronic delinquents, for their parents are often unmotivated or resistant to altering the family interactions that support illegal behavior.

Not all family counseling programs have been effective, but those which focus on improving family communication and teaching parents disciplining and

---

[108]William McCord and Jose Sanchez, "The Treatment of Deviant Children: A Twenty-Five Year Follow-Up Study," *Crime and Delinquency, 29,* no. 2 (April 1983), pp. 238–253.

[109]Gerald R. Patterson, *Coercive Family Process* (Eugene, Oregon: Castalia Publishing Company, 1982), pp. 304–306.

Exhibit 8-5 A proposed family intervention program

In considering the potential role of the family, the first step is to define a problem and consider when to initiate an intervention. Parents who have just experienced the initial arrest of one of their children are a clearly identifiable population for whom an intervention would seem appropriate.

The specific intervention that might be devised is to teach parents to implement a form of behavior contracting with their children. . . .

The theory underlying behavior contracting assumes several things that require further application of the template-matching procedure. First, the contracting is based on a *quid pro quo*—in this case meaning that the parents must have resources desired by their child. The resources need not necessarily be economic; e.g., they might consist of privileges that can be granted. The granting of privileges does imply a considerable degree of parental control over the child; the privilege of going out with friends can be granted only if the child cannot or does not go as he or she pleases. Thus families would have to be screened (probably by interview) to determine the availability of resources that might be used to foster the cooperation of the child. The parent-child relationship would have to be reasonably intact in that the parents would have to have enough residual control to initiate and enforce behavior contracts. Parents and the child must be sufficiently intelligent to understand the nature of the contracts and the processes that underlie them. Home life must be fairly stable. Thus families would also have to be screened for their understanding and stability, the latter reflecting fairly constant parental presence, personal stability (e.g., not psychotic or alcoholic), and the absence of major outside perturbations. Finally, the theory presumes that those involved in developing and enforcing the contracts are willing, motivated participants. Thus the program would be limited to families wanting help.

All the restrictions placed on the acceptance of families into the treatment program might seem to represent a prime instance of "creaming," selecting cases with such favorable characteristics that success is assured. We are recommending experimental tests of treatments, however, so that a control group with the same characteristics would provide a base against which to judge success. Far from representing creaming, the type of selection procedure described would result in a stringent test of the effectiveness of the intervention.

SOURCE: Susan E. Martin, Lee B. Sechrest, and Robin Redner, *New Directions in the Rehabilitation of Criminal Offenders* (Washington, D.C.: National Academy Press, 1981), pp. 140–142.

Issues for Discussion. What are the pros and cons of screening some youths out of the program? Is the proposed program based on evaluation research results?

decision-making skills have a good record, particularly compared with other treatment methods.[110] One short-term program of this type focused on:

1. assessing family interactions that maintain delinquent behavior;
2. modifying family communication to increase clarity, precision, and reciprocity;
3. instituting contingency contracting to promote alternatives to delinquent behavior within the home.

The recidivism rate for participants in this program was considerably lower than for participants exposed to other treatment methods or no treatment at all.[111] Another family-oriented program in San Diego was effective in reducing arrest rates for status offenders. The program operated in conjunction with the probation department. Lectures and follow-up discussions were used over a ten-week period to "improve the communication, discipline, and decision making skills of parents."[112] The lectures were about human growth and development. Evaluations of these and other family treatment programs reveal that, if the counselor spends a considerable amount of time with the family, the treatment is most likely to be effective.[113] Also, family intervention requires that the family not be so severely disorganized that members cannot use therapy.[114]

COMPARING GROUP METHODS

Just as we differentiated between individual treatment methods, we can differentiate between group methods by the degree of change that they attempt. Table 8-4 summarizes the various group treatment methods used with delinquents. Group psychotherapy, like individual psychotherapy, attempts the most complete personality change. Activity therapy, guided group interaction, and milieu therapy are oriented toward producing a less profound change. Group counseling, social group work, and intervention with families attempt to produce more immediate and concrete changes in peoples' behavior.

INTERVENTION METHODS FOR PURE PREVENTION

So far we have considered various treatment methods in the context of correctional programs. It is important to recognize that some of these methods also are used in prevention programs for youth who are not adjudicated as delinquent.

[110]Romig, *Justice for Our Children*, p. 93.
[111]James F. Alexander and Bruce V. Parsons, "Short-Term Behavioral Intervention with Delinquent Families: Impact on Family Process and Recidivism," *Journal of Abnormal Psychology, 81*, no. 3 (June 1973), pp. 219–225.
[112]Romig, *Justice for Our Children*, p. 91.
[113]Paul Gendreau and Bob Ross, "Effective Correctional Treatment: Bibliotherapy for Cynics," *Crime and Delinquency, 24*, no. 4 (October 1979), p. 471.
[114]*Ibid.*

Table 8-4 A Summary of Group Treatment Methods for Delinquents

TREATMENT METHOD	INTERVENTION USED TO PROMOTE CHANGE
Group Counseling	Group discussions to solve problems
Social Group Work	Assisting each group member to function effectively as a group member
Group Psychotherapy	Discussion to develop deep insight leading to personality restructuring and good reality testing
Activity Therapy	Play used to teach problem solving, self-control, and social responsibility
Guided Group Interaction	Discussion and analysis of group members' problems and their roles and relationships in the group
Milieu Therapy	Establishment of a total, 24-hour environment to bring about change, growth, and adjustment
Intervention with Families	Training parents to deal with their childrens' behavior problems

In many cases the prevention programs concentrate services on youth who are considered to be at high risk for delinquency, for example those who have serious school problems or who exhibit acting out behavior in the family or the community.

Parent training, for example, has been used as pure prevention in Seattle, Washington. Beginning in the first grade, all parents in some schools were offered the opportunity to receive parent training.[115] By offering the program to all parents, it was possible to avoid stigmatizing the families with predelinquent children. In the training sessions, the parents who were more effective in setting limits and providing appropriate discipline were available to serve as models for those who were less effective. Predelinquent youth were identified in the school, however, and special efforts were made to recruit them into the program.

The degree to which the program will prevent long-term delinquency is not yet known. However, there have been positive effects on school behavior, and many of the parents of high-risk children are receiving parent training. Because all children attend school, and because teachers can often identify the youth most at risk for becoming delinquent, school-based parent effectiveness training has the potential for being a far-reaching strategy for prevention.

The St. Louis experiment is a recent example of a pure prevention program that attempts to involve adolescents in a prosocial peer group.[116] Youths enter the program when they reach late childhood or early adolescence,

[115]J. David Hawkins, Richard F. Catalano, Gwen Jones and David Fine, "Delinquency Prevention Through Parent Training: Results and Issues from Work in Progress," eds. James Q. Wilson and Glenn C. Loury, *From Children to Citizens*, Vol. 3, *Families, Schools, and Delinquency Prevention* (New York: Springer-Verlag, 1987), pp. 186–204.

[116]Ronald A. Feldman, Timothy E. Caplinger, and John S. Wodarski, *The St. Louis Conundrum, The Effective Treatment of Antisocial Youths* (Englewood Cliffs, New Jersey: Prentice-Hall, Inc., 1983).

and they are referred to the program for repeated fighting or other similar antisocial behavior, which is a good predictor of involvement in the juvenile justice system.

Drawing on many different theories of delinquency, the designers of the St. Louis experiment concluded that

> optimum conditions for prosocial behavior change ought to occur in contexts where (1) only one or two antisocial youths are integrated into small groups that consist essentially of prosocial peers, (2) such groups concentrate on recreational, academic, work, and social activities that the youths are likely to encounter in their daily lives, and (3) the programs are located in community-based agencies whose public identity is recreational or educational rather than correctional or rehabilitative.[117]

As you can see, the design of the St. Louis program rests on several of the theories of delinquency that are discussed in Chapter 3. More than one theory identifies the peer group as essential in stimulating either legal or illegal behavior. Because it focused on activities that are common, the behaviors learned in the prosocial peer group could easily be transferred to other settings. Finally, the location of the program in community-based agencies would avoid stigmatizing the youths.

The St. Louis experiment was carried out in a suburban community center. More than 400 boys were referred into the program, and ten percent of them were integrated into existing groups of youths without a history of antisocial behavior. The rest of the youths were placed in groups with each other, that is, groups in which all of the participants had been referred to the program. For purposes of comparison, 625 boys who had not been referred for antisocial behavior but who were taking part in group activities were also studied. The experiment tried to determine the effect of several treatment conditions, including involvement in a prosocial as opposed to an antisocial peer group, experience of the group leader, and type of treatment method.

The greatest reductions in antisocial behavior occurred for boys with an experienced leader, in a group consisting primarily of prosocial peers. In these same groups, there were fewer adverse outcomes for the prosocial youths, who had not been referred into the program. The comparison of three treatment methods—traditional group work, the behavioral method, and minimal treatment—showed that there were very few differences. The greatest deterioration in behavior was among initially antisocial youths who were treated by inexperienced leaders using traditional groupwork methods.

The findings from the St. Louis experiment are quite promising, especially if we consider short-range changes. At the least, the study shows that treatment in groups of other delinquent youths, especially if carried out by inexperienced staff, is likely to be ineffective. Many of the programs that we discussed in Chapter 7 do provide treatment to groups of delinquents, and

[117]*Ibid.*, p. 46.

budgetary and other constraints may make it difficult to hire well-trained staff. The realities of current arrangements to handle delinquents leave us with perplexing questions. Is it possible to provide effective treatment in existing programs? In what types of programs are the most effective treatment methods likely to be used? How can we deliver the most effective treatment to the youths most in need, but still operate within constraints resulting from policies regarding secure placement and limitations on the amount of funding available?

CONCLUSION

This chapter has described some of the specific methods that are used in treating the juvenile. In some programs, the use of several of these methods at the same time has proven to be an effective strategy. Several of the methods are suited to a specific type of delinquent. Just because several methods have been described does not mean that all are successful in helping youths to adjust to their environment. In fact, we have pointed out that research has very often shown certain methods to be rarely effective. Many people take a pessimistic view of the many therapeutic techniques currently used. One author, for example, wrote:

> Treatment programs for delinquents have been notoriously unsuccessful, as indicated by the high recidivism rates usually reported. Efforts to keep delinquents free of crime are hampered by a strong peer culture which maintains the delinquent behavior. Even those treatments which are successful on a short-term basis have usually failed to document any long term difference over similar nontreated youth in such variables as number of offenses. As such, the treatment of delinquent youth represents one of the greatest challenges to the fields of psychology, psychiatry, and social work.[118]

Less pessimistic individuals have stressed the importance of carefully matching clients not only to the appropriate program, but also to the specific treatment methods used by the program. The best results occur when the needs of the juvenile are specifically addressed through the treatment. Comparisons of different treatment approaches tend to conclude that good results occur from treatments with specific behavioral goals rather than vague objectives and unstructured discussion. Thus, favorable results occur from treatments that develop skills to deal with peer pressure and other group dynamics, or that provide parents with specific skills in the areas of limit setting and discipline.[119] In comparison to deterence-oriented interventions, which of course do not try to meet individual offender needs, recidivism results are better for counseling and

[118]K. Daniel O'Leary and G. Terence Wilson, *Behavioral Therapy: Application and Outcome* (Englewood Cliffs, New Jersey: Prentice-Hall, Inc., 1975), p. 196.

[119]Donald A. Gordon and Jack Arbuthnot, "Individual, Group, and Family Interventions," *Handbook of Juvenile Delinquency*, ed. Herbert C. Quay (New York: John Wiley and Sons, 1987), pp. 290–324.

therapy approaches.[120] And when outcomes other than recidivism are considered, a number of different treatment approaches can produce at least some desirable outcomes.[121] Although treatment methods still require continued study and close attention must be paid to exactly which youth receive what services, there is increasing evidence that treatment continues to be a useful response to juvenile offenders and in the prevention of delinquency.

DISCUSSION QUESTIONS

1. Which treatment methods seem to be most effective for different types of delinquents?
2. Which of the most common treatment methods seem to be quite ineffective with delinquents?
3. What training, education, and personal characteristics are required for staff to be effective in applying the various treatment methods?
4. What are the theories of delinquency causation behind each of the treatment methods discussed?
5. What are the possible misuses of behavior modification?

PROJECTS

1. Attempt to identify the major treatment methods of the various agencies within your community.
2. Develop a list of the treatment methods which are most consistently effective. How could you combine these methods in one program?
3. Categorize the treatment methods in this chapter according to whether they are based on theories which are supported by research described in Chapters 3–5 of this book.
4. Taking the part of a person who believes that the juvenile justice system is primarily intended to punish offenders, argue for or against the various treatment methods. Identify the beliefs about the juvenile justice system and about offenders which underlie this position.

[120]Joanna M. Basta and William S. Davidson, III, "Treatment of Juvenile Offenders: Study Outcomes Since 1980," *Behavioral Sciences and the Law*, 6, no. 3 (Summer 1988), pp. 355–384.

[121]Carol J. Garrett, "Effects of Residential Treatment on Adjudicated Delinquents," *Journal of Research in Crime and Delinquency*, 22, no. 4 (November 1985), pp. 287–308.

9

An Example:
A Community-Based
Treatment Program

- HALFWAY HOUSES AND THEIR HISTORY
- A HALFWAY HOUSE IN MICHIGAN
- PROBLEMS IN OPERATING HALFWAY HOUSES
- EVALUATING THE HALFWAY-HOUSE PROGRAM
- RECOMMENDED GUIDELINES FOR THE HALFWAY HOUSE

LEARNING OBJECTIVES

1. To be knowledgeable of the advantages of providing treatment to delinquents in a half-way-house setting.
2. To be aware of the possible staff-related and other difficulties that occur in a halfway house, and to know of solutions to these difficulties.
3. To understand the training needs of halfway-house staff.
4. To be aware of the evaluation study of a halfway-house program.
5. To understand the complexity of the day-to-day operation of a halfway house, and recommend guidelines for the successful operation of such a program.

As noted in Chapter 1 of this book, several states have moved away from the use of large institutions for youth who are removed from their home environment, and instead are relying on alternative, community-based treatment programs. The most common types of community-based programs are the halfway house, for youth who have just left an institution, and the group home, which is often used as an alternative to institutional placement for youth on probation. Even before the renewed interest in community-based treatment, the group home and halfway-house programs were the most common type of facility in operation for children in custody. In the decade preceding 1984, boys' admissions to group homes and halfway houses increased by 85 percent (to 18,701 a year) while girls' admissions increased by 59 percent (to 10,335 a year).[1] Given the widespread use and renewed interest, the types of programs that operate in these settings take on increased importance.

A community-based prevention and treatment program can be defined as any program that attempts to mobilize the resources of the community in an effort to prevent and treat delinquency. Resources are based in the community, and most of the youngster's time is spent participating in community activities and utilizing those agencies and institutions that are a part of the community. The program that we will discuss specifically, a halfway house, is often indistinguishable from the group home, except that halfway house residents have previously been in institutions.

An example of a halfway house that is a community-based treatment and prevention program will facilitate the tying together of many of the principles that have been discussed so far. The establishing of a program is not a simple process, and more than a knowledge of delinquency causation is necessary (Chapter 3). We have seen that youths who break the law have the special needs which are shared by all adolescents (Chapter 5). It is necessary to understand both concepts, delinquent behavior and adolescent behavior, to understand the theories of causation. It also logically follows that knowledge of prevention programs (Chapter 7) and treatment therapies (Chapter 8) is necessary to best serve the clients.

Community-based treatment and prevention programs have become popular today, because, through research and observation, it has been determined that institutions are artificial and do not provide the type of atmosphere where the youngster can learn to work out problems in a realistic manner. Even though institutions are needed for some youngsters, as a last resort and final alternative, they have been utilized too frequently.

Vinter, Downs, and Hall, in their extensive study of juvenile corrections, point out that the states spent $300 million for the operation of juvenile correctional institutions, camps, and ranches during fiscal 1974. This was

> ten times the amount spent on community-based programs and over thirty times the amount spent on foster care. The average offender-year cost of these services was $11,657, with three states spending less than $5,000 and four spending over $19,000.
>
> . . . While it is apparent that the total number of group homes, halfway houses, etc., has greatly increased since the late sixties, community-based residential facilities are not—in the overwhelming majority of states—handling juvenile offenders on a scale consistent with either the recommendations of several national commissions and advisory bodies or the opinions of state correctional executives themselves. Our survey identified an aggregate average daily population of 5,663 in state-related community-based residential programs during 1974. This is about one-fifth the number of youth assigned to institutions.

[1]Office of Justice Programs, *Children in Custody, 1975–1985* (Washington, D.C.: Bureau of Justice Statistics, 1989), pp. 2, 38.

The average daily populations assigned to community programs ranged from 0 in six states and 3 in one state, to a high of 800. The average across the states was 110, compared with 560 for institutions, camps, and ranches. If we repeat the exercise of extrapolating hypothetical national average daily population figures for community-based facilities on the basis of states' highest and lowest rates, the two figures we arrive at are 41,658 and 0. Once again a remarkable variation.

The forty-three reporting states together spent slightly less than $30 million to operate their community programs during fiscal 1974. This sum is about one-tenth that spent on institutions, camps, and ranches, and clearly shows that these facilities are not receiving significant proportions of state juvenile corrections budgets. One state spent almost $5 million, but the overall average was $596,000, and half the states spent less than $300,000. Consistent with a basic argument of those who advocate wider use of this alternative, the offender-year cost averages less than half of that for institutions—approximately $5,500.[2]

Even though a greater emphasis was supposed to be placed on community-based programs, most states still assign more youngsters to residential-type facilities than to community-based programs. Furthermore, even when states utilize community-based programs, this does not necessarily mean that their institutional population will decrease.

Deinstitutionalization rates for the forty-eight reporting states indicated that only four states assigned as many youth to community as to institutional settings, that thirty-six states had rates of less than 25%, and that the average national rate was only 17.7%. Despite substantial deinstitutionalization achieved by states as varied as Massachusetts, South Dakota, Oregon, Maryland, and Utah, the majority have not embraced such a policy. . . .

. . . Overall there is *no* correlation between states' per capita average daily populations in institutions and those in community-based programs. This lack of relationship indicates that the increased use of community services is *not* accompanied by lower-than-average use of institutions. Naturally there are several exceptions, but generally as the number of offenders in community-based facilities increases, the *total* number in all programs also increases.[3]

Community-based control, treatment, and prevention programs can be much more effective in integrating individuals into their own communities and enabling them to adapt to the environment because treatment personnel will be familiar with the community resources available, such as educational and employment opportunities. Treatment can be based on the utilization of community resources. With help from professionals and volunteers, the offender can become acquainted with community resources and receive support and guidance in adjusting to the community and facing its pressures and responsibilities. The mobilization of community resources of both private and public agencies as well as the assistance of professionals and nonprofessionals will help integrate the delinquent into the community processes. In the artificial institution setting, the

[2]Robert D. Vinter, George Downs, and John Hall, *Juvenile Corrections in the States: Residential Programs and Deinstitutionalization*, A Preliminary Report, National Assessment of Juvenile Corrections, The University of Michigan, 1976, p. 68.
[3]*Ibid.*, pp. 73, 77.

delinquent more often than not loses touch with the community and the resources available and does not learn the problem-solving process that will contribute to personal and social adjustment.

In addition to academic and employment facilities, many resources within a community can help the youngster. Innovative approaches have been taken by local, state, and federal governments to help control, prevent, and treat delinquent behavior. For example, vocational rehabilitation provides academic, vocational, and on-the-job training services to persons who are culturally, economically, and socially disadvantaged, including persons convicted of crime or judged delinquent.

In sum, community-based treatment centers and other prevention, treatment, and control programs located near population centers permit the flexible use of community resources and enable the delinquent, in cooperation with treatment personnel, to establish new community ties which will assist him or her not only in becoming satisfactorily integrated into the community but also in developing new social, educational, and employment skills.

HALFWAY HOUSES

The use of halfway houses in delinquency prevention and treatment is becoming increasingly popular. The halfway house is a community-based program small enough to facilitate individualized treatment but still large enough to necessitate a knowledge of theories of causation, deviant and adolescent behavior, treatment therapies, prevention concepts, and procedures and methods for handling juveniles.

History

Even though halfway houses have only recently been used on a large scale, the halfway house concept is not a new one. As early as 1916 the Hebrew Orphan Asylum in New York established a home for adolescent girls who had been discharged from the asylum but were unable to adjust to their own homes, with foster families, or on their own.[4]

Although there have been exceptions, such as Pioneer House, established in Detroit in 1946, and Highfields, established in New Jersey in 1950, little actual development of this type of treatment facility took place until after 1960. In comparison with such other methods of treatment as the training school, aftercare, and probation, the halfway house is still in its infancy.

Halfway houses have been described in various ways. "The trend has been to name these facilities group homes, pre-release guidance centers, transitional homes and the like."[5]

[4]Martin Gula, *Agency Operated Group Homes*, U.S. Department of Health, Education, and Welfare (Washington, D.C.: U.S. Government Printing Office, 1964), p. 2.

[5]Kenneth Carpenter, "Halfway Houses for Delinquent Youth," in *Children*, U.S. Department of Health, Education, and Welfare, November–December 1963, p. 224.

The main idea behind the halfway-house concept is that it should help bridge the gap between the confinement of the institution and the total freedom of the community. The halfway house can be used for many different purposes. McCartt and Mangogna, in their federal government publication on guidelines and standards for halfway houses, describe the various clients that can benefit from this type of program.

Mandatory Releasee and Parolee. The mandatory releasee or parolee who is in need of a transitional center, and the range of services it offers has always been and still is being served by the community treatment center.

The Probationer. Many halfway houses are increasingly accepting persons placed on probation. Probationers are referred to a halfway house under two sets of general circumstances. First, the court may consider the individual too much of a risk to simply place them [sic] on probation to be supervised by an already overworked probation officer, who will be unable to give the needed time and attention to the prospective probationer. At the same time, the court may recognize that the individual in question does not need incarceration in the traditional institutional setting.

The Pre-releasee. For several years, Federal law, and more recently, the laws of several states, have allowed for the release of prisoners to halfway houses of community treatment centers prior to their actual mandatory release or release on parole.

Study and Diagnostic Services of Offenders. Depending on their level of sophistication, many halfway houses are now capable of offering study and diagnostic services to courts. Such services are rendered prior to final disposition in court.

The Juvenile-Neglected and Delinquent. Halfway houses, or group homes, as they are often called, are being utilized increasingly for the child who is neglected or delinquent. The establishment of such group homes has been increasing at an extremely rapid pace. Many times in the past, the neglected child was placed in detention facilities or training schools along with delinquent children, simply because there were no other resources to draw upon.

Use of Halfway Houses for Individuals with Special Difficulties, such as Drug Abuse, Alcoholism and Psychiatric Problems. Halfway houses or community treatment centers are being utilized for target populations with special difficulties such as drug abuse, alcoholism or psychiatric problems. Due to the nature of the problems being treated, the length of stay in such centers is usually much longer than in those servicing the general offender population, often for as long as eighteen months.

Use of Halfway Houses for Individuals Released on Bail Prior to Final Disposition. Bail reform has been spreading rapidly in the United States. Federal and many state and local jurisdictions have enacted bail reform measures.

Use of the Halfway House for Diversion from the Criminal Justice System. Halfway houses or community treatment centers can be utilized in the future to divert individuals from the criminal justice system.[6]

Types of Youth Served

According to Carpenter, the youths to whom halfway-house programs seem to give the most help are those

[6]John M. McCartt and Thomas J. Mangogna, *Guidelines and Standards for Halfway Houses and Community Treatment Centers,* U.S. Department of Justice, Law Enforcement Assistance Administration, Technical Assistance Division (Washington, D.C.: U.S. Government Printing Office, 1973), pp. 22–29.

who have no home to return to, those whose parents are sufficiently inadequate or rejecting to give them the necessary guidance and support for successful adjustment, those whose parents may be fostering their delinquent behavior or those whose parents live in neighborhoods in which the youth are unable to cope with the many pressures they would face upon return to their home community.[7]

Use of Structure

Structure is an important aspect of halfway-house programming. Rabinow lists some factors that must be considered in the structure of the halfway-house program:

1. A living situation that has limits to which the child can relate.
2. Adults who reflect maturity in their behavior.
3. A peer group that does not have too much extreme in age or behavior.
4. Living quarters that provide some degree of privacy.
5. Community resources such as schools, recreational facilities, and work opportunities that do not make overwhelming demands upon him.
6. Professional assistance to help in dealing with personal problems, family relationships, and peer relationships.
7. The security of knowing that food, clothing, financial aid, medical care, etc., are always provided for him no matter what his behavior.
8. The security of knowing that he will have competent assistance to aid in making plans for the future when he leaves placement.[8]

Personnel

Competent staff personnel are an important aspect of the total halfway house program and structure.

The opportunity to live closely with adults whose behavior can be a model to emulate and from which to take strength is a unique one for most of the adolescents in placement. Immature, undisciplined, and inconsistent behavior by house staff can have a most destructive effect.[9]

Location of the House

The location of a halfway house can have important ramifications and should be given careful consideration. The halfway house should be located in a metropolitan area near the resources of the community. It should also be located in a neighborhood where it will be accepted by the residents and where there will not be animosity between the community and the program.

[7]Carpenter, "Halfway Houses for Delinquent Youth," p. 224.

[8]Irvine Rabinow, "The Significance of Structure in the Group Release Program," *Journal of Jewish Communal Service*, 38, no. 3 (Spring 1962), p. 302.

[9]*Ibid.*, p. 301.

There should be schools and recreational facilities available and places of employment that are within a reasonable distance. Chapter 3, "Theories of Delinquency Causation," discussed the importance of the environment and institutions like the school in preventing delinquent behavior.

Economic Benefit

The halfway-house program is much less costly for the taxpayer than other programs. Even though the cost per resident may be the same as the cost at an institution, or even slightly higher, the halfway house returns the youngster to society soon, making the cost per individual treated much lower. In New Jersey eight out of ten releasees from the Highfields project were "successful" for one year after release as opposed to five out of ten releasees from the training school at Annandale. The costs per inmate per day were approximately equal. "On a strict per capita basis the Highfields project cost one-third as much as the traditional program for each boy treated."[10] The reason is that the average term of treatment at Highfields was approximately five months, whereas the average term of treatment at Annandale was slightly over a year.

Halfway Houses in Michigan

Because Michigan is one of the leaders in the nation in halfway-house development and utilization and also because one of the authors of this textbook was a director of a halfway house in Michigan for a period of time, the example presented will be taken from his experiences in the halfway-house program. Michigan halfway houses, which are called residential care centers, are operated by the Department of Social Services and serve children between the ages of thirteen and nineteen, with the average term of residence being four months.

The system of community care has grown considerably since the first halfway house was established in 1964. As of 1980, there were 14 halfway houses as well as 42 similar group home programs and 53 short-term programs. In Michigan, the group homes differ from the halfway houses, because group home parents actually live with residents and provide guidance and supervision just as natural parents would. The Michigan community programs have a capacity for accepting over 500 youths at one time and serving as an important alternative to secure detention and to institutionalization. Yet, there is still a need for more services to place "hard-to-place" youths, programs for youths requiring placement for more than one year, and programs for girls who are pregnant or who have recently given birth. For many years, one objective of the community residential programs has been to limit the use of institutions for all youngsters but those who are unable to tolerate the closeness and pressures of the communi-

---

[10]H. Ashley Weeks, "The Highfields Project," in *Juvenile Delinquency: A Book of Readings,* ed. Rose Giallombardo (New York: John Wiley and Sons, Inc., 1966), p. 530.

ty. However, experts continue to state that there still are many youths in institutions who could benefit from community placement.[11]

Administration and Programming

The halfway house that we will examine in depth was staffed by a caseworker, who also served as the director, and five child-care workers (boys' and girls' supervisors) who worked eight-hour shifts. As in other houses in Michigan, there was a capacity for eight wards, who were provided with both school and work experience if appropriate. In the *academic* program, those wards who were motivated and capable of further academic training were given an opportunity to continue their education. A ward also had the opportunity to enroll in a joint academic and work program, which allowed the child to continue an educational program, obtain some work experience, and achieve some financial independence. In the work program, wards who were not capable of, or not interested in, furthering their formal education were given the opportunity to work full time.

Although the halfway-house program that will be described was operated by the Department of Social Services, the development of new techniques and methods was highly flexible at the time the author was director because of the newness of the operation. The halfway house accepted boys. Halfway houses usually serve either boys or girls, but not both, except when dealing with very young children. A program for girls is described in Exhibit 9-1.

PROBLEMS INVOLVED IN OPERATING A HALFWAY-HOUSE PROGRAM

The Treatment-Custody Dilemma

The major problem that exists in correctional programs employing a wide variety of professionals is a communication breakdown between the college-educated and the noncollege-educated staff. This is merely a symptom of the age-old treatment-custody dilemma. This phenomenon occurs in a number of institutional and parainstitutional settings, and a review of the literature in this area reveals that this is a universal problem in the treatment of juvenile offenders, regardless of the type of facility.

This dichotomy usually exists because institutional staffs have historically been segregated—first by function, and second by training. On the one hand, the custody staff, who have the function of controlling (guarding) the clientele, usually have no formal training. On the other hand, the treatment staff, whose function it is to "treat" (however this is interpreted), usually have

---

[11]Office of Children and Youth Services, Michigan Department of Social Services, *Community Residential Care Services: State-Wide Plan* (July 1980).

Exhibit 9-1   A staff member's description of Argus, a group home for girls

At the beginning we chose girls because we liked working with them and because there were a greater number of girls than boys for whom proper placement was unavailable. Girls tend to be more difficult in residence than boys. They have been subjected to a double dose of discrimination—as females and as members of minority groups—and they tend to express their turmoil and rebelliousness by in-house acting out, where boys are likely to express theirs in street crime and antisocial acts in the community. Argus will shortly open a facility for twenty-four hard-to-place boys and we will have a better basis of comparison.

We take into consideration the fact that our youngsters and their families have been buffeted by migration, unemployment, ethnic and economic discrimination and the disintegration of their kinship and social networks. Many parents and family members have been caught up in drugs, alcohol and ill health. With little to lean upon, these children become overly self-reliant and are apt to mistrust adults. This requires patience and special handling. They can become enraged, depressed, dissociated or depersonalized, which frightens the staff and makes them think the kids are crazy. They act out also in the form of marijuana and alcohol abuse, promiscuity, destruction of property, theft, fire setting, assaultiveness and running away. In Argus, as these children become bonded to others in trust and affection, they experience remorse and welcome the opportunity to expiate their guilt in a group setting. Their maladaptive coping mechanisms generally are discarded in response to our process and the warm environment we try to maintain. I say "try to" because, given the obstacles in our path, including red tape, excessive paperwork, the perils of the job and the low salaries of people on the firing line, our effectiveness is constantly undermined, and we are forced to spend almost as much energy keeping a staff together as we do on the children. We recognize our obligation to protect and support the staff as well as the children.

Referral materials are sent to us from Special Services for Children, the Family Court and the voluntary child-care agencies. If there are no vacancies and none are anticipated, the materials are returned with a letter of explanation. If there are vacancies we fill them, accepting the youngster sight unseen. Our practice is that once we ask a girl to visit the program, she is free to accept or reject us, but we do not turn her away, for to do so would add another layer of pain and rejection to the burden she already carries.

SOURCE: Elizabeth Lyttleton Sturz, *Widening Circles* (New York: Harper & Row, Publishers, 1983), pp. 97–98. Copyright © 1983 by Elizabeth Lyttleton Sturz. Reprinted by permission of Harper & Row, Publishers Inc.

Issues for Discussion.   Exactly how could girls be affected by a double dose of discrimination? What special requirements should there be for staff in girls' programs?

extensive formal training. Also implied in the treatment-custody dilemma is the treatment staff's decision-making power in the institution. The custody individual is typified by the role of "watchdog" and "inhibitor of privileges," while the treatment individual is the "giver of privileges." Animosity can obviously exist in such a situation. This conflict of roles not only affects the relationship between the custody and the treatment personnel but also has implications in their relationship with the clientele. The dilemma affords a natural and opportune situation for the clientele to manipulate the staff and turn them against one another, which can have a decided negative effect on the total administration of the treatment program. Also, because of basic philosophical differences that often exist between occupational groups working in the juvenile justice system, the custodial staffs of institutions and even the noncollege-educated staffs of smaller programs like group homes and halfway houses are usually oriented criminologically to the classical school of criminology and the classical view of organization, whereas treatment personnel subscribe to the positive school of criminology and the human relations view of organization.

Several questions can be asked: Is the treatment-custody dilemma inevitable? Will it always exist because of the division of labor by function and training? What can an administrator do organizationally to alleviate this problem? These questions and others will be answered later in the chapter.

The Type of Clientele

Another problem that exists in correctional facilities is the type of clientele served. The clients of a typical group home or halfway house have many needs when they enter a program (see Exhibit 9-2). Persons adjudicated delinquent do not usually voluntarily seek treatment for their problems; on the contrary, they often attempt to perpetuate their condition. Unlike neurotics and psychotics who are plagued by anxiety and distress, some delinquents are unaware that they have problems. Because of their psychological makeup and learned social behavior, delinquents can be expert manipulators and effective con artists, and this is often an integral part of their value system. Manipulation is more than merely a prized and desired asset; it is a tool with which some delinquents "ply their trade." Hence, they have an extraordinary ability to manipulate people, and the treatment-custody dilemma plays right into their hands and perpetuates this pathological process.

Delinquents who are not classified as neurotics were described in Chapter 7 as power oriented or as passive conformists. As the California Treatment Project showed, the power oriented and to a lesser extent the passive conformists benefited more than the neurotics from placement in a residential, institutional program. In our discussion of Michigan halfway houses, we will focus on their use with the nonneurotic delinquent, since the neurotics seem to benefit from nonresidential treatment. Keep in mind that the treatment methods were chosen for use in the halfway house because of the particular needs and characteristics of the halfway-house residents.

Exhibit 9-2 Clients at Achievement Place, Lawrence, Missouri

Sixty-one percent of the youths were white; 29 percent black. American Indian (7 percent) and Mexican American (2 percent) youths made up the remainder. Achievement test scores placed the youths an average of two grade levels behind their actual grade levels and over half (57 percent) of the youths had already failed one or more grade levels. Sixty-five percent of the youths were suspended from school at the time they were admitted to Achievement Place. All had been adjudicated in juvenile court, 52 percent involving felonies. Two-thirds of the youths lived in homes lacking one or both natural parents, and slightly more than half of the families were receiving some form of public assistance for income.

SOURCE: John L. Levitt, Thomas M. Young, and Donnell M. Pappenfort, "Achievement Place: The Teaching-Family Treatment Model in a Group-Home Setting," *Reports of the National Juvenile Justice Assessment Centers* (Washington, D.C.: U.S. Department of Justice, 1981), p. 3.

Issues for Discussion.   What special difficulties do minority youths have in our society? Can community schools assist youths with the achievement problems of the residents of programs like Achievement Place? What type of family treatment, if any, should residents receive?

The delinquents in the halfway-house setting often lacked positive identification models who could transmit the values of the larger society. The result is that a social and moral void exists in some delinquents' conscience structure. hence, the attitude "take what you can get" and "it's only wrong or immoral if you get caught."

If, then, the delinquents in the halfway-house program we will discuss are different from the neurotic or the psychotic, what treatment techniques should be used? What types of personnel should be involved in applying these treatment methods?

Serving a Human Being

The "commodities" that are being produced and served in correctional settings are not inanimate objects, but human beings, and human beings have the innate ability to affect one another in many ways. For example, an assembly-line worker operating under classical organization theory receives instructions and orders from a supervisor and then performs the task of riveting the right front fender of a new automobile. The fender does not respond in a manner that can cause an emotional reaction in the worker. However, something quite different happens when the worker (the child-care staff member) is dealing with a human being (the delinquent). The worker may get instructions and advice from a supervisor, but a second element is involved in the process—the worker not only performs an action, but the object on which he or she performs the action is capable of producing a reaction in the worker. Thus a reciprocal emotional situation evolves. The delinquent can accentuate an emotional reaction in others because of aggressiveness and antisocial attitude. The delinquent often exhibits behavior that is boisterous, aggressive, and cocky to disguise feelings of worthlessness, fear, and insecurity. In effect, delinquent youths can actively attempt to antagonize society so that they will be rejected, thus reinforcing their self-concepts that they are worthless and social outcasts. Some youths who have been hurt emotionally do not want to take the chance of being hurt again. The dynamic of rejecting before being rejected is a defense against getting close to people. Because serving human beings is different from producing a material product, organizational assumptions have to be altered to consider the human factor, an important reason why classical organization theory cannot be easily transposed to situations where the "product" is human and not material.

The questions to be asked are: How can positive communications be facilitated between the staff and the youths? What effect does an emotionally charged situation have on both the youths and the staff? What techniques can be utilized to keep negative reinforcement and reactions at a minimum?

Personnel

Persons attracted to the correctional field can present certain problems. This is not to imply that all persons attracted to this field are negatively motivated, but it is important to mention that some of them are, and it is in reference to these individuals that this section attempts to raise some questions.

The child-care staff, since they are on the "firing line" and in constant contact with the youths, are in a position to exert a great amount of influence as identification and authority models. Whether this influence is positive or negative depends on the individual staff member.

People satisfy their emotional needs in a variety of ways. In some instances, delinquents are vulnerable to displaced hostility and negative reinforcement from persons working in correctional settings. An "energy surplus" exists in the work situation—the worker has more energy left than is needed to perform the job, and much of this energy is psychological and is manifested in the work group. Where the "product" is human, the surplus energy can be focused on the clients as well as on the work group. It is possible that some persons are attracted to this field because they can overassert their authority and direct their energy into negative channels.

Conversely, an individual can mask intense hostility by being overpermissive and oversolicitous even to the point of encouraging the delinquent to act out. A staff member who has a problem accepting authority can experience vicarious satisfaction when the delinquent acts out against society and specifically against the correctional administration. Deviant behavior by staff members in such instances can become commonplace.

Some questions to be asked at this point are: How do delinquents affect persons who are negatively motivated and attracted to the correctional field, and in turn how does this affect the treatment-custody dilemma? Do some staff members prefer and even perpetuate the treatment-custody dilemma? What are the ways in which staff members can be used most effectively?

The Treatment Concept

Another problem in correctional administration is defining of the word *treatment*. Many times treatment personnel are not clear as to what is meant by the concept and what it entails. Treatment varies with the treater and the situation. Many different approaches can be used, depending on the orientation of the agency and the academic and personal preferences of the therapist or the counselor (see Chapter 8). Can *treatment* personnel expect *custody* personnel to understand and accept the treatment concept if, in fact, it is not clearly defined and it changes like a chameleon depending on the circumstances? Does treatment mean being extremely permissive? Is treatment dependent on the treater's ability to use superfluous psychological jargon? Is it necessary that treatment be practiced in a clinical setting? Isn't the definition of treatment really a definition of the particular organization's purpose and goals? Isn't it possible to transform theoretical concepts into manageable and practical terms for the line staff?

Training

The area of training can present sizable problems for the administrator. The training concept has implications for the treatment goals. If the goals and purposes of the organization are clearly defined and if the staff understands the criminological and organizational orientation of their organization and the assumptions that its operation is based on, then the treatment techniques and the training methods needed will be a logical consequence. Exhibit 9-3 offers one example of training requirements established for a halfway house.

Just as training will have to fit the goals and purposes of the organization, so will the trainer have to be acquainted with the problems peculiar to that organization. It is one thing for the trainer to impart certain concepts, methods, and techniques on how to react in a certain volatile situation and another thing for the trainer to experience the actual aggressiveness. Can trainers, who are usually the college-educated treatment people, summarily chastise a staff member for reacting negatively to being called a derogatory name if they have not experienced the situation themselves? (This does not mean trainers have to agree with the negative reaction, but it is mandatory that the potential emotional ramifications be recognized.) Or should trainers stay away from the firing line so as not to taint their humanitarian image?

The Community

The relationship to the community can also pose certain problems. In the halfway house operated in Michigan, there was often a direct correlation

Exhibit 9-3 Staff training at Pine Lodge

The staff here at Pine Lodge shall be given 25 hours of ongoing training per year. All new staff members will be given 50 hours of orientation and training within their first year. The areas to be dealt with in the course of both ongoing and new staff members training shall include the following:

a) Developmental needs of children.
b) Child management techniques.
c) Basic group dynamics.
d) Appropriate discipline, crisis intervention, and child handling techniques.
e) The Direct Care workers and the Social Services workers roles in the institution.
f) Interpersonal communication.
g) Proper and safe methods and techniques of restraint.
h) First aid.

Training shall be accomplished by both on-site and off-site training opportunities. Staff here at Pine Lodge will be exposed to speakers who have expertise in the given areas listed above. Methods shall be developed to provide training in all these areas and the training time shall not be less than 25 hours for all ongoing staff per year and 50 hours for any new employees per year.

SOURCE: *Pine Lodge Manual*, 1985.

---

between the amount of aggression exhibited in the house and the amount of negative behavior exhibited in the community. Those boys who would verbalize and rebel in the house would not act out in the community. Therefore, our general philosophy was that it was better for the boys to act out in the house because the problem could be dealt with on the spot, and hence there would be less of a tendency for them to displace their aggression onto the community. This did not mean that the boys were free to express themselves in any manner they desired. They could not, for example, destroy the furniture; they could, however, express verbal anger and discontent to the staff.

Concomitant with this philosophy, our major emphasis was not on regimentation. On various occasions boys would rebel by not making their beds and not doing other assigned chores. The house, however, usually never looked any worse than it would have if a normal group of teenagers had been living in it. (Chapter 5, "The Adolescent," provided background on what is considered "normal.")

It was interesting to note that, even though visitors to the house seemed to accept our integrated organizational philosophy of "controls but not regimentation," they usually expected to see the "shiny institution" characteristic of classical organizational theory. Their disapproval and surprise could often be observed by staff members, who were presented with a role conflict that made them uncomfortable. On the one hand, they were attempting to play their roles according to the norms on which the program had been established but, on the other hand, they were being evaluated according to normative criteria with which the philosophy of the program did not adhere. What effect could this organizational paradox and role conflict have on the operation of the program? How could this situation be alleviated?

SOLUTIONS TO THE PROBLEMS: DEVELOPING A NEW ORGANIZATIONAL AND PHILOSOPHICAL (CRIMINOLOGICAL) SYSTEM

In the halfway house in Michigan, it was felt that the staff should not have to be dichotomized into treatment and custody. In other words, there did not have to be such strict division of labor and emphasis on specialization, two key principles of the classical view of organization. The same person could play the role of both "giver" and "taker," "controller" and "liberator." In effect, with adequate staff selection and training, one person could make the decision as to the proper treatment technique at any given time, which is congruent with the human relations view of participation in decision making.

Employing staff members who will perform what some people consider a dual function (treatment and custody) implies certain alterations in classical organizational theory concepts—namely, the decentralization of authority and decision making from the caseworker (administrator) to the line staff.

It was felt that if the new concept of decentralization of authority, which involved participation in decision making by the entire staff, were introduced into the halfway house program, the child-care staff would see their new role more favorably and would feel a part of, and identified with, the total treatment program, which would increase the congruent normative orientation of all concerned. This would specifically result in better communication between the caseworker and the staff, a more effective treatment program, and the solidification of the group—with corresponding social rewards for the group members.

It was also assumed that all staff members would be given authority commensurate with their responsibilities and that authority and communication would be a two-way process. Even though the major decisions would be made by the entire staff at the weekly staff meeting (group participation in decision making), day-to-day decisions would still have to be made by the particular staff members who were on duty. Their decisions would never be reversed by the caseworker, and if a difference of opinion arose, the problem would be discussed either privately or publicly at the staff meeting. In addition, the staff members were kept informed and were involved in every phase of both the house operation and the boys' status in terms of past, present, and future diagnosis, treatment, and planning. Hence the necessity for all staff to have knowledge of deviant behavior, theories of causation, therapies, and adolescent behavior.

Finally, because the boys had also witnessed the treatment-custody dilemma before coming to the halfway house, it was thought important that some tangible administrative responsibility (a form of division of labor and specialization) be given to each staff member to reinforce the concept that the entire staff was involved in decision making, and also to increase the status of the child-care staff. Each staff member was therefore given a major administrative responsibility; for example, one staff member was responsible for all monetary transactions in the house, and another staff member was responsible for programming all house activities.

Organization Structure

The organization chart took a new shape. Previously, the chart had resembled and had typified the classical organizational model shown in Figure 9-1. Under this system the head boys' supervisor did most of the actual staff direction, but the caseworker made most of the decisions. The decisions were meant to be categorized into treatment decisions (made by the caseworker) and house management decisions (made by the child-care staff). This was a very hazy line, however, and conceivably the caseworker could (and sometimes did) reverse a decision made by the child-care staff by rationalizing that it was a treatment decision. For example, if a boy was involved in a drinking escapade within the house and the child-care staff restricted him to the house, the caseworker could reverse the decision on treatment grounds (because he exercised his authority according to the classical principle) and allow the boy to go on a home visit because "the boy's drinking was the result of an excessive amount of pent-up frustration and anxiety." A situation like this can obviously affect the morale and the motivation of the child-care staff and the treatment of the boy.

Figure 9-1

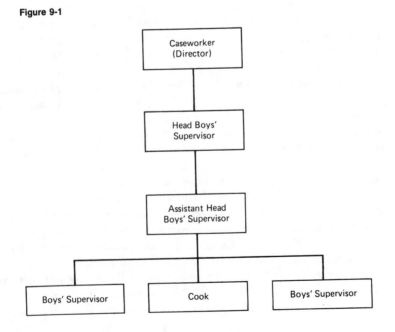

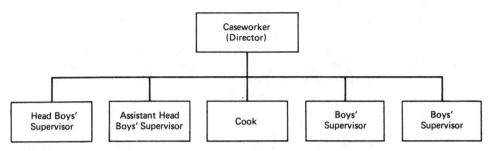

Figure 9-2

The staff would undoubtedly feel powerless in their roles, the boys would be able to utilize the situation for manipulating, and most important the normative bonds that have to exist for effective functioning would be nonexistent.

As seen in Figure 9-2, the new organizational chart of Pine Lodge was much more decentralized, with a "flattened" hierarchy. In this chart, the caseworker was the director and was responsible for supervising the staff, providing casework for the boys, and administering the total program. However, the total administrative and social structure of the house was considered the major therapeutic agent. This means that house management activities and house controls were considered as much a part of the treatment program as were direct casework services. There was an integrated approach to both the organizational structure (combining classical and human relations principles) and the treatment structure (combining positive and classical principles).

Differences in Treatment.   Treatment techniques in correctional settings have to be different because the clients are different. Treatment of the boys in the halfway house was a twenty-four-hour-a-day job. In a typical clinical or psychiatric setting, a client might tell the therapist that he was involved in a "beer blast" at home. The therapist would discuss the situation with the client and try to determine the etiology of the problem and the psychological dynamics present. In the halfway house, the staff did not have the luxury of merely discussing the problem in a secondhand manner. In addition to being concerned with the psychological dynamics of the client, the staff had to be concerned with controlling the client. Obviously, the boys could not be allowed to have a beer blast, especially on state property.

Because the treatment program was viewed as involving the boys' total life process within the organization structure, it was not feasible or desirable that the house staff be specialized into treatment areas and house management areas. Hence, decision making could not be dichotomized into decisions made by the caseworker and decisions made by the child-care staff. The entire staff had to participate in all decision making that affected the boy and the operation of the house.

This, however, did not necessarily mean that there was no division of labor or specialization of duties according to the staff members' positions as determined by their Civil Service classification. There was still a hierarchy of responsibilities, the head boys' supervisor having more responsibility, and so on. The responsibility, however, related to objective administrative functions, such as making out the staff payroll and being responsible for calling repairmen, not to decisions concerning the boys. The division of labor referred more to differences in responsibility for house management, not to differences in power or authority over the boys.

The more pronounced the hierarchical structure, the more the boys will have the opportunity to manipulate the "boss" against the "staff," and the more they will, in fact, manipulate. A flattened hierarchical structure with equal decision-making power for all eliminates much of this manipulation, and thus interrupts one of the boys' major pathological processes.

Even though treatment objectives should be specifically defined, the techniques for attaining these specifically defined goals should be kept flexible to encourage the staff to use their own initiative and personal assets. This would also facilitate decision making because the staff member would not have to be concerned about using the "right" technique. The right technique could apply in an industrial organization operation if under classical principles, but not in a situation where managing and dealing with human behavior was a major variable. Staff members could try innovative techniques, and this would eliminate their need to try new methods through devious means (see Chapter 8).

There were, however, specific guidelines under certain circumstances. For example, if a boy were placed on restriction by the entire staff, a staff member could not make the decision on another shift to allow the boy to go out on "free time." This, however, referred more to the concept of consistency in decision making than it did to flexibility in the particular technique applied. If an individual staff member deviated from the norms established by the rest of the staff, the informal sanctioning process was very effective. Because the size of the staff was small, and the problems the boys presented were difficult and frustrating, the individual staff member needed the support of other staff. Hence informal sanctioning by the staff, which many times meant withholding of social rewards (participation in social activities and other forms of socialization) was very effective. Formal sanctioning, like firing and administrative reprimand for deviations that were more serious, although infrequent, nevertheless had to be resorted to on occasion.

Another point should be clarified. Even though all staff members had the authority to make decisions about problems that would arise on their shift, they could always telephone another staff member for advice (usually the caseworker). At first the staff did this constantly, but when they became confident and comfortable with their decision-making ability and the normative orientation of the organization, consultation by telephone decreased.

Staff members were also informed that treatment did not necessarily mean a clinical setting and the use of psychological jargon. Treatment could be taking a boy shopping for clothes, giving him advice on dating, or helping him with his homework. Treatment could take place over a pool table or at the dinner table. In other words, treatment was considered anything that related to the boy's total life process. The importance of understanding all aspects of adolescent behavior was also emphasized. If staff members understood "normal" adolescent behavior, it was felt that they would be less critical of the boys when they manifested normal adolescent "symptoms" like being loud, boisterous, moody, secretive, and defiant.

The Treater: Facilitating Communication

People are attracted to certain types of work and organizations for many reasons, psychological, educational, monetary, social, and so on, and individuals working with juvenile delinquents are no exception.

It was mentioned earlier that since the delinquent at Pine Lodge was usually clinically different from the neurotic or the psychotic, it followed that the treater did not need the same clinical experience—the clinical difference between the delinquent and the neurotic or the psychotic was that the delinquent lacked an adequate conscience structure as a result of inadequate identification models. (Chapters 3 and 4 illustrated this.) At the halfway house it was felt that because positive identification models were so important, the major treatment device would not be the using of clinical jargon and knowledge to alleviate guilt and anxiety, since the client had a minimal amount of both, but would be the providing of positive identification models. Making this assumption would be a logical conclusion if the social learning and psychodynamic theories of delinquency causation were understood and made effective by translating them from theory into practice. Because positive identification models could be found in every walk of life, we did not look for persons with a particular educational background—according to our definition and requirements, formal education was not a prerequisite for being an effective therapist. Not emphasizing a particular educational background would facilitate the combining of the classical and positive schools of criminology because the person we were looking for had to be cognizant of social and psychological factors that contribute to delinquency (the positive school) but had to be practical with an emphasis on personal responsibility and free will (the classical school). In addition to being positive identification models, it was therefore mandatory that the staff be mature and understand their own personal dynamics as well as psychological and social dynamics contributing to human behavior. This would enable them to transmit an honest concern and to understand extenuating circumstances and variables. If a staff member's actions were inappropriate, it was important to determine if the staff member was displacing negative feelings from other persons or situations onto a youth. Staff members therefore had to understand psychological dynamics and be constantly introspective.

Persons were employed who liked children and had the ability to (1) tolerate and understand aggressive and demanding behavior, (2) give of themselves emotionally and mentally without expecting or demanding something in return, (3) work with other staff members, and (4) be understanding and flexible yet firm and consistent in the enforcement of house rules.

It was observed that certain boys were attracted to, confided in, and communicated with specific staff members. This natural attraction was encouraged because of the importance of the relationship with a positive identification model in helping the boy to modify his socially deviant behavior. This positive relationship with a particular staff member was beneficial because it not only accelerated the treatment process but also gave the boy someone he could emulate and please through socially acceptable behavior. In effect, we utilized and perpetuated the natural channels of communication, unlike the authority structure in classical organization theory with communication structured between layers, ranks, and positions. The caseworker would still provide supervision (unity of command principle) to the particular staff member, but the actual casework was being performed by the staff member the boy trusted and had chosen as his friend. The caseworker's supervision mainly involved interpreting the meaning of various behavior patterns and helping the staff member understand what dynamics were presented and operating in the boy. Because of the small size of the staff, span of control was not a factor.

Because one specific kind of formal education or one specific kind of personality was not required for work in Pine Lodge, the staff consisted of a variety of personality types. A person's positive personality characteristics were used to the program's best advantage. For example, an athletic staff member would program athletic events for the boys, and this could literally mean altering the organization to fit the employee. Altering the organization to fit the employee was done by choice in this instance, but it was also sometimes done by necessity. If some staff members had negative personality characteristics, these could also be utilized to the program's advantage. For example, a staff member who had difficulty exerting even minimal controls for fear of losing a "nice guy" image could be put on a shift that had the greatest amount of flexibility in regard to controls. The staff member could also be used effectively to perform duties that involved being "nice" to the boys. Conversely, a staff member who was excessively controlling could be used effectively in another phase of the program where, for example, the setting of the controls and limits would be beneficial to the program.

Like other delinquents, the boys at the halfway house had reached adolescence with many of the same likes, dislikes and pressures as normal adolescents, but they had fewer social, intellectual, and occupational skills. They had experienced little success in life. The staff attempted to intervene in their life process and acquaint them with positive life experiences.

Staff members were encouraged to react spontaneously. If a staff member was angry at something a boy had done, it was much better to express the anger than to suppress it, displace it, and have it come out in a subtle, punitive, passive-aggressive manner that the boy could neither accept nor understand. (Chapter 4 pointed out the negative effects of inconsistent discipline and passive hostility in child rearing.)

Staff members involved themselves personally. They took the boys job hunting and on recreational activities, and they gave advice on social amenities. Even when staff members were looking for a new car or shopping for clothes, they often took boys with them.

Because the boys were impulsive, hedonistic, and unable to tolerate much frustration, they needed constant support and encouragement to stay on their jobs, to stay in school, and to refrain from acting out behavior.

Staff members were always willing to give a boy a ride to and from work, advance money from the house fund until he received his first paycheck, and allow him much freedom in purchasing, with his pay, such items as record players, guitars, bicycles, and radios.

These actions not only supported the boy while he was experiencing the first few frustrating days on the job; it helped satisfy his need for immediate gratification and showed him that by means of employment it was possible to acquire pleasurable items legitimately. The staff should be aware of the clinical differences in some delinquents, such as their impulsiveness and low frustration tolerance level, because this understanding provides a basis for developing a treatment plan and orientation. Our constant support of the boys as they moved out into the environment was predicated on the clinical peculiarities of delinquents.

It was not naively assumed that a boy who had already utilized almost every state and local service available would suddenly succeed in the community because of some deep psychological insight into the nature of his behavior. If he refrained, for example, from shoplifting, it was probably because of the money in his pocket earned from a job to purchase the items rather than because of any insight into the nature of his "oedipal problem."

The approach with the boys was direct, always emphasizing the reality of the situation. The method of reality therapy was the basis of treatment (see Chapter 8). Reality therapy emphasizes individual responsibility for actions, which is similar to the classical school of criminology's concept of free will. Psychological and sociological variables, principles of the positive school of criminology, were considered, but these variables were combined with the concept of free will through the use of reality therapy. The unconscious was not probed, mainly because of the type of boy treated, with his impulsivity and need for immediate gratification. Time was also a factor.

If, for example, a boy had the urge to steal a car, the reality of the situation rather than the boy's "unconscious conflict with authority" was emphasized. Stealing the car was the important event. There was not time to—nor did the boy want to—look introspectively at the unconscious conflict. The present event and its consequences had to be dealt with because otherwise, unlike the neurotic who would have had an anxiety attack, the boy would have acted out in the community and would have been in conflict with the law.

It was also important for the boy to please an adult with whom he had a positive relationship (the identification process) so that if the adult was mainly concerned with obtaining information relating to the psychodynamics of the boy, then the boy would naturally attempt to please the adult by giving such information. If the adult was too eager to explain to the boy the reason why he went wrong, the boy might too eagerly accept this way of avoiding reality.[12] When the reality of the situation was emphasized, many of the boy's attempts to manipulate by means of psychological jargon in the interview were eliminated. The boy was encouraged to look at the situation and its consequences, and his guilt, which could have been a motivating factor for change, was not dissipated.

The structure of the house was constantly utilized in the treatment of the boys. There were not many rules, but the ones there were were consistently and firmly enforced using as a basis the works of many of the authors who were discussed earlier (see Chapter 4, "The Family and Juvenile Delinquency").

The boys also had the opportunity to go on home visits. This assisted them in experiencing home and community pressures in a less intensified manner. It gave them the opportunity to test out new skills and attitudes and then return to the halfway house to share their experience with staff members. The staff not only supported them in their responsible home behavior but also assisted them in seeking and implementing alternative socially acceptable solutions to problems. In addition, staff members involved themselves in community activities so that they could influence "social engineering" and help change environmental conditions that contribute to delinquent behavior.

Orientation

Prior to training staff members it is important to have an orientation procedure to familiarize the new staff member with the operation. McCartt and Mangogna have devised an appropriate orientation procedure. The following is extracted from their report on guidelines and standards for halfway houses:

A. *Orientation*
   1. *Introduction of the staff member,* student or volunteer to the immediate environment in which they will be working:
      a. To staff members who will be responsible for supervising them.
      b. To staff members with whom they will be collaborating.
      c. To clients with whom they will be working.
      d. To physical environment of the agency, and the neighborhood in which it is located.
   2. *Clear identification of new staff member's role* in agency:
      a. His responsibilities and duties, as outlined in a job description and job specification.
      b. The responsibilities and duties of other staff members in the agency, both those supervising him and those with whom he will be collaborating, as outlined in job descriptions and specifications.
   3. *Presentation of a thorough overview* of the agency and its functions. If the agency operates more than one program, the staff member must learn what relationships, if any, exist between the various programs and how he can utilize other components of the agency

---

[12]William Glasser, *Reality Therapy* (New York: Harper and Row, Publishers, 1965).

for the benefit of his clients. If the agency has an organizational chart, this will be helpful to the new staff member to gain insight into the agency's operations.

4. *Presentation of philosophy, goals, objectives and techniques* utilized by the agency.

5. *Introduction of basic policies and procedures* of the agency. This should include such matters as personnel and travel policies, intake policies and procedures, special requirements which may be imposed by law, funding or contract agencies. This section should also be used to introduce the staff member to the *shalls* and *shall-nots* established by the agency, and to give him a clear understanding of the latitude he has in which to function.

6. *Introduction to basic forms* the staff member will be required to use and some practical exercises in completing such forms.

7. *Introduction of the Criminal Justice System as a whole and corrections in particular.* Concurrently, the staff member must have a thorough understanding of the relationship of the halfway house to the Criminal Justice System and to the correctional system, including both its formal and informal relationships.

8. *Introduction to collateral agencies and community resources* with which the staff member will be working, and which he will be utilizing, including, but not limited to:

   a. Probation departments.

   b. Parole departments.

   c. Jails.

   d. Penal institutions.

   e. Courts.

   f. Mental health agencies.

   g. Medical agencies.

   h. Vocational training agencies.

   i. Educational facilities.

   j. Recreational facilities.

   k. Welfare agencies.

   l. Family service agencies.

   m. Employment agencies.

   n. Any other agencies utilized by the halfway house.

   It should be noted that the new staff member should not only be introduced to the services provided by these agencies, but also the method of obtaining such services for his clients, as well as methods for developing new resources to cope with unexpected problems. In addition, the new staff member should be introduced to workers at such agencies, at the line level, and given the opportunity to develop a relationship with them. It is important to start with line staff in collateral agencies, for they are usually responsible for intake and service delivery, on a day-to-day basis.

9. *Assignment of tasks* to the new staff member which are within his immediate capabilities and skills, with the assignment of increasingly complex and difficult tasks as his knowledge and skills grow. It is crucial that close supervision be provided to the staff member during the entire orientation period, and that orientation itself be goal- and task-oriented training, with intermediate objectives set out to attain those goals.

10. *Introduction to treatment framework* of the agency, if such a framework has been adopted. If not, then introduction into a few basic types of treatment modalities, acceptable and compatible with the agency's program.

11. *Planned opportunities* for the new staff member to give and receive feedback as well as to ask questions and clarify any issues which are not thoroughly understood. Feedback

should also include evaluation of the orientation program itself, by both the trainee and trainer. In retrospect, trainees can be extremely helpful in evaluating what was helpful to them, and what was not, what needed more emphasis, what less, what should have been included, and what should not.

> Once orientation has been completed, the process of training has only begun. Continuous in-service training, at regular intervals with continual supervision, is absolutely essential if the worker is to continue to grow in knowledge and skills, and be able to adapt to new situations and challenges.[13]

Training

Utilizing the personal assets of the staff also had implications for staff training at Pine Lodge. Even though staff training was usually geared to impart certain general principles and techniques for the entire staff, training also had to be geared to individual needs and abilities. In the halfway house some staff members had innate, intuitive, and empathetic qualities that assisted them in relating positively to the boys and reacting appropriately to emotion-laden situations. Others did not have these innate personal assets and in effect had to be "conditioned" to act in a certain manner even though they did not "feel like it." Of course, it was not merely a matter of either having the qualities or not having them. It should be viewed on a continuum, with some individuals having both more innate assets and a better ability to be introspective. Training can accentuate a person's positive traits and provide a person with new skills.

One of the trainer's major responsibilities should be the transforming of theoretical concepts into practical terms to make them more acceptable to the staff. Working with delinquent boys could be frustrating, and the staff might often need something tangible to look at in terms of their accomplishments. The trainer would be much more effective if he or she pointed out to the staff that a particular boy had improved a great deal because he was staying in school or on the job regularly for the first time in his life, instead of saying that the boy had increased "frustration tolerance" and "impulsive control." This would eliminate one of the major criticisms and problems of many theorists—namely, that they were impractical and that their propositions were not easily translated into practical application.

The trainer should also be realistic and able to empathize with the staff. The trainer should cover at least one shift a week so as to have an opportunity to observe what takes place "on the firing line." After having experienced various situations, at different times of the day and night, it is easier to be more tolerant and less judgmental of a staff member who might have reacted angrily in a particular situation. Such an experience affords the trainer new insights into the dynamics of human behavior and helps eliminate many of the problems inherent in staff-line relationships.

[13]McCartt and Mangogna, *Guidelines and Standards for Halfway Houses and Community Treatment Centers,* pp. 59–61.

In relation to the caseworker's covering a shift, many persons mistakenly believe that the "treatment person" should not become involved in the areas of disciplining and controlling. If the thesis concerning the staff (including the caseworker) acting as parental substitutes is extended, in how many families is one parent the "good guy" and giver and the other parent the "bad guy" and disciplinarian? The same parent can perform both functions effectively, and the child readily accepts and wants this. Why then can't parental substitutes perform the same dual function? It realistically illustrates to youths in halfway houses that adults play many roles and perform many functions, some pleasing and some displeasing, and it is an honest approach to child rearing (see Chapter 4).

Extending the analogy between parents and parental substitutes, just as teenagers in "normal" families "act up" and become aggressive, so do delinquent teenagers in a halfway house setting. The difference is that delinquents act up to a greater degree, and their acting up is much more difficult for the staff (parental substitutes) to tolerate because, even though the staff members are parental substitutes, there is not as great an emotional bond between them and the youths as there is between a parent and a child. Because of the different backgrounds and personalities of the youths and the staff, there is bound to be more of a chance for a personality clash than in a normal family. Different types of behavior will affect individual staff members differently. Hence, the necessity of staff members' understanding their own psychological dynamics and motivation as well as normal adolescent behavior.

Learning the System

After the boys had been in residence for a few weeks, they began to learn the organizational and social system. Some aspects of the Pine Lodge system were kept unpredictable (unlike classical organizations) because otherwise the boys would have spent much of their time trying to "beat the system" and little of their time trying to positively increase their social and personal functioning. The structure of the house, with its consistent enforcement of the rules, was an asset, but a system that was completely predictable could eliminate all anxiety and place a premium on conformity and "playing the game" to attain a release.

It is important to point out that the organization and the organization's system should be constantly evaluated in terms of the implications the system might have for the program.

In the case of the Pine Lodge system it was unlike that of the classical institution because a premium was not put on rationality, conformity, and regimentation. However, the boys quickly learned what was emphasized—namely, expression in the house rather than in the community—and some of them began "playing the game" in regard to this system. In other words, they were expressing themselves in the house so as to elicit the response, "Well, at least you must be improving because you are able to express yourself directly (in lieu of displacement) in the house." These same boys might also be "expressing" themselves in the community, however, and much of their energy might be expended in play-ing "our game." Thus the need for constant organizational evaluation, updating, and innovation.

Relation to the Community

It was mentioned that there were many community visitors to the half-way house. This in itself was not a problem. The problem arose when the visitors transmitted to the staff surprise and disappointment that there was not more uniformity and regimentation, which typifies most institutions that operate un-der the classical philosophy.

Quite naturally the staff wanted to operate within the philosophy of the program, but they were also concerned that the visitors would interpret the lived-in look as being a symptom of poor functioning. There was a role conflict.

Even though much of the negative communication from the visitors could not be dispelled, the problem took care of itself. As the staff became more identified with the treatment program and more committed to the philosophy of the program, they became less concerned with negative comments and more enthusiastic about the program and the special techniques that were used in the treatment of the boys. This increased enthusiasm, and *esprit de corps* and nor-mative transmission made a positive impact on the visitors, with the result that fewer negative comments were made about the lack of uniformity and regimen-tation. In other words, the visitors, because of good public relations work and commitment by the staff, began evaluating the program in terms of content rather than in terms of what could be seen (shiny floors, regimentation, and so on). This is not to imply, however, that the staff did not attempt to "tidy up" the house when a particular influential person who was "institution oriented" vis-ited. This is merely astute organizational management and perception of the reality of the need for public support if the program is going to succeed.

Conclusion

Throughout the chapter, involvement of the entire staff in the total program, and especially in decision making, has been emphasized. This does not mean, however, that there was not a central figure to give guidance and direc-tion. The caseworker (administrator) was responsible for directing and supervis-ing the staff. To be effective, the caseworker must be the "boss,' and must provide direction, guidance, and support, but must not be so "bossy" that individual initiative and thinking are squelched.

EVALUATION OF THE PROGRAM

Although some of the boys may not have developed any additional insight into the etiology of their behavior, they did experience some success and gratification in the areas of employment, education, and recreation. They were able, with the

Table 9-1 Results of the Pine Lodge Program

	NUMBER OF BOYS	PERCENT OF TOTAL
Returned to Boys Training School	11	13.7
Remained as residents of Pine Lodge	12	15.0
Released to the community	57	71.3
Boys involved in the evaluation of the program	80	100.0
Released to independent living arrangements	11	19.3
Enlisted in the armed forces	3	5.3
Released to previous home	27	47.4
Released to relatives or to foster homes	16	28.0
Boys who were released to the community	57	100.0
Number of boys who were reincarcerated	11	19.3
Boys who did not exhibit negative behavior	46	80.7
Boys who were released to the community	57	100.0

support of the staff, to delay immediate gratification and tolerate unpleasant situations even though the temptation to become involved in deviant behavior is always present.

In effect, the boys demonstrated to themselves that it is, for example, possible to go downtown without shoplifting because there are other means—namely, through employment—to acquire pleasurable items. Also, it is possible to get "chewed out" by the boss without quitting the job because the boys realize from previous experience that the paycheck received will be a source of much gratification.

During the evaluation period in the early stages of the program eighty boys were accepted by Pine Lodge. Eleven boys were returned directly to the Boys Training School after a short stay, twelve were residents at the time of the evaluation, and the remaining fifty-seven were released to the community. See Table 9-1.

Of the fifty-seven boys released from Pine Lodge to their home communities after an average stay of seven and one half months, eleven (19.3 percent) were released to independent living arrangements, three (5.3 percent) enlisted in the armed forces, twenty-seven (47.4 percent) were released home, and sixteen (28 percent) went to live with relatives or at a foster home.

Eleven of the fifty-seven (19.3 percent) had contact with law enforcement officials, necessitating a return to the Boys Training School or some other form of incarceration (an adult institution, a jail, etc.). The remaining forty-six boys (80.7 percent) did not become involved in future negative behavior in the community. At the time of the evaluation, some of the boys had been released for up to three and one half years.

The question will arise, and rightfully so, as to whether the positive results have taken place in spite of the program rather than because of it. This is possible, but it should be remembered that these boys had previously utilized almost every available state and local service, but to no avail. It must, however, be mentioned in all fairness to the various state and local facilities that a halfway house program has the advantage of being community based and able to maintain control over youths while providing them with extensive support and guidance as they move into the community to face its pressures and responsibilities. Furthermore, the program was established and operated on a sound framework, and a knowledge of deviant behavior, delinquency causation theory, organizational theory, adolescent behavior, clinical therapies, and prevention programs.

GUIDING PRINCIPLES FOR OPERATING A HALFWAY HOUSE

1. A competent staff dedicated to the philosophy that delinquents are persons worth helping.
2. Active involvement of the entire staff in the treatment process.
3. A sound administrative structure with clear lines of communication.
4. A minimum of rules and regulations; both the firm and consistent enforcement of the existing ones.
5. A refined selection process for accepting clients to the program. Each client's individual needs as well as the group interaction and the problems that can result from either overplacement or underplacement should be considered.
6. Adequate programming and good working relationships with such agencies as the police and the schools.

McCartt and Mangogna provide specific recommendations for standards and guidelines for community-based programs. The following are their recommendations:

RECOMMENDATIONS FOR STANDARDS AND GUIDELINES
FOR COMMUNITY-BASED PROGRAMS

Program

1. The community-based treatment center should be located in an area reasonably close to public transportation, employment and vocational opportunities, medical, psychiatric, recreational and other community resources and agencies to be utilized by the center for its clients.
2. The agency will clearly state in writing its purposes, programs, and services offered. This will be done in a form suitable for distribution to staff, clients, referral sources, funding agencies and the general public. Its program and services must have a direct relationship to its stated purposes as they appear in the agency's constitution, articles of incorporation, by-laws or statutes, if the agency is part of a public entity. The program and services must be based upon identified needs in the community in which it is located.
3. An agency operating a community-based treatment program will provide the following services:

shelter

food service

temporary financial assistance

individual counseling

group counseling

vocational counseling

vocational training referral

employment counseling and referral

4. The agency, if it does not provide the service itself, will see that its clients have ready access to:

medical services, including psychiatric and dental care

psychological evaluation

psychological counseling or therapy

vocational training

vocational and/or employment evaluation

employment placement

academic upgrading, e.g., G.E.D., college courses, etc.

any other services as needed by the type of program operated, and the particular need of an individual client

5. In general, the agency will provide clearly identified resources that are relevant and essential to the successful conduct of its programs and will utilize the resources of other agencies in order to provide services needed by its clientele but which cannot or should not be provided by the agency operating a community-based treatment program.

6. The agency will establish clearly defined and written intake policies and procedures. Such policies and procedures will state the type of client acceptable for admission to the program.

   Intake policies will be disseminated to all referral sources.

   Clearly defined age limits for admission to the program will be established by the agency. Any category or categories of potential clients not eligible for admission into the program must be clearly stated in the intake policies.

   Prospective clients ineligible for admission for services and their referral sources must be informed of the reasons for their ineligibility. When possible, the ineligible clients should be referred to other agencies for services.

7. Program goals and services to be offered will be discussed with each individual client.

8. The individual treatment program established will be done with a maximum degree of client involvement.

9. The agency will develop procedures for the evaluation of its clients in order to determine client progress in the program. Conferences, formal or informal, will be held regularly to review such progress and to alter or develop further treatment plans. For the greatest effectiveness, clients must be involved deeply in their own evaluation process.

10. The agency should participate actively in community-planning organizations as they relate to the agency's field of service and should conduct a program of public information, using appropriate forms of communication—such as the "news media," brochures, speaking engagements, etc., to encourage understanding, acceptance and support of its program.

11. The agency will maintain accurate and complete case records, reports and statistics necessary for the conduct of its program. Appropriate safeguards will be established to protect the confidentiality of the records, and minimize the possibility of theft, loss or destruction.

12. A single case record for each client admitted to the program or served by the agency will

be maintained so as to communicate clearly, concisely and completely, appropriate case information.

13. Individual case records will be maintained on a current basis, and will include:

identification data

reports from referral sources

pertinent case history

diagnosis when appropriate

problems and goals

referrals for service to other agencies

evaluation or progress reports

correspondence pertinent to client's case

record of any significant incidents, both positive and negative

signed release of information form, where appropriate

current employment data, including place of employment, date of employment, job title, rate of pay, record of client earnings

discharge report, including summary statement

other information necessary and appropriate to the program and/or individual client's case

14. Agencies operating community treatment center programs will establish methods and procedures for evaluating the effectiveness of the programs.

15. Evaluation must measure the outcome of the program and services in relation to the agency's stated purpose and goals. Program and service effectiveness must be measured by recognized evaluation techniques, and when possible, by formal research.

16. The results of evaluation and research should be reviewed on a systematic basis by the staff and governing body to determine:

the effectiveness of program and services in fulfilling the stated purposes and goals of the agency, and

as the basis for change, modification or addition to the program and services offered by the agency

Personnel

1. The agency must employ competent and qualified staff to provide the services essential to achievement of program goals and client needs.
2. The agency must provide competitive salaries and benefits in order to attract and retain competent personnel.
3. Minimum qualifications for professional staff will be four years of college plus two years of experience in social service, or a Master's Degree in one of the behavioral sciences. Experience may be substituted for educational background, but the ratio of such substitutions must be spelled out clearly in job qualifications. However, when standards of qualification have been established by recognized professional groups, the agency will not adopt less than those as minimum standards for its professional staff.
4. The agency will establish standards of qualification for its para-professional personnel.
5. When standards of qualification have not been established by an organization or group for a particular position, the agency must establish reasonable qualifications and an ongoing assessment of competence in job performance.
6. A balance of professionals, para-professionals and ex-offenders is the preferred staffing pattern.[14]

SUMMARY

Halfway houses are no panacea for the treatment of the delinquent. They cannot serve all children, especially those who need a good institutional treatment program with more stringent controls and at least partial separation from community pressures, but the halfway house does introduce a new resource that seems to be a better answer for certain children.[15]

There are some problems, however, in operating community-based programs, such as a lack of coordination both intraorganizationally and interorganizationally. Negative public attitudes can affect the operation of the program, and jurisdictional disputes between community agencies can hinder and even destroy the program. The next chapter will describe a process whereby these problems can be minimized and even alleviated.

DISCUSSION QUESTIONS

1. How can the treatment-custody dilemma be mitigated?
2. Why is proper personnel selection so important for agencies working with juvenile delinquents?
3. Why are programs for delinquents often very regimented?
4. Is a halfway house suitable for all youngsters?
5. Why do you think halfway houses were not utilized more in the past?

PROJECTS

1. Develop an approach for convincing community residents that a program like a halfway house will not "contaminate" them.
2. Develop a set of rules and regulations that could be implemented in a halfway house in your community.
3. Develop a detailed outline of the types of knowledge that a halfway-house director should have to run a successful program.
4. Using the model presented in Exhibit 1-1, show how theories about delinquency causation, the types of youths in a halfway-house program, and beliefs about delinquency and its treatment led to the use of certain treatment methods at Pine Lodge. Develop a model in which the theories, types of delinquents, and/or the beliefs are different, and describe the likely treatment method in such a situation.

[14]*Ibid.*, pp. 260–265.
[15]Gula, *Agency Operated Group Homes*, p. 29.

____10____

Delinquency Prevention Through Citizen Involvement

- THE NEED FOR CITIZEN INVOLVEMENT
- THE ROLE OF THE POLICE IN MOBILIZING CITIZEN INVOLVEMENT
- PLANNING AND ORGANIZING SUCCESSFUL CITIZEN EFFORTS

LEARNING OBJECTIVES

1. To understand the need for delinquency prevention by individual citizens and organized citizen groups.
2. To be aware of guidelines for organizing successful citizen prevention efforts.
3. To know of the great variety of ways in which citizens can be involved in delinquency prevention.
4. To know the steps involved in organizing citizen prevention programs.

Why, with all the resources and the theories from the many different disciplines available, have attempts at delinquency prevention been for the most part unsuccessful?

The answer to this question is not a simple one. The conditions that contribute to delinquency are complex, and long-range solutions to such problems as unemployment, inadequate housing, and unequal opportunity will not take place overnight. A massive amount of social engineering will be necessary, as well as a commitment to alleviate these social problems. It may be necessary to redefine the adolescent's role in a particular community setting or, more generally, in contemporary society.

Furthermore, it has been naively assumed that theories, manpower, and resources are automatically translated into action programs. For any program or organization to operate effectively, there has to be more than theories, resources, manpower, and good intentions; there must be an adequate *structure* to the program or organization, as well as a *process* that facilitates cooperation, integration of functions, and orderly procedure for goal achievement.

Developing an organizational structure, or even a process, is not difficult if the organization has well-defined specific goals. Establishing a *structure* and a *process* is not so simple, however, if goal achievement is dependent on a complex system of organizations.

Even though one of the stated goals of the organization and agencies of the juvenile justice system is delinquency prevention, the structures and processes of the individual agencies are often not conducive to interagency cooperation and goal achievement. The philosophical and operating ideologies of the various agencies often conflict with one another, and this leads to interagency bickering, attempts at boundary maintenance, and perpetuation of individualized approaches to delinquency prevention problem solving. The expertise of the numerous disciplines represented in the various agencies is not coordinated or integrated for the common good and welfare of the community.

The core of the problem is developing a *process* that will coordinate and involve the many agencies and community residents so that there will be a normative goal orientation to problem solving and a blending of ideas, expertise, and cooperative effort. The issue of developing and presenting a process that contributes to this end will be discussed shortly. First, however, some of the factors that have contributed to the need for a calculated and formal problem-solving process will be mentioned.

THE PRESENT INEFFECTIVENESS OF INFORMAL SOCIAL CONTROL

The importance of the family as an institution for transmitting the positive norms of the community and for teaching appropriate behaviors is readily acknowledged. Either directly or indirectly, the family influences the behavior of its members and can have a great impact on controlling their behavior. When many families are blended together to form a cohesive community, the impact of influencing the behavior of community members becomes even greater. Ideally, then, the community, through its natural interdependent processes that satisfy individual and group needs, is the most potent force for influencing behavior and preventing deviance.

Because of urbanization, mobility, and many other factors, present-day communities are not as cohesive as they were in the past. Hence, they no longer exert the degree of influence over individuals that they did in the past. Before the growth of our complex urban communities, much crime and delinquency was effectively prevented through informal normative influence. Even if the youngster did come in contact with a formal community agency, such as the police, the matter was often handled informally because the police officer on the beat knew the community and its residents.

One result of the complexity of present-day communities is the reduced impact and effectiveness of the police officer on the beat. The informal communication process between the police officer and the community no longer exists; and because of this lack of face-to-face contact, the police officer is no longer able to empathize with the community, understand the lifestyles of its members, or exert informal influence. We mention the police here not just as an example, but as an important part of the juvenile justice system that can be adapted to assist citizens in community-based prevention efforts.

In the past, most of the activities of the community residents revolved around community institutions like the family, the church, and the school. Most of the primary relationships and friendships were within the immediate boundaries of the community or neighborhood. The local businesspersons knew their customers and community members knew their neighbors, and public and private agency personnel lived in the community.

The interdependence and informal network of relationships that existed effectively complemented the formal institutions. Because of this network of interdependent relationships, youngsters who happened to become involved in some form of delinquent activity could easily be identified as community residents. Their actions would be made known to their parents, most of the time through informal channels, by the police officer or someone else in the community.

The police officer, or even a private citizen, knew that the youngster would usually be reprimanded by the parents. The community could also affect the youngster's future behavior through the influence it could transmit through its various institutions, of which the youngster was usually a member.

The preceding description of the community's power over the actions of its members does not mean to imply that crime and delinquency did not occur or that the social environment was devoid of unemployment, poverty, and discrimination. Crime, delinquency, and negative social conditions did exist, but these factors were often counterbalanced by the positive influence exerted by a strong, cohesive community and the effectiveness of its institutions of control.

Today, the same negative social conditions exist, but without the strong normative community bonds to counteract resulting delinquency. Furthermore, increased mobility and urbanization have contributed to the impersonality of both private and public service organizations. Community residents no longer feel that they can effectively exert influence through their community organizations and institutions. The present process of citizen influence usually has to be formal, impersonal, and time consuming, often with little assurance of success. This bureaucracy contributes to apathy and to an unwillingness of citizens to become involved in the community problem-solving process.

Many contemporary communities are not conducive to encouraging citizen involvement in problem solving or coordinating the efforts of the many community organizations for a common purpose or toward a common goal. The intracommunity and interorganization ties are no longer as binding. The community organizations and agencies have grown more independent and isolated from each other. Also there is usually a minimum of citizen input and involvement.

THE ROLE OF THE POLICE

Obviously, police themselves play a crucial role in crime and delinquency prevention. Equally obvious is that traditional forms of policing have often failed to meet the challenge. The prevailing strategy of relying exclusively on motor patrol units to prevent and solve crimes has failed to make citizens feel safe. However, many communities nationwide, now more than 300, have adopted a new form of policing, called community policing, that shows promise of providing an effective way to deal with fear of crime as well as crime itself.

Community Policing

Community policing is not intended to substitute for motor patrol. Instead, it provides a proactive form of police-citizen collaboration designed to supplement and complement motor patrol's reactive efforts. The community policing officer acts as a link to community resources, so that police and citizens work together toward the goals, wants, and needs of the community, both in terms of reducing the delinquency and crime rate and eliminating disorder. This keeps fear of crime within bounds; community policing becomes a force for positive change, offering the hope that cities will again be safer, more inviting places to live.

The community policing concept involves having the officer in closer contact with area residents, by freeing the officer from the isolation of the patrol car. In some communities, this simply means that the officer parks the car for part of the day, so he or she can walk a beat. In other programs, the community policing officer rides a motor scooter or patrols on horseback or on foot.

In some ways, contemporary community police efforts harken back to an earlier, safer era, when the local police officer walked a beat every day. But today's efforts are not reactionary, nostalgic attempts to recreate the past. While all share in common some tactic to put the officer in closer physical contact with the community, current efforts are far more sophisticated and far-reaching.

Yet, what is crucial about putting the officers in direct contact with residents is that this makes them visible symbols of police authority on the street. This helps reduce fear to manageable levels, so it can be translated into positive change.

Over the years, foot patrol as a viable form of police protection and crime prevention fell out of favor, partly because rising costs appeared to favor motor patrol, with its faster response time and its ability to cover large geographic areas. It can also be argued that using cars seems modern, while officers on foot seems antiquated—almost quaint.

It should also be noted that as motor patrol replaced foot patrol, after a brief lag, cities experienced a quantum leap in crime and delinquency. While the reduced use of foot patrol probably did not cause the increase, the relationship demonstrates that motor patrol alone cannot effectively meet the challenge of rising crime rates.

No doubt, when a situation demands immediate attention, sending a patrol car makes sense. But what is lost in the process is direct community contact. When motor patrol becomes the only kind of patrol, the community loses touch with its police. And crime reduction and prevention programs that fail to involve the community ignore a tremendous potential resource.

A police officer is only one person. Traditional forms of policing, specifically motor patrol, rely on the assumption that one person can intervene, from the outside, reactively, and make a difference in the community. What makes community policing unique is that one officer has a much more dramatic effect when the force of the community is behind that officer. If that lone officer enlists the aid and support of the community, they become the officer's eyes and ears twenty-four hours a day.

Community Policing Goals.   What makes community policing so dynamic is that goals can vary widely. The only common thread is that all provide a way to remove officers from patrol cars and put them into closer contact with community residents. Each method, however, requires a unique set of strategies to achieve desired goals. Instead of providing a monolithic model for how such efforts should be structured, community policing, by definition, invests each program with the flexibility and diversity to adapt to local needs. In most community policing efforts, residents who will be served are directly involved in the planning process. For example, before the Flint (Michigan) Neighborhood Foot Patrol Program began operation, a citywide series of meetings with residents was held to determine what the citizens wanted from the program, in terms of both goals and strategies.[1]

Most community policing efforts do not require additional funding. Both Houston and Newark had a one-year mandate from the National Institute of Justice to see what could be accomplished within existing police budgets.[2] Flint, Michigan, however, received a C. S. Mott Foundation grant for its initial three-year experimental Flint Neighborhood Foot Patrol Program. It was so popular that Flint's citizens have since voted three times for special millage increases to maintain and expand the program, the last time by an even larger margin than the other two elections. New York City's Community Patrol Pro-

---

[1]Trojanowicz, Robert, *An Evaluation of the Neighborhood Foot Patrol Program in Flint, Michigan,* National Center for Community Policing, Michigan State University, East Lansing, Michigan, 1982.

[2]Pate, Anthony M., *Reducing Fear of Crime in Houston and Newark: A Summary Report,* Washington, D.C.: The Police Foundation and the National Institute of Justice, 1986.

gram has also had additional funding, and like many programs, it benefits from special grants.[3]

Not all programs target delinquency or crime reduction as their primary goals; the Houston and Newark programs did not list crime reduction as a goal at all, but instead their stated goal was reduction of *fear* of crime. Reducing the crime rate does not necessarily mean citizens feel safer, nor does it automatically mean there is less illegal behavior. However, Flint's foot patrol program did succeed in reducing the crime rate 8.7 percent over the three years of the experimental program. Perhaps even more dramatic was the 43 percent reduction in the number of calls for service the police department received over the three years of the experiment. The Baltimore County COPE program also showed decreases in crime.[4]

All community policing programs attempt to make citizens feel safer. A survey done in Flint, for example, showed almost 70 percent of city residents polled said they felt safer as a direct result of foot patrol efforts. Many respondents qualified their statements further by saying they felt especially safe when the foot patrol officer was well known and highly visible.[5] In New York City, Community Patrol Officer sergeants conduct periodic interviews with residents. These interviews confirm that citizens not only feel safer but report they can "easily identify a visible change for the better in their community, which they attribute to the program."[6] Various "home-grown" fear reduction strategies used in Houston and Newark were targeted by residents as reducing social disorder, fear of personal victimization, worry about property crime, and the perceived risk of both personal and property crimes.[7]

The Houston and Newark programs also attempted to reduce physical disorder, through such efforts as a Signs of Crime campaign, though follow-up studies failed to confirm that these attempts made a statistically significant impact on community residents. In fairness, however, it should be noted that there were specific limitations inherent in the plan that may have precluded success.

Other efforts also focus on improving the relative safety of specific target groups, such as women, children, and the aged, through tactics ranging from giving crime prevention seminars at senior citizens' homes to organizing outings for inner-city children.

Juveniles constitute a twofold challenge for community policing efforts. Children need protection and juvenile offenders are the age group most responsible for today's high crime rates. In fact, many of the program strategies adopted essentially addressed both goals. For instance, by starting neighborhood athletic teams, Flint foot patrol officers organized supervised activities that not only served to keep potentially victimized children safe, but at the same time,

---

[3]Farrell, Michael J., *CPOP: Community Patrol Officer Program*, New York: Vera Institute of Justice, May 1986, p. 42.

[4]Cordner, Gary, *Fighting Fear: The Baltimore County COPE Project*, Washington, D.C., 1986.

[5]Trojanowicz, *An Evaluation of the Neighborhood Foot Patrol Program.*

[6]Farrell, *CPOP: Community Patrol Officer Program.*

[7]Pate, *Reducing Fear of Crime in Houston and Newark.*

provided disaffected, idle young people who might be prone to troublemaking with a life-affirming alternative activity.

Neighborhood Network Centers

Perhaps the biggest problem that dedicated Community Officers routinely face is finding the time and energy for all the worthwhile efforts that offer the promise of solving problems and improving the quality of life in their beat areas. No doubt, many think about how great it would be to work out of a storefront in the community, alongside other enthusiastic public and private social service professionals whose active support would bolster their efforts to reduce crime, violence, illicit drugs, and community disorder and decay. Far from being a dream, this new Neighborhood Network Center concept will soon become reality, as pilot projects begin.

As mentioned earlier, community policing reinvents the role of the old-fashioned beat cop, blending the best of the past with today's reality—combining high-touch with high-tech. Today's Community Officers are full-fledged law enforcement officers whose mandate requires them to serve as creative catalysts for positive change. They become, in effect, local community problem-solvers.

Yet when we look back at the past, we see that the old-fashioned beat cop was just one of a number of public service providers who worked directly in the community. Probation and parole officers personally made sure that ex-offenders followed the rules. Social workers and visiting public health nurses visited client families, where they could see for themselves whether the children suffered abuse or neglect. Truant officers often nipped problems in the bud, tracking down youngsters who played "hookey."

Chapter 2 emphasizes that juvenile violence and delinquency have been stable for years. Perhaps it is no coincidence that recent concerns about so-called gang and other delinquency in the inner city coincides with social service providers' leaving the community for offices downtown, as well as severe cutbacks in services for budgetary reasons.

Critics will no doubt suggest that Neighborhood Network Centers are mere nostalgia for a safer past that never truly existed—the same argument that is often leveled against Community Policing. And there were good reasons for removing these social service providers from their community, just as putting officers in patrol cars initially seemed like a tremendous stride forward. The problem is that these sweeping reforms may have inadvertently thrown out the baby with the bathwater.

In the case of foot patrol officers, the faster response of patrol cars to emergency calls implied improved efficiency. Linking the officers to the department by means of the police radio also allowed the department greater control and enhanced opportunities to monitor the officers' performance. Most of all, it seemed that the shift to patrol cars would reduce opportunities for corruption and abuse of authority.

The pressure to centralize other public social services stemmed from similar concerns. The primary goals were to improve efficiency and profession-alism and to eliminate the opportunities for abuse and fraud. With centralized supervision, no service provider could bend the rules to reward or to punish. Direct, face-to-face contact with people in the community seemed less like a plus and more like an unwarranted intrusion on the individual's right to privacy.

Over time, however, the drawbacks became increasingly apparent. The police, the only social service agency open twenty-four hours a day, seven days a week, whose representatives still made house calls, discovered that isolating of-ficers from direct involvement in the community threatened to rupture the all-important bond of trust and cooperation. A system that fostered having officers spend more time with each other than with the people they serve risked severing the department's link to the law-abiding people in the community—people whose participation and support are so essential in maintaining order and re-versing the spiral of decay.

Centralizing the other service providers also risked increasing deper-sonalization. Clients tended to become numbers, rather than people with prob-lems. The needs of the system threatened to overwhelm the needs of the people they were designed to help. It became increasingly clear that, instead of narrow-ing the gap between professional and client, centralization tended to promote the growth of an impersonal bureaucracy that could easily snarl clients in red tape.

As in policing, centralization and depersonalization of social service pro-viders also foster a system that measures performance by the numbers. Success is defined by the number of arrests made and clients processed, rather than on whether the problems are solved.

Developing New Models. Yet many will also argue that, even if there is merit in decentralizing and personalizing service to the community, our society can no longer afford the costs associated with the inherent inefficiencies of the past. When the police confronted this challenge, they recognized the need to update the role of the old-fashioned beat cop in ways that maintained the close community contact of the past, while recognizing the need to improve their efficiency and broaden the scope of their impact.

If we look at the beat cops of old, we see that the job required them to pound a beat and rattle doorknobs, in the hope that this would deter crime. Yet it was their unofficial duties, the elements that did not appear in a job description, that everyone missed so much when they left. Community Policing institu-tionalizes and enhances those aspects of the job, by challenging today's Commu-nity Officers to use their free patrol time to promote efforts to solve problems and to improve the overall quality of life in their neighborhoods.

Borrowing from that model suggests that the key to updating the role of the other social service providers requires restructuring their jobs to maximize their collective impact and involvement. This implies forging them into a new neighborhood-based team of problem solvers who can work together with the people in the community to address the issues that the people care about most.

Sometimes this will mean working on the specific problems of individuals and families. Perhaps a juvenile on parole needs drug counseling. Or the juvenile suspected of petty theft is also skipping school, which means the truant officer should become involved. Sometimes it could mean that code enforcement officials work with both social workers and the police on efforts to upgrade the living conditions for families in rental units.

But the goal is also to galvanize this new community-based team into developing creative long-term solutions to long-standing concerns. In some neighborhoods, this might mean developing an intervention to address the attitudes that promote violence among the young. It could mean using the Neighborhood Network Center for classes to help teen mothers learn how to nurture their young. Perhaps the most pressing concern is to develop an imaginative approach to reducing drug use among dropouts. The possibilities are bounded only by the needs and resources of the community and the creativity and enthusiasm of everyone involved.

The involvement of Community Officers is essential. Not only do they provide the other professionals with the protection and security that they need, Community Officers are also the only social service agent who can employ a full range of options, ranging from a pat on the back to pulling the trigger, depending on the specific problem that they face.

The plus for Community Officers is that they will receive much-needed direct help from the professionals. Community Officers are always looking for receptive individuals in various agencies who will assist with referrals. Working together in a Neighborhood Network Center not only formalizes the process, it also allows the team time together to develop broad-based, long-term efforts. Far too many Community Officers risk early burnout trying to do too much themselves.

Quite obviously, no one can yet know precisely how the new community-based teams will function in practice. Nor can anyone anticipate all the problems they may face. The research and evaluation component is vital in identifying what works and what doesn't—and why.

Nationally, community policing efforts have affected the neighborhoods and the families of many potential or active juvenile offenders. These efforts have resulted in direct interventions into the lives of these juveniles through such services as referral to counseling or recreational programs. The development of community policing provides an important example of how the difficulties of organizing citizen efforts to control delinquency can be overcome. In the next section of this chapter, we will present a more general understanding of the steps and difficulties involved in organizing citizens' delinquency control efforts.

ORGANIZING CITIZEN EFFORTS

As a result of poor organization many well-intentioned citizen efforts to combat delinquency have met with failure or died of attrition after initial successes.

Citizen motivation is, more often than not, sparked by some spectacular event—usually a particularly heinous crime. Initial response usually consists of forming an organization. It is appropriate to start a new organization only if there is none already in existence for this purpose. If a new organization to combat delinquency is perceived as essential after researching existing organizations, its organizers must proceed in full realization of the possible negative reactions to their efforts.

Since the mid-1960s, citizen participation has come to be identified with the civil rights movement; advocacy movements, such as the thrust to save the environment; and so on. The brand of political activism demonstrated by these movements has posed significant perceived threats to the interests of middle- and upper-class segments of society. The new community organization may elicit considerable negative reaction if it is construed as a challenge to established power relationships.

The difficulties involved in motivating large numbers of alienated citizens have been explored. Even when engendered, motivation and participation are difficult to sustain over extended periods of time. Public administrators seldom view citizen efforts, which they consider uninformed and amateurish, favorably. Foot-dragging, and even sabotage, can sometimes be expected from this quarter. The new effort will also have to deal with all the problems endemic to any organization: leadership and staffing concerns, funding problems, controls, red tape, and so on. The greatest problem of all is posed by the crime prevention effort itself. No single effort has been shown beyond reasonable doubt to be a foolproof method for preventing crime. There are efforts, to be sure, that show considerable promise. It is essential, though, that the citizen group will first have to identify an area of prevention on which it can realistically hope to have an impact. Objectives have to be narrow enough to make short-term successes possible; these will reinforce, and thus maintain, citizen motivation. The rationale or philosophy of the objectives should be nonjudgmental, and should be broad enough to appeal to many segments of society. Above all, the goals of the citizen group should not conflict with those of the professional crime fighters. To have any hope of success, the citizen effort must be buttressed by resources—both human and material—solicited from many sources. As such, it will be perceived as a complement, rather than a challenge, to the city administration.

A MODEL FOR ACTION: NORMATIVE SPONSORSHIP THEORY

The normative sponsorship theory approach to community problem solving has been used to assist communities in developing programs for the prevention and control of crime and delinquency. The theory was originated and developed by Dr. Christopher Sower, professor of sociology at Michigan State University.

Simply stated, normative sponsorship theory proposes that a community program will be sponsored if it is normative (within the limits of established standards) to all persons and interest groups involved. You will see that the community policing efforts described above illustrate many aspects of the normative sponsorship theory, a theory that would apply to a wide variety of different community prevention efforts.

In attempting to initiate community development and prevention programs, it is of major importance to understand how two or more interest groups can have sufficient convergence of interest or consensus on common goals to bring about program implementation.

Each group involved and interested in program implementation must be able to justify and, hence, legitimize the common group goal within its own patterns of values, norms, and goals. The more congruent the values, beliefs, and goals of all participating groups, the easier it will be for them to agree on common goals. The participating groups, however, do not necessarily have to justify their involvement or acceptance of a group goal for the same reasons.[8]

Whenever areas of consensus are being identified between groups with a different normative orientation, it is important not to deny the concept of self-interest, because it cannot be expected that all groups will have common or similar motivations for desiring program development. Self-interest is not dysfunctional unless it contributes to intergroup contests or opposition and diverts energy that should more appropriately be directed at problem solving.

Programs that follow the tenets of normative sponsorship will undoubtedly be more likely to succeed than those that do not. Violation of the normative sponsorship process usually results in apathy or even concerted subversion and resistance to program development.

An example of a community that has been successful in utilizing this approach will be given, and the normative sponsorship process will be explained. This method has been most successful in communities where there are several interest groups and a diverse orientation to problem solving and the expression of needs. For example, in describing a riot in Detroit, the Kerner Report states:

> As the riot alternately waxed and waned, one area of the ghetto remained insulated. On the northeast side the residents of some 150 square blocks inhabited by 21,000 persons had in 1966 banded together in the Positive Neighborhood Action Committee (PNAC). With the professional help from the Institute of Urban Dynamics, they had organized block clubs and made plans for improvement of the neighborhood. In order to meet the need for recreational facilities, which the city was not providing, they had raised $3000 to purchase empty lots for playgrounds (challenge instead of conflict).
>
> When the riot broke out, the residents, through the block clubs, were able to organize quickly. Youngsters agreeing to stay in the neighborhood participated in detouring traffic. While many persons reportedly sympathized with the idea of rebellion against the "system," only two small fires were set—one in an empty building.[9]

[8]Christopher Sower et al., *Community Involvement* (Glencoe, Illinois: The Free Press, 1957).
[9]*Report of the National Advisory Commission on Civil Disorders* (New York: Bantam Books, Inc., 1968), p. 96.

The PNAC neighborhood was organized and its positive programs developed by using the concepts of normative sponsorship theory. The excerpt illustrates that when people are actively involved in the community problem-solving process and have some control over their own destiny, they will respond positively and effectively to the implementation of community development programs.

The quotation also illustrates two other important concepts of normative sponsorship orientation to community development. First, the role of the Institute of Urban Dynamics was one of providing technical assistance. The technical assistance concept is different from many contemporary assistance roles. Too often assistance means (either directly or indirectly) paternalism or co-optation of community problem solving.

Effective technical assistance recognizes the vast amount of human resources within the community and the residents' willingness to develop positive community programs if their efforts are appreciated and if they are meaningfully involved in the problem-solving process.

Technical assistance, according to our definition, does not mean co-optation. It means making assistance readily available so that the community can "plug in" to *available* and appropriate resources. Technical assistance is provided only upon community request. After the specific assistance is rendered, the technical assistance unit withdraws until further requests are made. It is interesting to note that as the community becomes aware of available resources and learns the problem-solving process (which many of us take for granted), their requests for assistance decrease. It takes a special type of professional to operate effectively in a technical assistance role. Such professionals must be competent and knowledgeable in the areas of resource identification and problem solving, yet they must avoid a do-gooder or a paternalistic approach. They are not expected to save the world, but only to help make it run more smoothly.

The second important concept illustrated by the excerpt is that challenge is more effective than conflict as a means of program development. Normative sponsorship theory postulates that programs that challenge the skeptics through involvement, participation, and cooperative action will be more effective than programs that are conflict oriented. Not only do the skeptics and the cynics gain support when there is a conflict, interest groups polarize their positions. For example, the community may make unreasonable demands, while the community agencies react by overjustifying their positions and actions. The longer and more intense the conflict, the less chance there is to identify and develop consensus points from which viable programs can be implemented.

In sum, the technical assistance role is undoubtedly more conducive to community involvement and participation than contemporary approaches. Many contemporary "experts" who have attempted to provide "expertise" to community problem solving have "come under fire" from both the community and such community professionals as the police. The community feels that external experts often expect the community to act as a human laboratory. The experts, however, do not have a stake in the community and are frequently unconcerned about the frustration and disruption they create when they fail to keep promises.[10]

The police often feel that the outside experts, although teaching communication and stressing empathy, are themselves unwilling to empathize with the police and understand that the police are merely a reflection of the larger power structure of which the experts are also a part. The police, as well as other agency professionals, believe that if the experts would provide them with alternatives for action, rather than merely castigate them, they would be more receptive to constructive criticism and to "new and radical" ideas. A technical assistance unit should assume a *neutral* position in problem solving, emphasizing cooperative action, not disruptive verbalizations. Cooperation can be an elusive concept if normative sponsorship theory is not utilized as a model.

KEY ELEMENTS: A GUIDE TO ACTION

Every community is unique, and no one plan of action will guarantee success in all communities. Riedel's maxim that "the appropriate form of citizen participation is the one that works" is, in effect, a plan for community delinquency and crime prevention.

Program Organizers

The structure and specific role of the organization for crime prevention may be critical to the success of the effort. Who will comprise the initial cadre—city officials, community leaders, or an ad hoc committee of interested citizens? Are these individuals acceptable to the larger community (that is, do they have the social capability to motivate citizen participation in the initial stages of action, such as conferences and information gathering)? Where can the most innovative approaches be anticipated? Is consensus in the community strong enough so that broad goals can be stated with certitude? Does this apply to subgoals? Where does the direction and impetus for action in the community arise? How will the priorities of goals or subgoals be assigned?

In general, the organization that can remain most responsive to the perceived needs of citizens, that can act as a catalyst in promoting direct action at the citizen level, will probably have the most success. Such an organization should have as few levels as possible—usually a board of directors, program leaders, and volunteers. Programs that are established, coordinated, and directed from top levels will usually not promote the necessary citizen motivation and may, in fact, alienate many segments of the community.

[10]See also Robert C. Trojanowicz, "Police Community Relations: Problems and Process," *Criminology*, February 1972.

The theory of normative sponsorship assumes that the role of organizations in delinquency and crime prevention will be as enabling agencies—organizational leaders will coordinate and integrate the goals, needs, and capabilities of action groups; serve as a central information gathering and dissemination agency; provide a nexus for promoting official acceptance and cooperation with the various efforts; and plan for fund raising or logistical needs of the whole range of subgoal programs. The board of directors should be comprised of a wide mixture of private and official leaders, as well as representatives from many community areas. Its primary role should be to remain responsive to the information, material, and technical needs of the action groups. Procedures should be kept to a minimum in favor of action, and the entire community should have immediate access to the board. Ideally, a board of directors will prevent action groups from jumping at "glamor issues" in crime prevention and channel the actions of all groups toward goals they are most capable of attaining. The directorship of such an organization should, in short, determine the normative priorities of the community, and, within that framework, provide the action groups with the support necessary to translate those priorities into action.

Initial Steps

Step 1: Information Gathering. Crime and delinquency are talked about a great deal, but members of a community usually do not have any precise measure of the degree of delinquency and criminal behavior, its cost to the community, or the resources available to treat the problem. We described this problem fully in Chapter 2. Crime reporting can provide a beginning point, but it should be expanded to include an estimate, by area and by type, of unreported crime. This type of information can often be gained from neighborhood organizations, sampling of citizens, the medical profession, and church functionaries. Rape crisis centers, drug abuse "hotlines," and the like are excellent means of gaining a closer approximation of the real extent of crime in a community. For areas where victimization surveys have been carried out, these surveys are an additional source of information.

A comparison of crime rates in different areas with the physical realities of the areas often suggests immediate remedies, such as increased lighting, increased police patrols, block organizations, and citizen patrols. These apparently simple solutions should not be passed over on the assumption that any clear problems would already have been acted upon by public officials. Public officials operate in a climate of high demand and limited resources. They usually react only to blatant problems that immediately threaten public equilibrium. Action groups should be sensitive to this limitation and attempt to provide complementary action, if it is appropriate.

Step 2: Analysis of the Community. It is highly improbable that an outsider to the community could rationally organize a community crime prevention effort. It would first be necessary to become intimately familiar with the community, its history, its process of development and past conflicts, and its current politics and problems. All these factors influence the attitudes of the citizens and the acceptability of various problem-solving techniques. Consideration in analyzing the community should include the following:

1. Economic base:
   (a) Single-industry or business center base,
   (b) Expansion plans,
   (c) Community attitudes toward expansion.
   (d) Labor-management crises,
   (e) Present and future job market.
   2. Cultural aspects:
      (a) Single or multicultural community.
      (b) Class lines and prior conflict, if any,
      (c) In multiculture community, nature of equilibrium, if any, or strife,
      (d) Official response to cultural situation, in terms of favoritism, distribution of services, alignment of elected officials,
   (e) Mobility patterns.
3. Social organization:
   (a) Extent and nature of social, fraternal, and church organizations,
   (b) Conflict, cooperation, or coalition, if any, for common cause,
   (c) Reactive organizations, if any,
   (d) Political affiliations of organizations and attachments to particular social movements,
   (e) Existing social programs and projects,
   (f) Potential for creation of new organizations.
4. Official functions:
   (a) Punitive formal justice agencies,
   (b) Nonpunitive approaches created or supported by formal agencies,
   (c) History of attempts to create programs or supplement official crime prevention programs,
   (d) Current coordination and planning—fragmented or centrally assumed,
      (e) Inter- and intraagency conflict or cooperation; attitudes of formal justice and social agencies toward each other.
5. Crisis handling:
   (a) Natural disasters and social crises that have influenced attitude formation,
   (b) Racial strife and its resolution or nonresolution,
      (c) Sensational crime, by neighborhood or area; presence of organized crime, if any,
   (d) Public perceptions of adequacy of officials in responding to past crises, especially regarding major crime.

Step 3: Relevant System Identification. Before programs that necessitate cooperation of more than one group can be implemented, it is necessary to identify the relevant interest groups—the *relevant systems*. The major relevant systems concerned with delinquency prevention would be the community, the police, the court, the social work agencies, the legislature, and the other private and public agencies and business organizations in the community.

The technical assistance unit whose services are secured by the relevant systems is not a relevant system itself because it is usually not an integral part of the community. It is, rather, a *neutral external resource.*

In effect, all components of the community that can contribute any resources to delinquency and crime prevention should be identified. In addition to the official agencies, businessmen's groups, clubs, and church groups, special emphasis should be placed on gaining input from youth, neighborhood, block, occupations, drug and alcohol treatment, and informal interest groups. Press club representation is important for necessary publicity, as well as for the extensive contacts the press can activate in support of such a program. Ad hoc committees formed to deal with prior problems should be identified for potential reactivation. For the public agencies present in the community, information should be gathered about their charter or public mandate, jurisdiction, budget, current programs, physical and manpower resources, federal and state project endorsement, organizational structure, proposed future programs and budget requests, emphasis, expressed needs (media, budget requests), and operational limitations based on professional abilities, caseload, and past performance.

This list is a much abbreviated approach to the planning process. It must be complete and comprehensive to insure that false starts are avoided. With this information, a schema depicting social, economic, and normative links among various institutions, neighborhoods, and groups can be constructed. This schema should indicate the relative strength or potential strength of various positions to guide the planner in determining whether support exists for different tentative approaches to delinquency and crime prevention. Social situations are enormously changeable, however, and a prevention program must not only be founded on a thorough analysis of existing factors, but must also remain in touch with change. Modern communities are extremely complex social systems, which do not normally respond well to attempts at manipulation. The identification of an appeal to basic values holds out the greatest promise of effective community prevention. This is complicated to the extent that different groups hold different values. We discussed the extreme "right" and "left" value positions in Chapter 1 of this book.

Step 4: Identification of Leadership. There is no clear guide to the appropriate selection of leadership in prevention programs. In one community, civic, business, and government leaders may have the public support and confidence necessary to set goals and to execute action alternatives. In another, a high degree of skepticism will greet efforts by these leaders. In the main, it appears that most successful efforts at community delinquency and crime prevention utilize a coalition of established community leaders, who are genuinely interested in innovation and action, a leadership emerging from neighborhoods, and a variety of social groups. Research has shown that citizens who become active in crime prevention are not motivated so much by their own victimization or fear of crime, but rather by a general interest in neighborhood and community groups. Parents of small children and homeowners are also likely to become involved.[11] Persons identified from within the relevant system are better able to reflect the system's norms, values, and goals and are knowledgeable about how it functions. They also exert considerable influence, and their opinions and suggestions are respected and implemented.

They may hold a position in the formal structure of a community organization, such as officer in a block club, or they may hold a command rank in the police department or an administrative position in a social work agency. However, they may not have a formal position in either a community or a community agency, yet exert influence through the informal structure.

Identification of these leaders is accomplished through a process of sampling members of the relevant organizations and asking such questions as "Whom do you or most of the people in the organization go to for advice on problem solving?" and "Who in the organization is respected, has power and influence, and has the reputation for getting things done?"

After the sampling process is completed, it is possible to construct a list of those individuals whose names have been mentioned most often as leaders. The sampling process is important for leadership identification. It should not be assumed that sampling is not necessary because leaders are already known. Leadership is not static, and those persons *assumed* to be leaders because of their formal or informal position are not necessarily the major source of power or influence. The identification of true leadership is mandatory, if the process of program development and implementation is to be successful.

There are several groups not normally involved in community crime prevention that can supply leadership and volunteer services. Youth should be challenged to organize action programs in delinquency prevention, drug abuse treatment, and restorative education. The youth of any community usually have time to spend in such programs and are an invaluable source of creative thinking and energy. The aged also need desperately to be reintegrated into community life at all levels. Older citizens often possess the diplomatic abilities and strong sense of purpose that would lend great stability and status to a prevention program. Their experiences and commitment should be directly sought and extensively utilized. Prior offenders and citizens who profit from such action programs should also be encouraged to assume leadership and volunteer roles. They are in an excellent position not only to identify with those with social problems, but also to supply badly needed role models for offenders already being treated by the formal juvenile justice system.

Step 5: Bringing Leaders of Relevant Systems Together. After leaders have been identified in each relevant system, the next step is to bring the leaders

---

[11]Paul J. Lavrakas and Elicia J. Herz, "Citizen Participation in Neighborhood Crime Prevention," *Criminology, 20,* nos. 3 and 4 (November 1982), pp. 479–498.

together for a meeting. They should be told that they have been identified by their peers as influential leaders interested in the prevention of delinquency and crime. The initial meetings (the meetings are chaired by a technical assistance advisor) will be somewhat unstructured. The major objectives of the initial meetings will be to:

1. Facilitate the expression of feelings about the apparent problem.
2. Encourage relevant systems to exchange perceptions about each other. (There is often much suspiciousness between the agencies and between the citizens and the agencies.)
3. Produce an atmosphere conducive to meaningful dialogue so that the misperceptions can be identified and the constellation of factors contributing to the causation of the problem can be discussed.
4. Identify self-interest, pointing out that from the self-interest standpoint of all systems, cooperative problem solving to prevent crime and delinquency will benefit everyone. The community agencies will have smaller caseloads and more time to provide services; while the citizens will be better protected from threats and offenses against life and property.

It is not the purpose of the initial meetings to produce attitude changes or develop a "love relationship" between the relevant systems. Negative attitudes will change when positive perceptions between the relevant systems increase and when meaningful involvement and positive behavioral action is initiated and carried out through program development and implementation.

Whenever diverse interest groups assemble, they will often have biased opinions, misinformation, and negative perceptions toward one another. If there is extensive defensiveness by the relevant systems and if an atmosphere of freedom of expression does not prevail, the initial stages of the process will be hindered, and this can have unfavorable implications for future cooperation and program implementation.

In our experience with groups that have assembled to discuss delinquency prevention problems, initially many mutual accusations are made by the various relevant systems. The police, for example, are accused of authoritarianism and aloofness, while the community is accused of complacency and lack of cooperation. Agency professionals also exhibit intergroup hostility and negative perceptions. The social workers may call the police "hard-headed disciplinarians," and the police may retaliate by calling the social workers "permissive do-gooders." If there is too hasty denial of the accusation, if elements of truth in the accusations are not handled in an honest manner, if the constellation of factors that contributed to the perceptions are not identified, and if these perceptions are not discussed, then the communication process will be shallow and the total problem will not be understood.

Technical assistance advisors can play an important role in these early stages. They can help control the meetings so that they are not monopolized by one interest group or so that expression of feelings does not become inappropriate and offensive to the point of disruption and ultimate disbanding of the group. They can also help clarify the issues and provide insight into the problem and the reasons for its existence.

The admission of the obvious truth of some of the accusations by the relevant systems will be helpful in establishing an atmosphere of trust and credibility. This will facilitate understanding and cooperation.

The communication process between the relevant systems should be more than merely the denial or the admission of fact. It should include a discussion of the constellation of factors that can contribute to misperceptions. For example, the citizens could be informed of the policies of the various agencies and the effect these policies have on the delivering of services to the community. Insight in this area may be helpful in explaining that certain administrative considerations have to be weighed and certain priorities have to be established. Citizens could also share with the agencies the reasons why they become frustrated with the apparent lack of concern and impersonality of large agency structures. This will facilitate the agency personnel's empathizing with the citizens, and vice versa. Interagency misperceptions can also be neutralized through the process of sharing problem-solving approaches and reasons why an agency takes a particular orientation.

The increased empathy between relevant systems will help destroy misperceptions and provide the relevant systems with new insights into individual and organizational behavior. This will establish a basis for future understanding and cooperation.

The first few meetings are usually typified by (1) the unstructured expression of feelings and perceptions, (2) the admission of "reality facts," (3) the discussion of the constellation of contributing factors, (4) the facilitation of understanding, and (5) the increased number of positive perceptions. The sessions then begin to take a more focused and less emotional orientation. If the initial meetings have achieved their objectives, the stage is set for the next phase of the process, the identification of areas of consensus and disagreement in the prevention of crime and delinquency.

Step 6: The Identification of Areas of Consensus and Disagreement. In the third stage of the process, the matrix method is utilized for the identification of areas of consensus and disagreement. In dealing with this kind of methodology, Ladd has made an important contribution.[12] He obtained the following kinds of information for each of the major positions of the small society that he studied. This same information will be helpful in understanding the relevant systems involved in crime and delinquency prevention:

1. What are the prescriptions of expected behavior?
2. Who makes these prescriptions?
3. To what extent is there consensus about the prescriptions?
4. Who enforces them?

[12]John Ladd, *The Structure of a Moral Code* (Cambridge, Massachusetts: Harvard University Press, 1957).

5. What are the rewards for compliance?
6. What are the punishments for deviance?

As illustrated in Table 10-1, this kind of information, as well as additional information, can be assembled into a matrix pattern for the analysis of any system or set of systems.

This method serves as a vehicle for visually and objectively comparing the perceptions among and between relevant systems. For example, the perception the police have of their role can be compared with the perception the community has of the police role, and vice versa. This comparison can also be made with the other relevant systems—police with social workers, social workers with the community, and so on.

The perceived roles of the systems can also be compared with the actual behavior of both systems, and then an evaluation can be made regarding whether the behavior is deviant or normative, functional or nonfunctional. Finally, the statement of alternatives for problem solving of each system can be compared with the perceived expected alternatives. It may be learned, for example, that the alternatives contemplated by each system are not incompatible or as different from each other as originally perceived.

As a result of the intrasystem and intersystem comparisons, it is easy to compile the information about how each system expects and perceives both its own members and members of the other systems to behave. From this it is not a difficult research task to classify the categories of information as either normative (as they should be) or deviant (different than they should be) to the relevant systems.

The use of the matrix method results in the realization that many programs already exist and are unknown to much of the community, that there is more consensus than anticipated about basic values and needs, and that a good deal of honest effort fails because it occurs in isolation from the potential support of the larger community.

Comprehensive media coverage for the prevention project should be obtained. Normative priorities, goals and subgoals, proposed action programs, resources required, and calls for leadership and volunteers can thus be publicized. Even if some of the programs appear controversial, this should pique public interest and invite dialogue. Media coverage should challenge local community organizations to fund, organize, and take responsibility for action programs. Initial efforts might well be spent in pilot programs to determine the corrective potential of a particular approach, the extent of the resources that would have to be expended in such an effort, the normative priorities of the community, and the total known resources. Results of pilot programs should be presented in public forums and cooperation encouraged between citizens and groups throughout the community.

Step 7: Program Implementation. After areas of consensus and disagreement have been identified, a program can be developed that will incorpo-

Table 10-1 Diagram of the Matrix Method of Identifying Areas of Consensus and Disagreement

Norms and Behavior Perceptions Held By:	NORMS AND BEHAVIOR PERCEPTIONS HELD ABOUT:					
	The Police	The Community	Social Workers	Businesspeople	Legislators	Other Agencies and Organizations

The police	Self-Concept
	1. Perceived norms and expected behavior as it relates to delinquency prevention
	2. Description of actual behavior
	3. Defined as:
	  a. Normative
	  b. Deviant
	4. Statement of alternatives for problem solving
		1. Perceived norms and expected behavior as it relates to delinquency prevention
		2. Description of actual behavior
		3. Defined as:
		  a. Normative
		  b. Deviant
		4. Perception as to what alternatives the other systems will select for problem solving
			*	*	*	*

	Self-Concept				
The community (including youth groups)	Self-Concept	*	*	*	*
Social workers	*	Self-Concept	*	*	*
Business-people	*	*	Self-Concept	*	*
Legislators	*	*	*	Self-Concept	*
Other agencies and organizations	*	*	*	*	Self-Concept

Criteria for each cell:

1. Perceived norms and expected behavior as it relates to delinquency prevention
2. Description of actual behavior
3. Defined as:
   a. Normative
   b. Deviant
4. Perception as to what alternatives the other systems will select for problem solving

1. Perceived norms and expected behavior as it relates to delinquency prevention
2. Description of actual behavior
3. Defined as:
   a. Normative
   b. Deviant
4. Statement of alternatives for problem solving

*Use the same criteria that are presented in the cell showing the police department's perception of the community

rate the areas of consensus so that the program will be normative to *all* systems. The systems will not necessarily agree in all areas, but there will usually be enough common areas of agreement so that cooperation and sponsorship will be predictable.

It will be surprising and enlightening to the relevant systems, after the matrix method is used, to learn how many areas of consensus are present, which at first glance, after a subjective evaluation, may not be apparent. There generally will be consensus on major goals, such as the need for delinquency prevention programs, for more positive and effective communication, and for cooperation between the systems. Areas of consensus may decrease as specific techniques for problem solving are identified and alternatives for program implementation are suggested by each system. This will be a minor problem, however, because if the normative sponsorship process has been followed, an atmosphere of cooperation will prevail and compromise will be facilitated.

Step 8: Quality Control and Continuous Program Development and Updating.

As with any viable program, there is a constant need for quality control and continuous program development and updating. There should be meaningful feedback, the testing of new theories, and reciprocal involvement and program evaluation by the relevant systems, as well as individual and system introspection.

There is also a need for scientific research, not only on basic causes of crime, but also on the effectiveness of the system. Evaluation of each action program should be undertaken to determine its effectiveness. This may provide a guideline for the better allocation of official resources and an indication of which services the official juvenile justice system and the community can best provide. Considerations should include (relative to, for example, drug abuse among youth):

1. What is the drug overdose rate now in relation to when the program started?
2. What is the current and past arrest rate for trafficking and abuse? In this regard, make sure that the organizational posture of the official agencies is taken into consideration. The establishment of a special narcotics squad at the city or county level inevitably increases the arrest rate, even during an effective community attack on drug use.
3. What is the trend in drug use—from marijuana to amphetamines, to acid, and so on, or the other direction? Programs must insure that by attacking the use of marijuana (for example) they do not encourage drug abusers to turn to more dangerous substances.
4. What is the current state of drug use and trafficking in the local intermediate and high schools? Have sufficient youth been mobilized at those locations?
5. What is the current state of youth participation at the established drug abuse treatment clinics? Is the increase or decrease indicative of the effectiveness of the program? For example, an increase in the number of participants in a drug abuse clinic may be an indication that more youth are genuinely interested in decreasing their drug intake, or that, because of decreased availability "on the street," the drug rehabilitation center is the best place to make a "contact."
6. What effect has the problem had on the incidence of other crime (burglary, armed robbery, theft, and so on), if any, in the community, and by neighborhood?

7. What collateral problems have been discovered during the course of the program that indicate potential for treatment, and by whom?

8. Do the known or anticipated results justify the expenditure of resources, or could those resources (citizen time, funds, expertise, formal justice system emphasis, and so on) be better employed in another area? How can this be clearly shown to be the case?

9. What is the relative restorative effect of the citizen "prepunitive" efforts (for example) in relation to the punitive efforts of the police?

10. Are *all* the community efforts in the area of drug abuse providing a mutually complementary product, or are some aspects at "cross-purposes"? How can this problem be approached?[13]

These are but a few of the considerations relative to one subgoal—drug abuse—totally apart from the causation of drug abuse itself. Evaluation techniques must be devised to ensure effective programs by providing a rational basis for decision making and for the use of limited resources.

Exhibit 10-1   An Example of Delinquency Prevention through Citizen Involvement

From 1981 to 1986, a federally sponsored research and development program to prevent violent juvenile crime was implemented through neighborhood-based organizations in the Bronx, Chicago, Dallas, Los Angeles, New Orleans, and San Diego. Its goal was to reduce such crime in specific locations through resident mobilization to strengthen neighborhood cohesion and make local institutions more responsive. A conceptual framework was based on social control and learning theories. Each local version of the program involved an ongoing needs assessment through which neighborhood resident councils planned and revised their efforts. Each local program was required to include violent-crisis intervention, mediation, family support networking, and youth skills development. After thirty-six months of planning and implementation, serious juvenile crime decreased in three of the six target neighborhoods, compared to their respective cities. Most of the programs developed means of financial support to carry on all or part of the effort after federal funding ended. Community-led programs that emphasize advocacy and institutional mediation appear to be more effective than traditional social services in mobilizing residents to prevent juvenile crime and violence.

SOURCE: Jeffrey Fagan, "Neighborhood Education, Mobilization, and Organization for Juvenile Crime Prevention," *Annals of the American Association for Political and Social Sciences, 494* (November 1987), pp. 54–70.

[13]Developed by Forrest M. Moss and taken from Trojanowicz, Trojanowicz, and Moss, *Community-Based Crime Prevention.* (Pacific Palisades, California: Goodyear Publishing Co., 1975) pp. 128–130.

CONCLUSION

The normative sponsorship method can be used to link the university to the community through extension courses in the community. The extension course can serve the same general purpose as the community meeting, if the course has a wide variety of participants. The same type of problem-solving process, as it relates to delinquency prevention that was described earlier, can be facilitated in the classroom. The classroom is conducive to meaningful communication and the transmission of ideas and feelings because the organizational constraints and pressures that often inhibit the communication process in an interorganizational meeting are less evident. The instructor can function in the same technical assistance role described earlier. Community improvement projects such as crime and delinquency prevention can be initiated in the community through a cooperative team effort. The team (which is composed of representatives of all relevant systems) can return to the classroom periodically to provide feedback and receive inputs and an objective evaluation of their project by the instructor and class peers.

An effective prevention program results only through a cooperative firsthand experience of all relevant systems in the problem-solving process. A maximum of active involvement and a minimum of shallow verbalization will facilitate cooperation and mutual understanding among the relevant systems. Research has shown that general-purpose community organizations and the police play an important role in encouraging informal social control where it does not exist and strengthening it where it does.[14] Community crime prevention efforts are particularly effective in reducing fear of crime.[15]

The most effective means of motivating people is to transmit to them that their opinions will be valued, that they will have a voice in decision making, and that they will be involved in the problem-solving process. Programs will be sponsored and perpetuated if these criteria are adhered to, because the parties who comprise the relevant systems have a personal investment in the process. Involved action by the relevant systems will be mutually beneficial and will increase understanding and cooperation between them.

> The nature of the group (and group goal) serves to fulfill certain needs of its members, and the satisfaction of these needs is its function. Through the symbolic system of the group, its roles, role-systems, and norms, individual behavior is differentiated and at the same time integrated for the satisfaction of needs, and the fulfillment of its function.[16]

---

[14]Stephanie W. Greenberg, William M. Rohe, and Jay R. Williams, *Informal Citizen Action and Crime Prevention at the Neighborhood Level: Executive Summary* (Washington, D.C.: U.S. Government Printing Office, 1984).

[15]*Ibid.*

[16]Scott A. Greer, *Social Organizations* (New York: Random House, 1955), p. 24.

SUMMARY

Effective prevention includes more than a knowledge of theory, extensive resources, and good intentions. All of these are necessary, but they become translated into action only when there is cooperative involvement in the problem-solving process by the community residents and the maze of agencies and organizations both internal and external to the juvenile system. This chapter has presented a process that can facilitate the translation of theory, resources, and good intentions into action programs.

DISCUSSION QUESTIONS:

1. After reviewing appropriate sections of Chapter 3, Theories of Delinquency Causation, explain the connection of social control and learning theories with community interventions that stress advocacy and institutional mediation.
2. Use the information presented in this chapter to organize a citizen-based delinquency control effort. Develop a detailed plan for the program.

PROJECTS

1. Identify all the interest groups in your community that would have to cooperate for effective juvenile delinquency prevention, control, and treatment.
2. Develop a rationale for convincing adults that youngsters in the community should be actively involved in problem solving and decision making.
3. Set up a detailed plan for organizing groups with different beliefs about delinquency to take part in a joint citizen delinquency prevention effort.

═══════════ 11 ═══

Alcohol and Drug Abuse

- TYPES OF DRUGS
- THE IMAGE OF DRUG ABUSERS
- REASONS FOR DRUG ABUSE
- DRUG USE AND OTHER ILLEGAL BEHAVIOR
- HANDLING DRUG ABUSERS IN THE JUVENILE JUSTICE SYSTEM
- DRUG ABUSE PROGRAMS

LEARNING OBJECTIVES

1. To be familiar with the physical and psychological effects of the major types of drugs, including alcohol, which are used by adolescents.
2. To trace the changing image that the public and the criminologist have held of the drug abuser.
3. To know several theories which explain drug abuse among adolescents.
4. To understand the effects of alcohol and other drug abuse on tendencies to commit violent and property crimes.
5. To understand the connection between the juvenile justice system and the drug treatment system.
6. To be familiar with a variety of "pure" and other prevention programs which are used for adolescent drug and alcohol abusers.

An understanding of alcohol and other drug abuse is particularly relevant to juvenile delinquency control efforts. As we pointed out in Chapter 2, there is strong evidence that a majority of adolescents use alcohol and that many use other illegal drugs, particularly marijuana. Smaller numbers use heroin and cocaine, the drugs which we usually associate with the most severe problems of addiction. Because of this widespread use among adolescents, personnel in the juvenile justice system are likely to be called upon to arrest, prosecute, or treat youths who do use drugs.

Teenagers who use drugs become involved with police, court, and correctional programs in a number of ways. Alcohol and other drug use are in themselves illegal activities, as are selling and purchasing these substances. Beyond that, it is commonly believed that the use of these substances results in other types of criminal activity. Specifically, use can stimulate some people to be more violent, and the need to purchase expensive drugs can result in revenue-producing crimes. This causal connection of drug use with other illegal activity is not firmly established through research, and it will be explored in detail later in this chapter. Even if drug use does not cause other delinquent behavior, it is unquestionable that a large proportion of youths who are involved with the juvenile justice system are also regular users of drugs. Treatment and other control efforts aimed toward adolescents cannot be undertaken without knowledge of drug abuse.

In developing a knowledge base relevant to drugs, we will consider alcohol and drugs as similar substances. It is true that our society is much more tolerant of alcohol use, but alcohol is, strictly speaking, a potentially addictive drug which acts on the nervous system to bring about both physical and psychological changes. Also, the trend among teenagers who use alcohol is to use other substances as well—in other words, to be involved in polydrug use. It would be artificial to consider alcohol use as a separate problem.

Youths vary considerably in their patterns of drug use. Some are one-time or infrequent users, and particularly if they primarily use alcohol or the increasingly tolerated marijuana, these youths are not generally the target populations of treatment programs, or the focus of theories to explain abuse. Many people consider sporadic use by adolescents to be "part of growing up," and therefore normal behavior. Other youths are regular users who have incorporated drugs into their lives to meet social or other needs. These youths rely on drugs to produce a certain feeling or to help them take part in peer-group activities, and they are habituated to the drugs they use. It is possible to develop a tolerance to some drugs, in which case more of the substance is needed to achieve the same results. If a physical dependence develops, the youth is addicted. Tolerance and addiction do not develop for all kinds of drugs, but when they do, there is an increased chance that a person will ingest a physically damaging amount of the drug—a situation commonly called an overdose.

This chapter will focus on the problem drug abuser, that is, youths whose chronic use brings them into contact with the juvenile justice system or interrupts learning, work, and necessary developmental activities. We are also interested in problem behavior that is particularly dangerous to others, such as violence, or which is against the law, as it relates to drug use.

Table 11-1 Controlled Substances: Uses and Effects

	DRUGS	OFTEN PRESCRIBED BRAND NAMES	MEDICAL USES
Sedative-Hypnotics	BARBITURATES	Amytal, Butisol, Nembutal, Phenobarbital, Seconal, Tuinal	Anesthetic, epilepsy, sleep
	METHAQUALONE	Optimil, Parest, Quaalude, Somnafac, Sopor	Sedation, sleep
Hallucinogens	MARIJUANA	None	None
	HASHISH	None	None
	PHENCYCLIDINE (PCP)	Sernylan	Veterinary anesthetic
	LSD	None	None
Stimulants	AMPHETAMINES	Benzedrine, Biphetamine, Desoxyn, Dexe-drine	Hyperkinesis, weight control, narcolepsy
	COCAINE "CRACK"	Cocaine	Local anesthetic
	OTHER STIMULANTS	Bacarate, Cylert, Didrex, Ionamin, Plegine, Pondimin	Weight control
Narcotics	OPIUM	Dover's Powder, Paregoric	Analgesic, anti-diarrheal
	MORPHINE	Morphine	Analgesic
	CODEINE	Codeine	Analgesic, antitussive
	HEROIN	None	None
	METHADONE	Dolophine, Methadone, Methadose	Analgesic, heroin substitute

SOURCE: Most of the information for this table was taken from *Drug Enforcement* (Washington, D.C.: U.S. Govern-Government Printing Office, 1983).

TYPES OF DRUGS

Drugs can be classified into four main types: (1) sedative-hypnotics, (2) hallucinogens, (3) stimulants, and (4) opiate narcotics. A description of each will follow, with particular emphasis on examples of drugs which are either frequently used

DEPENDENCE POTENTIAL		USUAL METHODS OF ADMINISTRATION	POSSIBLE EFFECTS	EFFECTS OF OVERDOSE OR LONG-TERM USE
PHYSICAL	PSYCHO-LOGICAL			
High	High	Oral, injected	Slurred speech, disorientation, drunken behavior with odor of alcohol	Shallow repiration, cold and clammy skin, dilated pupils, weak and rapid pulse, coma, possible death
High	High	Oral		
Unknown	Moderate	Oral, smoked	Euphoria, relaxed inhibitions, increased appetite, disoriented behavior, faster heartbeat and pulse rate, bloodshot eyes	Fatigue, paranoia, possible psychosis, loss of motivation, problems in learning, effects on reproduction
Unknown	Moderate	Oral, smoked		
None	Unknown	Oral, injected, smoked, sniffed	Illusions and hallucinations; poor perception of time and distance; increased heart rate and blood pressure, dizziness, numbness	Drowsiness, convulsions; longer, more intense "trip" episodes, psychosis, possible death
Unknown	Yes	Oral	Same as PCP	Same as PCP
Possible	High	Oral, injected	Increased alertness, excitation, euphoria, dilated pupils, increased pulse rate and blood pressure, insomnia, loss of appetite	Agitation, increase in body temperature, hallucinations, convulsions, possible death
Possible	High	Injected, sniffed, smoked (free-based)		
Possible	Possible	Oral		
High	High	Oral, smoked	Euphoria, drowsiness, respiratory, depression, constricted pupils, nausea	Slow and shallow breathing, clammy skin, convulsions, coma, possible death
High	High	Injected, smoked		
Moderate	Moderate	Oral, injected		
High	High	Injected, sniffed		
High	High	Oral, injected		

ment Printing Office, 1975), pp. 20–21; updated with information in *Just Say No* pamphlets (Washington, D.C.: U.S.

by adolescents, or which may be particularly damaging to them. Additionally information about each drug type is summarized in Table 11-1.

Sedative-hypnotics. The sedative-hypnotics include the drugs which are commonly referred to as *depressants*. Depressants are sedative drugs that are manufactured for medical purposes to reduce tension and anxiety, as well as to treat epilepsy. Barbiturates are the largest group of sedatives, or depressants, and without medical supervision to avoid habituation the ultimate effects can be very destructive.

Because barbiturates depress the brain function and the central nervous system, they create a very powerful depressant. Continued use can produce tolerance and create a desire for taking them on a long-term basis. When barbiturates are combined and used with amphetamines, a chemical imbalance can result and can create a pleasant mood-elevating effect which entices a user to take increased amounts.

The majority of these drugs are used legally for tranquilizing purposes. Many of the drugs fall into illegal hands, however, and like the stimulant drugs, abuse can often start in the doctor's office as a result of a legitimate prescription.

Barbiturates can be dangerous when not taken under medical supervision, and death may result from an overdose. Withdrawal from the drug can cause many unpleasant physical symptoms—the withdrawal resembles delirium tremens. Like the stimulant drugs, sedative drugs are available only on prescription and are controlled by the Comprehensive Drug Abuse Prevention and Control Act of 1970.

> Tighter regulations and enforcement of law on the legitimate manufacture and distribution of barbiturates and tranquilizers are part of the answer. Because barbiturates and tranquilizers have sound medical usefulness, physicians must be wary of yielding to the demand of patients for increased amounts when, in fact, they may be manifesting tolerance. Widespread dissemination of information about the dangers of overusing these addictive drugs is essential.[1]

Like the other drugs we will mention, a great deal more has to be learned about the effects of sedatives on the body, brain, and nervous system. Consequently, research programs are under way to determine the entire scope of the use of sedatives, in both their positive and negative aspects.

Alcohol, which of course is illegal only for minors in our society, is the most commonly used sedative-hypnotic and in fact the most commonly used drug among youths. It is both physically and psychologically addictive, and heavy users can have an overwhelming urge to drink more and more alcohol.

Although we have classified alcohol as similar to a depressant, it does not act as a depressant in small doses. Bartol described the range of effects of alcohol:

> At low doses (two to four ounces of whiskey) alcohol appears to act as a stimulant on the central nervous system. The person may feel "high," euphoric, full of good cheer, and be socially and physically warm. At moderate and high quantities, however, alcohol becomes a central nervous system depressant. There is a

---

[1] *Sedatives, Some Questions and Answers,* U.S. Department of Health, Education, and Welfare, Public Health Service Publication no. 2098 (Washington, D.C.: U.S. Government Printing Office, 1970). Most of the descriptive information relating to the different types of drugs has been taken from documents provided by the U.S. Department of Health and Human Services, which was formerly the U.S. Department of Health, Education, and Welfare.

reduction in neuromuscular coordination, visual acuity, and perception of pain and fatigue. The ability to concentrate is impaired, and the ordinary restraints on speech and behavior are weakened. Very often, self-confidence is increased and the person becomes more daring, sometimes foolishly so. In general, alcohol at moderate levels begins to numb the higher brain centers which integrate information with judgment.[2]

It is the effects of alcohol in the higher doses which result in what is commonly called "problem drinking." That is, high doses of alcohol can result in the lack of judgment and inhibition which lead to crime. Just as serious in terms of developmental consequences for the adolescent, regular and high doses of alcohol can make it impossible to succeed in learning, work, and social settings. These undesirable consequences do not inevitably result from heavy adolescent drinking, for each person reacts differently to alcohol and people vary in their reactions to the same amount of alcohol.

Phencyclidine.   Phencyclidine (PCP) use is considerably less widespread than alcohol, but this drug was adopted as a "fad" by many youths at the end of the 1970s and it continues to be used by a small proportion. It is in the hallucinogen category, but it is very difficult to classify. It is sold under a wide variety of names, including dust, angel dust, crazy Eddie, tick, and erroneously as a derivative of marijuana, THC. Its primary legal use is as an anesthetic for monkeys and other primates. PCP is used by people either orally, or it is snorted, or it is smoked on other substances.

Depending on the dosage and the individual, PCP can produce a variety of effects, including excitation and stupor. These experiences are classified by users into four types:

> (1) "buzzed," (2) "wasted," (3) "ozones," (4) "overdosed." In the buzzed state, the user feels a mild euphoria and, rather than experiencing the drug as an anesthetic, experiences a stimulation so that activity is enjoyed. . . . When a user was in the wasted condition, the drug usually caused a body-wide anesthetic effect in which the user felt the sensations profoundly, especially in his or her legs and feet. Typically she/he found coordinating body movements difficult and speech somewhat slurred. Users, for example, described the action of walking as accompanied by the sensation that the ground had turned to sponge or marshmallows. In this state, users recognized that body movements were slowed, awkward, and unbalanced. In contrast to the outward awkwardness, users sensed a speeding up of thought processes and seemed to enjoy an odd sensation of being able to participate and observe themselves in what has been described as an out-of-body experience. The ozoned state is one in which the user becomes incoherent and immobile, although still conscious. And in the overdosed state, the user loses consciousness, a condition that most experienced PCP users did not believe was life threatening.[3]

[2]Curt R. Bartol, *Criminal Behavior: A Psychosocial Approach* (Englewood Cliffs, New Jersey: Prentice-Hall, Inc., 1980), p. 345.

[3]Harvey W. Feldman and Dan Waldorf, *Angel Dust in Four American Cities: An Ethnographic Study of PCP Users* (Washington, D.C.: U.S. Department of Health and Human Services, 1980), p. 9.

Although users do not apparently perceive the drug to be highly dangerous, there are estimates that in 1977, when its use was more common than now, PCP was involved in at least eighty deaths and more than four thousand hospital emergency room cases.[4] These most severe crises related to PCP use seem to result from taking a high dosage, which is difficult to regulate, and attempting some physical activity that results in harm to one's self. Chronic use does result in long-term memory loss, as well as impairment to physical coordination.

Hallucinogens. Hallucinogens are drugs that can have unpredictable effects on the mind. They include such drugs are marijuana, hashish, peyote, and mescaline, as well as LSD (lysergic acid diethylamide). Marijuana and hashish, which are derived from the Indian hemp plant, *cannabis sativa,* are the best known and most frequently used of the hallucinogens. *Cannabis sativa* grows wild in many parts of the world, including the United States. It can be used commercially in the production of fiber for ropes and birdseed. It varies greatly in strength, depending upon the concentration of the chemical, tetrahydrocannabinol (THC), which is found mainly in the resin of the plant. Hashish, which is produced by directly scraping some of this resin, has higher concentrations of THC than does marijuana, which is produced from the flowers, leaves, and stems of the plant. Hashish, for this reason, has a more powerful psychological and physical effect on users than does marijuana.

When smoked, marijuana or hashish enters the bloodstream, and within a very short time can affect the mood and the thinking of the user. The reactions that the drugs have on the mind are unique to each person, but may include feelings of tranquility, swings from hilarity to quiet moods, changes in perceptions, distortions in perceptions of time, and a loss of memory. Specific physical effects are reddening of the whites of the eyes, increased heartbeat, and sometimes coughing due to the irritating effects of the smoke on the lungs. The physical changes are quite constant during and immediately after use, but the psychological changes come and go, or in some cases do not occur at all.

Marijuana, which is not a narcotic, does not cause physical dependence as do heroin and other narcotics. Therefore, the body does not develop a tolerance to the drug, and withdrawal from marijuana does not usually produce physical sickness. Many scientists believe, however, that psychological dependence can develop. As to whether it leads to hard drugs, there is considerable agreement that a large number of marijuana users never progress to using other drugs, but that a person who is predisposed to abuse one drug is likely to abuse other drugs.[5]

Because marijuana use is relatively common, researchers have become

[4]Steven E. Lerner and R. Stanley Burns, "Youthful Phencyclidine (PCP) Use," in *Youth Drug Abuse: Problems, Issues, and Treatment,* eds. George M. Beschner and Alfred S. Friedman (Lexington, Massachusetts: Lexington Books, D.C. Heath and Company, 1979), p. 315.

[5]*Marihuana, Some Questions and Answers,* U.S. Department of Health and Education, and Welfare, Public Health Service Publication no. 1829 (Washington, D.C.: U.S. Government Printing Office, 1970).

interested in the subtle effects on motivation and other important characteristics of adolescents. A group of experts on marijuana agree that:

1. . . . the consistent use of marijuana by preadolescents and adolescents can affect mental functioning adversely. Furthermore, the participants agreed on many features of a syndrome of adolescent drug use that includes decreases in academic performance, alienation from parents and prevailing cultural values, loss of motivation to succeed at conventional tasks, feelings of isolation, and often suspiciousness and paranoia. There was general agreement that this syndrome is by no means a rarity and indeed occurs frequently among teenagers.
2. The family should be a central focus in the prevention and in the management of cannabis-induced emotional and cognitive disorders of children.
3. Much discussion focused on why adolescents appear to be more vulnerable than adults to the psychic effects of marijuana, and it was agreed that more information about the effects of intoxicants at different developmental stages is of utmost importance.
4. Much attention was paid to the problem of remaining accurate in communication while not obscuring the forest for the trees. Our public health responsibilities are weighty, and too often the presentation of carefully qualified scientific findings results in a severe dilution of the impact of the message concerning the health hazards of marijuana.

Furthermore

> It is particularly noteworthy that high school seniors perceive problems associated with marijuana use that correlate very well with the observations of the clinicians who participated in this workgroup. This conclusion is supported by the results of the 1979 and 1980 national surveys of high school seniors: Between 34 and 42 percent of daily marijuana users reported loss of energy (42.6 percent), deterioration of relationship with parents (38.6 percent), interference with ability to think clearly (37.3 percent), diminished interest in other activities (36.6 percent), and poor performance at school (34.0 percent).[6]

Marijuana does not have many of the physical effects of the harder drugs, but this is not to say that it has no impact on adolescent development. As shown in a pediatrician's report on marijuana use, there can be serious consequences (Exhibit 11-1).

LSD is a much stronger, though less often used, hallucinogen. It can be taken in the form of a capsule or it can be placed on other substances. LSD's effects are both physical and psychological. Enlarged pupils, flushed face, and rise in temperature and heartbeat are some of the common physical effects. Even though LSD is not a physically addictive drug, it can have psychological ramifications.

> Illusions and hallucinations can occur, and delusional thoughts are sometimes expressed. The sense of time and of self are strangely altered. Emotional variations are marked, ranging from bliss to horror, sometimes within a single experi-

[6]William Pollin, "Foreword," *Marijuana and Youth: Clinical Observations on Motivation and Learning* (Washington, D.C.: U.S. Government Printing Office, 1982), pp. v–vi.

Exhibit 11-1 A pediatrician's report on marijuana use

K.C., age 17: This girl is from a caring, interacting family without any marital problems. Her younger sister, age 14, is not on drugs. K.C. used to be an excellent student, always doing special projects, always active in sports. She started smoking marijuana at 15, and for the last 2 years has smoked daily. Her parents noticed increasing depression, with almost daily talk about suicide. She complained about poor concentration and loss of interest in her school activities because of constant fatigue. Mathematics and abstract thinking started to give her special problems. She gradually gave up all of her hobbies and sports. She started sleeping in, missing school, and taking naps in the afternoon. The family noticed that her physical appearance no longer mattered to her. She was irritable, moody, and difficult to get along with, becoming more and more withdrawn. She talked about dropping out of school and taking a job; her ideas for the future became totally unrealistic and impossible. She left home 3 weeks prior to her 18th birthday and dropped out of high school 2 months before graduation. She could not give any special reasons for her actions.

K.C. had had several counseling sessions with different people before I saw her. In these she was advised of the need to improve her self-image, but marijuana was not considered a problem. Because her parents felt marijuana smoking was merely a fad of today's youth, no attempts had been made to make her stop using it. After I saw her, she was able to discontinue her habit, and 2 years later she is completely off marijuana. She received her high school diploma and is in college, where she is working hard. She seems happy and gets along beautifully with her parents. She has resumed her previous hobbies and sports. At times she feels tempted to try marijuana again since most of her friends at college use it, but she has decided against it, remembering her previous depressions and inability to cope with her life.

SOURCE: Ingrid L. Lantner, "Marijuana Abuse by Children and Teenagers: A Pediatrician's View," in *Marijuana and Youth: Clinical Observations on Motivation and Learning,* ed. U.S. Department of Health and Human Services (Rockville, Maryland: National Institute on Drug Abuse, 1982), p. 89.

Issues for Discussion.   What type of research could tell us what proportion of adolescent marijuana users experience the types of difficulties described in the case study? After reading through this chapter, identify the program elements that would be most useful in treating or preventing the pattern of marijuana abuse described here. What role could pediatricians play in drug abuse prevention and control? How would the confidential nature of a doctor-patient relationship influence the appropriate role of the pediatrician?

---

ence. Because of the impaired time sense—a few minutes may seem like hours—such an experience can assume the proportions of a terrible nightmare from which one cannot easily awaken.[7]

[7]*LSD, Some Questions and Answers,* U.S. Department of Health, Education, and Welfare, Public Health Service Publication no. 1828 (Washington, D.C.: U.S. Government Printing Office, 1970).

The National Institute of Mental Health has attempted to determine the biological, psychological, and genetic effects of LSD on animals and humans. Research will continue until many of the questions about this drug have been answered. Many medical authorities believe that the chronic or continued use of LSD changes values and impairs the user's power of concentration and ability to think rationally. Up to now, it has not been proven, as some proponents claim, that LSD can increase creativity. In fact, because of lack of research, the actual workings of LSD in the body are not yet known.

> The strange sensations in clash of mood the drug causes can be frightening, even for a mature person. For young people who are still undergoing the process of emotional development, and who may lack the resilience to maintain the mental equilibrium under LSD, the effects can be even more frightening and confusing. The young, growing brain is more vulnerable to all mind-altering drugs than a brain in which metabolic activity is stabilized.[8]

Although LSD has not been used extensively for medical purposes, available evidence suggests that it may be useful, under controlled conditions, for neurotics and alcoholics. Although the drug may be a valuable tool in biomedical research, present indications are that its therapeutic value is limited. The penalty structure for illegal possession and distribution of LSD is delineated in the Comprehensive Drug Abuse Prevention and Control Act of 1970.

Stimulants.   Stimulants are drugs, usually amphetamines, that stimulate the central nervous system. They can increase alertness and are often used to combat fatigue, reduce depression, and control appetite. In addition to amphetamines, stimulants include cocaine, dextroamphetamine, and methamphetamine ("speed"). Stimulants are also known as pep pills. Coffee, tea, and caffeine are considered mild stimulants.

Abuse of amphetamines and stimulants can begin in the doctor's office as a result of a prescribed dosage which becomes abused and overextended. In some cases, over half of the legally manufactured supply of amphetamines finds its way into illegal channels for nonprescriptive use. In regard to the effects of amphetamine use,

> in ordinary amounts the amphetamines provide a transient sense of alertness, wakefulness, well-being and mental clarity. Hunger is diminished, and short term performance may be enhanced in the fatigued person. The drugs may increase the heart rate, raise the blood pressure, produce palpitation and rapid breathing, dilate the pupils, and cause dry mouth, sweating and headache—if use continues, however, a person can become psychologically dependent on the drug in a few weeks. The sense of power, self-confidence, and exhilaration artificially created by amphetamine use is so pleasant, and the fatigue and depression that follow discontinuance are so severe, that the user is heavily tempted to revert to the drug.[9]

[8]*Ibid.*

[9]*Stimulants, Some Questions and Answers,* U.S. Department of Health, Education, and Welfare, Public Health Service Publication no. 2097 (Washington, D.C.: U.S. Government Printing Office, 1970).

Amphetamines can be taken intravenously to produce a quicker and more pronounced "high." Prolonged use of "speed" has many negative ramifications, including psychological disturbances and the impairment of physical health as a result of body abuse and poor nutrition. Frequent abuse can result in brain damage that interferes with speech and thinking.

The stimulant, cocaine, including its more potent forms—crack and freebase—is one of the few drugs for which use has been increasing among adolescents and young adults.[10] Particularly in some inner-city neighborhoods, high proportions of delinquents have used it at least once, and there are estimates that in some areas nearly one third of delinquent youth have used crack on a daily basis.[11]

Cocaine is extracted from the leaves of coca plants. When it was first discovered, it was seen as having medical value in the treatment of a variety of psychiatric symptoms, for example depression. Freebase is a pure form of the cocaine that is usually dissolved in ether and then crystallized, crushed, and smoked. Smoking the drug makes it possible for larger amounts to get to the brain quickly. Crack is similar to freebase, but it is not made from pure cocaine. Crack's popularity rests on its low cost and the powerful high that it can produce when smoked.

Users who snort cocaine feel the most intense effects after 15 or 20 minutes, and when the drug is smoked, the effects are immediate. Common effects are dilated pupils, increased blood pressure and heart rate, and elevated body temperature. Users report a sense of well-being, energy and alertness, and the absence of hunger. Negative effects of the drug are restlessness, irritability, anxiety, and sleeplessness, and in some cases paranoia and hallucinations. An overdose can lead to death due to repeated seizures followed by respiratory and cardiac arrest. Death can result not only when the freebase form of the drug is used, but also from sniffing "street" cocaine.

Narcotics. The term *narcotic* refers to opium and pain-relieving drugs made from opium, such as morphine, paregoric, and codeine. Narcotics are used in medicine mainly to relieve pain and induce sleep. The narcotic abuser develops a physical addiction to the drug and, as the body develops a tolerance, larger dosages are needed to satisfy the craving. When the narcotic is withheld or when use has ceased, there are withdrawal symptoms and physical trauma such as sweating, shaking, nausea, and even abdominal pains and leg cramps. In

[10]Patrick M. O'Malley, Lloyd D. Johnston and Jerome G. Bachman, "Cocaine Use Among American Adolescents and Young Adults," in *Cocaine Use in America: Epidemiologic and Clinical Perspectives* eds. N. J. Kozel and E. H. Adams (Rockville, Maryland: National Institute on Drug Abuse, 1985); Arnold M. Washton and Martin S. Gold, "Recent Trends in Cocaine Abuse as Seen from the "800 Cocaine" Hotline," in *Cocaine: A Clinician's Handbook* eds. A. M. Washton and Martin S. Gold, (New York: Guilford, 1987), pp. 10–22.

[11]James Inciardi, "Beyond Cocaine: Basuco, Crack and Other Coca Products," paper presented at the Academy of Criminal Justice Sciences, St. Louis, Missouri, 1987; M. D. Newcomb and P. M. Bentler, *Consequences of Adolescent Drug Use: Impact on the Lives of Young Adults* (Beverly Hills, California: Sage, 1988).

addition to the physical dependence, however, psychological dependence results, and the individual who uses narcotics and becomes addicted attempts to handle his or her problems by using the narcotic drug.

Adolescent use of heroin is increasingly rare, with less than one percent of youths aged 12 to 17 estimated to have used it.[12] Heroine is usually adulterated and mixed with other substances, such as milk, sugar, or quinine. The drug makes a person believe that his or her problems have been eliminated, or that he or she can deal with life more adequately. Once the drug has worn off, however, the reality of daily responsibilities and pressures becomes even more acute, and as a result increased dosage is usually needed to "feed the habit."

Because of the cost of heroin and the fact that it often reduces hunger and thirst, addicts often become malnourished and physically emaciated, and therefore more susceptible to diseases like tuberculosis and pneumonia. Negative side effects, such as hepatitis and AIDS (from unsterile needles) and blood infections, are common.

In addition to the stringent penalties established under the Narcotic Control Act of 1956 and revised under the Comprehensive Drug Abuse Prevention and Control Act of 1970, treatment of the narcotic addict is often complicated and is generally a long-term process. One of the greatest difficulties is that when the individual has been released from the hospital (after going through withdrawal symptoms and the psychological problems associated with withdrawal), he or she often finds it impossible to remain off drugs and pursue a "conventional" existence in the community. Rehabilitation is complicated because not all addicts have the same problems, and therefore it is difficult to focus on specific methods of treatment. Also, many communities do not have facilities to help the addict who has been released from the protection of the hospital.

The Narcotic Addict Rehabilitation Act of 1966 (NARA) gives certain addicts a choice of treatment instead of prosecution or imprisonment. If addicts are not charged with a crime, they have the right to ask for treatment on their own initiative or it may be requested by a relative. Federal legislation also provides for a complete range of rehabilitation services to be made available to addicts in their own communities.[13]

Care of the addict after release from the hospital is a key aspect of treatment. Aftercare programs can provide continuing treatment for up to three years in the addict's own community. Besides treatment in a hospital or a therapeutic community, other drugs are often used in the treatment of heroin addiction. These include methadone, which is a substitute for heroin that allows people to continue to live productive lives, and narcotic antagonists, which block the "high" of opiates but do not produce a high on their own. When other drugs

[12]U.S. Department of Health and Human Services, National Institute on Drug Abuse, *National Household Survey on Drug Abuse: Main Findings 1985* (Washington, D.C.: U.S. Government Printing Office, 1988), pp. 18–20.

[13]*Narcotics, Some Questions and Answers*, U.S. Department of Health, Education, and Welfare, Public Health Service Publication no. 1827 (Washington, D.C.: U.S. Government Printing Office, 1970).

are used as part of the treatment, they are usually used in combination with counseling, vocational training, job placement, and other services.

Inhalants. Inhalants are the final type of drug that we will consider. Inhalants are common household products—for example, model airplane glue, nail polish remover, lighter and cleaning fluids, and gasoline.[14] Aerosol sprays, like hair spray, also are sniffed to produce a feeling of stimulation, less inhibition, and less control. Even in small doses, inhalants can produce such negative effects as nausea, lack of coordination, nosebleeds, and bad breath. In large doses, they can render the user unconscious. The unconscious person can vomit and death can occur from aspiration. In the case of some inhalants, death by suffocation or due to heart failure can occur on the first use. Even if death does not result, repeated sniffing can result in permanent damage to the nervous system and resulting harm to physical and mental capabilities. The likelihood of overdosing is increased because users do develop a tolerance, needing more each time to get the same effect.

The use of inhalants is of increasing concern, for most users are quite young, between the ages of 7 and 17.[15] Inhalants are often the only drug available to very young children, who do not have money to purchase other types. Boys are more likely than girls to use inhalants, with an estimate of about 5 percent of 12- to 17-year-olds having used inhalants in the last year.[16] Most users are experimental or transitional users, but some do become chronic users. The chronic users seem to come from the most unstable, disorganized, and problem-ridden families, to have alcoholic parents, and to have often been abused and/or neglected.

At present, inhalants are not covered under the Comprehensive Drug Abuse Prevention and Control Act of 1970, so there are no federal penalties for possession or selling of the substances. However, several states have passed laws prohibiting the sniffing of inhalants.

THE IMAGE OF DRUG ABUSERS

An examination of the different images of youths who use drugs since the 1960s provides an excellent illustration of several major themes in this book. This image has gradually changed from a picture of teenaged heroin addicts in ghetto areas, to one of self-seeking middle-class adolescents in the 1970s, to a picture of contemporary users as affected by various family and social conditions, but including youths from all social classes and racial groups. Parallel to this change in

[14]U.S. Department of Health and Human Services, *Inhalants: Just Say No* (Washington, D.C.: U.S. Government Printing Office, 1983).

[15]U.S. Department of Health, Education, and Welfare, "Inhalants, The Deliberate Inhalation of Volatile Substances," *Report Series, 30,* no. 2 (July 1978).

[16]U.S. Department of Health and Human Services, National Institute of Drug Abuse, *National Household Survey on Drug Abuse: Population Estimates 1985* (Washington, D.C.: United States Government Printing Office, 1987), pp. 18–25, 30–33.

the image of the adolescent, there have been major shifts in the theories developed to explain adolescent drug use and the programs to control the problem. At the same time, beliefs about the moral nature of the abuser also have changed.

As Frank Scarpitti and Susan Datesman note, drug abuse was associated in the 1960s with poor and minority youths who lived in the ghetto.[17] Very often, these youths were believed to be psychologically disturbed. For instance, in Cloward and Ohlin's opportunity theory, drug abuse resulted from two avenues of blocked opportunity. Legitimate opportunities to success were blocked as they were for many other ghetto youths. Also, even the illegitimate opportunities to join a gang subculture were unavailable because they were inept in relating to other subculture members.[18] This example from opportunity theory illustrates the depiction of drugs abusers as suffering from ghetto conditions coupled with individual inadequacies.

The change in the picture of the drug abusers was marked after the early 1960s. The middle-class youths who commonly used LSD and marijuana did not fit the image of the addict. They did not suffer from poverty, and appeared to have ample opportunity of the type described by Cloward and Ohlin. The widespread nature of use among college students made it difficult to accept any claim that these youths shared some major psychological inadequacy.

Today it is still true that the narcotic heroin is more commonly used by ghetto youths, and higher socioeconomic class youths more often use LSD. However, these tendencies are not extreme, and heroin and LSD are among the least often used of all the drugs. Marijuana, which is much more widely used, is used by all social classes, as is cocaine. Polydrug use, the switching between four or five different drugs depending on their availability and current popularity, is very common today. It is no longer accurate to depict drug users as the heroin addicts concentrated in poor areas, and therefore theories which focus on explaining the behavior of just this group are not adequate.

> . . . there appear to be, broadly speaking, two types of youthful drug users. On the one hand, there are the urban, largely minority, street users who remain committed to using various drugs. More recent studies of drug use in urban settings have found that many different patterns of use exist, however. Many habitual users avoid addictive drugs or are weekend users. Because the street dose of heroin is relatively low in potency, many addicts are able to control their habits. They may work or attend school and must exhibit energy and resourcefulness in order to support their drug use. Today, drug use is an integral part of the lives of many young urban residents who respond to the goals and beliefs of their drug subculture and in so doing gain status.[19]

[17]Frank R. Scarpitti and Susan K. Datesman, "Introduction," in *Drugs and the Youth Culture*, eds. Frank R. Scarpitti and Susan K. Datesman (Beverly Hills, California: Sage Publications, 1980), p. 14.

[18]Richard A. Cloward and Lloyd Ohlin, *Delinquency and Opportunity* (New York: The Free Press, 1960), pp. 178–186.

[19]Scarpitti and Datesman, "Introduction," pp. 17–18.

This picture is a far cry from the earlier view of the black ghetto youth who is completely dehabilitated by heroin addiction, or from the picture of the protesting middle-class youth who uses LSD to gain insight. The contemporary image reflects that many users attempt to manage their consumption so as to participate in some usual, legitimate teenage activities, and that use is varied and widespread throughout the adolescent population.

REASONS FOR DRUG ABUSE

How then can we explain the widespread and varied patterns of drug abuse? Some of the reasons that persons become involved in drug abuse and delinquency, or both, have already been discussed in Chapter 3, Theories of Delinquency Causation. Further, in the present chapter, we will see that many serious adolescent drug abusers are not involved in other forms of delinquency, a fact that suggests that the causes for these two forms of illegal behavior may differ, at least to some extent.

Unique Influences on Drug Abuse

Dealing first with unique influences on substance abuse, a variety of psychological variables play a part in substance abuse but not in delinquency. The psychological variables include such things as self-esteem, life distress, personality traits, psychiatric symptoms, and lack of inhibitions, and they are particularly influential on alcohol abuse, but also affect the use of other drugs.[20] In a study focused on cocaine use, the similar conclusion was that problematic drug involvement developed for youth experiencing psychological distress, for example negative self-feelings and feelings of being emotionally unsupported by other people.[21]

Lack of family support is often at the root of the psychological distress that contributes to substance use, as illustrated by a study of youths who used drugs other than alcohol and marijuana:

> Drug users felt rejected at home, that their parents did not trust them or genuinely care about them and that there was little to talk about in common with their parents. . . . Drug users' families exercise little or no control over the children's activities.[22]

[20]Helen Raskin White, Robert J. Pandina, and Randy L. LaGrange, "Longitudinal Predictors of Serious Substance Use and Delinquency," *Criminology*, 25, no. 3 (August 1987), p. 735.

[21]Michael D. Newcomb and Peter M. Bently, "Antecedents and Consequences of Cocaine Use: An Eight-Year Study from Early Adolescence to Young Adulthood," in *Straight and Devious Pathways from Childhood to Adulthood* eds. Lee N. Robins and Michael Rutter, (Cambridge: Cambridge University Press, 1990), p. 177.

[22]Richard C. Stephens, "The Hard Drug Scene," in *Drugs and the Youth Culture*, eds. Scarpitti and Datesman, p. 70.

Problem drinkers similarly tend to feel alienated from their families,[23] and heavy- and problem-drinking boys see their fathers as emotionally distant, uncaring, and unconcerned about them.[24] Heavy-drinking girls likewise felt emotionally and physically distant from their parents.[25] Combinations of lax control, rejection of the child, and tension in the parent-child relationship are even greater influences on regular adolescent drinking than the parents' own drinking behavior.[26]

The family does however exert some influence on drug use by directly teaching the patterns of use. Often, adolescents see their parents relying on barbiturates to help them sleep, stimulants and amphetamines to pep them up, tranquilizers to calm them down, and alcohol to have a good time. Consistent with social learning theory, research affirms that youths do model their parents' drug-using patterns. When both parents are heavy or problem drinkers, boys are heavy drinkers. Girls in families where the mother is a heavy drinker consume large amounts of alcohol during their adolescence, too.[27] Parents' drinking is a particularly important influence on youths' use of hard liquor.[28] Clearly, the prevention of drug abuse depends not only on whether parents maintain positive relations with their children, but also on the degree to which the parents themselves use drugs, thereby providing a model for use.[29]

Research provides considerable support for the conclusion that individual problems, often stemming from family dynamics, contribute importantly to substance abuse. Thus, even though some adolescents will require programming to prevent and treat both substance abuse and delinquency, programs will need to adapt to special needs of particular youth. That is, they will need to provide the resources directly, or coordinate with other services to make sure that a variety of personal and family needs are met.

[23]Gerald Globetti, "Problem and Non-problem Drinking among High School Students in Abstinence Communities," *International Journal of the Addictions, 7,* no. 3 (Fall 1972), pp. 511–523.

[24]Robert A. Zucker and F. H. Banon, "Parental Behaviors Associated with Problem Drinking and Antisocial Behavior Among Adolescent Males," *Proceedings of the First Annual Conference of the National Institute of Alcohol Abuse and Alcoholism* (Washington, D.C.: U.S. Government Printing Office, June 1971), pp. 276–296.

[25]Robert A. Zucker and Catherine I. DeVoe, "Life History Characteristics Associated with Problem Drinking and Antisocial Behavior in Antisocial Girls," in *Life History Research in Psychopathology, 4,* eds. Robert D. Wirt, George Winokur, and Merrill Roff (Minneapolis: University of Minnesota Press, 1975), pp. 109–134.

[26]Thomas J. Prendergast, Jr. and Earl S. Schaefer, "Correlates of Drinking and Drunkenness Among High School Students," *Quarterly Journal on the Studies of Alcohol, 35,* no. 1 (March 1974), pp. 232–242.

[27]Robert A. Zuker, "Parental Influences on the Drinking Patterns of Their Children," in *Alcoholism Problems in Women and Children,* eds. Milton Greenblatt and Marc A. Schuckit (New York: Grune and Stratton, Inc., 1976), pp. 211–238.

[28]Denise B. Kandel, Ronald C. Kessler, and Rebecca Z. Margulies, "Antecedents of Adolescent Initiation into Stages of Drug Use: A Developmental Analysis" in *Longitudinal Research on Drug Use: Empirical Findings and Methodological Issues,* ed. Denise B. Kandel (New York: Halstead Press, 1978). pp. 73–100.

[29]Richard Dembo, Gary Grandon, Lawrence La Voie, James Schmeidler, and William Burgos, "Parents and Drugs Revisited: Some Further Evidence in Support of Social Learning Theory," *Criminology, 24,* no. 1 (February 1986), p. 85.

The Influence of Peers and the Status of Adolescents

The National Youth Survey results alert us to a major similarity in substance abuse and delinquency. Exposure to deviant peers and access to deviant opportunity structures are key in causing, and therefore in controlling, both types of deviance.[30] It has long been recognized that there is often a great deal of peer influence involved in the use of drugs; using them can be considered the "in" thing to do. Aside from peer influence, bonds to legitimate institutions—especially to school and families—seem to help in the control of delinquency, primarily through protecting individuals once they are exposed to peer pressures and opportunities that might result in lawbreaking.[31] It is important to recognize that these bonds might have a critical, earlier influence by predisposing certain youth to avoid associations with substance-abusing peers in the first place.[32] Indeed, the connection of religion to lower levels of adolescent marijuana use occurs because religious youth generally avoid associating with others who use drugs.[33]

The extensive separation of youths from adults in our society often contributes to peers' considerable influence over other youths. For this reason, it is no surprise that in contemporary American society, the best predictor of one's drug use is often friends' use.[34] The earlier that adolescents are involved in peer group activities, such as meeting with friends, dating, attending parties, and driving around, the earlier that they begin to use hard liquor.[35] We should keep in mind that not all adolescents influence each other to use alcohol and drugs, and peer group activities are often a necessary and valuable influence on the development of interpersonal and other skills. In many cases, though, drug users seek out those peers who are similar to themselves in their feelings and behavior.[36] Although peer groups are not always a detrimental influence on members, those with a drug-using orientation can exert a powerful effect on members, particularly since contemporary adolescents are frequently isolated from individuals except for their peers.

[30]Delbert S. Elliott, David H. Huizinga, and Scott Menard, *Multiple Problem Youth: Delinquency, Substance Use, and Mental Health Problems* (New York: Springer-Verlag, 1989), pp. 201.

[31]*Ibid.* p. 201.

[32]Richard E. Johnson, Anastasios C. Marcos, and Stephen J. Bahr, "The Role of Peers in the Complex Etiology of Adolescent Drug Use," *Criminology*, 25, no. 2 (May 1987), p. 335.

[33]Steven R. Burkett and Bruce O. Warren, "Religiosity, Peer Associations, and Adolescent Marijuana Use: A Panel Study of Underlying Causal Structures," *Criminology*, 25, no. 1 (February, 1987), pp. 109–132.

[34]David A. Schultz and Robert A. Wilson, "Some Traditional Family Variables and Their Correlations with Drug Use Among High School Students," *Journal of Marriage and Family*, 35, no. 4 (November 1973), pp. 628–631.

[35]Kandel, Kessler, and Margulies, "Antecedents of Adolescent Initiation into Stages of Drug Use."

[36]Michael Spevack and R. O. Pihl, "Non-medical Drug Use by High School Students: A Three-Year Survey Study," *International Journal of the Addictions, 11*, no. 5 (October 1976), pp. 755–792.

In addition to the influences of peers and legitimate bonds, there are aspects of the adolescent status which contribute to drug use. In Chapter 5, we described the stressful experiences that are considered normal for youths in our society, such as the move toward independence and the choice of an occupation. Drug use is one way to escape from the difficulties of dealing with such normal stresses of life, at least temporarily:

> A number of researchers have noted that drug users seem ill equipped to cope with life's problems. . . . [C]ertain individuals have difficulty in coping with life's problems, become increasingly alienated, and turn to drug use to help them cope with these problems.[37]

Parents frequently teach their children to rely on drugs in coping with stress through their own behavior. Also, television has transmitted advertisements and popular programming displaying the ready accessibility of legitimate drugs and the "magical" way that they can solve problems and contribute to happiness in our fast-paced world.

It is possible that widespread drug use results, in part, from the general lack of meaningful activities available to adolescents in our society, and a related sense of boredom. Adolescents who do not feel a part of any of society's valued activities, such as work or relevant education, have no reason to avoid the use of drugs. They have no reason to remain straight, and drug use and the social interactions surrounding obtaining and using the drugs can be an exciting activity. This seems to be the reason for the use of PCP:

> Among those studied, there existed a kind of restlessness, an orientation for action, and a sense that life generally was uninteresting and lacking in recreational alternatives. Whether the setting was suburban Philadelphia where car and telephone connected the youth system or inner city Chicago where youth groups historically congregated on corners and milled around "mom and pop" sandwich shops, the theme of looking for action permeated. The core pastime of these collectivities of young people has not been simply taking drugs, but includes any activity that could dispel boredom and increase the pace of life.[38]

This explanation of some drug use as a reaction to adolescents' marginal status, and their resultant boredom, is further supported by research showing that youths who avoid drug use *are* involved with society's institutions. These institutions include religion and the family, as well as the educational system as a preparation for college.[39]

DRUG USE AND OTHER ILLEGAL BEHAVIOR

In this section we will shift our attention from the causes of teenage drug use to the connection between use and other types of illegal behavior. Other research

[37]Stephens, "The Hard Drug Scene," p. 72.
[38]Feldman and Waldorf, *Angel Dust in Four American Cities*, p. 3.
[39]Stephens, "The Hard Drug Scene," p. 73.

has shown that a majority of serious delinquents also are serious drug users, but only about one-third of serious users are serious delinquents.[40] The widespread use of drugs by serious delinquents is confirmed by survey findings that 60 percent of juveniles in state-operated institutions report using drugs regularly, and nearly 40 percent report being under the influence of drugs at the time of arrest.[41] Thus, juvenile justice practitioners are often faced with the need to provide drug treatment services to delinquents, particularly for older adolescents and for those who began using drugs at an early age.[42]

Researchers responsible for the National Youth Survey point out the importance of responding to adolescent drug abuse, in addition to other forms of delinquency:

> From a number of perspectives, multiple illicit drug use may be the more serious problem for our society. This form of problem behavior involves a larger proportion of the adolescent population, it is more likely to extend into the adult years, and it appears to represent a more permanent adaptation than delinquent behavior, with higher rates of continuity once youth enter the more serious levels of involvement. It seems clear that involvement in multiple illicit drugs is indicative of a greater commitment to a deviant lifestyle than is either delinquent behavior or mental health problems.[43]

Some people have suggested that the problems of adolescent delinquency, substance abuse, and mental illness are really just one problem and thus should be dealt with through similar programs targeted at the same group of youth. There is evidence that the degree of overlap is not this complete. Although most serious delinquents are serious drug users, particularly for girls, the majority of serious drug users do not commit other types of offenses,[44] and many of the youth reached by drug abuse prevention or treatment programs would not (and should not) be affected by more general delinquency programs.

There are some ways in which it is clear that certain types of drug abuse do result in specific kinds of delinquency. Committing violent acts is associated with being under the influence of alcohol, particularly in situations where the victim has been drinking heavily, too.[45] In a study of California adolescents who had been convicted of murder, manslaughter, or assault, over half were under

---

[40]Helen Raskin White, Robert J. Pandina, and Randy L. LaGrange, "Longitudinal Predictors of Serious Substance Use and Delinquency," *Criminology, 25,* no. 3 (August 1987), pp. 715–740.

[41]Allen J. Beck, Susan A. Kline, and Lawrence A. Greenfeld, *Survey of Youth in Custody, 1987* (Washington, D.C.: Bureau of Justice Statistics, 1988), p. 1.

[42]Delbert S. Elliott, David H. Huizinga, and Scott Menard, *Multiple Problem Youth: Delinquency, Substance Use, and Mental Health Problems* (New York: Springer-Verlag, 1989), pp. 200–201.

[43]Delbert S. Elliott, David H. Huizinga, and Scott Menard, *Multiple Problem Youth: Delinquency, Substance Use, and Mental Health Problems* (New York: Springer-Verlag, 1989), pp. 200–201.

[44]Helen Raskin White, Robert J. Pandina, and Randy L. LaGrange, "Longitudinal Predictors of Serious Substance Use and Delinquency," p. 735.

[45]Marvin E. Wolfgang, *Patterns in Criminal Homicide* (Philadelphia: University of Pennsylvania Press, 1958).

the influence of liquor at the time of their offense.[46] There are several theories to explain the association of violence and drinking, including those in which alcohol leads to aggression through physical effects on the brain. More psychologically oriented theories suggest that people expect alcohol to reduce their inhibitions, and this expectation leads them to act more aggressively.[47] Although these theories are partially supported by research, there is still some controversy over the specific way in which alcohol leads to aggression. What is widely accepted, though, is the fact that alcohol contributes to violent crime by some of the people who use it.

It is considerably less certain that claims that other drugs contribute to violent crime are true. As a matter of fact, in the case of marijuana, it has become increasingly clear that violence is not usually a result of use. Reversing many earlier government reports, the National Commission on Marihuana and Drug Abuse found:

> There is no systematic empirical evidence, at least that is drawn from the American experience, to support the thesis that the use of marihuana either inevitably or generally causes, leads to or precipitates criminal, violent, aggressive or delinquent behavior of a sexual or nonsexual nature. . . . If anything, the effects observed suggest that marihuana may be more likely to neutralize criminal behavior and to militate against the commission of aggressive acts.[48]

Although marijuana use does not cause increased illegal activity, except as directly related to obtaining and using the drug, many people who break laws unrelated to drug use do use marijuana:

> Delinquency and criminality tend to precede nonopiate drug use. The association between marihuana use and criminality is due mainly to the fact that persons with unconventional attitudes become involved in both delinquency and drug use—although the vast majority of smokers are not involved in crime.[49]

This underscores our point that a high proportion of youths who are involved with the juvenile justice system for breaking non-drug-related laws will be marijuana users, though this use is not an influence on their other illegal activities.

PCP is another drug which, according to some experts, results in violence. In one study, twenty regular users (three or more times per week) were interviewed, and some of this group did report becoming violent since they began taking the drug:

[46]Jared R. Tinklenberg, "Alcohol and Violence," in *Alcoholism: Progress in Research and Treatment*, eds. Peter G. Bourne and Ruth Fox (New York: Academic Press, Inc., 1973), pp. 195–210.

[47]For reviews of these and other theories see Bartol, *Criminal Behavior: A Psychosocial Approach*, pp. 346–351.

[48]National Commission on Marihuana and Drug Abuse, *Marihuana: A Signal of Misunderstanding*, Appendix, Vol. 1 (Washington, D.C.: U.S. Government Printing Office, 1972), p. 470.

[49]Bruce D. Johnson and Gopal S. Uppal, "Marihuana and Youth: A Generation Gone to Pot," in *Drugs and the Youth Culture*, eds. Scarpitti and Datesman, p. 95.

Chronic phencyclidine use has culminated in a picture of violent and aggressive behavior, paranoia, delusional thinking, and auditory hallucinations. In most cases, no known behavioral disturbance or psychiatric problems preceded phencyclidine use. The individual had used phencyclidine over several months or a few years with the same group of friends. For no apparent reason a sudden development of paranoia and auditory hallucinations were accompanied by violent, unpredictable behavior.[50]

The incidence with which PCP results in this type of violence is unknown. Feldman and Waldorf report that youths who considered themselves "successful" users did not require admission to treatment programs, and felt that it was unlikely that anyone under the influence of PCP would be physically capable of violent acts, since the drug brought about considerable physical disorientation.[51] These users, who ingested the drug once or twice a week, managed their dosage levels and the social situations in which they used PCP so as to minimize any difficulties. Only youths who valued "toughness" before they were acquainted with PCP seemed to act aggressively once they had used it. Users were more concerned with "burnout," which consisted of permanent lack of coordination and memory loss, than with possible violence.

Individuals who regularly use amphetamines have also become paranoid, and in that state may make threats and become aggressive and violent.[52] As with PCP, it is not known whether this occurs in a large number of instances, or whether the majority of users are able to manage their usage in such a way that they avoid any such difficulties.

Individuals addicted to costly drugs use a large amount of their income to obtain these drugs, and commit more crimes once addicted.[53] The income to purchase drugs can be obtained through illegal activity, as well as "nonpredatory crime, legitimate employment, public support, contributions from friends and/or family and miscellaneous hustling."[54] When young people, under twenty, rely on illegal activity to support an opiate habit, they most often commit property crimes, and then crimes against other people. Groups of adolescents and young adults involved in the crack cocaine market, in particular, tend to be involved in violence in the course of "doing business."[55] We can conclude that

[50]Lerner and Burns, "Youthful Phencyclidine (PCP) Users," p. 344.

[51]Feldman and Waldorf, *Angel Dust in Four American Cities*, p. 11.

[52]Jared R. Tinklenberg and Richard C. Stillman, "Drug Use and Violence," in *Violence and the Struggle for Existence*, eds. David N. Daniels, Marshall F. Gilula, and Frank M. Ochberg (Boston: Little, Brown and Company, 1970), pp. 327–366; and Frederick G. Hofmann, *A Handbook on Drug and Alcohol Abuse: The Biomedical Aspects* (New York: Oxford University Press, 1975).

[53]John C. Ball, "The Criminality of Heroin Addicts: When Addicted and When Off Opiates," in *The Drugs—Crime Connection*, ed. James A. Inciardi (Beverly Hills, California: Sage Publications, 1981), pp. 17–38.

[54]James A. Inciardi, "Drug Use and Criminal Behavior: Major Research Issues," in *The Drugs—Crime Connection*, ed. Inciardi, pp. 11–12.

[55]Jeffrey Fagan and Ko Lin Chin, "Violence as Regulation and Social Control in the Distribution of Crack," in *Drugs and Violence* eds. M. de la Rosa, B. Gropper and E. Lambert, (Rockville, Maryland: Alcohol, Drug Abuse and Mental Health Administration, forthcoming).

although not all youthful addicts are involved in other types of offenses, a large number do commit property and violent crimes as a way to raise the income for drug purchases.

In many instances, youthful addicts have delinquency records *before* they use drugs.[56] The association between drug use and other illegal activities occurs not because one causes the other, but because both have a common cause:

> Where high rates of opiate use are apparent, high levels of poverty, delinquency, and other social problems are likely to be found. The issue then becomes not one of a relationship between drug abuse and street crime, but rather, an interpretation of the conditions under which drugs and youth crime are likely to emerge and manifest themselves.[57]

At least insofar as the addicting opiates are concerned, it does not seem that reducing drug abuse would dramatically reduce other types of criminal activities. Instead, there is a need to attack more directly the root causes of both of these problems, which in many cases will be the same.

It is quite clear that, although alcohol abuse stimulates violent behavior, we are as yet uncertain that other drugs stimulate violent delinquent acts to any great extent. Even the necessity for raising funds to support a heroin addiction may not greatly influence delinquent activity, since addicts exhibit high levels of illegal behavior before they use drugs regularly. All of this leads us to question any causal link between drug abuse and most criminal activity, except perhaps in the case of alcohol and violence. However, there is an association between drugs and crime, since certain social conditions seem to stimulate both, with the result that many youthful offenders will commit a variety of crimes including drug abuse. In the next section we will discuss the ramifications of this overlap for handling drug users in the juvenile justice system.

HANDLING DRUG ABUSERS IN THE JUVENILE JUSTICE SYSTEM

Depending on the political climate, current beliefs, and popular theories, one of two extreme approaches can be taken to handling the drug abusers in the juvenile justice system. At one extreme, the "criminal model" can be used. With this model, drug abuse is seen as nothing other than a criminal activity to be deterred by punishment, and through law enforcement activities that limit the availability of illegal substances. At the other extreme, a "treatment model" can be used. With the treatment model, drug abuse is seen as a result of various individual and social difficulties, which can be controlled much like an illness. The causes can be removed, or at least modified, and this will bring an end to drug abuse. In reality, neither of these extremes is relied upon exclusively, and usually there is a

---

[56]James A. Inciardi, "Youth, Drugs, and Street Crime," in *Drugs and the Youth Culture*, eds. Scarpitti and Datesman, p. 194.

[57]*Ibid.*, p. 195; also see Elliott and Huizinga, *The Relationship Between Delinquent Behaviors and ADM Problems*, pp. 96–97.

mixed model, with joint use by juvenile justice and law enforcement personnel of both treatment and punishment for the drug-abusing teenager. As a result, there is considerable overlap between voluntary treatment programs and the formal components of the juvenile justice system. Individual youths may be referred from one to the other, or they may find themselves involved in both systems.

The overlap between drug treatment programs and the juvenile justice system is very clearly illustrated from a survey of 2,750 youths in 97 drug treatment programs. The survey is called the National Youth Polydrug Study, and is one of the most ambitious efforts to understand the experiences and psychological makeup of youths who abuse drugs. In the study,

> 73 percent [of the youths] had been picked up by the police; 36 percent had been incarcerated; and 32 percent were referred to treatment by the criminal justice system. Regardless of the criminal offense examined (that is, public or private property, drug use, possession, or drug sales), those youths who had used any of the substances examined were more likely to report involvement in criminal behavior, arrest for that behavior, and conviction.[58]

Not only are youths in drug treatment programs likely to have broken a variety of laws, but they have had considerable involvement with the juvenile justice system. In many cases, this involvement resulted in a referral out of the juvenile justice system for either required or voluntary treatment in a program specifically designed for drug abusers.

From an analysis of almost 393,000 cases processed in 696 courts in 15 states, the National Center for Juvenile Justice found that about 7 percent of cases involve a drug offense and 7 percent involve an alcohol offense. Exhibit 11-2 summarizes several of the key findings from the study, which confirmed that many of these cases are handled informally through referral to various treatment programs. However, there is tremendous variation between courts in how they respond to drug and alcohol cases—with one state prosecuting 12 percent of drug cases and another prosecuting 80 percent.

Despite the overall tendency to treat all but the repeat or trafficking drug offender informally, by 1987 there was enough of a shift towards a "criminal model" of treatment to account for a marked use in detention for drug offenders.[59] Although the number of drug cases increased one percent between 1985 and 1986, the use of detention increased by 21 percent. Because a high proportion of the drug offenders were black or Hispanic, the net result was a dramatic increase in the proportion of minority youth who were in detention facilities.

For those youths who are involved with the juvenile justice system, the

---

[58]Carl G. Leukefeld and Richard R. Clayton, "Drug Abuse and Delinquency: A Study of Youths in Treatment," in *Youth Drug Abuse: Problems, Issues, and Treatment*, eds. Beschner and Friedman, p. 225.

[59]Howard N. Snyder, *Growth in Minority Detentions Attributed to Drug Law Violations* (Washington, D.C.: Office of Juvenile Justice and Delinquency Prevention, March, 1990).

Exhibit 11-2   Juvenile Court and drug abuse

The Overlap between Juvenile Court Cases and Drug Abuse, 1984

- Juvenile courts handled three drug cases and three alcohol cases for every 1,000 youth ages 10 through 17 living within their jurisdiction.
- Drug cases were more common in large counties, but alcohol cases were more common in small ones.
- More than half the youth referred to juvenile court for a drug or alcohol offense had been referred to juvenile court at least once before.
- Juvenile courts responded formally to alcohol and drug cases much less often than to other delinquency cases.
- Courts were more likely to handle drug cases formally than alcohol cases.
- When drug and alcohol cases were handled formally, most youth were placed on probation or in residential facilities.
- Drug possession cases were just as likely to be processed formally by juvenile courts as were drug trafficking cases.
- Driving-under-the-influence cases were more likely to be handled formally than other alcohol cases.

SOURCE: Terrence S. Donahue, "Juvenile Courts Vary Greatly in How They Handle Drug and Alcohol Cases," *NIJ Reports*, no. 215 (July/August 1989), pp. 10–13.

National Institute on Drug Abuse has recommended that large numbers be referred into community-based treatment programs.[60] This is in keeping with the recognition that the juvenile and criminal justice systems are frequently the only formal agencies to identify drug abuse problems, and to alert youngsters to the need to take part in treatment programs. The referrals can be considered as a part of a diversion effort, or as conditions of probation. The use of the juvenile justice system to refer youths into treatment is not without its problems, however. Frequently adolescents who use drugs see treatment programs as an extension of the criminal justice system, and for that reason they avoid the programs. There are motivational problems too:

> Adolescents directed by the criminal justice system into treatment may demonstrate a lack of motivation or interest in participating in a serious and authentic way in the therapeutic process. Thus, the treatment experience may be a failure for a young drug abuser who views it only as "something better than jail."[61]

In spite of these difficulties, some youths who are initially unmotivated to participate in drug treatment programs do develop an interest once they are in the program, even if they attend as a result of pressure from police, probation officers, or other adults.[62] For this reason, referral should be considered as one

[60] National Institute on Drug Abuse, *Criminal Justice Alternatives for Disposition of Drug Abusing Offender Cases* (Washington, D.C.: U.S. Government Printing Office, 1978).

[61] David Smith, Stephen J. Levy, and Diane E. Striar, "Treatment Services for Youthful Drug Users," in *Youth Drug Abuse: Problems, Issues, and Treatment*, eds. Beschner and Friedman, p. 565.

[62] *Ibid.*, p. 565.

way to handle juvenile justice system clients, though it may not always be an effective strategy.

In the next section, we will review a number of programs which are available to adolescent drug users, and which can be used for youths who are involved in the justice system as well as those who are not.

DRUG ABUSE PROGRAMS

Drug abuse programs were initially developed on a large scale to serve adults addicted to opiates. You may recall that this is highly consistent with the early image of the addict as a heroin user from the ghetto. According to the Drug Enforcement Administration:

> Until recently, the public has regarded addicts as incurable. Once "hooked" there was no road back. This idea arose from the fact that so many opiate addicts relapsed to drug use, even after long periods of hospitalization. Not long ago, treatment for addiction consisted of little more than withdrawal from the drug and detoxification. When more ambitious programs were attempted, they had only limited success in terms of "cured" addicts, but each contributed to knowledge about the addict, the drugs he uses and the ways to effect his rehabilitation.[63]

Drug rehabilitation and prevention programs today encompass much more than withdrawal and detoxification, and extend to such community services as mental health clinics, educational facilities, and employment programs. Although drug treatment programs have changed rapidly to provide services in the community and to assist people who use drugs other than heroin, the initial program models which were used to treat addicts remain influential. These early programs, which are still used today, will be described in the next section.

Early Efforts to Treat Heroin Addicts

The Public Health Services Hospitals initially established treatment facilities for addicts at Lexington, Kentucky, in 1935, and at Forth Worth, Texas, in 1938. Addicts can voluntarily commit themselves to treatment at these hospitals or can be committed by the court. Treatment consists of decreasing dosages of morphine or methadone, as well as vocational and psychiatric care. Many times the positive gains that were made at these hospitals could not be maintained because of a lack of viable community programs to assist the addict after release back to the community. When specific community services are not provided, the chance for the addict to become a productive citizen is very limited. The Narcotic Addict Rehabilitation Act of 1966 has been very effective in helping to combat addiction. It specified that federal support could be given to states and commu-

---

[63]*Fact Sheets*, Drug Enforcement Administration, p. 12.

nities for training programs and for the construction, staffing, and operation of new addiction treatment facilities on a joint federal-state basis. Because of the increased resources provided by the federal government, many states developed programs in private hospitals, halfway houses, service organizations, and other community-based organizations.

A major advance in community treatment was the Synanon program, a private organization that focused on rehabilitating the narcotic addict. The Synanon program, initiated by Chuck Dederich, began in 1958 as an experimental project in response to the drug problem. The residents live, work, and interact in the "therapeutic community" of the Synanon program. Synanon, and other programs modeled after it, use a combination of treatment methods, including milieu therapy, reality therapy, and behavior modification (see Chapter 8). On a twenty-four-hour basis, residents are confronted with their own responsibilities and taught by staff to cope with day-to-day decisions in a constructive way. Rewards are frequently in the form of increased privileges, both within the program and in the larger community. Punishments can include removal of these privileges, as well as public admonishments for not facing up to one's responsibilities. In some cases, these punishments can be very harsh, and include forced wearing of a sign declaring some failure within the program, or even a shaved head to symbolize the failure. Staff are primarily previous clients of Synanon, and they are familiar with the destructive coping mechanisms commonly used by drug addicts. In order that clients are able to develop positive lifestyles, vocational skills are emphasized in the program, as well as healthy patterns of interaction with other people.

Numerous drug programs based on the Synanon concept exist in various communities today, and many of these accept adolescents. In some cases they have been developed to meet adolescents' special needs, such as the development of educational skills. Programs based on the Synanon concept are highly structured, and provide twenty-four-hour supervision. For that reason, youths who otherwise might require placement in state correctional institutions can be referred to them to provide more specialized help with a drug abuse problem.

The Public Health Service Hospital type of program is used considerably less today than when it first began, and has never affected large numbers of youths. The availability of community-based methadone maintenance programs has made it possible for addicts to remain in their communities while they reduce their physical dependence on heroin. Methadone is a synthetic pain killer which blocks the euphoric high from, and the physical cravings for, heroin.

Programs for Adolescents

Since the Synanon-type of program and the methadone maintenance programs began, a wide variety of other treatment approaches have been developed. It should be noted, however, that even though we have several different kinds of programs available, there are not enough in operation to fully meet the needs of adolescents.[64] In 1982, only 12 percent of the people entering a drug treatment program were adolescents, and many of them were in the programs designed for heroin use even though they were marijuana users. There also is a very serious lack of alcohol programs designed specifically for adolescents.[65]

Special alternatives for the adolescent drug abuser are necessary because, due to their developmental stage, youths have different needs than do adults:

> It has been learned that many treatment approaches, particularly the harsher forms of group therapy and behavior modification, are generally inappropriate for treating youthful drug users. These therapeutic approaches enforce a rigid standard of conformity that can stifle the personal growth and development so important in adolescents.[66]

Additionally, as we have already noted, most adolescent drug abusers are not primarily heroin users, whereas the Synanon program and methadone maintenance program are geared toward these addicts.

Our discussion of the reasons for drug abuse, as well as Chapter 4 on the family and juvenile delinquency, stressed the importance of parental attitudes and actions in influencing youths to take part in illegal activities. The majority of adults in drug treatment programs are independent of their parents, and treatment approaches are therefore aimed at helping them take responsibility for themselves or in some cases for their own spouses and children. Youthful drug abusers have a special need for therapy which helps them improve their relations with parents, and helps the family to become a positive influence on the youngster. A survey of youths in various programs confirms this, for nearly half of the clients reported that "family-related problems" were a reason for their seeking treatment. Only "substance-abuse problems" was a more frequently expressed motivation for seeking help.[67] In addition to a focus on parents, drug abuse prevention and treatment programs currently stress the involvement of peers and the development of alternatives to drug abuse.

Pure Prevention Programs. Drug education programs have been used extensively for adolescents. In fact, all fifty states have legislation which requires alcohol education programs in the public schools. There is now research evidence that youths can be convinced of the negative effects of drugs, and that they will respond with a decreased demand for illegal substances.

J. Michael Polich, Phyllis Ellickson, Peter Reuter, and James Kahan found that school-based programs reduced the number of cigarette smokers by

[64]J. Michael Polich, Phyllis L. Ellickson, Peter Reuter, and James P. Kahan, *Strategies for Controlling Adolescent Drug Use* (Santa Monica, California: The Rand Corporation, 1984).

[65]Claudia J. Kelly and Jean B. MacNeur, *Treatment Alternatives for Juvenile Alcohol and Drug Abusers: A Six-State Survey* (Sacramento, California: Center for the Assessment of the Juvenile Justice System, American Justice Institute, 1982).

[66]Smith, Levy, and Striar, "Treatment Services for Youthful Drug Users," p. 564.

[67]*Ibid.*, p. 565.

over one-third.[68] The successful programs first repeated the messages and arguments that peers, adults and the media use in favor of smoking. Then, the programs taught youngsters how to counter each argument. Youths practiced ways of saying that they did not want to smoke "gracefully." As further support for refusing to smoke, youths were told about the short-term effects of smoking, such as bad breath and discolored teeth. Long-term health effects, which seem uncertain and distant to most young people, were not the emphasis.

The lessons to be learned from the effective cigarette smoking education programs are reviewed by Polich and his coauthors. They suggest that it is most effective to use pure prevention programs aimed at seventh graders, who are just at the age when drug experimentation becomes common. Youth can be taught, for example, that marijuana impairs memory and motor skills, as well as leading to the longer-term health problems of lung disease and reproductive disfunctions. Such facts, coupled with practical assistance in the learning of techniques for resisting peer pressure, would be major components of a pure prevention effort.

The current thrust in the design of prevention programs is to involve peers, to emphasize parent involvement, and to empower communities to develop and operate their own programs. This thrust is consistent with research findings that a prevention program limited to the provision of information can have negative effects, but programs that rely on peer strategies, improvement of affective skills (communication skills, self-assertion skills), and experiences that promote positive experiences in areas like communication are most effective.[69]

There are several ways that peers can be involved in prevention programs. These programs include:

- *Positive peer influence* programs emphasize group interaction among peers and positive potential of peer intragroup and individual influence.
- *Peer teaching* programs emphasize the role of young people in conveying various kinds of information to their peers—about basic literacy skills or positive health practices, for example.
- *Peer counseling/facilitating/helping* programs focus more on the role of the peer group member as a helper of others. In many cases, research has repeatedly shown, the helper is the principal beneficiary of these kinds of programs; often the act of helping another person is the first opportunity a youth has to experience a sense of meaningful responsibility in the world outside the home.
- *Peer participation* programs focus primarily on creating new roles for youth within the school or the larger society by giving program participants decision-making powers and responsibilities that may place them on a peer level with adults. Peer participation programs tend to focus on older adolescents.[70]

[68]Polich, Ellickson, Reuter, and Kahan, *Strategies for Controlling Adolescent Drug Use.*

[69]Eric Schaps, Russell DiBartolo, Joel Moskowitz, Carol S. Palley, and Shoshanna Churgin, "A Review of 127 Drug Abuse Prevention Program Evaluations," *Journal of Drug Issues, 11,* no. 1 (Winter 1981), pp. 17–43.

[70]U.S. Department of Health and Human Services, *Adolescent Peer Pressure: Theory, Correlates, and Program Implications for Drug Abuse Prevention* (Rockville, Maryland: National Institute on Drug Abuse, Division of Prevention and Treatment Development, 1981), p. 55.

Exhibit 11-3   Peers in abuse prevention

Patty Basulto

Patty Basulto has always been a leader and speaks out about what she believes. Even so, her friends in the small town of Pittsburg, California, near San Francisco, where she is a junior in high school, were surprised when she started speaking out against drug use.

"A lot of my friends said, 'Wow, you're crazy doing this,' " Patty recalls. "They reminded me that I used to do it, and it's true—I did use drugs at one time. I told them, 'I'm trying to prevent it from happening to others. I was dumb for using whatever I used.' They said, 'Well, you still do it, don't you?' And I said, 'No, I don't. I don't mess around with drugs any more.' "

Some of Patty's friends put her down for not using drugs. Others agreed with her. As Patty recalls it, the put-downs didn't bother her. She'd made a decision not to use drugs, and she wasn't going to let peer pressure change her mind.

Now, as a member of the Youth Educator Program in her community, Patty has the first-hand knowledge to teach younger people about drugs and peer pressure. Through the program, sponsored by the Center for Human Development, Patty meets once a week with two classes of seventh-grade students to discuss information about alcohol and other drugs, why young people use drugs, and how to say "no" to peer pressure. Patty is learning a great deal about drugs herself through the program. She attends a class one night every week so she can gain increased understanding about the problem.

Patty was shocked when some of the seventh-graders told her they had started using drugs heavily in fifth grade. The seventh-graders said they'd used many different kinds of drugs and that they liked to feel "crazy" on drugs. But Patty was determined to teach them that you can make it through life a lot better without drugs.

One thing Patty found was that the peer pressure to use drugs in seventh grade was so strong that many of the students didn't want to participate in her class. "But then they'd take their papers home and do their homework and show it to me at the end of class," Patty says. "That way their friends wouldn't see that they'd done it." In Patty's opinion, the ones who got the most from the class were the students who thought they were cool and knew everything. Patty felt she'd really accomplished something when some of the "cool" seventh-graders told her they were learning new information about drugs they'd never known before.

Patty believes that if it hadn't been for the Youth Educator Program she might still be tempted to use drugs. Without the program, she says, it would have been a lot harder to resist the peer pressure. "This program has changed my life," Patty says. "It was like Boom! There it was, and I stopped using drugs."

Patty volunteered for the Youth Educator Program because she thought it would be interesting to work with younger kids. "A lot of my friends said, 'You know you're not going to get paid for it,' " she recalls. But that didn't bother her. "I told them that it was enough for me to know I was helping other people."

Exhibit 11-3 Cont.

Teaching about drugs and the problems that occur from drug use has become an important part of Patty's life. Still, sometimes she feels bad when she sees how many kids in her community are involved with drugs. "A lot of kids may have to find out about drugs the hard way," she says. "I tell my students in the program, 'What is it going to take? Is it going to take a death of one of your friends or even yourself to find out what harm drugs can do?' And I tell them what I've learned myself. You don't need drugs to be happy."

SOURCE: Tom Adams and Hank Resnik, *Teens in Action: Creating a Drug-Free Future for America's Youth* (Rockville, Maryland: U.S Department of Health and Human Services, 1985), pp. 8–9.

Issues for Discussion. What conditions are necessary in the peer group, the school, and the community for a peer group prevention program to work? What are the potential benefits and disadvantages of the Youth Educator Program to the peer educators and to other youths?

The peer strategies go beyond the education approach by trying to develop meaningful roles, activities, and opportunities for adolescents to take part in decisions that affect their own lives.[71] They also try to counteract negative peer pressure that encourages youth to take part in self-destructive activities, and to develop social and other skills that youths need to make sound decisions and resist peer pressure. As one part of the national effort to prevent drug abuse, the federal government has published information to give examples of the involvement of peers in abuse prevention (Exhibit 11-3).

Parents are important to the prevention of drug abuse, for they often are the most concerned community members, and therefore will invest their own energies and resources in program development and operation. Legislators have recognized the National Federation of Parents for Drug Free Youth, which is made up of several community groups of concerned parents.[72] In just the area of marijuana use, parent groups spread information from the new research on health hazards, lobbied against drug paraphernalia dealers selling to children in local stores, set up standard curfews and party rules, and worked directly to discourage drug use by their children. The federal government has encouraged the involvement of parent groups by supplying expertise and information, as well as many educational materials. One key element in the parents' efforts is involvement in public school by, for example, contacting the parents of absent children on a daily basis, monitoring school grounds, and chaperoning school events. Parents also have worked to change legislation, for example, the legal drinking age, and have formed their own peer pressure groups so that parents can present a united front to their children.

In addition to calling on peers and parents to prevent drug abuse, cur-

[71]*Ibid.*, pp. 48–49.

[72]Marsha Manatt, *Parents, Peers and Pot II: Parents in Action* (Rockville, Maryland: National Institute on Drug Abuse, 1983), p. iii.

rent federal programs emphasize state organizations and the private sector.[73] For example, in Texas the state agency concerned with drug abuse joined with ministers in black and Hispanic communities. Training materials and procedures were developed for ministers. Other community-based efforts have trained volunteers to make presentations to school children or have organized coalitions of existing community groups and leaders.

An idea that runs through much of the contemporary thinking on drug abuse prevention is that peers, parents, or even the community must provide alternatives to drugs as a source of recreation or status. The National Institute on Drug Abuse completed a survey to locate programs across the country which provide youths with alternatives to drug use. The project was called the *National Search for Youth Initiatives in Drug Abuse Prevention,* and it tried to locate community- and neighborhood-based projects in which youths themselves had an active and key role to play in managing the program.[74] Three examples of these programs follow:

[The *Community High School* sponsors an] . . . environmental action group . . . dedicated to working with industry and business to effect changes in attitude and behavior. Their first project has been the aerosol controversy, conducting consumer research, lobbying, public education, and contact with manufacturers. They have worked in elementary classes with slide presentations, published a newsletter and activities with local parties, environmental crusades, hospitals, child care, and volunteer work. The focus is on youth 13 to 19 and the groups work with young people, numbering from 30 to 129 at any given time.[75]

Gloucester Experiment is a community partnership project with broad agency participation. Its multifaceted alternative programming includes: career exploration, paraprofessional training, revitalization of lost crafts and trades, referrals, counseling, and restoration of colonial burial grounds and monuments. Since May of 1973 6 staff members and the 100 community volunteers have serviced 100 high-risk young people annually between the ages of 16 and 26. The youth participants are moving toward paraprofessional status; they accept responsibility and have input into the program.[76]

[The *Tierra Motorcycle and Small Engine Repair Institute* in El Paso, Texas] . . . provides youth and young adults with: (1) viable alternatives to drugs; (2) training in a marketable skill; and (3) training in the area of basic survival skills. These goals are accomplished by actual work in a motorcycle shop. Each individual is instructed over 500 hours and his/her final exam consists of breaking down a motorcycle and then putting it back together. Vocational counseling is done during the work period. There are two paid workers.[77]

Each of these programs gives participants a sense of control over their own lives and over the program itself and other institutions they come into contact with.

[73]U.S. Department of Health and Human Services, "Spotlighting Knowledge: Prevention Research and Knowledge Development, *Prevention Resources, 6,* no. 3 (Fall 1983), pp. 8–10.

[74]*Alternatives for Young Americans* (Washington, D.C.: U.S. Government Printing Office, 1979).

[75]*Ibid.,* p. 181.

[76]*Ibid.,* p. 34.

[77]*Ibid.,* p. 311.

The National Institute has published a catalogue of these and many other programs which can be considered as alternatives to drug abuse. The programs were identified by panels of experts along with representatives of youth groups.

The notion that we can prevent delinquency, including drug abuse, through the provision of alternative opportunities and through large-scale programs aimed at peers, parents, and community is not new to you. As you remember from reading Chapter 7, the early criminologists sought to organize the community to stop delinquency. Research does not provide us with a clear indication of whether or not the community-based strategies are effective. However, some program treatment methods appear to be better than others. In particular, peer and parent involvement seem to be essential ingredients in effective prevention programs.

Programs for Drug Abuser. The elements of effective programs for youths who are already involved in drug abuse do not differ significantly from the characteristics of effective pure prevention programs. In particular, institutionalized delinquents are most likely to reduce drug use during treatment when special services, such as contraceptive and vocational counseling, are provided. The most promising strategies for reduced recidivism after treatment are training in social and self-control skills, encouraging responsibility, and building peer groups that do not promote use.[78] More generally, effective drug programs for delinquents focus on family and peer interactions.

The *Juvenile Intervention Program* (JIP) was designed to treat youths with drug-related problems who are between the ages of thirteen and seventeen.[79] Unlike many other educational programs, JIP included parents in the educational effort. Six weekly two-hour sessions were held with the youth and the family participating in small groups, but not the same group. After the initial introductory sessions, other sessions were devoted to providing information about drugs, explaining relaxation as an alternate "high," improving family communication skills, and in other ways improving the family environment and interactions. The purpose of these educational topics was to improve the family atmosphere and thus improve each youth's self-esteem.

Most of the JIP participants were referred from the juvenile justice system, though 20 percent were self-referred and 20 percent were referred by schools. An evaluation of 111 of the youths who completed the program showed that the self-esteem levels of the juveniles, their family communication patterns, and their ability to communicate with their mothers significantly improved, but knowledge of drugs and communication with fathers did not. There was a decrease in contact with the juvenile justice system, and although the participants continued to use drugs, they did not use them as regularly.

[78]Richard F. Catalano, Elizabeth A. Wells, Jeffrey M. Jenson and J. David Haskins, "Aftercare Services for Drug-Using Institutionalized Delinquents," *Social Service Review, 63,* no. 4 (December 1989), pp. 553–577.

[79]Donald C. Iverson and Tom E. Roberts, "The Juvenile Intervention Program: Results of the Process, Impact and Outcome Evaluations," *Journal of Drug Education, 10,* no. 4 (1980), pp. 289–300.

The *Teen Challenge Program* had a religious orientation, and it attempted to convert the client to a "Born Again" Christian.[80] The program began in New York City in 1958, and by 1974 had grown to include eighty-eight branches in twenty-six states and jurisdictions. It involved a detoxification phase and then an eight-month to one-year placement in a therapeutic community that emphasizes spiritual support, vocational assistance, and education in a closely supervised setting. A follow-up period of reentry into the community provided further support once the youth left the residential placement. Throughout treatment, abstinence from drug use was tied closely to the religious beliefs of the group, and extended to all alcohol and tobacco. Participation in the religious activities of the faith of Pentecostal Protestantism was required to succeed in the program, and therefore the religious community could, in a sense, be seen as a major replacement for prior drug-related associations.

An evaluation of the Teen Challenge Program revealed few differences between the youths who were participants and those who took part in other similar drug abuse programs. In this study, of 336 youths in the program, staff considered 67 (18.3 percent) to be graduates of the program, and therefore to have successfully completed the treatment.[81] A follow-up interview confirmed that graduates were functioning more effectively than dropouts in terms of changes in arrest and educational status as well as employment. In addition, graduates made less use of alcohol and tobacco and were more optimistic regarding their state of health.[82]

The dropouts did seem to receive benefits from the programs, though, since they were less involved in heroin use than before their participation. As a result of the religious orientation of the treatment program, several graduates had become ministers or completed Bible College, and even a few of the program dropouts had accomplished these objectives.

The Teen Challenge Program seems to be most suited to youths who are religious before their involvement, and for those who become readily involved in the religious aspect of the program. Its overall success rate, as measured by the number of program graduates, is comparable to other similar programs. Although it is difficult to separate the effects of the religious component of the program from other parts, and from the effects of programs besides Teen Challenge that the participants might have attended, the evaluation suggests that involvement in a religious community is apparently an effective alternative to drug abuse for some youths.[83]

The Learning Laboratory is a final example of a promising treatment program for youths who abuse drugs.[84] It operated in New York City, and served youths ages 12 through 21. Most participants were dropouts and unemployed,

[80]"An Evaluation of the Teen Challenge Treatment Program" (Rockville, Maryland: Alcohol, Drug Abuse, and Mental Health Administration, 1977).

[81]*Ibid.*, p. 4.

[82]*Ibid.*, p. 8.

[83]*Ibid.*, pp. 12–13.

[84]U.S. Department of Health and Human Services, *The Learning Laboratory: The Door—a Center of Alternatives* (Rockville, Maryland: National Institute on Drug Abuse, 1980).

some used opiates, and most used nonopiate drugs frequently. Most of the participants had an arrest history, but few had been convicted and imprisoned. The objective of the program was to give youngsters who had failed in school and in life a chance to build self-esteem and competence in core life skills and academic and vocational skills. In addition to an individualized academic program, The Learning Laboratory ran theme-centered workshops on topics such as values clarification, problem solving, career education, and cultural studies. Two large companies and volunteers staffed prevocational skills training workshops in electricity, electronics, bookkeeping, accounting, and photography. Special projects and field trips focused on sexuality, family planning, the legal rights of minors, and other topics of immediate relevance to the youths. Weekly community meetings to resolve program issues, for example, being on time or making new youth welcome, and counseling also were important parts of the program. A before-and-after study showed that participants improved in educational progress, drug use patterns, and involvement in purposeful activities, but after the program ended, clients still required vocational skill training and experienced financial hardships.

Even though there are some promising strategies to be used with adolescent drug abusers, we are still in a stage of program development where there are many questions about the effectiveness of programs, particularly with certain subgroups. It would seem that an investment in prevention in the initial stages, for the "gateway substances of tobacco, alcohol, and marijuana," deserves continued attention. The National Institute on Drug Abuse has recommended this prevention strategy as an important complement to programs for youths who are already heavily involved in drug use.

The Adequacy of Drug Abuse Programs

Drug and alcohol abuse programs differ considerably from each other in their target populations, the type of drug abuse they are designed to control, and their choice of treatment strategy. This diversity makes it difficult to reach any general conclusions about the overall effectiveness of existent programs, though the examples which we have given above show that some programs are at least potentially effective. Even for some of these, however, we could not draw very firm conclusions, since there is often no well-designed evaluation study to provide solid evidence of program impacts over the long run.

A 1980 publication, *An Assessment of Evaluations of Drug Abuse Prevention Programs*, describes a comprehensive survey of the literature which located fifty-two studies.[85] These programs used one or more of four basic strategies: (1) providing information; (2) clarifying or changing values; (3) involving youths in alternatives to drug abuse; (4) counseling. Most of the programs were concerned with several types of drugs, which is consistent with youths' tendencies

---

[85]Richard L. Janvier, David R. Guthmann, and Richard F. Catalano, Jr., *Reports of the National Juvenile Justice Assessment Centers: An Assessment of Evaluations of Drug Abuse Prevention Programs* (Washington, D.C.: U.S. Government Printing Office, 1980).

toward polydrug use. Unfortunately, only nine of the studies had adequate research designs and measured the effect of the program on future drug use. Based on just these nine studies, the programs which emphasize value change and the provision of alternatives to drug abuse seemed most successful. Such a small number of evaluations is much too limited a basis for conclusions, but the *Assessment of Evaluations of Drug Abuse Prevention Programs* at least points out the need for more research and some promising directions for the development of programs.

The conclusion from a review of drug treatment programs is similar to the one regarding prevention programs:

> There has been a great diversity of services and modalities established to treat adolescent drug abuse, but thus far there has been a failure to design and test distinct treatment models that can be replicated in the field. Most youth programs in existence have not evaluated their services because of a lack of resources and research capability. The literature on the evaluation of treatment and rehabilitative methods and approaches for youthful drug abusers is limited. The result has been a reliance on hearsay and "plain common sense" in attempting to determine the most appropriate services for youngsters with drug problems.[86]

In addition to the lack of information, we have already mentioned the problem of locating programs which specifically meet the developmental needs of adolescents. The difficulty of locating adequate programs is compounded by programs which ignore the overlap between drug abuse and other delinquency, and attempt to treat just one of these problem areas, or restrict participants to those with a history of just one problem.

Females are at a particular disadvantage in being matched with a drug abuse program to meet their needs. Drug abuse programs are generally dominated by males, and therefore they use methods such as aggressive confrontation which are not necessarily well suited to females' patterns of behavior.[87] Drug abuse programs are frequently not designed to treat the causes of females' behavior:

> At the root of many adolescent female drug problems lie anxiety, concern, ignorance, and ambivalence about sexuality and reproductive functioning. A large number of young drug users are struggling with fears about homosexuality. Female sexuality and physiology are little understood by most men (who dominate the treatment scene) . . . and thus little emotional or medical attention is given to these problems.[88]

Within therapeutic communities, girls are forced into "female" activities, such as kitchen work, whereas boys have a greater variety of activities available to

---

[86]Smith, Levy, and Striar, "Treatment Services for Youthful Drug Users," pp. 566–567.
[87]George M. Beschner and Kerry G. Treasure, "Female Adolescent Drug Use," in *Youth Drug Abuse: Problems, Issues, and Treatment*, eds. Beschner and Friedman, p. 203.
[88]*Ibid.*, p. 203.

them.[89] In referring a girl to a drug abuse program, it is imperative that some attempt be made to ensure that the program meets her particular needs, some of which can be related to her gender, and that the problems described above be avoided to the extent that it is possible.

It also is important to take social class into account in the development of drug abuse prevention and treatment programs. The middle-class peer culture tends to emphasize competition and resulting groups of "winners" and "losers."[90] Losers are particularly susceptible to pressures towards substance abuse. A different dynamic operates in lower-class groups, where the street culture promotes a view of the entire community as an "out group." The pervasive problems of unemployment, poverty, and often racism must be dealt with in the program design, along with the typical peer group values that reflect an alienation from school and an identification of masculinity with aggression, bravado, and petty crime.[91] If the program is to use a peer group strategy, it might profitably draw on some of the principles of Positive Peer Culture (Chapter 8) that allow for a direct examination and reshaping of values. In lower-class communities, programs with the objective of offering youths alternatives to drug use must often develop the educational, recreational, and employment options.

We have described several promising drug abuse programs, and pointed out the inadequacies that exist in the treatment system of drug abuse programs for adolescents, particularly those who also are delinquent or female. The current state of our knowledge from research only suggests the program models which might be most effective, and more study is required to draw any sound conclusions regarding the most useful programs.

SUMMARY

In this chapter, we have discussed the effects of a great variety of drugs used by adolescents. These range from the frequently used marijuana and alcohol to the rarely used heroin. Between these drugs are substances such as crack, cocaine, and a variety of stimulants and depressants.

During the 1960s, drug-abusing teenagers were pictured as ghetto heroin addicts. This picture has changed markedly. By the 1970s, there was a recognition of the middle-class abuser who experimented with mind-altering drugs, and now there is the view that drug use is a common activity among youths of all social classes. Today we see that there are many patterns of use, only some of them being regular or disruptive to daily activities, and many youngsters are involved in polydrug use.

The family and the status of adolescents in our society are both contributing factors in causing abuse. Causes of drug use are often causes of other

[89]*Ibid.,* p. 204.
[90]U.S. Department of Health and Human Services, *Adolescent Peer Pressure,* p. 63.
[91]*Ibid.*

delinquency, and thus there is a close connection between these two types of problem behavior.

Although there are many different types of drug prevention and treatment programs in existence, and some of these are particularly promising for the adolescent, as a whole the drug treatment system does not fully meet the needs of youths. Youths who are delinquent and who are female are especially likely to lack adequate program resources. Juvenile justice system personnel must rely on the drug treatment system as a place to make referrals, and the problems created by the inadequacies of the system are compounded by the lack of good research to indicate which programs are most effective with certain types of youths.

DISCUSSION QUESTIONS

1. In what ways are the image of the drug-abusing teenager in the 1960s and the 1970s an inadequate basis for theories and programs today?
2. What are the major causes of drug abuse among teenagers?
3. Does drug use cause other delinquent activities? In your answer, be specific about the types of drug and the types of delinquency you are talking about.
4. What are the most promising strategies for drug abuse programs for teenagers?
5. What are the major inadequacies of the drug treatment system as a place to which juvenile justice personnel can refer delinquent youngsters?
6. Review each program described in this chapter and comment on the degree to which the program meets the developmental needs of adolescents described in Chapter 4.

PROJECTS

1. Design a comprehensive system of the different types of drug abuse programs that are needed to serve your community.
2. Adapt the most successful methods for the treatment of delinquency, as described in Chapter 8, to the treatment of drug abuse. Describe an ideal program that would use these methods.
3. Make a list of the family characteristics identified in Chapter 4 as contributors to delinquency which also contribute to drug abuse. Also note the factors that contribute to early sexual activity, a failure to use birth control, and adolescent pregnancy.

12

Child Abuse and Neglect*

- THE PROBLEM AND ITS HISTORY
- THE RELATIONSHIP OF ABUSE AND NEGLECT TO DELINQUENCY
- CAUSES OF ABUSE AND NEGLECT
- LAW ENFORCEMENT, JUVENILE COURT, AND CORRECTIONAL PROGRAMS
- CHILD PROTECTIVE SERVICES

LEARNING OBJECTIVES

1. To understand the evidence that supports a connection between delinquency and both child abuse and neglect.
2. To be familiar with several theories that explain child abuse and neglect.
3. To be aware of the involvement of law enforcement, juvenile court, and correctional personnel in the prevention, detection, and treatment of child abuse and neglect cases.
4. To be able to compare the role of personnel in the juvenile justice system with that of the protective services worker in handling the abused or neglected child's case.
5. To be familiar with child protective services' programs, and related community services, which can prevent and treat abuse and neglect.

*Susan K. Wright, a graduate student at Michigan State University, was responsible for the major portion of the revision of this chapter in the third edition.

Personnel who work in the juvenile justice system are often confronted with the problems of abuse and neglect in addition to delinquency in working with any individual child. The same youths who are abused may be delinquent, for abuse can lead to delinquency. The complex social conditions that result in one of these phenomena may also result in the other. Even when there is not any such overlap in abuse and delinquency within a particular family, the juvenile justice system is frequently expected to respond to child abuse and neglect. The juvenile court has historically handled these cases along with delinquency cases under the broad mandate of the *parens patriae* philosophy. The police are in many instances called when there is an act of abuse, or they can come upon such cases in the course of other investigations. Correctional programs are sometimes used as placement options for abused and neglected children, particularly when a full diagnosis of the children's problems reveals very little difference between these categories. All of these causal and practical connections between delinquency and both abuse and neglect underscore the necessity of having some familiarity with abuse and neglect in order to develop a full understanding of juvenile delinquency and the operations of the juvenile justice system.

In this chapter, we will emphasize the linkages between delinquency and juvenile justice system operations and abuse and neglect. First, though, we will provide an overview of the general problems of abuse and neglect, beginning with a historical perspective on efforts to protect children and a review of the scope of the problem.

HISTORY OF CHILD PROTECTION

Although society may never be fully capable of protecting its children from the harm of abuse and neglect, monumental progress has been made since that day in 1874 when visiting nurse Etta Wheeler, while making her rounds, stumbled upon a nine-year-old child named Mary Ellen. At the insistence of neighbors, Wheeler entered the apartment of Mary Ellen's parents to find the child chained to a bedpost. She had obviously been beaten often and was dangerously undernourished. Wishing to take legal action, Wheeler and other interested parties discovered that there was neither legislation nor a public agency which might empower them to move in such a case.

In desperation, the nurse and her friends appealed to the Society for the Prevention of Cruelty to Animals on the basis that Mary Ellen, as a member of the animal kingdom, qualified for their aid. The society perceived its legal jurisdiction and assisted in the removal of Mary Ellen from her home.

It was the case of Mary Ellen which dramatized the fact that the welfare of animals had been considered of more importance than that of human children. As a consequence of this sobering realization, the first Society for the Prevention of Cruelty to Children was organized in New York City in 1875. Many similar organizations sprang up in various parts of the country thereafter.

For decades, only the private sector concerned itself with child abuse and neglect.

In 1946, radiologist John Caffey reported on six infant patients with subdural hematoma and a combination of twenty-three fractures and four contusions of the long bones. As a possible cause of this combination of symptoms, he cautiously suggested the possibility of parental abuse and neglect. Widespread public acknowledgment of the problem of child abuse and neglect, however, was not to come for fifteen more years.

As a result of treating four infants in a single day who had been badly battered, Dr. C. Henry Kempe and his associates undertook a national survey to determine the frequency of cases of physical abuse in a given year. In discussing the results in the *Journal of the American Medical Association*,[1] he coined the new term, the "battered child syndrome." The survey uncovered a social malady of overwhelming dimensions. The publication and dissemination of the survey was largely responsible for the child protection legislation and corrective programs that will be discussed in this chapter.

THE PROBLEM

Although it is difficult to obtain accurate statistics on child abuse and neglect, there are indications that levels are quite high in the United States. According to a 1975 survey of households, it was estimated that there are between 1,400,000 and 1,900,000 cases of parent-to-child violence annually.[2] When the survey was repeated in 1985, the amount of overall violence against children was about the same, though there was a slight drop in the most severe forms. Despite the drop in severe abuse, which might be due to parents' reluctance to report on abusive behavior, there is no doubt that many children are affected.

In recent years, increased research attention has been focused upon child sexual abuse. David Finkelhor found that 6 percent of the males and 15 percent of the females surveyed in the Boston area reported sexual abuse before age sixteen by a person at least five years older.[3] In a survey of college students, Finkelhor found that 19.2 percent of women and 8.6 percent of men had been sexually victimized during childhood. Girls were most often victimized by a family member (43 percent) or an acquaintance (33 percent), and boys were more often victimized by an acquaintance (53 percent) or a stranger (30 percent).[4] With a survey in the San Francisco area, Diana Russell showed that 12

[1]C. Henry Kempe, "The Battered Child Syndrome," *Journal of the American Medical Association, 181*, no. 1 (July 1962), pp. 17–24.

[2]Murray Straus and Richard Gelles, "Societal Change and Change in Family Violence from 1975–1985 as Revealed by Two National Surveys," *Journal of Marriage and the Family, 48*, no. 3 (August 1986), pp. 465–479.

[3]David Finkelhor, *Child Sexual Abuse: New Theory and Research* (New York: Free Press, 1984).

[4]David Finkelhor, *Sexually Victimized Children* (New York: The Free Press, 1979).

percent of women reported having been sexually abused by a relative before the age of eighteen.[5] Taken together, the different surveys point to quite high levels of sexual abuse, particularly for girls.

The *Study of National Incidence and Prevalence of Child Abuse and Neglect* provides an alternative to parent and victim surveys in order to provide an indicator of child mistreatment.[6] It relies on three sources of information:

1. Records of both substantiated and unsubstantiated cases known to the official state Child Protection Services
2. Cases known to other investigatory agencies, including the police, the courts, and public health departments
3. Cases known to professionals in major community institutions, such as hospitals, schools, daycare programs, social service agencies and mental health agencies

In 1986, the abuse cases identified through the three sources totaled 10.7 per 1,000, or 675,000 nationwide, and the neglect cases totaled 15.9 per 1,000 children, or 1,003,600 nationwide.

The study of national incidence and prevalence confirms findings from victim surveys. Girls more often than boys experience serious sexual abuse. Also, levels of abuse and neglect seem to be fairly stable, but there is greater official reporting and professionals increasingly recognize the more moderate forms of abuse as requiring some response.

The various estimated numbers of neglect and abuse cases differ from each other for several reasons. There is a wide variation in the definitions of abuse and neglect that are used by researchers. When official and agency records are the source, estimates do not reflect the many unknown cases. When parents or children are asked to report on abuse and neglect, they may be hesitant to reveal the most serious abuse, including sexual abuse. Despite the range in estimates of the incidence of abuse, they all indicate a serious and widespread problem. It also should be noted that the number of cases of abuse and neglect that are formally reported to the authorities is increasing annually.

The United States Child Abuse and Prevention Act of 1974 defines abuse and neglect as "the physical or mental injury, sexual abuse, negligent treatment, or maltreatment of a child under the age of 18 by a person who is responsible for the child's welfare." Some authorities further define neglect as failing to provide for the physical, medical, or emotional needs of a child. Physical abuse is often easier to identify than either neglect or sexual abuse because of the overt nature of the act and the likelihood that there will be observable evidence of injury. What is referred to as emotional mistreatment is the most difficult to both define and identify, but generally it includes such things as parental rejection, coldness,

[5]Diana Russell, *Sexual Exploitation: Rape, Child Sexual Abuse, and Sexual Harassment* (Beverly Hills, California: Sage, 1984).

[6]National Center on Child Abuse and Neglect, *Study of National Incidence and Prevalence of Child Abuse and Neglect: 1988* (Washington, D.C.: U.S. Department of Health and Human Services, 1988).

cruel discipline and extreme inconsistency.[7] Most emotional mistreatment is handled outside of the juvenile court and protective services agencies unless it is accompanied by physical abuse or neglect.

Cases of abuse are often identified or diagnosed in a medical setting.

The maltreated child is often brought to the hospital or private physician with a history of failure to thrive, malnutrition, anemia, poor skin hygiene, irritability, a repressed personality and other signs of obvious neglect. The more severely abused children are seen in the emergency rooms of hospitals with external evidences of body trauma; bruises, abrasions, cuts, lacerations, burns, soft tissue swelling and hematomas. Inability to move certain extremities because of dislocations and fractures associated with neurological signs of intercranial damage are additional signals that should arouse the suspicion of the attending physician. Children manifesting the maltreatment syndrome give evidence of one or more of these complaints with the most severe of the maltreatment cases arriving at the hospital or at the physician's office in coma, convulsions or even dead.[8]

Both purposeful and neglectful maltreatment can cause the conditions described above that are all too familiar to health care professionals.

The neglected child may not be as easy to identify as the physically abused child but is of equal concern to the professional in the field:

It is difficult to demonstrate that neglect is a more serious problem than abuse considering the severity of harm inflicted. If one considers the number of fatalities as the most severe manifestation of harm, then an attempt can be made to demonstrate the severity of neglect. The National Clearinghouse Report published in October, 1976, shows that 631 children died in 1974 due to abuse. . . . By contrast, nobody has tallied the number of children who died due to lack of proper medical care, or who fell out of windows or down stairs, or ingested poisonous substances, or were hit by cars—all because parents neglected to take reasonable precaution and care.[9]

Neglect is characterized by omission rather than commission as in child abuse because the caretaker of a child is failing to provide for the essential needs of the child rather than intentionally harming the child.[10] In the case of neglect, blame must frequently be placed on the family as a whole. Parents as well as other family members share in the responsibility for neglect.

Like the neglected child, the sexually abused child is quite difficult to identify. Strong taboos against sexual involvement with children mitigate against

[7]J. Garbarino and A. Garbarino, *Emotional Maltreatment of Children* (Chicago: National Committee for Prevention of Child Abuse, 1986).

[8]Vincent J. Fontana and Douglas J. Besharov, *The Maltreated Child* (Springfield, Illinois: Charles C. Thomas, Publisher, 1977), p. 15.

[9]Alfred Kadushin, "Neglect—Is It Neglected Too Often?", in *Child Abuse and Neglect: Issues on Innovation and Implementation*, Vol. 1, eds. Michael L. Lauderdale et al. (Washington, D.C.: DHEW Publication No. (OHDS) 78-80147, 1978), pp. 217–218.

[10]Carolyn Hally, Nancy F. Polansky, and Norman A. Polansky, *Child Neglect: Mobilizing Services* (Washington, D.C.: Department of Health and Human Services, 1980), pp. 3–4.

open discussion of the topic, and a pervasive belief that family matters are private make it unlikely that abuse within the family will be disclosed. In recognition of the difficulty of detecting child sexual abuse, school programs have been designed to help children understand that they have a right to decline sexual advances, and to assist them in revealing victimization. For very young children, dolls and puppets are used to assist them in talking about their bodies and sexual acts. Older youths can be approached with discussions and audiovisual material.

In most cases, the natural parent is the perpetrator of maltreatment of children. This is shown by a study of the American Humane Association, which found that fathers made up 55 percent of the abusers, and mothers made up 68 percent of the neglectors.[11] David Gil similarly found that mothers and stepmothers accounted for 50 percent of abuse incidents, and fathers for 40 percent.[12] He concluded that fathers actually were more involved than mothers when it was taken into consideration that fathers were not present in 70 percent of the homes.

The psychological impact of abuse or neglect, including emotional mistreatment, may be as severe as the outward signs of physical abuse. Harold P. Martin and Martha A. Rodeheffer commented in the following manner on the psychological effect of physical abuse:

> All too often the psychological effects of the physical assault and the psychological overlay of the resultant brain damage are overlooked. A physical assault from the very person to whom the child looks for love, nurturance, and protection is in and of itself a psychic trauma of major proportions. Parental attack results in interpersonal ambivalence and a hypervigilant preoccupation with the behavior of others. The child's constant mobilizations of his defenses in anticipation of impending danger is reinforced by intermittent sudden attacks by a parent.[13]

Adolescents who are abused suffer a wide range of emotional as well as physical problems, and they rarely seek help or even talk to someone about their difficulties.[14] Youth who are severely punished feel very guilty and express their feeling that they deserved the punishment.[15] Females in particular are withdrawn and think the abuse was justified, and many adolescents respond with delinquency, running away, and thoughts or attempts of suicide.[16]

Although sexual abuse does not usually result in any physical injury,

[11]American Humane Association, *National Analysis of Official Child Neglect and Abuse Reporting (1978)* (Washington, D.C.: U.S. Government Printing Office, 1980), p. 22.

[12]David G. Gil, "Violence Against Children," in *Child Abuse and Violence*, ed. David G. Gil (New York: AMS Press, Inc., 1979), pp. 182–183.

[13]Harold P. Martin and Martha A. Rodeheffer, "The Psychological Impact of Abuse on Children," in *Traumatic Abuse and Neglect of Children at Home*, eds. Gertrude J. Williams and John Money (Baltimore: Johns Hopkins University Press, 1980), p. 256.

[14]Patricia Libbey and Rodger Bybee, "The Physical Abuse of Adolescents," *Journal of Social Issues*, 35, no. 2 (Spring 1979), pp. 101–126.

[15]Beulah Amsterdam, Mary Brill, Noa Weiselberg Bell, and Dan Edwards, "Coping with Abuse: Adolescents' Views," *Victimology*, 4, no. 2 (1979), p. 281.

[16]*Ibid.*, p. 282.

recent research has shown that there are serious immediate and long-term emotional impacts. Jon R. Conte and his colleagues evaluated the effects on 369 children by comparing the abused youth with those who had not been abused.[17] They found substantial differences. In addition to overt behaviors, such as somatic complaints, withdrawal from activities or aggression, there were the negative psychological effects of poor concentration, difficulty in working hard, regression to behavior typical of a younger child, and poor body- and self-image. One of the factors that meliorated the negative effects was family support for the child, and thus it can be of considerable help to the child to remain with the family rather than being removed if the abuser is either controlled or removed.

The circumstances of child abuse, in particular interactions with the abusive parent, often distort the child's sense of reality. The abused child is "brainwashed" into thinking that she or he is "bad."[18] Sexually abused children may be told that their father's attentions are normal and show that he loves them.[19] The resulting distortion feeds into the self-blame that victims often exhibit.

THE RELATIONSHIP OF CHILD ABUSE AND NEGLECT TO DELINQUENCY

There is a clear tendency for delinquent youths to have a history of child abuse and neglect. This was first demonstrated many years ago in a study comparing five hundred delinquent and five hundred nondelinquent boys.[20] In this study conducted by Sheldon and Eleanor Glueck, a large proportion, 86 percent, of the families of delinquents had a record of contact with agencies for child abuse and neglect concerns, but just half as many, or 44 percent, of the families of nondelinquents had a record. More recent studies confirm this finding. In one court jurisdiction, seven out of thirty-nine abused children were in court as juvenile delinquents after they had been reported as being abused.[21] Another study comparing 109 New Haven, Connecticut, delinquents with 109 nondelinquents provides somewhat different but supporting evidence that delinquent youths are disproportionately abused and neglected. In the New Haven study,

[17]Jon R. Conte, *Sexual Victimization of Children.* Unpublished manuscript available from University of Chicago, Social Service Administration, 969 E. 60th Street, Chicago, Illinois, 60637; 1985. Also see David Finkelhor and Angela Browne, "The Traumatic Impact of Child Sexual Abuse: A Conceptualization," *American Journal of Orthopsychiatry, 55,* no. 4 (October 1985), pp. 530–541; and Angela Browne and David Finkelhor, "Impact of Child Sexual Abuse: A Review of the Research," *Psychological Bulletin, 99,* no. 1 (January 1986), pp. 1–12.

[18]Finkelhor, Gelles, Hotaling, and Straus, *The Dark Side of Families,* p. 20.

[19]*Ibid.*

[20]Sheldon Glueck and Eleanor Glueck, *Unraveling Juvenile Delinquency* (Cambridge, Massachusetts: Harvard University Press, 1950).

[21]N. F. Chase, *A Child Is Being Beaten: Violence Against Children, An American Tragedy* (New York: McGraw-Hill Book Company, 1975), p. 117.

"8.6 percent of the delinquents, as compared with only 1 percent of the non-delinquents, had used the hospital services for the specific reason of child abuse."[22] A study in Oregon revealed that more than 50 percent of the juvenile delinquents reported experience with domestic violence, and delinquent girls were more likely to have been abused than boys.[23] Finally, a survey revealed that neglect and emotional abuse are related to offenses against persons and property as well as status offenses, but physical abuse is related only to offenses against property.[24] The studies mentioned here, as well as others that we have not used as examples, give us consistent evidence that youths who are adjudicated as delinquent or as status offenders tend to have a history of abuse and neglect. Thus, adolescents involved with the courts often require services to assist them with the resulting trauma.

It is unclear exactly how abuse and neglect are related to delinquency. Some experts see a direct causal linkage. Simmons, for instance, has written that "a brutal parent tends to produce a criminal child."[25]

A particularly compelling argument for the view that abuse leads to criminality is related to the learning of aggressive behavior. In Chapter 3 we described social learning theory, according to which children learn much of their behavior by imitating their parents. This certainly suggests that, if a parent is abusive, the child will learn to copy aggressive behavior. Timberlake confirmed this in a study of very young children, six and seven years old, who had been removed from their families as victims of either child abuse or neglect. In the foster families, the average abused youngster displayed aggressive behavior several times a day. The average neglected child was aggressive just several times a week.[26] A study of older children showed that children who were abused by both parents were particularly prone to violent acts of deviance, those abused by one parent were less prone, and those who were not abused at all were least prone.[27]

Although there is evidence that abused children are more violent than others, the link may not be extremely strong. Joan McCord compared four

[22]Peter Garabedian, "Appendix C: Synthesis of Literature on Linkage Between Child Abuse, Neglect, and Delinquency," in *A Preliminary National Assessment of Child Abuse and Neglect and the Juvenile Justice System: The Shadows of Distress*, eds. Charles P. Smith, David J. Berkman, and Warren M. Fraser (Washington, D.C.: U.S. Government Printing Office, 1980), p. 134.

[23]P. W. Rhoades and S. L. Parker, *Connections Between Youth Problems and Violence in the Home* (Portland, Oregon: Oregon Coalition Against Domestic and Sexual Violence, 1981).

[24]Stephen E. Brown, "An Analysis of the Relationship Between Child Abuse and Delinquency," *Crime and Justice*, 5, (1982), pp. 47–51.

[25]Harold E. Simmons, *Protective Services for Children*, 2nd ed. (Sacramento: The Citadel Press, 1970), p. 48.

[26]Elizabeth M. Timberlake, "Child Abuse and Externalized Aggression: Preventing a Delinquent Life Style," in *Exploring the Relationship Between Child Abuse and Delinquency*, eds. Robert J. Hunner and Yvonne Elder Walker (Montclair, New Jersey: Allanheld, Osmun, 1981), p. 45.

[27]Jane H. Pfouts, Janice H. Schopler, and H. Carl Henley, Jr., "Deviant Behaviors of Child Victims and Bystanders in Violent Families," in *Exploring the Relationship Between Child Abuse and Delinquency*, eds. Hunner and Walker, p. 97.

groups of boys who were similar in rates of poverty and in proportion from broken homes: neglected youths, abused youths, rejected youths, and loved youths.[28] Her forty-year follow-up study showed that more than one-third of the abused and neglected boys and more than half of the rejected boys had juvenile or adult criminal records. In contrast, just 23 percent of the boys raised by loving parents had a record. McCord concluded that child abuse and neglect have an impact on delinquency, but parental rejection is even more important. Consistent with social learning theory, the youths who were most affected by abuse and neglect had aggressive parents. Also, the youths least affected received the most education. Finally, it should be noted that a sizable group of boys from poor backgrounds, but with loving parents, had a record of breaking the law. As we have stressed throughout this book, individual and family tendencies in combination with social factors account for delinquency.

A study of substantiated physical abuse, sexual abuse, and neglect cases in a midwestern court jurisdiction between 1967 and 1971 also raises questions as to whether or not abused and neglected children become abusive adults.[29] Compared to a control group, men who had been abused or neglected as children had more frequent adult arrests for violent offenses. Women who had been abused or neglected were at increased risk for property, drug, and order offenses. Despite the increased risk for criminality, however, it is important to keep in mind that the majority (71 percent) of the abused and neglected children did not have criminal records later in life. There are many abused and neglected children who do not later appear as adult offenders.

Along with some relationship between delinquent acts and abuse, there is a relationship of status offenses to abuse. One study revealed that 35 percent of the offenses of abused children were such things as truancy and running away, which he called *escape offenses*.[30] Because involvement with the juvenile justice system is stigmatizing and can expose vulnerable youths to more serious offenders, there is a need for alternative programs, including shelter homes, hotlines, runaway programs, and family intervention on behalf of the adolescent.[31]

Despite the evidence of association between abuse and aggressive delinquency, some observers have cautioned that the relationship between child abuse and delinquency may not be one of direct causality. It is possible that child abuse and delinquency affect the same children because they are both caused by a similar set of conditions. Robert J. Bently concludes from an extensive review of the literature that severe parental discipline and marital discord result in both delinquency *and* abuse. He suggests that family disruption is common to large,

---

[28]Joan McCord, "A Forty Year Perspective on Effects of Child Abuse and Neglect," *Child Abuse and Neglect*, 7, no. 3 (1983), pp. 265–270.

[29]Cathy Spatz Widom, "Child Abuse, Neglect, and Violent Criminal Behavior," *Criminology*, 27, no. 2 (May 1989), pp. 251–271.

[30]James Garbarino, "Meeting the Needs of Mistreated Youths," *Social Work*, 25, no. 2 (March 1980), p. 124.

[31]Bruce Fisher and Jane Berdie, *Adolescent Abuse and Neglect: Issues of Incidents, Intervention, and Service Delivery*," *Child Abuse and Neglect*, 2, no. 3 (1978), pp. 173–192.

broken, and single-parent families and may result in both problems.[32] Abuse may be a contributing cause of delinquency or may be one of many influences leading to delinquent behavior. Regardless of the reasons that delinquency, abuse, and neglect are found to affect the same children, a full understanding of delinquency requires a knowledge of abuse. Prevention and correctional programs aimed at one problem cannot be effective unless the other is considered. In many cases where there is an overlap, the causative and resulting conditions are dealt with at the same time.

CAUSES OF ABUSE AND NEGLECT

Just as there are many different explanations of delinquency, there are different theories to explain abuse and neglect. When considerable attention was drawn to the problems of abuse and neglect nearly two decades ago, many of the theories identified the individual problems of parents as key. Extreme psychological disturbance and the intergenerational passing of abusive parenting were common explanations. As the problem is better understood, our explanations have changed to include the situational stresses that can confront a family as well as values and norms in our culture that provide an atmosphere conducive to child maltreatment.

Researchers who emphasize differences between individual parents have noted that neglecting and abusing parents have many similar characteristics:

> Both need and demand a great deal from their infants, and are distressed when met by inadequate response, so it is not surprising that we occasionally see an infant or child who is both neglected and abused. Yet there is a striking difference in these two forms of caretaker-infant interaction. The neglecting parent responds to distressing disappointment by giving up and abandoning efforts to even mechanically care for the child. The abusing parent seems to have more investment in the active life of the child and moves in to punish it for its failure and to make it "shape up" and perform better.[33]

A common characteristic of abusive parents is their failure to understand the limitations of very young children (Exhibit 12-1).

Fontana classifies abusing parents into the emotionally immature, neurotic or psychotic, mentally deficient or uninformed, disciplinarians, criminal-sadistic, and addictive.[34]

He defines emotionally immature parents as those who continue to place their own needs before those of their children. The child often gets in the way of

[32]Robert J. Bently, "Child Abuse, Cross-Cultural Childrearing Practices and Juvenile Delinquency: A Synthesis," in *Exploring the Relationship Between Child Abuse and Delinquency*, eds. Hunner and Walker, pp. 128–144.

[33]Brandt F. Steele and C. B. Pollock, "A Psychiatric Study of Parents Who Abuse Infants and Small Children," in *The Battered Child*, eds. Ray E. Helfer and C. Henry Kempe (Chicago: University of Chicago Press, 1974), p. 99.

[34]Vincent J. Fontana, *Somewhere a Child Is Crying* (New York: New American Library, 1976).

Exhibit 12-1   Abusive parents often fail to understand the limitations of very young children

---

[The abusive] parent emerged during our recent study of abused children. At one level, they seem terribly misinformed about what a 2- or a 5-year-old can do or needs to do. The behavior of the child is evaluated against standards that are more appropriate for an older child. For example, one mother explained that she had to beat her child because he refused to do what she asked him to do. She would make a request, then repeat it. The child she was beating was 13 months of age!

Another aspect of the problem is that the discrepancy between the child's behavior and the parent's expectations is viewed as a reflection of the child's *malevolent intentions*. The parent can become so preoccupied with negative attributions about the child that even his most innocent behavior is viewed as hostile. For example, when asked why she persisted in slapping her child's face, one mother explained that when her 18-month-old pursed his lips and blew, it meant that he was insulting her. She slapped him to teach him to be more respectful.

While many abused children have been observed to be highly coercive, some of them interact well within normal limits. Even within this subset of abused children, the parents seem to function with a kind of thought disorder analogous to projection. They take many aspects of their child's behavior very personally. This, combined with a profound ignorance of the intellectual and motor abilities for children of different ages, sets the stage for repeated misunderstandings. It is our clinical impression that many of these families can be helped.

SOURCE: Gerald R. Patterson, *Coercive Family Process* (Eugene, Oregon: Castalia Publishing Company, 1982), p. 302.

---

the quest for fulfillment of their childish needs. Others seek to bolster faltering egos by dominating the child or expecting him or her to meet unrealistic expectations, abusing and rejecting the child who cannot. Still others expect the child to fill an emotional void in the parent's life, turning upon the child who is unable to do so. Also in this group are untrusting, alienated people who have difficulty establishing meaningful relationships with anyone.

Fontana defines neurotic or psychotic abusers as those whose own upbringing and experiences have disturbed their personalities, attitudes, and values to the extent that they are unable to care about others and incapable of sharing of themselves. Their distorted spirits cause them to feel an unreal persecution at the hands of their children. They attribute to the child an adult capacity for organized, purposeful, and malevolent behavior, striking out at the child in an attempt to salvage what they can of themselves.

In some instances, the characteristics of the child may predispose the child to parental abuse. Fontana expands:

In all categories of maltreating parents we find that a "special kind of child" often triggers the maltreatment. He may be unlovable (because he is not cute), or difficult, or irritating, or finicky of appetite, or have a birth defect, or be a boy instead of a girl, or scowl instead of smile, or cry all the time, or have a particularly grating quality to his cry that drives his parents, or one of them, to distraction.[35]

Parents may simply be unable to cope with a child whose developmental pattern does not fit their expectations. Some individuals of less than normal intelligence may lack experience in child rearing or have difficulties learning to be effective parents.

Criminally sadistic child abusers, who kill and maim for the joy of it, are the ones who appear in the headlines. They draw public attention to child abuse, and their crimes often spur legislation concerning child abuse and neglect. Society must be protected from them but, fortunately, their numbers are small. Actions aimed at the prevention and treatment of child abuse and neglect must focus primarily on those more common abusers who are discussed in other parts of this section.

In studying characteristics that are associated with abusive parents, Elizabeth Elmer found that these individuals experience more medical and social stress than the majority of the population. Abusive mothers tend to perceive more pregnancy stress than do nonabusive mothers, and the rate of prematurity among abused children is considerably the norm. Abusive parents also have little support from neighbors, religious groups, and relatives.[36]

A study by Dr. Winifred J. Scott found that certain social history factors were indicative of a mother's predisposition toward abusing behavior. These indicators include:

1. separation from one or both parents or abuse in childhood,
2. delinquency or placement in a foster home or institution in adolescence,
3. psychiatric problems, drug or alcohol abuse, police involvement, illegitimate pregnancy, or assault by a significant male in adulthood,
4. temporary or long-term separation from one or more children prior to the abuse incident.[37]

Most of the indicators identified by Scott relate to the mother's own childhood, but she considers separation of the mother from a child due to hospitalization or some other reason also to be a contributing factor to abuse.

Recent research by Alfred Kadushin and Judith A. Martin suggests that the actual abusive incident is often initiated by an interaction between the parent and the child.[38] Although the parent certainly responds inappropriately in

---

[35]*Ibid.*, p. 62.

[36]Elizabeth Elmer, "A Social Worker's Assessment of Medico-Social Stress in Child Abuse Cases," in *Fourth National Symposium on Child Abuse* (Denver, Colorado: Children's Division, American Humane Association, 1975), pp. 88–90.

[37]Winifred J. Scott, "Attachment and Child Abuse: A Study of Social History Indicators Among Mothers of Abused Children," in *Traumatic Abuse and Neglect of Children at Home,* eds. Williams and Money, p. 141.

[38]Alfred Kadushin and Judith A. Martin, *Child Abuse: An Interactional Event* (New York: Columbia University Press, 1981).

harming the child, these researchers found that misbehavior or a rebellious action on the part of the child frequently preceded the abusive act. Kadushin and Martin noted that this finding has implications for the treatment of the entire family in which an abused child is identified.

David Finkelhor and his coauthors have described the growing awareness of a need to consider more than individual differences in parents and children as explanations of abuse, neglect, and sexual maltreatment:

> We need to understand, for example, how sexual abuse may be promoted by pornography, the sexualization of children in the media, the sexualization of power and dominance in the society as a whole, and the fact that males in our society are given little preparation for nurturant and affectionate interchanges with children which contain no sexual component.[39]

Similarly, Richard Gelles has criticized the focus on low coping skills and parent immaturity as the cause of abuse as a case of circular reasoning, for it is tantamount to arguing that poor parenting skills and immaturity result in behavior that demonstrates a lack of these same characteristics.[40] In recognition of the criticisms of the individual level explanation, there has been a trend to consider a wider range of variables.

There was a period when many researchers and practitioners agreed that poverty was not as strongly associated with child abuse as official statistics indicated, but it has become increasingly apparent that poverty can result in stress that contributes to child abuse, and it can contribute to neglect by making it difficult to meet a child's needs. It is true that official statistics overrepresent poor families, because poor families are already known to public agencies that are responsible for investigating abuse and neglect. Middle- and upper-class families can hide problems because they seek private medical care and because they more often live in single-family dwellings, away from the scrutiny of their neighbors. Yet even after we correct for the more frequent detection of abuse and neglect among the poor, there still is a connection. Leroy Pelton has noted that poverty can not only create stress on parents, but it can produce health and safety hazards in the living situation that contribute to injury when a child is hurt or neglected.[41] Horowitz and Wolock have observed that the influence of poverty is somewhat different depending on other family characteristics: Black maltreating families are more likely to live in the most extreme, materially deprived circumstances, and the most immediate source of stress seems to be poverty itself; white maltreating families often live in somewhat less extreme poverty, and inter- and intrapersonal problems seem to be a major source of stress.[42]

---

[39]Finkelhor, Gelles, Hotaling, and Straus, *The Dark Side of Families*, p. 86.

[40]Richard J. Gelles, "Child Abuse as Psychopathology: A Sociological Critique and Reformulation," *American Journal of Orthopsychiatry, 43,* no. 4 (July 1973), pp. 611–621.

[41]Leroy H. Pelton, *The Social Context of Child Abuse and Neglect* (New York: Human Sciences Press, 1981), p. 13.

[42]Bernard Horowitz and Isabel Wolock, "Material Deprivation, Child Maltreatment, and Agency Interventions Among Poor Families," in *The Social Context of Child Abuse and Neglect,* ed. Leroy H. Pelton (New York: Human Sciences Press, 1981), pp. 137–184.

Taking a somewhat different perspective on abuse, David Finkelhor has proposed that both physical and sexual abuse are related to power.[43] They involve actions that are carried out to compensate for a lack or loss of power. Thus, men tend to be sexually abusive when they are unemployed, men tend to be physically abusive when they feel impotent as parents, and mothers are abusive when they feel they have lost control of their children and their lives.

Many authorities feel that the very nature of contemporary society is a major contributing factor to the abuse and neglect of children. James Garbarino suggests that the isolation of families from "potent prosocial support systems" denies families the outside relationships which could assist them in times of crisis and serve as role models for child rearing. According to Garbarino, both "abuse and delinquency feed on privacy." Social isolation in combination with a stressful or crisis situation such as loss of employment may ignite an abusive situation.[44]

When child maltreatment first came to the attention of researchers, most of the studies focused on the characteristics of the child and parents and the situation which preceded the abusive incident.[45] The causal explanations for the problems of abuse and neglect that are derived from such investigations are diverse and often in conflict with one another. At one end of the spectrum, these explanations are grounded in theory that stresses the psychological characteristics of the abusing parent or person. Other explanations, however, emphasize environmental factors such as poverty and the inequitable structure of society. It would seem that the best explanation lies in the integration of the psychological and sociological perspectives:

> A psychosocial explanation which combines both the social stresses which might act as the "triggering context" for abuse, and the psychological factors which predispose the caretaker to resort to abuse as a selective response in dealing with child management problems, appears to be a more comprehensive interpretation.[46]

In addition to the individual and situational factors that promote child mistreatment, there are social and cultural variations that can increase its likelihood.

As was true for juvenile delinquency programs, programs to prevent child neglect and abuse differ depending on the underlying theory. The individual, psychological explanation has been criticized, for it leads to the use of programs that blame individual parents rather than programs that ameliorate the negative effects of poverty.[47] Programs directed at families in which sexual

[43]Finkelhor, Gelles, Hotaling, and Straus, *The Dark Side of Families*, p. 18.

[44]James Garbarino, "Child Abuse and Juvenile Delinquency: The Developmental Impact of Social Isolation," in *Exploring the Relationship Between Child Abuse and Delinquency*, eds. Hunner and Walker, pp. 120–122.

[45]Charles P. Smith, David J. Berkman, and Warren M. Fraser, *Reports of the National Juvenile Justice Assessment Centers: A Preliminary National Assessment of Child Abuse and Neglect and the Juvenile Justice System* (Washington, D.C.: American Justice Institute, 1979), p. 13.

[46]Kadushin and Martin, *Child Abuse: An Interactional Event*, p. 18.

[47]Pelton, *The Social Context of Child Abuse and Neglect*, p. 21.

abuse occurs can also be criticized for neglecting the broader social conditions that appear to sanction sexual activity with children and the treatment of females as "sex objects." There is no doubt that children and their families should be offered assistance directly, but it also is necessary to use education and other approaches to eradicate social causes.

Later in this chapter we will focus on child protective services, and specific programs intended to alleviate the problems of abuse and neglect. These programs can be considered against the standard of their dual focus on the social problems impacting on the family and the psychological needs of abusive parents. Before we discuss these programs, we will explain the role of law enforcement and court and correctional personnel in the steps leading up to eventual delivery of services to the abusing family.

LAW ENFORCEMENT AND PROSECUTION

In its early stages, child abuse legislation encouraged the reporting of cases of child abuse primarily to law enforcement authorities. Today, however, protective service divisions of social service agencies also are legally mandated to respond to child abuse and neglect so that corrective steps can be taken to help the parents as well as the child. Most commonly, attempts are made to salvage the family which is still considered to be the best milieu in which to raise and nurture a child. Several states recognize the shared functions of law enforcement and social service agencies by requiring that suspected child abuse cases be reported to both, and that the agencies report to each other.

In spite of the concentration of responsibility for child abuse in social service agencies, the public is accustomed to reporting cases of physical violence to the police and the police are in many instances the only public agency in the position to enter the child's home forcibly and take children into protective custody immediately. Thus, particularly in incidents of serious physical abuse, the law enforcement function in child protection is of major importance.

> The well-trained police officer armed with crisis intervention skills and a heightened awareness of objective indications of family dysfunction provides an invaluable case-finding and screening service. Police are routinely requested to handle family and neighborhood disputes, disturbances-of-the-peace violations, and situations involving drug or alcohol abuse. Children are frequently observed in undesirable circumstances during such routine investigations. The circumstances may not justify traditional police action. The referral of such children and families, however, to appropriate helping agencies may prevent crime and most certainly earns greater respect and trust for law enforcement within the community.[48]

[48]Jackie N. Howell, "The Role of Law Enforcement in the Prevention, Investigation, and Treatment of Child Abuse," in *The Battered Child*, 3rd ed., eds. C. Henry Kempe and Ray E. Helfer (Chicago: University of Chicago Press, 1980), p. 307.

Since the police may be involved in referring families to other appropriate agencies, it is essential that their training include a full understanding of community resources that are available.

The time factor is decisive in the police response to child abuse complaints. Often the complaint is lodged during the actual battering of the child or shortly thereafter. After evaluating the validity of the complaint, the primary duty of the police officer is the immediate protection of the child. Thus, the officer's first official act will be to get medical attention for the child. Most state laws require that an attempt be made to resolve the situation without removing the child from the home. It is, however, sometimes absolutely necessary to take the child into protective custody, especially if there is no reasonable assurance that the abuse will cease. There can exist no such assurance if there is not someone in the home who can prevent the abuser from indulging in violence in the future.

Second, as a law enforcement officer charged with upholding public standards and maintaining public order, the officer must determine whether or not the law has been violated, and, if so, whether there exists sufficient evidence to initiate a criminal action against the abuser. The officer must, therefore, conduct an investigation as would be done in any criminal case. If the investigation reveals sufficient evidence of a grave nature, the suspect will be taken into physical custody.

The National Center on Child Abuse and Neglect has set forth criteria to guide the police officer in making a decision about arrest.[49] According to the Center, arrest is justified only in the most serious cases, for example when

- injury to the child is very severe
- there is evidence of a serious crime
- the alleged abuser seems likely to leave the jurisdiction
- there is a disturbance of the peace
- the alleged abuser seems to pose a danger to others

One advantage of criminal processing is that, if the offender is placed on probation, which is the outcome for the vast majority, the criminal court can threaten incarceration if there is any violation of orders to stay away from the child or to obtain treatment.

Despite the coercive advantage of criminal prosecution, it should be used sparingly for several reasons. Some claim that abuse cases are too difficult to prove, and that the exculpated parents leave a court proceeding with increased bitterness, which subjects the victim to added danger. An unsuccessful prosecution may be viewed by the abuser as a vindication of the abuse. An experience of arrest and prosecution also can discourage abusive parents from seeking medical help if the child is injured in the future.

[49]National Center on Child Abuse and Neglect, *The Role of Law Enforcement in the Prevention and Treatment of Child Abuse and Neglect* (Washington, D.C.: Children's Bureau, Department of Health and Human Services, 1984).

Thus, even when there is an arrest, the prosecutor may decide not to proceed. Vincent De Francis and Carroll Lucht, themselves lawyers, write:

> An additional consideration is the fact that punishment of abusing parents through criminal prosecution does not correct the fundamental cause of their behavior. If we recognize the mental, physical and emotional inadequacies of these people then we must recognize that prosecution and punishment will not produce true change in their behavior. At best it can only produce surface compliance, with deeper motivational forces remaining untreated and emotional damage to their personality becoming greater as a result of the punitive experience.
>
> The decision of whether or not to prosecute in a given case should rest with the country prosecutor. In making this decision he must also consider what happens to children. No decision to prosecute parents can afford to overlook the necessity for adequate planning for the abused child and other children in the family.[50]

In deciding on prosecution, it is essential to weigh the potential pros and cons for the child.

Prosecution is a major problem in child sexual abuse cases, for parents and health and social services professionals are often afraid that the trauma of preparation and testimony in court will damage the child. Particularly in cases of incest, obtaining valid court testimony is problematic, for the child often is commanded by the parent to remain silent, and even if this is not the case, the child frequently feels responsible for "breaking up the family" if the testimony results in incarceration of the father. A recent study has identified a number of strategies for making prosecution more effective:

- Passage of statutes that abolish special competency requirements for children and that create special exception to hearsay for certain out-of-court statements of child sexual abuse victims.
- Laws permitting child witnesses to have a supportive person present during court proceedings, and offering the services of the court to explain the proceedings to the child, assist the family and child, and advise the court and prosecutor.
- Enhancing the child's communication skills through dolls, artwork, and simplified vocabulary.
- Modifying the physical environment—providing a small chair for the child, having the judge sit on a level with the child or wear business clothes instead of a judicial robe.
- Preparing child victims before their courtroom appearances—briefing them on the roles of people in the courtroom, introducing them to the judges, taking them for a tour of the courtroom, and allowing them to sit in the witness chair and speak into the microphone.
- Laws directing law enforcement, social service agencies, and prosecutors to conduct joint investigations in child sexual abuse cases, using a single trained interviewer.

[50]Vincent De Francis, J. D., and Carroll Lucht, J. D., *Child Abuse Legislation in the 1970s* (Denver, Colorado: Children's Division, American Humane Association, 1974), p. 4.

- Laws attempting to expedite the adjudication process by giving precedence in trial scheduling to sexual offense cases or to cases in which the victim is a minor.[51]

The recommended statutes and practices are intended to overcome children's special fear of testifying, communication difficulties, memory loss, and the problems in showing that a child is legally competent.

In the years following widespread public acknowledgment of the mistreatment of children, the role of law enforcement has increasingly been shared with other agencies. In many jurisdictions, police officers are required to refer complaints to social service agencies rather than directly to juvenile or family court as in the past. Particularly if parents are cooperative, social service agencies often handle the case without ever involving the police or, if the referral is from the police, without further police contact. Police and social workers may work together in more serious cases. When there appears to be sexual abuse, police usually conduct the investigation while the social worker attends to the victim.

As our knowledge of child abuse and its treatment has grown, large police jurisdictions have created juvenile units to respond to both delinquency and neglect or abuse cases. These units facilitate the extensive interagency coordination which is required for the effective sharing of responsibility.

THE JUVENILE COURT AND CORRECTIONAL PROGRAMS

Regardless of whether an incident of abuse or neglect results in an arrest or a criminal prosecution, the case is typically referred to a protective services agency. Protective services workers, sometimes in cooperation with the police, investigate and determine whether juvenile court involvement is needed. Basically, protective services screens cases for informal or formal court handling just as the intake division screens cases involving the charge of delinquency or status offense. The protective services agency can handle a case informally either because the problem is minor or not found to exist, or it can refer the case on for court involvement. If the criminal court is handling a charge against the adult involved, protective services, and usually the juvenile court, will also be involved.

For child abuse and neglect cases before the juvenile court, the parents have a right to counsel and in many states an attorney is also appointed to represent the child. In very serious cases, the child has been placed in emergency foster care or another facility as soon as the police or a protective services worker is made aware of danger to the child. The juvenile court has legal jurisdiction over the case, and thus must order that emergency care be continued. The court also has the authority to order that the child be placed in foster care or some other setting or that family members receive counseling once the hearing has been completed. These decisions will almost always be based on a social investi-

---

[51]Debra Whitcomb, *Prosecution of Child Sexual Abuse: Innovations in Practice, Research in Brief* (Washington, D.C.: U.S. Department of Justice, 1985).

gation of the situation provided by the protective services worker and, in some cases, a report from the police.[52]

There is another route through which the abused or neglected adolescent can become involved with the juvenile court, and eventually with juvenile correctional programs. The police do carry out a full investigation of many abuse and neglect cases, and for a high proportion of those involving adolescents, they file a petition with the juvenile authorities.[53] The intake division of the juvenile court then investigates the case further. Based on its findings, a petition can be forwarded to the court declaring that the child is "in need of supervision" or in some similar category of status offenders. This is accomplished under the same laws which allow the courts to assume jurisdiction over any status offender. If the neglected or dependent child is charged with a status offense, it is frequently a direct reaction to the family difficulties resulting in abuse or neglect.

> [C]harges brought against these youths were invariably related to their attempts to avoid the abuse and neglect they received at home. For example, a disproportionately large number of complaints made against them were "keeping late hours," "having an objectionable boyfriend," "associating with companions objectionable to parents," "avoiding their homes until late hours," and other allegations which reflected conflict with parents and other adults.[54]

Often, the youths who are charged as status offenders are detained until their hearing. The practice of charging and detaining the adolescent child who is abused and neglected as a status offender varies considerably between court jurisdictions, very often depending on the other resources available to deal with the problem. It occurs often enough, though, to demonstrate that the abused and neglected adolescent is frequently a client of the juvenile court, detention, and correctional programs.

The child's rights advocates, described in Chapter 5, have raised serious questions about the practice of charging and detaining youths as status offenders when they themselves are the victims of abuse and neglect. They maintain that these children have a right to avoid their homes and seek alternative living arrangements. Their argument is particularly convincing when applied to the runaway child, who in a large percentage of cases is escaping an intolerable home situation.[55] These youths are frequently arrested, detained, and charged with the status offense of running away. On the other hand, other people argue that the paucity of alternative resources necessitates that the juvenile court must

---

[52]Much of the information about court handling is informed by David Finkelhor, "Removing the Child—Prosecuting the Offender in Cases of Sexual Abuse: Evidence from the National Reporting System for Child Abuse and Neglect," *Child Abuse and Neglect*, 7, no. 2 (1983), pp. 195–205.

[53]Smith, Berkman, and Fraser, *A Preliminary National Assessment of Child Abuse and Neglect and the Juvenile Justice System*, p. 33.

[54]*Ibid.*, pp. 33–34.

[55]*Ibid.*, pp. 34–35.

somehow assume jurisdiction and responsibility for the adolescents who are abused and neglected, and that the status offense charge allows the court to do this in cases where the evidence of neglect or abuse is convincing but not legally sufficient. This argument assumes that the child's treatment by the court is relatively benign, and is highly consistent with the *parens patriae* philosophy of the original juvenile court. According to this philosophy, the court should assume responsibility for all youths who might become delinquent. In some communities, volunteers work with the courts to protect the rights of abused and neglected children (Exhibit 12-2).

Controversy about handling neglected and abused youths is even more complicated when a youth is delinquent *and* either abused or neglected, for then treatment for both related difficulties is needed. Few programs have been established to serve youths with both problems. If a comprehensive selection of such programs were available in a community, it would be preferable to use them and the child protective service agency for the abused and neglected adolescent which would free juvenile correctional programs to treat problems of delinquency. The function of the juvenile court would be limited to assuming legal jurisdiction over abused and neglected adolescents so that they could be treated in programs especially designed for them.

CHILD PROTECTIVE SERVICES

The role of child protective services in the investigation, prevention, and treatment of child abuse and neglect has developed rapidly since the enactment of child abuse and neglect reporting laws by state legislatures in the early 1960s. Mandatory reporting is required of professionals such as teachers, physicians, and social workers, and the agency to whom these individuals must report is most frequently the local social services department.[56] In response to a report of abuse or neglect, the social services department or other designated child protection agency is required by law to initiate an investigation. Most state laws specify that the investigating agency must *promptly* initiate its investigation of suspected abuse or neglect. Some states even require the child protective services worker to make contact with the family within twenty-four to forty-eight hours of the original complaint.

The numbers of cases referred to child protective services is staggering. By the mid 1980s, the estimate was 2,000,000 reports of child abuse alone, and nearly 300,000 children were in foster homes or other group care settings due to physical neglect, child abuse, abandonment, or parent incompetence.[57] Child protective services workers are responsible for investigating new cases; services

[56]Marlene H. Alderman, *Child Abuse and Neglect: State Reporting Laws* (Washington, D.C.: Department of Health and Human Services, 1980), pp. 17–19.
[57]Deborah Daro, *Confronting Child Abuse: Research for Effective Program Design* (New York: The Free Press, A Division of Macmillan, Inc., 1988), p. 75.

Exhibit 12-2   Volunteers work with abused and neglected children

In Spanish "casa" means "home." In today's juvenile justice system, CASA denotes a Court Appointed Special Advocate—a trained volunteer who advises the court about the best interests of a child whose home placement is being decided by the court—usually as a result of abuse or neglect. The CASA program tries to ensure that a child's right to a safe, permanent home is acted on by the court in a sensitive and expedient manner.

The CASA conducts an independent investigation of the case and submits a formal report advising the court about the best placement for the child. During the course of the investigation, the CASA will have talked with many people—the child, parents and family members, neighbors, doctors, teachers, and others—and will have reviewed all pertinent records and documents.

Only the court can appoint a CASA and only the court can dismiss a CASA for failure to meet responsibilities. Ideally, the appointment is made when a child's interests are first threatened and a petition is presented to the court. The appointment generally takes place during or immediately after the first hearing, which may be a shelter care or custody hearing.

The role of the CASA as a guardian *ad litem* is to investigate, evaluate, and recommend to the court what is truly in the child's best interests, both from a temporary and a long-term standpoint. The CASA serves as:

- *investigator*, determining all relevant facts through personal interviews and a review of records, documents, and clinical data;
- *advocate*, presenting the relevant facts before the court at hearings, through written reports and direct testimony;
- *facilitator* or *negotiator*, ensuring that the court, social services, and legal counsel fulfill their obligations to the child;
- *monitor* of all court orders, ensuring compliance by all parties and bringing to the court's attention any changes in circumstances that may require modification of the court order.

In essence, CASA's are the eyes and ears of the court, making independent, objective recommendations regarding the child's best interests. Judges have come to count heavily on the CASA's independent assessment and recommendations. However, since the CASA is only one of the parties providing recommendations to the court, the court may or may not accept the CASA's recommendations. Each case is determined on the facts presented by all parties and how those facts interface with case, State, and Federal law.

SOURCE: *National Institute of Justice Reports, Selective Notification of Information 192* (July 1985), pp. 7–8.

to parents and youth when there is no placement outside of the home; and working with service providers and the family when there is a placement. Some workers have caseloads of seventy or even more, and just like many prevention and correctional programs for delinquents, current economic conditions have resulted in shrinking resources for subcontracting services to private agencies.

In the highly demanding setting where protective services are carried out, a unique form of social work has evolved. In most social work situations, the client seeks the aid of the agency. The maltreated child is in no position to request aid, and thus the social worker must seek abused and neglected clients and their families. The child protective services worker must cope with the dual, and sometimes conflicting, roles of protecting the child from further harm and assisting the family to develop socially acceptable methods of child rearing. A delicate balance in this situation exists between the rights of the abused child and the rights of the parents.

Protective services workers represent that arm of the community that reaches out to take up the slack left when families are unable or unwilling to provide for the essential needs and care of their children. They carry the force of legal authority. The force of law requires that the child protection worker remain with a case until it is somehow resolved. This is an obligation that far exceeds that of the private agency whose responsibility is to the client alone rather than the community as a whole.

Child protective services workers frequently work in conjunction with a number of other agencies, depending on their availability in a given community. Their task, after having identified and assessed a case, consists largely in attempting to convert involuntary clients into voluntary ones who will actively participate in the treatment process. Portions of this process will often be the functions of other agencies to whom the problem family is referred.

The nature of the treatment process depends on the idiosyncratic needs of the child and the family. No two families exhibit the same needs, and experts agree that services must be individually tailored.

> Effective service provision is based on a thorough assessment of the family's strengths, weaknesses and needs, and the development of an appropriate service plan. The plan should reflect the family's needs and community resources available to meet those needs, should build on the family's strengths, and most important, should be designed to protect the child(ren).
>
> To implement the service plan, CPS [Child Protective Services] provides direct services and/or arranges for services for child protective clients. In rare cases, referrals to other service providers meet the children's and families' needs, and CPS involvement in the provision of direct services can be terminated. In the majority of cases, however, CPS has continued responsibility for ensuring the children's safety by *orchestrating* or *monitoring* the services provided by other agencies.[58]

The range of services that a child protection agency may obtain for its clients is immense and varied. According to Saad Z. Nagi, some of the more typical services provided to these families are marital and family counseling, counseling for the child, medical aid, treatment for alcoholism, homemaker services, financial aid, supervision in the home, and assistance to obtaining food

---

[58]Cynthia K. Ragan, Marsha K. Salus, and Gretchen L. Schultze, *Child Protection* (Washington, D.C.: Department of Health and Human Services, p. 1980), pp. 1–2.

and clothing.[59] Not infrequently, the child protection worker is also involved with the family as an advocate with the schools, in the provision of birth control information, or as an advisor regarding job counseling or vocational training.

As a last resort to protect the child from further harm, the child protection worker may initiate court action to remove a child from the home either temporarily or permanently. Requesting court jurisdiction of a child may occur immediately following the investigation stage of the process in extreme cases, or it may occur after a period of time in which other treatment alternatives have been unsuccessful. The court, however, may respond by ordering parents to use particular services.

The Varieties of Programs

Like delinquency programs, prevention and treatment programs for abusive and neglectful families are as diverse as the causal explanations of the problem, and either attempt to influence the parents' psychological functioning through therapy, or to reduce the stresses on the family which trigger abuse or neglect. In some cases, they try to do both of these.

Hawaii's *Children's Protective Services Center* was an early model that was emulated worldwide. Legislatively established in 1969, this program used a team approach. Team members included the public welfare social work supervisor, a pediatrician, a psychiatrist, and a psychologist. The team met weekly for two hours to provide diagnostic consultation on cases considered by social workers to be their most difficult. The social worker prepared a written summary of the case. The social work supervisor acted as conference chairperson and introduced the circumstances of the case. Other team members presented their findings and preliminary diagnoses. As needed, lawyers, public health officials, vocational rehabilitation counselors, and other agency representatives were team members. All members made suggestions concerning the most appropriate treatment plan. The social work supervisor then summarizes the collective recommendations. The ultimate choice of treatment plan and its implementation is, however, made by the social worker who submitted the case.

In the last two decades, both private and public agencies have developed a tremendous variety of intervention programs to control child abuse and neglect. Based on examination of the evaluation results for nineteen innovative programs (for examples, See Exhibit 12-3), Deborah Daro concludes:

- there is an increased understanding of the particular treatment needed for each type of mistreatment, that is physical abuse, sexual abuse, and neglect
- innovative programs increasingly provide multiple services both to the parents and the child

[59]Saad Z. Nagi, *Child Maltreatment in the United States* (New York: Columbia University Press, 1977), p. 80.

Exhibit 12-3   Examples of the nineteen treatment programs studied in the national
clinical evaluation study

PROGRAMS FOR SEXUAL ABUSE CASES

- Family Resource Center, Team III,
  Albuquerque, New Mexico
  serves: families with a substantial history of sexual abuse. Families tend to be disorganized, unable to communicate, lacking clearly defined parent-child roles
  theoretical model: a multidisciplinary approach, combining social support services and psychiatric/psychological therapy to improve family members' behavior and functioning
- Project Against the Sexual Abuse of Appalachian Children,
  Knoxville, Tennessee
  serves: mostly white, rural clients with a history of isolation, deficits in social and relational skills, and often using an adversary model of parenting in which children are seen as wild and evil
  theoretical model: combination of a social casework model with sex therapy, and a recognition that family life is valued even if there is dysfunction

PROGRAMS FOR ABUSE CASES

- Atlantic County Adolescent Maltreatment Project,
  Atlantic City, New Jersey
  serves: families where the stress of raising an adolescent results in physical or sexual abuse unique to the adolescent period
  theoretical model: juvenile delinquency and adolescent behavior problems are often due to maltreatment, which should be addressed through strengthening the family rather than breaking it up
- Children's Trauma Center,
  Oakland, California
  serves: physically abused children and their siblings from primarily low-income, minority families with parents often separated or in stressful marriages
  theoretical model: a theoretical preschool combines education and skill development with psychotherapy, while the program also works on parent-child interaction and the integration of child and adult services

PROGRAMS FOR NEGLECT CASES

- Specialized Treatment of Child Neglect Project,
  Auburn, Washington
  serves: Muckleshoot Indian families that are extremely poor, living in overcrowded, inadequate housing, and in which children suffer from lack of supervision, poor nutrition, and emotional neglect
  theoretical model: general mistreatment of Indians makes it difficult for them to provide for their children, and prior placement of many parents in schools outside the reservation during their childhood results in no support systems when they are adults. Individual project staff must take over the role of the elders and serve as extended family, teaching child care skills and resolving problems
- Child Neglect Demonstration of the Dallas Children and Youth Project,
  Dallas, Texas
  serves: primarily children under age 3 with medical problems due to poor nutrition or infections, socioeconomic problems, and cognitive delays
  theoretical model: to provide quality health services to all, a system of neighborhood clinics offers a team to provide a wide range of services and reach out to isolated mothers and their children

Exhibit 12-3   Cont.

SOURCE: Deborah Daro, *Confronting Child Abuse: Research for Effective Program Design* (New York: The Free Press, A Division of Macmillan, Inc., 1988), pp. 94–101.

Discussion Questions

1. To what extent do the problems addressed by the various programs listed above result from social ills such as poverty or from individual deficiencies such as poor parenting skills?
2. Describe the connection between a groups' culture and historical experiences and the types of services that may be required.

- the projects resulted in social work predictions of less risk to the children in the long run, particularly in sexual abuse cases
- serious child abuse and neglect often continue while the family is in the program despite early, thoughtful, and costly intervention
- the projects that most reduce abuse and neglect during the program intervention separate the child and parent, either by requiring that the parent leave the home or by placing the child in foster care[60]

One dilemma facing protective services agencies is that they are increasingly seeing families whose problems are caused or aggravated by larger social problems, such as inadequate housing or lack of money to meet basic needs.[61] Thus, the limited success of treatment programs results, in part, from the inability to fully correct the larger problems.

No consideration of the variety of abuse and neglect treatment models would be complete without a discussion of the use of foster care placements. Some experts claim that the emotional and social disruption resulting from removing a child from the family outweighs the benefits.[62] However, children who are removed tend to improve in problem behaviors, with abused children becoming less emotionally withdrawn and neglected children overcoming developmental delays.[63] We have already cited evidence that demonstration projects that separate the abuser from the child have the most positive outcomes. Children who stay in their homes often do not overcome problems, and many cases are referred for a second time to protective services.[64] It is necessary to carefully weigh the pros and cons of using foster care, considering the severity of abuse, the danger to the child, the availability of services if the child remains with the abuser, and the potential damage from a separation.

[60]Daro, *Confronting Child Abuse*, p. 121

[61]*Ibid.*, p. 320

[62]Douglas J. Besharov, "State Intervention to Protect Children," *New York Law School Law Review, 26*, no. 3 (November 1981), pp. 723–772.

[63]J. Kent, "A Follow-Up Study of Abused Children," *Journal of Pediatric Psychology, 1*, no. 2 (Spring 1976), pp. 25–31.

[64]John Laughlin and Myra Weiss, "An Outpatient Milieu Therapy Approach to Treatment of Child Abuse and Neglect Problems," *Social Casework, 62*, no. 2 (February 1981), pp. 106–109.

As previously mentioned, the causal explanations of abuse and neglect are complex and at times inconsistent with one another. Despite this lack of a definitive explanation, treatment modalities are frequently, either explicitly or implicitly, based on the assumed causes of the problem. For example, if it is assumed that abusive parents exhibit psycho-pathological traits, the logical mode of treatment would be some type of counseling. If environmental factors are considered to be most important in the explanation of abuse and neglect, income supplements and medical care would be perceived as appropriate treatments. Further complicating treatment concerns are issues of the availability of services and the necessity to protect the child from more harm. Although it may be desirable to treat the abusing or neglecting family as a unit in the natural home, adequate treatment services to do so may be unavailable, and the risk of further injury may be too great to keep the child in the home. On the whole, much of our treatment for abused and neglected children is based on common beliefs and resource availability rather than any empirical evidence of the causes of abuse or the success of particular programs.

Prevention

Because of the difficulty in responding to an established pattern of child neglect or abuse and the heavy demands on protective services workers, it is increasingly obvious that for real progress, the thrust must be in the area of prevention. Dr. Ray Hefner of the Michigan State University School of Medicine produced a major breakthrough in prevention by designing the Children's Trust Fund at the end of the 1970s. A majority of the states now have a Trust Fund that uses money from surcharges on personal documents obtained from the state—for example, birth certificates—or from a check-off system allowing contributions of a portion of tax refunds. Matching funds are available through the Child Abuse Prevention Federal Challenge Grant Program. Generally, the Trust Fund is used to promote "volunteerism, collaboration, community . . . support, evaluation, innovation, and . . . replication" of prevention efforts.[65]

Parenting education programs, similar to the ones used to prevent and control delinquency, are perhaps the most frequently emphasized prevention strategy,[66] and there is evidence of effectiveness. There were positive outcomes in a ten-year follow-up of children from low-income families that received child-care services plus support from a pediatrician teamed up with a social worker, psychologist, or nurse. The prevention program mothers obtained more education and were better off financially, and the children were better adjusted to school. It is worth noting that the families who were not in the program needed considerably more costly social services at the time of the follow-up than those who were in the program.

Home visits by a nurse or other support person generally appear to

---

[65]Daro, *Confronting Child Abuse*, p. 127.
[66]*Ibid.* p. 127.

reduce the potential for child abuse and neglect. This is particularly the case for new teenage mothers in a program that provided parent education in the area of prenatal and early infant development; encouragement of family members and friends to help with child care and other support for the mother; and referral of the mother to available health and social services.[67] Similarly positive results also are obtained when parent education and referral are provided in social services or health-care centers rather than during home visits.[68]

Prevention, in the strictest sense of the word, implies the identification of, and intervention with, families that are potentially abusive prior to an overt act of abuse or neglect. Some observers suggest that only major changes in the structure of our society will ease the problems experienced by families that may lead to abuse or neglect. This is similar to the idea that we presented in Chapter 5: that the structure of society itself contributes to delinquency. As Kenneth Keniston of the Carnegie Council on Children contends:

> If parents are to function in this role [as parents] with confidence, we must address ourselves less to the criticism and reform of parents themselves than to the criticism and reform of the institutions that sap their self-esteem and power. Recognizing that family self-sufficienty is a false myth, we also need to acknowledge that all today's families need help in raising children. The problem is not so much to reeducate parents but to make available the help they need and to give them enough power so that they can be effective advocates with and coordinators of the other forces that are bringing up their children.[69]

Although Keniston recognizes that there is a need for public agencies to intervene formally when children are at risk of serious injury, he believes that reorganization of our health care system, full employment, government income supplements, and other substantial changes in society would contribute to a reduction of the stresses and problems which are often precursors to abuse and neglect. These inequities in society may also contribute to delinquency, considering that a common population of youths often shares delinquent and abused or neglected characteristics.

SUMMARY

We began this chapter by noting that public outrage with the problems of child abuse and neglect has its origins in the case of a battered child by the name of Mary Ellen who was removed from her home in 1874 with the help of the Society for the Prevention of Cruelty to Animals. It was not until the early 1960s,

---

[67]David L. Olds, Robert Chamberlin, and Robert Tatlebaum, "Preventing Child Abuse and Neglect: A Randomized Trial of Nurse Home Visitation," *Pediatrics, 78,* no. 1 (July 1986), pp. 65–78.

[68]Daro, *Confronting Child Abuse,* p. 133.

[69]Kenneth Keniston and The Carnegie Council on Children, *All Our Children* (New York: Harcourt Brace Jovanovich, 1977), p. 23.

however, that legislation mandated the formal involvement of public agencies in the identification and treatment of child maltreatment.

The number of cases of abuse and neglect that are reported formally are increasing annually. Abuse is typically thought of as an overt act of physical, sexual, or emotional violence against a child. Neglect refers to the failure of the caretaker of a child to provide for the essential needs of that child. Many experts believe that a causal relationship exists between child abuse and neglect and delinquency and adult criminality. There is also considerable evidence that abused children are frequently involved in aggressive or delinquent behavior.

Abusive and neglectful families represent the entire socioeconomic spectrum, although neglectful families, in particular, are concentrated in the lower income brackets. Maltreatment occurs most frequently in broken or disintegrating homes. Typical situations resulting in child abuse are attempts at discipline, mental illness of the parent, crises that are either external or internal to the family, medical or social stress, and severe disruption in the parent's own childhood. A combination of parents' psychological problems and social stresses impinging on the family, as well as characteristics of our society, is the best explanation of abuse and neglect.

Reporting of suspected cases of abuse and neglect by certain professionals is required. The social services department is the agency most frequently designated as the child protective service, although the law enforcement, juvenile court, and correctional agencies often serve abused and neglected adolescents. Law enforcement agencies are most frequently involved with cases of physical and sexual violence. The juvenile courts are involved in cases involving legal jurisdiction over the child. Court and correctional services often work with youths who may be classified as offenders although they are neglected or abused.

Social casework is the primary method of treatment of child protective services. The nature of the healing process is based on the needs of the individual child and family. Many imaginative and innovative programs exist that are designed to improve the capabilities of families to meet the needs of their children in a socially acceptable manner, though in many communities there are not enough of these programs. If any real progress in resolving the problems of child abuse is to be forthcoming, the focus of public policy in the future should be in the area of prevention.

DISCUSSION QUESTIONS

1. Why is there wide variation in the reported incidence of child abuse and neglect?
2. How can a child be used as a pawn or a scapegoat by parents?
3. What is the difference between discipline and abuse? Explain your answers in detail.
4. Why is a child who is "different" often the object of abuse? Can you find examples of this phenomenon in society at large? Discuss them.
5. Review Chapter 4 on the family and identify the indicators of emotional and physical abuse that seem to contribute to delinquency and status offending.

6. What is the role of child protective agencies and law enforcement agencies in cases of child abuse and neglect?

7. Should child abusers be prosecuted? Give reasons for your answer.

8. Should juvenile court personnel routinely ask youth if they have been neglected or abused? Explain your answer by considering, among other things, the number of maltreated children who are likely to be involved with the juvenile court and the use of the information.

PROJECTS

1. Describe the roles of law enforcement, juvenile court, and protective services agencies in your community. Pinpoint and explain the need for joint action and the need for improvements in these agencies' responsibilities.

2. Which of the family circumstances and characteristics identified as causes of delinquency in Chapter 4 are also possible causes of child abuse and neglect?

13

Delinquency Control—A Look to the Future*

- LIBERAL AND CONSERVATIVE APPROACHES TO DELINQUENCY CONTROL
- LACK OF COORDINATION IN JUVENILE JUSTICE ADMINISTRATION
- IMPLEMENTATION OF POLICIES TO DEINSTITUTIONALIZE JUVENILE OFFENDERS, DIVERT YOUTHS, AND PROVIDE DUE PROCESS
- NEW AREAS OF CONCERN—DETERRENCE AND THE SERIOUS OFFENDER
- RESEARCH PROGRESS AND NEEDS

LEARNING OBJECTIVES

1. To understand the influence of political positions on juvenile justice policy.
2. To be aware of the progress, or lack of progress, in implementing deinstitutionalization, diversion, and due process reforms.
3. To know of the feasibility of implementing measures to deter juvenile delinquency.
4. To know about public beliefs and research findings pertinent to the serious offender.
5. To understand the influence of research on juvenile justice policy.

In this concluding chapter we will assess the major policies that currently influ-

*Note: Assistance with this chapter in the second edition was obtained from Bonnie Pollard, *Michigan FARMER*, Lansing, Michigan.

ence local efforts to control delinquency, and we will summarize progress in research that adds to our understanding of delinquency and its control. First, however, we will examine the political process through which policies are chosen, and the role of the general public in this process.

The difficulty of resolving the complex "delinquency problem" is intensified by a growing public fear of crime. To say that the general public views crime and delinquency as primary concerns is an obvious understatement. In many public opinion polls, crime is at or near the top of the list of domestic priorities.

Yet harnessing the citizens' fear of crime into support for prevention and control programs is increasingly difficult. As public fear of crime grows, existing programs appear to be failing. Despite evidence that delinquency is not increasing, there is increasing frustration based on the belief that society cannot stem the tide. This frustration manifests itself in anger and confusion that can turn into apathy—or extremism.

POSITIONS ON DELINQUENCY CONTROL

The Extremes

Extremism stems from the deep schism in society between the two opposing beliefs about how the offender should be treated, both positions being locked into a polarizing struggle for supremacy.[1] During the 1960s and early 1970s, the public was handed a great deal of information, sometimes supported by social science research, that contended that the solution to all crime problems lies in a humanistic approach based on the assumption that all offenders can be rehabilitated, and that crime will disappear if the root causes (poverty, urban blight, and so on) were eliminated by social action. According to this view, which is within the positive school of criminology, no individuals are inherently criminal, but social conditions cause them to break the law.

While proponents of this position argue persuasively that this approach was never adopted on a broad enough scale to get a fair trial, the apparent failure of this orientation in solving the problem has spawned an onslaught of criticism from vocal adherents of the opposite position who say punishment as a deterrent never had its fair trial either.

Gaining credence daily is the view that the crime rate is increasing due to the "coddling" of offenders as practiced by "bleeding heart liberals" during the 1960s and 1970s. The new conservatism that grew throughout the 1980s instead contends that crime can be controlled by the adoption of harsh methods, at whatever price necessary in terms of the loss of protection of individual rights.

[1]Walter B. Miller, "Ideology and Criminal Justice Policy: Some Current Issues," in *The Criminologist: Crime and the Criminal*, ed. Charles E. Reasons (Pacific Palisades, California: Goodyear Publishing Company, Inc., 1974), pp. 19–50.

This is reminiscent of the classical school of criminology, and it rests on the assumption that people are good only if the penalties for breaking the law are high enough to deter them from criminality.

In the center lies a confused and sometimes angry populace whose allegiance shifts between the simplistic solutions offered by both of these polar extremes in beliefs. Now the pendulum is shifting away from rehabilitation, back toward punishment, as evidenced by criticisms of the "rights" given to offenders or even to people charged but not yet convicted of an offense. There is growing public support for the use of incarceration, and a reduction of the age at which youths can be handled in the adult criminal courts.

The difficulty in resolving the delinquency problem lies in the fact that rational and realistic proposals, combining the best elements of both philosophies, are the least likely to be heard above the clamor created by the extremes. Since this middle position does not promise immediate results, it does not gain instant converts.

The Middle Ground

And there is a middle ground that contends that the approach to solving crime problems should be geared toward the person and the type of crime involved. There is indeed a small percentage of repeat violent offenders who are unlikely to respond to efforts toward rehabilitation unless they are removed from the community. On the other hand, the vast majority of juvenile offenders can potentially be reached by more humanistic approaches, and they should have the chance to change through interaction with alternative programs.

This sort of dual approach demands cooperation and support from the community to be successful, yet it is the polarization of the citizenry that allows this middle ground to get lost in the shuffle. For instance, it becomes almost impossible to achieve revision of the juvenile or criminal codes in most communities. Any move to legalize prostitution or betting on sports brings an outcry from both extremes. Legalizing marijuana is always a "hot" issue. Advocates of legalization or decriminalization argue positions that range from saying marijuana is no worse than alcohol to claiming it is beneficial. On the other side are vocal opponents who charge that marijuana is not only detrimental but sinful. To be in the middle urging substantive change to deal with the problem more effectively is to be virtually alone. Yet without grass-roots community support, change cannot occur.

Another obstacle in the path of gaining community support for efforts against crime is that fear of crime also means fear of contact with known offenders. Community-based treatment has proven to be one of the best alternatives currently available, yet many citizens react negatively if it means having offenders next door. These fearful citizens worry about further exploitation, as well as an increase in social problems and deterioration of the neighborhood. Yet it takes community support for such efforts to succeed.

In summary, there are innumerable studies that show citizens are concerned about crime, and suggestions about what to do are countless. There is nothing really new in the growing conservatism toward dealing with crime and criminal offenders. But the point to remember is that the public does see crime as a very serious problem, yet new and innovative programs will be difficult to initiate unless concern is translated into support. The community must be convinced that the program will indeed remedy the situation—but not at the expense of harm to people and property within the community.

In the remainder of this chapter we will focus on several key policy and research dilemmas that confront juvenile justice personnel, politicians, and the general public which is concerned with the control of delinquency. Ultimately, these dilemmas will be dealt with, whether effectively or ineffectively, through the political process. Legislators and lawmakers will favor some approaches to the juvenile delinquency problem over others, and this will be reflected in rules and laws as well as the resources allocated to prevention and other programs. If the dilemmas described below are to be resolved, it is essential that each of us understands the distortions which are introduced by the polarized beliefs about delinquency. Control efforts should be based on the recognition of the many factors that cause delinquency as well as the several different types of youths who are categorized as delinquent.

JUVENILE JUSTICE ADMINISTRATION

Agencies that handle juveniles are often referred to as *components of a system.* By calling this process a system, a certain coordination is implied as being an integral part of the system's operation and function. But, too often, that label is a misnomer. Coordination, and even cooperation, do not always exist.

Mason P. Thomas specifically points out that

> legislatures have passed laws to establish a separate court system for children under certain ages because youths should not be held accountable under the same standards as adults, and because there may be a better chance of reform or rehabilitation with young people. While these concepts contain assumptions that might be questioned, the separate system idea has never been tried with adequate resources and personnel—thus, while our separate juvenile corrections system may be more myth than fact, it seems clear that professionals involved must develop new strategies to work cooperatively as management teams. In the past, the judge has been the star, with the administrative control and other powers over the rest of the system. The challenge for today is whether the separate parts of the system, when available, can develop a team concept to help juvenile corrections to function as a system in a positive way upon the lives of those children who have no choice about being pushed through the various parts of the system.[2]

[2]Mason P. Thomas, Juvenile Corrections, Five Issues to Be Faced, Popular Government May 1971, Institute of Government, The University of North Carolina at Chapel Hill.

The juvenile justice system includes not only law enforcement, court, and correctional personnel, but also the numerous private and public delinquency prevention programs which serve adolescents who are potentially or presently law-breakers. The complexity of the system is even more apparent when one recognizes the overlap between the juvenile delinquent, the abused or neglected child, and the drug-abusing child. Because this overlap exists, child abuse and drug treatment programs are drawn into interaction with other parts of the juvenile justice system on a regular basis.

The Need for Coordination

Due to the system's complexity, there has been a need for a concerted effort at federal, state, and local levels to establish a system of justice more rational, consistent, and fair. In too many states, departments of welfare, education, and mental health, and divisions of probate courts act independently, with no common guidelines, facilities, or programs to exchange and share. Administrative responsibilities are fragmented, which leads to duplication of service. This creates a situation in which children can encounter various and conflicting methods of treatment throughout their exposure to the system. Competitive struggles among various departments occur too often, and there are often no separate bureaus of child welfare, of offices for family, children, or youth services, to provide a coordinated approach.

At the heart of the problem of lack of coordination in many juvenile justice systems is a lack of built-in accountability.

> The most important negative aspect of the diverse and complex organization of our services for children is an almost complete loss of accountability on the part of juvenile organizations. Individual components of the juvenile justice system have not been required either to give reasons for their decision making or to give accounts of their performance. Consequently, their activities often are not observed and the impact of their programs are rarely measurable.
>
> This lack of accountability is, in a sense, a function of the large amount of discretion which each component possesses. Each system—law enforcement, education, social service, and mental health—has the power to reject cases, divert them to nonjudicial process, or arrange for court hearings and judicially mandated treatment. As a result, large numbers of children may be dealt with by the various systems with little external control.[3]

Without a way to monitor such an unwieldy system, accountability and coordination are unlikely to be achieved.

In the past, the federal government, through the Office of Juvenile Justice and Delinquency Prevention, has attempted to establish a more rational approach to juvenile justice problems, processing, programming, and treatment.

[3]Paul Nejelski and Judith LaPook, "Monitoring the Juvenile Justice System: How Can You Tell Where You're Going, If You Don't Know Where You Are?" *American Criminal Law Review, 12,* no. 1 (Summer 1974), pp. 13–14.

Major problems identified included failure to provide consistency in treatment; housing status offenders in facilities with serious repeat offenders; lack of coordination among the several agencies that could be working with a single youth; and a lack of uniformity in procedures and programs, so that accountability in leadership often takes a back seat to expediency, system maintenance, and system perpetuation.

The 1974 Juvenile Justice and Delinquency Act (Public Law 93-415) mandates that the Office of Juvenile Justice and Delinquency Prevention insure a coordinated interagency and interdisciplinary approach to delinquency problems. Besides establishing overall objectives and priorities, the act also created both a coordinating council and an advisory committee on juvenile justice and delinquency problems.

There continues to be a problem in coordinating the various components of the juvenile justice system. This is particularly serious in the relationship between the court, protective services, and law enforcement agencies. The authors of a survey of seven jurisdictions concluded:

> Informal interviews conducted during the course of this study suggest that a good deal of ill will exists between intake and the police which has resulted in a lack of agreed upon criteria by which the police should select cases for referral to intake.[4]

In jurisdictions where the police and protective services workers do not agree with court intake staff on the handling of offenders, many youths will be referred by police or protective services staff only to be released with no action by the intake staff. This results in a misuse of resources, and inconsistent treatment of the child who is referred.

The trend toward conservatism and away from treatment programs for youths has intensified fragmentation within the juvenile justice system:

> In the last few years several states have "recriminalized" juvenile delinquency, redefining it as a crime rather than a social disorder. Prosecutors have been given more authority to deal with juvenile cases, and adult courts are playing a larger role as well. The problem is that the system still lacks uniformity of purpose and outlook and is therefore as unpredictable, if not more so, than it was several years ago. Different states may have procedures which bear no resemblance to each other. Needless to say, it is far from clear that this situation will provide a greater deterrent effect. At any rate, the present lack of predictability and uniformity undermines our ability to inculcate in our youth a respect for justice and the legal system.[5]

Although there has been a dual emphasis on treatment and on punishment within our juvenile system for some time, the confusion introduced by this

---

[4]Charles P. Smith, T. Edwin Black, and Fred R. Campbell, *A National Assessment of Case Disposition and Classification in The Juvenile Justice System: Inconsistent Labeling*, Vol. 3: Results of a Survey (Washington, D.C.: U.S. Government Printing Office, 1980), p. xxvi.

[5]Office of Juvenile Justice and Delinquency Prevention, *Juvenile Justice: Before and After the Onset of Delinquency* (Washington, D.C.: U.S. Government Printing Office, 1980), p. 49.

inconsistency is especially pronounced in recent years. This confusion results from the pressures to move away from a rehabilitation approach, while at the same time opposing forces support the maintenance of the rehabilitation approach insofar as possible.

Methods for Improving Coordination

In the 1980s there were federal efforts to solve problems, provide coordination, set priorities, and use more logical procedures. The national advisory committee on juvenile justice and delinquency problems issued guidelines to assist local communities in improving coordination. The advisory committee recognized that there are major differences between juvenile court jurisdictions across the country, and therefore the major responsibility for coordination should be held by a local community planning and coordinating group.[6] This group should include representatives of the schools, representatives of other agencies serving juveniles, members of citizens' groups, and youths. It would be responsible for developing a plan that is consistent with the state plan, and which addresses issues of system priorities and goals, as well as strategies for solving delinquency related problems. Coordination of local agencies would be an important part of this plan, as would coordination of the local and state services for delinquents.

Several states have used this approach to deal with the problem of local and state coordination of delinquency control efforts, though there is a continuing need to develop the method and its application further. Michigan, for example, established a juvenile service training council to provide a forum for key youth service system administrators to deal with training and related needs on a statewide basis. Through assistance, consultation, and coordination, services were provided to agencies and institutions. Money for training was also provided to staffs that work with delinquent and predelinquent youth.

The focus of this statewide system was to (1) identify gaps in youth service training, (2) eliminate unnecessary duplication of training efforts in youth service units, (3) establishing a central coordination and communication point for all youth service staff training in the state, (4) direct technical and financial support for training efforts to the areas of greatest need, and (5) subsidize training efforts and insure adequate quality and fiscal controls.[7]

Even though this Michigan effort focused only on training, delivery of services and programming could be handled on a statewide basis by using the same structure to provide accountability, coordination, and consistency of services provided to youths. Such a system, at both the state and the local level, makes decision making more rational and policies and programs more useful in

---

[6]National Advisory Committee for Juvenile Justice and Delinquency Prevention, *Standards for the Administration of Juvenile Justice* (Washington, D.C.: U.S. Government Printing Office, 1980), p. 73.

[7]Juvenile Services Training Council, Annual Report, 1974–1975, Michigan Department of Social Services, p. 1.

helping troubled youth. The point is that it takes a coordinated effort to deal adequately with the problem.

THE IMPLEMENTATION OF KEY JUVENILE JUSTICE POLICIES

Diversion, deinstitutionalization, and due process are three major national policy recommendations set forth in the 1970s. Federal funding and regulations, as well as the publication of information needed to implement these policies, were used to encourage local jurisdictions to adopt these approaches in the handling of juveniles. Although many localities have tried to implement them, there also have been many roadblocks and countervailing influences.

Progress and Problems in Deinstitutionalization

Federal guidelines have encouraged local law enforcement, court, and correctional personnel to avoid the use of institutions under a number of different conditions. First, the use of correctional institutions for nonoffenders (neglected, dependent, abused, emotionally disturbed, or retarded children) and status offenders is considered to be an overly restrictive approach to meeting their needs. Second, the use of jails for the detention of all juveniles is considered as inappropriate. Third, a wide range of community corrections alternatives is viewed as preferable for the treatment of the majority of adolescent offenders, and restrictive institutions are appropriate only for repeat offenders with a pattern of very serious delinquency.

There has been pronounced national progress in deinstitutionalizing status offenders, though the amount of progress varies considerably from state to state, and even between counties and cities. The national progress results from changes in law enforcement, detention, and court practices. Between 1975 and 1982, the juvenile courts handled 8 percent fewer cases, and the entire decline was due to a 37 percent reduction in status offense cases.[8] Following a similar trend, in 1975, 40 percent of all status offense cases involved secure detention, but this fell to 12 percent by 1982.[9]

Unlike the progress in deinstitutionalizing status offenders, there is no clear national gain in efforts to reduce the numbers of delinquent youths in correctional institutions. An increasing trend for delinquents to be committed to institutions, which we described in Chapter 2, reflects a combination of very dramatic increases in the use of institutions by some states while others, most notably Massachusetts, have all but abandoned institutions. Extensive use of institutions does not appear to reduce recidivism or to be related to the state crime rate, so there is no logical justification for a continued emphasis on this

[8]Howard N. Snyder, John L. Hutzler, and Terrence A. Finnegan, *Delinquency in the United States: 1982* (Pittsburgh, Pennsylvania: National Center for Juvenile Justice, 1985), p. 1.
[9]*Ibid.*, p. 2.

approach to delinquency control. Like many of the trends we have described in this chapter, it is likely to be related to the political climate and a shifting emphasis toward harsh treatment of the offender. We need to better understand and confront the difficulties in shifting to the more desirable system of community-based treatment in order to make progress in this area. These difficulties include the public's fear of the juvenile offender, and the problem of involving the community in delinquency control efforts.

The detention of delinquent and status offenders in jails and police lockups which were intended for adults is another unsolved problem pertaining to deinstitutionalization.

Particularly in rural areas, where there are no nearby juvenile facilities and the local economy often prevents the development of community resources, juveniles have been, and continue to be, confined in jails and lockups that primarily house adults. However, there are ongoing efforts to end the jailing of juveniles. The federal Juvenile Justice and Delinquency Prevention Act of 1974 established the jailing of juveniles as a national concern. Although this act discouraged the use of adult facilities, their use was allowed if the juveniles could be physically separated from the adults. Then a 1980 amendment took an even tougher stance, requiring that adult lockups and jails be completely closed to juveniles by 1985, a deadline that was later extended to 1988.

Legal actions have been another source of challenge to the confinement of youth in jails. Early cases focused on *habeas corpus* proceedings oriented towards the release of a particular child, but in recent years lawsuits for damages, and class actions challenging jail conditions and confinement as unconstitutional, have been most common.[10] Various cases concerning children have found jail confinement to constitute "cruel and unusual punishment" and denial of the "right to treatment." The particular types of experiences against which the court has ruled have included exposure to, and abuse by, adult inmates; unclean living conditions; lack of exercise; inadequate diet; and prohibition of contact between the youth and his or her family.[11]

Despite the federal mandate and legal actions, in 1985 there were still 1,629 juveniles confined in adult jails and lockups.[12] By the end of 1987, 29 states were still not in full compliance with the requirement of the federal law.

Nearly one-fourth of the adolescents confined to jails are girls. Their profiles are quite different than the profiles of confined boys. Almost 25 percent of girls in jail have committed a status offense, whereas only 5 percent of boys in jail are status offenders.[13] Also, compared with boys, girls more often have committed a status misdemeanor rather than a felony offense, they are younger,

[10]Mark Soler, "Litigation on Behalf of Children in Adult Jails," *Crime and Delinquency, 34,* no. 2 (April 1988): pp. 190–208.

[11]*Ibid.*

[12]Bureau of Justice Statistics, *Jail Inmates, 1985* (Washington, D.C.: Bureau of Justice Statistics, 1987)

[13]Meda Chesney-Lind, "Girls in Jails," *Crime and Delinquency, 34,* no. 2 (April 1988), pp. 150–168.

and they are held longer.[14] On the surface, the longer confinement of the younger and less serious offender appears to be inequitable, and the difficulty is even greater with the recognition that girls in jail have special problems of isolation, inadequate medical care, and sexual and physical abuse by male staff.[15]

Alternatives to Jail

The jailing of juveniles is often a result of a lack of alternatives rather than any preference for such treatment. For example, a study of Minnesota, which has a high rate of juveniles in jail, revealed that police, court, and other officials would use such alternatives as a 24-hour on-call crisis intervention and screening service, home detention, and shelter care homes if they were available and there were a means of transportation.[16] There has been a lack of attention to the problem of jailing juveniles, however, in part because of the lack of available services, but also because some key officials do not feel that the practice is problematic.

Because juveniles are still jailed in so many states, and often there is no state push to end the practice, the Office of Juvenile Justice and Delinquency Prevention has instituted the Jail Removal Initiative, which involves grants to states as an incentive to develop alternatives. States using the grants reported several reasons for not complying, including: lack of coordinated services for juveniles, overextended staff, failure to monitor jails and lockups, poor training of intake staff, no funds for alternatives, no 24-hour services, and judicial resistance.[17] A wide variety of alternatives to jail were implemented. For example, in Michigan the focus was on developing a network of nonsecure settings supplemented with home detention programs. Some states have legally prohibited the use of jails for juveniles, and others have set up transportation systems so that juveniles can be housed in youth facilities far from their homes.[18] These types of initiatives have had some clear impacts within selected states, though full compliance in all states has not been reached.

Issues in the Implementation
of the Diversion Policy

In 1973, the National Advisory Commission on Criminal Justice Standards and Goals recommended that all status offenders be diverted from juvenile court, and half of the remaining cases be diverted.[19] Since then, numerous

[14]*Ibid.*

[15]*Ibid.*

[16]Ira M. Schwartz, Linda Harris, and Laurie Levi, "The Jailing of Juveniles in Minnesota: A Case Study," *Crime and Delinquency, 34,* no. 2 (April 1988), pp. 133–149.

[17]Robert W. Sweet, Jr., "OJJDP Helps States Remove Juveniles from Adult Jails and Lockups," *NIJ Reports,* no. 220 (May/June 1990), p. 6.

[18]*Ibid.,* p. 7.

[19]National Advisory Commission on Criminal Justice Standards and Goals, *A National Strategy to Reduce Crime* (Washington, D.C.: U.S. Government Printing Office, 1973), pp. 23–25.

local programs have been funded and implemented as diversion efforts. The vast majority of these depart significantly from what would be considered to be pure diversion programs, for they do not allow youths freedom in seeking voluntary assistance. Most so-called diversion programs are extensions of the existing juvenile justice system, and many are housed in police and court departments.

> A salient unintended consequence of the diversion movement has been its substantial preemption by police and probation departments. In many areas they have set up in-house programs, hired their own personnel, and programmed cases in terms of their special ends and circumstances. This development is diametrically opposed to the main idea of diversion—that is, that diversion should be away from the juvenile justice system.[20]

Youths are usually required to attend program activities or they face more formal sanctions. As a result of the deviation from the initial conceptualization of diversion, the actual effect of these programs has often been to increase the number of youths in regular contact with the juvenile justice system. They also increase the amount of control over these youths, and the frequency of contact. While this is not the case with every program, it occurs often enough that even with the proliferation of diversion programs, there is no major net reduction in the proportion of delinquents involved with detention, court, and correctional facilities.

To further assess the implementation of the diversion policy, we must keep in mind that diversion programs tend to use the predominant treatment methods found in other delinquency programs. These are most often oriented toward changing the individual offender. Even though some methods are effective with certain youths, there is a need to carefully match the offender to the treatment method. The act of diverting a youngster to a new program does not replace this necessary act of choosing appropriate treatment methods for each youngster.

Just as diversion does not automatically result in the provision of appropriate treatment to each child, it does not automatically reduce stigmatization and the related depreciation of self-worth:

> Some diversion programs may recognize educational skills as being related to delinquency, but they may ignore the status problem and create conditions that lower status even more. For example, a diversion program concerned with education might provide extra classes at a different site for low status students without offering any credit courses that would enhance the student's school record. Although the diversion program means well, it could further contribute to the negative labeling of students involved. Their records would show that they were in a program for "problem boys" and hence would not be candidates for more academic courses or some of the other enrichments that high school could offer.[21]

[20]Lemert, "Diversion in Juvenile Justice," p. 40.
[21]James C. Hackler, *The Prevention of Youthful Crime: The Great Stumble Forward* (Toronto; Methuen, 1978), p. 136.

Hackler, a Canadian scholar concerned with this issue, recommends that diversion programs should increase status opportunities in the job and school setting, rather than focus on changing the offender.[22] This would be more in keeping with the diversionary objective of avoiding stigmatization, which is a common result of treatment methods that focus on delinquents' inadequacies by attempting to correct them through counseling and therapy.

In one sense, the national policy of diversion is highly successful. It has affected a multitude of police and court jurisdictions, and diversion programs are available to a majority of youthful offenders who are apprehended. In another sense, though, these programs did not achieve their major objectives of reducing the total numbers of youths involved with the juvenile justice system or decreasing stigmatization to a great degree. For this reason, a full understanding of the diversion policy and its actual implementation teaches us a very important lesson which should be applied to other policies that seemingly "sweep the country" as promised panaceas for the control of delinquency. Because the causation and control of delinquency are complex and are just partly understood phenomena, simple policy statements are inadequate guides to future action. Policy objectives must be spelled out clearly and in detail. Programs should be designed to anticipate and avoid undesirable but possible results, such as the increased stigmatization or judicial intervention. Since the juvenile justice system is itself fragmented, and differs considerably between cities and counties, program design must be adapted to each locality if national policies are to be implemented in such a way that national objectives are achieved.

Continuing Problems in Ensuring Due Process

In several of its rulings, the Supreme Court has confirmed the rights of juveniles who are arrested and are before the court to constitutional protection. From the moment of apprehension by the police, the juvenile is entitled to know his or her rights and legal protections are mandated to ensure due process. The actual implementation of these laws does not always conform to their intent, however. Rubin explains this inconsistency.

> We are now in the ninth year of the post-*Gault* era and, in my view, have lagged severely in implementing both the letter and the spirit of the mandate, particularly as to the rights of counsel. Despite the obvious conflict of interest, juvenile courts still allow the parents of a status offender to waive the child's right to counsel. Juvenile courts in many communities still actively discourage youth from exercising their right to counsel through a variety of approaches and with a variety of motivations.[23]

---

[22]*Ibid.*

[23]Ted Rubin, "The Juvenile Court's Search for Identity and Responsibility," *Crime and Delinquency, 23,* no. 1 (January 1977), p. 5; see also Harjit S. Sandhu and C. Wayne Heasley, *Improving Juvenile Justice: Power Advocacy, Diversion, Decriminalization, Deinstitutionalization, and Due Process* (New York: Human Sciences Press, 1981), pp. 164–181.

Exhibit 13-1 Pretrial conference

Intake Worker: He's 13-years 11-months going on 25.* [Six months ago] he was referred for assault with a deadly weapon and armed robbery. He continues to drive the school crazy. Now he's here on two assaults, both on school grounds, and for trespassing on school grounds. He was expelled from regular school. We have a complete workup for special school.

Judge: What did we do with the other ones [the other referrals]?

Public Defender: Witnesses weren't here so they weren't adjudicated [no finding of guilt].

Intake Worker: Clinical testing shows his behavior is disordered. . . . There are eight other siblings. Steven has moved in with a brother and sister-in-law.

They tell all sorts of untruths, give a wrong address, change one number in the telephone number.

The mother can't handle him. I think she's afraid of him. He denies everything even before you say it. He's slick, he's slippery.

Judge: We don't have jurisdiction? [We have not taken jurisdiction?]

Public Defender: No, you don't. I can't go along with a commitment to the Department of Corrections with a stay on two simple things from school.

[A joking exchange then occurs between the Public Defender and the Intake Worker.]

Intake Worker: Crockertown might be the place for the little booger. [Laughing.]

Public Defender: Your whole unit's getting vindictive. [Laughing.]

Intake Worker: He does what *you* say.

Public Defender: He *does*. Maybe *I* should be his supervisor.

Intake Worker: The police came over.

Prosecuting Attorney: I didn't ask them . . . Should we go with a commitment with a stay?

Intake Worker: I think we need it.

Prosecuting Attorney: He needs to be told. It's the "D.O.C. Express." [Brief phone call interrupts the discussion.]

Judge (to Public Defender): Well, you'll agree with jurisdiction but not commitment with a stay?

Public Defender: Right.

Judge (to Intake Worker): Would this make it impossible for you to work with him?

Intake Worker: No.

Prosecuting Attorney: He really needs to be laid into. [Public Defender goes into hallway to talk with the juvenile.]

Intake Worker: John Smaley [the probabtion officer who will get the case if jurisdiction is taken] says he wants a commitment with a stay. He says he can't supervise without it.

Judge: We can put one on the record vocally. If he doesn't go to school, shape up, he'll go to D.O.C. It's as good as putting it on paper.

[Public Defender returns after a four-minute conversation with the juvenile.]

Public Defender: He'll admit to one assault and the trespassing.

Judge: All right. Let's go in [to the courtroom].

*"Going on 25 (years)" is a common court expression used to suggest that the juvenile is more streetwise and sophisticated than most juveniles of the same age.

SOURCE: M. A. Bortner, *Inside a Juvenile Court: The Tarnished Ideal of Individualized Justice* (New York: New York University Press, 1982), pp. 49–51.

Exhibit 13-1   Cont.

Issues for Discussion.   What are the benefits and the disadvantages of the pretrial conference for the offender, the complainant, and society in general? Is a pretrial conference such as the one described here consistent with the law? What information should and should not be discussed at a pretrial conference? What are the benefits and the disadvantages of the pretrial conference for the judge, prosecuting and defending attorneys, and the intake worker?

Continued effort is required to ensure that laws granting youths legal rights are fully implemented in local court jurisdictions, for in many cases the actual practices in a juvenile court fall short of the ideal (Exhibit 13-1).

Another area of concern pertinent to due process guarantees is the rapid expansion of diversion programs. There is some question about whether the juveniles' rights during more formal procedures will continue to be protected in the informal diversion programs:

> Current discussion of diversion indicates that none of the recently won rights of juveniles will be applicable in diversionary hearings. One can anticipate hearing familiar justifications for the denial of notice, counsel, crossexamination, and other constitutional rights in informal, treatment-oriented diversion hearings.
>
> The reputedly therapeutic, nonpunitive nature of diversionary programs should not be permitted to serve as an excuse for the abridgment of fundamental constitutional freedoms. Placing properly adjudicated delinquents in these programs may be a commendable alternative to incarceration, but it would be a serious step backwards to permit diversionary placements without legal safeguards which assure that the community has a sound basis for any intervention at all.[24]

Many diversion programs are based on the *parens patriae* philosophy, according to which informality of procedures is consistent with the program's assumption of parental duties of caring for the child. This same reasoning, which was used to justify the informal handling of youths in juvenile court, has not been supported by the Supreme Court as a rationale for ignoring due process. Existing and new diversion programs should develop procedures which blend their assistance to the child with protection of the child's rights.

There have been continued efforts through the courts to protect juveniles' rights to due process throughout their contact with police, court, and correctional agencies. The extent of these protections, and the way that they will be provided, are less clear in the newly proliferated diversion programs. It is likely that the diversion programs will be subjected to court scrutiny, and the courts will set a standard for their operation.

Our review of the implementation of major national juvenile justice

---

[24]Bruce Billington, James Sprowls, Daniel Katkin, and Mark Phillips, "A Critique of Diversionary Juvenile Justice," *Crime and Delinquency, 24,* no. 1 (January 1978), p. 70.

policies—the decriminalization of status offenders, deinstitutionalization, diversion, and due process—reveals that there is some progress in each area, but many important questions and problems remain to be resolved. Looking into the future, we can expect continued attention in these areas, and continued debate about the most fruitful solution. Next we will discuss policy issues which have more recently come to the attention of the public and specialists, and which will no doubt be subject to the political debate surrounding delinquency control over the next several years.

NEW AREAS OF CONCERN FOR POLICYMAKERS

Unlike the deinstitutionalization, diversion, and due process approaches to reform of the juvenile justice system, more recently there is a demand to make the system "tougher." This demand rests on the beliefs that youths are not sufficiently punished for breaking the law, that juvenile delinquency is increasing, and that youths are becoming more violent. These beliefs are not necessarily grounded in fact. Ironically, in contrast to the view that we are not tough enough on juvenile offenders, despite policy objectives to reduce the amount of control exercised by the courts over youths, we maintain high levels of institutionalization and criminalization. Not only do we already institutionalize and process a large proportion of our youthful population, but as emphasized in Chapter 6, Handling the Juvenile Delinquent within the Juvenile Justice System, there is a conservative trend toward increasing this tendency.

Deterrence

Central to the position that we must make our juvenile justice system "tougher" is a belief in the effectiveness of deterrence and the failure of treatment for juveniles. Deterrence involves the increased certainty and severity of punishment, and is based on the idea that juveniles, as well as adults, weigh the probable costs (punishment) of breaking the law against the probable benefits. If the costs are high enough, the youths will be deterred from breaking the law. Therefore, if we improve law enforcement efforts to apprehend juveniles, and toughen the penalties, we will reduce the delinquency rate. The stress on the deterrence effect of the juvenile justice system is at odds with the strong treatment philosophy of the juvenile court and with policy recommendations to lessen controls over adolescents. It is, nevertheless, strongly advocated by those with a conservative view of the offender, and is an important influence on the current juvenile justice policies. For these reasons, it is important to examine the deterrence position closely.

In considering the usefulness of the deterrence approach, we must recognize that deterrence can occur only if people *perceive* that the certainty and the severity of punishments are increased. Even if they are increased, if youths are unaware of this, or do not think that it will affect them personally, deterrence cannot be effective.

The waiver of juveniles to adult court is a currently popular method of those who advocate the deterrence approach. Can waiver change youths' perceptions that penalties are serious? There is some evidence that it cannot:

> Although some legislators and other policymakers seem to have perceived adult courts as tougher when they acted to bring more youths under adult jurisdiction, some juveniles given the option do indeed elect to be tried as adults—either because they seek the more rigid due process provisions of adult court or because they seek to avoid the usually indeterminate nature of juvenile sentencing.[25]

Because due process constraints are not fully implemented in the juvenile court, and there is the rehabilitation rationale that sentencing should not be fixed, but should depend on progress in treatment, the juvenile justice system is more restrictive than the adult system in many jurisdictions. Juveniles themselves perceive the uncertainty of punishment by the criminal courts, and waiver to adult court is not in and of itself a deterrent.

Even if more procedures and punishments are changed to ensure more severe treatment of juveniles, this is unlikely to have a major impact on juvenile delinquency. According to Erickson and Gibbs, the certainty of punishment would be very hard to change, since arrest rates are so low that the chance of being punished is minimal to begin with, and public sentiment would mitigate against the extremely harsh punishments that would then be necessary to affect delinquent activity.[26]

> Thus the final question remains: With a limit to possible increases in severity of punishments for juvenile offenders and the low levels of certainty of punishment (objective and perceived) is it likely that efforts to broaden deterrence in the juvenile justice system will be successful? Based on what we now know, the prognosis must be pessimistic.[27]

Although deterrence seems, on the surface, to be a simple solution to the delinquency problem, a careful look at the process through which deterrence is achieved casts considerable doubt on the feasibility of implementing successful deterrence policies.

Another criticism of the widespread and immediate adoption of a deterrence approach to delinquency control is that this implies that sociological and psychological factors have little or no influence on a person's behavior relative to the costs of punishment. Can raising the costs of apprehension counterbalance the influence of family, community, and societal conditions on youths? Proponents of the deterrence approach do not generally attempt to integrate their theories of deterrence with other theories which research has supported, but

---

[25]Office of Juvenile Justice and Delinquency Prevention, *Juvenile Justice*, p. 50.

[26]Maynard L. Erickson and Jack P. Gibbs, "Punishment, Deterrence, and Juvenile Justice," in *Critical Issues in Juvenile Delinquency*, eds. David Shichor and Delos H. Kelly (Lexington, Massachusetts: Lexington Books, D.C. Heath and Company, 1980), pp. 200–201.

[27]*Ibid.*, p. 201.

instead they propose deterrence as a replacement. It would be more fruitful to accept that factors besides the severity and certainty of punishment have an influence on delinquency. Then efforts could be made to determine which youths, under what circumstances, are most likely to be deterred by punishment, and which respond more positively to various rehabilitative approaches to treatment.

In our discussion, we have identified some of the complexities involved in implementing a deterrence perspective on delinquency control. No doubt, as research progresses, we will gain a better understanding of how and when deterrence works. At this time, however, it cannot be accepted as either a simple or a sure solution to the delinquency problem. Many elements within the juvenile justice system would find the required punishment anathema to the notion of treatment, and these individuals would attempt to protect alternative methods of treatment. Rather than grasping deterrence as a substitute for other approaches, we should view it as one of several possible solutions to juvenile delinquency problems.

Serious Offenders

Closely related to the deterrence issue is contemporary concern about serious juvenile offenders, including those who are violent and who repeatedly commit major property crimes. Public opinion about the nature of the typical delinquent changes over time, and presently there is a tendency to equate juvenile delinquency with serious and dangerous lawbreaking. This ignores the very large group of offenders who commit one or two minor infractions, and it fails to provide an accurate picture of the status offender, who in many instances commits no other type of offense. Policies, such as the efforts to deter youths, are frequently designed for the serious offender, and then applied to a much larger group, because of the failure to differentiate between various types of delinquents.

We do not want to imply that there are no serious offenders who threaten public safety. However, their number is small. It is not only possible, but it is preferable, to reserve the most severe, and the most expensive, correctional resources for the serious offender. Several studies have shown that a small number of youngsters commit a large proportion of serious offenses, and the majority of youths involved with the courts commit just one or two relatively minor offenses. This relatively small group of youths contributes disproportionately to the rates of dangerous and property crime, and therefore it would be most fruitful to concentrate the most restrictive and intensive treatment on them.

Concentrating resources on the serious offender is compatible with decriminalization and true diversion programs which would remove minor offenders from the court and correctional programs. However, since we have been unsuccessful in achieving the objective of decreasing intervention with minor offenders, it is unlikely that increased resources will be available for the serious offender.

Even with increased resources, the question remains as to whether they will be concentrated on incarceration, treatment, or some combination of these approaches. At the root of this question are the polarized opinions regarding the appropriate method for controlling youths. This polarization becomes especially strong, and the issue becomes emotionally charged, when the serious offender is the topic.

On the liberal, or treatment-oriented side, arguments are for a direct attack on the social conditions which contribute to serious delinquency. These include poverty, child abuse, and racial discrimination. One representative of the liberal view presents evidence that there is a direct relationship between unemployment among black youths and their involvement in serious crime.[28] He describes the political controversy regarding the appropriate response to this problem:

> We have come to a fork in the road. We can accept the idea that there is something inherent in the black culture that produces criminals, and spend billions for additional prisons, or we can pursue the idea that crime by blacks is caused primarily by unemployment among black youths, and target concentrated job-producing programs on that particular subgroup of unemployed. The empirical evidence demonstrates that putting black youths in prisons neither rehabilitates nor deters. Furthermore, it is extremely costly. A reduction in unemployment among black youths would seem a much sounder goal to pursue. But it is apparent that, in today's political climate, sending more black youths to prison is much more popular than helping them to find satisfactory employment. It is imperative that informed criminal justice professionals do everything they can to make the crucial facts known, so that important social decisions can be based on reason rather than popular rhetoric.[29]

In Calvin's opinion, we should concentrate available resources on preventing serious delinquency by reducing unemployment. With this approach, if the causes of serious delinquency are eliminated, there is no need for increased incarceration as a deterrent.

On the conservative, or deterrence-oriented side, some states have passed legislation to make it easier, or even mandatory, to use incarceration and other severe penalties in an effort to deter youths. In California, Florida, New York, Colorado, Delaware, and Washington, for example, legislation facilitates the handling of serious juvenile offenders as adults, or it provides mandatory or determinate sentences to be used in the juvenile justice system.[30] Most states have not taken this punitive approach, and instead continue to provide for a wide variety of options in handling juveniles.[31]

We have already raised serious questions about the effectiveness of de-

---

[28]D. Calvin Allen, "Unemployment Among Black Youths, Demographics, and Crime," *Crime and Delinquency,* 27, no. 2 (April 1981), pp. 234–244.

[29]*Ibid.,* p. 244.

[30]Charles P. Smith and Paul S. Alexander, *A National Assessment of Serious Juvenile Crime and the Juvenile Justice System: The Need for a Rational Response,* Vol. 1: Summary (Washington, D.C.: U.S. Government Printing Office, 1980), p. 43.

[31]*Ibid.,* pp. 42–43.

terrence in controlling juvenile delinquency. The sparsity of treatment alternatives for serious offenders in most states raises questions about whether we are equipped to use the liberal approach to intervene in delinquency. As with all delinquency programs, those concentrated on the serious offender emphasize changing the offender rather than family, community, and social conditions. If Calvin is correct in attributing serious delinquency to factors such as unemployment, both deterrence and individual treatment efforts will have minimal effect.

> Even the individual treatment programs are severely limited in their variety: basically, correctional workers can provide remedial education, vocational training, recreation, and counseling. This last takes two main forms: one-to-one talk and verbal interaction within small groups. For violent, assaultive delinquents, of course, there must be added the medical remedies of psychotropic drugs, plus various restraining and stimulating techniques traditionally used in mental hospitals.[32]

Alternatives for the serious offender, such as peer-oriented programs, self-help groups, and even military academy programs, require further experimentation and study.

Our discussion of deterrence and its application to the serious offender confirms our conclusions regarding the policies of deinstitutionalization, diversion, and due process. Liberal versus conservative beliefs about the nature of juvenile delinquency have a major effect on public opinion about the "best" handling of juvenile delinquency. These beliefs influence the very nature of policies and laws, and the extent to which they are or are not successfully implemented at the local level.

As we have stressed throughout this book, these beliefs are not always grounded in research findings. Sometimes advocates of one position or another ignore research findings, and sometimes the necessary research is unavailable. Still, research does make its own contribution to shaping policies. New and needed directions in juvenile delinquency research are the topics for the next section.

RESEARCH IN DELINQUENCY PREVENTION AND TREATMENT

Vigorous research is necessary to identify the many variables related to the phenomenon of juvenile delinquency. Meaningful research can contribute to the establishment of theoretically sound treatment, prevention, and control programs. Research can provide a sound basis on which successful programs can be replicated in different environments and communities.

There are, unfortunately, serious deficiencies in research to evaluate prevention policies and programs. In many cases, useful evaluations are not carried out:

---

[32]*Ibid.*, p. 51.

As late as 1976, the National SPA [State Planning Agency] was proud that a mere 30 percent of state projects were being evaluated each year. Sarat testified that his research on the SPAs has revealed that "at the State level, evaluation is a sham. It is a joke." State planners told him that evaluation is nothing more than project monitoring. In its full-fledged 1978 review of LEAA evaluation activities the GAO [Government Accounting Office] found that the amounts and types of evaluations were inadequate, the quality of the research was "questionable," users' needs were "not being met," and management of evaluation needed improvement.[33]

Although we have cited a number of studies in our discussions of delinquency programs and treatment methods (Chapters 7 and 8), these are the exception. Most programs and methods are not evaluated so as to provide useful information about the success of control efforts.

Empey and Lubeck provide some helpful suggestions for carrying out useful research, and they list the following steps for an effective delinquency research process:

1. Define the target population. Decide whether it is to include the young children, a middle-range group, or older, convicted offenders.
2. Conduct a pilot study by which to identify and describe the particular children who fit the general characteristics of the target population.
3. Define objectives for the program. Include administrators, practitioners, and research people in the defining process.
4. Write a contract specifying the obligations and roles of each of these three sets of people.
5. Derive an intervention strategy based upon the general leads provided by the theory and the findings of the pilot study.
6. Establish a research strategy based on the same principles and guidelines and concerned with studying the characteristics of the subject population, the program itself, and its outcome.[34]

These steps are consistent with the model for understanding juvenile delinquency which we identified at the beginning of this book. Using this research process draws attention to the interconnections between (1) the target population (who are the delinquents?), (2) the theory that identifies the causes of delinquency to be changed by the program, and (3) program design and implementation. To be useful in practice, an evaluation must produce information in each of these three areas.

Much more effort has to be made toward more sophisticated evaluation and research procedures if successful programs are to be perpetuated and replicated and unsuccessful ones eliminated or improved. Evaluation and research should be an integral part of any program established to assist the delinquent.

[33]Richard S. Allinson, "LEAA's Impact on Criminal Justice: A Review of the Literature," *Criminal Justice Abstracts, 11,* no. 4 (December 1979), p. 646.

[34]Lamar T. Empey and Steven G. Lubeck, "Delinquency Prevention Strategies," U.S. Department of Health, Education, and Welfare, Social and Rehabilitation Service, Youth Development and Delinquency Prevention Administration, 1970.

It is obvious to anyone familiar with the field that delinquency treatment is not now simply a matter of the skilled application of demonstrably effective methods. Rigorous assessment of programs is rare, and the handful of studies that we have described almost exhausts the available literature on effective programs. The old saw that "more research needs to be done" is certainly true here. Ideally, every intervention effort should be regarded as experimental, imbedded in a rigorous research design that can demonstrate with fair assurance whether the method reduces delinquent behavior or not.[35]

Research means many different things to different people and often "strikes terror" into the hearts of practitioners when it is proposed. Research is merely a tool, which can take many different forms, to assist in defining problems and developing methods for their solution.

> Research is many kinds of activity. It is gathering and analyzing facts. It is conducting and evaluating operational experiments. It is searching for the motivations of human behavior. Obviously there is a need here for a wide variety of talents. Sociologists, lawyers, economists, psychiatrists, psychologists, physical scientists, engineers, statisticians, mathematicians—all these and more are needed. There is likewise opportunity for a wide variety of organizations and institutions. Too little is known about the various uses and limitations of different methods of organizing for research to permit the prescription of any one mold for future research efforts. Indeed it is essential that such efforts take many different forms.[36]

Since World War II, massive research efforts have been undertaken to determine the causes of and the solutions to crime and delinquency. Assumptions have been drastically modified, practices have changed, much has been learned, but the surface of the problem has hardly been scratched. Many promising courses have been embarked on only to be abandoned as time proved them ineffective, inefficient, too costly, or unpopular. No aspect of the criminal justice system has received more attention than juvenile and adult corrections. Yet there prevails at present a decidedly pessimistic attitude toward correctional research. In the words of Robert Martinson, "Correctional research is about nine-tenths pageantry, rumination, and rubbish, and about one-tenth useful knowledge."[37]

However pessimistic his statement, Martinson cannot but affirm the value of good research in problem solving. Moreover, crowded institutions, fear for public safety, budgetary problems, and the spread of new management methods into social agencies have all created strong pressure for evaluative research. The

[35]Martin Gold and Richard J. Petronio, "Delinquent Behavior in Adolescence" in *Handbook of Adolescent Psychology,* ed. Joseph Adelson (New York: Wiley-Interscience Publication, 1980), p. 523.

[36]Stanton Wheeler, Leonard Cottrell, Jr., and Ann Romasco, "Juvenile Delinquency—Its Prevention and Control," in The President's Commission on Law Enforcement and the Administration of Justice, *Task Force Report on Juvenile Delinquency and Youth Crime* (Washington, D.C.: U.S. Government Printing Office, 1967), p. 424.

[37]Robert Martinson, "California Research at the Crossroads," *Crime and Delinquency* (April 1976), p. 183.

public at large is demanding to know what is being done to reduce the crime rate, whether the measures employed are effective, and what they are costing them in tax dollars. The answers to these and other critical questions can come only from continued research. To be effective, however, the research of the future will have to proceed from a sound theoretical base, and be translated into practice by administrators open to experimentation and innovation.

History

Since adult and juvenile corrections have been the subject of such considerable research efforts, a summary of the history of correctional research will afford significant insight into the development of research in parallel components of the criminal and juvenile justice systems. Correctional research is, moreover, of particular relevance to juvenile delinquency. In addition, most of the early "vigorous" criminal justice research has been done in institutionalized correctional populations. This was done for the obvious reason of having the subject in a controlled setting.

Accounts and statistics have been maintained from the early nineteenth century in housekeeping, budgeting, and audit. These data were used as reports for funding sources and in planning for future needs. With an expanding offender population, the need for the increased accuracy of analytical techniques became acute. The advent of relatively accurate statistical analysis brought with it some penetrating questions regarding professional practice. The data suggested, for example, that the costs of imprisonment might be reduced by the increased use of probation and parole and other community treatment approaches. This raised the question of public safety. If relatively large numbers of offenders were to be set free or not incarcerated at all, small-scale experimentation had first to establish whether a considerable negative impact on public safety would ensue. The acceptance of the need for experimentation before large-scale changes in correctional practice could be undertaken established the principle of the continuity of statistical analysis.

For many years, the effectiveness of correctional programs has been evaluated by counting the convicted offenders who return to criminal behavior. This return is termed "recidivism," and understanding its scope is essential to operational control. The statistics on recidivism are extremely difficult to obtain, however; correctional agencies are, for the most part, not equipped to gather accurate data on recidivism. A greater hindrance to the collection of recidivism data is the fragmented nature of the criminal justice system: the police, the courts, and correctional agencies do not always cooperate effectively with one another.

Last, recidivism of this type is only the return to criminal behavior that is *officially* noted. In other words, officially noted recidivism is only a rough measure of objective recidivism, a certain percentage of which is always undetected.

Statistical data taken alone, however, by no means provide adequate information. They provide a numerical count or a numerical comparison. The numbers must be interpreted and strategies to improve results must be devised. Thus research and statistics are interdependent.

The earliest empirical research in corrections, that of Sheldon and Eleanor Glueck in the thirties,[38] examined the experience of offenders who had been exposed to various rehabilitative programs. Their basic approach has remained the one most frequently employed up to the present. A considerable amount of research data, which has had a significant impact on correctional programs, has accumulated. Perhaps the most dramatic finding of correctional research has been that incarceration cannot be shown to produce any positive effect on offender behavior. Thus incarceration seems incompatible with rehabilitation, regardless of the treatment program. This conclusion has been arrived at with amazing consistency and has led to an interest in developing community-based alternatives to incarceration. These offer more hope for rehabilitation and are also considerably cheaper. Present consensus maintains that institutionalization should be employed only in the cases of those offenders who pose a direct and obvious threat to the public. This position has resulted in the complete reorganization of juvenile correctional services in some states—for example, Massachusetts.

Experiments conducted since the 1950s have demonstrated the relative feasibility of various alternatives to incarceration such as community treatment, halfway houses, work release, and probation subsidy. Evidence seems to show that these programs do, in fact, reduce recidivism *if* the choice of the participant is fortunate—that is, if the appropriate type of offender is referred to the program. Establishing the objective criteria, however, which indicate that an offender is favorably predisposed to various treatment alternatives, constitutes a particularly critical need of research today, since if anything is obvious at this juncture it is that different offenders react in a variety of ways to treatment. Thus, the overall premise that a community-based, nonpunitive program is appropriate to *all* offenders is as erroneous as applying the age-old punitive and incarceration approach to *all* offenders.

Ongoing Research

The National Institute of Juvenile Justice, which is housed in the Department of Justice, as well as other public and private organizations, has taken important steps in improving the quality and quantity of juvenile delinquency research. The National Institute of Juvenile Justice has recently funded extensive research in three areas:

1. delinquent behavior and its prevention
2. the juvenile justice system (police, courts, and corrections), and
3. community-based alternatives to juvenile justice system processing.[39]

[38]Sheldon and Eleanor Glueck, *500 Criminal Careers* (New York: Alfred A. Knopf, Inc., 1930).

[39]National Institute for Juvenile Justice and Delinquency Prevention, *Annual Report Of NIJJDP, Fiscal Year 1979* (Washington, D.C.: U.S. Government Printing Office, 1980), p. 2.

In addition to funding universities and other organizations to carry out research in these areas, the institute has established several National Assessment Centers which compile the results of completed research and publish it in a form that is useful to policymakers and practitioners. These reports and the results of other federally funded research are available from the Juvenile Justice Clearinghouse.

In recent years, the nature of research has changed in many ways. It is widely recognized that, in program evaluation, recidivism by itself is a limited indicator of success or failure. Other program effects on the offender also must be considered. For example, an offender may not have been convicted of further crimes, but may be unemployed, lack job skills, and abuse drugs or alcohol. While technically not a failure, the youth is also not a success. Besides a variety of effects on the offender, program evaluation should consider effects on the rest of the juvenile justice system and the community. The value of evaluations of diversion programs lies not only in their pinpointing program effects on recidivism, but also in their showing that the programs increased the flow of youths into the system. This type of useful finding is most possible when the research studies a wide range of possible program effects on the offender, other individuals, and the juvenile justice system as a whole.

Another important shift in delinquency program evaluation is the increased recognition given to the value of controlled experiments. The controlled experiment evaluates a treatment experience by measuring differences in the outcomes for "experimental" and "control" groups. Because individuals are randomly assigned to one or the other of the groups, we can assume that they are similar at the start of the program. There is a strong likelihood that any difference between the groups at the completion of the program is due to the treatment. The controlled experiment maximizes the degree to which we can conclude that a delinquency program caused a certain outcome.

In many practical settings, it is possible to implement a controlled experiment. If there is a limit on the number of clients that a program can accept, which is usually the case, random selection from all those eligible is a fair way to choose those who will receive the services. Youths who are not selected make up the control group. This approach was used to justify the formation of a control group in an Oakland, California, work experience program:

> The Oakland project staff had considerable prior experience with youth work experience programs in Oakland and, in these earlier instances, had encountered criticism from community agencies and citizen interest groups over selection procedures and quotas. They were therefore quite open to our suggestion of using a random selection process and to the argument that this procedure was an equitable one which community agencies and interest groups would accept.
>
> The project staff correctly anticipated approximately six hundred eligible youth applicants for this program, which could accommodate a maximum of two hundred participants. Applicants were told that the actual selection of participants would be made randomly by a computer, and that each person's chance of selection was the same, approximately one in three.[40]

[40]Delbert S. Elliott, "Recurring Issues in the Evaluation of Delinquency Prevention and Treatment Programs," in *Critical Issues in Juvenile Delinquency*, eds. Shichor and Kelly, p. 247.

When practical and political considerations make it impossible to carry out a controlled experiment, other research designs must be used. In the many instances where a controlled experiment is possible, the increased training and understanding of program staff and evaluators make it possible to apply a very sound research design.

Another continuing concern in delinquency program evaluation is the need to relate success in some demonstrable way to a specific strategy or technique which is based on a theory of delinquency causation. As deterrence becomes more popular in the political arena, researchers will need to specify the ways in which increased certainty and severity of punishments actually affect youths. At the same time that a theory of the dynamics of deterrence is developed, evaluation should be conducted to show the impact of programs which are intended to deter adolescents.

Research with Impact

One of the objectives of research is to bring about change. Some research has had a broad impact on practice; other research has had none at all. Most of it could be placed somewhere on a continuum between these two extremes. In addition to stimulating change in criminal justice practice, research can have theoretical and methodological consequences, as well.

Following are some examples of studies that had impact: they resulted in change in the handling of offender populations.[41]

In 1956 the California Special Study Commission on Correctional Facilities and Services studied the sixty county probation departments in the state to evaluate the status of the probation process, to note problems and deficiencies in it, and to make relevant recommendations to the state legislature. A field survey design was employed; various types of instruments and strategies were used to secure descriptive and judgmental data from probation department staff and county judges. Research staff added their evaluations, which were based on generally accepted professional criteria.

One of the recommendations emanating from the survey report was that counties should be provided with a subsidy by the state to enable them to upgrade their operations so that they would better conform with professional standards.

This recommendation did not pass the assembly in 1957. A later survey, similar but on a smaller scale, stimulated the same recommendation. However, this time it was modified to tie payments to the county to rates of diversion of convicted offenders from state institutions to county correctional programs. This added incentive convinced the legislature, and the measure passed. It has been estimated that forty thousand adult and juvenile offenders were diverted from California penal institutions in the first eight years of its operation.

---

[41]These examples were taken from Stuart Adams, Ph.D., "Research with Impact: Six Case Studies," in *Evaluative Research in Corrections: A Practical Guide* (Washington, D.C.: U.S. Department of Justice, Law Enforcement Assistance Administration, National Institute of Law Enforcement and Criminal Justice, 1975), pp. 12–14.

In 1959 an exploratory study of the impact of the California Youth Authority's Preston School of Industry on its male delinquent inmates was undertaken. A series of interviews at two-week intervals were held with fifteen selected youths during a six-week stay at the Northern Reception Center Clinic and at two-month intervals at Preston. Delinquency identification, attitudes toward authority, peer relationships, values, goals, criminal language, and skills were examined with a view toward assessing the influence of the clinic and the training school on changes in these phenomena. At the completion of the study, the researcher judged that the net effect was probably unfavorable to the youths and to the communities to which they eventually returned. It was subsequently recommended to the Youth Authority that a controlled experiment be conducted to compare the effects of institutional and community treatments. The recommendation was accepted by the Youth Authority executives even though the results might prove the Youth Authority obsolete. This impact is indeed significant in view of the normal tendency of bureaucracies to reject anything that threatens their existence.

The decision to proceed with the experiment resulted in the now famous Community Treatment Project, which continued from 1961 to 1974 in three different phases, funded by the National Institute of Mental Health. The impact of the Community Treatment Project in the treatment and handling of juveniles has been momentous. It was largely responsible for rendering diversion and community treatment the wave of the future.

Most research does not result in this kind of impact. There are several reasons for low research payoff, regardless of the field. Research in high technology, for example, is successful only 5 percent of the time. There is no reason to believe that expectations for criminal justice research should be any more optimistic. Much research is of doubtful quality. There is often an incongruence between researcher styles and the pressing and practical needs of administrators; researcher priorities at higher levels of theory and purity of method clash with the administrator's need for advice in uncertain situations. Moreover,

> many administrators do not welcome change; their anxieties, personal views and preference for order and tranquility in their institutions may turn them against innovation, even when it appears reasonable, constructive and buttressed by scientific evidence. Others exist in precarious balance, and the operationalizing of new, even though tested, concepts increases the difficulty of their position. Still others have seen many promising new ideas come and go, leaving disillusion in their wake. Finally, new ideas may call for increased budgets, and the skepticism of legislative committees about budget expansion in correction cuts deeper than research ire.[42]

Research by itself does not lead to change. However, when it is disseminated and applied by individuals and groups with compatible beliefs and interests in the area of delinquency control, it can have considerable impact on policy.

[42]*Ibid.*, p. 34.

SUMMARY AND CONCLUSION

This chapter looked at many aspects of juvenile delinquency control with an eye toward existing policy dilemmas and what will happen in the future.

There was an examination of the influence of liberal and conservative opinion on juvenile justice policies. Efforts to improve the juvenile justice system are often blocked by the polarization of these two positions, as well as the fragmentation within the juvenile justice system itself. The highly publicized national policies of decriminalizing status offenders, deinstitutionalizing large numbers of delinquents, diverting many youths out of the system, and establishing regular practices to protect due process have not been fully achieved. In fact, rather than becoming more lenient, juvenile justice processing has become more punitive, as growing numbers of youths are brought into the juvenile justice system and its institutions.

Efforts should be made to tailor the juvenile justice system to the juvenile and the type of crime involved. Status offenders, first-time offenders, and those involved in less serious crimes should ideally be dealt with outside the stigmatizing formal system. The police officer should be the initial preventive agent who would deliver the offender to a social agency that could handle the specific problem on a voluntary basis. If this process of diversion is to work as intended, it will require more and varied programs within the community, along with improved follow-up and communication with the police.

But at the same time that this more liberal and humanistic approach shows the best promise of dealing effectively with the bulk of juvenile offenders, there is a pressing need to improve our methods of treatment for the serious and chronic offender. There is not at this time any convincing evidence that efforts to deter juvenile delinquency can be effective for the serious offender. Society must make the commitment to provide adequate treatment, and to explore a variety of treatment approaches. It may be necessary to remove the serious offender from the community for the protection of others, but at the same time there is a need to develop programs which can ensure some positive change in these youths' environments and in the youths themselves.

Going still deeper into the problem of how to handle juvenile crime and delinquency, it cannot be denied that the optimal method of attack is to get at the roots of the problem with primary prevention. This may involve working with families, or trying to alter the status of adolescents within our society. This preventive approach is the wisest course of action a civilized society can take, yet it would be naive not to admit that there are serious obstacles in the way.

Often parents are unwilling to allow an agency to intervene early, because intervention is viewed as interference. And typically the youngsters who will potentially have the most serious future problems come from families in which parents are the least willing to confront the situation responsibly.

Communities, too, show great reluctance in getting involved in primary prevention. It would mean identifying conditions and problems in the community and the larger society that show signs of leading to maladaptive behavior and then taking corresponding action early enough to prevent problems.

But many things must change before primary prevention stands a healthy chance of success. Legislative support and funding will be needed. Perhaps the most important component is cooperation and a spirit of compromise on the part of individuals and groups in society. Each must be willing to give up some short-term autonomy to gain long-term results.

Although the beliefs about delinquency which are expressed in the political arena and at the community level are strong influences on policy, research also can have some impact. Despite serious shortcomings, program evaluation can be expected to improve and provide increased insight into the most effective methods of delinquency treatment. Given the interest in deterrence, research in this area is likely to be of considerable practical importance in the future.

Every time a young person commits a crime, society loses. It is necessary, on the one hand, to improve services and systems needed to cope with today's teenagers in trouble, but it will take an even greater spirit of cooperation and support, on the other hand, to stand a chance of preventing tomorrow's problems before they begin.

Bibliography

INTRODUCTION

This bibliography attempts to provide the student of juvenile delinquency with a sample of recent literature relating to various aspects of the phenomenon. The works cited herein describe the problem in the United States and abroad, and discuss causes, treatment strategies, prevention, and professional training, among other topics. They reflect a number of differences of opinion in these areas, differences which are especially great in the areas of causes and ways of dealing with delinquency.

Special attention is paid to books that include very detailed descriptions and analysis of the youth who are involved in delinquency programs and the various types of programs and institutions that seek to prevent and control juvenile lawbreaking. Useful books on other nations are included, as well as books on topics that are receiving increased research attention, for example delinquent girls and contemporary gangs. Thus, the bibliography is a guide to literature that can be used for papers and other class projects to supplement the textbook, and to stimulate the interest of students who want to delve deeper into the subjects introduced in the textbook.

Most titles and accompanying descriptions are followed by the Library of Congress call number, which is utilized by large libraries.

The decision to include books published since 1970 was based on both an attempt to provide an in-depth treatment of the literature chosen and to focus on recent works. It is hoped that the selected titles and descriptions will aid in furthering the student's knowledge in the area of juvenile delinquency.

ACKLAND, JOHN W. *Girls in Care: A Case Study of Residential Treatment*. Hampshire, England: Gower Publishing Company Limited, 1982. 166 pp.

This book gives the reader an in-depth look at a residential program for girls in England. The structure and guidelines for the school are described, and the perceptions of staff and residents are measured with an interview schedule. One chapter is devoted to the system of control and discipline, and another to institutional reactions to runaway behavior. The book closes with the girls' and the staff's perceptions of relationships at the group home and implications for successful treatment.
HV9145.A5A34

AGEE, VICKI L. *Treatment of the Violent Incorrigible Adolescent*. Lexington, Massachusetts: Lexington Books, D.C. Heath and Company, 1979. 175 pp.
This book provides an in-depth review of the special difficulties as well as effective strategies relevant to the treatment of violent incorrigible adolescents. The background of these adolescents usually includes a series of institutional and community placements out of which the adolescent manipulates herself or himself. Agee draws on her knowledge of the Colorado Youth Services Institute, and she describes effective methods for working with both staff and clients. Several case studies are included in the book, and the results of a positive evaluation of the Colorado Youth Services Institute are summarized.
RJ506.V56A35

AHLSTROM, WINTON M., AND ROBERT J. HAVIGHURST. *400 Losers*. San Francisco: Jossey-Bass, Inc., 1971. 246 pp.
A report of a combined work-experience and modified academic program involving eighth-grade students who were studied until ages eighteen or nineteen. In addition to reporting specific experimental findings— mainly that the work-experience program was related to improved social adjustment in some of the boys— the book's main emphasis is on describing the actual life situations to which the boys successfully or unsuccessfully adapted.
HV9106.K2A64

APTER, STEVEN J. AND ARNOLD P. GOLDSTEIN, eds. *Youth Violence: Programs and Prospects*. New York: Pergamon Press, 1986. 301 pp.
The focus of this book is on programs to intervene in the lives of violent youths and the theories that explain their violence. Particular chapters focus on special education, neurological bases of youth violence, institutional treatment, psychological skills training and school delinquency. There also are chapters on ecological explanations of youth violence, social competence, the influence of television and film, legal concerns and youth violence in other cultures.
HV9104.Y686

ARMSTRONG, TROY L., ed. *Intensive Interventions with High-risk Youths: Promising Approaches in Juvenile Probation and Parole*. Monsey, New York: Criminal Justice Press, 1991. 464 pp.
Sixteen studies of intensive supervision programs for high-risk juvenile probationers and parolees provide an in-depth examination of the program designs and the outcomes. There is attention to the history of intensive intervention, theories of delinquency causation that underlie the programs as well as evaluation research. Employment, electronic monitoring, drug treatment, restitution and selective aftercare programs are covered. Guidance is provided for determining program philosophy and goals, caseload size and frequency of contact, and classification procedures and client targeting.

ARNOLD, WILLIAM R. *Juveniles on Parole: A Sociological Perspective*. New York: Random House, Inc., 1970. 177 pp.
Presents a sociological analysis of the parole system. Discusses the interrelationship of its components (parolees and their peers, parole officers and their peers, parents of parolees, and others), and the importance of the characteristics and roles of each. The author believes such analysis provides the best understanding of the behavior of those in the system in order to effect changes in that behavior. He suggests that the behavior of others in the system may need modification before parolees' behavior can be changed. Includes specific changes that might be made in the parole system to improve its effectiveness.
HV9104.A85

BAKAL, YITZHAK, ed. *Closing Correctional Institutions*. Lexington, Massachusetts: Lexington Books, D.C. Heath and Company, 1973. 186 pp.
The readings in this work present the case for closing correctional institutions, discuss some of the problems involved, and suggest specific alternatives. Contributors cite the failure of institutions to rehabilitate, and suggest that community-centered measures are more humane and effective as well as closer to the problem.
HV9069.C518

BAKAL, YITZHAK, AND HOWARD W. POLSKY. *Reforming Corrections for Juvenile Offenders.* Lexington, Massachusetts: Lexington Books, D.C. Heath and Company, 1979. 213 pp.
> *A detailed examination of delinquency and the archaic Massachusetts system of training schools is given. Once the Massachusetts training schools closed, a complex alternative system of care developed. New strategies of foster care, programs to assist youths in reintegrating into their communities and families, and special programs for serious offenders are described. The authors explain practical steps to be taken in staff training and evaluation for such a system of alternative care. Prospects and strategies for further change are reviewed, too.*
HV9105.M4B34

BAKER, KEITH, AND ROBERT J. RUBEL. *Violence and Crime in the Schools.* Lexington, Massachusetts: Lexington Books, D.C. Heath and Company, 1980. 295 pp.
> *A collection of articles relevant to four aspects of violence and crime in schools: (1) the history and extent of troublesome behavior, (2) the school as victim, (3) schools as contributors to the problem, and (4) vandalism. Many of these articles have practical implications for the prevention and control of school crime and violence.*
LB3013.3.V56

BARTOLLAS, CLEMENS, STUART J. MILLER, AND SIMON DINITZ. *Juvenile Victimization: The Institutional Paradox.* New York: Sage Publications, Halsted Press Division, John Wiley and Sons, Inc., 1976. 324 pp.
> *A description of the experiences of youths in an Ohio State Correctional Institution is provided. The authors show that many of the characteristics of a closed correctional facility victimize the inmates. Members of the inmate subculture exploit each other, and some youths are stigmatized by staff as even less desirable than others. Some youths can adapt so as to minimize such difficulties, but some, because of emotional or other problems, cannot. The book concludes with a strong condemnation of juvenile institutions.*
HV9104.B35

BASS, ELLEN, AND LOUISE THORNTON. *I Never Told Anyone: Writings by Women Survivors of Child Sexual Abuse.* New York: Harper and Row, 1983. 278 pp.
> *This anthology includes stories and poems that help the reader to understand female children's experiences of sexual abuse. The accounts are of abuse by fathers, by relatives, by friends and acquaintances, and by strangers. Additionally, the introduction reviews customs that support child sexual abuse.*
HQ71.115 1983

BEATTIE, JEANN. *And the Tiger Leaps.* Toronto: McClelland and Stewart, Ltd., 1971. 216 pp.
> *Personal narrative of a nonprofessional who becomes involved in work with delinquents and an antidelinquency group in Toronto.*
HV9108.B4

BLUM, RICHARD H. AND ASSOCIATES. *Horatio Alger's Children.* San Francisco: Jossey-Bass, Inc., 1972. 327 pp.
> *The authors focus on the link between family conditions and youthful drug use. They are able to identify predisposing conditions, and they present this information with the objective of helping parents, teachers, counselors, and community leaders concerned with teenage drug abusers.*
HV5825.B54

BENEDEK, ELISSA P., AND DEWEY G. CORNELL, eds. *Juvenile Homicide.* Washington, D.C.: American Psychiatric Press, 1989. 247 pp.
> *The clinical framework provides a common theme to the articles in this book. A typology of juvenile murderers, legal issues facing the examiner, transfer to adult court, and treatment options are considered.*
RJ506.H65J88

BORTNER, M. A. *Inside a Juvenile Court: The Tarnished Ideal of Individualized Justice.* New York: New York University Press, 1982. 283 pp.
> *This very readable description of the decision-making process in one juvenile court introduces the reader to the informal conversations that have a bearing on formal reactions to juvenile offenders. Numerous examples are provided of the pretrial conversations of attorneys, judges, and probation workers, and special chapters show the biases against social class, racial, and gender subgroups. Illustrations of conversation in the courtroom setting are also given. Difficulties involved in fairly delivering individualized justice are reviewed in the last chapter.*
KF9794.B67

BOTTOMS, A. E., AND FREDERICK H. MCCLINTOCK. *Criminals Coming of Age: A Study of Institutional Adaptation in the Treatment of Adolescent Offenders.*London: William Heinemann Ltd., 1973. 495 pp.
> *The population of closed correctional programs in England is described as exhibiting a multiplicity of problems. The borstal system, which is designed to correct these difficulties, is also plagued with problems. Instituting improvements met with a number of obstacles, and these are explained. Although some improvements were made in the program at one location, the effect on the recidivism rates was minimal at best.*
> HV6001.C3v.32

BREMMER, ROBERT H. (Ed.). *Children in Confinement.* New York: Arno Press, 1974. 324 pp.
> *Collection of five articles on the detention of youthful offenders in the United States, which was originally published in the years 1877–1944.*
> HV9104.C44

BRENNAN, TIM, DAVID HUIZINGA, AND DELBERT S. ELLIOTT. *The Social Psychology of Runaways.* Lexington, Massachusetts: Lexington Books, D.C. Heath and Company, 1978. 335 pp.
> *In this book the authors outline the serious nature of the runaway problem in the United States, and they describe the youths and their peer, family, and school relationships. Research showed that runaways were subjected to more stress and strain in the home and school than were other youths. Parents were not adequate role models, and the youths did not feel a strong bond with anyone in their environment. These and other findings are used to develop "early warning signals" that a youth will run away, and to set guidelines for intervention. The authors advance a strong argument for keeping runaways out of the juvenile justice system.*
> HQ796.B6882

BRENZEL, BARBARA M. *Daughters of the State: A Social Portrait of the First Reform School for Girls in North America, 1856–1905.* Cambridge, Massachusetts: The MIT Press, 1983. 206 pp.
> Daughters of the State *describes the first institution for adolescent girls who were judged to be in danger of becoming wayward and straying into prostitution and other forms of crime. The analysis of the school's history reveals the ideas behind the juvenile reform effort in nineteenth-century America as well as the prevailing attitudes toward females and the family. It also shows a change from the ideals of reform to a program of rigid training and custodial care. Finally, the historical material shows the class, age, and gender biases that influenced policies and programs intended to reform adolescents.*
> HV9105.M42S733 1983

BROWN, WALN. *The Other Side of Delinquency.* New Brunswick, New Jersey: Rutgers University Press, 1983. 188 pp.
> *Waln Brown, a successful professional, presents his own life experiences as a seriously delinquent youth. His unique story shows how an individual with a traumatic past can succeed in adulthood. The story reveals the insensitivity of regimes in juvenile institutions and the negative quality of psychiatric assessment in a state hospital. The great importance of the home environment in the causation of delinquency also is stressed. Brown's own recollections are contrasted with old case notes and assessments, which set forth the official views of the authorities.*
> HV9104.B77

BUTLER, SANDRA. *Conspiracy of Silence: The Trauma of Incest.* San Francisco, California: Volcano Press, Inc., 1978. 208 pp.
> *Sandra Butler has compiled extensive case materials on children affected by incest, the aggressors, mothers and other family members. In many cases, family members and victims tell their own stories, and this provides an in-depth understanding of all of the people involved. The problems and the successes in obtaining professional help are the topic of one of the later chapters, and the book ends with a collection of letters from the author to incest survivors, their family members, and others.*
> HQ72.U53B87

CAIN, MAUREEN, ed. *Growing Up Good: Policing the Behaviour of Girls in Europe.* Newbury Park, California: Sage Publications, Inc., 1989 256 pp.
> *Articles in this book reveal the role of stereotypes in shaping the personalities and lifestyles of girls who depart from the social norm and are involved in such activities as prostitution and drug abuse. There is information about the limits placed on girls behavior and the methods of policing the girls in ten European countries. Theories are developed to explain the girls' aspirations and practical suggestions are set forth to help girls with their problems. Surprisingly, there are many similarities between the experiences of girls in the ten countries, though the countries differ much from each other. Vivid accounts of girls' experiences in correctional institutions and alternative programs show how both male and female gender stereotypes are reinforced.*
> HV6046.G76

CARTER, ROBERT M., AND MALCOLM W. KLEIN. *Back on the Street: The Diversion of Juvenile Offenders.* Englewood Cliffs, New Jersey: Prentice-Hall, Inc., 1976. 368 pp.
> *Once diversion policies had been instituted throughout the United States, considerable discussion and research examined the effects of the change. Carter and Klein have assembled a number of articles pertaining to diversion. The first several of these set forth the basic philosophy of diversion, and following articles examine the labeling theory on which the policy is based. Additional sections of the book are devoted to guidelines needed by police and probation officers who implement the policy, examples of diversion programs, evaluations of programs, and tests of labeling theory.*
HV8104.B33

CASSERLY, MICHAEL D., SCOTT A. BASS, AND JOHN R. GARRETT. *School Vandalism.* Lexington, Massachusetts: Lexington Books, D.C. Heath and Company, 1980. 166 pp.
> *An in-depth analysis of the extent, nature, and control of school vandalism is given in this book. The major options for controlling school vandalism are explained, and several case studies of prevention programs are described. An outline is included to guide individuals through the process of designing a program.*
LB3249.C37

CHESNEY-LIND, MEDA AND RANDALL SHELDON. *Girls, Delinquency, and Juvenile Justice.* Pacific Grove, California: Brooks/Cole Publishing Company, 1991.
> *Drawing on research and new case material, the authors break the silence on girls and their problems. Both the similarities and differences in patterns and causes of girls' and boys' delinquency are covered. For girls, the connection between their own physical and sexual abuse in the family is a key explanation of their running away and other status offenses. The differential response of the juvenile justice system is an additional focus, with attention to the large proportion of girls who are arrested and placed in justice programs based on their involvement in status offenses. Throughout, the authors provide information to assist in "knowing what it is like" for girls with problems who because of their race, poverty, or a history of victimization find their way into the juvenile justice system. Historical information on the development of programs for girls and insights into needed policy and program changes provide additional insight.*

CLARK, TED. *The Oppression of Youth.* New York: Harper Colophon Books, Harper & Row, Publishers, 1975. 178 pp.
> *The author bases this book on his work as a counselor for adolescents, his friendship with the youths, and his own experiences growing up. He feels that many of youth's problems occur in their relationships with authority figures, and he challenges the idea that adolescents need to be controlled by adults. Many case examples are given of problems youths encounter in the family and school, and in sexual relationships.*
HQ796.C593 1975

COATES, ROBERT B., ALDEN D. MILLER, AND LLOYD E. OHLIN. *Diversity in a Youth Correctional System: Handling Delinquents in Massachusetts.* Cambridge, Massachusetts: Ballinger Publishing Company, Subsidiary of J. B. Lippincott Co., 1978. 228 pp.
> *An evaluation of programs which replaced the Massachusetts State Training schools shows that, on the whole, the community corrections alternatives provide a more positive experience for youthful offenders. Recidivism is not increased by any sizable amount once youths are placed in the community instead of in a closed program. The authors conclude that despite these advantages, community corrections programs can be further improved to increase youths' linkages to legitimate institutions and people in the area. There also is a need to advocate within the community on behalf of delinquent youths.*
HV9105.M4C6

COHEN, HAROLD L., AND JAMES FILIPCZAK. *A New Learning Environment.* San Francisco: Jossey-Bass, Inc., 1971. 192 pp.
> *Describes a project in "contingency management" carried out at the National Training School for Boys, in which boys were given monetary and material rewards for improved social behavior and academic performance. The project involved a twenty-four-hour learning environment and establishment of an economy based on academic achievement and work for the administration; essentially, it included choices and compensations available to wage-earning members of society. It was found that increased academic skills and positive attitudinal changes resulted.*
HV9106.W32N353

COLE, LARRY. *Our Children's Keepers.* New York: Grossman Publishers, 1972. 152 pp.
> *Cole is critical of juvenile correctional institutions, viewing them as both a result and a cause of problems. He traces the development of institutions, provides detailed portraits of several institutions, and presents*

specific cases through interviews with staff and inmates. Following this, he speculates on the reasons for the situation as it is and provides specific suggestions for positive change.
HV9104.C56

Committee on Mental Health Services Inside and Outside the Family Court in the City of New York. *Juvenile Justice Confounded: Pretensions and Realities of Treatment Services.* National Council on Crime and Delinquency. 1972. 124 pp.
Examination of the treatment services available to the court for children adjudged delinquent or in need of supervision. Concludes that resources are least available for those in greatest need of them. The court is faced with community "pathology," manifested through denial of treatment services, in addition to the pathology of the troubled child and family.
HV9105.N7A49 1972

CORTES, JUAN B. *Delinquency and Crime: A Biopsychosocial Approach.* New York: Seminar Press, 1972. 468 pp.
Review of biological, psychological, and social factors associated with juvenile delinquency and crime.
HV6025.C65

CREWDSON, JOHN. *By Silence Betrayed: Sexual Abuse of Children in America.* Waltham, Massachusetts: Little, Brown and Company, 1988. 267 pp.
Through a journalistic description of child sexual abuse, this book presents findings from interviews with the perpetrators, criminal justice personnel, mental health professionals, and researchers. Major topics are the amount and causes of child sexual abuse, the debate about whether pedophiles can be cured, and practical suggestions for effective prevention and prosecution. Detailed information is included regarding selected cases of child sexual abuse and about the reactions of the juvenile and criminal justice systems.
HQ72.U53C74

CRITES, LAURA, ed. *The Female Offender.* Lexington, Massachusetts: Lexington Books, D.C. Heath and Company, 1978. 230 pp.
Crites has assembled several articles on adult and juvenile female offenders. Of particular interest to the understanding of juveniles are articles about discriminatory bias in the juvenile law, girls in training school, and theories of female criminality.
HV6046.F373

CROW, RUTH, AND GINNY MCCARTHY, eds. *Teenage Women in the Juvenile Justice System: Changing Values.* Tucson, Arizona: New Directions for Young Women, Inc., 1979. 169 pp.
Written from a feminist perspective, the first several articles in this collection examine the changing role of young women, and implications for assisting them in the juvenile justice system. The authors of articles in Part II of the book are concerned with injustices against girls in the system, and the authors of Part III describe numerous constructive programs for the prevention and control of females' delinquency.
HQ1229.T43

DARO, DEBORAH. *Confronting Child Abuse: Research for Effective Program Design.* New York: Free Press, 1988. 356 pp.
This in-depth review summarizes what is currently known about child abuse, including individual and social factors that are causes. There is separate discussion of sexual abuse, physical abuse, neglect and emotional maltreatment. Based on an assessment of nineteen clinical demonstration programs that served more than 1,000 families across the U.S., the book outlines strategies for (1) public awareness campaigns; (2) crisis intervention efforts; (3) parent education; (4) day care and afterschool programs; (5) family support groups; and (6) childhood assault prevention training to be given in the schools.

DAVIDSON, WILLIAM S., II, ROBIN REDNER, RICHARD L. AMDUR AND CHRISTINA M. MITCHELL, *Alternative Treatments for Troubled Youth: The Case of Diversion from the Justice System.* New York: Plenum, 1991. 308 pp.
By focusing on the development of an innovation diversion program, the authors provide an awareness of the ingredients for promoting successful change in the juvenile justice system. Several models for diverting youth from serious court involvement are described in detail. For example, one program matched trained university students with delinquent youth; the university students provided a variety of carefully tailored services to assist the youth. The book highlights not only the programs and their design and implementation, but also the theories that explain both delinquency and the effectiveness of interventions. Background material is included on other intervention programs and on research strategies for program evaluation.
HV9104.A77

DEAN J. CHAMPION AND G. LARRY MAYS. *Transferring Juveniles to Criminal Courts: Trends and Implications for Criminal Justice.* New York: Westport, Connecticut: Praeger Publishers, 1991.
> *Consistent with the "get tough" policy that is juxtaposed to the rehabilitative approach in the juvenile courts, increasing numbers of juveniles are being transferred to criminal courts. This book is about the certification process through which the transfer (or waiver) takes place. Different social and legal definitions of delinquency are examined and the goals and functions of transfers are considered. The legal rights of juveniles as they pertain to transfer to juvenile court are an additional topic. The book provides discussion of the types of penalties that youth receive as a result of transfer and the degree to which these penalties are harsher, or in some cases less harsh, than those that are common in the juvenile justice system.*
> KF9794.C48

DEFLEUR, LOIS B. *Delinquency in Argentina.* Pullman: Washington State University Press, 1970. 164 pp.
> *The author's work was originally an attempt to "test," cross-culturally, Albert Cohen's formulations concerning the delinquent subculture, but it resulted in a new contribution. An important finding was that marginal participation in major social institutions may be a key factor related to juvenile delinquency. DeFleur concludes that theory must be built upon each specific society.*
> HV9130.C6D4

DEJONG, WILLIAM, AND CAROLYN STEWART. *An Exemplary Project: Project CREST, Gainesville, Florida.* Washington, D.C.: U.S. Government Printing Office, 1980. 74 pp.
> *This manual is written as a guide for courts which would like to establish a volunteer program like Project CREST. Project CREST uses carefully selected volunteers to provide intensive services to probationers, and to form close and meaningful relationships with them. The regular probation officer monitors volunteer activities and supervises the youngsters. The organizational structure and political support necessary to operate such a program are discussed, as are program costs and results.*
> J28.10:C61

ELDEFONSO, EDWARD. *Youth Problems and Law Enforcement.* Englewood Cliffs, New Jersey: Prentice-Hall, Inc., 1972. 128 pp.
> *This is a practical resource intended to aid in training police in the area of youth problems. Eldefonso feels that police are primarily responsible for enforcing the law and only indirectly responsible for resolving the social problem of juvenile delinquency. He presents legal and administrative definitions of juvenile delinquency; discusses differences between delinquents and nondelinquents, dependent, neglected, and abused children; methods of measurement; causes; the purposes, function, and operation of the juvenile court; juvenile law; and police handling of juveniles from arrest to disposition, with special emphasis on the problem of drug abuse.*
> HV9060.E52

ELLIOTT, DELBERT S., AND HARWIN L. VOSS. *Delinquency and Dropout.* Lexington, Massachusetts: Lexington Books, D.C. Heath and Company, 1974. 264 pp.
> *In an investigation of the problem of school dropout, the authors propose that delinquency and dropout are alternative responses to failure and alienation. They suggest, and the study supports, that delinquency leads to dropping out of school, and, further, that movement out of school reduces both frustration and delinquent behavior. The authors relate a number of variables to delinquency, not all of which are supported by the study, and question current antidropout campaigns.*
> HV9104.E44

ELLIOT, DOREEN. *Gender, Delinquency and Society: A Comparative Study of Male and Female Offenders and Juvenile Justice in Britain.* Brookfield, Vermont: Gower Publishing Company, 1988. 151 pp.
> *Gender bias at the point of contact with the police and then with the courts is studied in a small town and a large city. The book begins with a review of prior publications on women and crime. The conclusion is that the welfare oriented juvenile justice law produces a more punitive system. At some times the system is less punitive for females, but not always, and girls do not consistently benefit from chivalrous treatment.*

EMPEY, LAMAR T., ed. *The Future of Childhood and Juvenile Justice.* Charlottesville: University Press of Virginia, 1979. 422 pp.
> *These twelve articles are relevant to understanding the status of adolescents in American society, and the way in which this status can contribute to delinquency. Youths' rights and responsibilities are analyzed in relation to the philosophy of the juvenile court, which is questioned.*
> HV9091.F87

EMPEY, LAMAR T. (Ed.). *Juvenile Justice: The Progressive Legacy and Current Reforms.* Charlottesville: University Press of Virginia, 1979. 298 pp.

> *This collection of articles documents the historical events leading up to the founding of the juvenile court, and then resulting in contemporary questioning of the juvenile court philosophy and role. Tied to these changes are alterations in the definition of delinquency, and three articles are devoted to this topic. A final set of articles focus on the need for reform of the juvenile court and reform efforts in progress.*

HV9104.J873

EMPEY, LAMAR T., AND MAYNARD L. ERICKSON. *The Provo Experiment.* Lexington, Massachusetts: D.C. Heath and Company, 1972. 321 pp.

> *Report of one of the first attempts to provide a community alternative to incarceration for habitual delinquents. The authors present the underlying assumptions of the experiment, discuss the impact of the program on offenders, and describe the experimental operation.*

HV9106.P93E56

ERICSON, RICHARD V. *Young Offenders and Their Social Work.* Lexington, Massachusetts: Lexington Books, D.C. Heath and Company, 1975. 225 pp.

> *Young offenders' perceptions of police, sentencer, social worker, and institutional personnel are described. This descriptive information suggests that there is little evidence to support labeling theory. It further suggests that detention is a negative and nonproductive experience. Throughout the book numerous examples are given of youths' statements about their experiences in the juvenile justice system.*

HV9146.E75

FABRICANT, MICHAEL. *Juveniles in the Family Court.* Lexington, Massachusetts: Lexington Books, D.C. Heath and Company, 1983. 156 pp.

> *An in-depth study of the New York City juvenile court, which is described as being on the cutting edge of juvenile-justice reform, is provided. The breakdown of decision making, which results in long delays and a low rate of commitments, is attributed to the problems of a bureaucracy with a large and diverse workload. Detailed descriptions of working conditions in such a bureaucracy are a useful introduction for students interested in positions on intake or probations staffs. Another facet of the research focused on the importance of advocacy by lawyers in protecting client rights and in shaping juvenile law. Contrary to some prior research, the public defender is not ineffectual, but plays a central role in influencing court decisions. Concluding remarks focus on assessing public criticisms that the juvenile court does not protect the citizenry.*

KFN5116.6.F3

FARSON, RICHARD. *Birthrights.* New York: Macmillan Publishing Co., Inc., 1974. 248 pp.

> *A radical statement of the need to extend many rights to children. Among these are the right to leave the family for more desirable living situations, the right to avoid mandatory public education, and the right to sexual freedom. These and other rights are discussed in the context of conflicting, contemporary beliefs and values.*

HQ789.F37

FELD, BARRY C. *Neutralizing Inmate Violence: Juvenile Offenders in Institutions.* Cambridge, Massachusetts: Ballinger Publishing Company, subsidiary of J. B. Lippincott Co., 1977. 240 pp.

> *The study described in this book compared the youth subcultures in custody and treatment-oriented programs at Massachusetts state training schools. In cottages which were custody oriented, the youths were aggressive and violent toward each other. Treatment cottages were characterized by much more positive peer interactions, as well as by staff intervention to control difficulties. Staff behaviors which reduce violence are described in considerable detail.*

HV9105.M4F44

FELDMAN, HARVEY W., MICHAEL H. AGAR, AND GEORGE M. BESCHNER, eds. *Angel Dust: An Ethnographic Study of PCP Users.* Lexington, Massachusetts: Lexington Books, D.C. Heath and Company, 1979. 240 pp.

> *This book describes researchers' interviews and observations of young phencyclidine (PCP) users in four major cities scattered across the United States. The authors of the nine articles show how PCP gained in popularity and spread from city to city. They challenge the assumption that PCP is always a very dangerous drug by explaining how users developed a close-knit group to guard against harmful incidents and physical damage. Different groups of users have different reactions to the drug, and this depends on the group's predisposition.*

HV5822.P45A53

FELDMAN, RONALD A., TIMOTHY E. CAPLINGER, AND JOHN S. WODARSKI. *The St. Louis Conundrum: The Effective Treatment of Antisocial Youths.* Englewood Cliffs, New Jersey: Prentice-Hall, Inc., 1983. 320 pp.

Detailed descriptions are provided of a program to integrate antisocial and delinquent youth into prosocial community groups led by a treatment specialist. The program grew out of a comprehensive review of the literature on the treatment of antisocial children and on the causes of aggressive behavior. Statistical analysis of the study results, including numerous tables and graphs, are presented and discussed. The book ends with a discussion of the implications of the experiment for the design of future programs.

HV9106.S23F44

FERRACUTI, FRANCO, SIMON DINITZ, AND ESPERANZA ACOSTA DE BRENES. *Delinquents and Nondelinquents in the Puerto Rican Slum Culture.* Columbus: Ohio State University Press, 1975. 245 pp.

This book describes a study to compare the living conditions, family history, social, economic, and educational circumstances, and physiological and psychological variables of 101 delinquent and nondelinquent boys. The subjects of the study, Puerto Rican youths, differed from their United States counterparts in the absence of gangs, though drug abuse was common. Because the family and the school were important influences on the youths, the authors conclude that for youths from poor families school programs are the key to preventing delinquency.

HV9124.S25F47

FINKELHOR, DAVID. *Sexually Victimized Children.* New York: The Free Press, 1979. 228 pp.

This very readable book describes a survey of college students who were asked to report on their prior sexual victimizations as children. A brief review of major explanations, a nontechnical discussion of methodology and study limitations, and conclusions about explaining and responding to child sexual abuse also are provided. Specific types of sexual abuse considered include incest, victimization by family members other than parents, and victimization by people outside of the family.

HV6626.F56

FRIDAY, PAUL C., AND V. LORNE STEWART, eds. *Youth Crime and Juvenile Justice: International Perspectives.* New York: Frederick A. Praeger, Inc., 1977. 181 pp.

This collection of fourteen articles introduces the reader to an international perspective on juvenile delinquency. The juvenile justice systems in several affluent and industrialized countries, including Argentina, England, Scotland and Belgium, are described. The remaining articles focus on the causes of delinquency in Israel, prevention programs in Puerto Rico, and other topics related to juvenile delinquency.

HV9069.Y63

GARDINER, MURIEL. *The Deadly Innocents: Portraits of Children Who Kill.* New York: Basic Books, Inc., Publishers, 1976. 190 pp.

Several case studies of youthful murderers are presented from a psychoanalytic point of view. The background factors are traced for two different types of children, those who kill out of passion and those who kill with premeditated intent. The author also writes of her concern with the treatment of young offenders in prison, and their treatment by society after they leave prison.

HV6515.G37

GIALLOMBARDO, ROSE. *The Social World of Imprisoned Girls.* New York: John Wiley and Sons, Inc., 1974. 317 pp.

Report of a study which suggests that the inmate social system reflects the system of the outside society, not merely the values and attitudes of those who enter the institution. Further implications are that the goal emphasis of the institution has an impact on the inmate organization; thus, the informal social system can aid or hinder treatment.

HV9104.G5

GIBBONS, DON C. *Delinquent Behavior.* Englewood Cliffs, New Jersey: Prentice-Hall, Inc., 1970. 276 pp.

Gibbons uses existing data on delinquency to present a general overview of the problem. Although sociologically oriented, the work does identify ways in which psychological and sociological factors interact. Covers definitions, laws, statistics, police and court dealings with delinquents, "official delinquency," causes, forms of delinquency, international perspectives, and corrections. The author emphasizes that what is needed is further research aimed at a judicious combination of the various lines of thought into a coherent body of knowledge.

HV9104.G53

GLUECK, SHELDON, AND ELEANOR T. GLUECK, eds. *Identification of Predelinquents.* New York: Inter-continental Medical Book Corporation, 1972. 150 pp.
> *The book is an outgrowth of a session on identification of predelinquents at the Sixth International Congress of Criminology in 1970. Various facets of identification are explored in the articles. According to the editors, prediction is the most fruitful concept in criminology.*
> HV9069.G539

GLUECK, SHELDON, AND ELEANOR T. GLUECK. *Toward a Typology of Juvenile Offenders.* New York: Grune and Stratton, Inc., 1970. 203 pp.
> *The authors discuss the concept of "type," present a sample of typological approaches, and describe typology. In their view, the types can be arranged along a continuum from those whose prognosis is most favorable to the "core type" delinquent. Data from their earlier works are used as foundations for development of treatment strategies.*
> HV9069.G545

GOLD, MARTIN. *Delinquent Behavior in an American City.* Belmont, California: Brooks-Cole, 1970. 150 pp.
> *Report of a study conducted in Flint, Michigan, which attempted to obtain a clear picture of delinquent behavior. Gold stresses the distinction between delinquency and delinquent behavior, and concludes that present knowledge about juvenile delinquency may not apply to delinquent behavior. Furthermore, varying degrees of delinquency exist. Since almost everyone breaks the law, the idea of "the delinquent" is invalid.*
> HV9104.G63

GRIFFITHS, CURT TAYLOR, AND MARGIT NANCE, eds. *The Female Offender.* Vancouver, Canada: Simon Fraser University Press, 1980. 331 pp.
> *Papers presented at an international symposium on the female offender are included in this volume. Several of them are relevant to understanding and treating adult and juvenile offenders, but four are concerned just with juveniles. These papers pertain to the characteristics of the youths, juvenile prostitution, the use of contingency management with girls, and the use of guided group interaction for institutionalized juvenile females.*
> HV6046.G7

GRISSOM, GRANT R. AND WILLIAM L. DUBNOV. *Without Locks and Bars: Reforming Our Reform Schools.* New York: Praeger, 1989. 240 pp.
> *The authors of this book provide a detailed description of the transformation of a New Jersey state training school from a rarely used, expensive and destructive program to an institution with a prep school atmosphere. The management technique and the treatment philosophy that enabled the change are described, as well as the use of the treatment method, Guided Group Interaction. Youth discharged from the program regularly return without state aid, but "on scholarship," to complete academic and sports programs, and both staff and participant enthusiasm for the program are high. One chapter of the book is devoted to the results of evaluation of the program against several outcome measures, including recidivism.*
> HV9105.p22G544

HACKLER, JAMES C. *The Prevention of Youthful Crime: The Great Stumble Forward.* Toronto: Methuen, 1978. 252 pp.
> *Canadian examples as well as research are used to explain the research methods needed to advance delinquency prevention efforts. Information is presented about community programs, group-oriented programs, and those which try to change individuals' attitudes and behavior. Specific traditional programs which are discussed are forestry camps, training programs, probation, and parole. More innovative programs and the need for social change are additional topics. Although this book focuses on Canada, its examples and conclusions are highly relevant to prevention in both Great Britain and the United States.*
> HV9108.H32

HAGADORN, JOHN WITH PERRY MACON, *People and Folks: Gangs, Crime and the Underclass in a Restbelt City.* Chicago, Lake View Press, 1988.
> *This book is based on interviews with over 200 youths who were members of black, Chicano and white gangs in Milwaukee, Wisconsin. These interviews provide detailed descriptions of the involvement of these gangs in the use and selling of drugs and in violent activity, particularly fighting. Differences between the Milwaukee gangs and the gangs described in research on contemporary Chicano gangs and the Chicago gangs of earlier times are highlighted throughout the book. The authors stress that, unlike gangs studied in earlier periods, the contemporary Milwaukee gangs do not "mature out" when their members reach their*

early twenties and become involved in such legitimate activities as marriage and work. Instead, because of the dramatic changes in the economy in cities such as Milwaukee, young adults remain active in their gangs, shifting their activities from fighting to a focus on support for each other and economic survival. Largely as a result of desegregation efforts, which scattered black youths throughout the city, black gangs are alienated from their own communities, thus community social control efforts are ineffective. Serious inadequacies of more formal attempts at social control also are pinpointed.
HV 6439.U7 M554 1988

HANDLER, JOEL F., AND JULIE ZATZ, eds. *Neither Angels nor Thieves: Studies in Deinstitutionalization of Status Offenders.* Washington, D.C.: National Academy Press, 1982.
This book contains a collection of articles to evaluate efforts to remove status offenders from institutions. Three questions are addressed: What has happened to status offenders in terms of detention and placement in state correctional institutions? To what extent are status offenders handled by diversion programs? Where are status offenders going and what services, if any, are they receiving? In addition to an overview of the answers to these questions, detailed reports are provided for Arizona, Louisiana, Massachusetts, Pennsylvania, Utah, Virginia, Wisconsin, California, Illinois, and Texas. Special attention is paid to the role of social and political institutions in shaping public policy.
HV9104.N33

HARDY, RICHARD E., AND JOHN G. CULL. *Fundamentals of Juvenile Criminal Behavior and Drug Abuse.* Springfield, Illinois: Charles C. Thomas, Publisher, 1975. 258 pp.
The authors take a multidisciplinary stance in discussing current trends in rehabilitation of the delinquent, the delinquent's environment, reasons for his or her behavior, and specific case studies. Included is information on the types of drugs, their effects, and drug terminology.
HV9069.H316

HARDY, RICHARD E., AND JOHN G. CULL. *Psychological and Vocational Rehabilitation of the Youthful Delinquent.* Springfield, Illinois: Charles C. Thomas, Publisher, 1974. 248 pp.
The book includes articles by the authors and nine other contributors which describe the delinquent, types of delinquent behavior, and approaches to rehabilitation, including behavior modification, guided group interaction, and development of employment opportunities. It contains both theoretical and practical information, and is intended for both student and practitioner.
HV9069.H317

HARRIS, MARY G. *Cholas: Latino Girls and Gangs.* New York, New York: AMS Press, 1988. 220 pp.
Interviews were used to gather information from 21 girls who were or who had been gang members. They were part of female cliques in the male-dominated Latino gangs in the San Fernando Valley of Los Angeles. The girls were caught between the non-gang adolescent subculture and the Latino culture. They had joined the gang for a variety of reasons, including a desire for a common destiny, a sense of belonging and identity, and the need for group support. The gang served as a stronger reference group than either the family or legitimate institutions, like the school.
HV6439.U7 L73

HAWES, JOSEPH M. *Children in Urban Society.* New York: Oxford University Press, 1971. 315 pp.
Hawes traces juvenile misbehavior from colonial days to the present, emphasizing that juvenile delinquency is not a recent phenomenon. In attempting to present a complete narrative of American responses to the problem, he makes the following observations: (1) the trend toward more humane treatment is part of a general concern in Western countries; (2) the history of juvenile delinquency is basically a history of the city, since the city concentrates individual antisocial acts and lends increased visibility to them; and (3) government agencies and institutions and city government as a whole are inadequate to deal with the problem. Individual cases are presented to support these observations.
HV9104.H35

HELFER, RAY E., AND C. HENRY KEMPE, eds. *The Battered Child.* Chicago: University of Chicago Press, 1980. 440 pp.
The guiding philosophy of this book is that we must work to prevent child abuse, but at the same time protect parental freedoms and privacy. Several articles are included which apply our knowledge of child abuse to the development of services. The need for a wide variety of attractive and readily available services is emphasized. Specific treatment methods also are highlighted.
HV741.H4 1980

HIPPCHEN, LEONARD J.   *Ecologic-Biochemical Approaches to Treatment of Delinquents and Criminals.* New York: Van Nostrand Reinhold Company, 1978. 396 pp.
> *The author is a strong advocate of the biological approach to understanding and treating delinquency. Topics include the role of faulty nutrition and chemical toxins in causing deviance, alcoholism, learning disorders, and violence.*

HV6028.E28

HIRSCHI, TRAVIS, AND HANAN C. SELVIN.   *Principles of Survey Analysis.* New York: The Free Press, 1973. 280 pp.
> *An examination of published analyses of quantitative data on delinquency, which emphasizes that the most important part of a study is analysis. When approaching data the researcher is advised to be in the proper frame of mind, with objectivity, vigilance, and sympathy.*

HV9068.H55 1973

HOENIG, GARY.   *Reaper: The Story of a Gang Leader.* Indianapolis: The Bobbs-Merrill Co., Inc., 1975. 168 pp.
> *In-depth case history of a delinquent in Brooklyn which recounts the events leading to his gang involvement. Includes the author's comments on the social situation on the street.*

HV9106.N6H63

HUFF, C. RONALD, ed.   *Gangs in America.* Newbury Park, California: Sage, 1991. 351 pp.
> *This collection of nine papers exposes readers to information about a wide variety of gangs, including those made up of members who are white, Chicano, Afro-American, and Chinese. There is discussion of issues in defining a gang and changes in gangs since the beginning of the century. The final section of the book addresses policy and program strategies for confronting gang related delinquency. Special attention is paid to recent neighborhood and broader economic conditions that contribute to gang delinquency and that would need to be targeted in control programs.*

HV6439.U5G36

INTERNATIONAL PENAL AND PRISON COMMISSION.   *Children's Courts in the United States.* New York: AMS Press, Inc., 1973. 203 pp.
> *Reprint of the 1904 report of the International Prison Commission which was submitted to the U.S. Congress. The report strongly recommended and supported the juvenile court, citing its paternal attitude as an indication of a new spirit in corrections. Contains reports of courts established and operating in eight states at the time in addition to summaries of juvenile court laws in various states.*

HV9091.16 1973

JAMES, HOWARD.   *Children in Trouble.* New York: David McKay Co., Inc., 1970. 340 pp.
> *Through presentation of specific cases, James raises doubts about what the juvenile justice system is now doing to combat delinquency and offers recommendations. He is critical of institutions, viewing them as "damaging"; and of the process by which those employed in institutions come to see them as "normal" environments.*

HV9104.J34

JENKINS, RICHARD L. AND WALN K. BROWN.   *The Abandonment of Delinquent Behavior: Promoting the Turnaround.* Westport, Connecticut: Praeger Publishers, 1988. 238 pp.
> *This book challenges the common belief that early delinquency is sure to result in a life long involvement in illegal behavior. Experiences and individual differences that contribute to a "turnaround" are identified. Both personal and research perspectives are taken to show desired outcomes of juvenile court adjudication, following up previously adjudicated delinquents, the post-intervention experience, and treatment. The book provides many concrete examples of sensitive and effective court handling, people who "make a difference," and parole efforts that interrupt patterns of delinquency. A detailed bibliography suggests additional reading.*

HV9104.A615

JUSTICE, BLAIR, AND RITA JUSTICE.   *The Abusing Family.* New York: Human Sciences Press, 1976. 288 pp.
> *The book begins with a review of the influences on child abuse and several theoretical models. There is a lengthy discussion, and many examples, of treatment approaches for abusing parents and specific techniques of therapy. Programs to deliver these services to either a family involved in abuse, or one which is likely to become involved, are described.*

HV713.J87

KADUSHIN, ALFRED, AND JUDITH A. MARTIN. *Child Abuse: An Interactional Event.* New York: Columbia University Press, 1981. 304 pp.

> *The authors thoroughly review prior research on the extent of causes of child abuse. Based on this review and their own research, they describe the influences on the abuse as well as the actual event of child abuse. Their explanation rests on the understanding that the child and family members have a role to play in the interactions leading up to abuse. This viewpoint corrects the failure in previous research to take the child's actions which are antecedent to abuse into account, as well as the situation immediately preceding abuse. It suggests the need for social workers to attempt to fully understand the situation leading up to abuse, and the possibility of preventing abuse by changing the child's behavior and not just the parent's behavior.*
> HV713.K32

KASSEBAUM, GENE G. *Delinquency and Social Policy.* Englewood Cliffs, New Jersey: Prentice-Hall, Inc., 1974. 186 pp.

> *The book is concerned with the ways in which youths are defined as delinquent, the manner in which official agencies deal with them, and the resulting effects. Emphasis is on the social process by which juveniles are arrested, adjudicated, supervised, and instructed. Kassebaum feels that delinquency is built into society; most conflict which is labeled juvenile delinquency arises from child-adult conflict which cannot be understood apart from social conflict.*
> HV9069.K36

KENNEY, JOHN P., AND DAN G. PURSUIT. *Police Work with Juveniles and the Administration of Justice.* Springfield, Illinois: Charles C. Thomas, Publisher, 1978. 496 pp.

> *This textbook provides a basic knowledge of management in the juvenile justice system. Topics include the role of the police, team policing models, diversion, vandalism, judicial procedures, school relations, social agencies, and youth service bureaus. Standards of the National Advisory Commission on Criminal Justice Standards and Goals are presented.*
> HV9069.K3 1970

KHANNA, J. L., ed. *New Treatment Approaches to Juvenile Delinquency.* Springfield, Illinois: Charles C. Thomas, Publisher, 1975. 157 pp.

> *Contains papers given at a workshop on treatment approaches. The topics discussed include the extent of officially labeled juvenile delinquency; prediction and prevention; and contingency management of delinquent behavior. Participants discussed the use of token economies, the reversal of contingencies which maintain delinquent behavior, forms of behavior modification, and examples of new treatment approaches.*
> HV9104.N38 1975

KLEIN, MALCOLM W. *Street Gangs and Street Workers.* Englewood Cliffs, New Jersey: Prentice-Hall, Inc., 1971. 338 pp.

> *Klein presents current knowledge about gangs, information on gang workers and programs, and a report of a project carried out in California which combined action and research to gain more information about the gang. He believes that current approaches to reducing gang delinquency are unproductive; the gang member has numerous opportunities for getting into trouble, while the gang worker is almost devoid of resources necessary to reduce those opportunities.*
> HV7428.K6

KOBETZ, RICHARD W. *The Police Role and Juvenile Delinquency.* Gaithersburg, Maryland: International Association of Chiefs of Police, Inc., 1971. 264 pp.

> *The effects of recent Supreme Court decisions on police-juvenile operations and police roles in our society are the focus of this book. Information on police-juvenile operations was collected in a long-term research project funded by several government agencies. Policy guidelines which can be adopted by local police departments are set forth, along with examples of successful programs.*
> HV8080.J8K6

KOBETZ, RICHARD W., AND BETTY B. BOSARGE. *Juvenile Justice Administration.* Gaithersburg, Maryland: International Association of Chiefs of Police, Inc., 1973. 769 pp.

> *This comprehensive volume describes each component of the juvenile justice system in detail. Sections on the police, courts, probation, and community corrections outline standard operating practices as well as innovations and recommendations for improvement. The comprehensive overview is intended to foster coordination between the different parts of the system.*
> HV9104.K63

KORNHAUSER, RUTH ROSNER. *Social Sources of Delinquency: An Appraisal of Analytic Models*. Chicago: University of Chicago Press, 1978. 277 pp.

Drawing on a large number of studies, Kornhauser criticizes several major sociological theories of juvenile delinquency. These are opportunity theory, the "gang" theories, differential association theory, and in general the theories which attribute delinquency to membership in a subculture. She points out the strengths and weaknesses of each theory, and the direction for further research and theory development.
HV8069.K67

LAMPMAN, HENRY P. *The Wire Womb: Life in a Girls' Penal Institution*. Chicago: Nelson-Hall Publishers, 1973. 181 pp.

The author, who worked in a correctional institution for girls, recounts his observations and experiences. The special problems of a psychologist in such a setting are emphasized, as well as the many negative experiences of girls.
HV8738.L35

LE BLANC, MARC AND MARCEL FRECHETTE. *Male Criminal Activity from Childhood through Youth: Multi-level and Developmental Perspectives*. New York: Springer-Verlag, 1989. 228 pp.

The offense patterns of 1,684 Canadian boys are described in detail, with attention to both self-reported delinquency and official records. For youth who continued to break the law in their late teens and early adulthood, their offenses became more serious and the pattern began to resemble an occupation. The movement towards more serious delinquency did not occur by chance, but followed a predictable sequence. The book concludes with an agenda for future research as well as practical implications of the findings.
HV9069.L33

LEFKOWITZ, MONROE M., LEONARD D. EVON, LEOPOLD O. WALDER, AND L. ROWELL HUESMAN. *Growing Up to Be Violent: A Longitudinal Study of the Development of Aggression*. New York: Pergamon Press, 1977. 211 pp.

A longitudinal study of youths between the third grade and age nineteen showed that aggressive behavior is learned, and thus the study provides support for social learning theory. Other theories to explain aggression also are reviewed. The authors emphasize the methodology and findings of their research, but do discuss implications for both theory and practice.
BF723.A35G76 1977

LEMERT, EDWIN M. *Instead of Court*. Chevy Chase, Maryland: National Institute of Mental Health, Center for Studies of Crime and Delinquency, 1971. 95 pp.

Lemert feels that too many children are processed by the juvenile court and that the harm done to them outweighs any benefits. He examines a number of alternatives for diverting youth from the courts, among which are the school, welfare agencies, police, and community organizations. A major problem with these agencies is the phenomenon of labeling, whereby juveniles come to see themselves as delinquent and subsequently behave according to expectations. According to Lemert, new ways of perceiving the concept of prevention must be developed which consider the consequences of agency policies and actions. All children engage in delinquent behavior; therefore, efforts should be made to control rather than prevent such behavior. Forms of juvenile delinquency are defined into existence; therefore, they can be defined out of existence.
HV9065.L4

LEMERT, EDWIN M. *Social Action and Legal Change: Revolution Within the Juvenile Court*. Chicago: Aldine Publishing Co., 1970. 248 pp.

Account of the revision of California's juvenile court laws in 1961 and an analysis of the social action behind the revision. The study, conducted through interviews, committee reports, questionnaires, and examinations of files, was addressed to the question of how law develops, the specific processes which produce revolutionary change, and the extent to which legislation affects the direction of change.
KFC1177.L4

LERMAN, PAUL, ed. *Delinquency and Social Policy*. New York: Frederick A. Praeger, Inc., 1970. 488 pp.

Contains forty-two articles dealing with the major issues in prevention and control of juvenile delinquency—its definitions and legal basis, control and guidance of police handling of delinquents, assuring fairness in the administration of justice, correctional practices, and social planning to prevent and control delinquency.
HV9104.L37

LERMAN, PAUL. *Community Treatment and Social Control: A Critical Analysis of Juvenile Correctional Policy.* Chicago: University of Chicago Press, 1979. 254 pp.

> *This book provides a careful analysis of the California Community Treatment Project and Probation Subsidy Program. Both efforts were intended to increase community treatment of offenders, and thereby to lessen reliance on state institutions. A number of problems arose in achieving these objectives. For example, youths in the community were detained so often that some of the benefits of community treatment were eliminated; and people committed to state institutions were incarcerated for longer periods of time. The author concludes that sanctions are a more frequent response of the juvenile justice system than is treatment.*

HV9105.C2L47

LOBLE, LESTER H., AND MAX WYLIE. *Delinquency Can Be Stopped.* New York: McGraw-Hill Book Company, 1967. 148 pp.

> *The authors are highly critical of the leniency inherent in the present juvenile law, methods of dealing with juvenile offenders, and those who process juveniles through the criminal justice system. The law is seen as overly idealistic and obsolete; youths are treated as disadvantaged instead of criminal; and practitioners are ignorant of the effects of their permissiveness, the current juvenile "crime wave." The authors recommend that juvenile proceedings should not be hidden; that offenders should be made publicly answerable for their crimes; and that attention should be paid to the victims of crime. They emphasize that it is not society that is responsible for crime, but the offender who commits it.*

HV9105.M9L6

MCARTHUR, A. VERNE. *Coming Out Cold.* Lexington, Massachusetts: Lexington Books, D.C. Heath and Company, 1974. 131 pp.

> *The book is concerned with the situation confronting the offender who is released from a state reformatory. Through interviews with thirty-four youthful offenders and their mothers conducted from one week prior to release to four weeks after release, the author explores the problems of community reentry as experienced by the offenders and as shaped by institutional procedures. He concludes that the situation awaiting the released offender virtually insures that he will fail to become a productive, law-abiding citizen, and he raises serious questions about the criminal justice system's neglect of the people entrusted to it.*

HV9104.M18

MCEWEN, CRAIG A. *Designing Correctional Organizations for Youths: Dilemmas of Subcultural Development.* Cambridge, Massachusetts: Ballinger Publishing Company, Subsidiary of J. B. Lippincott Co., 1978. 246 pp.

> *The study described in this book focuses on designing correctional programs in such a way that a positive inmate subculture develops. The study conclusion is that not all programs can achieve the same correctional objectives, and therefore there is a need to have a variety of small programs available to delinquents. Such diversity has the further advantage of allowing youths some choice in their placement.*

HV9105.M4M2

MAHONEY, ANNE RANKIN. *Juvenile Justice in Context.* Boston, Massachusetts: Northeastern University Press, 1987. 181 pp.

> *Observations and court records provide the data for this study of a typical suburban court. The study reveals the degree to which the court is dependent on its environment for legitimation, resources and clients. It also reveals persistent problems in the areas of personnel turnover, difficulties creating new treatment programs, and lack of adequate funds. Youths in particular need of programming are repeat property offenders with no record of violence. Suggestions are made for restructuring the court to provide a potentially effective graduated approach to the treatment of juvenile offenders. Recognition and acceptance of a policy that emphasized a graduated approach would help the court to anticipate negative effects of changes in the community and the broader context in which the court operates.*

HV9104.M22

MANZANERA, LUIS RODRIGUES. *La Delinquencia de Menores en Mexico.* Mexico: Ediciones Botas, 1971. 343 pp.

> *Deals primarily with juvenile delinquency in Mexico City. Includes discussions of causes, kinds of delinquency, treatment, and prevention.*

HV9111.A5R6

MAYERS, MICHAEL O. *The Hard-Core Delinquent: An Experiment in Control and Care in a Community Home with Education.* Lexington, Massachusetts: Lexington Books, D.C. Heath and Company, 1980. 207 pp.

Based on a two-year experiment at a Community Home with Education in London, this book reports the results of a program for hard-core delinquents who would have been treated in institutions. The author's aim is to determine whether or not it is possible to treat some of the most disturbed, damaged, difficult, and delinquent boys in an open rather than a secure setting. The community home provided individual counseling, group therapy, and behavior modification. The boys did no worse than a matched comparison group in institutions, and on some measures they did better. However, there were special problems in operating a home for such serious delinquents, and staff found the work to be very taxing.
HV9146.L52A735

MENNEL, ROBERT M.   *Thorns and Thistles: Juvenile Delinquents in the United States 1825–1940.* Hanover, New Hampshire: The University Press of New England, 1973. 231 pp.
Traces the history of prevention, control, and explanation of juvenile delinquency in the United States from 1825 to 1940, with a very brief summary of developments since 1940. Concludes that economically disadvantaged youths have been stigmatized to a greater degree than the affluent; that institutions also stigmatize their population and lead them into adult criminal behaviors; and that change will occur only when the social structure is reorganized.
HV9104.M45

MILLHAM, SPENCER, ROGER BULLOCK, AND KENNETH HOSIE.   *Locking Up Children: Secure Provision Within the Child-Care System.* Westmead, England: Saxon House, 1978. 196 pp.
This book reports on a study of the children in a secure facility in Great Britain. It explores the tensions between custody and treatment, and it raises questions about the need for secure detention for troubled youths. Historical changes in the use of secure lockup for children are described and explored, and alternatives to lockup are discussed.
HV9145.A5M54

MOORE, JOE ALEX.   *First Offender.* New York: Funk and Wagnalls, 1970. 214 pp.
Describes a program in Royal Oak, Michigan, involving citizen volunteers who work with delinquents on a one-to-one basis under guidance of professionals.
HV9106.R62V65

MOSES, DONALD A., AND ROBERT E. BURGER.   *Are You Driving Your Children to Drink? Coping with Teenage Alcohol and Drug Abuse.* New York: Van Nostrand Reinhold Company, 1975. 235 pp.
The authors intended this book for use primarily by the parents of alcohol and drug-abusing youths. In straightforward language, they provide a psychological interpretation of the family's contribution to the problem and of symptoms that a child is abusing drugs. They describe one-to-one psychotherapy, group therapy, and concept therapy. Throughout the book, there is an emphasis on explaining things clearly and dispelling myths.
HV5801.M67

MUEHLBAUER, GENE, AND LAURA DODDER.   *The Losers: Gang Delinquency in an American Suburb.* New York: Praeger Publishers, 1983. 138 pp.
This book provides a description of overt hostility between police and adolescents in a well-to-do suburb of a large midwestern city. In addition to introducing us to the group interactions and specific incidents that lead up to the hostility, the authors point to the role of class conflict and cultural alienation. The influence of the schools on individual and group deviance also is considered. Throughout, the authors combine theory with description as they tell the story of the development of the delinquent subgroup of adolescents who chose to call themselves "The Losers."
HV9104.M82 1983

MUELLER, O. W.   *Delinquency and Puberty.* New York: New York University School of Law, 1971. 123 pp.
A study of "hidden" juvenile delinquency—law violations which do not come to the attention of authorities—which traces the movement of a fad involving theft across the United States.
HV9104.M8

MURPHY, PATRICK T.   *Our Kindly Parent—The State.* New York: The Viking Press, Inc., 1974. 180 pp.
A criticism of the juvenile justice system by a lawyer who maintains that the system does more harm than good. Murphy traces the history of the juvenile court, claims that numerous abuses exist, and cites specific cases to illustrate his charges.
HV9104.M87 1974

MURRAY, CHARLES A., AND LOUIS A. COX, JR. *Beyond Probation: Juvenile Corrections and the Chronic Delinquent.* Beverly Hills, California: Sage Publications, 1979. 235 pp.

> *This book describes and evaluates the Unified Delinquency Intervention Services (UDIS) program in Chicago. Youths in UDIS were involved in foster and group homes, wilderness programs, out-of-town placements, and intensive residential care. Some also received at-home services. Those not in the program were placed in a reformatory, were on probation, or received some other type of supervision. UDIS participants committed less delinquency than nonparticipants, though they did not withdraw from all delinquent activities.*

HV9106.C4M87

NEVARES, DORA, MARVIN E. WOLFGANG AND PAUL E. TRACEY, *Delinquency in Puerto Rico: The 1970 Birth Cohort Study.* Contributions in Criminology and Penology, no. 31. Westport, Connecticut: Greenwood Press, 1990. 248 pp.

> *The focus of this book is the results of a longitudinal study of delinquency for a sample of all of the adolescents born in San Juan, Puerto Rico, in 1970. Both girls and boys are studied. There is information on the number of contacts with the San Juan police departments, the number of repeat contacts, and differences from a similar study of adolescents born in Philadelphia in both 1945 and 1958. The book provides several suggestions for policy change as well as changes in the law.*

NEWCOMB, MICHAEL D. AND PETER M. BENTLER. *Consequences of Adolescent Drug Use: Impact on the Lives of Young Adults.* Newbury Park, California: Sage Publications, Inc. 1988, 288 pp.

> *The authors of this book address questions about the effect of adolescent drug use on later life. Particular attention is given to the influence of adolescent drug use on young adult family formation and stability, deviant behavior, sexual behavior, education, occupation, and mental health. Consideration is given to various types of drugs, including cocaine, alcohol, and PCP.*

HV5824.Y68N49

OFFER, DANIEL, RICHARD C. MAROHN, AND ERIC OSTROV. *The Psychological World of the Juvenile Delinquent.* New York: Basic Books, Inc., Publishers, 1979. 224 pp.

> *The researchers who conducted the study described here are psychiatrists and psychologists. They describe four types of delinquents: The Impulsive, The Narcissistic, The Depressed Borderline, and The Empty Borderline. Each type is characterized by certain psycho-pathological problems and conflicts. Delinquency, the authors conclude, is a reaction to these difficulties as well as outside pressures common in our society. Therefore, intervention strategies must include individual and group therapies as well as social change.*

RJ506.J88O33

PALMER, TED. *Correctional Intervention and Research.* Lexington, Massachusetts: Lexington Books, D.C. Heath and Company, 1978. 273 pp.

> *Ted Palmer explains and defends his position in the debate over whether correctional programs are effective. He presents evidence that certain programs do work for selected offenders, and that correctional programs can reduce recidivism.*

HV9275.P34

PALMER, TED, AND ROY V. LEWIS. *An Evaluation of Juvenile Diversion.* Cambridge, Massachusetts: Oelgeschlager, Gunn & Hain, Inc., Publishers, 1980. 384 pp.

> *This book presents the results of a three-year study of the effects of instituting several diversion programs in California. The results indicate that selected programs reduce recidivism for certain types of youths, and therefore there is a need for a variety of different programs. Diversion programs in California also resulted in a small financial savings and, though they increased program contacts for some youths, they reduced it for others.*

HV9105.C2P34

PARSLOE, PHYLLIDA. *Juvenile Justice in Britain and the United States: The Balance of Needs and Rights.* London: Routledge and Kegan Paul Ltd., 1978. 325 pp.

> *Parsloe compares the historical development and the current operational practices of the juvenile court in Britain and the United States. Her analysis of Britain includes sections on England and Wales, as well as Scotland. Final chapters discuss the roles of police, lawyers, social workers, and others who work in the courts in both countries, and the approaches used to control discretionary decision making. Innovative programs, such as the Youth Service Bureau in the United States, and problems of requiring treatment are also considered.*

K5575.P35

PEARL, ARTHUR, DOUGLAS GRANT, AND ERNST WENK, eds. *The Value of Youth.* Davis, California: International Dialogue Press, 1978. 318 pp.

> The Value of Youth *begins with a discussion of the status and value of adolescents in American society. Following are several articles on adolescents' alienation, and the deviance which can result. These articles describe a variety of social conditions which contribute to alienation, including the economic structure and the environment in which youths grow up. Another set of articles describes programs to help delinquents and others to become full participants in American social life, and thus to avoid alienation. The final chapter is a proposed national policy to change the status of youths in contemporary society, and in this way to reduce alienation and deviance.*
> HQ796.V27 1978

PETRIE, CAIRINE. *The Nowhere Boys: A Comparative Study of Open and Closed Residential Placement.* Lexington, Massachusetts: Lexington Books, D.C. Heath and Company, 1980. 184 pp.

> *Based in Scotland, this research compared boys in a maximum security program with a similar group in an open training school. Most of the study results reflect unfavorably on the continued use of institutions. The secure settings are not used for the "rotten apples"; they are not effective, and they are expensive to maintain.*
> HV9147.A5P47

PLATT, ANTHONY M. *The Child Savers.* Chicago: University of Chicago Press, 1969. 230 pp.

> *Platt links contemporary programs of delinquency control with the child-saving movement of the late nineteenth century. He studies the origins, nature, and achievements of the movement in an attempt to understand the relationship between social reforms and concomitant changes in the criminal justice system; the methods by which communities have an input in regulating crime; and the gap between the ideal and the actual in the implementation of change. Emphasis is placed on the development of the juvenile court in Illinois, theories of criminology, the value of punishment, and the civil liberties of youth.*
> HV9104.P53

POSTON, RICHARD W. *The Gang and the Establishment.* New York: Harper & Row, Publishers, 1971. 269 pp.

> *Poston describes an attempt by gang members to help other ghetto youths through elimination of poverty, establishment of job programs, day care programs, and so on. With support from private foundations, the Office of Economic Opportunity, business firms, city government, and police, the youths formed an organization aimed at constructive neighborhood development. The author tells of the problems associated with the attempt—which included failure to get neighborhood youth involved, infighting, and squandering of grant money—describes its ultimate failure, and gives suggestions for constructive use of grant funds.*
> HV6795.N5P68

POWERS, EDWIN, AND HELEN WITMER. *An Experiment in the Prevention of Delinquency.* Montclair, New Jersey: Patterson Smith, 1972. 649 pp.

> *Report of a study which investigated the idea that delinquency can be prevented through "sustained and directed friendship." Powers and Witmer suggest that a major cause of juvenile delinquency is the lack of such attachment, especially in the home. The study was longitudinal and offered one group of boys an additional measure of friendly and supportive counseling over the ordinary social services received by the other group.*
> HV9069.P73 1972

PRESCOTT, PETER S. *The Child Savers: Juvenile Justice Observed.* New York: Knopf, 1981. 244 pp.

> *This book presents the author's observations of a New York City Family Court over two years in the late 1970s. The descriptions of trials and the dialogue of judges, lawyers, and children present a discouraging picture of the frustrations and ineptitudes of court staff. About one-third of the book is devoted to Legal Aid attorneys who defend children ranging from the seriously abused to the violently delinquent. The lawyers consistently uphold the Constitution, even though the result is often withholding of relevant information and the return of dangerous children to the streets. Overall, the book provides insight into the daily experiences of judges, caseworkers, prosecutors, and lawyers in a busy urban court.*
> HV9106.N6P73

PURSUIT, DAN G. et al., eds. *Police Programs for Preventing Crime and Delinquency.* Springfield, Illinois: Charles C. Thomas, Publisher, 1972. 490 pp.

> *Seventy readings which deal with the following subjects: law enforcement's role in crime prevention,*

programs for community relations, prevention programs for specific offenses, educational programs, recreational programs, technological programs, and funding resources and requirements. The editors' criteria for selecting the programs included the following: the programs were innovative, used evaluative procedures, used officer time efficiently, involved volunteers and citizens effectively, were applicable to various communities, were applicable to youths of different ages, and/or tended to improve the police image.
HV8031.P58

RAPAPORT, ROBERT N.   *New Interventions for Children and Youth: Action-Research Approaches.* New York, New York: Cambridge University Press, 1987. 275 pp.
The author provides us with case studies of ten projects in which researchers worked along with practitioners to develop and study innovative programs for children. Each of the programs was aimed at improving mental health of the youngsters. Some of them operated in the juvenile court.
HV741.R36

RECKLESS, WALTER C., AND SIMON DINITZ.   *The Prevention of Juvenile Delinquency: An Experiment.* Columbus: Ohio State University Press, 1972. 253 pp.
The experiment described in this work consisted of four phases: development of theory—that self-concept acts as an insulator against delinquency—and testing of the theory; development of a school-based prevention program at the sixth-grade level in certain schools; implementation of the program at seventh-grade level in all inner-city schools; and evaluation through an annual follow-up of all participating students and home interviews with a sample of participants. The authors view juvenile delinquency as an inherent part of our social system and as an entity much affected by the family, the community, and the value structure. Findings showed few differences between participants and nonparticipants in the program. The authors offer possible explanations for such findings and suggest directions for further research.
HV9069.R413

RICHARDS, PAMELA, RICHARD A. BERK, AND BRENDA FOSTER.   *Crime as Play: Delinquency in a Middle Class Suburb.* Cambridge, Massachusetts: Ballinger Publishing Company, subsidiary of J. B. Lippincott Co., 1979. 259 pp.
This book considers the idea that delinquency is a result of the rational choice of enjoyable activities. Shoplifting and vandalism, for example, produce a maximum return of pleasure for the investment of time and energy. Results of a survey of three thousand middle-class youths are presented to support these ideas.
HV9104.R52

ROCHE, MICHAEL PHILIP.   *Rural Police and Rural Youth.* Charlottesville, Virginia: University Press of Virginia, 1985. 217 pp.
The focus of this book is on police handling of rural juvenile crime. The author draws on case studies and original data as the basis for an unusual and controversial approach for dealing with rural juvenile offenders. He proposes that most rural juvenile crime is extremely trivial, and that nonintervention is the best course of action. His argument centers on differences between rural and urban communities and on the negative effects of repressive measures currently used in dealing with juvenile offenders. In addition to the research and practical recommendations, there is a discussion of the relationship of the state and the family.
KF9779.R63

ROMIG, DENNIS A.   *Justice for Our Children.* Lexington, Massachusetts: Lexington Books, D.C. Heath and Company, 1978. 205 pp.
Romig thoroughly reviews research to evaluate delinquency treatment methods and programs. Based on his review, he develops an ideal program and model for the juvenile justice system. The ideal program would stress, among other things, help for specific problems, getting youths' attention and input, measurable goals, training for parents, and follow-up. Features of the ideal juvenile justice system are consistent goals and a capacity to deliver services in crisis situations.
HV9069.R65

ROSENHEIM, MARGARET K., ed.   *Pursuing Justice for the Child.* Chicago: University of Chicago Press, 1976. 361 pp.
In fifteen articles, the contributors to this collection provide a critical analysis of the major components of and practices in the juvenile justice system. Police operations, diversion programs, probation, and treatment are discussed. Chapters also are devoted to juvenile court philosophy, recordkeeping and privacy, the rights of children, neglected children, and juvenile justice systems in Europe.
KF9709.A2P87

ROTHMAN, JACK. *Runaway and Homeless Youth: STRENGTHENING SERVICES TO FAMILIES AND CHILDREN.* New York: Longman, 1991. 164 pp.

> *Each chapter of the book opens with an illustrative case study, and each closes with an example of a program that is designed to address key problems raised in the chapter. An historical perspective on the problem of runaway and homeless youth, their characteristics, programs, and the problem as manifested in Los Angeles are key topics. Interventions ranging in focus from the individual to the federal level are described. An appendix contains research methodologies, survey questions, and a list of participants in a survey of community experts.*
> HV1431.R67

RUBIN, H. TED. *Juvenile Justice: Police Practice and Law.* Santa Monica, California: Goodyear, 1979. 299 pp.

> *Detailed descriptions of all aspects of juvenile court operations are included in this book. Separate chapters are devoted to status offenders, police, detention, intake, and the court hearing. Issues related to the philosophy of the court, prosecutors and defense attorneys, abused children, and judges also are reviewed in detail.*
> KF9779.R8

RUBIN, SOL. *Crime and Juvenile Delinquency.* Dobbs Ferry, New York: Oceana Publications, Inc., 1970. 234 pp.

> *Discusses the definition of juvenile delinquency; the question of parental responsibility for delinquency; authority, procedures, and requirements of the juvenile court; treatment of youthful offenders; and the need for "scientific" research. Includes a criticism of* Unraveling Juvenile Delinquency.
> HV9104.R77 1970

SANDERS, WILEY B., ed. *Juvenile Offenders for a Thousand Years.* Chapel Hill: University of North Carolina Press, 1970. 453 pp.

> *Contains 124 readings tracing the handling of juvenile offenders from the year 688 to 1900 in England, Scotland, Australia, and the United States. Sanders concludes that children who have broken the law have generally been treated more leniently than adults.*
> HV9065.S25

SANDHU, HARJIN S., AND C. WAYNE HEASLEY. *Improving Juvenile Justice: Power Advocacy, Diversion, Deinstitutionalization, and Due Process.* New York: Human Sciences Press, 1981. 236 pp.

> *The authors explain their position that in our society there is a problem of overreaction to, overinstitutionalization of, and overcriminalization of juveniles. They review difficulties of implementing policies to counteract these trends. Diversion, deinstitutionalization, and due process are described as far from successful. Therefore, the authors recommend the use of power advocacy, which is a strategy for organizing relevant local individuals into an influential advocacy group for youths. Power advocacy makes it possible for local citizens to influence, monitor, and evaluate prevention and control policies and programs.*
> HV9104.S3154

SCARPITTI, FRANK R., AND SUSAN K. DATESMAN, eds. *Drugs and the Youth Culture.* Beverly Hills, California: Sage Publications, 1980. 320 pp.

> *This collection of readings provides up-to-date information about the use of many types of drugs, including heroin, marijuana, alcohol, and cigarettes. Descriptions of the extent of drug use among adolescents, as well as its causes, are provided. Reviews of drug education and treatment programs conclude that it is uncertain that education is effective, but that several treatment programs appear to be promising if not confirmed successes.*
> HV5824.Y68D78

SCHEFFER, MARTIN W. *Policing from the Schoolhouse—Police-School Liaison and Resource Officer Programs: A Case Study.* Springfield, Virginia: Charles C. Thomas, 1987, 101 pp.

> *This book is a thorough examination of the placement of police officers in public schools. The officers teach public safety and provide an understanding of criminal justice, they counsel students, and they conduct student investigations. The 17-year-old Boise, Idaho, School Resource Officer program is used as a case study. The details of program operations and methods for police to work with the students are described.*
> HV8079.25.S34

SCHUR, EDWIN M. *Radical Nonintervention: Rethinking the Delinquency Problem.* Englewood Cliffs, New Jersey: Prentice-Hall, Inc., 1973. 180 pp.

> *Schur feels that current policy on juvenile delinquency is ineffective. He advocates a radical change of major institutions and prevailing cultural values, and an acceptance of greater diversity in behavior. In*

his view, many youths engage in misconduct and lawbreaking but escape the delinquency label; the delinquent is the youth who is caught in this behavior. Schur further emphasizes that creation of programs for prevention should be based on research.
HV9104.S328

SCHWARTZ, IRA M. *(In)justice for Juveniles: Rethinking the Best Interests of the Child.* Lexington, Massachusetts: Lexington Books, 1989. 184 pp.
This essay reports on recent trends in U.S. federal and state juvenile justice policy. In the author's opinion, the "get tough" policies that were adopted in the late 1970s and early 1980s were poorly conceived. They resulted in increased detention center and training school populations. At the same time, the state and local facilities deteriorated because of neglect by both politicians and professionals. It has been difficult for federal juvenile crime control policies that stress deinstitutionalization to be effective until recent years when states concentrated in the west and the south began to reduce their reliance on incarceration for juveniles.
HV9014.S3286

SHANNON, LYLE W. *Criminal Career Continuity: Its Social Context.* New York, Human Sciences Press, 1988. 240 pp.
The author describes his well designed study of the transition from delinquency to adult criminal behavior. The study was done in a middle-sized Midwestern urban area, and it covers 1948–1976. Changes in social and economic conditions of the city resulted in different rates of delinquency and crime. The results of detailed interviews with the people who were studied give the reader an understanding of delinquency as a natural process in a complicated urban setting.
HV9105.W6S53

SHAW, OTTO L. *Prisons of the Mind.* New York: Hart Publishing Company, 1974. 243 pp.
Shaw stresses the importance of understanding and compassion in the treatment of maladjusted and delinquent boys. The diagnosis of each youth's problems must be supplemented by the removal of temptation. Specific cases described are drawn from the work of Red Hill School.
HV9148.E22R473

SHICHOR, DAVID, AND DELOS H. KELLY, eds. *Critical Issues in Juvenile Delinquency.* Lexington, Massachusetts: Lexington Books, D.C. Heath and Company, 1980. 347 pp.
The sixteen articles in this book report on several recent studies which contribute to our understanding of contemporary juvenile delinquency. Some of the specific topics are changing theoretical perspectives, changes in juvenile law, rural delinquency, female delinquency, and violence. The research that is described pertains to the influence of schools, the family, and gangs on delinquent behavior. Additional chapters are relevant to understanding status offenders, the effect of punishment, and programs and policies to control delinquency.
HV9104.C74

SLAVSON, S. R. *Reclaiming the Delinquent.* New York: The Free Press, 1965. 766 pp.
Slavson describes a study of group psychotherapy in residential treatment of delinquent boys. The study was designed to test Slavson's Activity and Analytic Group Psychotherapy, to obtain staff responses to such procedures, and to determine the effect of such procedures on the total institutional community. The author emphasizes the importance of discovering the underlying motives for and cases of delinquent behavior and feels that delinquents will reveal motives only when in therapy in the secure climate of the group. He includes case histories and recommendations for practitioners.
HV9069.S59

SORRENTINO, ANTHONY. *Organizing Against Crime: Redeveloping the Neighborhood.* New York: Human Sciences Press, 1977. 272 pp.
Sorrentino recounts his own experiences in an Italian-American neighborhood where he worked with youths and neighborhood groups in a crime prevention program. He organized gangs into clubs which engaged in positive experiences, and he attempted to increase legitimate opportunities for success of the neighborhood youths. Neighborhood redevelopment became a focal point for strengthening the community through organizing efforts.
HB9106.C4 S57

SPROWLS, JAMES T. *Discretion and Lawlessness: Compliance in the Juvenile Court.* Lexington, Massachusetts: Lexington Books, D.C. Heath and Company, 1980. 121 pp.
This book provides an evaluation of the degree to which juvenile courts in Pennsylvania comply with the provisions of the Pennsylvania Juvenile Court Act. The author describes his serious difficulties in gaining

access to data on juvenile courts. On the basis of the data that he was able to obtain, he concludes that there is very little compliance with the laws of Pennsylvania, and furthermore there is no evidence of compliance with Supreme Court decisions, including Gault. *The final sections of the book identify organizational and environmental factors that make it possible for the courts to avoid compliance with the law.*
KF9794.S65

STAPLETON, W. VAUGHN, AND LEE E. TEITELBAUM. *In Defense of Youth.* New York: Russell Sage Foundation, 1972. 243 pp.
A study of the role of attorneys in the juvenile court which combines legal analyses with social science methodology and interpretation. The authors discuss the history and philosophy of the juvenile court and maintain that the introduction of defense attorneys changed the proceeding into an adversary process. They also discuss the consequences of this process through observations from two cities.
KF9709.S7

STEPHENSON, RICHARD M., AND FRANK R. SCARPITTI. *Group Interaction as Therapy.* Westport, Connecticut: Greenwood Press, 1974. 235 pp.
The authors describe a program designed to intervene in the processes of juvenile delinquency and rechannel behavior into more acceptable dimensions. Using the Essexfields project as an example, they discuss the methodology of the project, its accompanying evaluative research, and comparative research on similar programs.
HV9275.S73

STRASBURG, PAUL A. *Violent Delinquents: A Report to the Ford Foundation from the Vera Institute of Justice.* New York: Monarch, 1978. 272 pp.
The author provides an overview of information about violent youths across the nation, as well as information from a study of those processed through New York courts. The youths are described, and their handling by the juvenile justice system is analyzed. An evaluation of treatment programs for violent offenders reveals that there is a need for more sophisticated research, but that programs should be supported. Recommendations are made for preventing violence, as well as for other strategies of control.
HV9104.S83

STURZ, ELIZABETH LYTTLETON. *Widening Circles.* New York: Harper and Row, Publishers, 1983. 334 pp.
The author of this readable book gives us a detailed description of a multifaceted program for abandoned, disruptive, and violent youth in one of the most depressed and disorganized areas of New York, the South Bronx. The adolescents who participate are primarily black and Hispanic, and they include both girls and boys. They do not have access to education or jobs, and they are negatively affected by labeling, mislabeling, and bureaucratic requirements. The program attempts to operate as an extended family, providing both nonresidential and residential services. Methods for putting together a positive peer group and for operating a girls' group home are explained. Throughout the book, the author recognizes that pressing community problems as well as individual difficulties affect the youths.
HV1437.B76588

TEITELBAUM, LEE E., AND AIDAN R. GOUGH, eds. *Beyond Control: Status Offenders in the Juvenile Court.* Cambridge, Massachusetts: Ballinger Publishing Company, Subsidiary of J. B. Lippincott Co., 1977. 330 pp.
A collection of nine articles provide an understanding of the historical development of legislation affecting status offenders, particularly in New York. Sex-based discrimination and other reasons for reform are discussed. Alternatives to handling status offenders in court are presented as an important step toward reform.
KF9712.A75B4

TRACY, PAUL E., MARVIN E. WOLFGANG AND ROBERT M. FIGLIO. *Delinquency Careers in two Birth Cohorts.* New York: Plenum, 1990.
The effects of growing up at different times, and the theories to explain differences in delinquency, are the focus of the research reported by the authors. The comparison is between males born in 1945 and 1958. The methodologically sophisticated longitudinal study sheds light on prevalence and incidence of delinquency, recidivism, offense specialization and escalation, and the types of police and court dispositions that youth receive.

TWENTIETH CENTURY FUND, TASK FORCE ON SENTENCING POLICY. *Confronting Youth Crime.* New York: Holmes & Meier Publishers, Inc., 1978. 120 pp.
In direct challenge to the individualized treatment philosophy of the juvenile court, this book sets forth

guidelines for fair and effective sentencing policies for youthful offenders. Confinement is recommended for a small number of violent offenders, whereas fines and supervision are recommended for property offenders. This system is intended to be more closely aligned with adult court operations, and to serve as a deterrent to youthful crime.
HV9104.T87

VEDER, CLYDE B., AND DORA B. SOMERVILLE. *The Delinquent Girl.* Springfield, Illinois: Charles C. Thomas, Publisher, 1970. 166 pp.
Veder and Somerville attempt to provide insight into the phenomenon of female juvenile delinquency. They report on a questionnaire sent to all state institutions for delinquent girls to ascertain the offenses which lead to institutional commitment, and discuss the results of the questionnaire. They also discuss theoretical considerations, briefly summarize the literature on female delinquency, and give case histories of females who were runaways, incorrigible, sex-delinquent, probation violators, or truant, the most common offenses of females.
HV6046.V4

VODOPIVEC, KATJA, ed. *Maladjusted Youth, An Experiment in Rehabilitation.* Lexington, Massachusetts: Lexington Books, D.C. Heath and Company, 1974. 275 pp.
Final report of a project concerned with the introduction of new methods of educating maladjusted and delinquent youths in a small institution in Yugoslavia. The staff developed a permissive and understanding relationship with inmates through the use of group counseling, individual therapy, and use of the entire setting as a therapeutic environment. The report stresses the importance of special training and counseling of staff. Vodopivec concludes that permissive educational methods do not result in inmates who are greater threats to society after release, and that institutions can deal with various kinds of disturbed inmates.
HV9191.6.D6M34

WADSWORTH, MICHAEL. *The Roots of Delinquency: Infancy, Adolescence and Crime.* Oxford: Martin Robertson, 1979. 150 pp.
A longitudinal study in England identifies early life events which influence the risk of delinquency later in life. It is the opinion of the author that even though we can use this information to identify a group of youths which includes most who will later become delinquent, we cannot reasonably subject this group to prevention programs. A large majority of the identified group would not become delinquents, but would react to stressful conditions in other ways.
HV9104.W33 1979

WEBER, GEORGE H. *Child-Menders.* Beverly Hills, California: Sage Publications, 1979. 223 pp.
Weber uses a series of vignettes to introduce the reader to the very human process of work with institutionalized delinquents. Some of the topics the author explores are youthful feelings of parental rejection, substance abuse, runaway behavior, staff disagreements, and different types of programs; throughout he captures the complexity of human behavior. There is evidence of counter-influences of staff, problems created by institutional procedures, and the seemingly insurmountable problems of serious delinquents.
HV7428.W4

WEISBERG, D. KELLY. *Children of the Night: A Study of Adolescent Prostitution.* Lexington, Massachusetts: Lexington Books, D.C. Heath and Company, 1985. 298 pp.
This book presents the results of research to uncover the cause of adolescent prostitution and to describe the prostitutes' lifestyles and their involvement with the juvenile justice system and social service programs. Special attention is given to the relationships of child abuse, neglect, and runaway behavior to prostitution, and the involvement of both girls and boys is considered. One chapter is devoted to a review of federal and state legislation that has a bearing on juvenile prostitution. The final chapter is devoted to program responses to adolescent prostitution, and several contemporary programs are described.
HQ144.W44

WENK, ERNST, AND NORA HARLOW, eds. *School Crime and Disruption.* Davis, California: Responsible Action, 1978. 237 pp.
The editors of this book have collected articles which provide several different theoretical explanations of the ways in which schools contribute to delinquency and an atmosphere of disruption. In many cases, there are practical steps which can be taken to reduce these problems. Negotiating methods, special programs, and training programs for school personnel are described in detail.
LB3249.S36

WEST, D. J., AND D. P. FARRINGTON. *Who Becomes Delinquent?* London: William Heinemann Ltd., 1973. 265 pp.

Report of a study which investigated the development of juvenile delinquency and compared delinquents with nondelinquents. A sample of boys was chosen, information about them was collected for ten years, and differences between those who became delinquent and those who did not were noted. Researchers concluded that differences did exist between delinquents and nondelinquents, noting especially that the family background and personal characteristics of delinquents were much less fortunate than those of nondelinquents. Some possible reasons for these findings are discussed, along with thoughts on prevention.
HV9069.W422

WILLIAMS, TERRY. *The Cocaine Kids: The Inside Story of a Teenage Drug Ring.* Reading, Massachusetts: Addison-Wesley Publishing Company, Inc., 1989.

The author of this book spent several years interviewing and interacting with the teenaged men and women who were part of a "crew" that dealt drugs in Washington Heights, New York City. His book includes detailed descriptions of the organization of the drug distribution trade and of the daily lives of the teenagers involved. There is some information on the effects of law enforcement efforts. The reader comes away from this book with a good sense of the family problems that the youths experienced, of the way they used their incomes, and of their plans for the future. The teenagers are relatively sophisticated business operators, who managed to support themselves and others over a period of time.
HV5833.N45W55 1989

WILLS, W., DAVID. *Spare the Child.* Baltimore: Penguin Books, 1971. 153 pp.

An account of the process of converting a British approved school into a therapeutic community, with emphasis on eliminating a hierarchical and repressive structure.
HV9146.W55

WOLFGANG, MARVIN E., TERENCE P. THORNBERRY AND ROBERT M. FIGLIO. *From Boy to Man, from Delinquency to Crime.* Chicago: The University of Chicago Press, 1987.

The authors build on the prior study of a 1945 Philadelphia birth cohort's delinquent activity by conducting interviews with 567 individuals once they were twenty-six years old. In order to obtain a full understanding of criminal behavior, police and FBI records were examined at the time of the interviews and again when the men were thirty years old. Empirical evidence is presented to describe the proportion of men who had broken the law as juveniles, as adults, and in both phases of their lives. Patterns of illegal activity for subgroups differing in age, race and social class are presented in detail. There also is description of the life events (e.g., marriage, changes in gang membership) that are helpful in understanding the seriousness and continuation of lawbreaking.
HV 9104.F76 1987

WOLFGANG, MARVIN E., ROBERT M. FIGLIO, AND THORSTEN SELLIN. *Delinquency in a Birth Cohort.* Chicago: University of Chicago Press, 1972. 327 pp.

The authors provide a statistical description of juvenile delinquency through studying the history of delinquency among a group of youths born in the same year. They analyze all available official data on nearly ten thousand boys from ages ten through eighteen, noting the age of onset of delinquency, and its progression or cessation. They then relate these data to personal or social characteristics of delinquents, and compare the characteristics with those of others in the cohort who have not become delinquent.
HV9106.P5W64

ZIMRING, FANKLIN E. *The Changing Legal World of Adolescence.* New York: The Free Press, 1982. 208 pp.

This book is an extension of the author's earlier analysis of the rights of adolescents. The book presents several examples of the types of legal dilemmas involved: Should the drinking age be arbitrarily set at 18, 21, or even 25? When can parents stop supporting their children? Should adolescents have the "right" to purchase contraceptives? Does a curfew ordinance violate the Constitution? With the aim of helping the readers think through such issues, the author analyzes recent court decisions that have a bearing on the rights of adolescents. Moreover, Zimring discusses the reasoning behind recent adolescent law reforms.
KF479.Z55

Index